NUMBER ONE

*The Nautical Archaeology Series*

# YASSI ADA

YASSI ADA

# YASSI ADA

## VOLUME I

### A Seventh-Century Byzantine Shipwreck

BY

GEORGE F. BASS and FREDERICK H. VAN DOORNINCK, JR.

With VAUGHN M. BRYANT, JR., D. E. DELWICHE, JOAN M. FAGERLIE,

JOHN A. GIFFORD, MICHAEL L. KATZEV, SUSAN WOMER KATZEV,

PETER IAN KUNIHOLM, ROBERT E. MURRY, JR., G. KENNETH SAMS,

J. RICHARD STEFFY, and KAREN D. VITELLI

*Published with the cooperation of the Institute of*

*Nautical Archaeology by*

TEXAS A&M UNIVERSITY PRESS

COLLEGE STATION

Library of Congress Cataloging in Publication Data

Bass, George Fletcher.
    Yassi Ada.

        (Nautical archaeology series; no. 1–   )
        Bibliography: v. 1, p.
        Includes index.
        Contents: v. 1. A seventh-century Byzantine
shipwreck.
        1. Yassi Island (Turkey)—Antiquities, Byzantine.
2. Underwater archaeology—Turkey—Yassi Island.
3. Shipbuilding—Mediterranean region—History.
I. Van Doorninck, Frederick H., 1933–   .
II. Title.   III. Series: Nautical archaeology
series; no. 1, etc.
DS156.Y37B37      956.2      81-40401
ISBN 0-89096-063-1 (v. 1)      AACR2

*Manufactured in the United States of America*
FIRST EDITION

To the memory of

Rodney Stuart Young

(1907–1974)

# CONTENTS

# FOLDOUT DIAGRAMS

# PREFACE

THIS book forms a final report on the underwater excavations I directed at Yassı Ada, Turkey, during the summers of 1961 through 1964 for the University Museum of the University of Pennsylvania. The excavation was the first to have been completed on the floor of the Mediterranean of a wreck with substantial hull remains. This pioneering work required the ingenuity, effort, and generosity of many people and institutions. I thank all of them here, however inadequately, by listing staff and sponsors of each campaign.

## 1961

STAFF. George F. Bass, director; Waldemar Illing, technical director and photographer; Herb Greer, photographer; Claude Duthuit, chief diver; Eric J. Ryan, artist; Kemal Aras, manager of boats and local arrangements; Charles Fries, physician; William Wiener, Jr., architect; Susan Womer, artist; Ann S. Bass, cataloger and conservator; Frederick H. van Doorninck, Jr., David I. Owen, and Lubiza Popovic, archaeology students; Robert Goodman, National Geographic Society photographer; Laurence T. Joline, diver; J. J. Flori, cinematographer; Jean Naz, mechanic; and W. J. Dixon, assistant conservator. Enver Bostanci and Hadi Altay served as commissioners from the Turkish Department of Antiquities and were assisted by Yüksel Eğdemir.

SPONSORS. The University Museum of the University of Pennsylvania, the National Geographic Society, the Catherwood Foundation, the American Philosophical Society, the Littauer Foundation with a grant through Colgate University, Bauer Kompressoren of Munich, the Main Line Diving Club of Philadelphia, and Nixon Griffis.

## 1962

STAFF. George and Ann Bass, Womer, Ryan, van Doorninck (in charge of underwater plans), Owen (in charge of barge operations), Illing, Joline (in charge of diving safety), Duthuit, Flori, Naz, and Aras. New members were Peter Hall, Pat Hall, and Louis Beauvy, physicians; Eric Carlson and Önder Seren, architects; Thomas Abercrombie (National Geographic Society) and Mustafa Kapkin, photographers; Oğuz Alpözen and Şeref Alkan, archaeology students; Jack Sofield, diving instructor; and Oktay Ercan, Agnes Beauvy, and André Morel, divers. Haluk Elbe was Turkish archaeological commissioner, assisted by Yüksel Eğdemir.

SPONSORS. The University Museum, the National Geographic Society, the American Philosophical Society, Nixon Griffis, the Catherwood Foundation, and the Corning Museum of Glass.

## 1963

STAFF. George and Ann Bass, van Doorninck (assistant director), Owen, Ryan, Womer, Alpözen, Joline, Seren, Duthuit, Illing, and Nixon Griffis. New members were David Leith, physician; Peter Fries, Ridge Kunzel, Geist Zantzinger, and Kiral Nalbantoğlu, students; Julian Whittlesey and Donald M. Rosencrantz, photogrammetry advisers; Avner Raban and Giora Raz, representatives of the Underwater Archaeological Society of Israel; and B. J. van Doorninck. Mehmet Turguttekin was in charge of boats and local arrangements, and Yüksel Eğdemir served as archaeological commissioner.

SPONSORS. The University Museum, the National Geographic Society, the Catherwood Foundation, Nixon

Griffis, the Corning Museum of Glass, and Mr. and Mrs. James P. Magill.

### 1964

STAFF. George and Ann Bass, Owen (assistant director), F. van Doorninck (in charge of hull studies), Womer, Ryan, Joline, Rosencrantz, Whittlesey, Beauvy, Alpözen, Seren, Illing, Turguttekin, and B. J. van Doorninck. New members were Bennett Jones, architect; William Beran, *Asherah* engineer; Rudolf Karius, photogrammetrist; Lloyd P. Wells, *Virazon* captain; Bates Littlehales and Robert Fuller, National Geographic Society photographers; Gerald Stern, mechanic; Frank Frost, historian; Michael L. Katzev, Mark Davies, and Sandy Fleitas, students; and Jean B. Wells and Susan Owen. Yüksel Eğdemir was Turkish archaeological commissioner.

SPONSORS. The University Museum, the National Geographic Society, William van Alen, the Catherwood Foundation, the Corning Museum of Glass, Nixon Griffis, the National Science Foundation, and the Rockefeller Foundation. The Office of Naval Research provided the *Virazon*, freighted to the Aegean by the Lykes Brothers Steamship Company.

### 1980

STAFF. Donald A. Frey, Merih Karabağ, Robin C. M. Piercy, and Tufan Turanli on *Virazon*, with volunteer deck hands Wayne Apostolik and Douglas Haldane; Netia Piercy, artist; and Robyn Woodward, conservator. Yaşar Yildiz was Turkish archaeological commissioner.

SPONSOR. The Institute of Nautical Archaeology

I am grateful to the authors of this book, which has been so long in preparation: John Gifford, University of Minnesota, Duluth; F. H. van Doorninck, Jr., Institute of Nautical Archaeology and Texas A&M University; Karen D. Vitelli, Indiana University; Joan Fagerlie, Wilson Library, University of Minnesota, Twin Cities; G. Kenneth Sams, University of North Carolina, Chapel Hill; Michael L. Katzev, Institute of Nautical Archaeology; Peter Kuniholm, Cornell University; Susan Womer Katzev; D. E. Delwiche, General Electric Company; and Robert E. Murry, Jr., and Vaughn M. Bryant, Jr., Texas A&M University.

Susan Womer Katzev also is responsible for most of the object drawings in the book; several were done by Gündüz Gölönü of the Istanbul State Academy of Fine Arts and by Netia Piercy and Sema Pulak. Diagrams and sketches of excavation techniques in chapter 2 are mostly the work of Eric J. Ryan. Object photographs were taken by Donald A. Frey, Waldemar Illing, Donald M. Rosencrantz, and Herb Greer, among others, but they are not responsible for those taken by the inexperienced hand of this writer. Most of the underwater photographs are by Herb Greer and Jack Sofield.

Lisa Shuey, Sheila Matthews, Cemal Pulak, and Sheli Smith gave considerable help in inking, lettering, and arranging plans and plates, and Lisa Shuey, Paul Hundley, and Cemal Pulak spent long hours in the darkroom printing the photographs for publication; all are graduate students in nautical archaeology at Texas A&M University. In proofreading my several typed drafts of the entire book, I was aided by my sons, Gordon and Alan Bass, and especially by Ann Bass, whose other contributions are recognized below; Diane Foley and Kenneth Cassavoy of Texas A&M have given a fresh eye to the final version.

Special Byzantine Greek characters and symbols used in the chapters on coins and weights are reproduced from Philip Grierson's *Catalogue of the Byzantine Coins in the Dumbarton Oaks Collection and in the Whittemore Collection*, vol. II, part 1, *Phocas and Heraclius (602–641)*, by permission of the Dumbarton Oaks Library and Collection.

I was greatly aided over the years by correspondence with Kazimierz Majewski of the University of Warsaw; G. M. A. Hanfmann of the Fogg Art Museum; Jean-Pierre Sodini of the Sorbonne; B. F. Kukachka of the Forest Products Laboratory of the U.S. Department of Agriculture; Francis Croissant of the French School of Archaeology at Athens; Gerhard Kapitän; Jean Pouilloux; Judith Perlzweig of the American School of Classical Studies at Athens; A. J. Parker of Bristol University; and Thomas P. Hoving of the Metropolitan Museum of Art. I can only apologize to those I may have neglected to mention here and below.

The wreck was first brought to my attention by Peter Throckmorton through John Huston of the Council for Underwater Archaeology in San Francisco. I first dived on it in September, 1960, accompanied by Mustafa Kapkin and Rasim Divanli, partners in Mr. Throckmorton's earlier exploration. The wreck had been dated for Mr. Throckmorton, on the basis of its amphora types, by Virginia Grace of the American School of Classical Studies. To all I am grateful.

I owe special thanks to Dr. Froelich Rainey, Director of the University Museum, and to the Board of Managers of the Museum for their foresight in encouraging me to pursue the new field of underwater archaeology. I owe equal thanks to my wife, Ann Singletary Bass, for devoting most of the years of the excavation to its success, in all aspects of its organization both in America and Turkey, and to Laurence T. Joline for his meticulous care in organizing necessary diving equipment.

The project could not have been accomplished without permission of the Turkish Directorate of Antiquities and Museums, which has since displayed the finds in a special museum for underwater archaeology in Bodrum.

A sabbatical year from the University of Pennsylvania in 1969–1970, supported in part by a grant from the American Council of Learned Societies, allowed me to spend a year at Cambridge University, where I wrote most of my chapters of this work; Professor Glyn Daniel had kindly invited me to be a visiting scholar at St. John's College, and Professor R. M. Cook provided me with an office in the Museum of Classical Archaeology. During that year I was able to visit Rumania to examine numerous parallels for the Yassi Ada artifacts after Joan du Plat Taylor of the Institute of Archaeology, London University, had led me to published Rumanian examples. My productive trip was greatly aided by the hospitality of Dr. A. Radulescu and Mikai Bucovala at the Regional Museum of Dobrudja in Constanţa; Dr. Maria Coja, of the Institute of Archaeology in Bucharest, at her excavation of Argumum; A. Suceveanu, who showed me the site of Histria; Dr. D. Tudor; and Dr. Barnea, who guided me through the remains of Adamclisi.

In England I received invaluable information from Drs. John Boardman and Hector Catling of the Ashmolean Museum; Professor R. M. Harrison of the University of Newcastle-upon-Tyne; Dr. John Hayes, now of the Royal Ontario Museum; and Philip Grierson, Fellow of Gonville and Caius College.

During the sabbatical year I also received the chapters on coins, weights and balances, lamps, and miscellaneous finds. The long delay between the completion of most of the chapters on artifacts and the completion of the entire manuscript was based on the difficulty of reconstructing the hull and galley of the ship accurately, for such a reconstruction had not previously been attempted from seabed remains. Work begun by van Doorninck at the University of Pennsylvania and the American School of Classical Studies at Athens was continued at the University of California, Davis Campus, and became a collaboration, largely by transcontinental correspondence, with Steffy.

In 1973 I formed the American Institute of Nautical Archaeology (now the Institute of Nautical Archaeology) with a Mediterranean headquarters on Cyprus; for a few months in 1974, van Doorninck (on sabbatical leave), Steffy, Gifford, Susan Womer Katzev, Michael Katzev, and I were able to work together on a daily basis, but the Cyprus War ended that ideal situation.

At the suggestion of Carl J. Clausen, then state underwater archaeologist for Texas, Texas A&M University invited the institute to be based at College Station in 1976, bringing van Doorninck, Steffy, and me together on its faculty. A unique affiliation between the university and the institute provides nautical archaeology faculty the time for institute-supported research, writing, and travel free from normal teaching duties. This freedom, finally, has allowed completion of the book.

The Institute of Nautical Archaeology also allowed us to have a year-round staff in Bodrum, Turkey, where all of the finds from the Byzantine shipwreck remain. This staff, in addition to its work on other projects, made new discoveries for this study, both from further conservation of artifacts and from a few additional dives at Yassi Ada in 1980. The new information is included here, although some of it was added only days before the book went to press.

In closing, I should note that both excavation and publication of the Yassi Ada Byzantine shipwreck were largely the work of University of Pennsylvania graduate students. I completed my doctorate only at the beginning of the final excavation campaign, and van Doorninck wrote his dissertation on the ship's reconstruction; Vitelli, Sams, M. L. Katzev, Kuniholm, and S. Womer Katzev wrote their chapters during or following a seminar on ancient seafaring I offered at the university. All of us were students of Professor Rodney S. Young, chairman of the Department of Classical Archaeology. By treating students and senior colleagues with equal respect, Rodney Young inspired our best, teaching us something more valuable than anything we learned in classes. It is to his memory that this book is dedicated.

GEORGE F. BASS

*College Station, Texas*
*January 10, 1981*

# ABBREVIATIONS

### REFERENCES

| | |
|---|---|
| AA | *Archäologischer Anzeiger* |
| AJA | *American Journal of Archaeology* |
| ANSMN | *American Numismatic Society, Museum Notes* |
| ANSNNM | American Numismatic Society, Numismatic Notes and Monographs |
| ArchEph | *Archaiologike Ephemeris* |
| AthMitt | *Mitteilungen des deutschen archäologischen Instituts, Athenische Abteilung* |
| BCH | *Bulletin de correspondance hellénique* |
| BIABulg | *Bulletin [Izvestia] de l'Institut archéologique bulgare* |
| BMC | W. Wroth, *Catalogue of the Imperial Byzantine Coins in the British Museum* |
| BonnJbb | *Bonner Jahrbücher* |
| BSA | Annual of the British School at Athens |
| BSAE | British School of Archaeology in Egypt, Publications |
| BSR | British School of Archaeology at Rome, Papers |
| BZ | *Byzantinische Zeitschrift* |
| CahArchSub | *Cahiers d'archéologie subaquatique* |
| CMH | *Cambridge Medieval History* |
| CRAI | *Comptes rendus de l'Académie des inscriptions et belles lettres* |
| Deltion | *Archaiologikon deltion* |
| DOC | *Catalogue of the Byzantine Coins in the Dumbarton Oaks Collection and in the Whittemore Collection,* Vols. I and II. |
| DOP | *Dumbarton Oaks Papers* |
| Epet | *Epeteris Hetaireias Byzantinon Spoudon* |
| Expedition | *Expedition, Bulletin of the University Museum of the University of Pennsylvania* |
| IJNA | *International Journal of Nautical Archaeology and Underwater Exploration* |
| ILN | *Illustrated London News* |
| JdI | *Jahrbuch des deutschen archäologischen Instituts* |
| JOAIBeibl | *Jahreshefte des österreichischen archäologischen Institutes, Beiblatt* |
| JRS | *Journal of Roman Studies* |
| KJVuF | *Kölner Jahrbuch für Vor- und Frühgeschichte* |
| MCA | *Materiale si Cercetari Arheologie* |
| MM | *The Mariner's Mirror* |
| MonAnt | Monumenti Antichi pubblicati a cura della Accademia Nazionale dei Lincei, Rome |
| MonPiot | Foundation Eugène Piot, *Monuments et mémoires publ. par l'Académie des inscriptions et belles lettres* |
| NatGeo | *National Geographic Magazine* |
| NSc | *Notizie degli Scavi di Antichità, Accademia dei Lincei, Rome* |
| NumCirc | *Numismatic Circular* |
| OIP | Publications of the Oriental Institute, University of Chicago |
| ÖJh | *Jahreshefte des österreichischen archäologischen Institutes* |
| RA | *Revue archéologique* |
| RE | *Paulys Real-Encyclopädie der klassischen Altertumswissenschaft* |
| REG | *Revue des études grecques* |
| RendLinc | *Rendiconti della R. Accademia dei Lincei* |
| RIN | *Rivista Italiana di Numismatica* |
| RStLig | *Rivista di Studi Liguri* |
| SBMünchen | *Sitzungsberichte der philos.-philol. und* |

der hist. Klasse der K. B. Akad. der
Wiss. zu München

SovArch     Sovetskaia arkheologiia
ZSchwAKg   Zeitschrift für schweizerische Archae-
ologie und Kunstgeschichte

### CATALOG ABBREVIATIONS

| | |
|---|---|
| Æ | copper coin |
| An | anchor |
| aper. | aperture |
| approx. | approximately |
| A͞ | gold coin |
| B | balances and accessories |
| CT | cover tile |
| diam. | diameter |
| est. | estimated |
| Fe | iron |
| g | gram |
| Ger. | German |
| Gk. | Greek |
| h. | height |
| HT | hearth tile |
| IB | iron bar |
| Inv. No. | inventory number |
| L | lamp |
| l. | length (preceding number) |
| l | liter (following number) |
| LW | lead fishing weight |
| max. | maximum |
| MF | miscellaneous find |
| min. | minimum |
| MT | miscellaneous tile |
| P | pottery |
| pres. | preserved |
| PT | pantile |
| sect. | section |
| St | anchor stock |
| th. | thickness |
| Turk. | Turkish |
| w. | width |

W3     Wreck 3, the original designation given to the seventh-century Byzantine shipwreck by Peter Throckmorton during his survey of Yassi Ada in 1958.

Find-spot sectors are given in parentheses, as (6C).
Seabed identification letters precede find spots, as MCA (6C).
Seabed identification letters for joining fragments are denoted by +, as BEI+KTT.
Seabed identification letters for single objects that were inadvertently given two sets of letters are denoted by ≡, as KAA≡KQP.
Measurements in catalogs are given in meters, as 0.123.

### INITIALS OF ILLUSTRATORS AND PHOTOGRAPHERS

| | |
|---|---|
| BB | Bobbe Baker |
| DAF | Donald A. Frey |
| DF | Debbie Faul |
| DMR | Donald M. Rosencrantz |
| EBS | Elizabeth B. Shuey |
| EJR | Eric J. Ryan |
| FHvD | Frederick H. van Doorninck |
| FM | Freya Mechanic |
| GFB | George F. Bass |
| GG | Gündüz Gölönü |
| GKS | G. Kenneth Sams |
| HG | Herb Greer |
| JRS | J. Richard Steffy |
| JS | Jack Sofield |
| LTJ | Laurence T. Joline |
| MK | Mustafa Kapkin |
| NP | Netia Piercy |
| SS | Sheli Smith |
| SWK | Susan Womer Katzev |
| UM | staff of the University Museum of the University of Pennsylvania |
| WI | Waldemar Illing |

# YASSI ADA

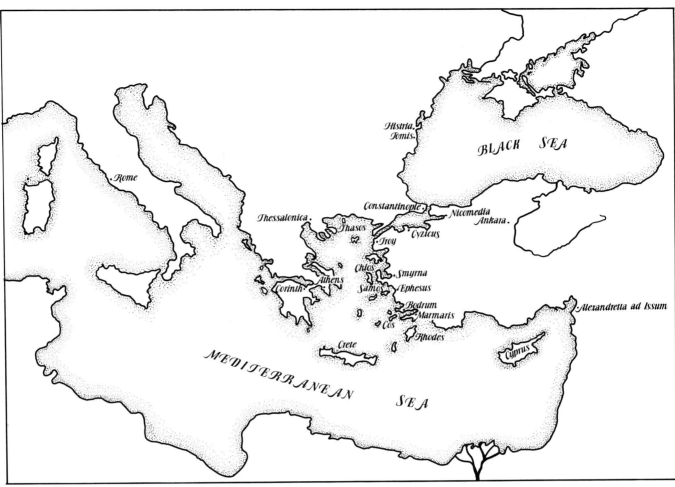

FIG. 1-1. The central and eastern Mediterranean. SS

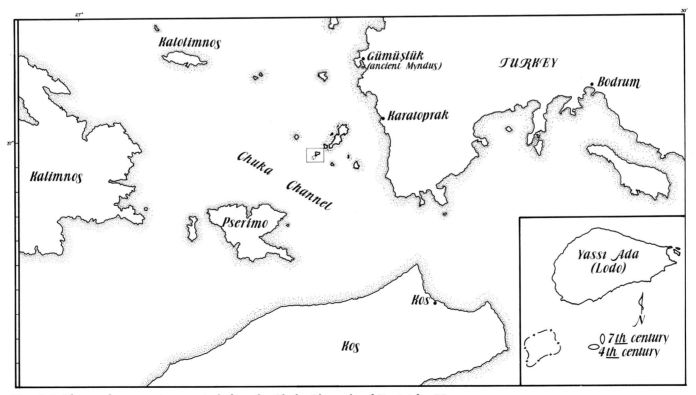

FIG. 1-2. The southeastern Aegean, including the Chuka Channel and Yassı Ada. SS

# I

# THE SITE

## George F. Bass and John A. Gifford

Yassı Ada or Yassıada (27°11′45″ E, 36°59′30″ N), meaning simply "Flat Island," is one of several islands bordering the Chuka Channel in the southeastern Aegean Sea (Figs. 1-1, 1-2). It lies near Bodrum, Turkey, in the province of Muğla and should not be confused with at least one other island of the same name nearer Istanbul. Yassı Ada (also called Lodo) is properly spelled with the Turkish undotted ı, but for convenience we will Anglicize it hereafter as Yassi Ada, although it is pronounced Yahs-suh Ah-dah.[1]

Of the islands in the area, Yassi Ada is exceptional in possessing a reef extending west-southwest for about 200 m from the southwest side of the island. The *Sailing Directions for the Mediterranean* mention this reef and warn that it "should be given a wide berth."[2] The sketch map of Fig. 1-3 illustrates the reason for this warning: the reef is saddle-shaped, with its highest points (within 2–3 m of the surface) occurring at the southwest extremity, at the greatest distance from Yassi Ada.

A sediment-trapping basin is formed by the curve of the reef and the island from the southwest around to the east. The bottom slopes steeply away from the south shore of the island, reaching an angle of almost 40° between the 15- and 35-m contour lines; east-southeastward from the reef the slope is somewhat less steep. At the 40-m contour, the angle of slope suddenly decreases to less than 10°, producing a flat, featureless sediment plain that continues into deeper water to the southeast. Three shipwrecks have been located near this 40-m slope break at a spot about 80 m due south of the southernmost point on Yassi Ada. The sites shown in the sketch map of Fig. 1-3 locate two of these wrecks—a fourth-century cargo vessel excavated by the University Museum of the University of Pennsylvania during the summers of 1967 and 1969,[3] and the seventh-century Byzantine shipwreck described in this book; the approximate position of the latter was added to the map several years after the completion of its excavation.

The discovery by Peter Throckmorton of the Byzantine shipwreck at Yassi Ada has been detailed previously. The wreck was only one of many he charted off the Turkish coast while sailing and diving with Bodrum spongers during the summers of 1958 and 1959.[4] George Bass had visited the site, accompanied by Mustafa Kapkin and Rasim Divanli of Throckmorton's original survey team, only once before the excavation, in October, 1960, so he relied heavily on descriptions given to him by Throckmorton and Honor Frost, and these proved to be remarkably accurate.

Experience at Cape Gelidonya in 1960 had demonstrated that improved methods of underwater excavation were required.[5] The decision to begin work at Yassi Ada the following year was based not entirely on hopes of significant archaeological results, but also on a desire to develop new techniques. Thus, the Byzantine wreck

---

[1] U.S. Department of Defense, Defense Mapping Agency Hydrographic Center, N.O. Chart no. BHA 54418. We have chosen, arbitrarily, the Latin spellings of most ancient place names in the text, but some inconsistencies do appear. Cos, for example, is spelled Kos on one of the maps because the map imitates a modern nautical chart.

[2] U.S. Naval Oceanographic Office, *Sailing Directions for the Mediterranean*, vol. V, *The Aegean Sea*, pp. 506ff.

[3] G. F. Bass and F. H. van Doorninck, Jr., "A Fourth-Century Shipwreck at Yassi Ada," *AJA* 75 (1971): 27–37.

[4] P. Throckmorton, *The Lost Ships*, pp. 1–71; G. F. Bass, *Cape Gelidonya: A Bronze Age Shipwreck*, pp. 14–15; H. Frost, *Under the Mediterranean*, pp. 158–173.

[5] Bass, *Cape Gelidonya*, chap. 2.

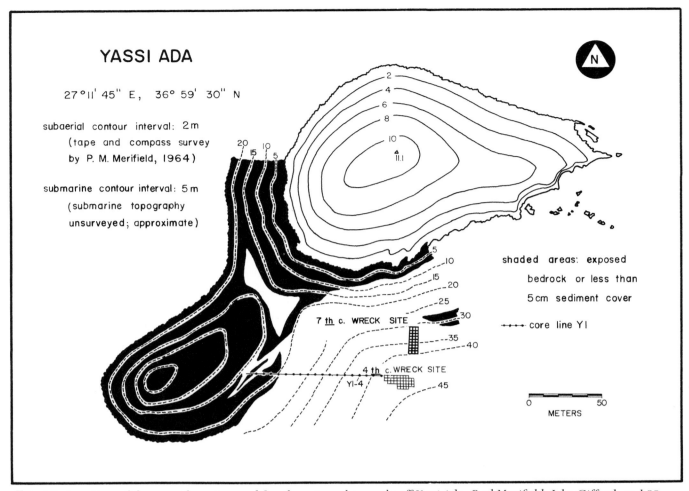

FIG. 1-3. Locations of the seventh-century and fourth-century shipwrecks off Yassi Ada. *Paul Merifield, John Gifford, and SS*

was selected from a number of ships sunk by Yassi Ada's reef more on the basis of its depth and condition than its date. Wrecks high on the reef had been badly damaged by wave action, and those lying only slightly deeper had settled onto nearly bare rock, with little sediment to cover and protect their wooden hulls from marine borers. The two best-preserved sites lay much deeper, about 100 m east of the reef and only 10 to 15 m apart. These two were visible as compact mounds of amphoras, 16 to 17 m long and 9 to 11 m wide, protruding from what appeared to be a thick sediment cover. Virginia Grace dated the amphora shapes tentatively for Throckmorton; one site was dated to the seventh century on the basis of its globular amphoras, and the other was thought at the time to be a century or two older (it was dated to the end of the fourth century by the excavations begun in 1967).[6]

The more recent wreck lay on a slope with its higher end about 32 m deep and its lower end at 39 m, as measured with a taut wire from a surface float on a calm day with little or no current. The older wreck was between 38 m and 42 m deep.

The seventh-century ship was chosen for primary excavation not only for its lesser depth, which allowed longer working dives, but also because Throckmorton had uncovered traces of its timbers just beneath the sand and because it was more intelligible from the outset: a stack of concreted iron anchors, lying across the cargo at its upper end, suggested the forward part of the ship pointing up the slope, toward Yassi Ada, while a mass of broken terra-cotta tiles and cooking ware suggested the galley—and, presumably, the stern—at the deeper end of the site (Fig. 1-4).[7]

[6] Bass and van Doorninck, *AJA* 75 (1971): 34–37.

[7] Frost, *Under the Mediterranean*, fig. 33 on p. 166.

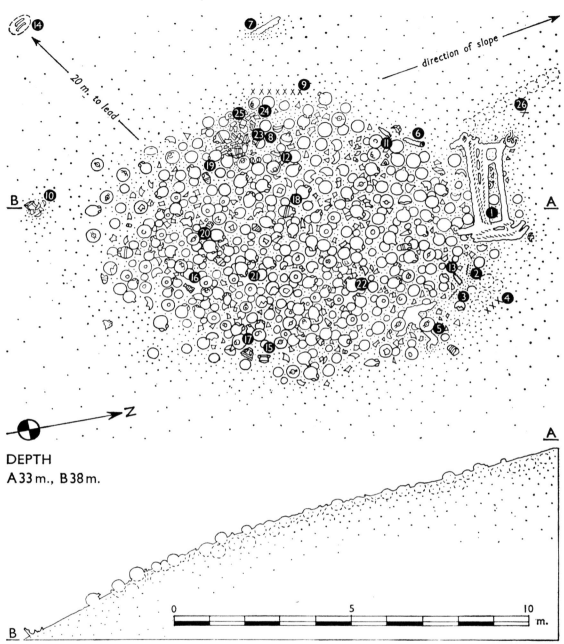

DEPTH
A 33 m., B 38 m.

F<small>IG</small>. 1-4. Sketch plan of the wreck made by Honor Frost in 1959: "(1) A pile of concreted iron; possibly anchors with movable flukes. (2) and (3) 'Steps' of concreted metal in the sand. (4) A line of probes made in the sand with a metal rod between points 3 and 4. The rod struck pottery, then (at the crosses) a substance of the consistency of waterlogged wood. (5) Small iron anchor; the kedge? (6) Tapered bronze pipe loose on the sand. Merchant ships of the period being armed, it was suggested that this pipe may have been connected with Greek fire. (7) Iron bar 1 metre long emerging from the sand at an angle of 45°. (8) Galley area containing kitchen utensils, roof and floor tiles. (9) Timber located by probes; a sample length of 40 centimetres (section 20 centimetres square) was raised; it contained remains of iron nails, and one facet bore traces of a protective covering like paint. (10) Roof-tile and sherds. (11) One of the elongated amphorae. (12) and (13) Small pieces of concreted metal emerging from the sand. (14) One of the sponge divers said he had taken two small lead bars from this area; possibly connected with the wreck. (15) Cooking-pot. (16) Pottery vase. (17)–(22) Amphorae representative of the main cargo (dated by similar specimens from a land excavation at Chios). (23) Copper baking tin. (24) and (25) Roof and floor tiles. (26) Probe striking wood at X." (From H. Frost, *Under the Mediterranean*, pp. 166–168.)

# GEOLOGY AND SEDIMENTOLOGY

## John A. Gifford

Both Yassi Ada and its reef are composed of a compact, light grey globigerinid-bearing limestone. Although a large-scale geologic map of this area is unavailable, the limestone seems to correlate with similar deposits of Upper Cretaceous age that are shown on the Regional Geologic Map of Greece (approx. 1:1,000,000) as forming the bedrock of all the Greek islands surrounding Yassi Ada (Kalolimnos, Kalymnos, and Pserimos). Erentoz notes that Upper Cretaceous deposits in south Anatolia are characteristically of Cenomanian or later age, with rudistid-bearing reef limestones that are replaced upsection by radiolarites, deep-water limestones, marls, marly limestones, and shales.[8] On Yassi Ada this limestone is extensively faulted and jointed. Hydrothermal quartz and calcite fill many of the larger fault zones; iron-rich quartz veins fill the narrower joints. Two major sets of faults and joints are evident. One trends northeast-southwest; the other is less well defined, but trends approximately north-south.

Only one other rock type was identified on the island: a breccia of angular bedrock fragments in a fine-grained reddish matrix. Most cavities and solution holes on the island are filled with this distinctive red breccia; these fillings are probably lithified residual pockets of a once more extensive Late Pleistocene soil of the *terra rossa* variety. Much of the island above the 3-m contour is covered by a few centimeters of *AC*-type rendzina soil, which is produced in the Mediterranean climate predominantly by bedrock weathering, with little organic matter being contributed.[9]

Bedrock has exerted little influence on the topography of Yassi Ada except along the present shoreline. There, differential solution has removed the more soluble limestone from around the iron-rich quartz joint fillings, leaving reticulate patterns of what, at first glance, appear to be rusted iron objects embedded in the rocky shore. The reef southwest of Yassi Ada has been shaped by the same process of differential solution, resulting in wall-like vertical outcrops of resistant quartz oriented parallel to the trends of the major sets of faults and joints. This jagged, steplike topography is especially well developed on the southeast side of the reef at depths of 10–15 m, as indicated on the sketch map of the island (Fig. 1-3).

No positive indications of subaerial weathering were observed anywhere on the reef. Features such as solution pits, associated *terra rossa* infillings, and horizontal solution notches might have delineated lower stillstands of sea level dating from the late Pleistocene-Holocene epochs; it is possible that intense abrasion and solution have removed all traces of these features or that they are presently buried under recent sediment accumulations.

During August, 1969, eighteen short cores were taken at 5-m intervals along a transect from the fourth-century wreck, then under excavation, westward to shallow water on the southeast flank of the reef. The core line and core locations are shown on the island sketch map (Fig. 1-3); cores are designated Y1-1 (nearest to the wreck) to Y1-18 (nearest to the reef).

The cores were taken with a diver-operated corer based on the design of Sanders,[10] in which a 2-m length of expendable plastic tubing is driven into the bottom with a sliding lead weight, the upper end is sealed, and the tube is pulled out of the bottom, with each core being taken with a new length of plastic tubing. The cores are transported and stored in the tubing until they are extruded for study. Few of the cores were a full 2 m long when extruded because of packing of the sediment; also, bedrock lies under less than 2 m of sediment from location Y1-12 westward to the reef.

Field analysis of the cores was limited to a description of stratigraphy; samples of the different sediment types were obtained from the even-numbered cores. Upon my return to the United States, a qualitative study of the samples was done by microscopic examination and identification of components in the size fraction coarser than 0.062 mm, followed by dissolution of a split of each sample in 10 percent hydrochloric acid and recovery of the insoluble residue for further examination.

The sediment between the wreck site and the reef may be described as a medium- to coarse-grained calcareous sand of predominantly biological origin with a small contribution of limestone fragments eroded from the island of Yassi Ada and its reef. Residues from the acid digestion of sample splits usually comprised 3–4 percent of the original sample weight and never exceeded 6 percent. Two distinct trends in sediment char-

[8] K. Erentoz, "A Brief Review of the Geology of Anatolia (Asia Minor)," *Geotectonics* 2 (1967): 92.

[9] K. W. Butzer, *Environment and Archaeology*, p. 95.

[10] J. E. Sanders, "Diver-operated Simple Hand Tools for Coring Nearshore Sands," *Journal of Sedimentary Petrology* 38 (1968): 1381–1386.

acteristics were noted in moving from location Yl-1 to Yl-18: the median grain size of each core increases towards the reef, and the percentage of nonbiogenic calcareous material (limestone fragments) also increases toward the reef. These trends are easily explained by proximity to higher energy conditions and to the source area, respectively.

Molluscan shell fragments make up the largest component of the sediment fraction of biological origin. Next in abundance are foraminiferal tests from both benthonic and planktonic species, whole micromollusc shells, and echinoderm and bryozoan skeletal fragments, with calcareous sponge spicules contributing the least to this fraction. The relatively great abundance of benthonic foraminifera and micromolluscs is a reflection of the dense growths of the marine grass *Poseidonia oceanica* that carpet the steep slopes around the wreck sites, since those organisms encrust blades of the grass.

The limestone fragments that make up the nonbiogenic calcareous fraction of the sediment are coarse and angular. As noted above, the contribution of these fragments to the total sediment mass is greatly influenced by wave activity on the reef: more waves mean more mechanical abrasion of the bedrock and therefore more limestone fragments. Of the noncalcareous sediment fraction (insoluble residue), wind-blown soil and rock particles from Yassi Ada are the largest contributors, though some quartz grains 1–3 mm in diameter are unmistakably derived from abrasion of floating pumice fragments. In addition to these sources, siliceous sponge spicules constitute a small noncalcareous biogenic contributor to the insoluble residue.

A very uniform stratigraphy was observed in cores Yl-1 through Yl-18: an upper layer, 20–40 cm thick, of dark grey, fine-grained sand smelling strongly of hydrogen sulfide (characteristic of a reducing environment resulting from decomposing *Poseidonia*); a middle layer, 60–100 cm thick, of coarse calcareous sand having less organic debris but still grey from staining by hydrogen sulfide; and a bottom layer, extending to bedrock, composed of a coarse calcareous sand of brownish grey color, with no decomposing organic debris and therefore no odor of hydrogen sulfide (indicating an oxidizing environment). Such uniform stratigraphy is not too surprising in a depositional environment where sediment influx is uniform and constant, affected principally by the annual life cycle of the *Poseidonia* beds.

Theoretically, it seems that the introduction of a shipwreck into a sedimentary environment such as that off Yassi Ada (*in situ* sediment production with little current winnowing) would alter that environment in the manner described by Dumas—the wreck itself would provide a hard substrate and even nourishment for calcareous organisms otherwise unlikely to settle on a flat, sandy bottom.[11] This change in the living faunal community (biocoenosis) would effect an observable change in the constituent composition of the faunal community's skeletal remains (thanatocoenosis) in the immediate vicinity of the wreck. This variation in sediment composition is of little practical significance, as it would probably not extend far enough from the wreck site to enable it to be located through analysis of cores.

[11] F. Dumas, *Deep-Water Archaeology*, p. 12.

FIG. 2-1. Yassi Ada viewed from the northeast in 1967, with the diving barge moored over the fourth-century wreck at the far left. *Charles R. Nicklin, Jr.,* © National Geographic Society

FIG. 2-2. The diving barge as viewed from Yassi Ada in 1967. *Bennett Jones*

# II

## THE EXCAVATION

### GEORGE F. BASS

EXCAVATION required the four summers of 1961 through 1964.[1] Many of the techniques devised during that time have since been used in other underwater excavations, and their evolution, of interest for the history of nautical archaeology, is best understood if they are described in the order in which they were developed.

### 1961 Season

A larger staff than had been used at Cape Gelidonya was required at Yassi Ada, for the greater depth meant less time per day for each excavator to work on the site.[2] The dozen members who regularly dived included three archaeology students, a physician, two draftsmen, an architect, a photographer, three experienced divers (two from the Cape Gelidonya staff), and a cinematographer, who dived in order to make a documentary film of the excavation, which seemed worthwhile since visitors cannot watch an excavation in progress under water as they can on land.[3] Most of the staff were chosen for skills other than diving ability, and several were taught to dive only after reaching Turkey. A mechanic and a cataloger did not dive.

The larger staff and greater quantity of equipment demanded a larger diving platform than the decks of the sponge boats I had used at Cape Gelidonya. We therefore positioned a rented wooden barge, about 15 m long and 6 m wide, directly over the site and pointing into the waves driven almost constantly over the reef by the *meltem*, the seasonal northwest wind (Figs. 2-1, 2-2). One barge cable ran to an anchor on the reef, another to Yassi Ada itself, and a third to a stern anchor for protection against the possibility of a southwest wind (*lodos*), which rarely blows in summer. Although Yassi Ada protected us from the full force of the prevailing *meltem*, 1961 was an unusually windy summer, and the cold air offered an unexpected hardship, especially after dives. The flat deck of the heavy barge, however, provided a steady living and working area even on the worst of days.

The otherwise annoying wind did carry out to sea—away from air intake hoses of diving compressors—the dangerous exhaust fumes of the engines mounted across the barge stern. These engines included two portable Bauer four-stage compressors and one Siebe Gorman compressor for filling tanks, a large (3-ton) road-work

---

[1] A popular, illustrated account of the excavation may be found in G. F. Bass, *Archaeology Beneath the Sea*, chaps. 4–8. The first two campaigns are described in G. F. Bass, "Underwater Archaeology: Key to History's Warehouse," *NatGeo* 124, no. 1 (July, 1963): 138–156. Brief preliminary reports by G. F. Bass appear in *National Geographic Society Research Reports* for 1961–1962, 1963, and 1964, with a fuller report of the first campaign in G. F. Bass, "Underwater Excavations at Yassi Ada: A Byzantine Shipwreck," *AA* 77 (1962): 537–564. The excavation methods are described more briefly in G. F. Bass, *Archaeology Under Water*.

[2] A diver drains the air from his breathing tanks more quickly at greater depths, and longer decompression periods are required after dives of the same length at greater depths. For a good introduction to diving, consult Conference for National Cooperation in Aquatics, *The New Science of Skin and Scuba Diving*, frequently revised, or the U.S. Navy *Diving Manual*, NAVSHIPS 250-538.

[3] A closed-circuit television system, with the camera mounted over the site and a monitor installed on the barge, was used during the excavation of the fourth-century Yassi Ada wreck in the 1974 campaign; it proved invaluable for nondiving archaeologist visitors.

FIG. 2-3. The *Sanane* in the Chuka Channel in 1961. *Robert B. Goodman*, © National Geographic Society

compressor to supply air to our air lift, and two generators to provide electricity for the underwater floodlights used in filming.

Lack of fresh water on Yassi Ada, and a population of rats that had plagued Throckmorton and Mustafa Kapkin on an earlier visit, made the island undesirable for an expedition camp that first season, and nearby villages on the unsheltered coast would have been difficult to reach by boat in bad weather. Thus, we made our expedition headquarters in two rented houses in Bodrum, although that city was a 16-mile sail from the site. Two or more staff members slept on the barge each night, along with two Bodrum sailors, as guards.

Every morning at 6:00 A.M. we sailed from Bodrum in the motor sailer *Sanane* (Fig. 2-3), captained by Kemal Aras, so that diving might begin about 8:00 A.M., when light conditions on the wreck were adequate for photography. The first dives of the morning and afternoon work shifts were often reserved for photography, since excavation had not yet disturbed the clarity of the water. Photographs were developed and enlarged each

evening in our Bodrum darkroom for use in planning work during the daily voyages to Yassi Ada.

We dived twice a day, in pairs or slightly larger groups, with normal scuba equipment.[4] The first team was generally chosen from those who had remained on the barge overnight, for they could be suited and ready to dive upon arrival of the *Sanane*. The exact time they left the surface was noted by the physician, who also signaled the end of their dive by hammering on a metal bar hanging partly in the water from the barge; in addition, at least one member of each team wore a diver's watch. The second team was prepared to dive as soon as the first surfaced and commented on what they had accomplished. For each dive the physician recorded in a permanent log the time of descent, the time of ascent (the hammered signal), the time of arrival at the decompression stop beneath the barge, and the time of surfacing.

The decompression stop was a concrete block, hung exactly 10 feet deep, to which divers could hold while decompressing to avoid the bends (decompression sickness); in 1961 few dives were long enough to require a first stage of decompression at 20 feet. Each team normally dived for 25 or 30 minutes in the morning, followed by appropriate periods of decompression.[5] Afternoon dives usually were shorter, as repetitive diving tables take into consideration residual nitrogen left in divers' systems in any given day.

Equipment was so sparse that the same neoprene rubber suit and fins were usually shared by several divers, and this sharing had to be taken into consideration when team members were assigned; two "size large" divers could seldom either dive together or follow one another into the water.

At the beginning of excavation the amphoras and other visible items on the wreck were partly obscured by sea growth (Fig. 2-4), much of which we removed with ordinary scrubbing brushes. At the same time, we began the process of labeling every object with a white plastic tag, 6 to 8 cm long, inked by marking pen with a different combination of two or three letters. Each tag was punched near one end with two holes through which we attached a "stem" of fairly stiff wire 15 cm long or more. The stem was tied to an artifact and bent so that a surface of its tag faced upwards, making its identifying

[4] See G. F. Bass, *Cape Gelidonya*, pp. 22–25; or Bass, *Archaeology Under Water*, chap. 2, for descriptions and theory of diving and equipment.

[5] Decompression times, of course, depended on which parts of the sloping site we were working on. Decompression tables used were those published in the U.S. Navy *Diving Manual*.

FIG. 2-4. Part of the cargo of amphoras before removal of sea growth in 1961. *HG and WI*

letters clearly legible to an excavator or photographer (see Fig. 5-1).

After taking preliminary measurements of the site with meter tapes, we followed the independent suggestions of Laurence T. Joline and William Wiener, Jr., by beginning to map it with plane tables (their first use for underwater surveying). The plane tables were a pair of wooden tables about 1 m square, each with three wooden legs attached by hinges so that the table could be leveled. The alidades, or sights, were lengths of pipe

about 25 cm long and 6 cm in diameter with cross-wires welded into their ends; each pipe was supported above an angle-iron base by vertical brackets (Figs. 2-5, 2-6). Everything was made in Bodrum blacksmith shops.[6]

The tables were positioned on either side of the wreck, and the distance between them was measured

[6] E. Ryan and G. F. Bass, "Underwater Surveying and Draughting: A Technique," *Antiquity* 36 (1962): 255–256, with fig. 2 and pl. XXXIII(*a*). Color photographs of the plane tables are in Bass, *NatGeo* 124, no. 1 (July, 1963): 140–141.

FIG. 2-5. One of the pair of plane tables in use in 1961. *HG*

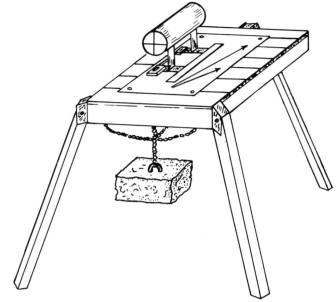

FIG. 2-6. A plane table. *LTJ and EBS*

with a meter tape. Their use required three surveyors: divers A and B at the two tables and diver C to carry a ranging rod or surveyor's pole. Each plane-table operator affixed a sheet of mat-surfaced, or "frosted," plastic drawing film to his tabletop with thumbtacks and sighting on the other table, drew a line along the straight angle-iron base of his sight with a solid graphite pencil (ordinary wooden pencils having been found to disintegrate too quickly under water); this vector was labeled accordingly. The alidades were then pointed at a base point at the top of the wreck, and the procedure was repeated. Next, diver C placed his surveying pole, buoyed by an air-filled can tied to its top, on an object —for example, the middle of amphora APQ. He noted "1—APQ" on a sheet of plastic drawing film attached to a clipboard. The plane-table operators sighted on the pole, drew their vectors, and labeled each "1" (Fig. 2-7). Then diver C moved his finger slowly up the pole until it was level with the horizontal cross-wire in one of the alidades (*always* the same one), at which time that plane-table operator signaled with his arms to stop (Fig. 2-8). Diver C read the elevation where his finger rested on the pole, recorded it on the paper after his earlier notation, and moved to the next object.

We had decided that a scale of 1:10 would be most suitable for our plans of the site, allowing us to add small artifacts with relative ease. Wiener, the architect, therefore laid the sheets of plastic over his plan on his drafting table one-tenth the distance apart that the plane tables

had been measured on the seabed, lined up the "back bearings" so that they pointed to one another and to the base point, and, using a long straightedge, extended the vectors onto his plan until they crossed. Each crossing marked the position of a surveyed point. These points usually signified only the centers of plotted amphoras and would not have produced a meaningful plan without the aid of vertical photographs taken directly above the wreck. The photographs allowed the architect to draw each amphora with its body, neck, and handles properly oriented. Larger objects, such as anchors, were plotted with several points. Smaller objects often could not be drawn on the plan until they were raised (with their identification tags still attached), cleaned, and studied in more detail.

The disadvantages of plane-table surveying under water are obvious: the method is slow (especially if one wishes to plot all corners of every tile fragment), it requires three divers at a time, it is subject to the clarity of the water (often clouded by amphora removal or actual digging), it requires supplemental photographs to be effective, and it allows great chance of potential error when an object lies more or less directly between the two tables. Further, some of our earliest bearings, or vectors, were so wildly impossible that we suspect at least one operator was more subject to nitrogen narcosis (a dulling of the brain, increasing with greater depths, caused by breathing air under pressure) than were others; the errors ceased, in time, but we were never able to explain their cause.

Nevertheless, plane tables allowed us to make an

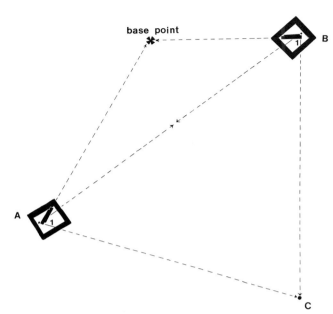

FIG. 2-7. Method of drawing vectors with plane tables. *EJR*

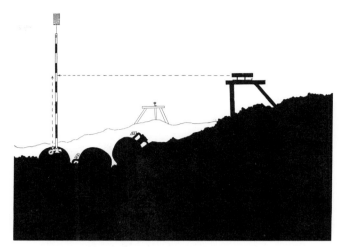

FIG. 2-8. Method of taking elevation measurements with plane tables. *EJR*

overall survey of the wreck and to begin plotting some of its components; they later proved valuable in positioning other mapping devices described below. Our system would have been better had the sights been of larger diameter and had we used an underwater light to supplement diver C's moving finger in taking elevation measurements.[7]

After we had plotted the positions of amphoras in a strip about 2 m wide across the wreck, we removed the amphoras, tagged those beneath, and repeated the process until, under three layers, we encountered wood, which we covered with sand. I hoped we might remove all of the cargo before uncovering fragile wood remains, and this trial trench was mainly to establish the presence of wood and determine where to expect it. We also hoped to learn something about the stacking arrangement of the cargo by studying the sides of the trench.

Plotted amphoras were sent to the surface at first by holding them upside down and forcing air into them from a diver's mouthpiece; most of them arrived safely on the surface, where they were collected by swimmers and towed through the waves to the barge.[8] This dramatic and photogenic procedure was often most time-

consuming, however, for many of the wine jars were full of tightly packed mud that had to be displaced by the air. Further, if an apparently sound amphora contained hairline cracks, the rapidly expanding air inside would burst it on its upward journey, showering mud and sherds back down on the wreck.

Amphoras, and later other artifacts, were carried more surely to the surface in a large wire basket used with one or more lifting balloons from Cape Gelidonya (Fig. 2-9).[9] Balloons were filled with an air hose from the barge or from a tank carried for that purpose (an early practice of filling balloons from divers' air tanks proved hazardous; more than one diver accidentally drained his entire air supply in this manner).

When a representative sample of the approximately nine hundred amphoras had been brought to Bodrum and studied, duplicates were carried to one side of the site and left on the seabed. Even this simple practice contained risks to the diver. The large, mud-filled vessels were heavy, even under water. One diver became so exhausted by his work that he could no longer draw sufficient air through his regulator. He surfaced directly, gasping for breath, without stopping for decompression. Although he eventually was able to return to the decompression stop and suffered no ill effects, I then limited the number of amphoras that any excavator could remove on a single dive to six.

Our next trench ran directly through the area of the galley called at that time (and in early publications) the "captain's cabin." For plotting the hundreds of items in this area we turned to a mapping frame suggested by

[7]Plane tables have since been used effectively elsewhere, especially on large objects, such as sarcophagi, in clear, shallow water. See P. Throckmorton and J. Bullitt, "Underwater Surveys in Greece: 1962," *Expedition* 5, no. 2 (Winter, 1963): 16–23; and P. Throckmorton et al., *Surveying in Archaeology Underwater*, pp. 1–20.

[8]This technique is illustrated in P. Throckmorton, "Thirty-three Centuries Under the Sea," *NatGeo* 117, no. 5 (May, 1960): fig. on pp. 692–693.

[9]Bass, *Cape Gelidonya*, pp. 29–30. It is most important that the bleeder valve be on top of the balloon and not on the side, as on some manufactured models.

FIG. 2-9. Using a lifting balloon to raise artifacts. *HG*

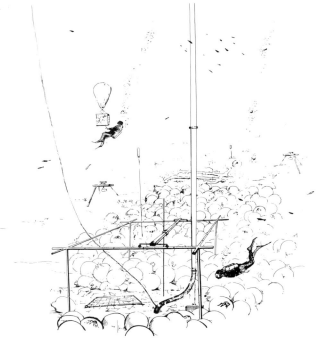

FIG. 2-10. Mapping frame, plane tables, grid, air lift, and lifting balloon used in 1961. The grid lies in the galley area of the wreck. *EJR*

Frederic Dumas and built by Claude Duthuit for use at Cape Gelidonya; it had not been used there, however, which I now regard as an error in judgment.[10]

The frame was a 5-m square of yellow-painted pipe supported at its corners by telescoping pipe legs that enabled us to level it horizontally up to 2 m high (Figs. 2-10 to 2-12). Metal pins, chained to the frame to avoid their loss, were thrust through matching holes in the telescoping sections of the legs to lock them in position after we had insured that the frame was horizontal with an ordinary carpenter's level. Metal plates under the pipe legs prevented them from sinking far into the sand.

Riding across the top of the frame was a metal beam with a pair of wheels at either end to fit on the horizontal pipe sides; it could be moved back and forth as if on tracks (Fig. 2-11). A vertical metal rod was yoked to the beam so that it could slide back and forth on the beam and, at the same time, could be raised or lowered by loosening a thumbscrew that locked it in place. The two sides of the frame on which the beam rested, the beam itself, and the vertical rod were all painted with numbered centimeter calibrations. When the beam and rod

[10]G. F. Bass and P. Throckmorton, "Excavating a Bronze Age Shipwreck," *Archaeology* 14 (1961): 81.

were positioned so that the bottom of the rod rested on an object in the wreck, therefore, it was possible to record on a sheet of frosted plastic the coordinates and elevation of that object.

We lowered the mapping frame to the wreck in sections and assembled it over the galley area (Fig. 2-10). With the plane tables we then plotted the positions of the frame's four corners, or legs, and marked them on our plans.

A most useful mapping frame could be made along the same general lines, but the model at Yassi Ada, although used throughout the summer, had serious deficiencies. It was so large and cumbersome that one diver could not move the beam evenly across the frame. Thus, two divers, one at either end of the beam, were needed for each of the moves between hundreds of measurements, and one of these divers (or even a third) had to swim continually from one side of the frame to the other in order to read and record the small numbers painted on the pipes. As with the plane tables, photographs were an essential supplement to the recorded information.

Architect Wiener suggested that mapping could be improved by a series of wire grids placed directly on the wreck. He built three frames of angle-iron and strung

FIG. 2-11. Divers using the mapping frame in 1961. *WI*

FIG. 2-12. Mapping frame in use, showing cross-beam calibrations. *HG*

each with cross-wires 20 cm apart; the frames were 1, 2, and 3 m square (Fig. 2-13). The wires were numbered in sequence across the top of the frame and lettered down the sides. (The grid wire was replaced in later years with white elastic cord that cannot be bent permanently out of position.)

The grids were laid almost randomly wherever we were working on the site. If this happened to be under the mapping frame, the position of the grid was recorded by it; if elsewhere on the wreck, the corners of the grid were plotted with the plane tables or by triangulation with meter tapes from the mapping-frame legs.

Each diver now carried a clipboard bearing a sheet of plastic drawing film marked and labeled in ink with an identical grid at one-tenth the scale of that with which he was working.[11] We hovered over the grid wires and, taking extreme care to remain over each 20-cm square in turn, made accurate scale drawings of the cargo and other remains beneath; each object was identified on its drawing by the letter combination on its plastic tag. The drawings were more accurate than photographs because a diver can avoid parallax by moving constantly to remain above what he is drawing; photographs remained helpful in providing details on the plan. Elevation measurements were taken with meter sticks from the grid wires to objects beneath (Fig. 2-14).

At first we attempted to level the grids over the sloping wreck, but this leveling increased the possibility of errors through parallax and caused an apparent diminution in the sizes of objects farther downhill than others. We then allowed the grids to rest directly on the site, although this meant that their four corners might be in four different planes. Elevations of the corners were measured with either the plane tables or the mapping frame. With these elevation measurements, Wiener was able to reconstruct, on paper, a side view of each grid, regardless of its position, showing the pattern of the grid wires. With this drawing he could correct elevation measurements taken from the grid wires on the seabed.

One further mapping experiment was made when we reached wooden hull remains under the ceramic finds of the galley. We laid a large sheet of clear plastic directly on the timbers, which we then traced at full scale with a grease pencil. The method is theoretically sound, but large sheets of flexible material are unwieldy under water, and the technique was abandoned after its first trial (Fig. 2-15).[12]

Wood remains were badly fragmented and easily moved from their original positions. In order to keep them in place until they were recorded, we pinned them to the sand by driving two or more sharpened bicycle spokes through each piece. The upper ends of the spokes had been bent at right angles to form "heads,"

[11] We used Cronaflex drafting film in 1961. Today we usually use Mylar with a mat surface.

[12] Ryan and Bass, *Antiquity* 36 (1962): 257 and pl. XXXIII(*b*).

FIG. 2-13. Artist drawing labeled amphoras through 3-m-square wire grid. *HG*

FIG. 2-14. Artist taking an elevation measurement from the grid wire. *HG*

FIG. 2-15. Tracing wood fragments at full scale on a plastic sheet. *HG*

FIG. 2-16. Excavators using the air lift to remove sediment from the site. *HG*

and one spoke on any given fragment held a plastic identification label similar to those wired to objects.

To remove sand from over the wreck, we used an air lift, which is a long, more or less vertical pipe. Air introduced toward its lower end, by means of a hose from a surface compressor, expands as it rises through the pipe, drawing water with it and creating a suction effect at the bottom of the pipe. The air lift at Yassi Ada was the larger of the two air lifts used previously at Cape Gelidonya,[13] but with two improvements. We feared that we might inadvertently suck up a small object and lose it in the air-lift discharge above, even while working carefully with two divers, one holding the flexible lower end of the tube and the other fanning sand gently toward its mouth (Fig. 2-16). At Cape Gelidonya we had sometimes placed a net bag over the lift's upper end, but Duthuit now designed a wire basket and bolted it directly to the top of the air-lift pipe. (There was no thought of running the top of the air lift above the surface, as is done in calmer waters, because wave action would have affected

[13] Bass, *Cape Gelidonya*, p. 31; and Bass, *Archaeology Under Water*, chap. 7, contain descriptions of air lifts used elsewhere. We have since abandoned heavy metal air lifts with flexible lower ends in

favor of lighter models made easily and cheaply from polyvinyl chloride (PVC) irrigation piping; in this we followed the example of M. Katzev at Kyrenia, Cyprus.

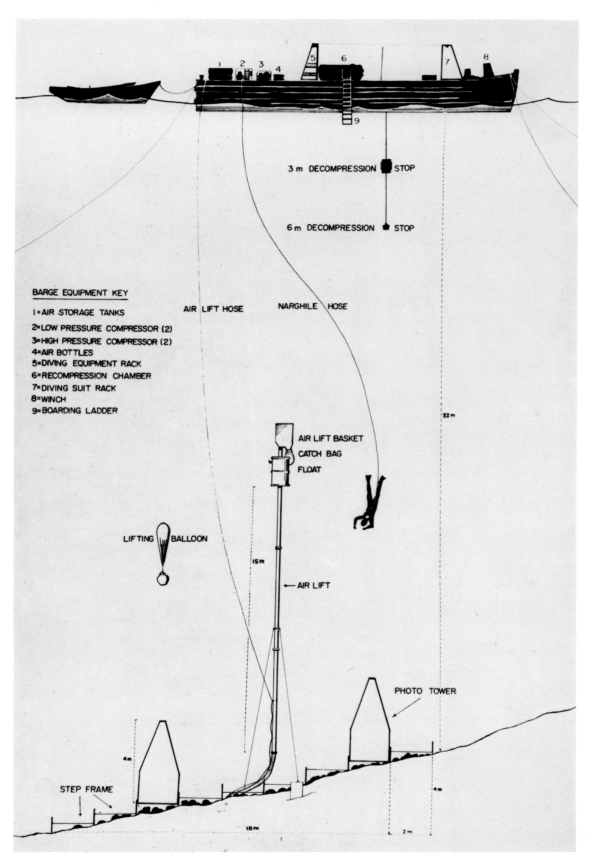

BARGE EQUIPMENT KEY

1 = AIR STORAGE TANKS
2 = LOW PRESSURE COMPRESSOR (2)
3 = HIGH PRESSURE COMPRESSOR (2)
4 = AIR BOTTLES
5 = DIVING EQUIPMENT RACK
6 = RECOMPRESSION CHAMBER
7 = DIVING SUIT RACK
8 = WINCH
9 = BOARDING LADDER

3 m DECOMPRESSION STOP

6 m DECOMPRESSION STOP

AIR LIFT HOSE          NARGHILE HOSE

32 m

AIR LIFT BASKET
CATCH BAG
FLOAT

LIFTING BALLOON

15 m

← AIR LIFT

PHOTO TOWER

STEP FRAME

4 m

4 m

18 m          2 m

Fig. 2-17. Excavation and mapping methods used in 1962. *EJR*

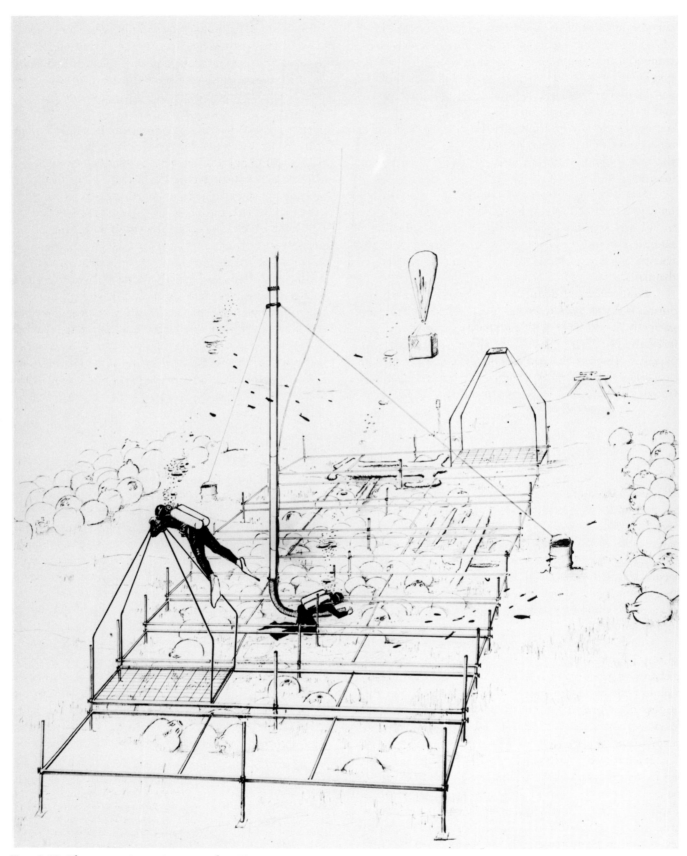

FIG. 2-18. The excavation as it appeared in 1962. *EJR*

its entire length.) The basket allowed the current to carry away most of the sand and mud through the mesh of its wire, but even relatively small objects were trapped inside and funneled down into a cloth bag hung just below (Fig. 2-17). The bag, when full, was replaced and hauled to the barge, where it was emptied on deck and its contents, usually gravel and broken shells, were searched carefully for finds. We did not like to discover objects in the bag, for we knew only the general area of the wreck that had produced them, and not their exact locations.

The other improvement, simple but most important, was to attach the air lift's guy lines high on the 20-m-tall air-lift tube, thus allowing considerable movement of the air lift's lower end over the site without any change in the positions of its anchors (rock-filled oil drums).

The hazards of diving were brought home vividly during our first season at Yassi Ada. Joline, following a perfectly timed dive with proper decompression, suffered the bends (or, possibly, an embolism) and became paralyzed below the waist. Although we had borrowed a portable recompression chamber from the National Geographic Society, we were not adequately prepared for such an emergency; we had neither an air bank nor a compressor suitable for supplying pressure and ventilation to the chamber on the barge. Additionally, Dr. Charles Fries had just returned to the United States, but we had all decided to continue excavation for a few weeks without a physician. Joline was taken to Bodrum, where a similar portable chamber had been left in a customs warehouse the previous year by Peter Throckmorton. He was treated in that chamber for eight hours, with air supplied through a hose from the compressor of a local sponge boat moored at the Bodrum dock. Collapsible, portable chambers of this type cannot, however, withstand the necessary pressures needed for treating such serious cases of diving illness, and no improvement was noted in the patient. Meanwhile, arrangements had been made by telephone with the U.S. consulate in Izmir for a small military plane. Joline was driven through the night to the Izmir airport and then flown to Istanbul, where a Turkish navy speedboat was waiting to rush him to a large chamber at the Turkish Navy Diving School. After 38 hours in this chamber, Joline was hospitalized for several days. His recovery was never complete, some weakness remaining still in one leg.[14]

## 1962 Season

All of the mapping methods devised in 1961 proved useful, and most have seen service on later underwater excavations. None, however, seemed suitable for making a plan of the hull remains that had begun to appear in 1961, a plan that would show nail holes and cuttings as accurately as if made on land. During the months between the 1961 and 1962 diving campaigns, therefore, Joline and I considered numerous possibilities for a new approach.

Controlled photographs seemed to be the basis for all our ideas. Aids were needed to make the taking of pictures as precise and automatic as possible; even with a plumb line and bubble level attached to his camera and targets placed on the wreck beneath him, it is difficult for a swimming photographer to take pictures with the accuracy we required.

If a wreck lies on a slope of 1:4, useful pictures cannot be taken from a horizontal plane, for the camera will be nearly 10 m above one end of the wreck and only 3 m above the other. Ideally, then, we would have photographed the Byzantine wreck with a series of pictures taken from a plane parallel to the slope, with the lens and film of the camera always parallel to the wreck.

First we considered a series of taut wires, from which a camera could be suspended at the proper angle, running the length of the wreck at a fixed distance above it. Practical considerations prohibited our ideal concept, for we also wanted a grid in each photograph for control; the physical difficulty of positioning such a grid parallel to both the plane of the film and that of the wreck seemed to be too great. It seemed more sensible to build the grid into the base of a photographic tower that would insure that the film and the grid, at least, were always parallel. Experience in 1961 had showed that pictures encompassing a 3-m-square grid were too distant and lacked necessary detail, whereas 2-m-square areas were photographed with acceptable clarity. Thus, we imagined a photographic tower with a 2-m-square base; the

[14] Bass, *Archaeology Beneath the Sea*, pp. 87–91; Bass, *NatGeo* 124, no. 1 (1963): 153–156. Because of this accident we began in 1962 to use a new diving schedule suggested by a leading hyperbaric specialist in the U.S. Navy: we always read the diving tables for the next deeper depth and the next longer time than that required by the tables and decompress accordingly. In well over five thousand decompression dives since then, we have not suffered another case of the bends.

focal length of the lens in our Roleimarin camera required the tower to be just over 4 m high for complete coverage of its grid base.

We wanted to keep the wire grid as close to the wreck as possible to avoid parallax, and ideally we could have done so by erecting tracks, 2 m apart, directly on the wreck for movement of the tower. Again, practical considerations ruled out this idea, although theoretically it would have been the best solution to the problem.

We compromised and decided that our pictures would be taken vertically, using the simplest angle to control; the relatively small differences in scale of objects higher or lower on the slope in any 2-m-square area could be corrected easily in drawing plans from the photographs. We realized that the forthcoming plan would be foreshortened, but this is true of most archaeological plans.

To insure verticality of photographs, and to enable the photographer to return precisely and repeatedly to the same areas during the course of excavation, we planned for the tower to rest on horizontal metal frames 2 m wide and 6 m long, each supported by pipe legs. Nine of these frames, running up the slope like giant steps, we believed, would cover the site almost completely (Figs. 2-17, 2-18).

Final construction of the frames was dictated by the materials we could afford and by those readily available in Bodrum. Each frame, or step,[15] was made of angle iron, 2 cm on a side, with six short, vertical pipe collars, 4 cm in diameter, welded outside its long sides (one at each corner and one in each center). Each collar was pierced and threaded for a simple thumbscrew.

The nine steps were lowered from the barge to the seabed upon our return to Yassi Ada in 1962, and the lowest was positioned on the site. Six pipe legs, each 2 m tall, were dropped through the pipe collars, within which they fit fairly snugly. The upslope edge of the step was allowed to rest directly on the ancient cargo and was leveled by two divers with an ordinary carpenter's level;[16] the thumbscrews were then tightened to lock the step in place. Next, the two short sides of the step were leveled and locked into position, leaving the second long side to be leveled by minor adjustments. The second

step was then dropped into position, its upslope edge again resting directly on the wreck and its downslope edge sharing the three upper legs of the lowest step. It was leveled and the procedure was then repeated on up the slope.

Following this simple procedure exactly is of the utmost importance in erecting the scaffolding. Using the same steps on the fourth-century wreck in 1967, we forgot our own experiences and erected the entire scaffolding in a roughly level position before making final adjustments. By then the nine steps were bonded as one, and it proved impossible to move any of them without jamming the legs, which became so frozen in place that we could neither move nor remove them, even with a sledgehammer. After breaking several of the welded collars, we abandoned attempts to level or dismantle the framework, which still rests on the seabed.

There was also a minor flaw in the design of the steps. The collars had to be attached outside each step to allow the photo tower to be slid from end to end without being obstructed by the pipe legs. Thus, the steps were separated by 4 cm (the diameter of the collars), which had to be taken into consideration in using the photographs.

To conserve precious diving time, we constructed two photo towers, one usually left near the shallower end of the site and the other lower down. The base of each tower was an angle-iron square, drilled and strung with wires 20 cm apart. The wires, as in 1961, were numbered across the top of the square and lettered down the sides. The tower itself was formed of four tall rods of soft metal (concrete reinforcing rods), bent so that they would not appear in the photographs. Their tops were bolted to a smaller angle-iron square, about 30 cm on a side, that enclosed a flat wooden top in which was cut a hole to receive the face of the Roleimarin camera. Taking pictures from the top of the tower proved to be remarkably simple, for the camera fit in only one position, the distance from the camera to the grid was always the same, the light level changed little throughout the day, and the stability of the tower allowed longer exposures than could be taken by a swimming diver, with a resultant greater depth of field. Each step of the scaffolding below had been divided into three equal squares by wooden strips bolted beneath, and thus it was also simple to position the tower, whenever desired, directly over any of the twenty-seven 2-m-square areas into which the site was now divided. The steps were numbered 1 through 9 from top to bottom; the 2-m squares of each step were labeled A, B, and C, from left to right when facing upslope (Fig. 2-19).

---

[15] In all staff discussion, and in prior publications, we have referred to these tools as frames; because of possible confusion in a book of this sort with the meaning of the word *frame* in ship construction, I have tried to refer to them as steps wherever possible—a practice that should be continued.

[16] For another method of leveling under water, see P. Merifield and D. Rosencrantz, *Limnology and Oceanography* 11, no. 3 (1966): 408–409; D. M. Rosencrantz, "Underwater Photography and Photogrammetry," in *Photography in Archaeological Research*, ed. E. Harp, pp. 280–283; and Bass, *Archaeology Under Water*, figs. 25a and b.

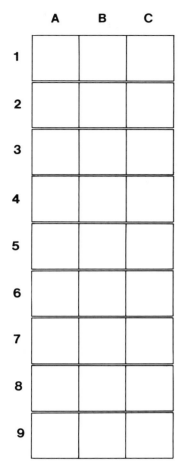

FIG. 2-19. Plan of the step frames as first set up in 1962.

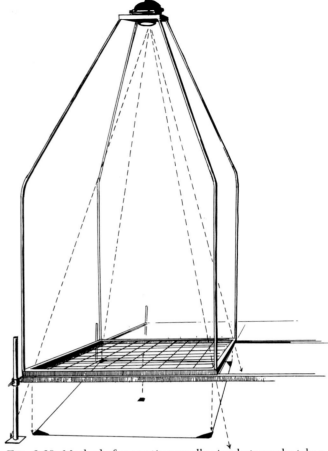

FIG. 2-20. Method of correcting parallax in photographs taken from the camera tower. The triangles mark true grid corners on the seabed. *EJR*

The towers, as constructed, were far from perfect. Because their light metal rods proved to be too flimsy, allowing them to sway at first, we stiffened them by tying air-filled gasoline cans above their tops by pairs of wires. Photographers had to place their heads between the wires, however, and one became entangled, with his air-intake hose pinched, until he was freed by an alert diving partner.[17]

Photographs taken from the towers could not, of course, be traced directly onto site plans, even if they were enlarged and printed at the same 1:10 scale. Three factors were involved:

1. *Pincushion distortion*. This "pillowing" effect, causing the sides of the squares to bulge outwards in pho-

tographs, was caused by the difference between the index of refraction of water and that of air.[18]

2. *Parallax*. Except for objects in the centers of photographs, the objects on the seabed did not appear in a true relationship to the grid wires above them.

3. *Scale*. Objects such as amphoras appeared to be smaller if they lay downslope, being farther from the camera.

Corrections were made by insuring that the *true* corners of each 2-m-square area of the wreck appeared in all photographs (Fig. 2-20). Plumb lines were dropped from the four corners of the grids, and white markers were placed where the plumbs hit the seabed. These markers were joined on photographs by pencil lines that, although forming irregular quadrangles, in fact de-

---

[17] An improved tower of angle-iron, with air-filled floats built into its top, was used with success in 1967; see G. F. Bass, "New Tools for Undersea Archaeology," *NatGeo* 134, no. 3 (September, 1968): figs. on pp. 410 and 412. The recent development of a 15-mm lens for underwater use, allowing the photographer to cover large areas from a short distance, has made photo towers obsolete.

[18] This distortion was overcome in later years by the use of correction lenses designed by A. Ivanoff; see R. Karius, P. Merifield, and D. Rosencrantz, "Stereo Mapping of Underwater Terrain from a Submarine," in *Ocean Science and Engineering*, p. 1169.

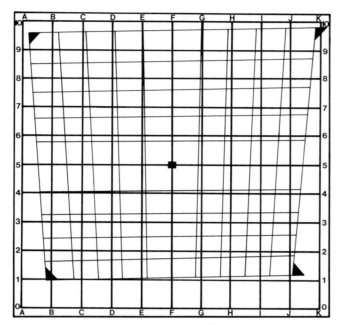

FIG. 2-21. Method of correcting parallax and scale distortion on grid photographs. *EJR*

FIG. 2-22. Elevation measurement being taken from the grid base of the photo tower resting on a step frame. *JS*

lineated the true boundaries of the square seabed areas. Each side of a resultant quadrangle was next divided into ten equal lengths, which were joined by pencil lines (Fig. 2-21). Using these new grid lines (which were seldom parallel) as guides, it was possible to draw the material in the photograph on a fresh, rectangular 1:10 grid, and this drawing could be traced onto the plan. The method would not have produced accurate results had there been deep depressions or high rises within squares, but the slope of the seabed was fairly regular.

Elevation measurements were taken with plumb lines from the wires of the photo towers' gridded bases; elevations of the steps on which the bases rested were known from a datum plane (Fig. 2-22).

The step-frame system of mapping, as we called it, worked remarkably well. Not only did mapping progress smoothly, but the steps offered excavators support as they worked on delicate hull fragments. Generally we removed our fins on the site and moved over it by walking on the steps,[19] for even the movement of a diver swimming some distance above the wreck was capable of creating currents that moved wood pieces before they were pinned into place by the thousand-odd bicycle spokes that we used during the summer. Furthermore, pairs of divers would be assigned to specific 2-m squares,

responsible for their excavation day after day. Most importantly, we could discuss work in terms of the squares ("Clear area 3B for photography"; "Move the air lift into area 8C"; and so on).

The air lift was used with decreasing frequency. Even its flexible lower end, moved carefully over the site, endangered the hull. Excavators became adept at lying on the steps and fanning sand downslope by hand. Fortunately, the current usually ran in approximately the same direction, carrying much overburden completely away from the site. Mounds of fanned sand, when too heavy to move easily by hand, were finally removed with the air lift.

Work was further facilitated by more efficient diving methods and improvements to the diving barge. Much of the diving in 1962 was by means of "hookah" or "narghile" equipment:[20] air was provided to divers' regulators through hoses from two low-pressure compressors, built in Istanbul under Duthuit's direction, mounted on the barge. Hookah divers were not limited by the amount of air in tanks, but simply by the lengths of time they could reasonably decompress. A small, rock-filled metal drum with vertical handles welded to its sides was hung below the barge to provide a more comfortable decompression stage; a concrete block ten feet below this

---

[19] We now consider working at this depth without fins to be a potentially dangerous practice and have discontinued it in normal circumstances.

[20] Bass, *Cape Gelidonya*, pp. 24–25; Bass, *Archaeology Under Water*, chap. 2.

FIG. 2-23. Diver at the decompression stop preparing a sketch to be raised to the barge. *HG*

served as the now necessary twenty-foot decompression stop, the result of longer dives.

In order that time between dives not be wasted by these longer periods of decompression, two new procedures were implemented:

1. A writing board and pencil were hung near the main decompression stop by a string attached to a bell on the barge. As soon as divers arrived at the stop, they wrote briefly what they had accomplished on their dive and rang the bell by pulling the string. The message, hauled to the surface, was relayed immediately to the next team, already prepared to dive (Fig. 2-23).

2. If the next team planned also to dive with the hookah, the decompressing divers removed their hookah harnesses and allowed their hoses and regulators to be hauled up to the barge while they continued decompressing by breathing from shorter hoses lowered to the decompression stop. The procedure was necessitated by our having only two lengths of hose capable of reaching the wreck from the barge.

Such practices might seem too minor to warrant mention, but they allowed us almost to double daily work time on the wreck with a minimum of expense.

Another seemingly unimportant improvement was the design and construction of a comfortable boarding ladder by Joline, who also designed equipment racks that allowed greater work space on the barge. Such things have an incalculable effect on the morale of divers who spend long hours daily in cramped quarters, climbing often into and out of the water. Finally, the barge now held a rigid, one-man Galeazzi recompression chamber, luckily never needed on this project.[21]

Certainly the greatest increase in efficiency in 1962 came from the decision to build a camp on Yassi Ada for our larger staff. Poison held the rat population under control; remaining rodents did not try to enter our tents. We also constructed a large dormitory/workhouse by laying a concrete floor 5 m wide by 15 m long, building a stone wall 2 m high along one long side to block out the constant northwest wind, and enclosing the other three sides with screen wire; the roof was of canvas. A smaller building similarly constructed served as kitchen and darkroom. The entire staff was now only minutes from the site, avoiding the four hours a day spent previously in commuting from Bodrum.

During the course of excavation we had tagged and plotted the positions of hundreds of pieces of amorphous concretion. In camp we cut several of these open with a hacksaw to reveal what was inside: sometimes it was only rock, but more often it was the residue of a corroded iron object.

The ability to cast replicas of disintegrated iron objects by cutting concretions into open sections, washing out the small amounts of iron oxide, and filling the resultant molds with plaster was already known to marine archaeologists.[22] We tested the method on small concretion molds of nails and tacks.[23] The brittle nature and stark appearance of plaster of Paris (see Fig. 3-30, Fe 69) made it a poor casting material, however, especially for extremely thin objects, so we decided to seek a better casting method.

At the end of the summer, the site was covered with a thin layer of sand for protection; we repeated this procedure each year.

[21] We have made a practice of having double-lock chambers on our deep-diving projects since 1967. Such a chamber allowed successful treatment of a diver stricken by an embolism in 1969; Bass, *Archaeology Beneath the Sea*, pp. 185–191.

[22] G. Barnier in *Atti del II Congresso Internazionale di Archeologia Sottomarina, Albenga, 1958*, pp. 310–314; H. Frost, *Under the Mediterranean*, pp. 59–60.

[23] Bass, *NatGeo* 124, no. 1 (1963): 142.

## 1963 Season

The third campaign lasted from mid-June until the beginning of September, with staff members diving in pairs twice a day for six days of each week. Each dive normally lasted twenty-five minutes in the morning and eighteen in the afternoon.

Excavators often dived with hoses running to their regulators (hookah or narghile diving) as in 1962, but each now wore at the same time a small air tank with its own one-hose regulator; in one case this spare air supply allowed a new diver to avoid potential danger when he lost his normal air supply through a loose hose clamp. Additional air for such emergencies was supplied on the seabed by extra tanks and regulators placed on the wreck each day and by hoses and regulators lowered from air tanks on the barge to the 20- and 10-foot decompression stops when diving was in progress.

Excavation in 1962 had showed us that the scaffolding of step frames did not cover large parts of the starboard side of the wreck that had been buried when the steps were installed. Thus, we moved several of the lower steps 3 m to the right, a distance chosen mostly because of the spacing between the pipe collars in which the steps' legs were placed. The shifted 2-m squares, in their new positions, were relabeled *A'*, *B'*, and *C'* (Fig. 2-24). At the same time, a new mapping technique was tried.

Mapping under water by photogrammetry, the art of the aerial surveyor, had been suggested independently by Duthuit in 1960 at Cape Gelidonya and by Wiener in 1961. Now, anxious to save still more valuable work time on the seabed, we began our first attempts at photogrammetry, although mapping by the step frames continued to be effective. We later learned that similar experiments were being conducted by the U.S. Navy, but at the time we received neither encouragement nor advice from the cartographic departments and aerial survey firms we contacted and were left to devise our own methods of duplicating airborne techniques beneath the sea.

I knew only that aerial surveys were made by an airplane flying in a level path over the ground, taking sequential and overlapping photographs to form stereo pairs that could be used to produce three-dimensional maps. It seemed to me that the flight of an airplane could be imitated by sliding a camera along a horizontal bar over a shipwreck, but I depended on new expedition members Julian Whittlesey and Donald Rosencrantz to develop that concept into a working system.

We positioned a horizontal bar about 6 m above the

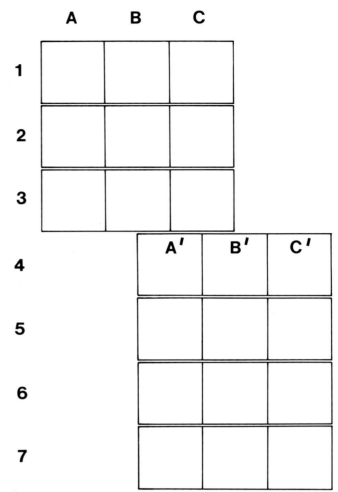

FIG. 2-24. Plan of the step frames as set up in 1963.

Byzantine wreck, using concrete blocks as anchors and air-filled cans as buoys for the guy wires that passed through pipe valves just below the bar; the valves were tightened on the wires when the bar had been leveled, holding it securely in place (Fig. 2-25). Three metal rods with lead weights screwed to their threaded ends were attached to a ring around the glass plate of a Rolleimarin camera; by screwing the weights in and out while viewing a bull's-eye level on the camera, a diver could balance the camera so that it hung vertically from the bar on gimbals made from hinges (Fig. 2-26). He then slid the camera from one side of the wreck to the other, taking a picture whenever the top of the gimbals reached one of a sequence of marks filed into the bar 1.20 m apart; a cable release for the camera, made from a Jeep choke cable, allowed sufficient exposure for great depth of field.

The resultant overlapping pictures formed a series

FIG. 2-25. Method of stereophotogrammetric mapping used in 1963. *EJR*

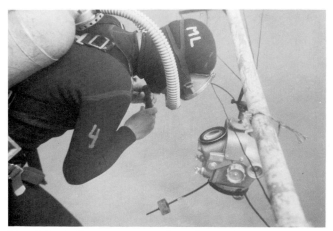

FIG. 2-26. Rolleimarin camera hung by gimbals from the horizontal bar for stereo mapping. *DMR*

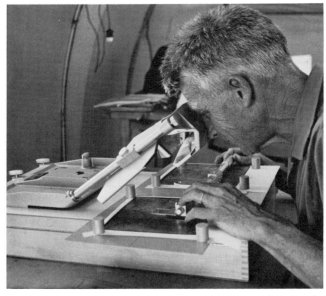

FIG. 2-27. Measuring parallax on a pair of stereo photographs under a Zeiss stereoscope. *GFB*

FIG. 2-28. Trench wall showing depth of burial of amphoras farther forward on the wreck site than the highest step frame. *JS*

FIG. 2-29. Hull fragments being carried to the surface in a wire basket. *MK*

of stereo pairs that gave a three-dimensional image of the wreck when viewed through a Zeiss stereoscope (Fig. 2-27). More important for mapping, it was possible to measure the parallax in stereo pairs with a micrometer and to calculate the distance from the camera to any object by using the formula $(f \times b) \div p = H$, where $f$ is the focal length of the lens, $b$ (base) the distance between camera positions on the bar, $p$ the parallax, and $H$ (height) the distance from camera to object. Thus, a three-dimensional map could be produced without the time-consuming elevation measurements taken from

grid wires with plumb lines in previous years; a few such measurements were necessary, however, as control data for proper analyses of the stereophotographs. A slight distortion in the photographs, caused by the difference between the indices of refraction of water outside the camera and air inside the camera, prevented accurate results in 1963; the problem was overcome in 1964.

We had thought at the beginning of the summer

FIG. 2-30. Hull fragments being placed into a holding tank filled with water on Yassi Ada.

that the excavation of the wreck was nearly complete. We discovered, however, that the bow cargo extended much farther and deeper under the sand than anticipated (Fig. 2-28). Most of the 1963 campaign, therefore, was devoted to cutting with knives through sand tightly impacted with seaweed roots and digging deeper with the air lift. No wood was preserved here, for the bow had originally been held out of the protective sand by a rock outcrop and had been devoured by teredos (shipworms).

Oinochoai, cooking pots, lamps, coins, and lead fishing weights continued to appear in the galley area near the stern and were carried to the surface, as in previous summers, by hand. Small fragments of wood from completely excavated areas were also raised by hand, and larger pieces were, at first, hauled slowly to the barge with ropes. The latter method, however, sometimes caused damage to fragile hull remains. A 6-m-long wire basket, long enough to hold the largest timber fragments, was then fabricated. The basket had three handles on either side, and four or six divers, wearing tennis shoes instead of fins, placed timbers into the basket and walked with it up the slope to a beach on Yassi Ada about 150 m away (Fig. 2-29). To prevent the timbers from drying out, they were stored on the island in a long trough made of oil drums cut in half, welded together, and lined with tar (Fig. 2-30).

Casting of corroded iron objects in their natural molds of marine concretion continued with improvements (see chapter 11). Experiments were made with a number of substitutes for plaster of Paris, with best

FIG. 2-31. Mending tiles from the ship's galley roof. *DMR*

results obtained from polysulfide rubber compounds (Smooth-On Flexible Mold Compound No. 100 for small, thin objects, and No. 300 for larger objects). Not only did casts with these compounds preserve the finest details of the molds, but a thin layer of iron oxide adhering to the surface of each cast also gave them the appearance of actual iron objects.[24]

An electric rotary saw with a diamond-edged blade greatly speeded the cutting of concretions. Still, because of the time needed to cut open concretions, remove the residue of iron oxide, prepare cardboard shims to compensate for the amount of each mold destroyed by the thickness of the saw blade, glue the shims in place like gaskets, pour the rubber compound, and, finally, break away the concretions from their casts, few artifacts were reconstructed in 1963.

By the end of the summer, most of the site had been cleared of sand, and van Doorninck was kept increasingly busy in the workhouse on Yassi Ada, fitting together and recording fragments of the wooden hull, while Ann Bass mended roof tiles (Fig. 2-31).

[24] L. T. Joline and F. H. van Doorninck, Jr., were responsible for the development of our casting techniques. Casts made with Smooth-On have proved to be short-lived, however, and the reader is referred to D. L. Hamilton, *Conservation of Metal Objects from Underwater Sites: A Study in Methods*, chap. 6, for improved methods.

## *1964 Season*

The fourth and final campaign on the Byzantine ship-wreck was devoted largely to raising the remaining hull fragments; making a final search for artifacts; examining the amphora dump for possibly important sherds; casting scores of iron concretions;[25] improving the technique of photogrammetric mapping with corrective lenses;[26] and completing object catalogs, drawings, and photographs. Wood was stored for further study in a concrete water tank in the Bodrum castle, where a museum has since been built to display our finds.

At the same time, experiments were made with the *Asherah*, the first submarine designed and built for archaeology, and with methods of mapping photogrammetrically from it.[27] These experiments were conducted mostly on the slightly deeper fourth-century wreck at Yassi Ada and will be described in the publication of its subsequent excavation. The submarine's surface tender *Virazon*, lent by the U.S. Office of Naval Research, was used on the seventh-century site, however, to lift heavy concretions of iron anchors.

By this time, most of the compressors and generators used in 1961 had been replaced by larger, more permanent equipment.

At the conclusion of excavation, a vast cavity lined on either side with discarded amphoras was the only trace of the Byzantine shipwreck; the step frames remained in place until 1967, when they were removed to the fourth-century wreck nearby. Dives in 1974 revealed that the cavity had scarcely changed in a decade, remaining a light sandy patch in the midst of dark sea growth.

## *1979–1980*

Conservation, photography, and drawing of artifacts excavated between 1961 and 1964 were all accomplished during academic summer vacations, often under relatively primitive camp conditions. The formation of the Institute of Nautical Archaeology since then, however, has allowed a permanent INA presence in Turkey, where van Doorninck and I have alternated academic years, along with other institute staff members, at the Bodrum Museum. Although most of the 1979 and 1980 stays in Turkey were devoted to the study of more recently excavated materials from other wrecks, the opportunity to improve this study of the Yassi Ada Byzantine ship was not lost.

Van Doorninck made a last, thorough search through all Yassi Ada pottery and metal fragments in the museum storerooms and was able to find a few additional joins which led to a better understanding of some of the shapes, with resultant new drawings, photographs, and additions to catalogs.

Don L. Hamilton in the summer of 1979 began an institute program of artifact conservation in the Bodrum Museum laboratory, a program which was continued through the spring of 1980 by Robyn Woodward and still later by B. J. van Doorninck and Sheila Matthews. Cleaning of metal vessels and weights from Yassi Ada brought out previously invisible details which required new drawings and photographs.

Donald A. Frey, during this time, rephotographed some of the Byzantine shipwreck artifacts. Using backlighting through a curved, translucent background, he was able to produce crisp object photographs without shadows, and these new pictures have replaced many more old-fashioned prints already mounted for this book (Fig. 2-32). Unfortunately, time did not allow Frey to rephotograph more.

These years led also to the institute's outright purchase of the *Virazon*, which had been only borrowed in 1964. We outfitted the vessel in 1980 with double-lock recompression chamber, darkroom, drafting table, and all necessary diving compressors and equipment, making it possible, for the first time, to visit Yassi Ada or other deep sites for just a few dives without spending weeks preparing a diving barge or camp. Thus, after we learned on excavations subsequent to our work at Yassi Ada that organic remains can be extracted from mud-filled amphoras, I was able to send an institute team

---

[25] M. L. Katzev and F. H. van Doorninck, Jr., "Replicas of Iron Tools from a Byzantine Shipwreck," *Studies in Conservation* 11, no. 3 (1966): 133–142.

[26] Karius, Merifield, and Rosencrantz, *Ocean Science and Engineering*, p. 1169. See also Rosencrantz, *supra* n. 16.

[27] G. F. Bass and D. M. Rosencrantz, *A Diversified Program for the Study of Shallow Water Searching and Mapping Techniques*; G. F. Bass and D. M. Rosencrantz, "Submersibles in Underwater Search and Photogrammetric Mapping," in *Underwater Archaeology: A Nascent Discipline*, pp. 271–283; and G. F. Bass and D. M. Rosencrantz, "The Asherah—A Pioneer in Search of the Past," in *Submersibles and Their Use in Oceanography and Ocean Engineering*, ed. R. A. Geyer, pp. 335–351.

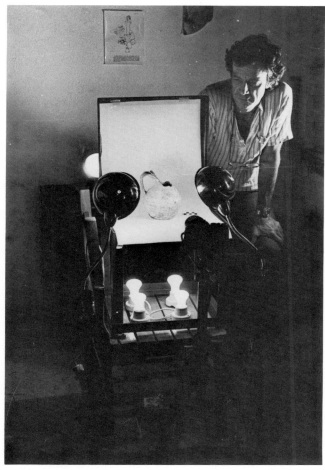

FIG. 2-32. Method of rephotographing objects in 1980. *DAF*

back to Yassi Ada in late 1980 to raise a dozen or more amphoras and inspect their contents. This book, ready for the printer, was delayed while I awaited telephoned results from Turkey.

In these latest dives, Donald Frey, Robin Piercy, and Tufan Turanli found hundreds of amphoras just as they had been discarded on the side of the excavated area sixteen and more years earlier. Only amphoras of the larger, globular type remained, as all smaller amphoras had been easily raised and cleaned during the excavation. Sixteen large amphoras were lifted intact to the surface, where their mud and sand contents were first screened and then searched for seeds by flotation, using methods devised for us by Donald H. Keith several summers earlier.

Piercy reported that nine of the amphoras contained grape seeds. Other amphoras contained, additionally, olive pits, which may represent contamination from the careless habits of divers and others who ate meals on decks directly over the wreck in 1961 and earlier. Piercy noted other seeds which he felt were ancient but which he could not identify. Rather than delay this overdue book by additional months while awaiting laboratory analyses, I prefer to state that forthcoming seed identifications will be submitted to the *International Journal of Nautical Archaeology* for publication. A very small sampling of the organic material was studied at Texas A&M University, with results given in Appendix E.

## Efficiency and Costs

For consideration in planning future underwater excavations, van Doorninck made an efficiency study based on our diving logs and field notebooks. This study revealed that we had spent a total of 1,244 man-hours on the seabed in 3,533 individual dives on 211 diving days during four summers. Total *necessary* work time (discounting hours spent making a film, taking publicity photographs, doing unnecessary tagging, taking unnecessary elevation measurements, and the like) was 1,083 hours and 46 minutes.

Total necessary work time was spent as follows: 204 hours, 24 minutes, or 19 percent of the total, making site plans; 693 hours, 34 minutes, or 64 percent of the total, removing sand, shell, and other debris (469 hours, 51 minutes sweeping sand by hand, and 223 hours, 43 minutes using the air lift); 115 hours, 21 minutes, or 11 per-

cent of the total, removing amphoras, anchors, ballast stones, and small finds; 41 hours, 10 minutes, or 4 percent of the total, raising hull remains; and 23 hours, 40 minutes or 2 percent of the total, on other necessary activities, such as anchoring the barge, pinning wood to the seabed, and covering the site with sand at the end of each campaign.[28]

Although the average number of individual dives per day over the four years was 16.7, as many as 30 indi-

[28] This efficiency study was used to great advantage in planning our next excavation at Yassi Ada; Bass, *Archaeology Beneath the Sea*, chap. 10; Bass, *Archaeology Under Water*, pp. 147–148; Bass, *NatGeo* 134, no. 3 (1968): 402–422; G. F. Bass, "The Turkish Aegean: Proving Ground for Underwater Archaeology," *Expedition* 10, no. 3 (Spring, 1968): 3–10; G. F. Bass and M. L. Katzev, "Tools for Underwater Archaeology," *Archaeology* 21 (1968): 165–173.

vidual dives were made on some days, and on several occasions 14 group dives (comprising 2 or more individual dives) were made on a single day. July and August, 1963, with twenty-seven and twenty-five diving days, respectively, produced a total of 1,034 individual dives, giving an average of 20 individual dives per day.

The total cost of the excavation was approximately ninety-five thousand dollars; most staff members, including the director, were unsalaried students or volunteer technicians. Financial reports for the first two campaigns indicate how funds were spent throughout the four years.

### 1961 FINANCIAL REPORT

Expenses for Personnel:

| | |
|---|---|
| Salaries (one diver, doctor, mechanic, cook, houseboy, guard) | $2,556.61 |
| Travel (American personnel, $300 to $800 each; European personnel, $200 each) | 4,126.92 |
| Food ($5 or less per person per week) | 1,083.46 |
| Houses (rent and furnishings) | 792.72 |
| Hotels | 134.38 |
| Communications (telegrams, letters, overseas telephone calls) | 329.02 |
| | $9,023.11 |

Expedition Expenses:

| | |
|---|---|
| Equipment (for diving, mooring, drafting, object photography) | $3,530.06 |
| Hire of boats and Turkish crew | 2,031.78 |
| Fuel and repairs for engines | 1,158.60 |
| Shipping | 731.82 |
| Customs (duty and broker's fees) | 598.06 |
| Barge (rent, towing, repairs) | 606.16 |
| Photo developing (three sets of black-and-white photographs in Turkey) | 200.00 |
| Miscellaneous (medicine, Jeep insurance, | |

| | |
|---|---|
| archaeological books, etc.) | 342.72 |
| | $9,199.20 |
| 1961 Total | $18,222.31 |

### 1962 FINANCIAL REPORT

Expenses for Personnel:

| | |
|---|---|
| Salaries (one senior diver, doctor, mechanic, cook, houseboy) | $4,371.27 |
| Travel (American personnel, $300 to $800 each; European personnel, $200 each) | 7,245.47 |
| Food ($5 or less per person per week) | 1,493.47 |
| Insurance for all divers | 1,478.52 |
| Housing and camping facilities | 850.24 |
| Hotels | 453.58 |
| Communications (telegrams, letters, overseas calls) | 298.17 |
| | $16,190.72 |

Expedition Expenses:

| | |
|---|---|
| Equipment (for diving, mooring, drafting and object photography) | $6,648.67 |
| Hire of boats, barge, and Turkish crew | 1,772.27 |
| Fuel and repair for engines | 762.99 |
| Shipping | 221.43 |
| Customs (duty and broker's fees) | 456.29 |
| Miscellaneous (medicine, photo developing, archaeological books, Jeep insurance) | 384.93 |
| | .$10,246.58 |
| 1962 Total | $26,437.30 |

Total expenses in 1963 were $25,754. Costs of the 1964 campaign were about the same, but they can only be estimated from the total cost of that summer's work, which included unrelated, but expensive, experiments with the submarine *Asherah*.

## In Retrospect

Most of this chapter was written in 1969, with supplementary information added over the years. A retrospective view from 1981 is useful. The Byzantine shipwreck at Yassi Ada was the first wreck with substantial hull remains to have been excavated completely on the seabed.[29] In future years, many or all of the techniques used then will seem as old-fashioned as the techniques

of early land excavations seem today; some, as noted, are already out of date. Three decisions made on the project might be questioned, however, even by contemporary standards.

First, we did not raise hundreds of duplicate amphoras, after inspecting them on the seabed, because no adequate storage space remained in the Bodrum Museum and because raising them would have required an additional campaign of some expense. We thought them safe under water, where they had remained for thirteen centuries, and this proved to be the case still in 1980,

[29] Cape Gelidonya was the first shipwreck site to have been excavated in its entirety on the seabed, but that site represented more a sunken cargo than an actual wreck, as almost all traces of wood had disappeared.

despite rumors that some or all had been removed and sold by local divers. Had we raised all of the amphoras during the course of excavation, we might have noted more of the graffiti which we learned existed on the shoulders of some only in 1980. On the other hand, we would have lost all traces of amphora contents, for we made only a cursory examination of the mud washed from the amphoras raised between 1961 and 1964 instead of screening it carefully as we learned to do only on later excavations in Italy and Turkey. Thus, we were fortunate that uncleaned amphoras still existed when we returned to Yassi Ada in 1980 to look, successfully, for seeds.[30] Similar screening of the pantry wares might have revealed the shipboard diet.

Second, we did not conserve the wood remains after they were documented thoroughly by van Doorninck. Although today he wishes he could recheck certain measurements and observations, we did not think at the time that the enormous expense of chemical conservation was justified by the fragmentary nature of the wood (there was no chance of restoring the hull for display as was later done with the much better preserved Kyrenia ship).[31] As he digs deeper on land, the archaeologist routinely destroys evidence, stratum by statum, after recording it, although he might spend the time and money to move and reassemble every mud-brick or rubble wall and trace of paving. We followed that example, in a sense, even though we left the wood in fresh water in the Bodrum castle.[32] The question of just how much wood from similar wrecks ought to be conserved should be the subject of scholarly debate. Kuniholm informed me in 1981, for example, that a piece of pine planking might have been better for his dendrochronological study than the dried piece of keel furnished to him; alas, the planking no longer exists (see Appendix D).

Third, because we could date the sinking of the ship with some precision by coins found during the course of excavation, we did not have less precise radiocarbon dates of the wood made. Such dates, however, might have given us an approximate age of the hull before it was wrecked.

Probably the most dramatic change in underwater archaeology since 1969 has been the shift in emphasis from means to ends.[33] The 1960's were devoted largely to the development of techniques that could produce the safest, most accurate, and most efficient results. These developments led to greater complexity of equipment. More recently, largely through the work of van Doorninck, Steffy, and Katzev, a far greater understanding of priorities has been attained. And this knowledge, in turn, has led often to greater simplicity of underwater techniques.

Many of the hundreds of elevation measurements taken on the Byzantine wreck, for example, proved to be unnecessary for its final analysis, although there was no way of knowing that at the time. Many hundreds of man-hours spent changing, raising, and inspecting the air-lift catch bag proved fruitless, as very few objects were found to have been sucked up inadvertently over the four summers. Detailed mapping of hundreds of amorphous lumps of concretion, on the other hand, proved, after they had been opened and cast, to be more valuable than we could have guessed. If we erred, at least it was on the side of caution.

A better understanding of ancient ships' hulls has led to a better understanding of what seabed measurements are necessary and what can best be learned from the wood after it has been raised to the surface.

Our most recent excavation, of a well-preserved eleventh-century shipwreck at Serçe Liman, Turkey,[34] is as accurate as that of the Byzantine ship. Yet it is being accomplished without step frames, photo towers, 20-cm grids, stereophotogrammetry, plane tables, water jets, large air lifts, or a submarine. This reduction in apparatus demonstrates that each underwater site demands its own methods of excavation and suggests that "underwater" archaeology, with its emphasis on technique, has matured into "nautical" archaeology.

---

[30] For present and past examinations of amphora interiors, see A. Tchernia, P. Pomey, and A. Hesnard, *L'Épave romaine de la Madrague de Giens*, p. 13; D. Frey, F. Hentschel, and D. Keith, "Deep-water Archaeology: The Capistello Wreck Excavation, Lipari, Aeolian Islands," *IJNA* 7 (1968): 289.

[31] S. W. Katzev and M. L. Katzev, "Last Harbor for the Oldest Ship," *NatGeo* 146, no. 5 (November, 1974): 618–625.

[32] After several years the water in the basin was simply allowed to evaporate, with the result that the wood disintegrated. Although this loss occurred during winter months when our staff was away, I am not critical of the decision of the Bodrum Museum director; had we strongly urged him to renew the water, I am sure he would have done so.

[33] In the admirable report on the Roman wreck at Giens, A. Tchernia writes: "Nous ne nous étendrons pas sur la technique de fouille: des progrès suffisants ont maintenant été réalisés en archéologie sous-marine pour que les problèmes de méthode cessent d'occuper la place majeure qu'ils ont souvent tenue" (Tchernia, Pomey, and Hesnard, *L'Epave romaine*, p. 11).

[34] G. F. Bass and F. H. van Doorninck, Jr., "An 11th Century Shipwreck at Serçe Liman, Turkey," *IJNA* 7 (1978): 119–132; G. F. Bass, "Glass Treasure from the Aegean," *NatGeo* 153, no. 6 (June, 1978): 768–793; and G. F. Bass, "A Medieval Islamic Merchant Venture," *Archaeological News* 7, nos. 2 and 3 (1979): 84–94.

# III

# THE HULL REMAINS

### Frederick H. van Doorninck, Jr.

INITIAL probings of the seabed on the seventh-century wreck site in 1958 indicated that the hull had come to rest on a soft, muddy sand bottom and was relatively well preserved.[1] Bedrock was not detected, and wood was encountered at points 4, 9, and 26 on Frost's plan of the wreck (Fig. 1-4). Throckmorton traced the timber located at point 9 for a distance of 3 m along the port edge of the wreck and raised a 40-cm-long section of it which was reported to be 20 cm square in cross-section and to contain traces of iron nails. This timber, if located accurately in Frost's plan, was most probably part of the ship's port gunwale.[2]

Excavation revealed a somewhat different picture. The ship had come to rest on a steep slope with her bow pointing up the slope toward Yassi Ada. She had listed to port upon hitting the seabed, and both keel and port bilge had come to rest on exposed bedrock that only later became deeply buried under sand and mud, after the process of wreck formation had been completed. The steepness of the slope was sufficient to cause the ship to slide farther downslope toward an area where the

bedrock was already well covered by a layer of sand. The ship continued downslope until the after part of the keel and port bilge began to dig into sand (Fig. 3-1), but her forward half remained in an area of extensive out-croppings of exposed bedrock (Wreck Plan I); the result was that nothing whatsoever of her unprotected bow survived.

All but the very smallest surviving hull fragments to port and within 1 m to starboard of the keel and stern-post appear on Wreck Plan II. A small scattering of planking fragments occurring for an additional distance of about 1 m to starboard were too fragmentary and dislocated to warrant being mapped.

Since the ship had come to rest on her port bilge, the starboard hull bottom received no support or protection from the seabed before the hull collapsed, and the hull's starboard side fell in upon the cargo of amphoras when collapse occurred. Thus, very little of the hull to starboard was preserved at any point along the ship's length. The keel was well preserved at two points where it was at the outset partially buried in sand and thus protected from wood-consuming teredo worms, and it was partially preserved in immediately adjacent areas (Fig. 3-1). A fairly deep furrow in the sand, formed by the sternpost as the ship slid downslope, helped to preserve a substantial portion of the post almost to waterline level. The bottom planking to port was either resting on or was suspended only a few centimeters above the sand, prior to collapse, for a distance of about one meter forward and aft of the juncture of keel and sternpost and at the point farther forward where the keel was immediately buried in the sand. Almost all this planking was soon supported and covered by sand and was exceptionally well preserved, but a deep depression on the

---

[1] H. Gültekin and P. Throckmorton, "Preliminary Report of Exploration for Ancient Wrecks in the Turkish Aegean" (unpublished manuscript), p. 11.

[2] Although this sample was preserved in water at the Bodrum Museum until as late as 1962, it has since disappeared, and apparently no drawings were made of it. We found only very fragmentary wooden remains in the general area where Frost's plan of the wreck located this timber. However, since her plan has proven to be highly reliable in every other instance where a check could be made, I am inclined to believe that the timber suffered breakup and dispersion between 1958 and 1961. A documented example of such rapid breakup and dispersion occurred on the wreck during the course of excavation: some well-preserved wood of substantial size uncovered in step sector 4A in 1961 (Fig. 3-7) had become badly broken and had partially disappeared by 1962.

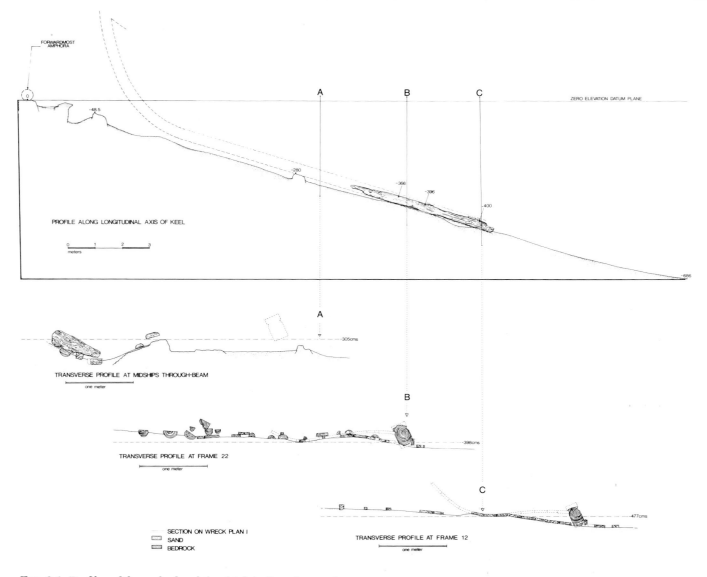

FIG. 3-1. Profiles of the seabed and the ship's hull on the wreck site.

seabed prevented planking preservation in the intermediate area (Wreck Plan I). Framing within the hull bottom was not quickly covered with sand in any area and perished almost entirely. A substantial portion of the ceiling strakes lining the hull floor to port did survive, however, in step sectors 3 and 4, for reasons that are not clear. The after third of the port bilge had dug down somewhat into the sand when the ship slid downslope (Fig. 3-1, sections B and C). Planking and framing there consequently were buried quickly in sand and largely survived.

When the hull's port side collapsed outward, the planking in the immediate area of maximum curvature along the port bilge was pulled apart and greatly fragmented. The side had been more or less intact when it collapsed, and that portion of it that soon became firmly supported by sand in large part survived. Very little of the side just above bilge level was preserved even where there was sand, however, due to another depression on the seabed; the depression underlay this part of the hull

along the entire middle third of the ship (Wreck Plan I), and was most pronounced where midships lay (Fig. 3-1, section A).

Wood did not survive as a general rule whenever it was not soon both firmly supported and buried by sand. Inner hull members were for this reason rarely preserved in areas where the outer hull survived, denying them contact with the sand. Members that were well supported but were not soon covered by sand often did escape destruction in areas where the wood was in close proximity to iron and became highly impregnated with iron oxide.[3] One general area where this often occurred was in the immediate vicinity of the ship's anchors. Another area was where portions of the outer hull just above and below deck level were preserved; here, iron

___

[3] While most wood on the wreck was so soft that one could easily reduce it to a pulpy mass, wood well impregnated with iron oxide had the hardness of sound wood even before it had dried. Wood impregnated with iron oxide also resists teredo worm attack (C. Davis, *The Ship Model Builder's Assistant*, p. 205).

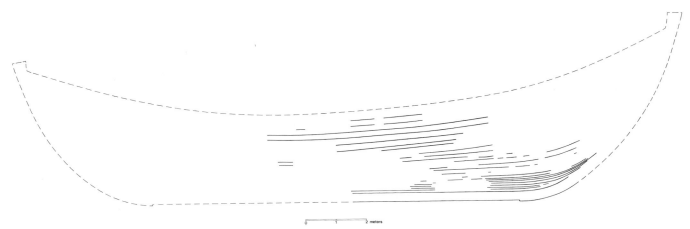

FIG. 3-2. General extent of surviving sections of the hull's port side. *FHvD*

oxide from large numbers of bolts employed in fastening this part of the hull contributed to an often excellent preservation of framing and shelf strakes. The general extent of outer hull survival to port is illustrated by Fig. 3-2.

## Mapping and Drawing the Hull Remains

Since the hull's metal fastenings had been of iron that had long since rusted away, no surviving hull remnants were still held together, and it proved necessary to devise a way of fixing each fragment in place as it was uncovered. Sharpened bicycle spokes were used to pin the wooden remnants together and to the seabed, and thus all hull remains of any substance appearing in Wreck Plan II are definitely *in situ*.

Almost all of the hull remains in Wreck Plan II are clearly visible in grid photographs like Fig. 3-3, and numerous close-up photographs like Figs. 3-4 to 3-6 establish with certainty the precise locations of remains that do not show up well in the grid photographs. For example, a portion of the port edge of the timber just to starboard of step sector 2C is visible in a grid photograph taken from that step, and the timber is completely visible in stereophotographs taken of that part of the wreck.

Some hull remains were uncovered and photographed in sector 4A (Fig. 3-7) and sectors 6B, 6C, 7B, and 7C (Fig. 3-8) during the 1961 season. About half of that wood was no longer *in situ* or had disappeared by 1962 when grid photographs were taken of these areas from the steps, but by comparing the 1961 photographs with the grid photographs, it was possible to determine the original position of every piece of wood that had disappeared or was no longer *in situ*.

An attempt was made to raise all of the hull remains, other than the starboard planking remnants, so

that detailed drawings of them could be made on land. Quarter, half, and whole timbers were placed in a large wire basket and were carried up to the island by four divers (Fig. 2-29). No serious difficulties were encountered in removing and raising these timbers. The removal and raising of the planking, on the other hand, was not easily accomplished, for even the relatively well preserved planks had been fragmented into fairly small-sized pieces. Regardless of the care exercised, these pieces usually broke into still smaller fragments when they were lifted from the seabed. In order to overcome this problem, close-up photographs were taken of each length of planking before its removal (Fig. 3-9). Points of weakness were noted, and the length was then purposely broken into smaller fragments at these points. A coded tag was attached to each fragment to indicate its relative position within the length before all the pieces were raised carefully to the surface in a small wire basket. It was later possible to reassemble the fragments by referring to the close-up photographs and the coded tags (Fig. 3-10). Once perfected, this procedure proved to be highly satisfactory.

Detailed drawings were made of all timbers raised and of all planking raised that could be reassembled. These pieces are the unshaded hull remains appearing in Wreck Plan II. Detailed drawings could not be made of the shaded remnants, but general measurements in those areas, including measurements of the positions of

FIG. 3-3. Hull remains on the seabed.

FIG. 3-4. Detail of hull remains, showing frame 17, ceiling strake 11, and wales 1 and 2.

FIG. 3-5. Detail of hull remains, showing frames 7 and 9 and planking strake 6.

FIG. 3-6. Detail of hull remains, showing through-beam; planking strake 19; ceiling strakes 13, 15, and 16; and wale 2.

visible nail holes, had been made under water. Such remnants were also used in making a reconstruction of the hull.

All wood drawn in detail was raised during the 1963 season except for a few small fragments brought up in 1961 and 1962. Each piece was drawn within a few weeks of its recovery, having meanwhile been stored in water to keep it from shrinking and causing errors in measurement. Representative examples of the wood drawings are illustrated by Figs. 3-11 through 3-14. A plan view was drawn of almost all the wood raised. When quarter, half, or whole timbers were involved, cross-sections were made at frequent intervals. Side views were drawn of wood belonging to the hull's skeletal framework: keel, sternpost, frames, through-beam, and hanging knees. Preserved original faces were noted on the drawings, and particular care was taken in determining the extent of such surfaces when the side views of remnants of frames and the sternpost were drawn. All surface deposits of interest, score lines, mortises and other cuttings, nail holes, bolt holes, and impressions of nail and bolt heads on surfaces were included in the drawings. All measurements made were also recorded.

Wreck plans and reconstruction drawings were done at a scale of one-tenth actual size, and all wood

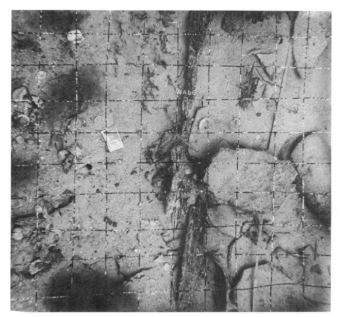

FIG. 3-7. Hull remains in sector 4A uncovered in 1961.

FIG. 3-8. Hull remains in sectors 6B, 6C, 7B, and 7C uncovered in 1961.

FIG. 3-9. Planking strakes 16 and 17 on the seabed.

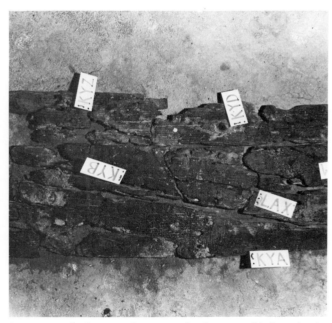

FIG. 3-10. Planking strakes 16 and 17 reassembled on land. *DMR*

drawings originally made at a different scale were redone to this scale. It was rarely possible, however, to transfer directly a plan or side-view drawing of a wooden member at this scale directly to Wreck Plan II, since few of these members had been lying in a horizontal plane on the seabed. It was usually necessary, therefore, to determine first the attitude of a piece of wood on the seabed relative to a horizontal plane and then to draw a special

oblique view of the piece in that attitude. The elevation, relative to a datum plane, of at least several points on all wooden members of any appreciable size had been recorded during excavation, making close estimates of their attitudes on the seabed possible. The principles of descriptive geometry were then applied to make the oblique views that were required. This procedure

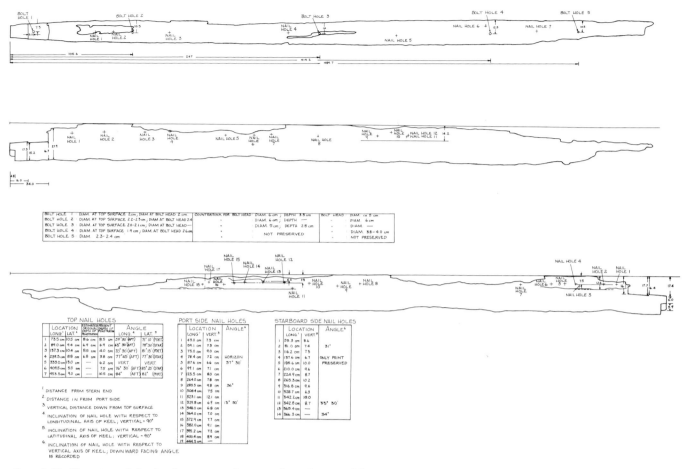

| BOLT HOLE | 1 | DIAM. AT TOP SURFACE 2 cm ; DIAM AT BOLT HEAD 2 cm | COUNTERSINK FOR BOLT HEAD : DIAM. 6 cm ; DEPTH 3.5 cm | BOLT HEAD : DIAM. 4-5 cm |
|---|---|---|---|---|
| BOLT HOLE | 2 | DIAM. AT TOP SURFACE 2.2-2.3 cm ; DIAM AT BOLT HEAD 2.4 | - | DIAM. 6 cm ; DEPTH - | - DIAM. 6 cm |
| BOLT HOLE | 3 | DIAM. AT TOP SURFACE 2.0-2.1 cm ; DIAM AT BOLT HEAD — | - | DIAM. 5 cm ; DEPTH 2.8 cm | - DIAM. — |
| BOLT HOLE | 4 | DIAM. AT TOP SURFACE 1.9 cm ; DIAM AT BOLT HEAD 2.6 cm | - | NOT PRESERVED | - DIAM. 3.8-4.0 cm |
| BOLT HOLE | 5 | DIAM. 2.3-2.4 cm | | | NOT PRESERVED |

**TOP NAIL HOLES**

| | LOCATION | | ESTIMATED PRESENT ORIGINAL DEPTH OF DEPTH OF PENETRATION | ANGLE | |
|---|---|---|---|---|---|
| | LONG. | LAT. | | LONG. | LAT. |
| 1 | 73.5 cm | 10.5 cm | 8.6 cm / 8.5 cm | 59°30'(AFT) | 71°10'(PORT) |
| 2 | 89.0 cm | 9.4 cm | 6.9 cm / 6.9 cm | 65°30'(AFT) | 78°30'(STAR) |
| 3 | 137.3 cm | 10.4 cm | 8.5 cm / 4.0 cm | 70°30'(AFT) | 81°15'(PORT) |
| 4 | 233.3 cm | 8.8 cm | 6.8 cm / 3.8 cm | 77°45'(AFT) | 77°30'(STAR) |
| 5 | 333.0 cm | 13.0 cm | — / 6.2 cm | VERT. | VERT. |
| 6 | 407.5 cm | 5.0 cm | — / 7.5 cm | 76°30'(AFT) | 85°25'(STAR) |
| 7 | 453.5 cm | 9.0 cm | — / 10.5 cm | 84°(AFT) | 82°(PORT) |

**PORT SIDE NAIL HOLES**

| | LOCATION | | ANGLE |
|---|---|---|---|
| | LONG. | VERT. | |
| 1 | 43.0 cm | 7.3 cm | |
| 2 | 64.1 cm | 7.3 cm | |
| 3 | 75.0 cm | 9.0 cm | |
| 4 | 78.4 cm | 7.2 cm | HORIZON 57°30' |
| 5 | 87.6 cm | 6.4 cm | |
| 6 | 99.1 cm | 7.1 cm | |
| 7 | 125.5 cm | 8.0 cm | |
| 8 | 264.0 cm | 7.8 cm | |
| 9 | 283.3 cm | 4.8 cm | 36° |
| 10 | 308.4 cm | 7.5 cm | |
| 11 | 323.1 cm | 12.1 cm | |
| 12 | 329.8 cm | 6.9 cm | 13°30' |
| 13 | 348.0 cm | 6.8 cm | |
| 14 | 364.0 cm | 7.0 cm | |
| 15 | 372.9 cm | 7.7 cm | |
| 16 | 382.0 cm | 9.1 cm | |
| 17 | 388.2 cm | 7.2 cm | |
| 18 | 400.4 cm | 8.9 cm | |
| 19 | 444.5 cm | | |

**STARBOARD SIDE NAIL HOLES**

| | LOCATION | | ANGLE |
|---|---|---|---|
| | LONG. | VERT. | |
| 1 | 33.3 cm | 8.6 | |
| 2 | 81.0 cm | 7.4 | 31° |
| 3 | 116.2 cm | 7.5 | |
| 4 | 157.6 cm | 6.7 | ONLY POINT PRESERVED |
| 5 | 186.6 cm | 10.0 | |
| 6 | 210.0 cm | 9.6 | |
| 7 | 224.9 cm | 8.7 | |
| 8 | 265.3 cm | 10.2 | |
| 9 | 516.8 cm | 9.6 | |
| 10 | 528.7 cm | 6.3 | |
| 11 | 542.2 cm | 10.0 | |
| 12 | 542.8 cm | 8.7 | 33°30' |
| 13 | 565.4 cm | — | |
| 14 | 566.3 cm | | 34° |

1. DISTANCE FROM STERN END
2. DISTANCE IN FROM PORT SIDE
3. VERTICAL DISTANCE DOWN FROM TOP SURFACE
4. INCLINATION OF NAIL HOLE WITH RESPECT TO LONGITUDINAL AXIS OF KEEL; VERTICAL = 90°
5. INCLINATION OF NAIL HOLE WITH RESPECT TO LATITUDINAL AXIS OF KEEL; VERTICAL = 90°
6. INCLINATION OF NAIL HOLE WITH RESPECT TO VERTICAL AXIS OF KEEL; DOWNWARD FACING ANGLE IS RECORDED

FIG. 3-11. Drawing of the keel remnant, showing three faces and locating major features.

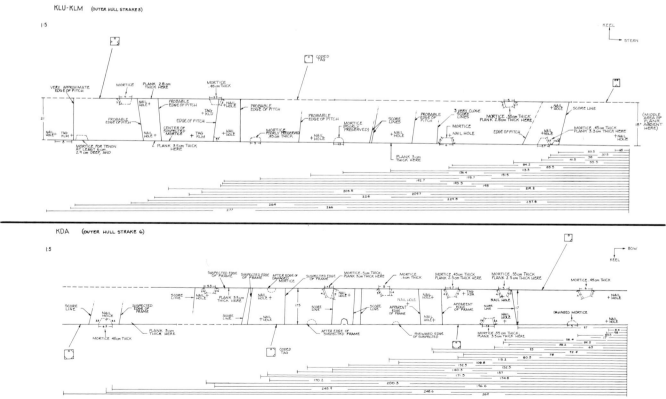

FIG. 3-12. Drawing of main remnants of outer hull planking strakes 5 and 6.

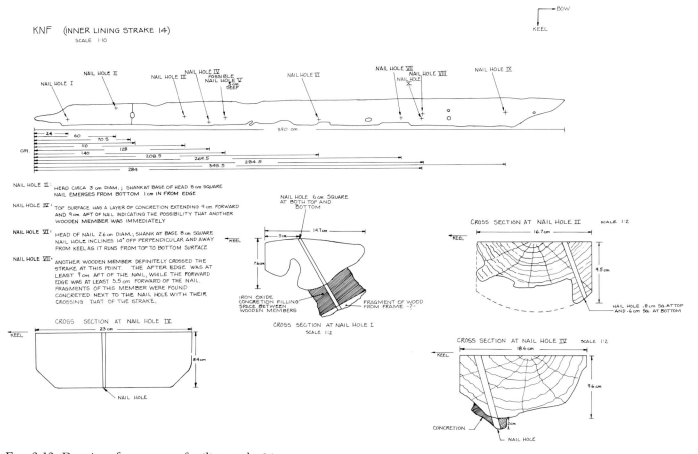

FIG. 3-13. Drawing of a remnant of ceiling strake 14.

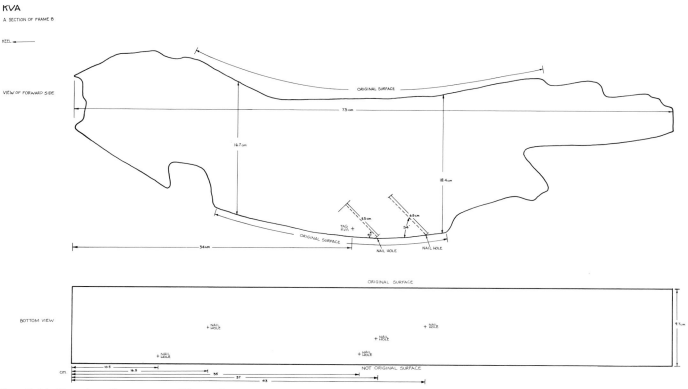

FIG. 3-14. Drawing of a remnant of frame 8.

proved to be rather complicated when long strakes were involved, since the slope of the seabed on which they had lain frequently increased or diminished to a marked degree.

A precise placement of the drawing of each wooden member on Wreck Plan II was usually made possible by features included in the drawing that were also clearly visible in a grid photograph, and thus the cumulative error in the relative positions of hull remnants on the plan is normally well under 10 cm. In the case of some strakes, however, only an approximate correlation between drawing and photograph could be made with respect to the wreck's longitudinal axis. It is not likely that the resultant error in placement ever exceeds 5 cm, but the cumulative error in the relative placement of some strakes, due to errors in placement plus general plan error, may approach 20 cm.

## A Two-Dimensional Reassembly of the Remains

The first step in reconstructing the hull was to reassemble on paper those surviving remnants whose original positions within the hull could be accurately determined. Those remnants included all but four surviving members (marked with an X on Wreck Plan II) of any import on the hull's port side. A master reassembly drawing was made, but for the sake of clarity it is reproduced here in the form of three separate reassembly drawings: the surviving portions of framing are shown in Reassembly Drawing I; the surviving portions of planking strakes, wales, and a through-beam in Reassembly Drawing II; and the surviving portions of ceiling strakes and hanging knees in Reassembly Drawing III. In the drawings, each planking strake, wale, ceiling strake, and frame bears an identifying number indicating its relative position within the hull. The numbering of strakes and wales runs out from the keel; the numbering of frames runs forward from the stern.

The hull remnants were of necessity reassembled in a horizontal, two-dimensional plane, since a determination of the hull's original shape could not be attempted until after such reassembly had been completed. It is, of course, impossible to lay out substantial portions of a three-dimensional structure embodying complex curved surfaces in a two-dimensional plane without introducing elements of distortion and dislocation. In the present case, however, these elements have been carefully controlled. Such control was not difficult, since very little of the hull where surface curvatures were both fairly complex and of a substantial magnitude had survived.

The reassembled hull remnants are shown in their original positions within the hull, which has been flattened out so that all of the planking lies in a single horizontal plane. This flattening was done in such a way that the surviving portions of hull strakes have not been subjected to distortion and the original orientation of each frame with respect to the ship's longitudinal axis has not been altered at any point along the frame's length. Frame distortion due to flattening was controlled by first graphically reducing the thickness of the frames to zero. Every feature on each frame's inner face was graphically projected down perpendicularly onto the frame's outer face, which when then flattened out lay in the same plane as the planking. Consequently, linear distances along the inner face within any particular section of frame have been increased in direct proportion to the degree of inward (upward) curvature, if any, that the section originally possessed,[4] and the ceiling strakes which overlie the inner faces of the frames in the immediate area of the strongly incurving bilge appear to be slightly more widely spaced in Reassembly Drawing III than they actually were. (Compare, for example, the space between ceiling strakes 7 and 8 midway between frames 25 and 26 in Reassembly Drawing III and in the reconstructed hull [Fig. 3-18].) In this way, however, the original positional relationship between the outer hull strakes and the ceiling strakes has been maintained in the reassembly drawings.

Distortion resulting from the flattening out of the curving sternpost was controlled by graphically projecting all surviving structural features perpendicularly to the post's inner face. For the sake of clarity, both bolt and nail holes have been drawn as if their axes were exactly vertical when the sternpost is flattened out (Reassembly Drawing I), although this actually was true only in the case of the nail holes.

There are in the reassembly drawings some minor dislocations in the positions of strakes relative to the lon-

---

[4]The three-dimensional reconstruction of the hull will show that the frames below bilge level had an outward rather than an inward curvature. This outward curvature was not taken into account in the reassembly drawings, since there were no frame remnants from this part of the hull sufficiently well preserved to pose a problem in this regard.

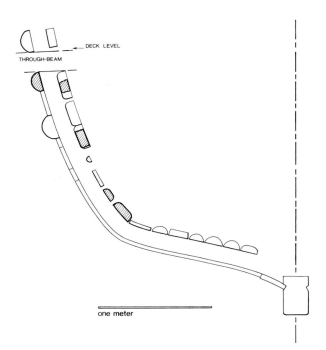

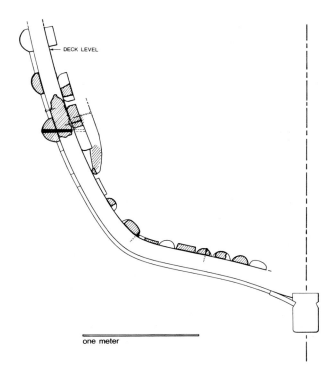

FIG. 3-15. Hull section at the through-beam at midships (be-tween frames 32 and 33).

FIG. 3-16. Hull section at frame 29.

gitudinal positions of the frames. The largest surviving portion of wale 2 constitutes the most extreme example (Reassembly Drawing II). As did all strakes located along the hull's sides, this strake had curved in towards the ship's longitudinal centerline at either end. It had been bolted to frames 15 and 32, among others, and when the hull is flattened out, the straight-line distance between these two bolt holes in the wale, as measured along the ship's longitudinal axis, is slightly increased by virtue of the fact that the wale is no longer incurving but straight. The straight-line distance between the two correspond-ing bolt holes in frames 15 and 32, as measured along the ship's longitudinal axis, has at the same time remained unchanged, since the original distance between the frames has been maintained throughout their lengths. When the hull reconstruction was completed, the dis-location proved to have been only about 3 cm; the bolt hole passing through wale 2 at frame 15 most probably passed through the frame about 3 cm closer in toward the frame's centerline than the reassembly drawing indi-cates. Dislocation is not as great for the other strakes belonging to the hull side, since none of the other sur-viving portions are as long as the longest surviving por-tion of wale 2. At the very stern of the ship, where the sides of the hull curved in at a rapidly increasing rate, only very short lengths of planking from the side of the

hull were preserved, and here dislocation was mini-mized by placing the surviving portions of each plank slightly closer together than they actually were when the plank was intact.

The hull bottom between the bow and the stern was virtually flat in the forward-aft direction, while the hull bottom planking aft of the keel curved upward in the forward-aft direction at essentially the same rate as did the sternpost. Thus, there is no measurable dislocation of the hull bottom strakes relative to the longitudinal positions of the frames in the reassembly drawings.

The greatest dislocations in the reassembly draw-ings occur in the positions of the surviving sternward extremities of planks relative to the sternpost. The far-ther out the plank had been from the keel, the greater its dislocation. Remnants of planking which had been in close proximity to the sternpost have been placed on Re-assembly Drawing II so that they are not distorted in shape and so that the frames at the stern maintain their original lateral orientations throughout.

The positions of forty-five consecutive frames are shown in Reassembly Drawing I. The original widths of twenty-five of these frames (4, 6–13, 15, 17–22, 25–29, 31, 37, 39, and 43) are known at one or more points along their lengths. They varied in width from 12 cm to 16 cm, and thirteen of them were 14 cm wide. It is highly prob-

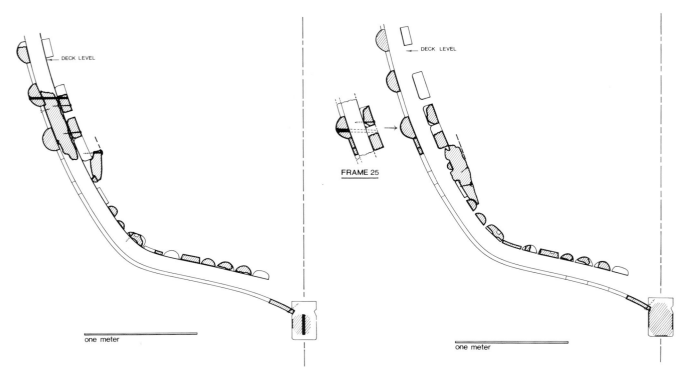

FIG. 3-17. Hull section at frame 27.

FIG. 3-18. Hull section midway between frames 25 and 26, with detail at frame 25.

able, therefore, that almost all, if not all, of the frames whose actual widths are not known were within 1 or 2 cm of being 14 cm wide, and this is the width to which they have been restored.

Determination of the spacing between most of these forty-five frames proved to be the most difficult problem encountered in reassembling the hull remains. The keel was drawn first on the master reassembly drawing. The major surviving portion of the port garboard could also immediately be drawn in its original position when attached to the keel, since both parts of a nail hole made by a nail fastening garboard to keel at frame 22 had survived and could be matched (Fig. 3-19). Plan-view drawings to scale were then made on transparent plastic drawing film of each portion of the ceiling and outer hull strakes that had survived between frames 13 and 45 and that had been drawn in detail on land. These drawings were cut out, and each was placed on the master reassembly drawing in the approximate position indicated for it by Wreck Plan II. After these cutouts were in place, the alignments of holes made by nails and bolts used to fasten strakes to frames and of lines scored on the inner surfaces of planks to mark the intended positions of frames emerged that revealed the certain existence and approximate positions of frames 13 through 37 and frame 39.

When different parts of the same bolt or nail hole

had been preserved in a strake remnant and in a frame remnant, a cutout drawing of the frame also was made and attached to the cutout drawing of the strake so that the hole or holes matched. The precise original positions of frame 17 with respect to the surviving portion of planking strake 16; of frames 20 and 29 with respect to the surviving portion of wale 1; and of frames 23, 27, and 32 with respect to the largest remnant of wale 2 were established in this way. The precise original positions of frame 27 with respect to the largest remnants of both ceiling strakes 14 and 15 and of frame 32 with respect to the other remnant of ceiling strake 15 that was drawn in detail also were established in the same way. The frame 27 and 32 remnants further served to join together the remnants of ceiling strakes 14 and 15 and of wale 2 to which they had been fastened. Thus, the positions of these strake remnants with respect to the ship's longitudinal axis could be adjusted as a unit while the spacing of the frames was worked out.

Adjustments were made in the relative positions of the plastic cutout drawings with respect to each other and to the keel until all of the nail and bolt holes associated with any particular frame were located as close as possible to an imaginary line running perpendicular to the keel representing the theoretical centerline of that frame. Score lines associated with a particular frame

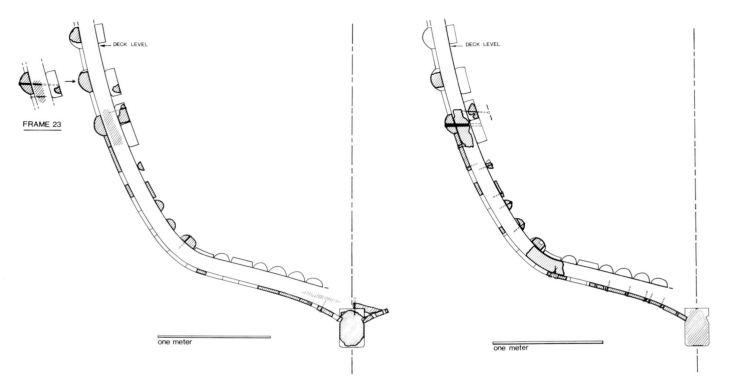

FIG. 3-19. Hull section at frame 22, with detail at frame 23.

FIG. 3-20. Hull section at frame 20 or frame 21 (see p. 59).

were positioned so that they fell at the proper distance to one side or the other of the frame's theoretical centerline, and a frame remnant whose placement with respect to a strake or strakes was fixed was positioned so that it was bisected by its theoretical centerline. The positions within the hull of frames 13 through 37 and frame 39 were determined in this manner. The position assigned to frame 43 is in accordance with the find spots of its one surviving portion and of the bolt which served to fasten wale 1 and ceiling strake 13 to it. The bolt appears in Wreck Plan II. The position assigned to frame 45 is in accordance with the find spot of its one remnant.

Frames 38, 40, 41, 42, and 44 have been hypothesized in order to achieve a frame spacing forward of frame 36 equal to the normal frame spacing farther aft in Reassembly Drawing I. It appears likely that all of these frames actually did exist, but they did not necessarily have the regular spacing given to them in the reassembly drawing. It is possible that there were a few frames farther aft as well that perished without leaving any clue to their existence or location.

With the exception of frames 20 and 21, the spacing of frames 13 through 45 is in part based on the assumption that the centerline of each of these frames ran perpendicular to the ship's longitudinal axis throughout the frame's length. In reality, it is quite possible that some of

these frames were not altogether straight. We have several good examples of frames in the hull of this ship that were quite crooked (frames 9, 12, 14, 20, and 21), and frame crookedness is probably the cause of some of the apparent variation in the intervals between consecutive frames in the drawings. In most cases where these variations are in excess of 5 cm, however, we can be certain that there was an actual fundamental variance in frame spacing.

The positions within the hull of frames 6 through 12 were revealed, often in considerable detail, by the portions of planking strakes 2 through 8 that had survived in that area. Much of the inner surface of this planking was in an excellent state of preservation and was well coated with pitch except in those areas where frames had been in contact with it. These areas are outlined by striated lines on Wreck Plan II and Reassembly Drawing II. Numerous score lines also showed where the frames had been placed. These features made possible a reassembly of all of this planking in which each remnant is in its precise original position with respect to the other remnants near it. A plastic cutout drawing of this reassembled planking was made and placed on the master reassembly drawing so that frames 8 and 11 were in proper alignment with the bolt holes for these frames in the keel and sternpost and so that nail holes associated with frames 13 and 14, whose general positions had already been determined, fell under these frames. The fact that this reassembly could be done suggests that any error in the placement of frames 6 through 12 can be only slight.

That portion of the sternpost extending from frame 8 to frame 5 broke up into several pieces as the stern of the ship was flattened out on the seabed, and the pieces were pulled apart. The total dislocation with respect to the ship's longitudinal axis was about 40 cm, as a comparison of Wreck Plan II and Reassembly Drawing I will show. The port planking aft of frame 5 also parted and pulled away from the planking forward of frame 6. The surviving planking aft of frame 5 has been placed on the reassembly drawing so that the two separated portions of strake 4 join. Thus, the assumptions were made that there was not an intervening section of planking missing in strake 4 and that the dislocation between the planking aft of frame 5 and the planking forward of frame 6 was the same as that suffered by the sternpost remains in this area. That these assumptions are in all probability the case is indicated by the fact that when the remnants of strake 4 are so joined, the interval between frame 6 and frame 5 is the normal one for the frames.

Remnants of planking strakes 4 through 8 were preserved aft of frame 5. The position of frame 4 was clearly marked on the inner surface of the remnants of each of these strakes, and here again, a reassemblage was possible in which each remnant is in its precise original position with respect to the adjoining remnants. This reassembled planking reveals what the original spacing of frames 3, 4, and 5 was in the immediate vicinity of the sternpost. The evidence for frames 1 and 2 is sufficient to make their existence certain but does not give us a precise indication of what the intervals between frames 1, 2, and 3 were. In the absence of such evidence, these frames have been given the same spacing within the reconstructed hull as frames 3, 4, and 5.

It is reasonably certain that the total width given to planking strakes 1 through 17 at frame 16 in Reassembly Drawing II is within 5 cm of what their total width at that point actually was. Although strakes 1 through 7 were not preserved at that point, their total width is known at frame 13 through direct measurement. Between frames 21 and 22 the total width of strakes 1 through 4 is known through direct measurement, and the distance between the outer edge of strake 4 and the inner edge of strake 8 can be calculated from a grid photograph. Calculation error cannot exceed 2 cm, and the distance is valid for our purposes, since both strake 4 and strake 8 were resting on the seabed before the hull collapsed (Fig. 3-1, section B). The width of strake 8 at frame 16 is known through a direct measurement made under water. Although strake 9 was not preserved to its original width at any point, holes made by nails driven through it into frames 7, 8, 13, 15, and 18, preserved in remnants of these frames, permit us to make a very close estimate of the strake's original width from frame 7 to frame 18. It is highly doubtful that the error in the restored width of strake 9 at frame 16 exceeds 3 cm. The widths of strakes 10 through 17 are known through direct measurement either at frame 16 or within 50 cm forward or aft of that frame.

Such an accurate determination of the original total width of strakes 1 through 17 unfortunately cannot be made at any other point. It can be demonstrated, however, that the total width indicated for these strakes in Reassembly Drawing II at frame 21 is their most probable total width at that point. The original total width of strakes 1 through 11 at frame 21 is known with the same degree of certainty that it is known at frame 16. The original total width of strakes 14 through 17 at frame 21 is, moreover, precisely known. Uncertainty about the total width of strakes 1 through 17 at frame 21 is caused primarily, therefore, by the lack of known widths of strakes 12 and 13. The distance between strakes 11 and 14 at frame 21 in Reassembly Drawing II has been made equal to the distance between these two strakes at this point on the seabed according to the grid photograph of sector 4B. There was no discernible dislocation between strakes 11 through 14 on the seabed midway between frames 15 and 16, the one place where remnants of all four strakes were preserved (Wreck Plan II). If there was no dislocation between these strakes at frame 21, the error in the total width of reassembled outer hull strakes 1 through 17 at that frame is certainly within a few centimeters of what it is at frame 16.

It is the total width of strakes 1 through 17 at frames 16 and 21 reassembled which has in turn determined the orientation of the surviving portion of wale 1 with respect to the keel's longitudinal axis in the reassembly drawing, but this orientation is the very same as the one this strake remnant had with respect to the keel on the seabed.

When the port side of the hull collapsed, surviving portions of it up to and including wale 1 had quickly come into contact with the sand. Above wale 1, however, the side continued for a time to remain suspended above the sand. As Wreck Plan II and Fig. 3-1, section B, reveal, the upward inclination from the seabed of the upper part of the side was retained by the remnants of wale 1 and ceiling strake 14 and frame remnants sandwiched between these two members. The outer hull strake and frame remnants above wale 1 appear to have collapsed in turn more or less as a unit. Wales 2 and 3 were still connected together by frames when this collapse occurred. Small pieces of these connecting frames appear on Wreck Plan II, particularly in the vicinity of the remnants of wale 2. Note that the small remnants of wale 3 that survived were located at what proved to be the point of maximum width in the hull, thus having had a better chance of becoming buried in sand before being destroyed than did the remainder of the strake. Ceiling strakes 14, 15, and 16, on the other hand, broke loose and slid down within the hull toward the keel before or during this final collapse, even though ceiling strake 15 had been bolted to wale 2 and ceiling strake 16, in all probability, to wale 3.

No recognizable fragments of planking strake 18 survived. Nail holes made by nails driven through this strake into frames 23, 26, 27, 29, and 37 and preserved in remnants of these frames reveal that the strake did exist and was planking, and although its exact width— the exact original spacing between wales 1 and 2—is not known, it must have been at least 22 cm at frame 25. Wale 1 and ceiling strake 13 had been bolted together at various frames, including frame 25 (Fig. 3-18, insert). Ceiling strake 14 was well preserved at that point, and the bolt did not pass through any part of it. We also know the exact positional relationship between wale 2 and ceiling strake 14 at frame 27 (Fig. 3-17). This relationship could not have differed by more than a centimeter or two at frame 25, and had the distance between wales 1 and 2 been less than 22 cm, the bolt fastening wale 1 to frame 25 would have passed through the lower edge of ceiling strake 14. If ceiling strakes 13 and 14 were set edge to edge in the hull without intervening space, the distance between wales 1 and 2 could not have been greater than 22 cm at frame 25 either.

The insert in Fig. 3-18 illustrates the situation. Ceiling strake 13 has been given a restored width in the insert equal to that possessed by the well-preserved portion of this same strake located farther forward in the hull and has been set right up against ceiling strake 14. That this remnant of ceiling strake 13 had such a width was indicated by the heart of the timber within the remnant, which becomes centrally located only if we assume that the timber originally had the same width here that it had farther forward. The assigning of a distance between wales 1 and 2 greater than 22 cm would necessitate a corresponding shift upward in the position of both ceiling strake 14 and ceiling strake 13 if contact between the two strakes were maintained. But if ceiling strake 13

had been set only 1 cm higher, the bolt fastening wale 1 to frame 25 would have passed through the remnant of strake 13 located there, and it did not. It is possible, however, that there was a slight space between ceiling strakes 13 and 14 at frame 25. In view of the spacing between the nail holes made by nails driven through planking strake 18 into frames 26 and 37 (Reassembly Drawing II), it is also doubtful that the spacing of the wales exceeded the minimum of 22 cm by more than a few centimeters at most. In Reassembly Drawing II, wale 2 has been set at the minimum possible distance from wale 1 and has been given the same orientation as wale 1 with respect to the keel.

One small fragment of planking strake 19 survived, but neither plank edge was preserved. We can be reasonably certain, however, that the original distance between wales 2 and 3 was about 19 cm. Not only was this the distance between the remnants of these wales on the seabed, but it also was the thickness of the through-beam that projected out through the hull side between them just forward of frame 32. Reference to Wreck Plan II will show that the surviving portion of the through-beam was overlying remnants of both wale 2 and ceiling strakes 13 and 15 (no part of ceiling strake 14 appears to have survived forward of frame 32) and was underlying a remnant of ceiling strake 16. This position indicates that the through-beam had projected out through the hull side above the level of wale 2 and ceiling strake 15 and below the level of ceiling strake 16. Since both of the bottom two wales girdling the hull sides were bolted at regular intervals to frames and to massive half-timber clamp strakes—wale 1 to ceiling strake 13 and wale 2 to ceiling strake 15—we may be confident that the next wale, wale 3, which was also bolted to frames, was bolted to a half-timber clamp strake as well. Unless this strake was set between ceiling strakes 15 and 16 and has disappeared without leaving a trace, it must have been ceiling strake 16, another massive half-timber. If wale 3 was in fact bolted to ceiling strake 16, the through-beam must have projected out between wales 2 and 3. There is other independent evidence which leads one to the same conclusion (p. 52).

As noted above, ceiling strake 13 was bolted to wale 1 at regular intervals, and the positional relationship between the two strakes is known within a few centimeters at frames 25, 34, and 39. The bolt hole passing through ceiling strake 13 at frame 25 was not preserved, since the strake had not survived to its full width at that point. However, the strake very probably had the same width there that it had throughout its length between frames 33 and 40, where it had survived virtually intact, and if

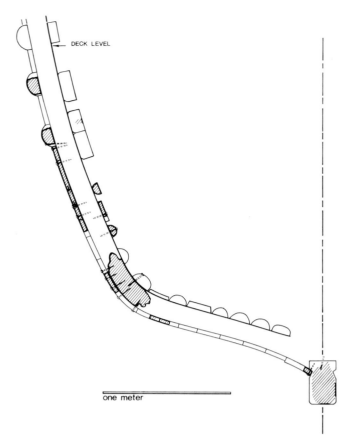

FIG. 3-21. Hull section at frame 18.

this was the case, wale 1 and ceiling strake 13 must have had a positional relationship at frame 25 very close to that shown by the insert in Fig. 3-18. Wale 1 was not preserved forward of frame 30. Nevertheless, we are reasonably certain of the positional relationship between the two strakes at frames 34 and 39 to within a few centimeters by virtue of the fact that in every case where we have a bolt hole passing through an outer hull strake preserved, the shipwright started his hole somewhere within a few centimeters of the center point in the strake's width. The two strakes had run parallel to one another. Ceiling strake 15 had been bolted to wale 2, and as discussed above, the positional relationship between these two strakes, as well as between wale 2 and ceiling strake 14, is known at frame 27 (Fig. 3-17). Ceiling strake 16 was almost certainly set just above the level of the through-beam between frames 32 and 33 and in that position would undoubtedly have been bolted to wale 3 at regular intervals.

Notches cut into the under faces of remnants of hanging knees located at frame 27 (Fig. 3-17) and between frames 25 and 26 (Fig. 3-18) reveal the original spacing between ceiling strakes 12 and 13 at frame 27 and between ceiling strakes 11, 12, and 13 between frames 25 and 26.

Ceiling strake 8 curves in toward the keel both forward and aft of midships, while all of the strakes farther out from the keel than strake 8 curve away from the keel both forward and aft of midships. This fact in itself suggests that strake 8 most probably had been set at the turn of the bilge—that is, at the point of transition from bottom to side where each frame underwent its maximum degree of curvature. Certainly it had not been set anywhere above that level. Sufficient portions of frames along the line of the turn of the bilge survived so that we can trace this line accurately as far forward as frame 20, and by placing the surviving portion of ceiling strake 8 on the reassembly drawing in accordance with its position on the wreck, it falls into precise alignment with the line of the bilge insofar as the latter can be traced. Furthermore, we cannot set the forward end of the strake 8 remnant more than a few centimeters farther away from the keel, for in doing so we would no longer leave sufficient room for ceiling strake 10. It is not likely, on the other hand, that the remnant's aft end had been any more than a few centimeters closer to the keel, since the nail hole preserved in the upper face of the surviving portion of frame 18 was most probably made by a nail fastening ceiling strake 8 to that frame (Reassembly Drawing III and Fig. 3-21).

Wreck Plan II shows that all surviving portions of ceiling strakes 1 through 7 had the same orientation, which differed from that of the keel and other strakes belonging to the hull bottom. Two of the surviving portions of strake 7 were found, moreover, completely overlying strake 8. It is clear, therefore, that the surviving portions of ceiling strakes 1 through 7 shifted considerably as the hull flattened out on the seabed. The fact that they all had the same orientation further indicates that they were all still attached to the same frame or frames when this happened. Their original longitudinal positions within the hull, about 36 cm forward of their final positions on the wreck, were revealed by the spacing of the two surviving nail holes in both strake 4 and strake 5.

Although there was only one portside remnant of ceiling strake 5, a portion of the corresponding starboard strake was preserved farther forward and appears on Wreck Plan II just to starboard of sector 2C. It had the identical width and the same distinctive trapezoidal cross-section as did the portside remnant of ceiling strake 5. This strake remnant has been placed on the reassembly drawing in accordance with its position on the wreck but for convenience has been transposed to the corresponding portside position. The other remnant of strake 5 has been placed at the same distance out from the keel, and since this was the distance out from the keel at which the midpoint of its preserved length lay on the wreck, the error in the placement of both remnants is probably slight.

The other remnants of ceiling strakes have been placed at what seemed to be their most probable distances out from the keel in view of their locations on the wreck. Ceiling strakes 1 through 4 have been set closely together, leaving a space of 15–20 cm between the inner edge of strake 1 and the keel. The existence of limber boards covering this space has been hypothesized in the hull reconstruction. These boards would have been removable so that the limber holes on either side of the keel for the drainage of bilge water could be periodically cleaned out. Such removable boards could easily have disappeared in their entirety.

### Preliminary, Three-Dimensional Reassembly

Now that the hull remains have been reassembled within a two-dimensional plane, we can proceed to an examination of the excavational evidence which will assist us in determining the hull's original three-dimensional form. As this evidence is presented, it will be illustrated graphically by eleven tentative and sometimes only partially reconstructed hull sections on the port side between frames 33 and 4 (Figs. 3-15 through 3-25). A tentative and partial reconstruction of the sternpost will also be made (Fig. 3-26).[5]

We may best begin with the evidence for the shape of the hull bottom forward of the sternpost. Rabbets cut into the sides of the keel, for seating the garboards, were best preserved at two points along the keel remnant where frames 12 and 22 had been fastened to it. Drawings of the keel in cross-section at these frames show the angle at which the garboards had been seated in the rabbets at these points (Figs. 3-19 and 3-23).

In addition to this slight bit of direct evidence, there is considerable indirect evidence for the shape of the hull bottom forward of the sternpost. An outcropping of bedrock lying within a small amphora-free area appears on Wreck Plans I and III just downslope from the anchor pile. This outcropping had a single, well-defined peak that projected far enough above the surrounding seabed to leave no doubt whatsoever that the port hull bottom between frames 32 and 33 came to rest upon it. Fig. 3-1, section A, shows a profile of the seabed at the time of the shipwreck that runs perpendicular to the hull's longitudinal axis and through the high point of this outcropping.

As already noted, the port bilge toward the stern end of the ship dug into sand just as the downslope movement of the ship was arrested. The resultant furrow on the seabed constituted a mold of that portion of the port bilge which came to rest within it. (Such a statement can safely be made due to the basic shape of most hulls, including certainly the present one: the distance of the turn of the bilge out from the keel progressively lessened sternward after midships. Thus, we can be certain that the shape and depth of the furrow at any point along its length was formed by that part of the bilge which came to rest directly in it and not by some portion of the bilge farther aft.) The furrow most clearly emerged in cross-section in transverse profiles of the seabed made at frame 22 (Fig. 3-1, section B) and at frame 12 (Fig. 3-1, section C).

The keel's top face was well preserved at two points: where frame 19 had been bolted to it and where frame 12 had been nailed to it. Two series of measurements of the slope of the top face to port at each point were made on two different dives. All measurements made at frame 19, where the surface was unfortunately badly concreted by iron from the bolt, consistently yielded 19.5° of slope. Those made at frame 12, where the surface was free of concretion deposits, consistently yielded 24° of slope. The readings at frame 12 were preferred over those taken at frame 19 in view of the better surface condition at frame 12. The measurements were made with a simple plastic protractor to which was attached a thin line tied to a flashbulb float which provided the vertical axis. The measurements were taken when there were no bottom currents to deflect the line from a true vertical.

We will make an initial assumption that the angle of 24° was in fact the actual degree of port list taken by the ship when she came to rest on the seabed and tentatively reconstruct the hull bottom between frames 32 and 33, at frame 22, and at frame 12 so that it would have rested

[5]Original versions of these hull sections appear in F. H. van Doorninck, Jr., "The Seventh-Century Byzantine Ship at Yassi Ada: Some Contributions to the History of Naval Architecture" (Ph.D. diss., University of Pennsylvania, 1967), figs. 10–20. These original drawings have been modified to better illustrate the present text, but the hull curvatures have remained unchanged in Figs. 3-15 through 3-24. In Fig. 3-25, an error in the original drawing made while graphically determining the lateral rise of the hull bottom at frame 4 has been corrected. The tentative and partial reconstruction of the sternpost remains unchanged.

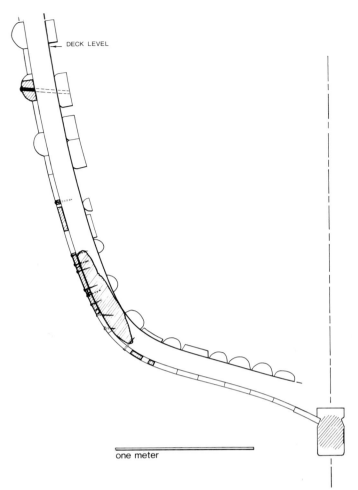

FIG. 3-22. Hull section at frame 15.

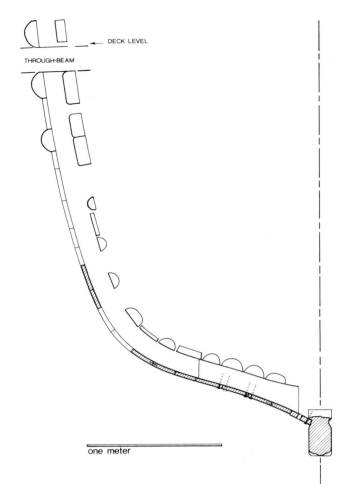

FIG. 3-23. Hull section at frame 12.

on the high outcropping of bedrock and would have made the furrow in the sand that was in fact made with the keel in the position in which it was found (Figs. 3-15, 3-19, and 3-23). Note that the keel was not preserved as far forward as frames 32 and 33 where the hull bottom rested on the high outcropping of bedrock. The keel's original position at this point can be projected with certainty, however, since it clearly had been resting on an outcropping of bedrock just forward of this point (Wreck Plan I and Fig. 3-1).

The tentative graphic reconstruction of the hull bottom at frames 22 and 12 indicates that the ship's list to port when it first came to rest on the seabed must indeed have been very close to 24°. The transverse seabed profiles in Fig. 3-1, sections B and C, will serve to illustrate the fact that the less the ship's list to port had been, the farther to starboard would have been the position of the rabbet cut into the keel for the port garboard and, consequently, the farther to starboard would have been the final position on the seabed of the hull's bottom planking on the port side. Conversely, the greater the list to port, the farther to port would have been the final positions

on the seabed of the bottom planking. A partial superimposing of the hull sections at frames 22 and 12 (Figs. 3-19 and 3-23) onto the transverse seabed profiles at frames 22 and 12 reveals, however, that the bilge planking in the tentative reconstructions of the hull bottom at these frames would have assumed the same position within the furrow (where the hull was already resting firmly on the seabed at the very outset) that the remnants of this planking did in fact assume.

Turning to the very stern of the ship, we find that there is also evidence for hull bottom shape at frame 4 (Fig. 3-25). In this case the hull bottom must be restored so that the stern end of planking strake 4 will be properly seated in the sternpost's portside rabbet. Although the rabbet is not preserved at this point, both the sternpost's overall width here and the extent to which the rabbet overlapped the inner surface of planking strake 4 at its stern end are known. The rabbet overlap was clearly defined on the strake's inner surface, since the rabbet's contact with this surface had prevented as great a buildup of iron oxide deposits from nearby rusting nails as had occurred elsewhere on the plank's surface. The

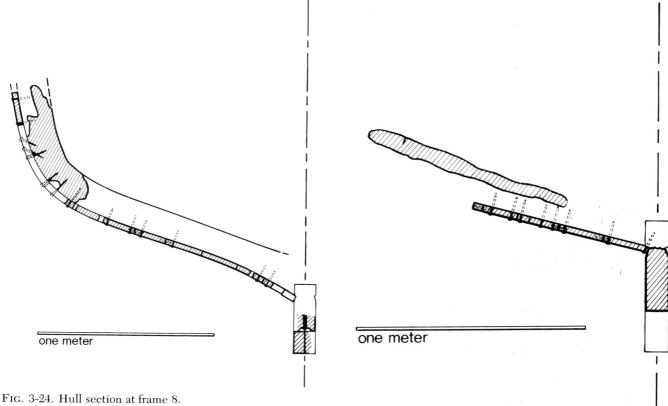

FIG. 3-24. Hull section at frame 8.

FIG. 3-25. Hull section at frame 4.

extent of this overlap has been indicated in Reassembly Drawing II. The hull bottom at frame 4 should also be restored so that frame 4 will be set perpendicular to the sternpost. It has been noted above that the position of frame 4 was clearly marked on the inner surface of remnants of the first five portside planks. It is clear from this evidence that the section of frame passing over this planking was quite straight. Consequently, there can be but little doubt that this section of frame had run nearly perpendicular to the sternpost throughout its length. The conditions just outlined require that the sternpost at frame 4 have a particular altitude and slope and that the hull bottom at frame 4 have a particular degree of lateral rise. The modeling described in chapter 4 will best determine precisely what all these must have been, but for our present purposes of examining and illustrating the evidence, close estimates can be made.

We must first attempt to establish the altitude and slope of the sternpost at frame 4. Three major portions of the sternpost complex survived between the keel-sternpost scarph and frame 5. Two of these remnants belonged to the main sternpost, and the third remnant belonged to an outer false post nailed to the main post. The false-post remnant had been nailed to both main-post remnants, and both nail holes were completely preserved. Careful measurements of the positions of the nail holes and of the angles at which the nails had been driven revealed the original positional relationship of the three remnants. A few small areas of original surface belonging to the keel-sternpost scarph, as well as a section of the port garboard rabbet, preserved in the forwardmost main-post remnant further revealed the original positional relationship between the three remnants of the sternpost complex and the keel (Fig. 3-26). Thus, it was possible to make a completely accurate determination of the curvature of the sternpost as far aft as frame 5. We have no direct evidence for the sternpost's curvature between frames 5 and 4, but since the distance between these frames along the sternpost's axis was only a matter of some 40 cm, our estimate of the altitude and slope of the sternpost at frame 4 cannot be very far off if we hypothesize, for the present, that the sternpost had the same rate of curvature between frames 5 and 4 that it did between frames 6 and 5. The correctness of this hypothesis will, of course, be tested in chapter 4 when the model is discussed.

Referring again to the planking remnants at frame 4 and to the score lines on them marking the position of a section of this frame, note that the score lines are not

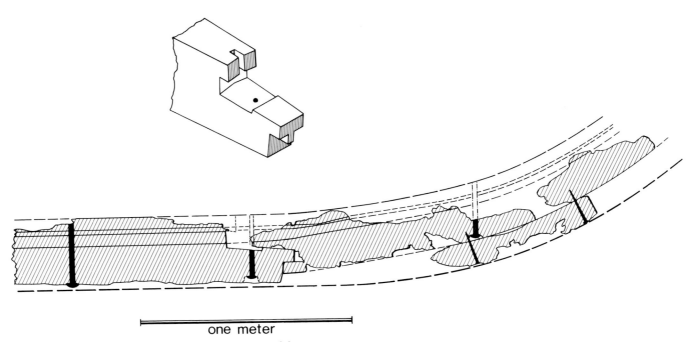

one meter

FIG. 3-26. Reassembly of major surviving portions of the sternpost and restoration of the scarph joining sternpost to keel.

perpendicular to planking strake 4's stern end. Had the
sternpost and planking, when fastened together, all lain
in a flat, horizontal plane, these lines would not have run
out from the sternpost perpendicularly in plan view but
slightly in a sternward direction instead. Because of the
stern's upward slope and the hull bottom's lateral rise,
however, the planking remnants had both a forward and
an upward tilt within the assembled hull. This twofold
tilting of the planking would have changed the plan-view
orientation of the score lines with respect to the sternpost by moving their outer ends both upward and *forward*. If at frame 4 we give to the sternpost the slope we
have hypothesized for it here, and to the hull bottom the
general lateral rise shown in the hull section of Fig.
3-25, the score lines—and thus the frame section whose
position they mark—will assume within the reassembled hull a plan-view orientation that is perpendicular to
the sternpost. It should be noted that the required degree of rise is directly dependent on the sternpost's slope
at this point. If the slope was actually greater than has
been estimated, the general rise shown in Fig. 3-25
would be too steep; if the slope was less, it would not be
steep enough.

The available evidence for a reconstruction of the
hull bottom has proven to be slight, but fortunately it is
well spaced along the hull's after half and permits us to
graphically develop tentative lines for the hull bottom all
the way from frame 4 to frames 32 and 33. The fact that a

hull bottom with coherent lines and with an essentially
horizontal fore-aft inclination within what was certainly
part of the middle body of the hull can be developed on
the basis of this evidence without even minor adjustments being necessary suggests that the results are
basically sound.

Turning to evidence for the shape of the bilge, we
find that well-preserved portions of frames 20, 18, 15,
and 8 survived at the turn of the bilge. Additional hull
sections based on the tentative lines of the hull bottom
must now be begun at these frames in order to present
and evaluate this evidence in proper context (Figs. 3-20
through 3-22 and Fig. 3-24). The positions within the
hull of the frame remnants are fixed precisely by preserved nail holes made when planking was fastened to
the frames, and the original distance out from the keel of
all this planking is known to within a few centimeters.
When restored to their original positions in Figs. 3-20,
3-21, and 3-22, the remnants of frames 20, 18, and 8 reveal what the curvature of these frames had been from
the outer limit of the hull bottom up through the turn of
the bilge. Thus, these hull sections can be continued up
through the turn of the bilge without encountering any
problem. In the case of the hull section in Fig. 3-22,
however, the remnant of frame 15 reveals only the curvature of the upper part of the bilge, making it necessary
to restore the curvature of the lower part in conformity
with the known curvatures at frames 18 and 8.

There is no direct evidence for the shape of the bilge forward of frame 20, but its distance out from the keel is defined by the position of ceiling strake 8, which was set at the turn of the bilge. Nor is there direct evidence for bilge shape aft of frame 8, but we do have evidence regarding the location of the turn of the bilge at frame 4. Wreck Plan II shows that a relatively long but rather poorly preserved section of frame 4 had survived and was found lying in precise alignment with the surviving score lines marking its position. We can be reasonably certain, therefore, that the frame remnant was found in what had been its original position relative to the planking underlying it. By restoring it to this position in Fig. 3-25, we establish an approximate minimum possible distance out from the sternpost for the turn of the bilge at this point.

Although several well-preserved frame remnants belonging to the hull side to port were recovered, none had survived to any great length, and thus they yielded little direct evidence for the shape of the hull sides. There is, however, some indirect evidence to assist us here. As discussed in the previous section, bolts were used in fastening wale 1 and ceiling strake 13, wale 2 and ceiling strake 15, and wale 3 and ceiling strake 16 to intervening frames. A measurement was made wherever possible of the angle at which these bolts had passed through the three members they fastened together, and it proved possible to make a very exact determination of this angle for the bolts that had fastened together wale 1 and ceiling strake 13 at frames 20 (Fig. 3-20), 25 (Fig. 3-18, insert), and 29 (Fig. 3-16) and for the bolts that had fastened together outer wale 2 and ceiling strake 15 at frames 23 (Fig. 3-19, insert) and 27 (Fig. 3-17). It also proved possible to determine quite closely the value of this angle for the bolts that had fastened together wale 1 and ceiling strake 13 at frames 34 (Fig. 3-27b) and 39 (Fig. 3-27c) and for the bolt that had fastened together wale 2 and ceiling strake 15 at frame 36 (Fig. 3-27a). Only a rough estimate could be made of this angle for the bolts that had fastened together wale 2 and ceiling strake 15 at frames 15 and 19 because of poor preservation; since the estimated angles of these bolts were so completely at variance with the measured angles of the other bolts, they have been discounted.[6]

Let us assume for the moment that all the bolts with measurable angles had had a perfectly horizontal attitude within the hull. If we attempt to complete a tentative reconstruction of the hull between frames 33–32

[6]Contrary to the statement in van Doorninck, ibid., p. 61, a determination of this angle for the bolt that had fastened together wale 1 and ceiling strake 13 at frame 43 could not be made.

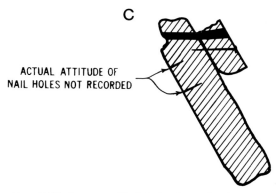

ACTUAL ATTITUDE OF
NAIL HOLES NOT RECORDED

FIG. 3-27. Section of bolt holes for wales forward of midships: (a) wale 2 at frame 36, (b) ceiling strake 13 at frame 34, and (c) frame 39 and ceiling strake 13.

and frame 8 (in which the five bolts are in a horizontal attitude and the line of the bilge between frames 33–32 and frame 20 follows that of ceiling strake 8), making additional hull sections at frames 29, 27, and 25 (Figs. 3-16 through 3-18) so that the bolt holes at these frames can be incorporated into the reconstruction, we find that we can make a reconstruction with coherent lines throughout; four of the bolts then have precisely horizontal attitudes, and the bolt at frame 23 slopes downward toward the keel at an angle of only 2°.

Looking ahead for a moment, we will find that the model has confirmed that forward of midships the bolts at frames 34 and 36 also will have horizontal attitudes and that the bolt at frame 39 will slope downward toward the keel only 2°. The success met in attempting to complete a hull reconstruction between frames 33–32 and frame 8 on this basis cannot be considered as a matter of coincidence; too many bolts are involved, and the angles at which they passed through the hull side vary too much for this to be possible. The fact that the hull side between frames 33–32 and frame 8 can be reconstructed with good lines on this basis only indicates, of course, that all these bolts originally had virtually the same attitude within the hull. The fact that the shape of the bilge between frames 33–32 and frame 22 can on the same basis be reconstructed to be in harmony with its known shape between frame 22 and frame 8 further indicates, however, that this common bolt attitude must have been horizontal. We may be confident, therefore, that the completed tentative reconstruction of the bilge and hull side between frames 33–32 and frame 8 is basically correct.

There was ample evidence to show that the hull had largely been decked, even though the deck had perished in its entirety. Approximately 3 m forward of the through-beam set between frames 32 and 33, seven iron anchors and some movable stocks had been stacked on the deck, while aft of the through-beam, at frames 21, 24, 27, 29, and 31 and between frames 25 and 26, component parts of the support system for the deck survived (Reassembly Drawing III, locations A through F). We will examine these component parts more closely in the final section of this chapter. We are presently interested, however, in determining the level at which the deck was set. In approaching this problem, we might begin by considering what evidence we have for through-beams and the level at which they were set.

The through-beam between frames 32 and 33 had a width equal to the interval between the two frames: 32 cm. Thus, it would not have been necessary to cut away part of the through-beam or part of one or both frames in order to fit the through-beam in place. Aft of this through-beam there had been a comparable spacing between frames at only two points: between frames 12 and 13 there had been an interval of about 34 cm, and between frames 15 and 16 there had been an interval of about 35 cm. This spacing between the two sets of frames, which was much greater than that between all other frames except frames 32 and 33, suggests that two other through-beams had projected out through the hull sides at these points. The positions involved are roughly 1 and 2 m forward of the beginning of rise in the sternpost, and we find a pair of through-beams so located in the contemporaneous Pantano Longarini ship.[7] Perhaps looms for steering oars had been fastened between a pair of through-beams at this location in both ships; such a method of mounting steering oars was employed throughout antiquity.[8]

A fairly contemporaneous ship representation is also informative in regard to these through-beams: the mosaic in the church of S. Apollinare Nuovo at Ravenna which depicts the city and port of Classis. Three ships appear in the mosaic, their steering oars mounted in boxlike structures formed by two projecting timbers, the hull side, and an outer crosspiece.[9] The interval of about 55 cm between the two through-beams in the Yassi Ada hull supports the hypothesis that they were used in a similar fashion. Moreover, note that there was hardly any spacing between intervening frames 13, 14, and 15 (there was, in fact, as can be seen in Reassembly Drawing I, clear evidence that frames 14 and 15 touched at one point where the aft face of frame 15 had bulged out slightly), and frame 14 was one of the frames that had been bolted to the keel. The shipwrights obviously anticipated that the hull would undergo some unusual stress at this point.

We have established that the through-beam set between frames 32 and 33 had projected through the hull sides above the level of wale 2, most probably between wales 2 and 3. Moreover, the run of ceiling strake 14 would hardly have permitted through-beams to be set lower between wales 1 and 2. On the other hand, it is difficult to see how the through-beams could have been set above wale 3. They would not have been set above deck level, but if the deck had been set above the level of wale 3, the sheer would have been much too high for the hull's beam, assuming, that is, that our tentative hull sections are essentially correct.

Let us suppose, then, that all three through-beams were set between wales 2 and 3 and that they functioned in part as deck beams. Through-beams were normally used as deck beams throughout the long period in which they were employed in Mediterranean hull construction. The juncture between the deck and the sides of the hull would have run along the lower edge of wale 3. The position on the wreck of this strake's portside lower edge has been indicated by a broken line on Wreck Plan III. This line has been projected both forward and aft of the surviving portions of wale 3 and is based on the position on the wreck of the wale 2 remnants. It would appear to be more than just coincidence that the positions of the

---

[7] P. Throckmorton and J. Throckmorton, "The Roman Wreck at Pantano Longarini," *IJNA* 2 (1973): 264 and fig. 15, sections 4 and 5, fig. 18, and figs. 20–22.

[8] L. Casson, *Ships and Seamanship in the Ancient World*, figs. 81, 91, 117, and 178; and L. Casson, *Illustrated History of Ships and Boats*, fig. 98.

[9] For a clear illustration of the three ships, see van Doorninck, "Byzantium, Mistress of the Sea: 330–641," plate 18, in *A History of Seafaring Based on Underwater Archaeology*, ed. G. F. Bass. The mosaic was somewhat altered just after A.D. 561, but the ships undoubtedly belong to the original mosaic, which dates to shortly before the death of Theodoric in A.D. 526. The hulls of the bottom two ships in the mosaic have undergone extensive repair, but the original design of all three ships would appear to have remained essentially unchanged (G. Bovini, "Principali restauri compiuti nel secolo scorso da Felice Kibel nei mosaici di S. Apollinare Nuovo di Ravenna," *Corsi di cultura sull'arte Ravennate e Bizantina* 13 [1966]: 93ff.).

port edge of the pile of seven anchors and of an iron bar labeled St 3, which was probably an anchor stock, fall on this broken line. It will be remembered that the hull had a list of 24° to port on the seabed. It would have been natural enough, therefore, for even heavy objects lashed down on the deck, upon eventually breaking loose, to slide across it and come to rest against the port bulwark, and the most probable final position on the wreck of such objects would have been the line of juncture of the deck and the port bulwark. We also find that only a handful of amphoras came to rest to port of the broken line on Wreck Plan III. Here, again, the most probable portside limit of cargo amphoras on the wreck would have been the line of juncture of the deck and the side of the hull to port. Thus, the evidence for the level of the deck, although limited, supports well the supposition that the three through-beams partially functioned as deck beams and projected out through the hull sides between wales 2 and 3.

Tests made with a hull model have shown that the steering oars would have functioned well when mounted between the two after through-beams (see p. 85). The tests further indicate, however, that the helmsman could not have steered from deck level. We have therefore hypothesized the existence of a helm deck located above the steering through-beams. Since no evidence of storage facilities forward of the galley complex was found, it is likely that this helm deck took the form of a light-timbered, open deck shelter with a flat roof. Such deck shelters appear in several representations of Roman merchantmen, and their location suggests that each roof probably served as a helm deck.[10] Some small nails and a finishing nail recovered from the wreck may have been used in the shelter's construction (see pp. 56–57).

A preliminary three-dimensional reassembly of the hull's remains has now been completed. However, some evidence concerning the hull's overall length remains to be considered. A few small sternpost fragments that could not be reassembled survived between frames 2 and 5. The forwardmost of these pieces preserved part of the hole for a bolt which fastened frame 4 to it. Nothing of the sternpost remained aft of frame 2, but despite this absence of wooden remains, the final position on the wreck of the middle section of the sternpost before its breakup and dispersion was marked. When the stern began to flatten out on the seabed, objects that had been

stowed within the hull aft of frame 4 or that had rolled downslope into this part of the hull from farther forward piled up inside the hull in the general area where the two sides of the hull had their juncture with the sternpost's middle section. Wreck Plan III reveals that these objects included cargo amphoras from the hold. Smaller objects had fallen to either side of the sternpost so that as the process of breakup and flattening of the stern continued, this material came to be deposited on the seabed just to either side of the sternpost, thereby forming two distinctly separate concentrations of objects (Fig. 3-28). The complete disappearance of the intervening portion of the sternpost itself suggests that it never came to rest securely on the seabed but broke up and was dispersed while still suspended, at least for the most part, at some distance above the seabed. The distance certainly was slight, however, for otherwise the smaller objects lodged on either side would not have been deposited in two distinctly separate areas. It is also clear that the sternpost's middle section would not have collapsed inward upon the stern ends of port hull strakes, causing them to double over on themselves. The relatively steep slope on which the ship had come to rest, coupled with a substantial weight of objects piled up within the hull at the stern, would have prevented that.

The final position on the wreck of the sternpost's middle section, as revealed by the evidence just presented, is indicated on Wreck Plan II. The post must have had a curvature such that the middle section could not have attained a final position any farther down slope than that indicated without to some degree or other breaking away from the rest of the hull. This analysis establishes for us a maximum possible extension of the middle section aft. Its minimum possible extension aft is established by the existence of frames 1 and 2, for the sternpost must be restored so that there will be at least adequate space within the hull for them. It should be noted, however, that the two frames might have been set a bit closer together than indicated by the reassembly drawings.

There also is evidence to indicate the minimal upslope extension of the hull. The distribution of amphoras (Wreck Plan III) shows that all had been stowed below deck within the hull. As we have noted, only a handful came to rest at a very slight distance to port of the line along which the deck had its juncture with the hull's port side. Nor did amphoras escape from the hold as the ship sank, for none were found in any real sense isolated from the main deposit. If the forwardmost amphoras on the wreck had been inside the hull when the ship came to rest on the seabed, therefore, the hull must have ex-

---

[10] For some examples, see G. Becatti, *Scavi di Ostia*, vol. IV, *Mosaici e pavimenti marmorei*, plate CLXXXII, figs. 1 and 2; and Casson, *Ships and Seamanship*, fig. 154.

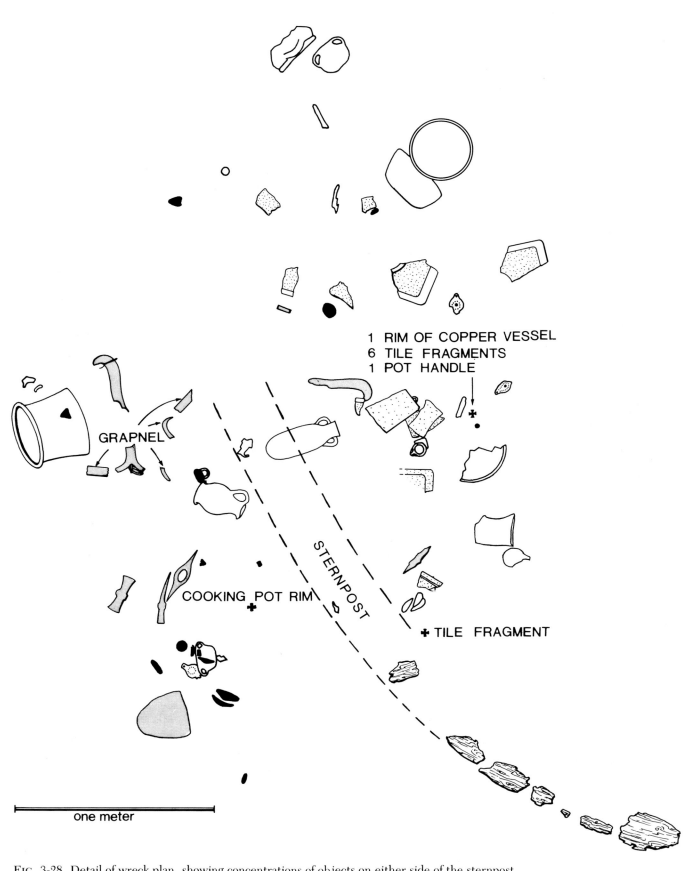

1 RIM OF COPPER VESSEL
6 TILE FRAGMENTS
1 POT HANDLE

GRAPNEL

STERNPOST

COOKING POT RIM

+ TILE FRAGMENT

one meter

FIG. 3-28. Detail of wreck plan, showing concentrations of objects on either side of the sternpost.

tended far enough forward so that they could have made their way from within the hull to their final positions on the seabed as the hull broke up. The position of the forwardmost amphora on the wreck is indicated on the drawing of the seabed profile along the keel's longitudinal axis (Fig. 3-1). It is obvious that, due to the general nature and slope of the seabed at this point, this amphora could not initially have been deposited on the seabed any farther aft than it was found. Thus, the hull must have had at the very least an overall length which conceivably would have permitted this amphora to make its way to its location had it been the forwardmost

amphora within the hold and had the stem been flattened out to its full length when the hull broke up. Stem shape is one factor determining what this extreme minimum length would have been.

Finally, mention should be made of the slotted ends of two bolts found *in situ* about 50 cm to port of the keel's longitudinal axis near the top of sector 1C (Fe 77 and Fe 78 in Wreck Plan II and chapter 11). Their find spots suggest that both bolts quite possibly had been used in the keel and had been set not very far apart somewhere between frame 45 and the keel's forward end.[11]

## *Preliminary Observations on Hull Construction*

The hull remains gave evidence concerning materials of construction, types of fastenings, scantling, and construction procedures and techniques that were taken into account when the hull was reconstructed. In presenting this evidence, I will first describe the types of wood and fastenings employed and then examine those hull members and construction procedures and techniques that are directly documented by the remains, attempting to follow as closely as possible the original sequence of hull assemblage. Additional information and insights on construction developed by the reconstruction of the hull will be set forth in the next chapter.

Cypress (*Cupressus sempervirens*) was used for the keel, sternpost, wales, through-beams, and larger-sized ceiling strakes; pine for the planking, the false sternpost, and the hanging knees; elm for the frames; and white oak for the tenons.[12] Fasteners were limited to three types: mortise-and-tenon joints, iron nails, and iron bolts. Evidence of dowels or treenails was not found.[13]

Bottom planking was edge-joined with mortise-and-tenon joints. The joints (Fig. 3-29) were small. Mortises cut into the edges of planks were normally only 5 cm

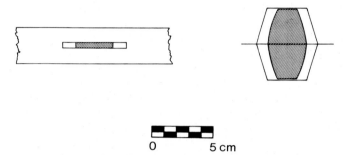

FIG. 3-29. Typical mortise-and-tenon joint as used on this ship.

wide at the surface, 3.5 cm deep, and 0.5 cm thick; the tenons had a maximum width of barely 3 cm. The joints were rather widely spaced. Within the stern area, where most of the surviving outer hull planking was found, they were set at intervals ranging from 35 cm to 50 cm from center to center.[14] What little evidence we have suggests that within the middle body of the hull the joints were set farther apart but at intervals not normally exceeding 90 cm. A closer spacing of joints would have been required in the stern area, where hull curvatures were at a maximum. Tenons were much smaller than the mortises into which they were inserted, and both mortises and tenons were strongly tapered. Thus, it was not necessary that the mortises be in perfect alignment in joints; very often when the fitting of two strakes together was completed, there was considerable overlap between the two mortises in each joint (Reassembly Drawing II). Once a strake had been fitted, tenons were not fastened in place with dowels, nor would it have been practical to do so, for in many cases the position within the joint of

---

[11] In the initial study of the hull remains, van Doorninck, "Seventh-Century Byzantine Ship," pp. 33–34, the presence of one bolt end was overlooked. The other bolt end was associated with frame 45, but in view of the slope on which the wreck lay and the fact that the keel had been suspended some 20–30 cm off the seabed toward its forward end, frame 45 should only be considered the aftermost possible limit for the location of this bolt.

[12] The wood was identified by Mr. B. Francis Kukachka of the Forest Products Laboratory, U.S. Department of Agriculture, Madison, Wisconsin. Mr. Kuchachka states that the elm may have been *Ulmus robur*. It was impossible to determine even the general type of pine used.

[13] A dowel and dowel hole earlier reported in G. F. Bass, "Underwater Excavations at Yassi Ada: A Byzantine Shipwreck," *AA* 77 (1962): 551, proved to be a knot and knothole.

[14] Thus, the spacing between joints ranged from 30 to 45 cm. See van Doorninck, "Seventh-Century Byzantine Ship," p. 90; and Casson, *Ships and Seamanship*, p. 216.

FIG. 3-30. Cast replicas of (*left to right*) nails and spikes Fe 46– Fe 50, Fe 58, Fe 55, Fe 59, Fe 60, Fe 63, Fe 64, Fe 66, and Fe 69. These fasteners are described in greater detail in chapter 11.

the small-sized tenon could not have been determined with sufficient precision. These joints were designed primarily to facilitate as much as possible the task of fitting the strakes together and shaping the hull, and their contribution to outer shell strength was both slight and incidental to their primary function.

Iron nails in a wide range of sizes were used extensively in the ship's construction. All apparently had round heads 2–3 cm in diameter and anything from moderately curved to flat in section; their shafts were 0.5–1.0 cm square in section. A representative sampling of nail replicas cast in concretion molds recovered from the wreck is illustrated in Fig. 3–30, and the nail replicas are individually described in chapter 11 under the catalog designations Fe 39– Fe 69.

Some of the largest nails were employed in fastening frames to the keel. We have no complete example of such a nail, but in most recordable instances they penetrated the top surface of the keel to a depth of from 7 to 9 cm. If they were driven in from the top surface of the frames, their shafts must have been about 26 cm long. A nail at frame 26 penetrated approximately 20 cm into the keel, but this depth of penetration is only an estimate, for the top surface of the keel was no longer preserved at that point. Since the axis of the nail hole was only about 9° off vertical, it is quite possible that the nail was driven from the top surface of frame 26. If so, its shaft must have been about 37 cm long.

Nails of this same general size were used to fasten wales to frames temporarily before the insertion of bolts. These nails were driven from the inside and clenched on the wale's outer face. Two examples of such temporary fastenings were detected. One was located in wale 1 at frame 20, and the other was located in wale 2 at frame 19. In the latter case, the nail had a shaft about 28 cm long, with the outermost 2 cm clenched. The largest of our completely preserved nail replicas, 17.5 cm long, had the outermost 1.5 cm of its shaft clenched (Fig. 3-30, Fe 69). It was found within the starboard half of sector 3A, where the port wales lay in sector 3, but the shaft seems a bit too short for use in fastening a wale to a frame. No other evidence for clenched nails in the hull's construction was found.

Nails with shafts about 14–16 cm long were used in fastening half-timber ceiling strakes to frames; we recovered one complete example of this general size (Fig. 3-30, Fe 66). Nails used in fastening planking to frames normally had shafts 8–12 cm long. Consequently, they often barely penetrated halfway through the frames. Most of the nail replicas are either of this general size (Fig. 3-30, Fe 50, Fe 55, Fe 58– Fe 60, Fe 63, Fe 64) or are of a slightly smaller size with shafts 6–8 cm long (Fig. 3-30, Fe 46– Fe 49).

Five tack replicas (see Figs. 11-17 and 11-18) form a distinct and interesting group. Their heads are 2.1–2.5 cm in diameter; their shafts are 3–4 cm in length and

5–6 mm square in section. As we will see, tacks were sometimes used in keeping bolt assemblies tight. However, the fact that the four of these five tack replicas whose find spots are known were all recovered from either sector 5 or sector 6 raises the possibility that some or all of them were employed in the construction of the hypothesized light-timbered helm deck or deck shelter located topsides of the steering through-beams. Perhaps a headless nail found between remnants of frames 10 and 11 in sector 6B was used as a finishing nail in this structure. Concretions probably representing four separate sacks of nails were recovered from the wreck. These sacks had been stowed with the tools for shipboard repairs in a storage compartment located just forward of the galley (pp. 92 and 96) and are described in Chapter 11 under catalog designations Fe 70–Fe 73.

Iron bolts normally had round heads that, like the nail heads, ranged from moderately curved to flat in section. Preserved heads ranged in diameter from 3.6 to 6 cm, but most had diameters of 4–5 cm. The bolt in the sternpost at frame 4 was unusual in that it had an ovoid head measuring 6.3 × 4.7 cm (Reassembly Drawing I). Bolt shafts were round in section and tapered. Their maximum diameter, occurring at the base of the head, ranged in surviving examples from 1.8 to 3.5 cm but was normally from 2 to 2.4 cm. The shafts tapered gradually to a diameter of 1.4–2 cm near the end. The fact that the tapered shafts fit snugly in their holes throughout their length indicates that the bolts had been hammered in. The largest bolts, those used in the keel, were perhaps as long as 72 cm; wale bolts were about 40 cm long.

The bolt shafts were rectangular in section at their extremity and were furnished with a slot for a key.[15] An iron ring was placed over the shaft end to serve as a washer, and a tapered key was inserted into the slot and then bent so that it would not slip out. Some replicas of these bolt-end assemblies are illustrated in Fig. 3-31 and are described in chapter 11 under catalog designations Fe 40, Fe 43, and Fe 74–Fe 81. In one of the best preserved examples of such an assembly, Fe 74, a tack was used to help hold the key tightly in place. It is likely that an iron ring and a tack found concreted together in sector 8B (Fe 40 and Fe 81) were part of another such as-

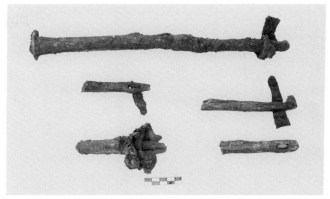

FIG. 3-31. Cast replicas of bolts and bolt-end assemblies. *Clockwise from top:* Fe 76, Fe 78, Fe 77, Fe 74, and Fe 79. These bolts are discussed in greater detail in chapter 11.

sembly, particularly since the ring involved was of the same size as the rings belonging to other assemblies. A ring and a tack possibly found together in sector 5A (Fe 43 and Fe 80) also may have belonged to a bolt-end assembly; the ring was again the same size as other assembly rings.

The washers employed in the bolt-end assemblies are of particular interest because two different types occur. One type (Fig. 3-31, Fe 74 and Fe 81) took the form of a closed circle, but the other type (Fig. 3-31, Fe 75, Fe 76, and Fe 80) had open ends that overlapped slightly. The one end was set about 0.5 cm higher than the other so that the ring had the form of a crude spring washer. The upper end was blunt, but the lower end terminated in a sharp point. The iron probably did not have sufficient spring for these open-ended rings to have functioned as true spring washers, but their design enabled them to be turned up tight against a key's underside after its insertion. The sharp point of the lower end would have helped to hold the ring in the desired position by digging down slightly into the surface of the underlying wood. One wonders why these open-ended rings were not used in every case in view of their superior design. Perhaps the shipwright had made do with whatever was at hand, or perhaps the closed rings are replacements used after assemblies had loosened or component parts had broken as the hull worked under stress. The ring for the bolt that passed through wale 1, frame 34, and ceiling strake 13 apparently had in this way been lost and not replaced, for the key in this bolt had eventually cut down into the surface of the ceiling strake due to the absence of a ring (Reassembly Drawing III). The tacks sometimes used to hold keys in place may

[15]The presence of slotted bolts has been noted on several Mediterranean ships dating to the beginning of the Byzantine period: the fourth-century Yassi Ada ship (F. H. van Doorninck, Jr., "The 4th Century Wreck at Yassi Ada: An Interim Report on the Hull," *IJNA* 5 [1976]: 124); the Pointe de la Luque B ship (B. Liou, "Direction des recherches archéologiques sous-marines," *Gallia* 33 [1975]: 578); and the Port Vendres I ship (B. Liou, "L'Épave romaine de l'anse Gerbal à Port-Vendres," *CRAI*, 1974, p. 420).

FIG. 3-32. Top view of the keel's after end.

FIG. 3-33. Oblique side view of the keel's after end.

have served to tighten loosened assemblies. In the case of Fe 74, for example, the assembly appears to have been repaired at some time during the ship's life after the large end of the key had broken off. The broken end of the remaining part of the key had then been wedged against the inside of a closed ring, and the key was held in this position by the tack.

The keel, which when built must have been set up on stocks high enough to permit the insertion of keel bolts from underneath, was a straight member with a molded height of 35.5 cm and a width of 22 cm aft to a point 3.3 m forward of the sternpost scarph. There it began tapering gradually to a 17-cm width 40 cm from the scarph and then rapidly to a 13-cm width where it met the sternpost. A hook scarph, fastened by a bolt, joined the keel to the main sternpost (Figs. 3-11, 3-26, 3-32, and 3-33). The keel's upper part and the main sternpost's lower part were cut back to form the scarph. The aftermost face of the keel presented a T-shaped tenon which fit into a 5-cm-deep mortise of corresponding shape in the main post. The forwardmost face of the main post presented a similar tenon which fit into a mortise in the keel. Nothing of the main post tenon and only a portion of its mortise survived. Enough of the mortise was preserved, however, to show that it extended the full width of the keel in the lower half of the joint and did not extend into the upper half of the joint along the port side of the keel (Figs. 3-11, 3-32, and 3-33). Thus, the tenon must have taken the shape of an inverted T. The overall length of the scarph, including the tenons, was 32 cm.[16]

The main sternpost had a molded height of 27.5 cm.

[16]There is a very similar scarph joining the keel and stem on the fourth-century B.C. Kyrenia ship (S. W. Katzev and M. L. Katzev, "Last Harbor for the Oldest Ship," *NatGeo* 146, no. 5 [November, 1974]: 623). Other similar scarphs have been found on Roman-period

After the stern frames had been installed, an outer false sternpost with a molded height of 12.5 cm was fastened to the main post. The two posts were 11.5 cm wide (13 cm at the scarph) and had a combined molded height of 40 cm (35.5 cm at the scarph) at least as far aft as frame 4. Beyond that point no evidence for their dimensions survived. The false post was not joined to the keel in any way, and iron nails alone were used in fastening the false post to the main post. Two nail holes were preserved in the one surviving section of the false post; they had a spacing of 55 cm and only penetrated the main post 5–6 cm (Fig. 3-26). Thus, the false post would have torn away easily under a severe impact, thereby minimizing damage to the main post or keel.

When the longitudinal spine of keel, stem, and sternpost had been properly braced and plumbed, the shell was begun by rabbeting in garboards that had a maximum width of 24 cm and a thickness of 4.2 cm. The bearding line occurred 6 cm below the top of both keel and sternpost wherever it survived. Apparently a few widely spaced nails were driven into the keel sides at the

vessels: the Lake Nemi barges (G. Ucelli, *Le Navi di Nemi*, p. 157, fig. 158, and pl. VIII); the "Caesar's galley" (C. Varoqueaux, "L'Épave du Musée des Docks à Marseille," *Publications universitaires des lettres et sciences humaines d'Aix-en-Provence: Études classiques* 3 [1968–70]: 36, fig. 9); the Pointe de la Luque B ship (J. Negrel, "Une Coque du Bas-Empire dans la rade de Marseille," *Archéologia* 55 [February, 1973]: 60, 62); the Gruissan ship (B. Liou, "Direction des recherches archéologiques sous-marines," *Gallia* 31 [1973]: 575, 576, fig. 6); and the ship at Monaco (F. Benoît, *L'Épave du Grand Congloué à Marseille*, p. 146, fig. 79). A hook scarph joined the two timbers that formed the keel of the second-century B.C. Punic ship at Isola Lunga in Sicily, but details about the scarph are not yet available at this writing (H. Frost, "The Punic Wreck in Sicily: 1. Second Season of Excavation," *IJNA* 3 [1974]: figs. 1, 4). The keel-sternpost scarph on the fourth-century ship at Yassi Ada was not a hook scarph (G. F. Bass and F. H. van Doorninck, Jr., "A Fourth-Century Shipwreck at Yassi Ada," *AJA* 75 [1971]: 30).

base of the rabbets so that the garboards could temporarily be set in place when desired during the fitting of garboards and rabbets. This would appear to have been the function of the nail that made starboard-side nail hole number 11 in Fig. 3-11. When the fitting was completed, the garboards were joined to the keel by a few mortise-and-tenon joints set at intervals of well over 2 m and were then securely fastened in place by nails driven up into the rabbet overhang at roughly 30-cm intervals (Reassembly Drawing II and Figs. 3-17 through 3-19, 3-21, 3-23, and 3-25). Only one of the mortise-and-tenon joints, located to port directly under frame 26 (Reassembly Drawing II), was detected, and since the keel rabbet at this point was entirely gone, only the garboard half of the joint survived. The port garboard's inner edge was well preserved for a distance of 2.25 m aft of the joint. Farther aft, neither rabbet nor garboard was preserved for a distance of 1.3 m. Another joint may have occurred there.

After the garboard was fastened to the keel, the next strake was then fitted and edge-joined by mortise-and-tenon joints to the garboard on either side. Assemblage of the shell was continued in this way until strake 16 had been installed. Strakes 2 through 16 all consisted of planking 3.5 cm thick and, excepting strakes 11 and 16, 13–21 cm wide. Strake 11 rapidly narrowed as it ran forward, and strake 16 had a width of about 25 cm.

The sections of planking that made up any one strake had diagonally cut butts. In some cases two strake sections were scarphed together before either section had been installed. When butts were made, they were fastened together by a nail driven in from either edge of the plank. Naturally, the nail with its head on the plank's inner (lower) edge must have been driven in before either section had been installed. Examples of this kind of scarph occurred in strakes 6 and 9 (Reassembly Drawing II). Other butts were scarphed together by a single mortise-and-tenon joint. Apparently this method was employed when one of the sections had already been installed. Examples of this kind of scarph occurred in strakes 2, 7, and 12. We can be reasonably certain that mortise-and-tenon joints were not used in the scarphs in strakes 6 and 9 and that nails were not used in the scarphs in strakes 2 and 7. There is uncertainty about the scarph in strake 12, since only a portion of it was raised.

Shell construction ceased when strake 16 had been installed port and starboard and the shell had attained the waterline amidships. Mortises were not cut into the upper edge of this last shell strake.

A detailed and certain reconstruction of the framing is impossible, and even the general framing pattern is not immediately apparent. No recognizable frame-section end survived, nor was any evidence for an overlapping of section ends detected. The frames, normally 14 cm square, were fastened to the shell planking by nails driven from the outside; nails often damaged mortise-and-tenon joints, as in strake 3 under frame 10, strake 6 under frames 7 and 12, strake 11 under frame 15, strake 12 under frame 15, and strake 13 under frame 14. Guidelines were scored on the inner surface of the shell planking to show where frames were to be placed (Reassembly Drawing II and Fig. 3-12). In almost every case in which a frame had passed over a section of planking belonging to one of the sixteen shell strakes, where the inner surface of the plank was still well preserved and not obscured by deposits of pitch, such lines were found. All remnants of strakes 13, 14, and 15 were, unfortunately, so poorly preserved that it was impossible to tell whether or not they originally had been so marked, but a great deal of the inner surface of the remnant of strake 16 was well preserved, and it bore scored guidelines marking the positions of frames 19, 20, and 21. A close examination was made, therefore, of the equally well preserved inner surface of the strake 17 remnant. No lines were found. The absence of guidelines there appears to indicate that strake 17 was not installed until sometime after frames 19, 20, and 21 had been inserted.

Most frames extended in to the spine of keel, stem, and sternpost, and many of them were fastened to the spine. Two exceptions on the port side appear to be frame 13 and either frame 20 or frame 21. Frame 13 began at outer hull strake 7, where the irregularity of the scored lines marking the position of the frame's forward side suggests that the shipwright may have had a little difficulty in starting his line. That frame 13 did not extend any closer to the keel on the port side is demonstrated by the fact that the inner surface of strake 6 was well covered with pitch in this area. Pitch did not occur on the planking where frames were located. However, the starboard counterpart of port frame 13 appears to have reached and to have been nailed to the keel.

Two remnants of side framing belonging to frames 20 and 21 were found set against one another without intervening space in the interval between frames 19 and 22. Nail holes in the forward remnants of planking strakes 2 through 4 clearly marked the location of a single frame midway between frames 19 and 22, while pitch on the planking in this area revealed that only one frame between frames 19 and 22 had extended all the way in to the keel. Either frame 20 or frame 21 had been a partial frame. Frame 20 was restored as the partial frame in the reassembly drawings, but frame 21 has been made the partial frame in the final reconstruction of the hull.

Roughly one out of every four frames was bolted to the spine after the bottom framing had been completed and the keelson was in place. The bolts were inserted from beneath the spine, and the heads were countersunk 1 to 4 cm in from the spine's under face. These bolted frames occurred where exceptionally sturdy frames were desirable, and they were undoubtedly floors. At least one of them, frame 25, had been both nailed and bolted to the keel. Most other frames were fastened to the spine by a single nail, but they were not necessarily floors.[17]

The keel remnant extended from frame 11 to frame 28, and traces of nail holes made by single nails fastening framing to keel were found at frames 12, 13, 15, 18, 22, 25, and 26. Frames 11, 14, 19, 25, and 27 were bolted to the keel. The top part of the keel at frames 16, 17, and 28 was so poorly preserved that all traces of nail holes in the keel's top surface probably would have been completely obliterated. This leaves frames 20 and 21, one of which was a partial frame, and frames 23 and 24. A sequence of four out of five frames in a row not fastened to the keel seems rather odd. Perhaps one or more nail holes escaped detection there. The practice of fastening only one of a pair of half-frames to the spine occurs in the contemporaneous Pantano Longarini ship,[18] and, as just noted, one of a pair of half-frames appears to have been nailed to the keel at frame 13.

Only one small portion of frame that passed over the keel survived (Fig. 3-19). This remnant, belonging to frame 22, was not well enough preserved to show how high the frames were above the keel, but it does give us a general idea of the size and position of the limber holes which must have been located just to either side of the keel to permit bilge water to drain into a central sump. The little protuberance on the remnant's bottom face is a knot. Since knots were normally found preserved to their original cut length in hull remnants, the frame's bottom face probably did not extend any farther down than the knot's protruding end.[19] On the basis of this

evidence, triangular limber holes measuring about 5 cm on a side can be restored that would be very close in size, shape, and placement to those found just beyond either end of the keel in the fourth-century ship, about 19 m long, at Yassi Ada.[20]

After the framing had been completed, save for top-timbers, but before the ceiling strakes were installed, a thick coating of pitch was applied to the interior and, perhaps nearer launching time, to the exterior of the shell below the waterline.[21] The method of sealing the shell's interior presents an interesting contrast to that employed in the fourth-century Yassi Ada hull, wherein pitch was applied to the under faces of the frames at the time of their insertion rather than to the planking between frames after frame insertion. The method employed in our seventh-century hull was less time-consuming and was probably preferred by the builder.

A keelson and the first twelve ceiling strakes were next installed. The reason for assuming the presence of a keelson is given in the next chapter, p. 77. The fact that no traces of a keelson were found does not, in this case, constitute evidence that one did not exist. Only remnants of frames 9, 22, and 23 survived in general proximity to either keel or sternpost, and only in the case of frame 22 had a remnant actually rested on the keel. We could not expect, therefore, that any portion of a timber overlying the frames where they passed over the keel would have survived, especially in view of the fact that this timber would have been entirely boxed in on either side by amphoras that would have kept it suspended well above the seabed even after the hull had been flattened out.

Most of the ceiling strakes were no more than rough half-logs. What appeared to be traces of bark were visible on one or two of them when they were first uncovered. They had a maximum diameter of from 13 to 16 cm except for strake 12, whose maximum diameter was 10 cm. Strakes 5 and 8 were somewhat larger and, as we will shortly see, apparently supported stanchions. Strake 5 was a finished timber 18 cm by 5.2 cm, trapezoidal in section, while strake 8 was a partially flattened half-timber with a maximum width of 21.5 cm. Strakes 7

---

[17] The realization that half-frames may have played a significant role in the framing of the hull has been late in coming. In the initial study of the hull's construction, it was assumed that all of the frames fastened to the keel were floors (van Doorninck, "Seventh-Century Byzantine Ship," p. 94). That assumption led to subsequent statements implying that almost all of the frames were floors with futtocks (Casson, *Ships and Seamanship*, pp. 207, 216; and van Doorninck, supra n. 9, pp. 143 and 144).

[18] Throckmorton and Throckmorton, *IJNA* 2 (1973): fig. 4.

[19] J. Richard Steffy has pointed out that knots in the Kyrenia ship

hull remains were also found intact. It may be that teredo worms avoid knots because of their high resin content.

[20] These limber holes are illustrated in Bass and van Doorninck, *AJA* 75 (1971), by the floors of frames B-21 and A-7 in fig. 4 and by fig. 5.

[21] Specimens of the coating on both the inner and outer surfaces of shell planking were analyzed by Mr. A. Eric Parkinson of the Applied Science Center for Archaeology at the University Museum of the University of Pennsylvania. They were identified as being of a resinous or pitchy material. Hulls were usually smeared with pitch or with pitch and wax in antiquity (Casson, *Ships and Seamanship*, pp. 211–212).

and 11 were merely boards 2.8 cm thick. Strake 11 had been nailed fast; strake 7 was probably removable.

Once the hull below the waterline was completed, the shipwright was able to put on the heavy side timbers. He began with the lower two wales, large half-timbers roughly 20 cm in diameter. The wales were not edge-joined to the adjoining planking. The actual existence of the three mortises cut into the upper edge of wale 1, as indicated in Reassembly Drawing II, is highly suspect. They may have been nothing more than deep cracks in the wood. Although tenon fragments were recovered from almost all surviving mortises in the shell planking, no traces of a tenon were detected within any of these possible mortises. The absence of mortises above the lower edge of strake 16 cannot be explained as being due to a lack of well-preserved outer-hull strake remnants above this level. The upper edge of strake 16 was well preserved for a continuous length of 2.2 m, and within this distance the lower edge of strake 17 was well preserved for a continuous length of 2.0 m. The lower edge of wale 1 was well preserved for a continuous length of 3.45 m, while both sides of the major wale 2 remnant were well preserved for a continuous length of about 3 m. The utmost care was taken in examining all these edges, and nothing that even remotely looked like a cutting was found.

Apparently the wales were first fastened in place at wide intervals by nails driven from the inside through frame and wale and then clenched. Wale 1 within its preserved length was so fastened at frame 20; wale 2 within its preserved length, at frame 19. Note that a bolt was added at each of these points later. Much of the side framing was then fastened to one or both of the wales by nails also driven from the inside but not completely through the wales. Any top timbers involved in the framing pattern would now have been put in and fastened in the same way. The shipwright normally did not fasten to either of the lower two wales framing that was later bolted to one of these two wales, except when initially using clenched nails. Perhaps he avoided doing so in order to be sure that he would not run into nails when he later drilled his bolt holes. One exception to this avoidance occurs at frame 25, but even there the frame was not nailed to the same wale to which it was later bolted.

We know that frames 17, 22, and 30 were neither nailed nor later bolted to either of the lower two wales. That frames 17 and 30 were not fastened to either wale is particularly interesting in that a single scored guideline detected on the inner face of the wale 1 remnant occurred at frame 30, and the only definite guideline detected on the inner face of the wale 2 remnants occurred at frame 17. A second scored line detected on the inner face of the main wale 2 remnant may have been a guideline, but its abrupt change in direction as it crossed the wale and its location midway between two frames (18 and 19) leave its purpose in doubt. One wonders if there might be some direct connection between the presence of guidelines on the wales at frames 17 and 30 and the fact that these frames were not fastened to either of the wales.

Ceiling strakes 13, 14, and 15 were next installed. These clamp strakes backing the lower two wales were partially trimmed half-timbers with maximum dimensions of about 25 cm by 10 cm. After the clamp strakes were nailed in place, each wale was fastened to its backing clamp by bolts passing through wale, frame, and clamp. Surviving hull remnants show that wale 1 was bolted to ceiling strake 13 at frames 20, 25, 29, 34, 39, and 43 and that wale 2 was bolted to ceiling strake 15 at frames 15, 19, 23, 27, 32, and 36. The bolts in each wale were set about midway between the bolts in the other wale in every case where their locations can be documented. Thus, it is likely that wales 1 and 2 were also bolted at frames 16 and 41, respectively.

The through-beams were next laid across the solid shelves formed by wale 2 and ceiling strake 15, and the overlying wale and clamp strake, wale 3 and ceiling strake 16, were then installed. Perhaps, as in the Pantano Longarini ship, the through-beams' under and upper faces were notched where the wales, just below and above, came into contact with them so that the beams would become locked in place when the above wale was installed.[22] Unfortunately, our single through-beam remnant was not well enough preserved to shed any light on this point. Wale 3, also a half-timber roughly 20 cm in diameter, was bolted through frames to ceiling strake 16. Traces of only one of these bolts survived, at frame 28. What were possibly remnants of a second bulwark wale, again with a width of roughly 20 cm, may have been uncovered in 1958 (p. 32).

The bolt holes in the lower wales were spaced at intervals of every four or five frames, and the known bolt hole in wale 3 was fastened to a frame to which neither of the lower wales was bolted. Perhaps, then, there were four wales, each bolted at regular intervals so that no more than one wale was bolted to any one frame.

Installation of planking adjacent to the wales and of deck framing and planking was the major remaining

---

[22]Throckmorton and Throckmorton, *IJNA* 2 (1973): fig. 15, section 4, and fig. 22.

task. The side planks appear normally to have been fastened to each consecutive frame by either one or two nails, depending on planking width. The nails were driven from the outside. The sole piece of this planking to survive, a remnant of strake 19, had the same thickness of 3.5 cm that the shell planking had.

Nothing of the deck framing or planking survived. However, component parts of the deck support system that survived between frames 21 and 31 provide us with a partial picture of how at least some deck beams were supported and possibly give evidence for the existence and location of a main hatch giving access to the hold. All of these components appear in Reassembly Drawing III at the locations labeled A through F.

A total of seven small rectangular mortises were found cut into the upper surfaces of remnants of ceiling strakes 5, 8, and 10. They varied in width from 3.5 to 4 cm; in length from 4.5 to 7 cm; and in depth from 2 to 3.5 cm. Two were found in strake 5, four in strake 8, and one in strake 10. Of the four mortises in strake 8, one was located at frame 21, one at frame 24, one halfway between frames 25 and 26, and one at frame 27. The two mortises in strake 5 were in precise lateral alignment with the two middle mortises in strake 8. The mortise in strake 10 was located between frames 30 and 31. These mortises, then, were at five different locations (labeled A through D and F in Reassembly Drawing III) along the hull's length.

At locations B, C, and D, timber remnants were preserved that had been laid down over the side ceiling strakes. These timbers had been set perpendicular to the keel's longitudinal axis and had cross-sectional dimensions comparable to those of the frames. Their under surfaces had been notched so they would fit securely in place over the ceiling strakes (Figs. 3-17 and 3-18). The remnants have been placed on the reassembly drawing of the ceiling strakes in strict accordance with their positions on the wreck as shown by Wreck Plan II. When so placed, they are in lateral alignment with the mortises in ceiling strakes 5 and 8 at locations B, C, and D. It should also be noted that a nail hole in ceiling strake 14 at frames 20 and 21 seems to have been made by a nail used in fastening another such overlying timber to this strake, and this timber would have been in lateral alignment with the mortise cut into ceiling strake 8 at location A. These alignments indicate that there had been a structural relationship between the mortises and the timbers, and there seems to be only one likely way in which they would have been so related. The timbers were probably hanging knees which had served as braces for deck beams at their juncture with the hull's port side,

and the mortises probably were for tenons at the bottom ends of stanchions for these deck beams.[23] Since ceiling strake 5 was located in the hull bottom and ceiling strake 8 ran along the turn of the bilge, it seems likely that stanchions tenoned to strake 5 would have been upright deck-beam supports, and that stanchions tenoned to strake 8 would have been diagonal deck-beam supports. Unfortunately, a measurement of the angle at which the mortises had been cut was made only in the case of that cut into strake 8 at location D, and since the remnants of strakes 5 and 8 no longer exist, the angles at which the other mortises had been cut will never be known. The angle at which the mortise was cut into strake 8 at location D (Fig. 3-17) does indicate, however, that a stanchion there would have been diagonally set.

Remnants of what was apparently yet another hanging knee survived at location E, but no mortises had been cut into the upper surfaces of either strake 5 or strake 8 at this location, nor did mortises occur in the remnants of these strakes at any place forward of location D. This fact suggests that stanchions resting on strake 5 at locations B and C and on strake 8 at locations A through D would have had some special function and that deck beams were not normally supported by stanchions resting on these strakes. Moreover, since these were the only two heavy half-timber ceiling strakes with flat upper faces in the hull bottom, it is not likely that deck beams would normally have been supported by stanchions that had rested on any of the other ceiling strakes. Indeed, unless we postulate beams that were extremely light in comparison to other hull timbering, or poor deck framing techniques, the deck beams in our hull with an overall breadth of only 5 m would not have required stanchion support under most circumstances. Why, then, did the deck beams at locations A through D require such support? A comparison of hull breadth in Figs. 3-15 through 3-24 will show that the hull attained its maximum breadth within this part of the hull. Thus, it might be supposed that the deck beams there required more support because they had a greater distance to span than did the others. Yet, as noted, the maximum

[23] In the Pantano Longarini ship there were through-beams braced by a pair of riders, one set on either side of the beam (ibid., figs. 4, 20, 21). Examples of mortises for deck-beam stanchions occur in the Isola Lunga Punic ships (H. Frost, "First Season of Excavation on the Punic Wreck in Sicily," *IJNA* 2 [1973]: 38); in the two Lake Nemi barges (Ucelli, *Navi di Nemi*, plates II, VI, and VIII); in the smaller Fiumicino barge (O. Testaguzza, *Portus: Illustrazione dei porti di Claudio e Traiano e della citta di Porto a Fiumicino*, p. 131); and in the County Hall ship (P. Marsden, "The County Hall Ship," *Transactions of the London and Middlesex Archaelogical Society* 21 [1965]: 110, 115, and figs. 1 and 4).

span is not very great, nor would such a supposition appear to explain adequately the presence of uprights tenoned to ceiling strake 5 at locations *B* and *C*.

There is, however, another factor to be considered. If most of the hull was decked, there must have been a hatch or hatches to provide access to the hold, and one of the most practical locations for a main hatch would have been where the hold attained its maximum breadth. Deck beams would not, of course, have spanned the entire width of the hull wherever a hatch was located. Perhaps stanchion support for deck framing in the hatch area was considered desirable. And a possible partial function of the two stanchions tenoned to ceiling strake 5 might have been that of furnishing uprights for a permanent ladder giving access to the hold. Just how a system of stanchion support between locations *A* and *D* might have been structurally related to a hatch opening will best be demonstrated by the model. For the moment it may be noted that the forewardmost possible extent of such a hatch would seem to be limited by the deck beam at location *E*, which apparently spanned the entire width of the hull, there being no mortises cut into either ceiling strake 5 or ceiling strake 8 at that location. Direct evidence suggesting the aftermost possible extent of such a hatch, on the other hand, appears to be lacking.

The spacing of deck beams at locations *A* through *E* suggests that the next deck beam forward most probably would have been located in close proximity to frame 31, and there was a nail hole in ceiling strake 14 at this frame, apparently made by a nail fastening an overlying timber to it. It is possible, therefore, that there had been a hanging knee bracing a deck beam there. If there was a deck beam at location *F*, the mortise cut into ceiling strake 10 between frames 30 and 31 may have been for a diagonal stanchion supporting it. Again, we must wonder why a deck beam there would have required this unusual arrangement of support. One possibility is that the ship's mainmast had been boxed between a deck beam at *F* and the through-beam at midships. A mast in this position would have worked against both the through-beam and the deck beam. Thus, some special arrangement of additional bracing for the deck beam might have been desirable.

## Ballast Stones

A small quantity of ballast stones was uncovered between frames 28 and 35 on the port side of the wreck (Wreck Plan II). Many were found in close proximity to the surviving remnant of the midships through-beam (Fig. 3-34). Virtually all of the stones uncovered were raised. Some were inadvertently lost in transit to the Bodrum Museum, but not before all had been photographed while piled together on the beach at Yassi Ada. We have estimated on the basis of the photographs and the weight of the stones not lost that those raised had weighed only about 300 kg; it is unlikely that the total weight of the stones uncovered was substantially greater.

It would appear that the stones were all originally located in the port bilge between frames 28 and 35, for the amphoras within the hold would have prevented them from appreciably shifting in position.[24] Although it is not unusual for a captain to ballast one side of his ship heavier than the other when he anticipates favoring a certain tack on a voyage, the paucity of stones and their concentration within a small area in the present case is puzzling. Even if we were to suppose that our estimated

FIG. 3-34. Ballast stones on the seabed. The large timber at right center is the midships through-beam.

[24]Contrary to van Doorninck, "Seventh-Century Byzantine Ship," p. 83, it is highly unlikely that the stones could have made their way from an original location immediately above the keel.

weight of the stones raised equals only about one-half the weight of all the stones that were in the hold, the stones by themselves would not have been anywhere near sufficient ballast for a ship of our vessel's size and high, narrow hull design, particularly if she were lateen-rigged. However, evidence suggesting the possible presence of any other type of ballast, such as sand or gravel, was not detected. It seems reasonably certain that the ship was not heavily ballasted when she sank. Apparently, then, the lower part of her hold was heavily laden with cargo at the time.

An analysis of the stones was made and is given in Appendix A. Unfortunately, the nondistinctive nature of the stones and the possibly ephemeral nature of their source make them useless for any study of their provenance or the possible origin of the ship.

# IV

## RECONSTRUCTING THE HULL

### J. Richard Steffy

An initial examination of the material set forth in the preceding chapter produced many feelings of doubt. Iron planking nails penetrating only halfway through frames, half-log wales above deck level, strange framing patterns, and poorly fitting mortise-and-tenon joints were but a few aspects of the hull remains that would have perplexed anyone steeped in the traditions of good shipbuilding. However, the intervening years have produced results which have explained many of these perplexing aspects of the ship's construction. Other excava-

tions in the interim have yielded helpful comparative material, but more important have been new insights and understanding derived from the construction of various types of models. While admittedly a slow and tedious procedure, an application of the excavated evidence to three-dimensional study generally produced valuable disclosures. The results of these efforts, based on the evidence outlined in the preceding chapter, are presented in this chapter.

### Developing the Ship's Lines

Inspection of the hull reassembly drawings indicated that there was a good distribution of inner and outer planking with enough nail and bolt evidence to develop the lines over a large part of the ship. The first step in determining the lines was to make 1:10 scale replicas of all the wood that had been recorded with the exception of frame fragments. Nail and bolt holes were indicated, and when the angle of a fastener was known, a hole was drilled through the strake at that angle. Thin strips of veneer were cut to represent inside and outside frame faces, and fastener locations were marked on these strips. The strips were then bent to various shapes until the pieces of model planking were properly aligned with respect to nail holes, pitch marks, and so on. Outside planking and frame faces were aligned first, then ceiling strakes and clamps were attached to their veneer strips wherever practical.

The inner and outer strake assemblies were next aligned to each other by using known bolt angles at wale

level, distances to the keel centerline, and, in two cases, frame thickness. Inner and outer assemblies were first shimmed apart at the estimated 14-cm frame thickness, which was then varied until the maximum amount of evidence was satisfied. Fig. 4-1 illustrates the method described above. The wooden strips running perpendicular to the frame sections were braces along which the assemblies could be moved and clamped in various positions. This method was a tedious one, indeed, but it was the most accurate one we could devise to satisfy such a small amount of excavated evidence.

Once the research model assemblies were carried as far as was practical, hull sections could be drawn from them. These sections could be determined over most of the hull between frames 45 and 4 and were drawn for locations every 25 cm within this distance. A "mold-and-batten" model, illustrated in Figs. 4-2 and 4-3, was chosen instead of simple drafting to project the ship's lines from these hull sections. The decision to use such a

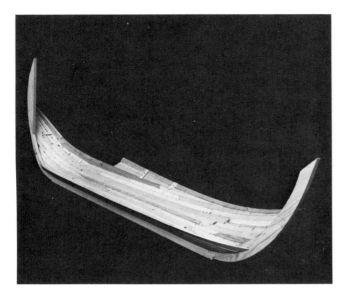

FIG. 4-1. Research model used to determine planking shapes. Veneer frames have been removed for clarity. *UM*

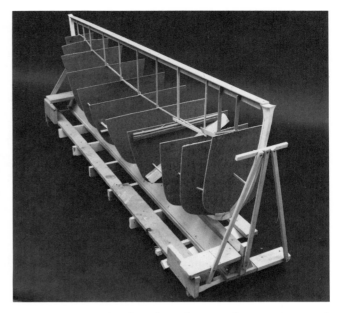

FIG. 4-2. Movable hardboard molds on an adjustable base used to determine hull lines. *UM*

FIG. 4-3. Bow view of the mold model. *UM*

model was based largely on the fact that the battens used in drafting the ship's lines could be inadvertently persuaded into false shapes. A three-dimensional model on which the battens could be seated was less likely to permit such distortion.

A keel of the same scale width and thickness as the original, but considerably longer, was fastened to a substantial base. A temporary stem and a temporary sternpost were then mounted so that they could be slid back and forth along the keel at any angle in order to determine the location and angle of the stem and the sternpost with relation to the various body shapes acquired from the previous experiment.

Molds of the hull section shapes were placed at their assigned locations along the keel. Battens, thin strips of wood longer than the anticipated length of the ship, were laid along the edges of the molds. All molds were then trimmed or shimmed out to produce a fair batten curve. The battens were also used to determine fair and complimentary hull lines into the stem and stern.

It should be noted here that in most respects virtually no adjustment had to be made in the preliminary hull section shapes developed in chapter 3. Only the turn of the bilge proved to be too tight and had to be slightly softened. This softening at first glance appeared to clash with the evidence provided by the surviving remnant of frame 8. However, a reexamination of the original drawing of this remnant (Fig. 3-14) revealed that a more complete preservation of its outer face had been assumed in developing the hull section at that frame than was necessarily the case.

When a satisfactory set of lines in agreement with as much of the evidence as possible was produced, the battens and posts were fastened at their proper locations and angles. Hull sections were then taken from the model at scale 50-cm distances, and a set of drawings of the ship's lines was produced from them (Fig. 4-4).[1] While these published lines drawings were largely correct for the area of the ship below the waterline, they were not satisfactory in the bow and stern areas above

[1] First published in F. H. van Doorninck, Jr., "Byzantium, Mistress of the Sea: 340–641," in *A History of Seafaring Based on Underwater Archaeology*, ed. G. F. Bass, pp. 140–141.

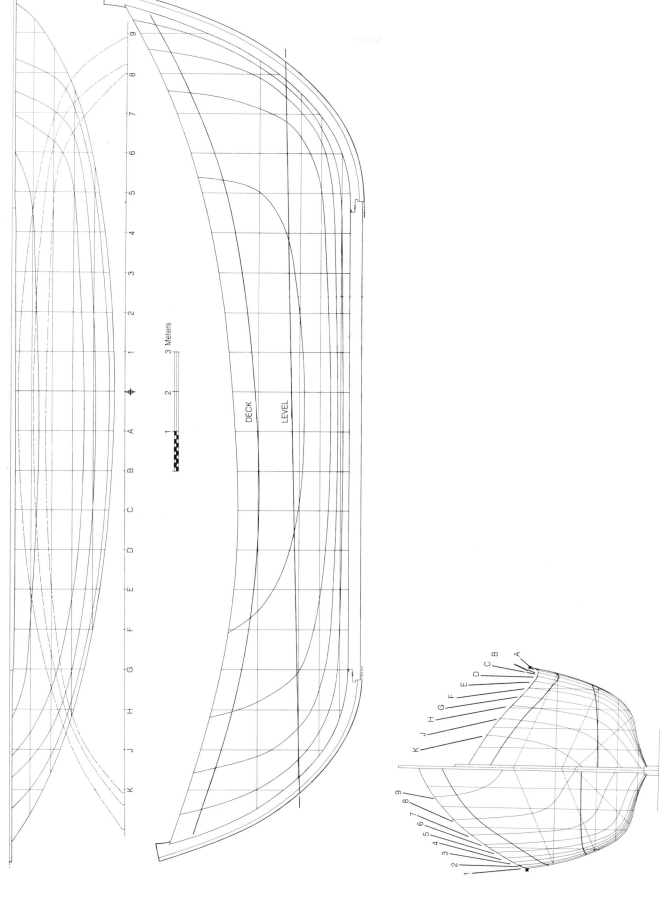

Fig. 4-4. Ship's lines developed for use in modeling.

that point. They were merely the expression of the maximum amount of information which we could glean from the evidence and knowledge available to us at the time. Certain factors caused us to reevaluate our findings and continue our study. One of these factors was a highly detailed 1:10 scale model which was built to determine the accuracy and practicality of our previous results. We did not have to carry the model beyond the seventh strake of planking before fallacies developed. The initially envisaged framing plan, in which most frames had floors, was found to be doubtful and impractical, while the projected planking, although it seemed to satisfy the evidence of the surviving planking, did not appear mechanically feasible where it entered the stern rabbet. Another disturbing fact was that with the bow restored the way it was, the forwardmost amphora on the wreck would have lain more than half a meter upslope from the farthest extent of collapsed bow.

Information produced by two ship excavations became available at about that time which contributed to a resolution of these problems. As already noted in the preceding chapter, the first detailed publication of the Pantano Longarini ship remains led to a profitable reex-

amination of the slight evidence for our own hull's framing plan. The other helpful excavation was that of the Kyrenia ship, directed by Michael Katzev.[2] This remarkable find, dating to the fourth century B.C., was well preserved throughout three-fourths of its hull and has been physically preserved and reconstructed in the Crusader Castle, Kyrenia, Cyprus. The Kyrenia ship has nearly full runs of planking preserved and has shed considerable light on many of the mysteries surrounding ancient shell-first construction. Despite many differences in construction, a number of basic shell-construction techniques used in forming the Kyrenia ship's hull were quite obviously used in the Byzantine hull as well, and it now has become possible to develop a complete and mechanically sound planking plan for the Byzantine hull on the basis of its surviving planking and a better understanding of these techniques.

New lines and construction plans have evolved out of this new information from countless additional hours of research and model building, and many of the elusive problems of the past have been overcome. While the bow area is still largely conjectural, there is now at least a basis of fact for it.

## *Plans and Models*

The section on construction immediately following will continuously refer to the plans and the models. The ship's lines, Fig. 4-4, have been kept as simple as possible, and many of the features normally found on line drawings (deck structures, wales, and so on) are assigned to other plans. The station lines in Fig. 4-4, represented by letters forward from midships and numbers aft, do not necessarily represent any particular frame centers since frames were too crooked and spacing too irregular to base the stations on frame centers. The midship flat was located at the point of greatest surface area, and stations were spaced at 50-cm intervals fore and aft of that point. While the development of this set of drawings will be more thoroughly studied in the section on hull analysis, it is useful here in determining the scope and dimensions of the hull.

The Construction Plan illustrates construction details. It is a port-side elevation with frame outlines added. The frame numbering system, while not standard, is the one first used during excavation and described in detail in chapter 3, and it has been retained here to avoid confusion. The deck view of Fig. 4-5 locates the various topside appointments described in this and following chapters. More elaborate interior con-

struction details will be found in Fig. 4-6, a scaled sectional view (not isometric) of the stern, and Fig. 4-7, a side construction view of the stern interior. These drawings show the aft runs of ceiling strakes, the galley complex, and other construction aft of the cargo hold.

The model shown in Fig. 4-8 is one of two highly detailed 1:10 scale replicas which were built to gain additional insights related to hull construction. The first model, a full-hull model, duplicated every nail and mortise-and-tenon joint found in the original hull; it contributed greatly to the original drawings published in 1972. A more recent half-model was constructed only on the port side so that its interior was accessible for study and photography. With the exception of a few statements about starboard and full-hull construction, which refer to the earlier full-hull model, the step-by-step construction of the hull explained on the following pages is that followed on the half-model, and all illustrations pertaining to construction were photographed during the building of the half-model. The variations in a few minor details between the drawings and the model indicate attempts to analyze parallel building methods.

[2]S. W. Katzev and M. L. Katzev, "Last Harbor for the Oldest Ship," *NatGeo* 146, no. 5 (November, 1974): 618.

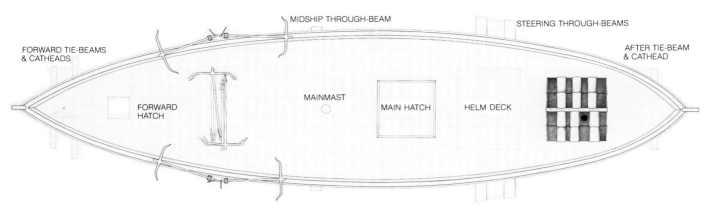

FIG. 4-5. Deck plan of the seventh-century Byzantine ship.

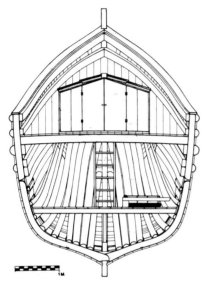

FIG. 4-6. Stern section of the ship at the forward galley bulkhead. *JRS and SWK*

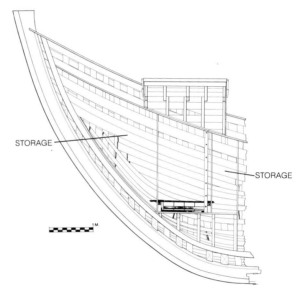

FIG. 4-7. Side interior view of the stern of the ship, showing storage areas. *JRS and SWK*

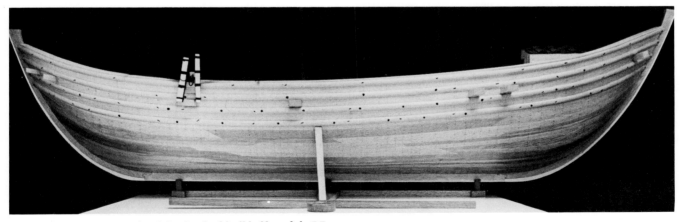

FIG. 4-8. Exterior port side of the finished hull half-model. *BB*

## KEEL AND POSTS

One can only speculate on the nature of a seventh-century shipyard—the arrangements for cutting and storing timber, the smithy, and the ways upon which the ship was built. Possibly these yards were not too much different from many of the small yards still to be seen along the shores of the eastern Mediterranean. A few stages for sawing and adzing timber, perhaps an open shed for

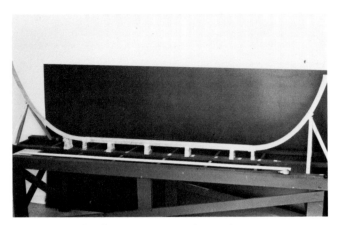

FIG. 4-9. Keel and posts set up on the stocks. *JRS*

storing wood, and a simple set of stocks close to the shore of some sheltered inlet may have been the scene for the birth of our humble merchantman.

Whatever the surroundings, the keel would have been set on stocks high enough to insert the frame bolts and work the bottom planking (Fig. 4-9). Being only slightly more than 12 m in length, sided 35.5 cm, and molded a maximum 22 cm, the keel was probably hewn from a single log of cypress. The keel tapered at the stern end, as described in the previous chapter, and a short box scarph was cut at that end. The bow end, for which no evidence could be found, was similarly treated on the model for reasons of planking symmetry which will be described later.

No evidence of a shoe, or false keel, could be found on the surviving portion of the keel, but its condition was such that whatever nailing evidence of a lightly fastened shoe remained could easily have escaped detection. We assumed the existence of a shoe and fitted one on the model. There were several reasons for this assumption. First of all, shoes are known to have already existed in the fourth century B.C., for the Kyrenia ship had a shoe still attached along the length of its keel. It hardly seemed likely that our ship, sporting a false sternpost, would not also have had protection for the keel, especially desirable when hauling the ship out for repairs. Second, in referring to Fig. 3-26, one can see how the false sternpost would have had to diminish rapidly in thickness at the scarph if there were no shoe. If the false post maintained its existing thickness throughout, a keel shoe 4.2 cm thick would have been used. A third argument for existence of a shoe lies in the fact that some sort of covering should have been present over the keel bolt recesses. These recesses, cut to house the heads of the keel bolts, could have been plugged and caulked, but a shoe would have afforded them much more protection.

We attached the model's shoe to its keel temporarily with two partially driven nails since it had to be moved aside later to allow installation of the bolts. The stem and the sternpost were made next and, being rather small posts, could have been cut from single select pieces of naturally curved timber. Although the curvature of the sternpost could not be determined from excavated remains aft of frame 8, some hint of its length and curvature could be derived from the planking. The rabbet of the sternpost used on the model was the minimum length which would permit all strakes to be seated if they continued their existing shapes and curvatures to the rabbet. There was sufficient preservation of the after ends of the first four strakes to make a precise determination of their run into the sternpost, while half of the remaining strakes survived far enough aft to preclude any possibility of a radical change in their width or curvature beyond the point of survival. The curve of the sheer was established as far aft as frame 12, and it is doubtful that the heavy wales would have radically changed their natural curve beyond that point. Thus, the sternpost height and curvature cannot have varied much from its dimensions indicated on the plans.

The shape of the stem is hypothetical but is based on a planking pattern discussed later. The false posts were not fitted until the floor bolts were inserted. Scarphs were cut in each of the posts to match their keel counterparts. The posts were then fitted to the keel simply by sliding them together and driving home the locking key.

It should be stated here that the scarph is unusually short and therefore weak when compared with latter-day keel scarphs, which were usually made to lengths equal to five times the keel height. Perhaps the shipwright felt that he did not need such strength at this joint, since the cargo hold terminated aft at the scarph and probably did likewise in the bow. Thus, no heavy load was carried aft of the scarph to cause hogging. After the posts were scarphed to the keel, each post was securely braced and blocked. The rabbet was then roughly cut on both sides of the keel and posts, and the shipwright was ready to start planking.

### PLANKS BEFORE FRAMES

At this stage a latter-day shipbuilder would have begun erecting his frames. Such was not the case with our ship. For all practical purposes this ship was shell-built in the tradition of earlier vessels. Several facets of construction are apparent which imply the use of shell-first construction.

Perhaps the best indication of the older construction technique is the use of diagonal scarphing as opposed to butt joining of the planking strakes.[3] The model has taught us that diagonal joining of the strakes requires infinitely more time and skill than butt joining. Had the frames already been in place, it certainly would have been more advisable to butt join the planking ends.

The planking exhibits configurations characteristic of shell-first construction. The Kyrenia ship had presented us with a detailed picture of how, in shell-first construction, hull shape is determined by variations in the widths of the strakes, their edge angles, and their curvature with relation to adjacent strakes. We shall not go into the details of these methods here, but a short explanation is necessary.

When planks are set up on preerected frames, they can be applied with great force by drawing them against the frames and their adjacent strake with clamps, jacks, and brute force. Thus, except for the ends of the ship and the garboards, where some shaping is needed, such planking is cut to its desired thickness and fairly straight on one edge, forced into the proper contour, and held in position with several treenails or bolts in each frame. To be sure, a strake may have to be broadened somewhat to fill a large hull area, but not in great amounts. When extra surface area does need to be filled out, stealers are worked in. Not so with shell construction. Stealers were difficult to use, inherently weak, and avoided whenever possible. The shipwright, shaping the hull with each strake as he went, was obliged to change the width of the strake as his eyeball evaluation of the ship's lines demanded. Thus, planking widths doubled and trebled through the length of the hull, while both edges were altered to change strake width. Since the planks could not be pulled against frames, they were often shaped to their required lateral curvature and thickness to prevent excessive resistance around bends. In summary, planking applied to preerected frames is designed to offer the least resistance when bent in natural curves around the contours of those frames, while shell-type planking is designed to offer the least resistance to its adjacent strake edges. Reassembly Drawing II and the Construction Plan well illustrate these characteristics of shell construction. Notice, for example, how strake 4 widened as it rounded the stern and strake 11 doubled its width every few meters, their edges often producing strange humps and hollows. Such fitting of strake edges was extremely difficult, generally required the aid of edge fas-

[3] The few cases in which scarphed planking was used with frame-first construction, notably nineteenth-century American river steamers and local fishing boats, do not apply as an argument here. In most of these exceptions scarphing was the result of some construction variance unique to these types.

tenings, wasted a good deal of timber, and would have been totally unnecessary if preerected frames had existed. Undoubtedly the system lost favor when mold lofting was developed.

Mortise-and-tenon joints over frame faces are a good indication that the frames could not have been present when the joints were set up. As one who gained considerable experience in mortise-and-tenon joinery during the past few years, I can attest to the fact that the cutting of such a mortise only 1.5 cm from the frame face, especially in bottom planking, is virtually impossible. Yet in a number of such cases in evidence, the lay of the planking is such that the cutting of upper-edge mortises had to be done when the strake was already on the ship. Additionally, a number of tenons had a nail driven directly through them, attesting to the fact that the shipwright did not know where they were by the time he installed his frames; nor did he care. The tenons had performed their intended task, that of holding the planking edges in line until the frames could be inserted.

The scribe marks coinciding with frame locations on the inside surfaces of the hull planking would not have been necessary had the strakes been fastened to existing frames. Even if the shipbuilder found it expeditious to scribe a reference line for fitting his strake, he needed only to scribe one line. This is the suspected reason for the scribed line on the inner surface of wale 1 (p. 61). If the hull planking were already in place, however, and the carpenter intended to fit frames to its contours, he certainly would have found it to his advantage to scribe lines along the sides of the frame he was shaping and onto the strakes so that he could always hold the frame at the same location when checking its shape. Thus, the double scribe lines could be interpreted as some sort of difficulty the carpenter had in starting his lines, but they more likely indicate the possibility that he had cut too much wood from his frame faces at some stage and had to move the frame farther aft to compensate for his error.

Evidence exists for the use of half-frames, some not reaching the keel, while a total lack of evidence for an overlapping of frame-section ends suggests that floors and futtocks probably were unconnected. In such a case, only floors could have been preerected. A preerection of floors only, as opposed to full frames, would have gained nothing in lining out the ship and seems unlikely unless the builder was unable to assemble full frames. Since he did know how to fabricate longer strakes and the keel-sternpost complex by scarphing, we must rule out his inability to construct full frames.

While it is clear that our ship was essentially shell-built, the question remains whether or not molds or one

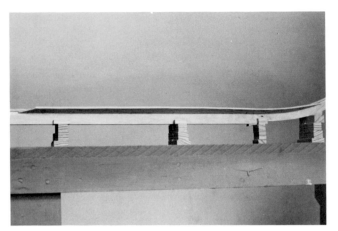

FIG. 4-10. After half of the port garboard resting in its rabbet during final fitting. *JRS*

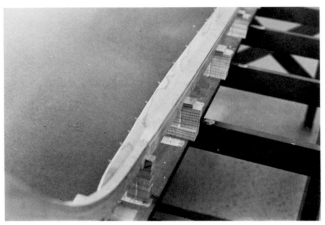

FIG. 4-11. Port garboard in place, with tenons set to fit strake 2. *JRS*

to several preerected frames were used in the construction. However, this is a question that may best be considered after all other aspects of the hull's construction have been thoroughly discussed.

### THE GARBOARDS

Each of the garboards on the model was made from two pieces of planking (Fig. 4-10). Single-piece garboards may have been more desirable, but they were found to be extremely difficult to install, and they wasted considerably more timber without greatly increasing hull strength. Possibly the original garboards were also fabricated in this manner. They were roughly cut to size and shape, then fitted to the rabbet while resting on nails driven just below the rabbet line. Although spacing between mortises in the keel could not have been less than 2.25 m (p. 59), the mortises in the keel and garboard of the model were spaced about 2.5 m apart simply because that seemed to be the maximum desirable spacing to maintain garboard alignment. The fact that the mortise spacing was so much greater along this straight edge than along the contoured edges of the upper hull is a good indication that the shipwright only cut as many mortises as he deemed necessary to keep his strake edges in alignment.

The width of the garboards was determined by scribing a line 1.5 cm above the top faces of stem, keel, and sternpost. This height was maintained from a point 60 cm aft of the keel to a point approximately the same distance forward of it. Beyond these points the garboards curved sharply into the rabbet. The pieces were then removed, the mortises cut, the rabbet finished, and the strake dressed off with the exception of final trimming, which was probably done on the ship.

Because of the diagonal scarph joints and the careful

fitting of strake edges, all the pieces making up a strake of planking were undoubtedly fitted on the ship at the same time, although they did not need to be finally installed as a single piece. The fitting of strake edges was an infinitely more demanding skill on shell-built vessels since the tightness of the hull depended solely on the seams. Mortise-and-tenon construction did not permit driven caulking, and a coating of pitch was the only means of seepage protection available to our ship. Thus, the seams had to be made tight enough to prevent seepage without relying on driven caulking at all.

The planking on the model was always laid port side first. The nails which held the garboard during fitting were pulled, and the after half of the strake was slipped down over the tenons inserted in the keel mortises and nailed through the rabbet. We had to be extremely careful with the narrow end at the sternpost. This problem was solved on the model by avoiding mortise-and-tenon joints in the posts to prevent edge splitting and by cutting this end of the strake from a board which had a natural grain curve at the end to reduce tension at the end of the plank. When the after portion of the garboard was firmly seated, the forward half was given a final fitting, and two mortise-and-tenon joints were cut into the scarph. It was not an easy task to get a perfect fit at these angle scarphs, so the joints helped align the strakes for the final trimming. The forward portion of garboard was installed in the same manner as its mate, the entire strake was then dressed to a smooth finish, and mortises were cut into its edge (Fig. 4-11). The process was repeated for the starboard garboard.

### BOTTOM PLANKING

Starting with the second strake, the expertise of the ancient shipwright really came to the fore.[4] Strakes 2 and 3 carried the curve of the garboard throughout—that is, their outer edges ran more or less equidistant from the outer edge of the garboard. From the evidence at hand, it appears our shipwright laid his strakes alternately from the bow and stern. This alternation was important, as it caused the scarph angles to reverse, thus avoiding patterns of weakness. More than that, it permitted the shipbuilder to fair off his curves from both directions and reduce chances of error, much as one changes directions occasionally when troweling cement or brushing on paint. Thus, strake 2 would have been fitted in two pieces, with the forward piece installed first, as indicated by the existing scarph. Strake 3 would have been installed stern first.

Most ancient hulls excavated to date have had pegged tenons. Once the pegs were driven, the seams stayed tightly together. This sort of construction permitted the installation of all strakes right to the rail cap before a single frame was inserted, if the builder so desired. The mortises on the Byzantine ship, however, are larger than the tenons, and the tenons are left unpegged. This looseness facilitated a slight shifting of the strakes while fitting them but did not keep the seams from pulling apart. The tenons did fit the mortises tightly with respect to their thickness and thus afforded some resistance to strake separation, but the builder had to overcome seam separation during construction by shaping his strakes so that there was no tension along the seam or, where this shaping was impractical, by using some bracing or clamping arrangement. Obviously, these techniques did not permit planking of the entire hull before framing. It is our conclusion that the builder most probably overcame this problem by arranging the framing so that it could be inserted gradually as the planking progressed.

The method of planking and framing hypothesized and described below is that which was worked out on the model. While every conceivable framing sequence and planking method was tried, both individually and in combination, the arrangement of short floors, long

FIG. 4-12. Stern with five strakes erected. Note widening of strake 4 near rabbet. *JRS*

floors, and half-frames shown on the Construction Plan seems to be the only one which satisfies all excavated evidence and structural considerations. Within the sequence of forty-five frames worked out in the preliminary reassembly of the hull remains, eight frames have been added on the Construction Plan: frames 15A, 26A, 28A, 30A, 32A, 36A, 40A, and 42A. Some of these frames may not in fact have existed, but all of them have been hypothesized at points where additional framing appeared structurally desirable, and their addition also serves to regularize the framing pattern.

Strakes 2 and 3 were held to each other and the garboard by their attachment to stem and sternpost, the mortise-and-tenon joints, and probably the help of a bit of bracing amidships. These strakes defined the bottom shape by following the line of the garboard. Strake 4, however, began to define the stern shape, as this strake became considerably wider aft in an approximate ratio to the increased stern area the builder hoped to achieve. Strake 5 roughly followed this new line but was narrowed somewhat aft of the fullest section of the stern (Fig. 4-12). Thus, the shipwright had now expressed his approximate desired hull contour in the upper edge of strake 5. He had also reached a stage at which it was necessary to permanently fasten the strakes thus far installed. On the model, at least, it would have been extremely difficult to start rounding the bilge with planking if some framing had not been put in. Sometime during the installation of strakes 5, 6, or 7, the short floor timbers were probably installed. Being inexperienced in the ancient tradition, we chose strake 5 on the model, but we suspect the ancient craftsmen could have maintained a tight fit until strake 7 was installed.

The short floors, occurring at every third frame, were flat enough to be cut from straight timber. They

[4]The planking of the Byzantine ship was not sufficiently well preserved to permit detailed conclusions regarding the method of shaping and fitting strakes, and in much of the description of the shaping and fitting of strakes 2 through 16 I rely heavily on my experience in studying and reassembling the physical remains of the Kyrenia ship. It was this experience that made possible an otherwise indeterminable planking plan for the Byzantine ship. It also should be understood that the planking plan forward of hull section C, although based on evidence further aft, could in fact have been somewhat different for reasons of wood condition or bow construction unique to that period that are unknown to us.

FIG. 4-13. Short floor timbers being installed. *JRS*

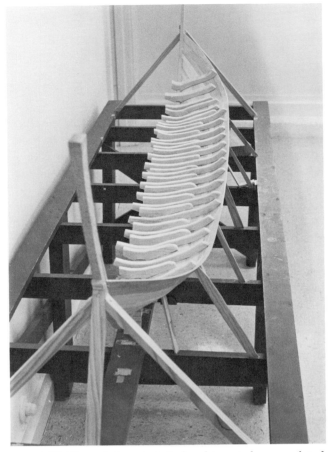

FIG. 4-15. Floor timbers installed and ten strakes completed. View from bow. *JRS*

FIG. 4-14. Nine strakes erected on the model before installation of long floor timbers and short end floors. *JRS*

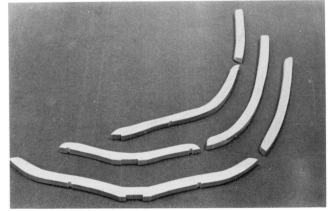

FIG. 4-16. Three common frame assemblies believed to have been used alternately in the Yassi Ada seventh-century hull. *JRS*

would have been hewn to a fine finish with iron adzes, the builder first making a rough cut and then holding the floor against the inside of the hull to mark its exact shape. When the roughly cut frame was fitted, a mark was scribed on the planking along each frame edge to note the location for checking its curvature as it was

being shaped. Small flats were cut into the bottom of each frame at its junction with the keel in order to form a triangular limber hole on either side of the keel. When the floor face was considered finished, it was nailed to the keel and the planking was nailed to the floor with iron nails (Fig. 4-13). This procedure was followed, start-

32    33  34  35    36    37    38    39    40    41    42    43    44    45

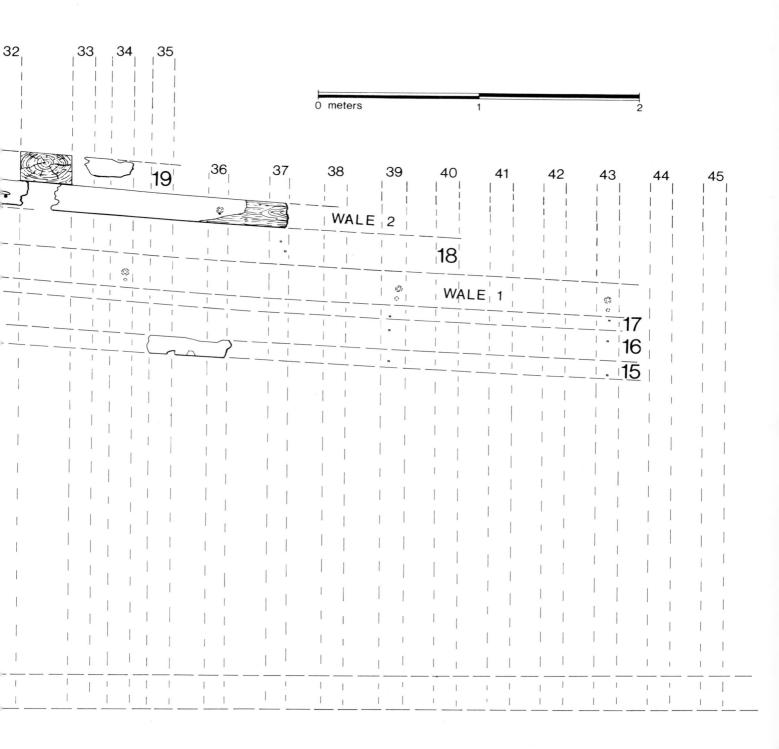

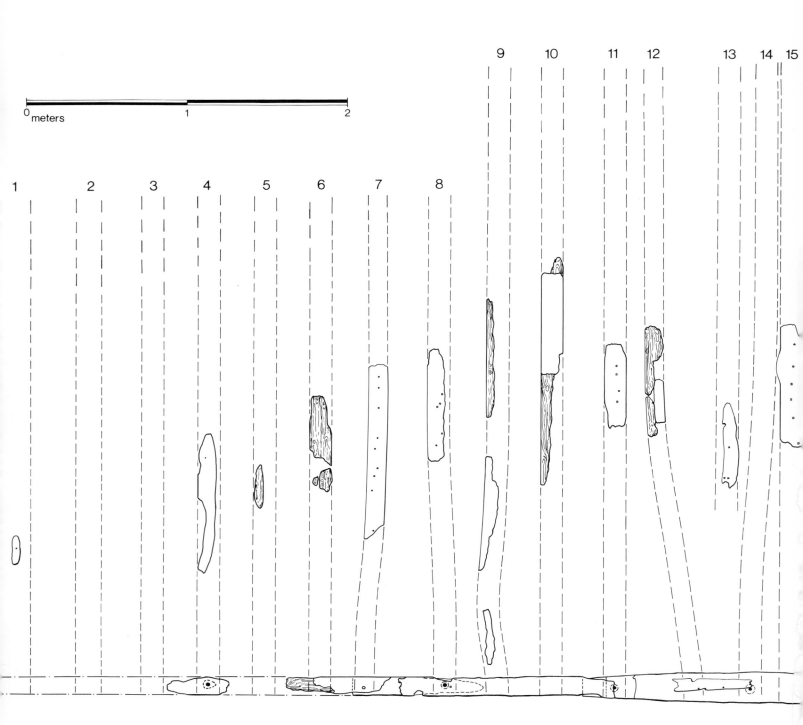

# REASSEMBLY DRAWING I. Keel, Sternpost, and Frames

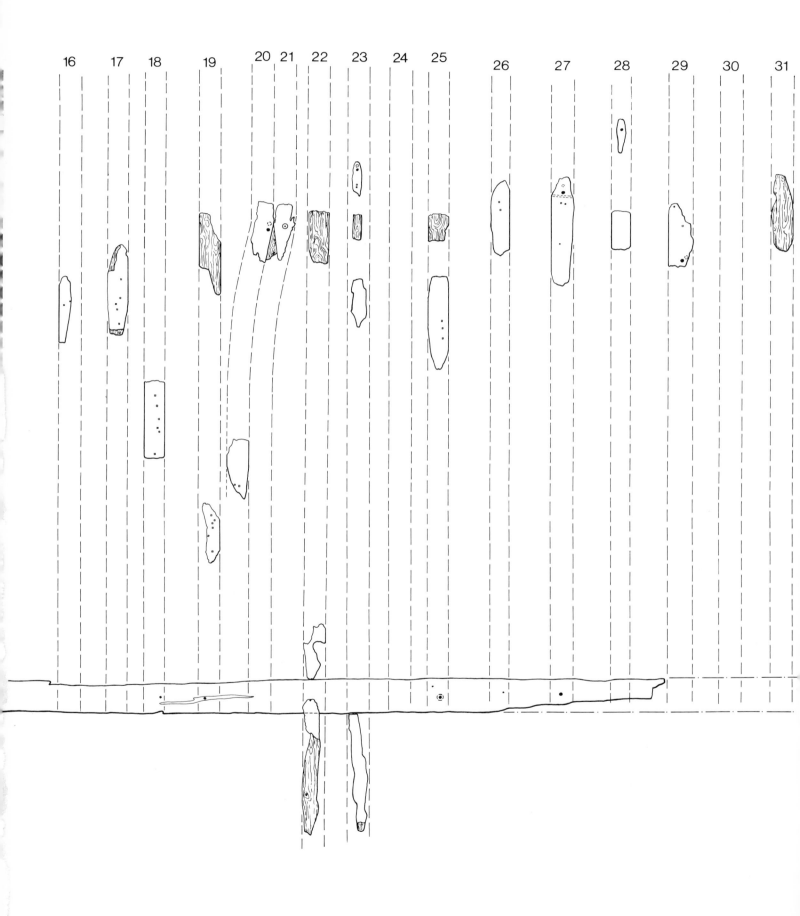

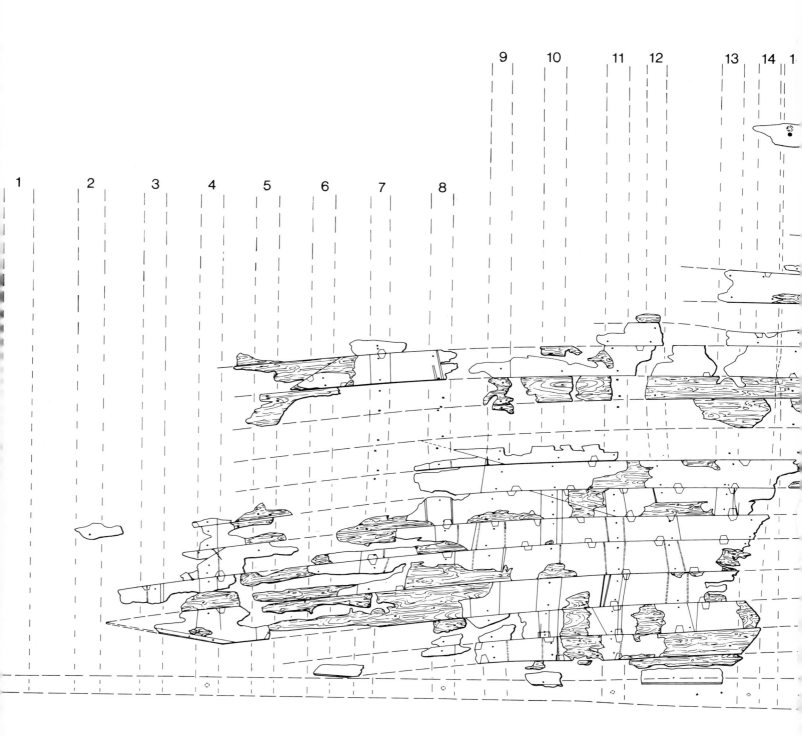

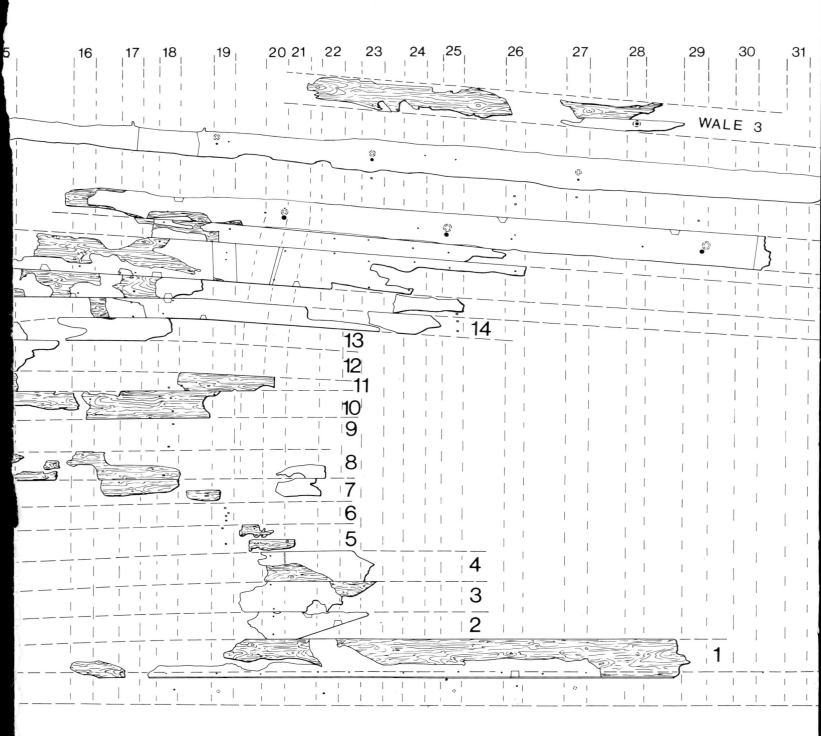

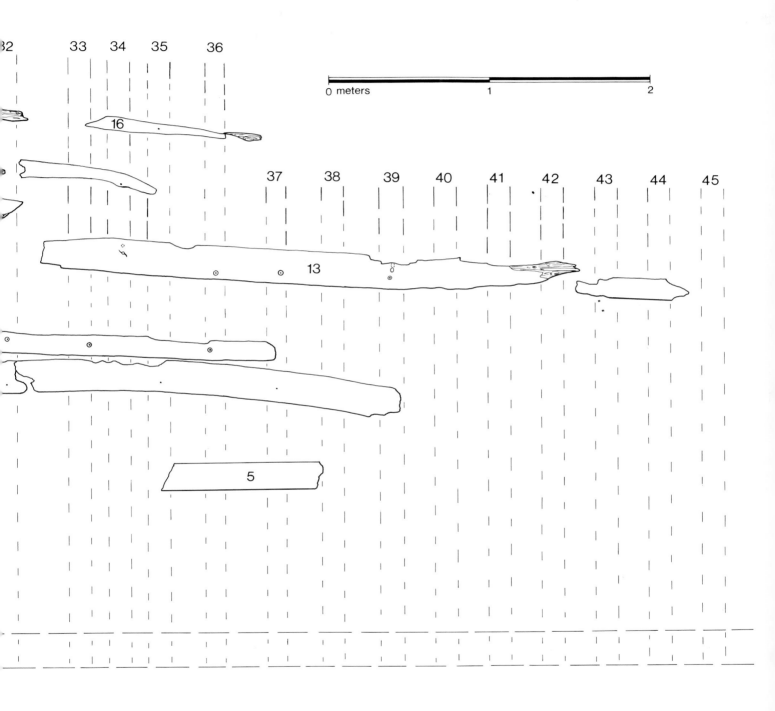

0 meters  1  2

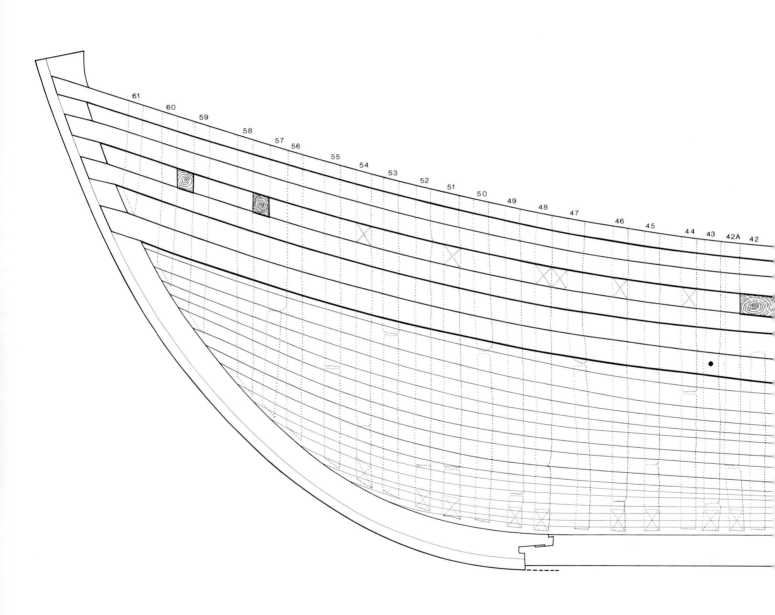

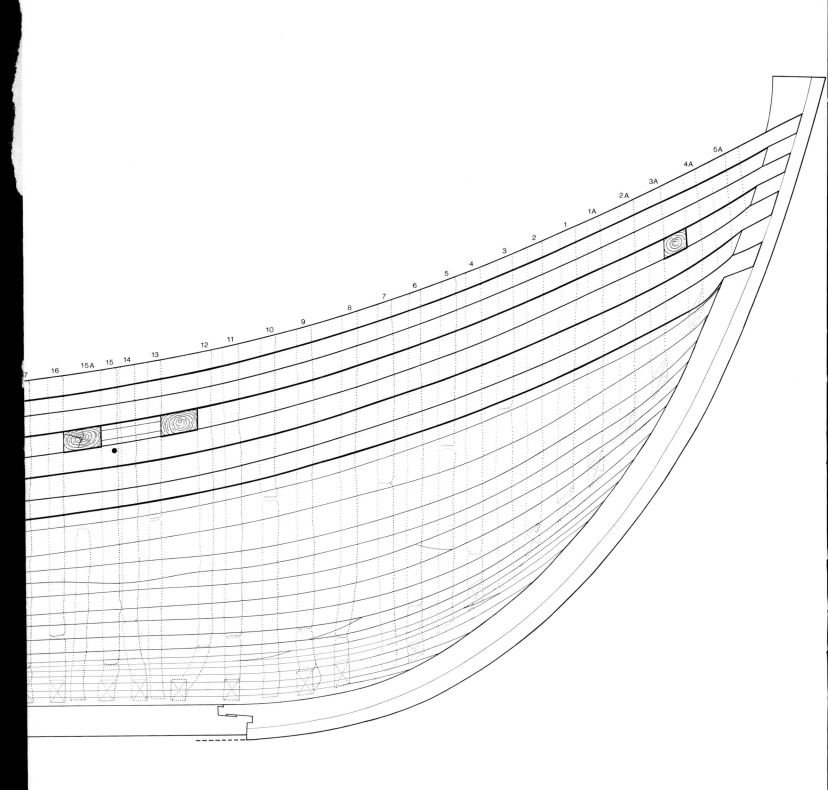

# CONSTRUCTION PLAN

0        1        2        3 Meters

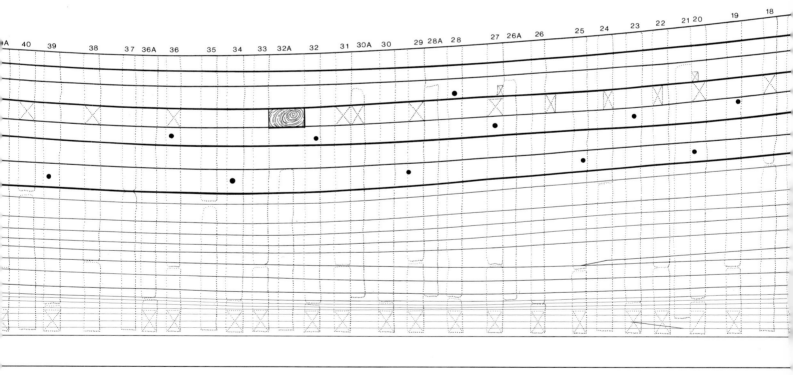

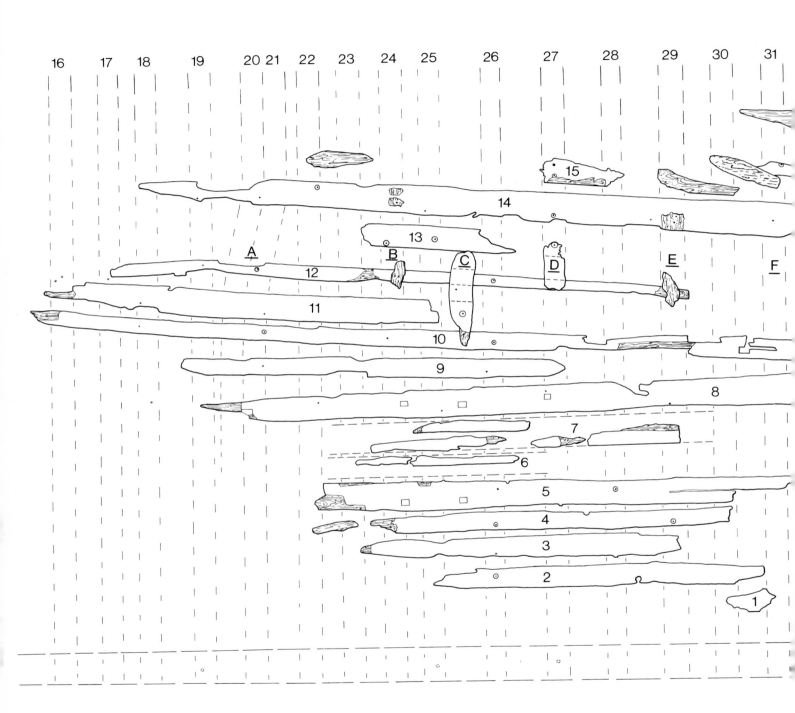

FIG. 4-17. Completed shell before being adzed smooth. Note the stealer, strake 11, just above the floor timbers and the difficult curvature of strake 12 above it. *JRS*

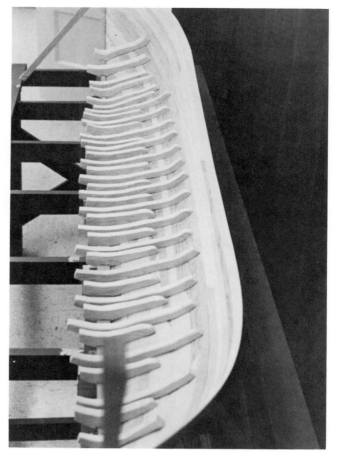

FIG. 4-18. Shell completed, ready for installation of half-frames. *JRS*

ing with frame 28 and alternately working aft to frame 15 and forward to frame 49. Fore and aft of these points it was found more convenient to install short floors on nine strakes, especially in the stern where the bottom was flatter (Fig. 4-14).

Strakes 6, 7, 8, and 9 progressively filled out the sheer line the shipwright hoped to achieve. As each strake rounded the bilge further, the shape of the bottom yielded to that of the sheer in the form of an ever-increasing sweep. The original ship was probably built to include strake 10 before the long floors were set. However, we found it advantageous to set long floors with only nine strakes in place and use the slightly extending floor arms amidships to help steady strake 10, which had a tendency to pull in here (Fig. 4-15).

The long floors were fitted in the same manner as the short floors. Similarly, they had triangular limber holes cut in them, and we also hypothesized a second set of watercourses along the seam of strakes 4 and 5 (Fig. 4-16). Every second long floor was nailed to the keel, and the strakes were then nailed to them. The intermediate long floors were not nailed to the keel so that they could later be drilled for bolts. An exception was frame 25, which had been nailed off-center to allow for drilling. This extra bolt was probably thought necessary to brace the stresses in the hatch area. No drilling or bolting was done at this stage.

### SIDE PLANKING

Hull strake 10 was broadened considerably in the stern area, but the necessity of a stealer became apparent here in order to simplify side planking. This long stealer,

strake 11, was the only one used on the ship, the rest of the filling out being done simply by varying strake widths (Fig. 4-17). A nail was required on the model to hold down the forward tip of strake 11 against the edge of strake 10.

Strake 12 was carefully fitted to the upper edges of 10 and 11. The shipwright simplified his work by placing his strake 12 scarph rather far aft where the planking curvature became difficult. Unlike strakes 6 and 9, whose scarph ends were nailed together, allowing them to be applied as single units, the forward end of strake 12 was fitted and installed first. It was necessary to fit the after end of this strake separately, inserting a tenon into the diagonal scarph. Pieces of planking such as the after section of strake 12 had to be exactly shaped from a much larger piece of timber. For this reason, we have come to the conclusion that considerably more wood was used to plank a shell-first hull than was used for a similar-sized frame-first vessel.

Strakes 13 and 14 illustrate the expertise of the ancient shipwright when it came to fitting outer planking.

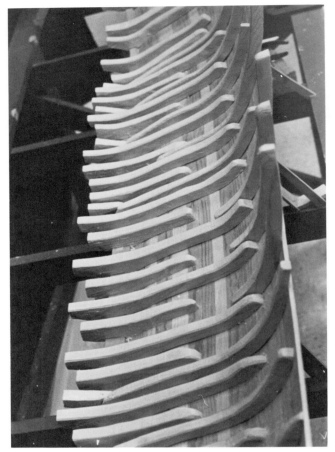

Fig. 4-19. Half-frames being installed. *JRS*

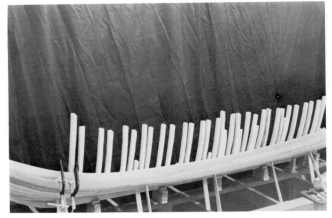

Fig. 4-20. Futtocks being clamped for nailing. *JRS*

We have surmised that the upper edge of strake 13 between frames 16 and 12 split away after installation or was deliberately cut away due to its erratic grain or a knot. Rather than remove strake 13 and lose his investment in time and timber, the builder simply fit strake 14 to 13, concave edge and all. Such a process would have been inadvisable when standing frames and driven caulking were used, but with planking shaped like this, it was possible and apparently practical.

Strakes 15 and 16 completed the shell-first construction. Strake 15 was a narrow strake whose main function was to fill out the stern area, where it reached a breadth of 29.2 cm. Strake 16 was a broad plank which made up the difference between the upper edge of strake 15 and the desired sheer. No mortises were cut in the top edge of strake 16 (Fig. 4-18).

### LINING THE HULL

After the first sixteen strakes were fitted, the shipwright turned to another task—that of stiffening the hull. His first effort was directed toward the installation of half-frames which apparently partially crossed the keel. From the evidence at hand it appears that only one side of the frame was nailed to the keel, when it was nailed at all, and for this reason we have drawn the assumption that the half-frame pairs met in some sort of diagonal butt that may have been nailed together (Fig. 4-19). The practice of nailing only one of a pair of diagonally butted half-frames occurred on the Pantano Longarini ship, and off-center nails in our own keel were noted for frames 13 and 18.

The portside half-frame 13 was extended all the way in to the keel on the model, despite some evidence set forth in the previous chapter (p. 59) suggesting that it may not have extended any closer in than strake 7. The model has indicated that extension to the keel was necessary to maintain continuity of strength. No nailing evidence for frame 13 existed in the bottom six portside strakes, but the frame may not have been nailed to these strakes because of its close proximity here to frame 14. Such an absence of nailing could have made it possible for some pitch on the inside of the planking to seep in under the frame. Finally, there was a scribe mark on strake 3 that may have been made to mark the position of frame 13.

Frame 21 did not reach the keel and probably had the function of a rider or futtock that doubled frame thickness in an area of stress where the after limit of the hatch was located. We have hypothesized such partial frames at three other points as well: frame 26A, where the forward limit of the hatch was located; frame 28A, where a deck-beam almost certainly occurred which would have carried great weight, since cargo would have been stacked in this area before being passed down the hatch; and frame 30A, where the after end of the partner for the mast, which we have located just forward of frame 32 on the model, would have required double bracing.

When all half-frames, from 3 to 59, were installed, the shipwright completed the installation of the futtocks

FIG. 4-21. Keelson and inner posts bolted in place and ceiling installation begun. *JRS*

FIG. 4-22. Lower ceiling at after end of hold. *JRS*

extending above the floors. These were simply clamped in place, and the planking was nailed to them. The method used on the model was to clamp the middle of the futtock to strake 16 and to force the bottom of the futtock against the planking by a brace wedged between opposing members (Fig. 4-20). The half-frames were similarly braced and clamped for nailing. Futtocks ran all the way to the rail but were left longer on the model at this stage and cut off later. Remaining floors in bow and stern were also now applied.

No hint of the nature of the short frames in the ends of the ship existed, and they could have been cant frames, floors, half-frames, or solid timbering. On the model we hypothesized half-frames butted and nailed together on the center of the posts. This method was used only because it was the simplest means we could find to achieve the required stiffening. It must be understood that no basis for construction existed forward of the stem scarph or aft of frame 1 other than that suggested by the known areas.

After all framing was in except the top-timbers above half-frames (which had no place for attachment yet), internal longitudinal stiffening began. The shoe was slid out to one side past the keel centerline to allow for working the bolts, and the outside of the hull was better braced now that nailing was completed. The keelson and inner posts were then worked in. Nothing remained of these members, but their existence is hypothesized because of the relatively advanced stage of other internal scantling. On the model, the keelson was squared to the width of the keel amidships (22 cm), and this height was maintained throughout the lengths of the posts. The widths, however, duplicated the width of the keel and posts throughout. Inner posts were diagonally scarphed to the keelson about 1 m aft and forward of the outer

scarphs to avoid points of weakness. All three members were nailed to the floors wherever the floors were nailed to the keel. At every long floor (and floor 25) holes were drilled for bolts through keelson, floor, and keel. Recesses for bolt heads were cut in keel, stem, and sternpost, and the bolts were installed (Fig. 4-21). Bolts at frames 11 and 48 stiffened the scarphs as well. One of the two bolts found near the top of step sector 1C has been assigned to the scarph at frame 48, and the other, to a long floor at frame 45.

The shoe was now replaced and nailed fast on the model. The false stem and false sternpost could be fastened at this stage, and these parts were cut from naturally curved wood and nailed on. The model had become considerably stiffer by this time, so we could remove some of the stem and stern bracing and use it for ceiling.

The use of half-logs for ceiling and wales on this ship is odd indeed. Still, one cannot doubt their comparative strength and the economy of simply sawing a log in half to acquire two important timbers. A half-log has the comparative strength of a squared timber taken from a much larger log. The main objections one could raise to the existence of half-log timbers on our ship are that their appearance was not as pleasing to the eye as that of standard wales, especially since their widths kept changing, and that their rounded surfaces were probably inconvenient to walk on and store cargo upon where they were used as ceiling.

Ceiling strake 1 was laid first, leaving room along the keelson for limber boards. Ceiling strakes 2, 3, and 4 were installed in turn. All four strakes were carried forward and aft to the ends of the ship, where they met the upper ceiling clamps. There does not seem to have been a definite nailing pattern in fastening these ceiling strakes, nor was a convenient one found. The nailing

FIG. 4-23. Completed ceiling, looking aft. *JRS*

FIG. 4-24. Completed ceiling, looking forward. Note the convergence of upper ceiling strakes and the open area along the keelson where limber boards were removed. *JRS*

pattern adopted for the model is such that at least one of these strakes was nailed to each frame, thereby giving the hull a very stiff bottom.

Ceiling strakes 5 and 8 both had flat bearing surfaces that extended far beyond the limits of the hatch (Fig. 4-22), and there is the possibility that additional mortises existed in ceiling strake 5 outside the hatch area. Thus, we must assume that possible uses of these bearing surfaces could have included support for temporary decking, cargo partitioning, or cargo bulkheads. Such bearing surfaces would not have been needed beyond the limits of the hold, and for this reason ceiling strakes 5 and 8 were terminated at frames 11 and 48 on the model. (It should be noted here that the deck-beam stanchions hypothesized for the mortises in ceiling strakes 5 and 8 seemed unnecessary and much in the way on the model, but we may have made the hatch opening wider than was the case.)

Ceiling strakes 7 and 11 were flat filler boards with no structural strength and were also terminated at the ends of the hold. Ceiling strakes 6, 9, and 10 were struc-

tural, however, and were carried to the ends of the ship (Fig. 4-23). Finally, ceiling strake 12 was a reversed half-log which had little or no structural function other than to serve as a bearing surface for the knees. It was terminated on frames 11 and 48, where deck load became necessarily light aft and beams so narrow forward that knees were not necessary (Fig. 4-24).

### THE TOPSIDES

With the installation of the ceiling planking, the shipwright had completed all scantling below the waterline and was prepared to tackle the heavy timbers above—the wales, clamps, and beams. The wales were cut from logs which averaged 30 cm in diameter, but they by no means held this dimension. Within limits of evidence, the wales varied in width from 17 cm to 22 cm. It is quite obvious from Reassembly Drawing II that no attempt was made to change uneven cross-sections or the natural taper of the logs. It is equally obvious that these timbers

FIG. 4-25. Clench nails on stempost fastening port wales. Chocks were inserted for further bolting of wales. *JRS*

FIG. 4-26. Wales and through-beams in place. Nail cap being treenailed in place. *Donald H. Keith*

were placed with their broad and narrow ends alternating in progressive strakes. Thus, wale 1 had its broad end toward the bow and narrowed as it went astern, wale 2 was broad in the stern and narrowed toward the bow, and so on. These wales, averaging more than 25 m in length, were not likely to have been made of single timbers, although such lengths probably would have been available to the shipwright. We used single timbers on the model to avoid hypothesizing scarph joints, but the drawing shows the timbers broadening again at the ends. In any case, the same log possibly contributed halves of the same wale on each side of the ship.

Before the wales were attached on the full-hull model, frames on opposite sides of the ship were braced by spawls (cross-braces) set between their upper ends and temporary cross-braces over ceiling strake 12. A mark was scribed across the inside of wale 1 at its midpoint in length, and the wale was held against the port side of the ship so that this mark lined up with the forward edge of frame 30 and the bottom of the wale was 10 cm above strake 16. From that point toward the ends of the ship the wale was then drawn in by brute force or whatever equipment the builders of that day employed, and it was clamped and clench-nailed about every second long futtock. Between the clench nails, the frames were nailed to the wale. In both nailing and clench nailing, the nails were driven through the frames and into the wale, never the opposite. It took quite a bit of persuasion to draw the ends of the wales into the posts, and their final end finishing was done just before they reached that point. On the full-hull model a similar procedure was followed for starboard wale 1. On the model we attached the ends by first clench nailing the port wale to the posts, then clench nailing the starboard wale to the post and the port wale. We then let little chocks in

against the wales and posts and ran bolts through wales and chocks (Fig. 4-25).[5] Rather than rely on the rabbet alone, we also let the wales of the model feather out over the posts, making for an easier fit and more fastening area.

The second wales were mounted in the same manner as the first, leaving a space of approximately 20 cm between the two amidships. Note that the space between the wales and between wale 1 and hull strake 16 varied according to the thickness and shape of the wales, but always the sheer shape dictated by the upper edge of strake 16 was adhered to as closely as was practical.

After wale 2 was in place, the top-timbers above the half-frames were nailed to the two wales. The clamps, strong internal timbers which had a reverse force to that of the wales and completed the clamping effect at the top of the hull, were installed. Two clamps, ceiling strakes 13 and 14, were combined at the waterline and formed the backing for wale 1. Mere half-logs could not be used for the clamps since bearing surfaces for knees and/or riders were needed. The clamps were drawn tightly against the inner frame faces, then nailed to about every third frame. The bolts fastening together wale 1 and ceiling strake 13 were also inserted at this time. The next clamp, ceiling strake 14, was the backing clamp for wale 2 and was installed in the same manner as the previous clamps. It was also the shelf clamp, supporting through-beams and deck beams alike.

The through-beams were installed at this stage, and then the upper two wales and their corresponding clamps were put on (Fig. 4-26). The reader may question the wisdom of using wales above deck. The model

[5] Bolts were used to fasten the ends of wale pairs to posts in the fourth-century ship at Yassi Ada (G. F. Bass and F. H. van Doorninck, Jr., "A Fourth-Century Shipwreck at Yassi Ada," *AJA* 75 [1971]: 31).

FIG. 4-27. Decking being laid. *JRS*

FIG. 4-28. Deck, clamps, and cap in place. *JRS*

FIG. 4-29. Deck view of completed half-model. *JRS*

shed some light on this problem by indicating that the upper wales did help to form a sort of box structure, absorbing some of the stresses transmitted through the frames and therefore adding to the strength of the whole. However, great care had to be taken to equalize the strain of wales and clamps when applying them to the model.

Another problem was the proximity of wale 3 and its clamp to the deck. Since wale 3 was at deck level and the clamp nearly touched the deck, the method of locating scuppers to drain off deck water and of deck framing and fastening were questionable. While the evidence points rather strongly toward a deck at this precise level, we shall not hypothesize the nature of the deck construction.

Since a deck had to be installed on the model to show other features, we proceeded as follows. After the through-beams were mounted and the top wales and corresponding clamps were installed, the deck framing was put in, including hatch coamings and deckhouse lining (Fig. 4-27). The ancient shipwright, of course, could have reversed this procedure, laying all beams and deck-

ing first and then working the top wales and clamps from the comfort of the deck. Deck beams were crowned 5 cm amidships. The deck was laid as straight, caulked planks, and it was fitted to small waterways mounted along the clamps (Fig. 4-28). The space between the clamps was then boarded shut to prevent water from

Fig. 4-30. Bottom view of completed half-model. *JRS*

Fig. 4-31. Stern view of completed hull. *JRS*

running between the frames and into the hold.

After the decking was completed, the excess lengths of frames were sawed off, and the rail cap was mounted to seal off the openings. Strakes 17, 19, 21, and 23 were now carefully fitted and nailed to the frames. Finally, the stem and sternpost were cut to their proper heights and shaped. This completed the hull construction.

## JOINERY

The joinery work within the hull and the deckhouse remained to be completed. No forward bulkhead was assumed in the hold, since some of the amphoras apparently wedged in the forepeak when the ship sank, indicating that they had free intercourse with the entire bow area. Probably a little platform forward on which to store anchor cables and gear was the extent of forward accomodations, and we placed a small hatch on the

model's foredeck to provide access to this area. Evidence for the main hatch was well documented in the preceding chapter, but the manner of framing and coaming was a matter for speculation. The steering deck was the subject of considerable experimentation, for it was found that the helmsman could not have steered from deck level, nor could he have steered from aft of the paired through-beams. The matter is further discussed later in this chapter, but we may note here that a suggestion of such a deck exists in a sixth-century representation.[6] Because of their conjectural nature, neither helm deck nor quarter rudders (or steering oars) were installed on the model.

Sufficient coverage will be given the galley, anchors, and small finds in their respective chapters, so it is not necessary to discuss them here. The model's galley was supplied with roof tiles and a hearth, but artifacts and hearth gratings were left out to better illustrate this area in the next chapter. Figs. 4-29 through 4-32 show the completed model from various angles.

[6] The cave frescos at Ajunta, India. A good reproduction exists in the South Kensington Museum, and a good model is in the Commercial Museum, Philadelphia.

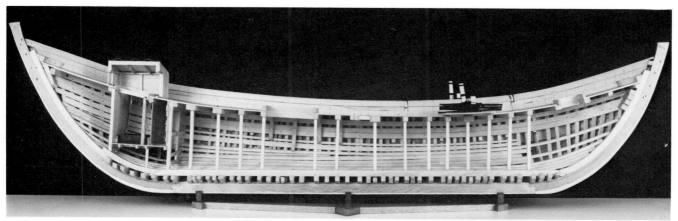

Fig. 4-32. Interior view of completed half-model. *BB*

## *In Retrospect*

Before we turn away from the analysis of construction, a popular dispute should be considered. Discussions on the shell-first building technique are frequently spiced with arguments concerning the use of molds or various types of frames in assembling the strakes.[7] There were simply not enough remains, especially of frames, to determine the precise, detailed sequence in assembling this hull. We have, therefore, investigated all possible methods of construction and have used the one which we deem most likely in building the model.

The shape of all hulls is to some extent predetermined. Nineteenth-century American frigates were precisely planned by drafts, mold lofts, models, and specifications from which the shipwright took his measurements and built his hull. Only minor details were left to the discretion of the builder. At the other end of the scale are early vessels such as the Kyrenia ship, for which the shipwright used no mechanical aids in shaping his hull. But even here, some predetermination of hull shape must have been involved. Certainly the builder had to know what size and type of hull he was to construct. He would have had the hull shapes figured out in his mind, and their application would then have been controlled by experience and the materials at hand. Somewhere between these two extremes lies the method used to determine and control the shape of the Byzantine hull.

Although ours was essentially a shell-built hull, the use of control frames cannot necessarily be ruled out. During the last few centuries control frames have been used for many reasons, but the most common purpose was to avoid elaborate drafts or mold lofting. Smaller yards engaged in the building of local craft often used this method. A few of the more critical hull shapes were taken from a half-model, rough drawing, or even the builder's mind. Frames were made to these shapes and set up on the keel, and the whole assembly was faired with battens to assure good hull contours. The planking was then applied to these widely spaced frames, and the intermediate frames were inserted after the hull was planked. Such a method of building required less preparation and technology than that employed by more conventional methods but was usually limited to designs with which the builder was familiar. It can be argued

that the Byzantine hull could have been so framed, the wales bent on, and the planking laid up in succession for the first sixteen strakes. The hull could then have been finished off by inserting the four filler strakes adjacent to the wales and adding the intermediate frames. The possibility of such a method cannot be flatly denied, but it was avoided in the building of our exhibition model for the following reasons.

First, a control frame should be sturdy and well braced to withstand the pressures of applying planking as heavy as that of the Byzantine hull. It should be fairly straight and plumb to the keel to perform a proper job. If a control frame had been necessary anywhere in this hull, it would have been in the area of the sternpost scarph. There is no evidence to substantiate the existence of such a frame among the surviving hull members in this area. On the other hand, scribe marks, mortise-and-tenon joints over frame faces, indications of crooked frames, and nonattachment of frames to the keel occur in sufficient combination to indicate that control frames were probably not used within the area where the hull remains were in good condition.

Second, mortise-and-tenon joints should not have been necessary unless control frames were spread extremely far apart. It would have been much easier to set a few more control frames than to make all those mortise-and-tenon joints. It can be argued that these joints were traditional and therefore a construction habit, but to those who have cut such joints in quantity, such an argument seems preposterous. The models have shown us that these joints did add some strength to the hull. Thus, they conceivably could have been used in conjunction with control frames to compensate for the fact that the strakes were so lightly nailed to the frames. However, we have come to the conclusion that the joints were not a compensation for, but instead permitted, the light nailing of strakes to frames. After all, most of the excavated Mediterranean ships that predate this one exhibit considerably stronger nailing methods. The combination of light nailing and mortise-and-tenon joints employed here seems to have been yet another economy measure on the part of the builder. Since the joints were already there, he could use a lighter nailing pattern without fear of individual strakes pulling away under stress. By driving adjacent nails at different angles, as he often did, additional holding power was achieved.

Third, the shapes of the planking strakes were not those which could be expected to be used with control

---

[7]The use of molds by some present-day builders, especially around the Persian Gulf and in Scandinavia, is usually suggested as a reason for the need for molds. These forms of construction do not follow that of the Byzantine shipwright and therefore are irrelevant.

frames. Certainly a builder with enough expertise to construct a vessel using control frames would have known how to cut planking edges so they would fit more naturally around the face of a frame. Again, this strake pattern seemed to work well only when the strake being applied was free-standing and bent to its curvature before application. In other words, the pattern is one suited more to naturally curved or prebent strakes than to strakes forced around some sort of form.

Finally, the use of control frames would suggest a degree of technology not elsewhere apparent in this hull. Since the ability of this shipwright to develop the surfaces of control frames is at least questionable, we have not deemed it advisable to assume such an ability.

Molds and temporary frames used as methods for controlling the shape of this hull are even more difficult to confirm or deny. Molds or widely spaced temporary frames could have been used to express the shipwright's intended hull shapes without the involvement of formal naval architecture. He still may have needed his time-tested method of edge fastening the strakes, and also diagonal planking butts, if molds were spaced far apart or used only to express the midship bend. The lay of the planking is the lone argument one could present against the use of molds or temporary frames. It is not my intention to flatly state that molds or frames were not used in the construction of this hull, but rather to suggest, on the basis of experience gained from the models and knowledge of other ancient hulls, that molds or frames would not have been needed and were better dispensed with. Thus, we selected the simplest method that satisfied all the evidence. Frames were added after each few strakes of planking, sometimes with both operations occurring almost simultaneously, but with the planking always controlling the shape of the frames.

One final suggestion should be made here for the reader's consideration. The fact that the shipwright used edge-fastened strakes on the lower part of the hull but not topsides indicates that he approached these two areas with differing degrees of percipience. It was infinitely more difficult to determine hull shapes below the waterline than above it. The lines drawings of Fig. 4-4 indicate the comparative complexity of lower hull shapes. The upper 2 m of hull, on the other hand, had relatively flat sides with a smooth, naturally curving sheer. It is quite possible that this ship was representative of a stage in shipbuilding history at which builders were just learning to set frames and to properly shape frame faces before erecting planking. A natural beginning for such a step would have been in this elementary area of the up-

per hull, and, without the technology or frame strength to apply heavy quarter-sawn wales to this sheer, half-round timbers were used for simplicity. Lacking experience at mounting half-round timbers on frames, we experimented and found that they were much easier to apply to a sheer curve like that found on the Byzantine hull than were quarter-sawn timbers of the same size.

The ceiling strakes which structurally braced the hull interior may be similarly considered. If used in great lengths, they would have gone in under tension and would have been much more expeditiously applied in their half-round state, especially if the frames were as weak as we have hypothesized. Therefore, economy may not have been as great a factor in the composition of these timbers as was structural convenience.

One may question why the clamps which backed the wales were not so rounded. The shipwright needed a flat bearing surface on these timbers to accommodate bolt washers and knees and/or riders and perhaps for additional reasons unknown to us. However, even here the edges adjoining the frames were somewhat rounded. The clamps could have been shaped before installation. They could also have been installed by pulling straight timbers against the inside of the frames along the flatter portions of the hull sides and scarphing short, bent pieces to their ends where hull curvature was extreme, a practice not uncommon in latter-day shipbuilding. Whatever the method, the installation of these members was greatly simplified, since the presence of the wales had made the upper part of the hull quite rigid.

Whether or not one accepts the theory that the installation of the topsides of this hull represents an early step toward frame-first construction, it cannot be denied that two separate techniques of hull construction were represented here. This hull, with its loosely and partially tenoned strakes, represents a faster and more economical method of construction than that of earlier vessels, whose excavated remains reveal rigidly tenoned hulls throughout. Nor can it be denied that the structural components of this hull show an advanced knowledge of the elements of fabrication on the part of the builder. The transition from shell to skeletal construction must have happened slowly. The fact that at least part of this hull had been built onto existing frames is an indication that the transition was well under way in this period. The time when frames were set before strakes, mortise-and-tenon joints were eliminated, and the projection of hull lines was mastered could not have been far off.

## An Analysis of the Hull

It cannot be denied that the ship models played a very helpful role in the reconstruction of this ship. Although they undoubtedly failed in some cases to resolve problems and left a multitude of questions unanswered, their three-dimensional scope very often served to suggest solutions that now seem elementary but were not immediately evident without the benefit of three-dimensional construction.

A major reason for building the experimental models was that the ship seemed to violate so many sound practices of naval architecture. We had thought that perhaps they would show us another hull shape or an error which would change the curvature of some member. Largely they did not do this. The deep, narrow hull and the erratic framing plan have been confirmed, while the bulwarks still look as if the ship were plowing through a logjam.

To work on the models was to understand one point clearly: the construction of this ship was not as awkward as outward appearances suggest. The planking runs were graceful and relatively easy to install. They made good sense looking aft along the bilge. And when one learned to cock the saw a bit near the ends of the wales, one could appreciate that, with a little practice, half-round wales may be easier to install than square ones and infinitely less expensive. If the models helped us form conclusions, not the least of these was the realization that this ship was not a freak at all, but rather another design from another age with which we had not been familiar.

To understand the reasons for the design of our ship, we must have at least a little knowledge of the conditions under which she sailed. During the seventh century, maritime trade played an indispensable role in Byzantine economic life, for many land routes linking the various regions of the empire had become severed, or virtually so, because of territorial losses and greatly reduced population levels resulting from famine and plague. At the same time, territorial losses and reduced population levels meant that the total volume of trade within the empire decreased. The large merchant ships and state-financed merchant fleets of the Roman period disappeared, and a maritime trade reduced in volume, but even more vital than before, came to be served by independent owners of small merchantmen.[8]

These shipowners were frequently men of relatively

moderate means who simultaneously played the roles of shipowner, captain, and merchant. Even so, they became an important and influential class in Byzantine society during the seventh century. They codified the customary practices under which they operated in the Nomos Nautikos or Rhodian Sea-Law, which, among other things, strictly regulated the sizes of crews, cargoes, and even budgets of ships. Our own ship suggests that their vessels often reflected considerable pride in status, but a very practical pride as well.

It is likely that new developments in ship construction played an important role in the rise of these middle-income shipowners, for many of the methods employed in the construction of our seventh-century ship are more economical than those of earlier periods. We might do well to summarize these more economical methods here.

Mortise-and-tenon joints were smaller and more sparsely situated than those noted on earlier hulls. The oversized mortises were much more quickly cut, and pegs no longer were employed to lock the joint on either side of the planking seam. Above the waterline, the shipwright had learned to eliminate these joints entirely. Large clench nails and wooden treenails employed on planking of earlier ships were replaced by a light, fast nailing system. The use of half-logs for wales and ceiling has been previously discussed, but the fact that they were not faced off or dressed in any manner suggests the priority economy had over appearance.

Perhaps the lines of the ship best illustrate the trend of construction in this period. No frills adorned the existing portions of the hull. In fact, the design is such that complex methods of construction were completely avoided. Easy planking runs and frame shapes eliminated reverse curves and difficult contours. The hull, deep and narrow, was probably fast and seems designed to produce the extra voyaging needed to turn larger profits.

If our ship seems too lightly timbered, we should remember she was not an Atlantic courier. In fact, she was probably not intended for heavy weather at all. Available literature indicates that sailing schedules were, if anything, a bit more restricted than they had been in the Roman period. In other words, Byzantine sailors were probably fair-weather sailors, keeping their ships in port when the strong winds blew from the north during the winter. They were never too far from a landfall, and their knowledge of trade winds and currents has been established.

Our ship seems perhaps too sharp in the bow, but

---

[8] For a general discussion, see R. S. Lopez, "The Role of Trade in the Economic Readjustment of Byzantium in the Seventh Century," *DOP* 13 (1959): 69–85.

literary sources indicate that slimmer, swifter vessels were developed in this period because of increased insecurity at sea,[9] and a brief analysis of the hull's lines and statistics may help to determine whether or not she is an awkward ship. It should be stated at the outset that much thought and experimentation went into the design of the hypothetical bow. The mold models were primarily built for this purpose. The planking and framing patterns existing aft were carried out forward, and excavated evidence dominated the fairing of all lines. Buttock lines were extended forward as projections from the known areas. The sheer is debatable from amidships forward, but it, too, was strongly influenced by other factors such as concentration of cargo and a minimum possible hull length dictated by cargo dispersion on the seabed. Any real increase in length, on the other hand, would have produced impossible coefficients and lines.

The vessel had an extremely fine entry, one considerably finer than might have been expected for this period. Her garboard was slightly hollow, and for the greater extent of the hull this hollow carried to the third and fourth strakes. Whether intended or not, this concavity increased stability. Since there were no frames to draw in the planking, the only possible hollow in a ship with this type of construction is that made with an adze. Elsewhere, the hull was composed of a rather graceful series of convex curves. The bottom rose rather sharply but curved easily into a side which continued its overhang to the stern. The full stern, which housed a galley, rapidly diminished into a high sternpost.

Students of the architecture of latter-day sailing ships may be surprised to see the plan of a ship with a midship section located well into the after half of the vessel. In fact, the maximum hold area occurred 1 m still further aft. However, the exceptionally well-preserved Kyrenia ship has a similar heavy afterbody and fine bow. This may possibly have been a characteristic of shell construction, at least with certain rigs and steering locations. Ancient representations offer little help in determining hull cross-sections, but some of them do seem to indicate very full hulls aft of amidships.

The steering oar is another factor that affects hull performance, and it produces results quite different from those of a stern-mounted rudder. This ship had her steering oars mounted rather far forward, but they probably canted aft to nearly the location of the sternpost scarph. Although the models and tank used were crude, experiments were conducted to study the effects of steering oars on hull performance. These tests indicated that the ship had a tendency to pivot on her keel center when turning sharply at low speeds, a condition largely brought about by the fine bow and heavy afterbody. Instead of swinging the stern about as a rudder normally does, the ship was pushed sideways in the original direction, with subsequent loss of control. However, at increased speeds or less degree of blade, the control was improved. When a rudder was temporarily hung on the stern, the bow seemed even less responsive under all conditions.

While the steering tests are inconclusive because we have no direct evidence for the characteristics of the ship's rig or the shape of her steering oars, they do suggest certain probabilities, one of which is that the location of the steering oars, in this case relatively far forward, was strongly dependent on hull shape. Also, a helmsman steering with two oars must have had an infinitely more demanding task than one steering with a rudder. All manner of responses could be attained by varying the amount of blade immersed or by assigning different angles to each blade. The design of the oars must have been every bit as critical as that of a rudder. Finally, although our tests were extremely limited in technology, we found the hull to sail better under a fore-and-aft rig (lateen) for the given locations of mainmast and steering oars. Furthermore, the tests proved beyond a doubt that if it had been square-rigged the vessel must have had a foresail such as an artemon. Some may argue that the mast location we have selected is too far forward to accommodate a square rig, but the effect of the steering oars on the center of lateral resistance must be taken into account. Not only do these oars create a leeboard effect under certain conditions, but they also bring the turning effort of the hull considerably farther forward. Thus, the lead of the mainsail cannot be calculated for this hull as it can on later designs.

The final matter to be dealt with is the ship's waterline. We have shown her sitting by the stern. This was the trim at which she seemed to ride best and to follow when load was proportionately distributed. But whether she trimmed level or down by the stern, her load waterline must have been anticipated near strake 16, as this was where the shipwright stopped his shell.

The tonnage for this ship has been previously published as "some 40 tons." Using preliminary data, the tonnage was calculated from an old customhouse formula where tonnage = (length of keel × beam × depth of hold) ÷ 94 and all dimensions are represented in feet. Calculating the tonnage with the dimensions given in this chapter would yield a burden of 51.5 tons. In an-

[9] Ibid., p. 71.

other popular formula, tonnage = (length of keel × beam × ½ beam) ÷ 94, and by this formula our ship would have a burden of 58 tons. These formulae actually determine volume tonnage and were fairly accurate when used on the full-proportioned hulls of the seventeenth and eighteenth centuries, for which they were intended. They do not necessarily determine the payload which could be carried by spoon- or crescent-shaped ancient hulls or by those ships whose keels had no relation to the length of their holds.

The listed tonnage of this ship was determined by calculating its total displacement and subtracting the effective weight of ship and gear. Displacement calculations are too lengthy and involved for inclusion here, and those interested in learning the process are advised to consult a good textbook on naval architecture. Total displacement was determined to be 72.86 tons at the waterline indicated on the sheer plan. For the purpose of our calculations, effective weight of ship and gear were estimated at 20 tons. Thus, the tonnage of the Byzantine ship was approximately 53 tons at the indicated waterline. Sailing the Mediterranean during calm summer months, she could have safely carried closer to 60 tons, and so we have rated her a 60-tonner. The ship was carrying approximately nine hundred amphoras when she went down. These amphoras, if filled, would have weighed just over 37 tons. On the shell models we observed that the vessel could have stowed as many as twelve hundred such amphoras below decks, though this was loading her a bit tightly. Such a burden would have weighed slightly over 50 tons, so the tonnage formulae in this case proved reasonable.

Time and new comparative material will undoubtedly yield additional information on this ship. For the present, however, we must take her for what we know of her—a step between the art of the ancient Nile builder and the not far distant draughts of the early architect. In the meantime, the ship model has found a new role as a tool for the archaeologist.

## Statistics

| | | | |
|---|---|---|---|
| Length on deck | 20.52 m | Displacement (indicated waterline) | 72.86 tons |
| Length (indicated waterline) | 18.22 m | Beam-to-length ratio | 1:4 |
| Length of keel | 12 m | Keel and posts | cypress |
| Beam (maximum) | 5.22 m | Frames | elm |
| Beam (molded) | 5.02 m | Planking | pine |
| Depth in hold | 2.25 m | Fastenings | iron |
| Tons burden | 60 tons | | |

# V

## THE GALLEY

### Frederick H. van Doorninck, Jr.

Although fragments of tiles not constituting parts of cargoes have been found on many ancient Mediterranean shipwrecks, evidence adequately explaining their presence had not yet been brought to light in 1958 when Frost and Throckmorton first examined the seventh-century Byzantine shipwreck at Yassi Ada. Consequently, a small, amphora-free area filled with tile fragments found at the wreck's stern quickly became the chief focal point of interest. The fragments belonged for the most part to roof tiles (both pantiles and cover tiles) and to hearth tiles, and since the area in which they lay appeared to be fairly well defined, there seemed to be an excellent chance of determining their original function. We excavated this area, therefore, with particular care.

Wreck Plan IV shows that most of the tile fragments recovered from the wreck lay within an area measuring roughly 1.5 × 2.5 m located within the confines of step sectors 6A, 6B, 7A, and 7B. Reference to Wreck Plan III will further show that amphoras did not occupy a major portion of the same area. We will call this area the tile area. Its spatial limits have been indicated in outline on Wreck Plans II–V.

A few tile fragments and a copper tray (MF 7) had been removed from the tile area by Frost and Throckmorton, but they made a careful record of the pieces and their find spots and left the area otherwise untouched;[1] we found no physical evidence that the area had ever been significantly disturbed. It should be noted, however, that while many of the area's tiles were partially or completely exposed to view before excavation was begun, such was not the case with any of the many pottery vessels found here, despite the fact that there was but little overburden present. It is difficult to understand why this was so unless one supposes that exposed vessels within the tile area had been removed previously by sponge divers or other early visitors to the wreck.

A photograph taken of the tile area on July 25, 1961 (Fig. 5-1) shows its appearance after all visible tile fragments had been labeled. A slight amount of cleaning around tile edges had made them more clearly visible. During the course of this cleaning, a surviving portion of hull frame 7 was uncovered. It appears in the center of the photograph, bearing the tag CE. Most if not all of the objects appearing in the photograph were definitely *in situ*.

Other objects recovered from the tile area consisted almost entirely of cooking utensils, tableware, lumps of partially fired clay, and fragments of small iron bars, leaving little doubt that the area marked in some way the location of the ship's galley.

The tile area lay on the port side of the wreck between hull frames 4 and 8. Although only one small portion of either frame had survived, the known positions on the seabed of other hull remnants from the stern has made possible a close approximation of what must have been these frames' general positions on the seabed throughout the better part of their length after the hull had flattened out. These approximate positions have been fully indicated on Wreck Plan IV (see the discussion of their positions on p. 44). They reveal that a little over three-quarters of all the tile fragments recovered were found between the two frames. Only two small

---

[1] H. Frost, *Under the Mediterranean*, pp. 166–168, reprinted in our Fig. 1-4, nos. 23, 24, and 25; H. Gültekin and P. Throckmorton, "Preliminary Report of Exploration for Ancient Wrecks in the Turkish Aegean" (unpublished manuscript), pp. 11, 83–85, nos. 35 and 36. These tile fragments are included in the tile catalogs and galley restorations presented in this chapter.

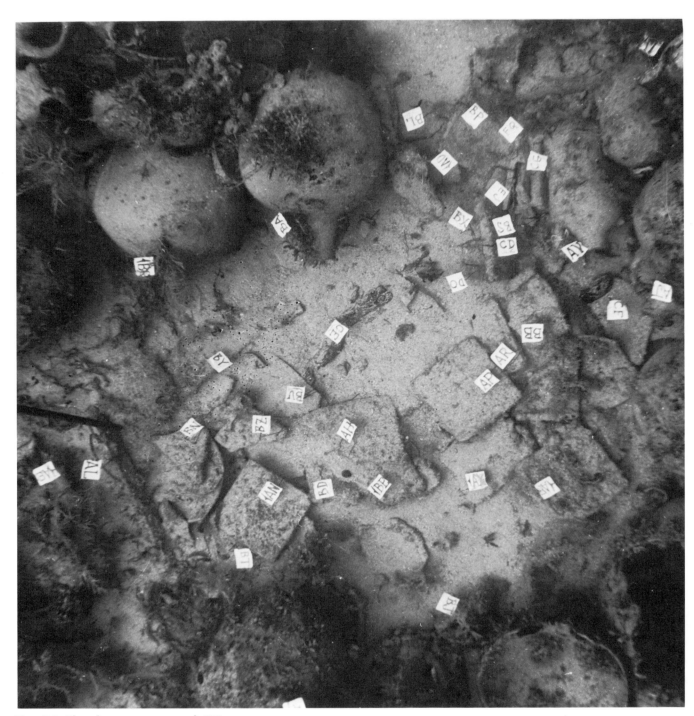

Fig. 5-1. The tile area as excavated. *WI*

fragments were found forward of frame 8, and one of these (PT 11*i*) was not *in situ* when its position was recorded. The remaining fragments were found loosely scattered aft of frame 4, with all but three between frame 4 and the sternpost's final position on the seabed.

The tile area's starboard edge was well defined. Reference to Wreck Plan II will show that it overlay remnants of planking strakes 8 through 11. These strakes covered the turn of the bilge at the point of transition from the bottom to the side of the hull. Thus, the tile area overlay hull remnants between frames 4 and 8 whose positions within the hull had been at or above the turn of the port bilge. The tile area extended out almost as far to port as objects were found in sector 7A, but this edge of the area was rather poorly defined.

Wreck Plan III shows that although there was considerable intrusion of amphoras into the port half of the tile area, the starboard half was almost entirely free of amphoras. Certainly it was not the deposit of tile fragments and other materials within the area that was primarily responsible for preventing amphoras from intruding into it. Such an explanation reasonably could be given for the absence of amphoras from the area's after-starboard part, where the concentration of tiles was the heaviest. But along the forward edge of the area's starboard half, where the amphoras were most effectively excluded, there had been only a thin covering of sand and shell and a loose scattering of tile fragments over the surviving hull remnants. It also is obvious that the amphoras were not responsible for holding the tile fragments within such a clearly defined area. We can only conclude that there had been some kind of substantial barriers interposed between the tiles and the amphoras along the forward, starboard, and after edges of the tile area. Since nothing in any way approaching substantial barriers was found in these locations, we can safely assume that they were wooden structures that did not survive.

In attempting to identify these wooden structures, we can best begin with the one that had constituted a barrier along the tile area's starboard side. This structure must have been the floor for the ship's galley, set down within the stern somewhere near the turn of the bilge. We have already noted that the tile area overlay hull remnants whose positions within the hull had been either at or above the turn of the port bilge. Many of the tile fragments within the area were from a roof for the galley's superstructure, which rose above deck level (this will become evident in a later section of this chapter). When the roof collapsed under the weight of the tiles at an early stage in the process of wreck formation, a major portion of the tiles fell to the galley floor, which was at

the time more or less intact. The floor had a moderately steep inclination to port due to the ship's port list on the seabed. The tiles consequently piled up on the floor over against the port side of the hull. Almost all the elements of the galley hearth, upon breaking up, came to be piled up over against the port side of the hull as well. The floor thus prevented any of the roof tiles (except for a few small fragments that do not appear on Wreck Plan IV) or hearth tiles from eventually coming to rest in the area where the remnants of the stern from below the turn of the bilge were found.

As we shall see shortly, substantial numbers of cargo amphoras rolled downslope into the wreck's stern area aft of frame 8 at a later stage in the process of wreck formation. However, portions of the galley floor at its juncture with the hull's port side apparently still remained when this shift in the cargo occurred, and the floor prevented amphoras from intruding into the tile area itself along the area's starboard side.

Wreck Plan IV shows that the pileup of hearth and roof tiles was particularly heavy in the after-port corner of the galley floor because of the slope of the seabed on which the ship had come to rest. The final disposition of the tiles suggests further that those tiles in the pile that had come to rest primarily against the side of the hull spilled out to port when the hull's port side collapsed outwardly, while those tiles in the pile that were resting primarily on the galley floor remained concentrated together within a small area. The latter tiles had as a group the same inclination as the galley floor on which they had come to rest, and many retained this inclination either fully or partially even after the disappearance of the floor. Note in Fig. 5-1 how these tiles, which appear in the upper right-hand part of the photograph, are to varying degrees tilted up on end. If our analysis of the tiles' disposition is essentially correct, the juncture of the galley floor with the port side of the hull occurred somewhere just to port of this main concentration of tiles within the tile area.

Our evidence is much too imprecise and hazardous to permit a really close determination of what the galley floor's level had been. It does indicate, however, that the floor very probably was set some short distance above the turn of the bilge. Guided by this general conclusion, Steffy has set the floor in his reconstruction of the ship at a level that best satisfies principles of sound construction. As a point of interest, we have indicated with a dotted line on Wreck Plan IV the idealized final position on the seabed of the juncture of the galley floor, as reconstructed, with the hull's port side; it falls along the port edge of the main concentration of tiles.

The galley floor, as reconstructed, extends aft only

as far as frame 4, since the inner lining of the hull bottom rises above the floor at this point (Fig. 4-7). This would appear to be the fundamental reason why very few of the tiles which came to be piled up on the galley floor finally came to rest on the seabed aft of this frame.

The fact that only one, or perhaps two, tile fragments came to rest forward of frame 8 indicates that the galley floor did not extend forward of this frame. Just forward of frame 8 a bulkhead partitioned off the galley from the hold. The breakup of this bulkhead as the hull flattened out allowed amphoras from the hold to move downslope into that part of the wreck aft of frame 8. However, portions of the bulkhead at its juncture with the port side of the hull apparently survived long enough to effectively prevent amphoras from intruding into the tile area along its forward edge, particularly in the region closer to the bilge, where the hull's outer shell was from the outset closer to the seabed and not subject to as great a degree of dislocation. The bulkhead left other faint but unmistakable traces of its existence and general location. Wreck Plan III shows that throughout most of the area between midships and frame 8 the cargo amphoras overlying that portion of the hull extending from the port to the starboard bilges were stacked three deep. One will note, however, that this density of amphoras overlying the hull bottom drops off rather suddenly just a slight distance forward of frame 8. Aft of this frame the amphoras are rather thinly scattered, except where they are piled up along the sternpost (see p. 53). The great majority of small finds, on the other hand, were found aft of frame 8 (Wreck Plans V*a* through V*f*). The remaining small finds, some eighty in all, had for the most part come to rest between frames 8 and 10, while no more than twenty were found forward of the latter frame. We have concluded that the bulkhead between hold and galley had been set at frame 10 and that aft of the bulkhead at frame 8 a lightly timbered partition had been constructed, thereby creating a storage area between frames 8 and 10. The evidence for this conclusion will be presented in greater detail in the next section of this chapter.

We have yet to consider what significance, if any, the general location of the tile area's rather poorly defined port edge may have. The farthest extent to port of cargo amphoras in the middle part of the wreck coincided very closely with the known final position on the seabed of the deck's juncture with the port bulwark, indicated by a broken line on Wreck Plan III. Portions of the deck at this juncture within the hull's middle body apparently had survived long enough to prevent amphoras from spilling out any farther in this direction when the side of the hull collapsed outwardly. Such control may have happened to a lesser degree farther toward the stern as well, despite the fact that there the incurving side was initially suspended higher off the seabed and must have suffered major dislocations when it flattened out. We have indicated with a dotted line on Wreck Plan IV what would have been the final position on the seabed of the juncture of the deck as reconstructed with the port bulwark between frames 4 and 8 had the side of the hull there somehow escaped severe breakup and dislocation when it collapsed. Interestingly, the dotted line defines the tile area's port edge fairly well. Only three small tile fragments were found to port of the line, and very close by. It is conceivable, then, that there had been some deck remnants constituting something of a confining barrier along the tile area's port edge.

The evidence for the galley's location and size set forth above indicates that it was quite a large structure of more than ample dimensions. The floor, roughly trapezoidal in plan due to the incurving stern, had maximum dimensions of about 3.2 × 1.2 m. The mean clearance between floor and deck beams was just about 2 m.

## *General Layout and Storage Arrangements*

The seabed distribution of small finds (Wreck Plans V*a* through V*f*) shows that almost all of these objects had been kept either in or immediately adjacent to the galley. Their distribution also has yielded some general information concerning where within the galley area their various categories had been stowed.

Any distribution of objects on a shipwreck is, of course, to some extent random. Shipboard objects are usually well secured when a ship is under sail and often will remain in place should the ship be wrecked and sink. However, many of these objects will eventually be released from their confinement and undergo some random movement during the process of wreck formation that follows. The primary directions of this movement in the present case were downslope and to port due to the seabed slope and the hull's list. Cargo amphoras moving downslope after the breakup of the bulkhead between galley and hold undoubtedly caused further displacement of galley objects.

Despite a definite random element in the seabed

distribution of the objects from the galley area, significant patterns in their distribution do emerge. Various categories of objects have distributions and areas of concentration that often markedly differ from each other, so it can reasonably be inferred that different kinds of objects had been stowed in different locations within the galley complex, and it has proven possible to ascertain the general nature of these storage arrangements.

We will begin by considering the basic layout of the galley itself. Almost all remnants of the galley hearth were found within the tile area's confines. Only four small hearth tile fragments (HTa 17c, HTa 20a, HTa 21a, and HTb 10b on Wreck Plan IV) lay outside this area between frame 4 and the sternpost, and three of these were found in very close proximity to frame 4. Although four small roof tile fragments were found on the starboard side of the wreck, two in sector 6B' and two in 6C', not one hearth tile fragment was found anywhere to starboard of the tile area. (Note that the step-frame identifiers marked with a prime ['] are those that were shifted one and one-half sectors [3 m] to starboard after excavation in 1962 had revealed the wider dispersal of artifacts than had been originally estimated. See chapter 2, p. 24.) Clay employed in constructing the hearth was also found only within the tile area or along its immediate periphery. Remnants of iron bars used to reinforce the hearth were again found only within the confines of this area. Most remnants of an iron grill for the hearth, on the other hand, were found outside the tile area. Possible reasons for this exceptional distribution will become evident in a later section devoted to the hearth. We need only note for the moment that but one fragment of this grill (IB 2a on Wreck Plan IV) was found over on the starboard side of the wreck (at frame 8 near the wreck's starboard edge), and it belonged to a removable element. The hearth was of such a size that it must have been a heavy structure fixed in place on either the port or the starboard side of the galley floor. Thus, even though the ship had a port list on the seabed, one would have expected to find some slight remnants of the hearth, beyond a single removable element, on the wreck's starboard side if the hearth had been located there. The absence of such remnants points to a port-side location for the hearth.

The distribution of cooking utensils on the wreck (Wreck Plan Va) appears to confirm this deduction. Well over one-half the utensils for the preparation and cooking of food recovered from the wreck were found either in the tile area or within half a meter of it, while almost all the rest were found scattered directly downslope from it. Only one cooking pot and one cooking pot frag-

ment were found farther to starboard than the demarcation line between B and C grid sectors. The cooking pot (P 58) is no. 15 on Frost's plan of the wreck (Fig. 1-4). A comparison of her plan with our Wreck Plan III reveals that this pot was probably found within the area of our sector 6C', some slight distance forward of frame 8. The cooking pot fragment was found well forward of frame 8 in sector 5B'.

The distribution outlined above indicates that most utensils used in preparing and cooking food must have been stowed on the galley's port side either between frames 4 and 8 or in close proximity to one or the other frame. We should, of course, keep in mind the ship's port list on the seabed in our analysis. The great majority of the galley objects were found to port of the sternpost, and it will become evident as our analysis proceeds that some of these objects had been stowed on the ship's starboard side. Even so, a substantial minority of galley objects were uncovered to starboard of the sternpost. Thus, the fact that not one utensil used in preparing and cooking food was found on the wreck's starboard side aft of frame 8 makes it highly unlikely that any significant number of such utensils had been stowed on the galley's starboard side. We have concluded, therefore, that the hearth had been located on the galley's port side and that most utensils used in the preparation and cooking of food had been kept in close proximity to it.

The spouted jars, the jar lids, the cups, and most plates and dishes also appear to have been stowed on the galley's port side; their distribution on the wreck has been included on Wreck Plan Va. Of the six spouted jars recovered, only P 39 and possibly P 36 (recovered from sector 8A or 8B) came to light farther to starboard than the tile area's starboard edge, but even these were found to port of the demarcation line between B and C sectors. The find spot of jar lid P 41 is not known, but the lid may very well have belonged to spouted jar P35, found within the tile area. The other lid, P 42, was uncovered just forward of the tile area near the wreck's port edge. All cups recovered were found well over on the wreck's port side near the demarcation line between A and B sectors, with P 32 in sector 6A, P 33 in sector 8B, and P 34 in sector 9A.

The main concentration of the nine plates and dishes cataloged occurred just on or downslope from the tile area's after edge. This concentration included P 5 and P 6 and major fragments of P 7, P 10, and P 12. The one fragment of P 9 with a known find spot probably can also be included here, since the fragment was found somewhere in sector 8B. The origins of P 8 and P 11 are uncertain. There remains P 13. The two fragments of this dish with known find spots were recovered in sectors 6B′ and 6C′. As we shall see, the find spots indicate that the dish may have been stowed on the hull's starboard side in a storage compartment located just forward of the galley.

Wreck Plans V*b* and V*c* show the distribution of most of the various categories of objects that we have concluded had been stowed in the forward storage compartment located between frames 8 and 10. The great majority of the some eighty small finds uncovered between frames 8 and 10 consisted of coins and tools. The overall distribution of these two categories of objects provides much of the evidence for the existence and location of this storage facility.

The find spots of sixty-nine of the sixteen gold and about sixty copper coins recovered from the wreck are known.[2] Forty were found between frames 4 and 8, but twenty-three were found farther forward between frames 8 and 10, thirteen of these having come to rest against the forward face of frame 8. Two of the remaining six coins were found next to sternpost remnants just aft of frame 4. The other four were widely scattered farther downslope. Also noteworthy is the fact that while the distribution of the coins recovered from between frames 8 and 10 extended the full width of the wreck, all of the coins recovered from between frames 4 and 8 and from just aft of frame 4 were found to starboard of the galley floor juncture with the hull's port side.

According to maritime law of the period, the ship's captain was responsible for the safekeeping of all money turned over to him during a voyage. He was not responsible, on the other hand, for what happened to money not entrusted to his care.[3] That all or almost all of the coins found on the wreck were in safekeeping when the ship sank is revealed by several points of evidence. For one thing, no "small change" is involved. All of the copper coins are 40-nummi pieces, the largest denomination for coins of that metal. Furthermore, all but two of

the fifteen gold coins and all but seven of the fifty-four copper coins with known find spots were in either case found concentrated within a roughly 2-m-square area. Forty-four of the copper coins were found contained within four masses of concretion, the number in each mass ranging from six to twenty-one coins.

The area within which the copper coins were concentrated occurred roughly 3 m to starboard of the area of gold coin concentration. At the same time, however, both groups of coins had very similar overall distributions on the wreck. In either case, some were found between frames 8 and 10, most were located between frames 4 and 8 to starboard of the tile area, and a few were found scattered farther downslope. It would appear, then, that the gold coins and the copper coins had been kept within the same general area but in separate containers.

The distribution of the copper coins is particularly instructive. The location of their area of concentration indicates that if they were initially all together, they must have been kept well over on the hull's starboard side and forward of frame 8. Some of the coins eventually came to rest on the seabed there; even more made their way a short distance downslope and to port as the hull broke up. If the two copper coins found in sector 6A were in fact initially together with the others, the copper coins must have been kept somewhere above the level of the galley floor. Otherwise it is difficult to imagine how the two coins could have possibly made their way over to the hull's port side.

The gold coins aft of frame 8 appear to have made their way downslope and to port from a location forward of frame 8 about midway between the two sides of the hull. It well may be, of course, that the container of gold coins initially had been kept farther over toward the hull's starboard side.

Iron tools were found in two distinct areas, one forward and one aft of frame 4. We shall have more to say about the after group later. For the moment we are concerned with the tool distribution forward of frame 4 (Wreck Plan V*b*). Just fewer than fifty tools, as well as two sacks of nails and a folded sheet of lead for repairs (MF 38), were uncovered in this forward area. Four of the tools were found at some distance from the rest, scattered across the wreck's entire width in sector 5. Most of the other tools and one sack of nails (Fe 73) were found in the immediate vicinity of or between frames 8 and 10. A remaining six tools, the other sack of nails (Fe 70), and the folded lead sheet were found between frames 4 and 8.

If the six tools in sector 5, which possibly had been

---

[2] Included in this number are one gold coin and one copper coin that do not appear on Wreck Plan V*b*. They were both deposited in the air-lift bag during air lifting between frames 4 and 8 just to starboard of the tile area where the main concentration of gold coins occurred. The other gold coin which does not appear on Wreck Plan V*b* also was deposited in the air-lift bag possibly during air lifting in this same area. Another copper coin that does not appear on Wreck Plan V*b* was recovered from sector 6B. The find spots of about one-half dozen very badly corroded copper coins were not recorded.

[3] W. Ashburner, *The Rhodian Sea-Law*, p. 3, ιδ′; p. 62, no. 14; p. 19, ιγ′; p. 94, no. 13. It is generally held that the Rhodian Sea-Law, or Nomos Nautikos, was compiled between A.D. 600 and 800 (p. cxii). R. S. Lopez ("The Role of Trade in the Economic Readjustment of Byzantium in the Seventh Century," *DOP* 13 [1959]: 79) believes it was most probably compiled in the seventh century.

out on deck at the time of the ship's sinking, are excluded, the distribution of the forward group of tools, nail sacks, and folded lead sheet closely parallels that of the coins, particularly the copper coins. Apparently, then, these objects also had been stowed on the starboard side forward of frame 8.

The find spot of a large concretion containing at least eight tools, just aft of frame 10 in sector 6C, offers further evidence concerning the storage facility involved. Although this concretion was large, measuring about 60 × 25 cm, it was found with its entire undersurface resting directly upon hull planking remnants, and it had been overlain by a two-layer-deep deposit of amphoras.[4] This position can best be explained by supposing that the ship's hold actually had extended only as far aft as frame 10 and that at some time before the bulkhead between the hold and the galley gave way, permitting cargo amphoras to move farther downslope, the group of tools in the large concretion had fallen down to the hull bottom from some higher location between frames 8 and 10. It should further be noted that Steffy has independently concluded from his own research on the hull's construction that the stern had probably not been designed for heavy loading beyond the keel's after end (see p. 70). We think, therefore, that the hold was terminated at frame 10 by the galley bulkhead, and we further hypothesize a light partition aft of the bulkhead at frame 8. This partition would have had incorporated within it means of access to the intervening space, which was used for storage.

The distribution on the wreck of weighing implements (Wreck Plan V*c*) leads us to conclude that this category of objects also had been stowed in the forward storage compartment. Steelyards B 1 and B 2 were found along with their counterweights where the main concentration of gold coins occurred, while steelyard B 3 apparently came to rest somewhere near the lighter end of B 1. Bronze fittings B 8 and B 9 and steelyard weight W 10 were also found where the gold coins were concentrated. Six of the eight bronze disc weights recovered (W 1–W 4, W 7 and W 8) and bronze hinge strap (?) MF 12, which possibly belonged to the wooden box housing the disc weights, were again recovered from this same area.[5] Disc weight W 5, a small fragment of

the wooden box, and disc weight W 6 were found fairly close by in sector 7A′ (of these, only W 6 appears in Wreck Plan V*c*). B 5, a steelyard weight, was found just 1 m from W 6, farther downslope and to port.

A few parts of weighing instruments were found widely scattered in the aftermost part of the wreck. Bronze pan B 4 and ten links of bronze chain were found together in sector 10B, bronze hook B 6 was found in sector 9B, bronze hook B 7 was in 9C, and lead weight W 11 was in 8B. Perhaps bronze fragment MF 14, found slightly downslope from steelyard B 1, should be added to this list, since it may belong to a balancing instrument. These objects had probably been stowed with the other weighing implements. Pan B 4 and accompanying chain apparently belonged to a pan balance with which the disc weights would have been used. Bronze hook B 7 was found with copper pitcher MF 5. As we shall see, it is quite probable that this pitcher had been stowed forward of frame 8.

Eleven of the fourteen conical and teardrop-shaped lead weights recovered from the wreck have a distribution suggesting that they had been kept in the forward compartment (Wreck Plan V*e*). Two (LW 9 and LW 15) were found within a meter forward of the tile area, six (LW 1, LW 2, LW 4, LW 5, LW 7, and LW 10) were within the tile area and/or in close proximity to steelyards B 1 and B 2, and two (LW 3 and LW 13) were not far downslope from the tile area. Another conical weight (LW 12) was recovered from sector 7A′, the same sector in which LW 10 was found. The rather restricted distribution of these pieces suggests that they had been stowed together. They probably became dispersed from a point just forward of frame 8 well over toward the hull's port side. It is worth noting that the two conical weights found forward of the galley on the starboard side of the wreck, LW 6 and LW 8, are somewhat larger than the others.

Glass and fine metal vessels also appear to have been stowed in the forward storage compartment (Wreck Plan V*c*). Bronze censer MF 1 and cross MF 2, copper pitchers MF 6*a* and MF 6*b*, and bronze or copper vessel MF 9 were all found in close proximity to steelyards B 1 and B 2. Bronze or copper vessel fragment MF 8 was found together with disc weight W 5 in sector 7A′. Bronze or copper pitcher MF 5 was uncovered far downslope in sector 9C in the same spot where bronze hook B 7 came to light, but the mouth of this vessel (MF 5*a*) was found between frames 4 and 8 in sector 7C.

[4] I overlooked this important fact in my original study, where I concluded that the tools had been stowed on the starboard side just forward of frame 8 but up at deck level (F. H. van Doorninck, Jr., "The Seventh-Century Byzantine Ship at Yassi Ada: Some Contributions to the History of Naval Architecture" [Ph.D. diss., University of Pennsylvania, 1967], p. 118).

[5] The field notebook reports that steelyard B 3 was found "above frame [sector] 8 to the right of the keel [sternpost]." B 8, W 7, W 8, and MF 12 were deposited in the air-lift bag while air lifting was being done in the area of gold coin concentration.

Glass bottle MF 61 was uncovered near MF 5a. Glass fragment MF 62 may have been recovered from the same sector or from either sector 7B or 6A. (MF 62 was found in the air-lift bag after air lifting had been done in these three sectors.) All three sectors favor an origin forward of frame 8 for the fragment.

A majority of the lamps had a distribution on the wreck that closely paralleled that of the coins and tools (Wreck Plan Vb).[6] The remaining lamps, unlike either the coins or the tools, were concentrated within or just aft of the tile area. There were, in fact, two distinctly separate concentrations of lamps on the wreck, one on the starboard side and the other on the port side. The lamps appear to have been stowed forward of frame 8 in two separate groups, one on either side of the hull. Seven of the eight lamps bearing definite signs of use (L 11, L 12, L 15, L 16, L 19, L 22, and L 23) belonged to the portside group. (The other lamp showing definite signs of use, L 18, is from sector 6B'.)

The area between frames 8 and 10 directly forward of the hearth probably constituted a storage place separate from the main forward storage compartment. We ought not to suppose, however, that cooking utensils had been kept beyond the hearth to port, thereby forcing someone to lean directly over the hearth in order to reach them. Further, there was little room for stowage directly aft of the hearth due to the sharply incurving side of the hull as it approached the sternpost, although some utensils possibly had been stowed there fairly high up where space was available; plates and dishes, found primarily near the tile area's after-port corner, may have been kept there. Most of the cooking and food preparation utensils, then, were probably stowed forward of the hearth in a cupboard or the like accessible from the hearth. Perhaps the spouted jars, jar lids, cups, and some of the lamps, including many of those then in use, had been kept with them.

The storage compartment for shipboard valuables and finer or more fragile utensils probably extended little more than halfway across the ship from the hull's starboard side. As the hull was flattened out and its two sides were forced farther apart and down onto the seabed, objects stowed in the more starboard reaches of the compartment, including tools, the copper coins, and some glass vessels and spare lamps, were conveyed in large part to the wreck's starboard edge. Some of these objects subsequently made their way short distances farther

downslope as the process of wreck formation continued. A breach in the partition between storage compartment and galley, which perforce took place as the hull was flattened out, released from confinement objects located midway between the two sides of the hull in the more port reaches of the compartment. These objects had either been stowed on the compartment's port side or had made their way there after shipwreck because of the ship's port list on the seabed. They included weighing implements, the gold coins, and most of the fine metal vessels. Virtually all of this material spilled out through the partition breach into the galley itself. One consequence of this pattern of spillage was that no small finds were uncovered between the port and starboard bilges just forward of frame 8. A handful of objects stowed in the forward compartment did apparently find their way to the wreck's starboard side: some copper coins and iron tools, some small lead weights, and perhaps one or two lamps.

The tiles and other material which had accumulated on the galley floor over on the port side during the early stages of wreck formation must have undergone their final heavy concentration along the juncture of the floor and the hull's port side when the two sides of the hull were forced apart and down onto the seabed. The weighing implements, gold coins, and fine metal vessels were not included in this concentration and, therefore, must have spilled out into the galley only after the two sides of the hull had been forced apart and the galley floor had been breached. Since the galley floor no longer intervened, these objects fell down into the hull bottom and piled up in the port bilge, which was located right beneath the galley floor at its juncture with the hull's port side. Consequently, some of the objects in this deposit, such as steelyard B 2, the Athena counterweight, and the bronze censer (MF 1), were found (at a distinctly lower level) under tiles delimiting the starboard edge of the tile area. At an intermediate level and just to port of steelyard B 2 and the censer, a group of pottery vessels consisting of three cooking pots, a pitcher, and a spouted jar was uncovered. These vessels apparently had fallen behind the hearth into the after-port corner of the galley floor before the dissolution of the hearth had occurred.

Mention should also be made here of three slabs of stone (S 1–S 3) found within the port bilge beneath the galley floor in the bottommost stratum of finds (Wreck Plan Vf). The original location of these slabs within the galley is uncertain, but one possibility is that they had been situated from the outset in the hull bottom beneath the galley floor.

There is no evidence to indicate that any other ob-

---

[6] L 21, which does not appear on Wreck Plan Vb, was recovered from the air-lift bag after air lifting had been done in the general area where the main concentration of gold coins occurred.

jects had been kept in this part of the hull. We have concluded for this reason that all of the space aft of frame 10 and below the galley floor level had not been used in any important way. Steffy informs me that such areas of dead space are commonly encountered in ships of more modern times.

A few of the objects that spilled out through the partition breach, such as disc weights W 5 and W 6 and steelyard weight B 5, made their way downslope into the area between frame 4 and the sternpost. A wooden padlock (MF 51) was found in this same area only half a meter downslope from the bronze censer. It is likely that this padlock had been used to secure the valuables within the forward storage compartment.

We have not yet considered where glazed wares, pitchers, and pantry storage jars may have been kept. Their distributions on the wreck are shown in Wreck Plan V*d*. The glazed-ware bowls and bowl fragments with known find spots were found widely scattered over a large area ranging from sectors 6 to 9, A to C. There were no concentrations of glazed ware. Noteworthy are the find spots of the two major fragments of P 3. Although P 3*a* came to light well downslope in sector 9B, fragment P 3*b* was found midway between frames 4 and 8 in sector 7C. The two fragments do not join but appear to belong to the same bowl. The find spot of fragment P 3*b* suggests that the bowl probably had been stowed in the forward storage compartment. Perhaps P 1 from sector 6A had been kept there as well. However, the fact that it was found almost one and one-half meters forward of frame 8 raises the distinct possibility that it had been located forward of the galley complex at the time of the ship's sinking.

Thirteen of the fourteen pitchers with known find spots, out of a total of eighteen recovered, were found in one of two areas.[7] Seven came to light near the after-starboard corner of the tile area. Five of these tile-area pitchers were uncovered within 1 m of the corner; two (P 27 and P 31) were found about 1.5 m away. The other six pitchers were found downslope from the sternpost; these include P 24, not shown on Wreck Plan V*d*, from sector 8A. Five of the downslope pitchers were lying directly downslope from the after-starboard corner of the tile area, four of them within 1.5 m of the sternpost. The sixth pitcher (P 24) may have been uncovered quite near the last four. It is quite possible in view of this distribution that all or most of these thirteen pitchers had been stowed together. Perhaps they had been kept aft of the hearth just starboard of the plates and dishes.

The find spots of fifteen out of seventeen complete or partially preserved storage jars recovered from the wreck are known. Two of these, alabastron P 67 and amphora base fragment P 68, came to light well forward of the galley. P 67, no. 11 on Frost's plan (Fig. 1-4), was probably found within our sector 3A. P 68, not shown on Wreck Plan V*d*, was found in 4C'. Another amphora base fragment (P 69) was uncovered slightly less than 1.5 m forward of frame 8 near the wreck's port edge. Seven of the twelve remaining storage jars were found to starboard of the tile area, five between frames 4 and 8 and two (P 81 and P 83) either between frames 4 and 8 or slightly aft of frame 4. P 81, no. 16 on Frost's plan (Fig. 1-4), appears to have been found within our sector 7B'; P 83 was recovered from sector 7A'. Only two of the other five storage jars were found farther to port than the demarcation line between sectors A and B. These are P 70 from the after-port corner of the tile area and P 77, not shown on Wreck Plan V*d*, from 8A. Two of the remaining three storage jars (P 72 and P 75) were found between frame 4 and the sternpost. P 79 was uncovered farther downslope at the bottom of sector 8B.

Since the principal area within which these storage jars were found was to starboard of the tile area between frame 8 and frame 4 or slightly aft of frame 4, and only one isolated fragment of an amphora not belonging to the cargo was brought to light anywhere immediately forward of frame 8, it was initially concluded that pantry storage jars had been kept in front of the hearth on the galley's starboard side.[8] However, we are now inclined to think that most of the food to be consumed on the ship had been secured in the forward storage compartment. First, over half of the storage jars recovered were found in areas where objects that clearly had been kept in the forward compartment also came to light. Further, it seems unlikely that the cook would have had ready access to the food stores. Certainly it has been customary in more modern times to keep food stores on ships well secured in a place apart from the galley itself, and this appears to have been a practice at least as early as Roman times.[9] It would appear, then, that most of the stor-

---

[7] The other pitcher, P 17, was found well forward of the galley in sector 4A.

[8] van Doorninck, "Seventh-Century Byzantine Ship," p. 186.

[9] My thanks to J. R. Steffy for reminding me of this fact. The Chrétienne C ship, a small merchantman (length 15 to 16 m) dating to the second quarter of the second century B.C., had a galley with a tile roof in the bow and what was probably a main cabin in the stern. Four food storage amphoras recovered were all found in the stern (J.-P. Joncheray, *L'Épave "C" de la Chrétienne*, pp. 93–94 and figs. 7, 9, and 10). On the Dramont D ship, another small merchantman dating to the middle of the first century, the main storage compartment for water and food was located in the bow, while most of the cooking utensils recovered were found near the stern (J.-P. Joncheray, "Étude de l'épave Dramont D, dite 'des pelvis,'" *CahArchSub* 3 [1974]: 26–28; and "Étude de l'épave Dramont D: IV, les objets métalliques," *CahArchSub* 4 [1975]: wreck plan).

age jars recovered had been secured in the forward compartment and in a location far enough to port so that they spilled out through the partition breach into the galley. It is doubtful, on the other hand, that the water pithos (P 82) with its great size could have been stowed anywhere other than on the galley's starboard side.

The find spot of the grapnel and the seabed distribution both of the tools uncovered aft of frame 4 and of the fishing equipment remain to be considered (Wreck Plan V*e*). Most of these objects—including the grapnel; the spherical, triangular, sphendonoidal, and crescentic fishing weights; and needles for repairing fishing nets[10]—were found within a roughly 2-m-square area immediately downslope and to starboard of the sternpost.

The iron tools from this area are axes Fe 9 and Fe 11, mattock Fe 12, billhook Fe 3, adze Fe 14, and spade Fe 1. Billhook Fe 4 and knife blade Fe 91, found immediately unslope just on the other side of the sternpost, knife blade Fe 90 from sector 8B, and billhook socket Fe 8 from sector 8A should also in all probability be associated with this group of tools.

The other two tools and two sacks of nails recovered aft of frame 4, none of which appear on Wreck Plan V*e*, can be associated with the tools kept in the forward compartment. One of the nail sacks (Fe 72) and file Fe 85, both found in 8C, undoubtedly represent a further extension of the tools scattered downslope from frame 8 on the wreck's starboard side. This is probably also the case with billhook socket Fe 7 from sector 9C. The other nail sack (Fe 71) was recovered from either sector 8B or sector 9B but was clearly not *in situ*.

None of the tools that can be associated with the grapnel and fishing equipment are of a type that would have been used exclusively for carpentry work, while all would have been useful on land in setting up a temporary camp or in foraging for water and firewood.

Only four or possibly five of the thirteen folded lead strips with known find spots were found with the spherical, triangular, sphendonoidal, and crescentic fishing weights,[11] while one other (LW 38) came to light further downslope in sector 9C. Two folded lead strips (LW 25 and LW 27) were found well forward of frame 8 in sectors 5A and 5B, respectively, and probably had not been located within the galley when the ship sank. However, three or possibly all four of the remaining strips undoubtedly had been stowed in the forward storage compartment. The three strips (LW 28–LW 30) came to light on the wreck's starboard side just forward and aft of frame 8; the fourth (LW 31) was found somewhere in sector 7A'. The small, square lead sheet (LW 32), found toward the wreck's starboard side between frames 4 and 8, possibly should be associated with this last group of strips. As we have seen, a number of objects found downslope from the sternpost, such as coins, copper pitcher MF 5, and parts of weighing implements, had undoubtedly made their way there from the forward compartment. Perhaps some of the folded lead strips, such as LW 38, found near steelyard hook B 7 in sector 9C, and LW 33 and LW 35, found near steelyard hook B 6 in sector 9B, did so as well.

It is difficult to believe that the close seabed association of fishing equipment, grapnel, and tools is accidental, particularly when it involves an assemblage of equipment entirely appropriate for a boatswain's store used in conjunction with the ship's boat. We have considered and rejected the idea that the fishing equipment, grapnel, and associated tools had all been kept in the forward compartment. One cannot imagine how all this material could have in this case retained such a relatively compact distribution on the seabed, particularly if some of the tools had been hafted.[12] The evidence therefore points to a boatswain's locker located aft of the galley. A few folded lead strips may have been included among its stores; others were kept in the forward compartment, perhaps to provide, along with the large folded lead sheet, lead for shipboard repairs.

Since there would not have been ample room for a locker low down within the hull aft of the galley, we think that it was probably set fairly high in the stern and accessible from the deck by means of a hatch. We further hypothesize that the starboard planking pulled away from the sternpost as the hull was flattened out, thus permitting most of the contents of the locker, as well as many of the cargo amphoras and galley objects that had made their way aft into the stern, to spill out onto the seabed immediately downslope from the sternpost.

The picture of the galley's storage arrangements that has emerged through our analysis of the seabed distributions of galley objects, although beset by a number of uncertainties, is undoubtedly correct in the main. It is clear that objects of similar or like nature normally had been stowed together as a group in an appointed place. Most utensils for preparing, cooking, and serving food had been kept on the galley's port side in close proximity to the hearth, while a locker for valuables and stores had

---

[10] Two needles (Fe 94 and Fe 95) were found, both in sector 8A. Only Fe 95 appears on Wreck Plan V*e*.

[11] Four of the folded lead strips are LW 33 and LW 35–LW 37. Folded lead strip LW 34, not shown on Wreck Plan V*e*, was found in sector 8C.

[12] Although no traces of handles were found with any of these tools, a nail to fix the handle in place was found concreted to the haft hole of axe Fe 9.

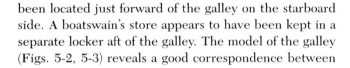

FIG. 5-2. Side view of the galley on the model. *DAF*

FIG. 5-3. Top view of the galley on the model. *DAF*

been located just forward of the galley on the starboard side. A boatswain's store appears to have been kept in a separate locker aft of the galley. The model of the galley (Figs. 5-2, 5-3) reveals a good correspondence between

required and available storage spaces, and one is left with the impression that the galley not only had been well appointed but also had been well ordered and practical in its layout.

## The Roof and Roof Tiles

Almost all of the roof-tile fragments found on the wreck can be assigned with reasonable certainty to one of sixteen pantiles and thirteen cover tiles on the basis of fabric and thickness. The wide variety of fabrics exhibited by the tiles has been particularly helpful in determining the number of individual tiles represented by the fragments. Thus, there will be some emphasis on fabric in the roof-tile catalogs. The fabric color of joining fragments often differed somewhat due to the differing chemical environment in which each had lain on the wreck. Color variations that could be attributed to this factor are not included in the description of fabrics, and this factor was taken fully into account when fragments that did not join were assigned to any particular tile on the basis of fabric.

### PANTILES

Pantiles have been given the designation PT. Two types can be distinguished. Type 1, to which PT 1–PT 6 belong, is of unusual design in that the raised rim bordering the two sides continues across the top. The rim is in section essentially rectangular along the sides but roughly triangular across the top, where it tapers to a

thin, rather carefully terminated outer edge. Although the rim is generally about 1 cm higher on the sides than across the top, the height transition is gradual and smooth. Consequently, this type would not have permitted the lower edge of a pantile in a next higher row to rest securely in place upon its upper end. These tiles, then, were probably designed for placement in an uppermost row of tiles on either a shed or a gable roof. Five of them (PT 1– PT 4 and PT 6) possess very similar fabrics with rather prominent surface grit and a brick red to bluish red surface color. The outer, visible faces of all five tiles bear traces of what appears to be a pale olive yellow slip and are decorated by bands of shallow grooves made by from one to three extended fingers of one hand. Most of the decorative pattern on PT 3 can be discerned. Five bands of grooves run down the tile's length. The outer two bands are in fact one continuous band running around three sides of the tile just inside the rim. How and to what extent the other three bands were interconnected is not clear. If the pattern of grooves on PT 2 was a balanced one, then it was very similar to that possessed by PT 3. Those small, surviving portions of the decorative patterns on poorly preserved PT 1, PT 4, and PT 6 parallel well the more completely preserved patterns on PT 2 and PT 3. It is quite possible, then, that all five tiles possessed very similar decorative patterns. The other type 1 tile, PT 5, has less prominent surface grit and a buff to brick red surface color. Decorative finger grooves do not occur on the tile's surviving portion, nor were any traces of a slip detected on its outer face. PT 5 is further distinguished by a smoke hole approximately 23.5 cm in diameter set in its center; a raised collar around the edge of the hole prevented water from running down into it.

Type 2 pantiles are of a commonly encountered design. A low, thin ridge, which prevented water from seeping between the tile's top edge and the bottom edge of the pantile in the next higher row, runs across the tile about 4 cm below the top edge. That upper ridge is from 1 to 3 cm lower than the side rims, permitting the next higher tile's bottom edge to rest securely in place. PT 8, PT 10, PT 11, PT 13, PT 15, and PT 16 possess such ridges either entirely or partially preserved. All have fabrics that can readily be distinguished from one another. Decorative finger grooves do not occur on the surviving portions of PT 8, PT 11, and PT 13, but the right half of PT 10 bears a single, S-shaped finger groove, and a wavy hairpin pattern consisting of three parallel finger grooves adorns the entire outer face of PT 15. A small, isolated fragment (*d*) belonging to the bottom half of PT 16 also bears part of a finger-groove design.

PT 7, PT 9, PT 12, and PT 14 cannot with certainty be classified individually as type 1 or type 2 pantiles. However, at least one and probably more were of the second type. PT A, a large, ridge-bearing pantile fragment photographed on the wreck but then lost, could not have belonged to PT 8, PT 10–PT 11, or PT 13–PT 16 but could have been a part of PT 7, PT 9, or PT 12. PT 9 and type 2 PT 16 may well have been of identical manufacture and design. They have very similar fabrics and are not markedly dissimilar in thickness. The partially preserved finger-groove design on PT 16*d* is perhaps more fully represented by the V-shaped pattern on PT 9, as a comparison of the drawings of these tiles will show. The design in both cases adorns the tile's bottom half. A substantial part of what may have been a V-shaped pattern is also preserved on the bottom half of PT 14. Type 2 tiles PT 8, PT 10, and PT 15, and PT 12 and PT 14, are noticeably thicker than all the type 1 pantiles. PT 7, PT 12, and PT 14 have in each case a distinct fabric, each of which is closer to the fabrics of type 2 pantiles than to the brick red fabrics of type 1.

PT 3, the best-preserved type 1 pantile, has an overall length of 57 cm and a maximum width of 48 cm. PT 2 is almost identical in size, PT 4 has the same width, and PT 5 can be restored to the same width and length if we assume that the smoke hole was exactly centered. PT 8 and PT 10, the two best-preserved type 2 pantiles, have overall lengths of 58 cm and maximum widths of 49 cm. PT 15 has an overall length of 59 cm. PT 16, however, has a maximum width of only 44 cm. All of the overall length and width measurements that could be made, then, are virtually the same with the exception of the width of PT 16. It probably would have been necessary, therefore, to cut down slightly one or both of the bottom corners of the pantile that was placed above PT 16 and, possibly, PT 9, if all sixteen pantiles were employed together in the same roof.

There are two fragments in addition to PT A that may or may not belong to one of the sixteen pantiles. PT B may have been a part of PT 16, and there is a remote possibility that PT C is the missing center portion of PT 3. An additional handful of fragments recovered were too small and concreted to be assigned to individual pantiles and are not included in the pantile catalog. One of these, PT D, appears on Wreck Plan IV in sector 9B.

PT 1.  Figs. 5-4 and 5-5. Th. of fragments 0.018–0.022. Four pieces. Only two fragments join. Most of top edge, two top corners, and small portion of bottom edge preserved. Fragment *c*, found in sector 6B', does not appear on Wreck Plan IV. Coarse, gritty fabric. Core colors: buff, brick red, and lavender. Light buff grit predominates in core; white and buff grit on surface. Also some black grit throughout.

PT 2.  Figs. 5-4, 5-5, and 5-7. L. 0.58; th. 0.018–0.02. Twelve pieces, all joining. Top and bottom right-hand corners missing. Find spot of fragment *j* not known. Fragment *f* appears in grid photograph taken on August 20, 1961 (Fig. 5-7), but was not recovered from wreck. Scale drawing made from grid photograph indicates that fragment probably could be joined to PT 2 in position shown by Fig. 5-5. Coarse, gritty fabric. Surface colors: orange red, brick red, and bluish red. Surface grit: white and light buff grit predominant; also some black grit.

PT 3.  Figs. 5-4 and 5-5. L. 0.57; max. w. 0.48; th. 0.018–0.023.
Eleven pieces, all joining. Top right-hand corner and other minor fragments missing. Find spots of fragments *d*, *h*, and *j* not known; *h* probably recovered from tile area. Coarse, gritty fabric.

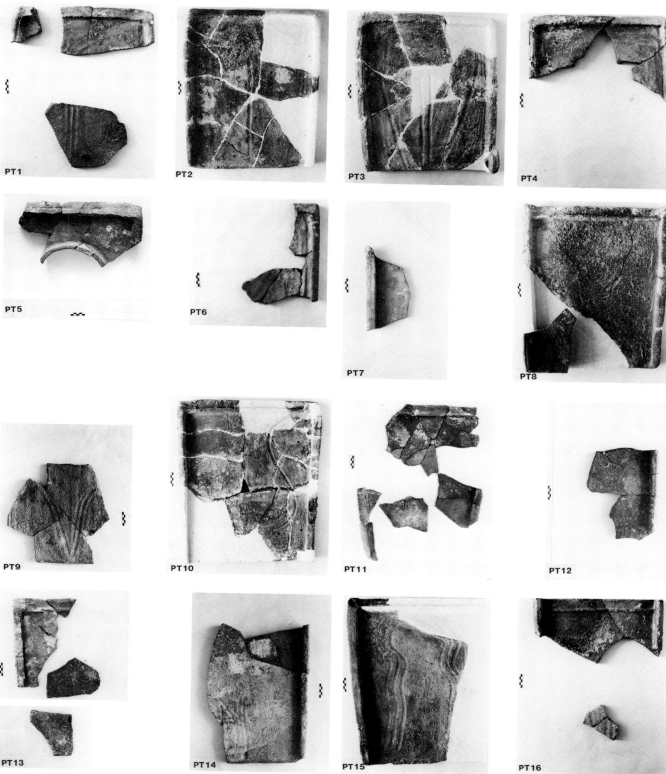

Fig. 5-4. Recovered remnants of pantiles PT 1 through PT 16.

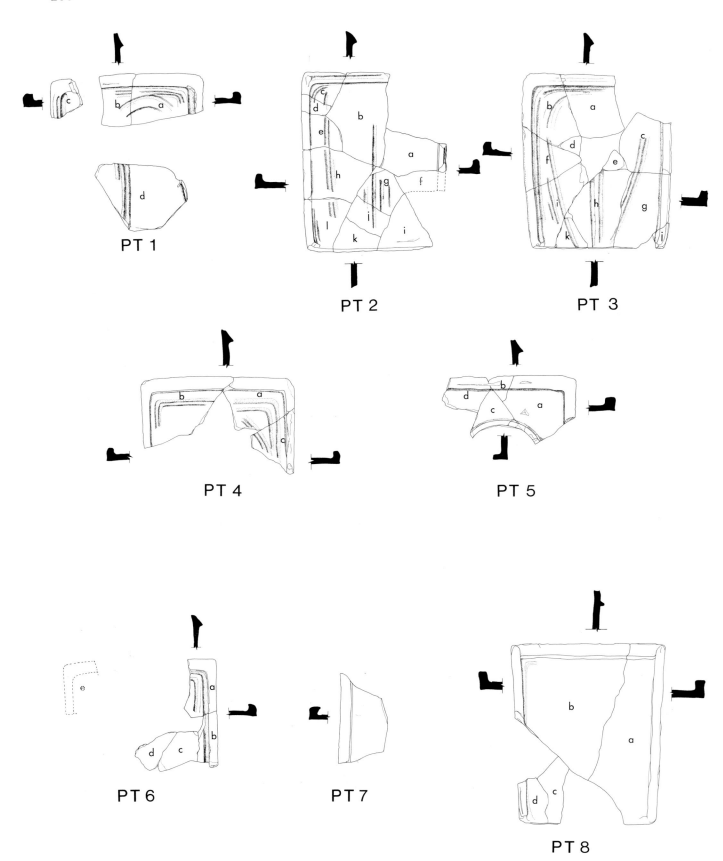

FIG. 5-5. Pantiles PT 1 through PT 8, with cross-sections of rims. 1:12. *LTJ and DF*

Core color: orange red. Surface colors: buff to brick red, with some bluish areas. Grit: white, buff, and black, with white predominating on surface.

PT 4.  Figs. 5-4 and 5-5. Max. w. 0.48; th. of fragments 0.02–0.021.
Three pieces, all joining. Top edge, top corners, and about half of each side preserved. Coarse fabric with large particles of grit. Core color: orange red to brick red. Surface color: buff, with some bluish red. Core grit: white, buff, and black. Surface grit: buff predominates.

PT 5.  Figs. 5-4 and 5-5. Th. of fragments 0.019–0.021.
Five fragments (one without alphabetical designation), all joining. Most of top edge and top right-hand corner preserved. Approx. one-third of a smoke hole with a collar around its edge preserved; original diam. of hole 0.235. Coarse, gritty fabric. Core color: reddish to bluish grey. Surface color: buff to brick red. White and black grit throughout.

PT 6.  Figs. 5-4, 5-5, and 5-8. Th. of fragments 0.014.
Five fragments, all but one joining. Top right-hand and left-hand corners preserved. Fragment *e* appears in grid photograph taken on August 9, 1961 (Fig. 5-8), but was not recovered from wreck; it is partially hidden by an overlying amphora sherd in the grid photograph, but a scale drawing could be made of visible portions. Upper left-hand corner of pantile with broad, raised rim running along top edge is involved; 0.11 of edge is preserved. If there were only six type 1 tiles and PT 5 had a normal width, fragment *e* could only have belonged to PT 6. It and four fragments that join all lay between the sternpost and frame 4. Coarse, gritty fabric. Core color: brick red, with tinges of bluish red. Surface color: brick red, with tinges of orange red and bluish red. Core grit: white, light buff, and black, with light buff and black predominating.

PT 7.  Figs. 5-4 and 5-5. Th. 0.015.
One fragment. Slightly over one-half of one side preserved. Moderately coarse fabric with small particles of grit. Core color: buff. Surface color: cream buff to orange buff. Core grit: white, a little buff, and black. Surface grit: white, brick red, and black, with brick red predominating.

PT 8.  Figs. 5-4 and 5-5. L. 0.58; max. w. 0.49; th. 0.02–0.024.
Four pieces (fragment *a* broken into two after recovery), all joining. Portions of bottom and left-

hand side missing. Fragment *b*, recovered from tile area in 1959 (Fig. 1-4, no. 25), and fragment *c*, found in sector 7B, do not appear on Wreck Plan IV. Coarse fabric with small particles of grit. Core colors: orange buff, brick red, and reddish grey. Surface colors: orange buff, red buff, and grey, with red buff predominating. Core grit: light buff, brick red, and black. Surface grit: inconspicuous.

PT 9.  Figs. 5-4 and 5-5. Th. 0.016.
Three fragments, all joining. Portion of bottom edge and very small portion of rim running along left-hand side preserved. Find spot of fragment *a* not known. Coarse, gritty fabric. Core color: light orange buff. Surface color: light orange buff to buff. Core grit: white, buff, and black, with black predominating. Surface grit: white, buff, and black, with buff predominating.

PT 10.  Figs. 5-4 and 5-6. L. 0.58; max. w. 0.49; th. from 0.016 at top to 0.024 at bottom.
Ten pieces, all joining. Middle portion of top edge, most of bottom left-hand quadrant, and very small piece of bottom right-hand corner missing. Find spots of fragments *c* and *i* not known. Coarse fabric with small particles of grit. Surface color: orange buff, buff, and bluish grey. Surface grit: some white, buff, and black.

PT 11.  Figs. 5-4 and 5-6. Th. of fragments 0.015–0.016.
Nine pieces (fragment *a* broken into four pieces, fragment *c* into four pieces, and fragment *d* into two pieces after recovery). Fragments form four separate portions of the tile that do not join; undersurface of fragment *g* is face up in Fig. 5-4. Top left-hand corner, top half of left side, middle portion of right side, bottom edge, and bottom right-hand corner missing. Fragments *a*, *b*, and *d* do not appear on Wreck Plan IV. Fragments *a* and *d* probably recovered from tile area; fragment *b* recovered from sector 8A. Coarse, gritty fabric. Core colors: orange buff, brick red, and reddish brown. Surface colors: orange buff and reddish brown. Core grit: white and black, with a little buff. Surface grit: white, buff, brick red, and black.

PT 12.  Figs. 5-4 and 5-6. Th. of fragments 0.024–0.025.
Three pieces, all joining. Slightly over half of one side preserved. Coarse, gritty fabric. Core colors: buff and reddish brown. Surface colors: buff, orange buff, and reddish brown. Core grit: buff and black, with a little white. Surface grit: some brick red and black; even less white.

PT 13.  Figs. 5-4 and 5-6. Th. 0.012 and 0.018.

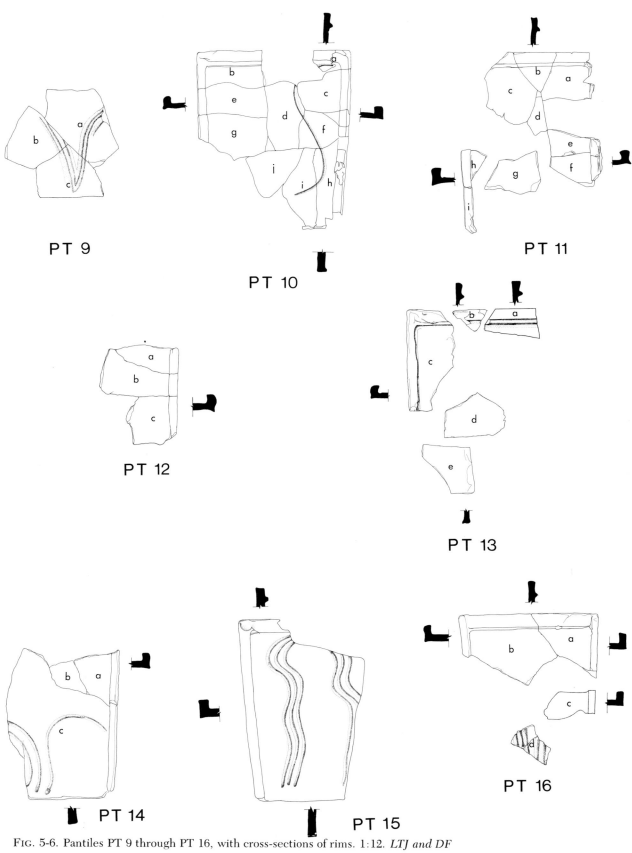

Fig. 5-6. Pantiles PT 9 through PT 16, with cross-sections of rims. 1:12. *LTJ and DF*

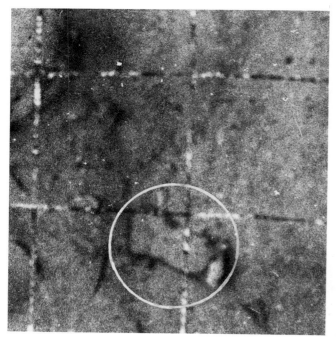

FIG. 5-7. Pantile fragment PT 2*f* on the seabed.

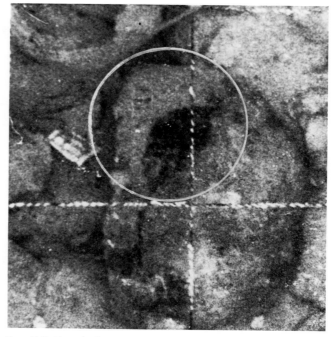

FIG. 5-8. Pantile fragment PT 6*e* on the seabed.

Five pieces (fragment *c* broken into two pieces after recovery). Present location of fragment *a*, recovered from tile area in 1958, is not known, but it was both photographed and drawn by Throckmorton.[13] His drawing indicates that fragment might join with fragment *b*, and his photograph reveals that surface of fragment tends to exfoliate, as does surface of all PT 13 fragments; surface exfoliation does not occur on any other pantiles. All of the fragments together form three separate portions of the tile that do not join; undersurface of fragment *d* is face up in Fig. 5-4. Most of top edge, top left-hand corner, a little over half of left-hand side, and a small part of bottom edge preserved. Fragment *e* includes very small portion of left-hand rim as well as preserved part of bottom edge. Find spots of fragments *b* and *d* not known. Coarse, gritty fabric. Core and surface color: orange buff to buff. Core grit: some white, buff, and black. Surface grit: white, buff, grey, and black.

PT 14. Figs. 5-4 and 5-6. Th. 0.024–0.029.
Three pieces, all joining. Most of right side, bottom right-hand corner, and well over half of bottom edge preserved. Coarse, gritty fabric. Core and surface color: orange buff. Core grit: white, brick red, and black, with black predominating.

Surface grit: white, buff, brick red, and black, with white predominating.

PT 15. Figs. 5-4 and 5-6. L. 0.59; th. 0.025–0.027.
One piece. Top and bottom left-hand corners, entire left side, and well over half of bottom edge preserved. Coarse fabric with small particles of grit. Surface color: orange buff to grey buff. Surface grit: white, buff, and black, with black predominating.

PT 16. Figs. 5-4 and 5-6. Max. w. 0.44; th. of fragments 0.017–0.022.
Four pieces (fragment *d* broken into two pieces after recovery). Present location of fragment *c*, recovered from tile area in 1958, unknown, but it was both photographed and drawn by Throckmorton, who describes it as being "yellowish coarse ware."[14] Comparison of the drawn profile of fragment *c* with the profiles of the sixteen pantiles reveals that it is highly improbable that this fragment belonged to any pantile other than PT 9 or PT 16, and with "yellowish coarse" fabric it could have belonged to either. Unfortunately, there is no way of knowing what the side profiles of PT 9 were like. However, as Fig. 5-6 reveals, the side profile of fragment *a* is close to that of fragment *c*, and it is much closer to this profile than to that of the other side of PT 16 or of any

[13]Gültekin and Throckmorton, "Preliminary Report," no. 35.

[14]Ibid., no. 36.

FIG. 5-9. Pantile PT A on the seabed. White arrow points to the ridge.

FIG. 5-10. Pantile PT B.

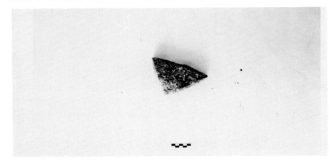

FIG. 5-11. Pantile PT C.

other pantile. For this reason fragment *c* has been assigned to the right side of PT 16. All of the fragments together form three separate portions of the tile that do not join. Top edge, top corners, and about half of right side preserved. Find spot of fragment *d* unknown. Coarse, gritty, but relatively light fabric. Core colors: orange buff and pinkish grey. Surface colors: orange buff. Core and surface grit: white, buff, and black.

PT A.    Fig. 5-9.

Fragment, partially buried in sand, appears in grid photograph taken September 16, 1962, but was not recovered from wreck. Thin ridge, indicated by arrow in photograph, reveals that fragment belongs to type 2 pantile.

PT B.    Fig. 5-10.

Fragment measuring 0.085 × 0.09; th. 0.022. Found concreted to fired clay in which IB 4*b* was embedded (pp. 118–120). Moderately coarse, gritty fabric. Core colors: orange buff and brick red. Surface color: orange buff. Core grit: white and black, with black predominating. Surface grit: a little black.

PT C.    Fig. 5-11.

Triangular fragment measuring 0.15 × 0.12 × 0.105; th. 0.023.

Found in sector 8B; fragment does not appear on Wreck Plan IV. Coarse, gritty fabric. Core color: reddish brown. Surface color: reddish grey. Core grit: brick red predominant. Surface grit: buff to brick red. Fabric does not really seem to match that of any of the sixteen pantiles.

## COVER TILES

Cover tiles have been given the designation CT. Two basic types can be distinguished. Type 1 cover tiles, to which CT 1–CT 8 and CT 10 belong, are curved, Laconian tiles. Only one of them, CT 1, is virtually complete; it is 56 cm long and has a maximum width of 30 cm. None of the other type 1 cover tiles have either one or both overall dimensions preserved. The outer face of CT 1 is decorated by a single large **S**-shaped finger-groove pattern. Only one finger groove occurs in the lower half of the pattern; three parallel grooves are in the upper half. There are three parallel finger grooves on the outer face of the surviving lower left-hand corner of CT 3. They run diagonally from the corner and quite possibly were part of an **S**-shaped pattern similar to that on CT 1. There is a slightly curving finger groove on the outer face of CT 5*c* and a short terminal section of a finger groove on the outer face of CT 8*a*. Finger grooves do not occur on the fragments of CT 2, CT 4, CT 6, CT 7, and CT 10, but it should be noted that only small portions of these tiles are represented by their fragments. Of the nine type 1 cover tiles, only CT 1 and CT 7 have similar fabrics.

Fig. 5-12. Recovered remnants of cover tiles CT 1 through CT 13.

The type 2 cover tiles, to which CT 9 and CT 11–CT 13 belong, are flat with flanged edges. Although these tiles originally may have been designed to serve as pantiles, they are here designated as cover tiles since they seem to have served as such on the ship. The best-preserved tile of this type, CT 9, has a maximum width of 35 cm across its bottom edge. If we assume that the tile had a uniform rate of taper throughout its length and that it would have overlapped snugly another tile of identical size and shape, we must restore to it a length comparable to that of CT 1. None of the other type 2 cover tiles have either overall dimension preserved. Decorative finger grooves do not occur on any of the fragments of these tiles, and all have fabrics that can readily be distinguished one from the other. The fabric of CT 9, however, is very close to that of CT 7.

CT 1.  Figs. 5-12 and 5-13. L. 0.56; max. w. 0.30; normal th. 0.018 (bottom) to 0.028 (top).

One piece. Small part of bottom right-hand corner missing. Coarse, gritty fabric. Surface colors: buff, brick red, and brown. Surface grit: white and black, with black predominating.

CT 2.  Figs. 5-12 and 5-13. Th. of fragments 0.022–0.031.

Three pieces, all joining. Top left-hand corner preserved. Find spot of fragment c unknown. Coarse fabric with numerous large particles of fibrous grit. Core color: brownish buff to brick red. Surface color: brownish buff to greyish red. Grit: brown.

CT 3.  Figs. 5-12 and 5-13. Th. 0.02–0.027.

One piece. Bottom left-hand corner and a little less than one-half of left side preserved. Coarse fabric with much grit, some micaceous. Core color: brown. Surface color: buff to brown. Grit: white, buff, brown, and black, with black predominating.

CT 4.  Figs. 5-12 and 5-13. Th. of fragments 0.018–0.028.

Three pieces. Fragments do not join. Top corners and a little more than one-half of left side preserved. Find spot of fragment b unknown. All three fragments have finely striated and pockmarked surfaces. Coarse, gritty fabric. Core color: light bluish red. Surface color: orange buff to bluish red. Core grit: white and light red. Surface grit: white, buff, and black.

CT 5.  Figs. 5-12 and 5-13. Th. of fragments 0.02–0.027.

Three pieces. Fragments do not join. Placement of fragments in illustrations is random. Small portions of one or both sides preserved in fragments a and b. Find spots of fragments b and c unknown. Coarse fabric with large particles of grit. Core color: reddish brown. Surface color: reddish brown to greyish brown. Core grit: white, brown, and black, with black pebbles predominating. Surface grit: white and black, with large particles of black grit predominating.

CT 6.  Figs. 5-12 and 5-13. Th. of fragments 0.023–0.031.

Two pieces. Fragments do not join. Top left-hand or bottom right-hand corner and about two-thirds of either top or bottom edge preserved in fragment b. Find spot of b unknown. Coarse, gritty fabric. Core and surface color: orange buff to greyish red. Grit: white, red, and black.

CT 7.  Figs. 5-12 and 5-13. Th. 0.028–0.032.

One piece. Top left-hand corner preserved. Coarse, gritty fabric. Core and surface color: buff. Core grit: white and black. Surface grit: white and black, with black predominating.

CT 8.  Figs. 5-12 and 5-13. Th. of fragments 0.015–0.018.

Three pieces. Fragments do not join. Undersurface of fragments is face up in Fig. 5-12. No edges or corners preserved. Find spots of fragments unknown. Very coarse fabric with much grit. Core and surface color: greyish buff. Grit: white and black.

CT 9.  Figs. 5-12 and 5-13. Max. w. 0.35; th. 0.01–0.025.

One piece. Bottom edge, bottom two corners, and about one-half of each side preserved. Coarse, gritty fabric. Core color: orange buff. Surface color: orange buff to brown. Core grit: white and black. Surface grit: white and black, with black predominating.

CT 10.  Figs. 5-12 and 5-13. Th. of fragments 0.013–0.017.

Two pieces. Fragments do not join. No edges or corners preserved. Find spot of fragment b uncertain; found in either sector 6B' or, more probably, sector 8A. Moderately coarse fabric with small particles of grit. Core color: orange buff. Surface color: orange buff to brick red. Core and surface grit: white, brown, and black.

CT 11.  Figs. 5-12 and 5-13. Th. 0.02–0.025.

One piece. Bottom left-hand corner and about one-half of bottom edge preserved. Coarse fabric

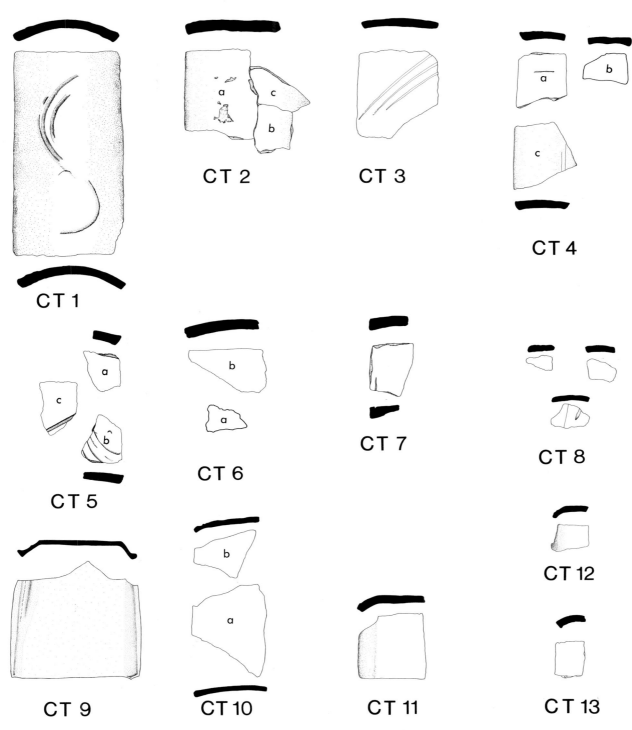

CT 2

CT 3

CT 4

CT 1

CT 5

CT 6

CT 7

CT 8

CT 12

CT 9

CT 10

CT 11

CT 13

Fig. 5-13. Cover tiles CT 1 through CT 13, with cross-sections. 1:10. *LTJ and DF*

with small particles of grit. Core color: greyish brown. Surface color: dark buff to greyish brown. Grit: white and black.

CT 12.  Figs. 5-12 and 5-13. Th. 0.012–0.015.
    One piece. Small portion of one side preserved. Coarse fabric with relatively little grit. Core and surface color: light brick red. Core grit: white. Surface grit: inconspicuous.

CT 13.  Figs. 5-12 and 5-13. Th. 0.018–0.022.
    One piece. Small portion of one side preserved. Coarse, gritty fabric with some large particles of grit. Core and surface color: brick red. Grit: white and grey, with some buff-colored pebbles.

### RECONSTRUCTION OF THE ROOF

One might first suppose from the seabed distribution of roof tiles (Wreck Plan IV) that they had been within the galley on the port side, perhaps as a part of the hearth complex, since most of their recorded fragments were found within the tile area. However, the tiles are simply too large and too numerous for this to have been the case, and their seabed distribution differs appreciably from that of the hearth tiles.

All of the hearth tiles with known find spots, except for four fragments, were found within the tile area. The remaining fragments came to light between frame 4 and the sternpost and, in most cases, much closer to the former than to the latter. Moreover, three of the fragments belong to hearth tiles whose major parts were found within the tile area. In the case of the roof-tile fragments, on the other hand, a substantial number were found between frame 4 and the sternpost, one was found *in situ* somewhat forward of frame 8, four small fragments (not on Wreck Plan IV) came to light over on the wreck's starboard side (two in sector 6B' and two in sector 6C'), and two cover-tile fragments were uncovered in sector 9 between 2 and 3m aft of the sternpost.[15]

In addition to these finds there was a deposit of roof-tile fragments at the wreck's very stern end. This deposit has not been recovered from the wreck but appears on Frost's wreck plan a slight distance aft of the aftermost amphoras visible in 1959 (Fig. 1-4, no. 10). The tile fragment in the deposit shown standing on end on the 1959 plan apparently constitutes a substantial portion of the upper edge of a type 2 pantile. Neither Frost nor Throckmorton reported the removal of this fragment from the wreck site. During a dive on July 12, 1961, David Owen and I examined a deposit of terra-cotta frag-

ments at the wreck's stern end. These fragments were for the most part standing on end and included at the very least several pantile fragments with rims or ridges. An entry was made in the field notes that there seemed to be two tile areas on the wreck. The deposit was located roughly 1 m to port of a stake driven into the seabed at the wreck's stern end at the very beginning of the 1961 season.

As the first season's work progressed, these tile fragments became buried under sand from farther upslope and have not been seen since, even though an effort was made to relocate the deposit in 1964. Our search was hampered by the fact that the stake had been removed in 1962 when mapping frame 9 was placed on the wreck. The position of this stake had been measured in 1961, but we had neglected to plot its position in relation to mapping frame 9 in 1962, and the 1961 and 1962 plans had not yet been integrated in 1964. Thus, we did not know exactly where the stake had been located when the search was made. Furthermore, since the plan of the bottom part of the wreck had not yet been completed, we could not properly correlate it with Frost's plan of the area. Since then, however, we have been able to determine on the final plan of the wreck (Wreck Plans III and IV) the approximate position of the stake and the approximate position of the tile deposit as indicated by Frost's plan. A comparison of Frost's plan with our own shows that the tile deposit was about 1 m to port and 50 cm aft of the stake. Thus, Frost's placement of the deposit is in essential agreement with my own visual estimate in 1961 that it was roughly 1 m to port of the stake. We can be confident, therefore, that the placement of the deposit on Wreck Plans III and IV is fairly accurate. The deposit is just outside the excavated area, which extended no farther to port than the sternmost five amphoras appearing on Wreck Plan III.

The seabed distribution of the roof-tile fragments can best be explained by assigning these tiles to the roof of a deckhouse for the galley. The fact that the tiles were not found scattered over broad areas of the wreck indicates that this roof had still been more or less intact when the ship came to rest on the seabed. When the deckhouse roof finally did give way under their weight, the tiles fell into the galley, mostly piling up on the galley's port side upon and among the hearth tiles. Since most of the roof tiles in the pile overlay hearth tiles, and most of the uppermost tiles in the pile eventually came to rest on the seabed within the tile area's port half, the great majority of the tiles found in that part of the tile area were roof tiles. A number of fragments belonging to tiles that had fallen into the galley eventually made their

---

[15] PT D was not *in situ* when found and originally may have lain farther forward on the wreck.

way into the area between frame 4 and the sternpost. These fragments very probably had been among the uppermost tile fragments within the heavy concentration of tiles in the after-port corner of the galley.

Many roof tiles apparently broke at the moment when the roof collapsed, so parts of some tiles fell outside the deckhouse onto the deck. This appears to have happened, for example, to PT 5. The five recovered fragments of this tile, which were found widely scattered within the tile area and between the tile area and the sternpost, all joined to form most of the top one-third of the tile. Not one fragment belonging to any other portion of the tile was found, yet most of these fragments would have been eye-catching because of the presence of the smoke hole in the tile. The only reasonable conclusion that can be made from these facts is that a major portion of the bottom part of this tile was not present within the excavated area of the wreck. It is also probable that substantial portions of PT 4, PT 6, PT 9, PT 14, and PT 16 and of many of the cover tiles were not present within the excavated area. But if substantial portions of these tiles were not present within the excavated area, then certainly they had not come to rest within the confines of the galley when the deckhouse roof collapsed. One might think that these tiles had not been complete when the ship sank, but how can we explain the presence of so many partial tiles carried on board?

A satisfactory explanation is that many of the missing portions of these tiles had fallen outside the deckhouse onto the sternmost part of the deck, as did, in all probability, the two pieces of cover tile recovered from sector 9. Some of these pieces undoubtedly constitute the deposit of tiles at the wreck's after end shown on Frost's plan. Other major portions of tiles not recovered may also lie beyond the extent of the excavation just within and outside sectors 8 and 9.

Pantile fragment PT 3f, found just over 50 cm forward of the tile area, and the four small roof-tile fragments found in sectors 6B' and 6C', may have fallen to the deck just forward and to starboard of the deckhouse. It is equally possible, however, that some or all of these fragments had fallen down into the galley.

Note that more major portions of cover tiles than of pantiles are missing. This discrepancy is probably due to the cover tiles having overlain the pantiles on the roof. Thus, pieces of cover tiles would have more readily fallen outside the deckhouse when the roof collapsed than would have pieces of pantiles.

Although a great many of the missing parts of the roof tiles would appear to be still on the wreck in unexca-

vated areas, quite a number of fragments that are missing undoubtedly had been lying within the excavated galley area. Three pantile fragments that were photographed but not recovered have already been noted: PT A, PT 2f, and PT 6e. An additional half-dozen unrecovered tile fragments with unmistakable raised rims or ridges appear in various other wreck photographs and drawings. These have not been included in the pantile catalog, however, because their sizes, shapes, or specific identities are not certain. Many roof-tile fragments were unwittingly carried to the sherd dumps along either side of the wreck. I personally recovered six pantile fragments, most with raised rims, from a sherd dump during a single dive on August 13, 1961. No other attempt to locate tile fragments in the dumps was made. One suspects that the dumps would be especially fruitful in yielding fragments of the relatively thin type 2 cover tiles, for it was difficult under water to distinguish between such fragments and amphora sherds. Moreover, the existence of this type of tile was not recognized until the very end of the second season when CT 9 was found. A conscious effort to recover type 2 cover-tile fragments consequently was not made until the 1963 season. In addition to the many tile fragments that were seen but not recognized by the excavators, there very probably were a few tile fragments hidden among piles of amphora sherds that were removed *en masse* from the wreck, and quite a few smaller tile fragments undoubtedly remain in small unexcavated pockets within the excavated area.

Our reconstruction of the galley deckhouse (Figs. 4-5, 4-6, 5-2, and 5-3) is highly conjectural but nevertheless serves to illustrate that our roof tiles as complete tiles would have been sufficient in terms of numbers, size, and types to roof a deckhouse large enough to shelter the galley and provide it with both easy access and adequate illumination and ventilation. At the same time, it will be seen that a deckhouse roofed with these tiles need not have been so large that it would have impeded passage along the deck into the stern.

The deckhouse as reconstructed has a gable roof. The sixteen pantiles at our disposal have been arranged in two rows of four on either side of the roof. Type 1 pantiles have been assigned to the upper rows; type 2 pantiles, to the lower rows. Ideally, there would have been eight type 1 and eight type 2 pantiles in the roof as reconstructed, and it is possible that our sixteen pantiles did consist of eight tiles of either type. There is no need, however, to rule out the possibility that there had been one or two type 2 pantiles in the roof's uppermost rows of pantiles. The roof tiles present us with a great variety of fabrics, two types of cover tile, and a variant size of pantile. Clearly the tile roof either had been from the start a somewhat makeshift affair constructed out of tiles collected from a number of different sources, or it had undergone repairs from time to time, with broken tiles being replaced with whatever was at hand.

The tile roof as reconstructed would have required eight type 1 and four type 2 cover tiles. While the complete type 1 cover tile, CT 1, is of a size and shape perfectly suited for general use with the pantiles, cover tiles of this type would have been a little too wide to fit properly when placed over the lateral joints between the pantile with the smoke hole, PT 5, and the adjoining pantile to either side. This misfitting is due to the presence of the smoke hole's raised collar. The type 2 cover

tiles would have fit PT 5, however, since unlike the type 1 cover tiles, they can be set off-center in relation to the lateral joints of the pantiles beneath. We have placed PT 5 in our reconstructed roof so that it is located directly above the hearth. When so located, it is one of the two inner pantiles in its row. Consequently, the roof requires four type 2 cover tiles, one on either side of PT 5 and one on either side of the pantile directly below PT 5. We are left with one more type 1 cover tile than is needed for our reconstruction. Perhaps a piece of tile put to some secondary use is involved here, or perhaps one or more of our type 1 cover tiles had, in fact, functioned as ridge tiles.

## The Hearth

All other tiles and tile fragments recovered from the wreck can be associated with the galley hearth. The majority of them, twenty-seven in all, have been assigned with reasonable certainty to the group of flat, square tiles designated HTa. In addition, another ten fragments, thicker than the first group, have been designated HTb, and two miscellaneous fragments are also considered to have been pieces of hearth tiles. Finally, a large number of amorphous clay lumps and several iron bars found in the galley area were parts of the hearth.

### HTA TILES

These hearth tiles (Fig. 5-14), 23–24 cm square when complete and 1.8–3 cm thick, are smooth and finished on one side but with the other side rough and with raised edges made when the clay was cut. Before HTa 3 was baked, it was trod on by an infant, who left behind a footprint (Fig. 5-15). Thirteen of the tiles (HTa 1– HTa 11, HTa 13, and HTa 15) are complete. Of them, HTa 13 was recovered in two pieces and HTa 5 was broken into three pieces after recovery. Six other tiles (HTa 12, HTa 14, HTa 16, HTa 18, HTa 19, and HTa 22) lack single corners. HTa 12 was recovered in two pieces and HTa 18 in three pieces. Large pieces of HTa 17, HTa 20, and HTa 21 are missing, but all four corners of HTa 20 and substantial portions of all four sides of HTa 17 and HTa 21 were recovered. Thus, it is probable that all three tiles were originally complete. Note that the four fragments of HTa 20 are nonjoining portions of the tile. Similarly, the pieces of HTa 21 form three nonjoining parts. The fabric of the two tiles were sufficiently different and their profiles such, however, that the as-

signment of the fragments to, and their approximate relative positions within, either tile are certain. HTa 23 through HTa 27 are partially preserved tiles that quite possibly were not originally complete. Of all the pieces, only the small fragment HTa 23*b* may not belong to its parent tile. Both HTa 25 and HTa 27 have neither edges nor corners preserved.

The find spots of HTa 17*b*, HTa 18*b* and *c*, HTa 21*b* and *d*, HTa 23*b*, HTa 25, and HTa 27 are unknown. HTa 1 was recovered from the tile area in 1959 and appears on Frost's plan (Fig. 1-4, no. 24). The fabrics of just over half of the HTa tiles are visible for examination; at least six different fabrics can be distinguished.

HTa 3, 5, 7, 9, 10, 15, 16. Coarse, gritty fabric. Surface color: reddish brown. Surface grit: some white and black.

HTa 17. Coarse, gritty fabric. Core color: grey. Surface colors: orange buff, greyish green, and grey. Core grit: very large black particles predominant; also white and grey grit. Surface grit: large black particles predominant; also white, grey, and brown.

HTa 18. Coarse, gritty fabric. Core and surface color: light brown. Core grit: white, black, and brown. Surface grit: white, brick red, and black.

HTa 20, 21. Coarse, gritty fabric. Core colors: buff, reddish brown, and brown. Surface color: light orangish buff to greyish brown. Core grit: white, brown, and black, with black predominating. Surface grit: white, brown, and black.

HTa 11. Coarse, gritty fabric. Surface color: burnt ochre

FIG. 5-14. Hearth tiles HTa 1 through HTa 27.

to ochre. Surface grit: white, brown, and black. Core not visible, but fabric possibly the same as that of HTa 20 and HTa 21.

HTa 25. Coarse, gritty fabric. Core and surface color: very light brick red. Core grit: white, red, and black; also a few small pebbles. Surface grit: white, brown, and black.

HTa 27. Coarse, gritty fabric. Core color: reddish brown. Surface color: dark buff to reddish brown. Core grit: large brick red particles and brown; also some white and black. Surface grit: white, brown, and black.

On the whole, the fabrics of the HTa tiles tend to be coarser and more poorly baked than those of the roof tiles. The nature of the fabric is such that these tiles would not long have endured as floor tiles. They are perfectly suited to serve as hearth tiles, however, and their association with other materials, described below, leaves no doubt that this was their function.

The variety of fabrics possessed by the HTa tiles suggests that they, like the roof tiles, may have been obtained from several different places. Moreover, small deposits of mortar containing tiny pebbles adhering to the rough side of HTa 13, HTa 14, and HTa 19 and to both sides of HTa 2 and HTa 3 indicate that at least some of the HTa tiles had seen earlier use, since mortar was not found in the tile area.

## HTB TILES

Almost all of the tile fragments not yet described belong

FIG. 5-15. Hearth tile HTa 3, showing imprint of infant's toes.

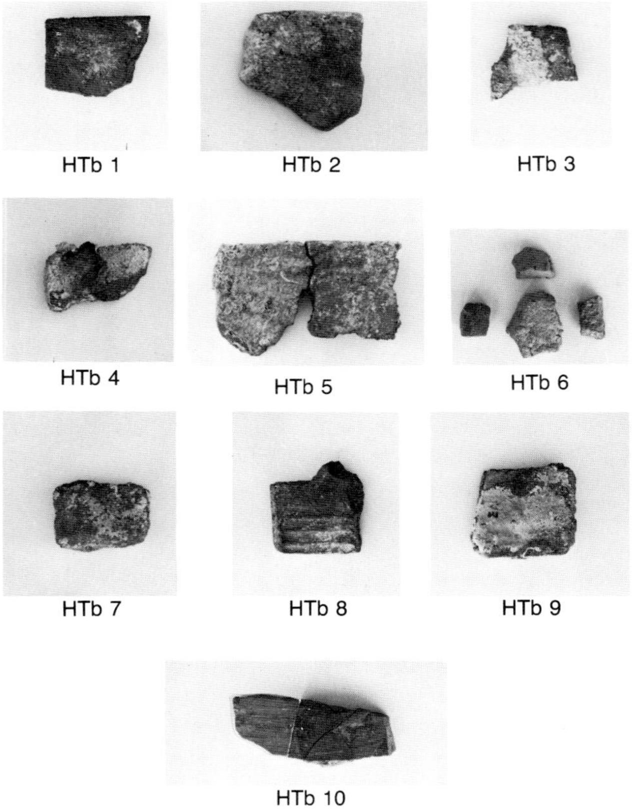

FIG. 5-16. Hearth tiles HTb 1 through HTb 10.

to flat tiles with thicknesses ranging from 2.9 to 3.9 cm. Ten fragments of such tiles were recovered (Figs. 5-16 and 5-17) and have been designated HTb. The find spots of HTb 1, HTb 3, and HTb 6 are unknown. The precise find spots of HTb 10*a* and *c* are also unknown, but these fragments were recovered from a small area, where HTb 10*b* was found, about 35 cm aft of frame 4. HTb 2, HTb 4, and HTb 5 were found together just inside the tile area's starboard edge and about 55 cm aft of its forward edge. HTb 7, HTb 8, and HTb 9 were found within the tile area 25–35 cm forward of frame 4.

HTb 1. Figs. 5-16 and 5-17. L. 0.137; w. 0.108; th. 0.03–0.033.

One corner of tile preserved. One edge chamfered almost to corner. Coarse, gritty fabric. Core and surface color: brick red. Core and surface grit: very large brick red and grey particles predominant; also white, buff, and black grit.

HTb 2. Figs. 5-16 and 5-17. L. 0.139–0.16; w. 0.112–0.16; th. 0.033–0.037.

One corner of tile preserved. Coarse, gritty fabric. Core and surface color: orange buff to greyish brown. Core grit: white predominant; also some buff and black. Surface grit: white, brown, and black.

HTb 3. Figs. 5-16 and 5-17. L. 0.108; w. 0.087; th. 0.029–0.03.

No edge or corners preserved. Coarse, gritty fabric. Core and surface color: orange buff to brownish red. Grit: same as in HTb 1.

HTb 4. Figs. 5-16 and 5-17. L. 0.14; w. 0.08; th. 0.039. One corner of tile preserved. Coarse, gritty fabric. Core color: light buff to greyish brown. Surface color: light buff to orange buff. Core and surface grit: white and brown predominant; also some white, brick red, and black.

HTb 5. Figs. 5-16 and 5-17. L. 0.21; w. 0.13; th. 0.033–0.038.

One corner of tile preserved. Coarse, gritty fabric. Core color: buff to grey brown. Surface color: buff to orange buff. Core grit: brick red predominant; also a little white and black. Sur-

HTb 1

HTb 2

HTb 3

HTb 4

HTb 5

HTb 6

HTb 7

HTb 8

HTb 9

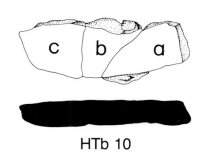

HTb 10

FIG. 5-17. Hearth tiles HTb 1 through HTb 10, with cross-sections. 1:5. *LTJ and DF*

face grit: small white, buff, and black particles.

HTb 6.    Figs. 5-16 and 5-17. L. 0.09; w. 0.07; th. 0.034.
No edges or corners preserved. Coarse, gritty fabric. Core color: buff to pinkish buff. Surface color: orange buff to pinkish buff. Core grit: white, brick red, and grey; also some black. Surface grit: white, buff, and grey. Three small tile fragments with the same fabric appear with HTb 6 in Fig. 5-16.

HTb 7.    Figs. 5-16 and 5-17. L. 0.12; w. 0.095; th. 0.032–0.034.
No edges or corners preserved. Fabric: same as that of HTb 4.

HTb 8.    Figs. 5-16 and 5-17. L. 0.125; w. 0.092–0.115; th. 0.029–0.031.
Corner of tile preserved. Four shallow, flat, and uniformly spaced grooves separated by narrow ridges run along one edge of tile and terminate 0.015 from other edge. Coarse, gritty fabric. Core color; brownish red. Surface color: light brick red. Core grit: white, grey, and black. Surface grit: white, brown, and grey.

HTb 9.    Figs. 5-16 and 5-17. L. 0.12–0.137; w. 0.115–0.12; th. 0.029–0.033.
One edge, and probably second edge and corner, preserved. Four shallow, flat, and uniformly spaced grooves separated by narrow ridges run along the certain edge and seem to terminate about 0.022 from the probable edge. Coarse, gritty fabric. Core color: very light brick red. Surface color: orange buff to brick red. Core grit: brick red predominant; also some white. Surface grit: white, brown, and black.

HTb 10.   Figs. 5-16 and 5-17. L. 0.22; w. 0.09; th. 0.032–0.035.
Three fragments that join. No edges or corners preserved. Fabric: same as that of HTb 6.

All of these tile fragments are somewhat rectangular in shape, certainly five and probably six of them being corner fragments. Most have very similar dimensions. The maximum dimensions of HTb 1, HTb 3, HTb 4, HTb 7, and HTb 8 and the minimum dimensions of HTb 2 and HTb 9 are within 2 cm in either dimension of measuring 12 × 9.5 cm. An attempt seems to have been begun, but not completed, to cut HTb 5 into two fragments, each measuring again about 12 × 9.5 cm. Fragment pairs HTb 1 and HTb 3, HTb 4 and HTb 7, and HTb 6 and HTb 10 are in each case very probably non-joining fragments from the same tiles. While the fabrics

FIG. 5-18. Recovered remnant of miscellaneous tile MT 1.

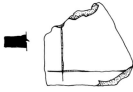

FIG. 5-19. Miscellaneous tile MT 1, with cross-section.

of HTb 8 and HTb 9 differ, primarily in that brick red grit is present in the core of HTb 9 but is absent from the core of HTb 8, they otherwise appear to be quite similar, and it is very possible that these two fragments also originally belonged to separate portions of the same tile. In view of the above, it would appear likely that the ten fragments, for the most part at least, are the product of purposeful rather than accidental breakage.

## MISCELLANEOUS TILE FRAGMENTS

Two pieces of tile whose uses cannot be identified are designated MT.

MT 1.    Figs. 5-18 and 5-19. L. 0.185; w. 0.175; th. 0.026.
One corner of tile preserved. A depressed margin, 0.03–0.035 wide, runs along the two original edges on one face, reducing the tile's thickness to 0.023. Moderately coarse, gritty fabric. Core color: light brick red. Surface color: buff to light brick red. Grit: white, brick red, buff, grey, and black, with large brick red and black particles predominating on the surface.

MT 2.    Photograph or drawing not available. L. 0.075; w. 0.068; th. 0.053.
No edges or corners preserved. Light brick red, fine but gritty fabric that tends to crumble easily.

## CLAY

A large amount of clay with consistent, fine-textured, and impurity-free fabric was found within the tile area and along its immediate periphery and in no other area of the wreck. This clay had been subjected to varying

FIG. 5-20. Samples of fired clay from the hearth (described in text).

FIG. 5-21. Polysulfide rubber replica of iron bar IB 1*a* concretion.

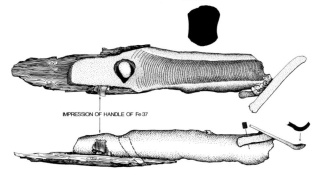

IMPRESSION OF HANDLE OF Fe 37

FIG. 5-22. Concretion of iron bar IB 1*a* and associated wood and iron pieces.

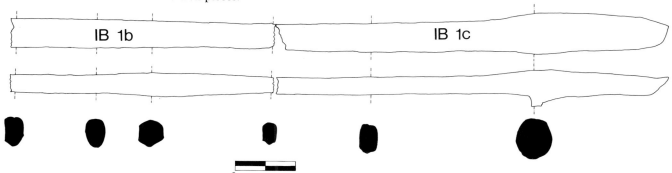

IB 1b

IB 1c

0      10 cms

FIG. 5-23. Arrangement of IB 1*b* and IB 1*c*, with cross-sections.

degrees of heat and normally occurred in the form of amorphous lumps. Three samples of clay in this form are shown in Fig. 5-20. Sample *a* shows only slight signs of exposure to heat and has a greyish green color which is fairly uniform throughout. Sample *b* has been exposed to a higher degree of heat, for its core has a buff grey color with tinges of pink. One side of the lump had been exposed to a much higher degree of heat than the other, with the result that one face has much the same color as the core. Sample *c* has been fairly well fired throughout and has a reddish brown surface color that approaches a brick red color in the core.

## IRON BARS

Fragments of a number of iron bars belonging to the hearth were recovered. We shall first consider the largest of them.

A piece of concreted metal emerging from the sand appears on Frost's plan near the forward-starboard corner of the tile area (Fig. 1-4, no. 12). A polysulfide rubber cast made of this concretion revealed the end section of a large iron bar, IB 1, that was essentially elliptical in cross-section (Figs. 5-21, 5-22, and 5-23). This end section, IB 1*a*, had broken off from the bar at some time after the process of oxidation and formation of the concretion had begun, but since the broken end had come to rest against the face of HTa 6, the concretion resealed itself and was for this reason in an excellent state of preservation. The bar had been fastened to a large wooden timber by means of an iron bolt running through a hole located 9 cm from the bar's end. Part of the timber to which it had been fastened had been covered over and preserved by iron concretion.

Two pieces of concretion, IB 1*b* and *c*, apparently representing a middle portion and the other end of the bar, had not resealed at their broken ends, and their interiors were somewhat eroded. However, the condition of the concretions was generally good, and the broken ends were not at all fragile. It proved possible to reconstruct in general outline on paper the shape and size of these two sections of bar (Fig. 5-23). There had been a protuberance on one face of IB 1*c* 21.5 cm from its unbroken end. This protuberance almost certainly had been a bolt that was a counterpart to the bolt at the bar's other end.

IB 1*c* diminishes in width toward its broken end; one end of IB 1*b* exhibits the same rate of taper and has the same cross-sectional size and shape as the broken end of IB 1*c*. Thus, while a perfect joining could not be made between the two concretions, it is doubtful that more than a centimeter or two of concretion is missing. The broken end of IB 1*a* and the other end of IB 1*b*, on the other hand, differ somewhat in cross-sectional size and shape, IB 1*a* having a larger cross-sectional area. However, the difference is not so great that it would introduce doubt that IB 1*a* is actually a part of the same bar as IB 1*b* and *c*. IB 1*a* decreases in size at a rapid rate in the vicinity of its broken end; IB 1*b* increases in size at an equally rapid rate at the end that does not join with IB 1*c*. If the bar continued to decrease in size at the same rate beyond the broken end of IB 1*a* and continued to increase in size at the same rate beyond the broken end of IB 1*b* that does not join with IB 1*c*, then only relatively small fragments of concretion may be missing. The minimum length to which the bar can be restored is 1.46 m. When the bar is so restored, the distance between the centers of the bolts at each end is 1.15 m. The bar may have been a bit longer, but there is no reason to believe that any substantial part of it is missing.

Two sections of a very small iron bar, IB 2*e*, can be seen in Figs. 5-21 and 5-22 adhering to the broken end of IB 1*a*. The longer of the two sections curves down slightly at the broken end which projects forward of the broken end of IB 1*a*. The other end was not properly cast, but the section cannot have been more than 1 cm longer than its preserved length. The shorter section

also was not properly cast and may have been several centimeters longer than its preserved length. The two sections have the same rectangular cross-section and undoubtedly had been adjacent parts of the same bar. Eight other iron bar fragments that were recovered had rectangular cross-sections of a similar size.[16]

IB 2*a*.  Figs. 5-24, section A, and 5-25, bottom. L. 0.26; cross-sectional measurements 0.018 × 0.006 at broken end; 0.016 × 0.005 at other end.

End piece. Polysulfide rubber replica made. End has rounded corners and curves in vertical plane to form hook. Bar tapers toward end, becoming smaller both in width and thickness. Found overlying frame 8 on wreck's starboard side; appears on Wreck Plan IV.

IB 2*b*.  L. ca. 0.08. Cross-sectional measurements 0.021 × 0.01.

Found somewhere in sector 9C.

IB 2*c*.  L. 0.105. Cross-sectional measurements 0.021 × 0.008 at one end; 0.018 × 0.008 at other.

Fragment tapers, changing in width. Concretion which formed around fragment is highly friable.[17] Find spot unknown.

IB 2*d*.  L. 0.06. Cross-sectional measurements 0.017 × 0.007.

Highly friable concretion. Found in corner common to sectors 9A, 9B, 10A, and 10B; appears on Wreck Plan IV.

IB 2*e*.  Two pieces. L. of one piece 0.13; l. of other piece 0.05; cross-sectional measurements 0.015 × 0.007.

IB 5*a*.  Figs. 5-24, section B, and 5-25, top. L. 0.065; cross-sectional measurements 0.015 × 0.004.

End piece. Polysulfide rubber replica made. End has rounded corners and curves in vertical plane to form hook. Found somewhere in sector 8B.

IB 5*b*.  L. 0.075; cross-sectional measurements 0.015 × 0.004 at one end; 0.017 × 0.005 at the other.

Fragment tapers, changing in both width and thickness. Highly friable concretion. Fragment

---

[16] A tenth bar, IB 5*d* (van Doorninck, "Seventh-Century Byzantine Ship," p. 180), very probably belongs to padlock MF 27.

[17] I initially assumed that the highly friable nature of the concretion that had formed around this fragment and fragments IB 5*b* and *c* was due to the presence of a high percentage of clay in these concretions (van Doorninck, "Seventh-Century Byzantine Ship," pp. 179–180). However, there were no distinct deposits of clay within these concretions. Such friable concretions sometimes form around iron when the objects involved are quite small. Further, concretions formed on unburied iron objects are generally thinner than those covered by sand. Thus, if these were grill bars, their concretions could have formed before the bars came into contact with the seabed.

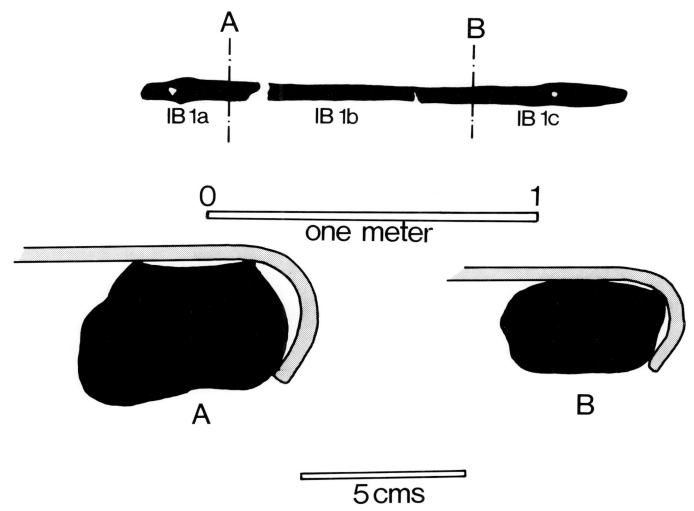

A

B

IB 1a          IB 1b          IB 1c

0          1

one meter

A

B

5 cms

FIG. 5-24. Reconstruction of IB 1 and relative positions of IB 2a (section A) and IB 5a (section B).

concreted to lead weight B 5, found in sector 8A; appears on Wreck Plan IV.

IB 5c. L. 0.105; cross-sectional measurements 0.017 × 0.006 at one end, 0.019 × 0.006 at other.
Fragment tapers, changing in width. Highly friable concretion. Found in sector 9B; appears on Wreck Plan IV.

IB 5e. L. 0.095; cross-sectional measurements 0.016 × 0.005.
Concreted to nail sack (Fe 71) found (not *in situ*) in either sector 8B or 9B.

IB 2a and IB 5a are end fragments terminating in hooks. IB 2e, with its half-preserved hook, also can be considered an end fragment. Thus, these nine fragments are portions of at least two separate bars. In view of the extremely fragile nature of the iron concretion that had formed around many of the fragments, we must assume that large portions of iron bar of this size probably did not survive, so it is quite possible that more than two bars are involved.

None of the eight IB 2 and IB 5 fragments whose find spots are exactly or approximately known were found forward of frame 8. These bars, therefore, are probably to be associated in some way with the galley. All three sections of IB 1 also were found aft of frame 8. Moreover, IB 2e, which has a partially preserved hook at one end, was concreted to IB 1a at the latter bar's broken end. Experience with other material recovered from the wreck serves as a warning that this association of the two fragments could be accidental. In the present case, however, we have good reason to believe it is not, for if we attempt to fit the hooked end of fragment IB 2a

FIG. 5-25. Polysulfide rubber replicas of IB 2*a* (*bottom*) and IB 5*a* (*top*).

over IB 1*a* near the latter's broken end, we find that the hook fits perfectly (Fig. 5-24, section A). If we attempt to fit the hooked end of fragment IB 5*a* over IB 1*c* anywhere near its broken end, we find that it, too, fits perfectly (Fig. 5-24, section B). When we reverse the general positions of the two hooks, however, we find that they do not fit well. It is very possibly not without significance, therefore, that IB 1*a* and IB 2*a* were both found along the forward edge of the galley area, whereas IB 1*c* was found just forward of frame 4 and IB 5*a* somewhat aft of that frame. Finally, we may note that although the hook at one end of IB 2*e* is only about half preserved, it probably would have fit well near or at the point at which it was concreted to IB 1*a*, but rather loosely along most of IB 1*c* and the better part of IB 1*b*. We have good reason to believe, then, that IB 1 and many or all of the nine IB 2 and IB 5 fragments were part of a single structure located aft of frame 8.

Seven fragments of iron bars with a larger rectangular section measuring 32 × 7 mm were also found. The precise find spots of only two of these are known, but it is certain that all seven were recovered from the tile area. Four of the fragments are end pieces. Thus, two or more bars are involved. Certainly one and probably at least two of the end pieces had been nailed to something. The other three fragments, broken at either end, were embedded in clay that had been subjected to varying degrees of heat.

IB 3*a*. L. 0.035.
    End piece with rounded corners.
IB 3*b*. L. 0.19.
    Fragment partially embedded in greenish grey clay covered over by iron concretion.
IB 3*c*. L. 0.085.
    Pockets of greenish grey clay within concretion around fragment.
IB 3*d*. Fig. 5-26. L. 0.12.
    End piece with rounded corners. Polysulfide

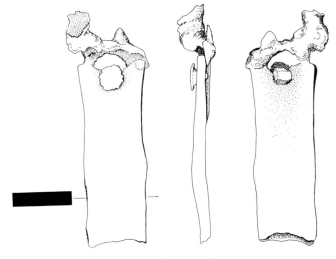

FIG. 5-26. Three views of iron bar IB 3*d*. 1:2.

FIG. 5-27. Iron bar IB 4*b* with tiles HTb 8 and PT B in place over clay bedding.

FIG. 5-28. Iron bar IB 4*b* with tiles HTb 8 and PT B removed to show clay bedding.

rubber replica made of fragment. Bar had been fastened to something by iron nail driven through hole located about 0.02 from preserved end. Fragment appears on Wreck Plan IV.

IB 4*a*. L. 0.06.
    End piece with rounded corners.
IB 4*b*. Figs. 5-27–5-29. L. 0.19.
    Fragment embedded in clay fired to a deep brick

## IB 4b

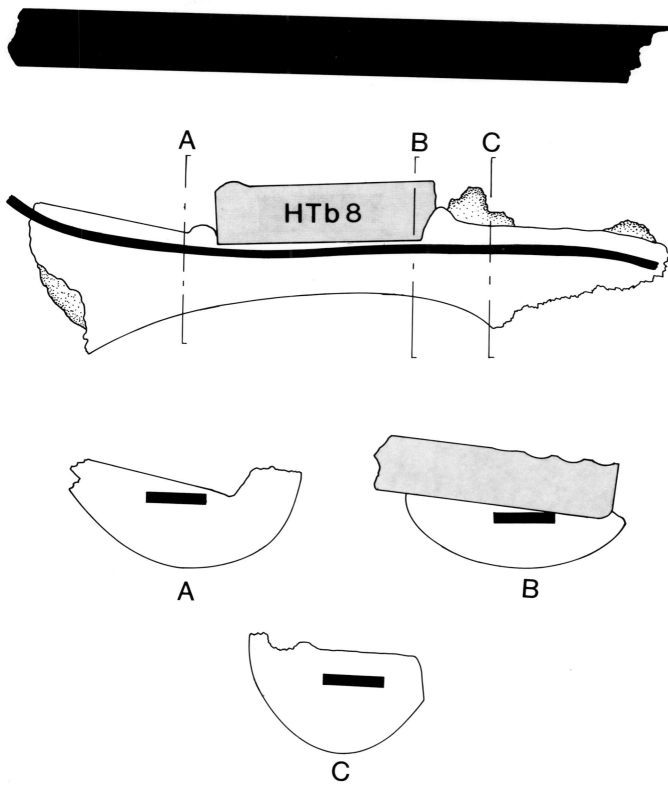

FIG. 5-29. Views and sections of iron bar IB 4b, clay bedding, and tile HTb 8.

red color throughout. Fragment appears on Wreck Plan IV.

IB 4c.  L. 0.055.

End piece with rounded corners. Apparent hole through bar about 0.02 from preserved end.

Fragment IB 4b is particularly noteworthy. The fragment, when viewed from the side, bends near either end, forming a long S-shaped curve. The surrounding clay, which has been exposed to high temperatures, had been applied in layers to either side of the bar and more thickly on one side, particularly toward either end of the fragment. The clay on this side had then been molded by hand into a curved surface roughly semicircular in section.

On the other side, tile fragment HTb 8 had been pressed down into the clay midway along the fragment's length until it came into contact with the bar (Fig. 5-29, section B). The tile fragment was found in this position firmly set in the fire-hardened clay. Another flat-surfaced object had been pressed down into the clay next to HTb 8 at one end of the fragment (Fig. 5-29, section A). Roof-tile fragment PT B was found concreted to the surface of the clay here, but the tile's outline did not closely correspond with the impression made by the flat-surfaced object (Figs. 5-27 and 5-28). Thus PT B's association with IB 4b was possibly accidental. Yet another flat-surfaced object may have been pressed down into the clay on the other side of HTb 8 (Fig. 5-29, section C). Unfortunately, concretion deposits have somewhat destroyed the clay surface here, leaving the issue in doubt.

### RECONSTRUCTION OF THE HEARTH

The hearth tiles, iron bar fragments, and fired clay described above provide us with only a general notion of the hearth's appearance and construction. The hearth itself, built of the HTa tiles, was probably some form of firebox practical for shipboard use.[18] This firebox had been reinforced and/or supported by iron bars embedded in clay that to varying degrees became exposed to heat from hearth fires. The IB 3d fragment with its iron nail suggests that these iron bars had also served to anchor the hearth structure. It would appear that the HTb tiles were in some way employed in conjunction with the iron bars embedded in clay. Certainly this was the case with HTb 8. All surviving elements of the firebox

were found either within the tile area or slightly down-slope from it.

The IB 1, IB 2, and IB 5 fragments appear to be the remains of an iron grill set over the firebox. The dimensions of IB 1 and the find spots of its three fragments suggest that this bar had spanned the distance between frames 4 and 8 somewhere roughly midway between the two sides of the hull. The distance between the two bolt holes in the bar when restored to its minimum possible length is equal to what had been the center-line distance between frames 4 and 8. Furthermore, IB 1a was found in actual contact with frame 8 remnants, and the broken end of IB 1c was found only 15 cm forward of frame 4. IB 1b overlay frame 4. It is rather unlikely that the bar had originally been located well over toward either side of the hull. While IB 1a was found just inside the tile area's starboard edge, IB 1c overlay sternpost remnants.

As already noted, the IB 2 and IB 5 fragments almost certainly belonged to two or more small-sized iron bars with ends that hooked around IB 1. These smaller bars must have lain in a horizontal plane, for there is no evidence that the hooked ends were fastened in any way to IB 1, and if the smaller bars had hung down from IB 1, the hooks surely would have extended further around the larger bar than they did.

How the smaller bars terminated at their other ends is unknown, but it would appear that they were not supported by another iron bar like IB 1. Such a large iron bar could hardly have disappeared without a trace. Perhaps the starboard side of the firebox was not quite as high as the other three sides so that the fire could easily be fed when the smaller grill bars were in place. Only the one larger bar would have been needed to support the smaller bars of the grill. The smaller bars could have been supported at the other end by the back part of the firebox.

The smaller bars may have hooked only partly around IB 1 so that they could be shifted in position or removed. The fact that the seabed distribution of their fragments was much wider than that of the other hearth elements may in part have been a result of their not being fastened down.

The reconstruction of the hearth on the model, as illustrated in Figs. 5-2 and 5-3, is highly conjectural. Since we do not know precisely how the clay-embedded bars and HTb tiles were employed in the hearth's construction, these elements have been omitted. The reconstructed firebox consists of twenty-six complete HTa tiles, but partial tiles would have been used on the starboard side if it was not as high. The hearth as reconstructed is of an ample but practical size. The firebox has overall dimensions of $1 \times 0.73$ m, and the grill is just large enough to have accommodated both of the large caldrons on board.

---

[18] The hearth as initially reconstructed (van Doorninck, "Seventh-Century Byzantine Ship," pp. 162–191) is quite impractical and is in any case not in complete accord with the evidence. The reconstruction was undertaken before it was possible to complete a detailed study of the hearth remains. Peter Kuniholm first suggested that a firebox would have been a more practical form of hearth, and further study of the evidence has borne this out. The initial reconstruction also appears in G. F. Bass, ed., *A History of Seafaring Based on Underwater Archaeology*, p. 142, fig. 10; and G. F. Bass, "Underwater Archaeology: Key to History's Warehouse," *NatGeo* 124, no. 1 (July, 1963): 418–419.

# VI

## THE ANCHORS

FREDERICK H. VAN DOORNINCK, JR.

PRIOR to excavation, a large mass of iron concretion marked the forward, upslope limit of the visible shipwreck (Fig. 1-4, no. 1). Both Frost and Throckmorton had identified this mass correctly as a pile of concreted iron anchors and had estimated that there were about five anchors in all. However, the anchors' actual appearance and design were not clear since they were in large part concreted together and heavily overgrown with marine life.[1] Indeed, it was only after the overgrowth had been removed during the first week of the 1961 season that their general appearance emerged clearly for the first time (Fig. 6-1).

A general plan of the anchor pile was made at the end of the 1961 season showing the presence of six anchors. A more detailed plan was made the following summer by means of photo tower grid photographs (Fig. 3-3), and finally, during the 1963 season the anchor pile was included in three of the six series of stereo photographs taken of the forward half of the wreck (Fig. 6-2).

In order to raise this enormous mass of concretion, as many anchor arms and rings as possible were first broken off, and the remaining mass was then cut with hammer and chisel into two parts. Even so, the weight of either part severely taxed the lifting capacity of the University Museum's research vessel, *Virazon*, and the attempt to raise the two sections was very nearly abandoned. The task was finally accomplished at the close of the 1964 season (Fig. 6-3).[2]

FIG. 6-1. Anchor pile at an early stage of the excavations.

The two major sections and the dozens of smaller pieces that had been broken off were then reassembled. Only a few small and relatively unimportant fragments proved to be missing. As the job of reassembly progressed, sections were drawn of rings, shanks, and arms at the various breaks. When all the pieces had been put in place, detailed measurements were made of each anchor wherever possible, and the exact position of each anchor within the concretion complex was superimposed on the stereo photographs of the complex. A final

---

[1] H. Frost, *Under the Mediterranean*, p. 173.

[2] The success of this extremely difficult operation was in large part due to the efforts of David I. Owen and Lloyd P. Wells. Owen was in charge of the recovery of the anchors from beginning to end and was field director during the last third of the 1964 season. Wells was the very able captain of the *Virazon*. In spite of bad weather and high

waves, they made one last attempt to raise the two large masses of concretion at the very end of the season and, happily, on that attempt succeeded.

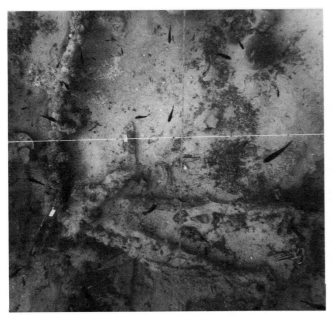

FIG. 6-2. Anchor pile at a late stage in the excavations. The ring and most of the shank of anchor An 8, the forward arm of An 8 and An 10, almost all of An 5, and the after arm of An 6 have been removed. A hammer and saw used in detaching some of these parts appear at the pile's starboard end (*lower right*). Anchors An 1 and An 3 are partially visible just to port of the pile. *DMR*

FIG. 6-3. Concretion of anchors being raised by the *Virazon*. © National Geographic Society

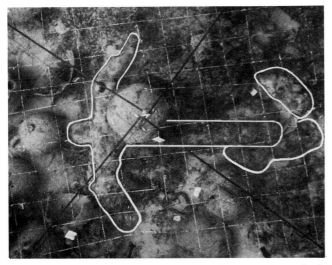

FIG. 6-4. Grid photograph with outline of An 2 on the seabed.

plan of the anchor pile was then made and placed in its proper position on Wreck Plan III.

During the course of this work, a previously undetected anchor was discovered at the bottom of the pile, well concealed by the anchor immediately above it, making a total of seven anchors (An 5 through An 11) in the pile.

One other anchor (An 2) was readily visible on the wreck before excavation, lying well over on the starboard edge of the wreck and slightly downslope from the pile of seven anchors. The upper portion of its shank had broken off and had in turn broken into two pieces. There apparently had not been sufficient unoxidized iron remaining within these pieces to permit a resealing of their open, broken ends through a continuing buildup of concretion, and since their interiors were exposed to the scouring action of current and sand, they had been reduced to severely eroded, hollow concretion shells, which lay partly concealed in the sand next to the broken end of the lower portion of the shank (Fig. 6-4). Some substantial amounts of unoxidized iron, on the other hand, did still remain within the lower portion of the shank when the upper portion broke off. As this iron then continued to oxidize, the broken, open end of the lower portion became so completely and uniformly covered over with concretion that it appeared to be the original upper end of the shank. Consequently, it was initially thought that the anchor had been smaller than those in the pile, and Frost suggested that it might have

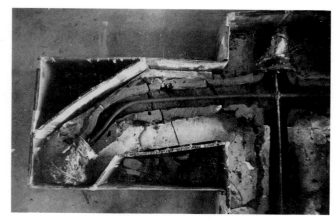

FIG. 6-5. *Left*: Concretion of bottom part of An 2 opened and cleaned to form a mold. *Right*: Iron armature inserted to rein-

force the polysulfide rubber cast.

FIG. 6-6. Concretion being broken away from polysulfide rubber cast of An 2.

FIG. 6-7. Rubber cast being removed from concretion mold.

been a kedge anchor.[3] Its true configuration and nature were not recognized until the end of the 1964 season, when the two concretion shells were identified as the upper portion of the anchor shank.

The concretion mold of the bottom half of An 2 was in perfect condition and was used to make a polysulfide rubber replica (Figs. 6-5–6-8) now on display at the Bodrum Museum. Since the other two pieces of concretion were severely eroded, the overall length of the anchor is uncertain. It was possible, however, to make accurate measurements and drawings of the upper end of the shank.

Approximately halfway between this anchor and the pile of seven anchors Frost noted the presence of "concreted metal emerging from the sand" with "'steps' of concreted metal in the sand" on either side (Fig. 1-4, nos. 2, 3, and 13). Excavation revealed these "steps" to be the bottom half of the shank and the arms of still another anchor (Fig. 6-9). The top half of the shank of

this anchor (An 4) was found, once again broken into two pieces, deeply buried in the sand in the upper right-hand corner of sector 4C, about 3 m directly downslope from the rest of the anchor.[4] The open, broken ends of these two pieces had not been resealed by concretion, and the interior iron oxide had been entirely washed away. There was, however, no appreciable erosion of the concretion shells themselves, probably because they were buried in sand at an early date. A sufficient amount of concretion had formed over the open, broken end of the bottom half of the shank to protect it from erosion as well. While the three sections of shank no longer fit together perfectly, there did not appear to have been any significant loss of concretion between them, and the overall length of the shank given in the anchor catalog below may be considered as quite close to its original length.

Two other anchors were found lying along the port

---

[3] Frost, *Under the Mediterranean*, p. 166.

[4] These pieces were not photographed or drawn *in situ* and do not, therefore, appear on Wreck Plan III.

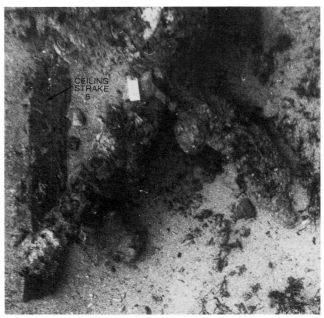

FIG. 6-9. Bottom section of An 4 and starboard remnant of ceiling strake 5 on the seabed.

FIG. 6-8. Polysulfide rubber replica of the bottom section of An 2.

side of the wreck, one (An 1) alongside the port edge of the pile of seven anchors and the other (An 3) immediately forward of the first (Fig. 6-10). Although these anchors had been completely hidden in sand until they were uncovered during the 1962 and 1963 seasons, the presence of something substantial buried at this point had been noted by Frost (Fig. 1-4, no. 26).[5]

The concretion shell of the forward anchor (An 3) was well preserved almost throughout. However, the ring had been broken away at an early date, save for a small section which remained in place within the ring aperture at the head of the shank. Thus, the diameter of the ring is not known. The concretion shell which formed around the bottom half of the shank and the arms of the anchor was very thick and has not been broken or cut into sections. The drawing of this part of the anchor is based solely on the shape of the surrounding concretion shell, and the overall dimensions given for the anchor in the anchor catalog are only approximate.

The concretion shell of the other portside anchor (An 1) was perfectly preserved, and since it was free of any other masses of concretion, we were able to cut it into small sections with a lapidary saw. Surprisingly, substantial amounts of unoxidized iron were found within

the shell in the area of the juncture of the shank and the arms and around the stock aperture (Fig. 6-11). An analysis of a sample of this iron taken from one of the arms will be found in Appendix B. At the time the shell was sectioned in 1964, work was begun on making a polysulfide rubber replica of the anchor, but when it then proved impossible to remove the unoxidized iron without shattering the surrounding concretion, the project was abandoned. It was possible, however, to make accurate drawings of the anchor that are faithful to the original in every detail (Fig. 6-12). The unoxidized iron was easily removed from the concretion shell in 1970, for in the intervening years the concretion had separated from the iron while drying out.

The following catalog of the eleven anchors lists for each anchor the overall length of the shank, including the projecting crown (l.), the distance from fluke tip to fluke tip (w.), the outside diameter of the ring (ring diam.), and the cross-sectional diameter of the ring (ring sect., with two dimensions given if the ring had an elliptical cross-section). Each anchor has an elliptical aperture for a movable stock below the anchor-cable ring at the head of the shank. For the first four anchors in the catalog, precise measurements of one or both diameters of the aperture (stock aper.) are given. All other stock aperture measurements, based on the outer configuration and dimensions of the surrounding concretion shell, are approximate but almost certainly accurate to within 1 cm. Cross-sectional measurements made of the shank

---

[5] Frost's plan shows a row of amphoras buried under the sand at this point. However, no amphoras were found in this area. The wood found here by Frost is almost certainly the piece of wood concreted to An 1 that appears on Wreck Plan II.

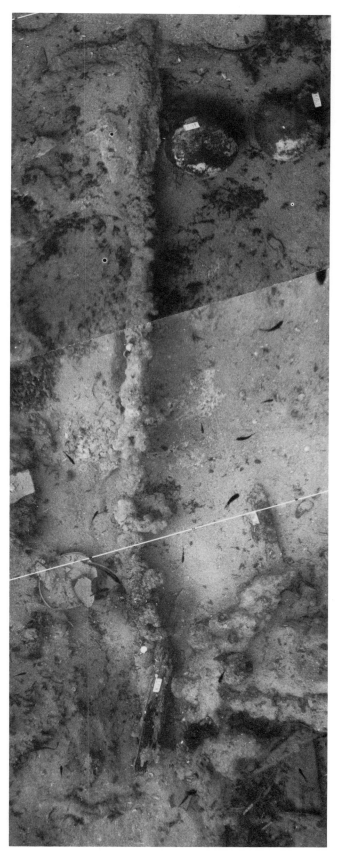

FIG. 6-10. Anchors An 1 and An 3 on the seabed. The port arm of An 1 is just visible at the bottom of the picture. The port end of the anchor pile appears at the bottom right.

FIG. 6-11. Unoxidized iron from An 1. *Above*: shank head; *below*: juncture of shank and arms. Arrow points to source of analyzed sample.

and arms of each anchor are given on the individual anchor drawings. The anchors are listed in order of their general accessibility for use at the time of the shipwreck. Measurements are given in meters.

An 1.  Fig. 6-12. L. 2.14; w. 1.405; ring diam. 0.26; ring sect. 0.026; stock aper. l. 0.062; stock aper. w. 0.06.

Complete. Portions of original anchor preserved (Appendix B).

An 2.  Fig. 6-13. L. ——; w. 1.345; ring diam. 0.32; ring sect. 0.021; stock aper. l. 0.096; stock aper. w. 0.077.

Shank broken in two places. Concretion shell representing two upper sections of shank severely eroded. L. of bottom section of shank 1.47; l. of middle section approx. 0.31; l. of upper section approx. 0.55. Polysulfide rubber replica made of bottom part of anchor.

An 3.  Fig. 6-14. L. approx. 2.19; w. approx. 1.29; ring diam. ——; ring sect. 0.026; stock aper. l. 0.072 ± 0.002; stock aper. w. 0.06.

Ring missing except for portion passing through aperture in shank. A few centimeters of one fluke tip may be missing; otherwise, anchor is complete.

An 4.  Fig. 6-15. L. approx. 2.04; w. 1.58; ring diam. 0.27; ring sect. 0.023 × 0.025; stock aper. l. 0.066+; stock aper. w. 0.065.

Shank broken in two places. Concretion representing bottom section of anchor in excellent condition. Concretion representing two upper sections of shank in fairly good condition.

An 5.  Fig. 6-16. L. 2.375; w. approx. 1.525; ring diam. 0.28; ring sect. 0.021 × 0.017; stock aper. l. approx. 0.063; stock aper. w. approx. 0.046.

Complete. Only upslope arm could be measured

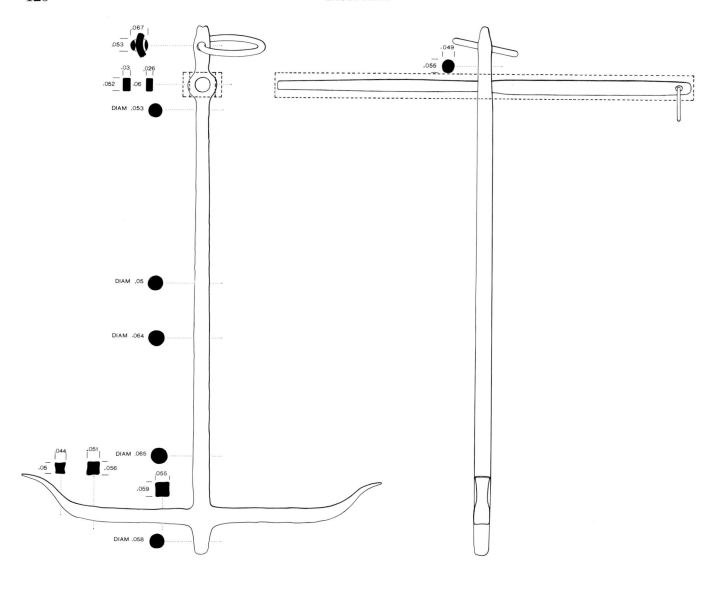

FIG. 6-12. Anchor An 1 and iron stock St 1, with cross-sections. (All measurements in meters.)

in detail. Overall width is estimate based on stereo photographs of concretion on wreck.

An 6.    Fig. 6-17. L. 2.565; w. 1.42; ring diam. 0.25; ring sect. 0.023; stock aper. l. approx. 0.06; stock aper. w. approx. 0.048.
Complete.

An 7.    Fig. 6-18. L. 2.25; w. approx. 1.35; ring diam. 0.24; ring sect. 0.022; stock aper. l. approx. 0.056; stock aper. w. approx. 0.045.
Complete. Only downslope arm could be measured in detail. Overall width given is estimate based on stereo photographs.

An 8.    Fig. 6-19. L. 2.465; w. 1.57; ring diam. 0.38; ring sect. 0.032; stock aper. l. approx. 0.08; stock aper. w. approx. 0.068.
Complete.

An 9.    Fig. 6-20. L. approx. 2.00; w. approx. 1.535; ring diam. 0.25; ring sect. ——; stock aper. l. approx. 0.082; stock aper. w. approx. 0.066.
Direct measurements of overall dimensions could not be made. Overall length and width given are estimates based on stereo photographs. A precise measurement of ring's outside diameter was made, but large masses of concretion surrounding the ring made it impossible to obtain a cross-sectional measurement.

An 10.   Fig. 6-21. L. approx. 2.405; w. approx. 1.50; ring diam. ——; ring sect. ——; stock aper. l. approx. 0.085; stock aper. w. approx. 0.069.
Complete. Direct measurement of overall length could not be made; measurement given is estimate based on stereo photographs. However, di-

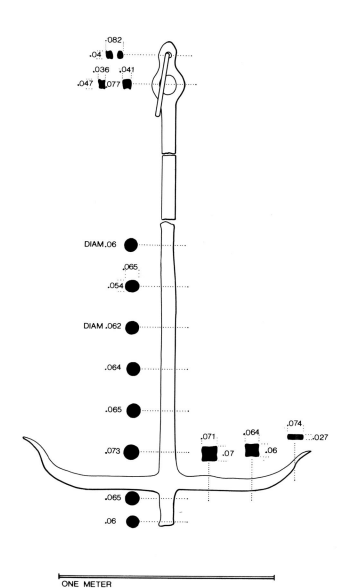

ONE METER

FIG. 6-13. Anchor An 2, with cross-sections. (All measurements in meters.)

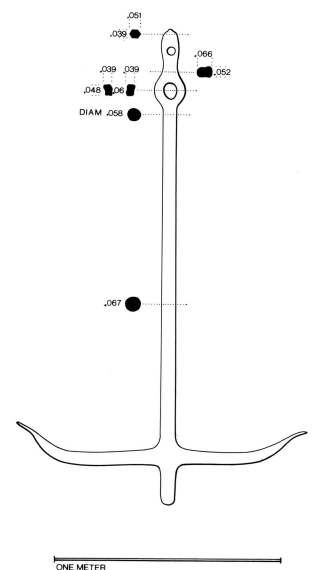

ONE METER

FIG. 6-14. Anchor An 3, with cross-sections. (All measurements in meters.)

rectly measured distance from crown to center of stock aperture is 2.19. Only upslope arm could be measured in detail. Overall width given is estimate based on stereo photographs. Ring was inaccessible and could not be measured.

An 11. Fig. 6-22. L. approx. 2.415; w. approx. 1.55; ring diam. 0.375; ring sect. 0.026; stock aper. l. approx. 0.076; stock aper. w. approx. 0.064.

Complete. Direct measurements of anchor's overall dimensions could not be made. Overall length and width are estimates based on stereo photographs.

All of the anchors are identical in basic design. One is immediately struck by the thinness of both their shanks and arms, but this is a common characteristic of

early forged anchors. There is no evidence whatsoever to suggest that the anchors might have been sheathed with wood.[6]

The anchors are cruciform. In every case the longitudinal axes of the two arms, out to the point where they begin to curve upward, join together to form a single, straight line which for eight of the anchors is perpendicular to the longitudinal axis of the shank, thereby forming a cross. In the case of An 5 and, to a lesser degree, An 4 and An 6, however, the axis of the arms is somewhat off the perpendicular, a fact that led me to

[6]J. van Houhuys, "The Anchor," *MM* 37 (1951): 43–44.

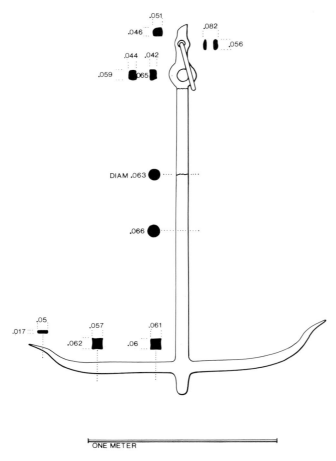

FIG. 6-15. Anchor An 4, with cross-sections. (All measurements in meters.)

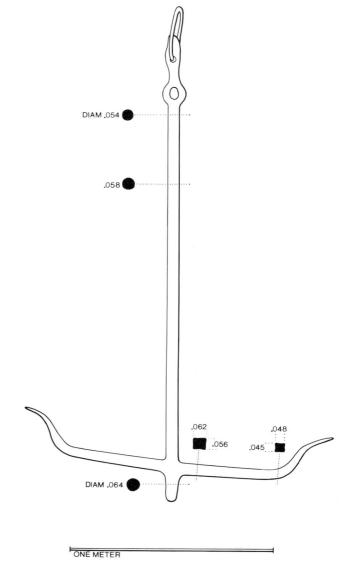

FIG. 6-16. Anchor An 5, with cross-sections. (All measurements in meters.)

conclude that the arms of each anchor might have been made from a single piece of iron which was forge-welded to the shank. A reexamination of the unoxidized iron from the juncture of the shank and the arms of An 1 in 1981 has revealed, however, that either arm had been individually welded to the shank and that both the shank and the arms had been made from a number of pieces welded together. A new study of the anchors will be undertaken to learn as much as possible about their manufacture and will be published in future issues of the *International Journal of Nautical Archaeology.*

The arms turn up and then out at their ends, tapering down in thickness to a rounded edge at the same time. As the arms turn up, they also narrow down to about three-quarters of their maximum width and then widen again to form the flukes as they turn out (Fig. 6-12). The flukes are very poorly developed, being no wider than the main body of the arms, nor do they possess what might properly be called palms, since they do not have flat upper surfaces.

Although the anchor crowns are not equipped with rings, they extend a good distance below the base of the arms, providing ample purchase for a cable to disengage

the anchor if it became hung up on a rocky bottom. Examination of the rings at the heads of the anchor shanks did not reveal any traces of anchor cables, indicating that the cables were made of some perishable fiber and not of iron chain. Indeed, not a link of iron chain was found anywhere on the wreck.

We were especially puzzled at the end of the 1961 season by the fact that nothing had been uncovered that could be interpreted as having to do with stocks for the anchors.[7] During the 1962 season, however, two perfectly preserved concretion shells of iron stocks (St 1 and St 2) were uncovered during the course of excavating along the upslope side of the pile of seven anchors (Fig.

[7] G. F. Bass, "Underwater Excavations at Yassi Ada: A Byzantine Shipwreck," *AA* 77 (1962): 546.

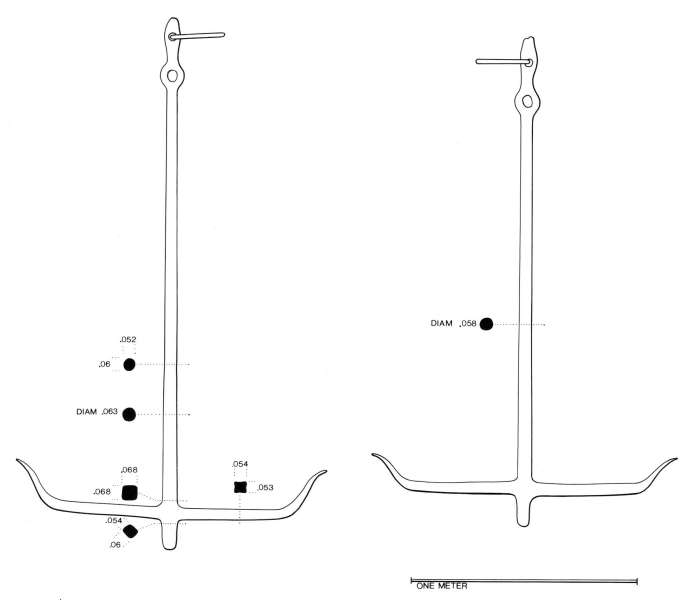

FIG. 6-17. Anchor An 6, with cross-sections. (All measurements in meters.)

FIG. 6-18. Anchor An 7, with cross-sections. (All measurements in meters.)

6-23). The positions of the stocks were fixed, since both were concreted to the anchor pile. The portion of the concretion shell of each stock that projected from the anchor pile was broken off and raised separately. The projecting portion of St 1 broke off cleanly and was recovered in its entirety, but the shell of St 2 shattered at the break, and a section of the shell, approximately 8 cm long, was lost. Even so, it was possible to determine very closely the original overall length of the stock, since the exact relative positions of the heavy ends of St 1 and St 2 and of the heavy end of St 1 and the light end of St 2 are all known through direct measurement. Consequently, the restored length of St 2 cannot be in error

by more than a few centimeters at most.

The presence of another piece of concreted metal lying loose on the sand on the port edge of the wreck just below the anchor pile had been noted by Frost, who carefully left it in place (Fig. 1-4, no. 6). It was found in the same position in 1961, was raised the following summer, and proved to be a partially preserved but eroded concretion shell that had formed around a solid iron bar roughly circular in cross-section.[8] We judge from the find spot and the bar's general diameter that it probably

[8]The attractive suggestion that the concretion had to do with a slightly tapered copper tube for Greek fire (Frost, *Under the Mediterranean*, p. 173) is therefore no longer tenable.

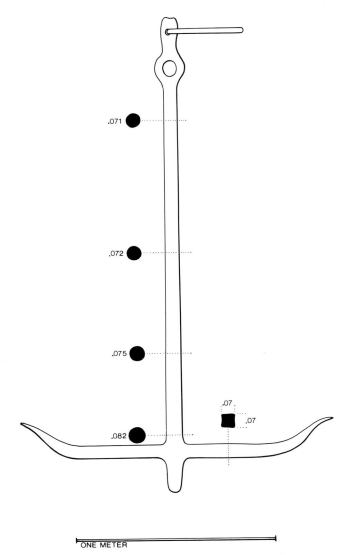

FIG. 6-19. Anchor An 8, with cross-sections. (All measurements in meters.)

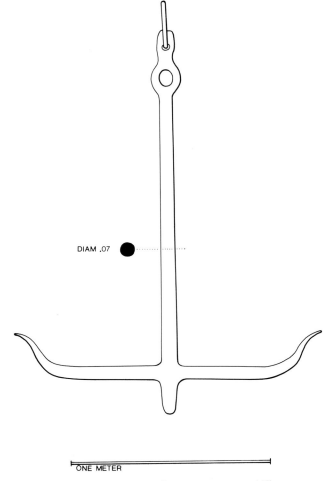

FIG. 6-20. Anchor An 9, with cross-sections. (All measurements in meters.)

was another iron stock (St 3). Off the wreck on the port side, another large iron bar, about 1 m of its length projecting up out of the sand, was also noted by Frost (Fig. 1-4, no. 7). It turned out, however, that this bar had nothing to do with the seventh-century Byzantine shipwreck.[9]

[9]Underwater examination of this bar suggested that substantial amounts of iron within it remained in an unoxidized state, and an effort during the 1963 season to uncover its buried portion quickly led to the discovery that it belonged to another shipwreck. The placement of the bar on Frost's plan is quite accurate and gives one a good idea of how close that shipwreck was to the seventh-century Byzantine wreck. Despite its close proximity, it probably would have remained undetected for several more years had it not been for the projecting iron bar, eloquently attesting to the inherent difficulty in visually locating on a sandy or muddy bottom the wrecks of ships that were not carrying bulky cargoes of imperishable material. The wreck was partially excavated in 1967 and has been dated to the sixteenth century by a silver coin of Philip II of Spain (1556–1598) recovered in 1969 (G. F.

Remains of certainly two and probably three iron stocks, then, were recovered from the wreck. Their measurements are given in meters.

St 1. Figs. 6-12 and 6-24. L. 1.615; ring diam. 0.14; ring sect. 0.015.
    Complete.

St 2. Fig. 6-24. L. approx. 1.45.
    Ring and section approx. 0.08 long from middle portion of bar missing.

St 3. Wreck Plan III, sector 3A. Pres. l. 0.88.
    Concretion shell broken away at either end and eroded. Cross-section roughly circular with a more or less uniform diam. of 0.055. Possibly a swelling approx. 0.02 wide 0.3 from one end of the bar as preserved, giving it a max. diam. of perhaps as much as 0.08, but this is very uncertain.

Bass and F. H. van Doorninck, Jr., "A Fourth-Century Shipwreck at Yassi Ada," *AJA* 75 [1971]: 37; uncleaned coin misdated).

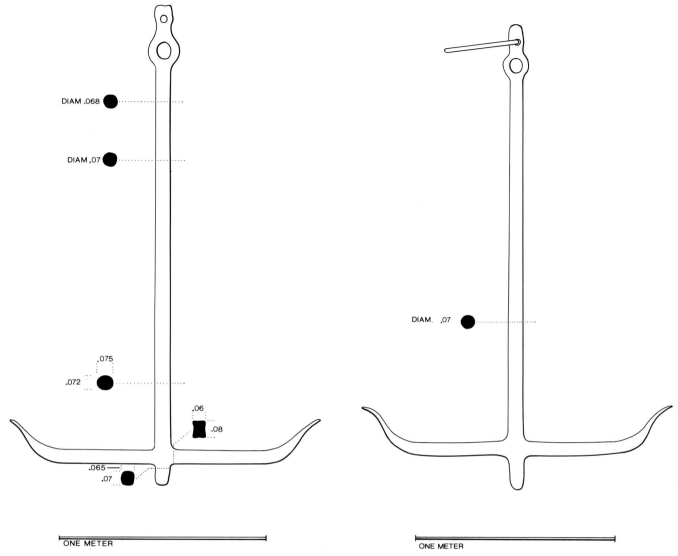

DIAM .068

DIAM .07

.075
.072

.06
.08

.065 —
.07

DIAM. .07

ONE METER

ONE METER

FIG. 6-21. Anchor An 10, with cross-sections. (All measurements in meters.)

FIG. 6-22. Anchor An 11, with cross-sections. (All measurements in meters.)

## Size and Weight

The anchors vary from approximately 2 m to 2.565 m in length and from approximately 1.29 m to 1.58 m in width. These overall measurements, while useful in revealing the amount of deck space required for anchor stowage, are not reliable indicators of the actual variances in the total volumes and weights of the anchors, for shanks and arms vary in cross-sectional size and not necessarily in a direct ratio to their overall dimensions. An 9, for example, which is only about 2 m long and approximately 1.535 m wide, must have weighed considerably more than An 4, which is approximately 2.155 m long and 1.58 m wide. As we will see, there is also a good deal of variation in the overall dimensions of some of the

anchors which seem to have had equal weights. Such variations in overall dimensions are, of course, to be expected in forged anchors.

An 8, An 10, and An 11, however, are virtually identical, not only in their overall dimensions, but also in the cross-sectional dimensions of their shanks and arms. While it is true that the crown of An 10 projects little more than half as far as do the crowns of An 8 and An 11, the anchor had an overall length only about 1 cm shorter than that of An 11 and about 5 cm shorter than that of An 8. It is also true that An 11 seems to have had a slightly more slender shank than the other two anchors, but this difference may be more apparent than real,

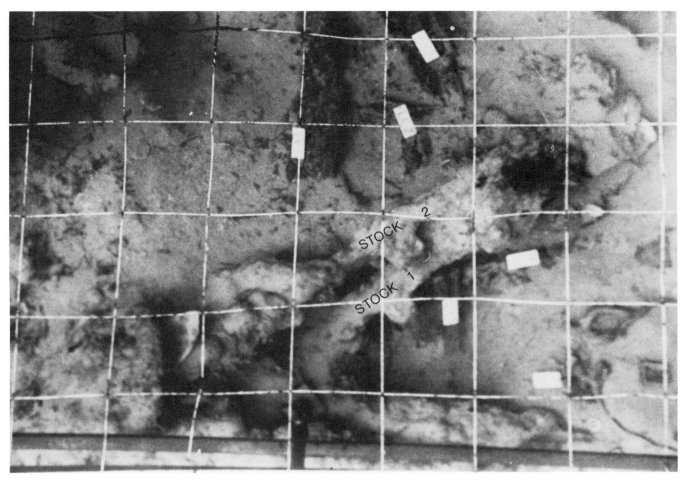

FIG. 6-23. Grid photograph showing concretions of iron anchor stocks St 1 and St 2 on the seabed.

since a direct measurement of the shank diameter of this anchor was possible at only one point. In any case, even the apparent difference in the size of this shank is too slight to warrant any supposition that An 11 was significantly lighter in weight than the other two anchors, while it is absolutely certain that all the remaining eight anchors were considerably lighter in weight. It is also noteworthy that the rings of An 8 and An 11 are much larger than the other anchor rings of known size. Unfortunately, the size of An 10's ring cannot be determined without causing extensive damage to surrounding concretion.

An 8, An 10, and An 11, then, can be put together in one weight group. Of these three anchors, the dimensions of An 8 are known in the greatest detail, and a calculation of the total volume of this anchor based on these dimensions has yielded the figure of 17.82 l. That volume was for the most part mathematically calculated by dividing the anchor into sections with the shapes of reg-

ular solids. Since the outer portions of the anchor arms could not be divided like that, scale clay models of these portions were made and the volume of clay used was then measured. The same procedure was followed in arriving at the approximate volumes of An 1, An 2, and An 9.

The shanks of An 1, An 3, and An 7 are virtually identical in size. To these three we may also add the shanks of An 5 and An 6, for while the latter shanks are a bit more slender, they are roughly equal in volume to the other three shanks because of their correspondingly greater lengths. Turning to the arms of these five anchors, we find that the arms of An 1 and An 7 are virtually identical in size. One of the fluke tips of An 3 seems to have been corroded away, and in all probability the arms of this anchor were also originally of the same size. The arms of An 5 and An 6 are somewhat smaller in cross-section, but this is fully compensated for both by the higher upsweep of their arms as they curve up and

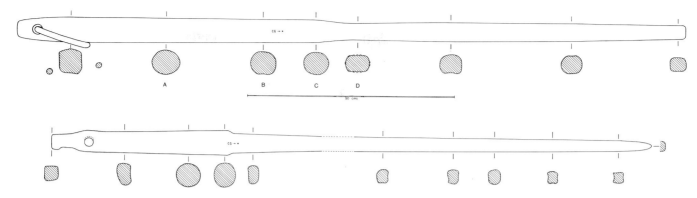

Fig. 6-24. Iron stocks St 1 (top) and St 2 (bottom), with cross-sections.

out to form the flukes and by the slightly greater span of their arms. To An 1, An 3, An 5, An 6, and An 7 we may also add An 4. The shank of An 4 has the same cross-sectional size as the shanks of An 1, An 3, and An 7, but it is about 10–20 cm shorter than these shanks. The arms of An 4, on the other hand, have a span about 20–30 cm greater than the arms of An 1, An 3, and An 7. About 10 cm of this difference, however, is due to the relative shallowness of the curve of the arms of An 4 as they turn up and then out to form the flukes. The volume deficiency in the shank of An 4, therefore, is roughly equal to the volume surplus in the arms. An 1 and An 3–An 7, then, can be put in a second weight group. Of these six anchors, the dimensions of An 1 are known in the greatest detail, and a calculation of this anchor's total volume has yielded the figure of 10.19 l.

An 2 and An 9 remain. A close estimate of the volume of An 2 cannot be made because of the uncertain length of its shank. It is clear, however, that its volume was greater than that of the small anchors and less than that of the large anchors. Its arms have a span which is less than that of the large anchors but comparable to that of some of the small anchors, while the cross-sectional size of its arms is greater than that of the small anchors and comparable to that of the large anchors. The shank is larger in cross-section than the shanks of the small anchors but smaller in cross-section than the shanks of the large anchors. An estimate of the volume of An 2 based on the total length of the surviving sections of the shank (2.33 m) has yielded a minimum figure of 13.33 l. A volume estimate based on a restored shank having the same length as the exceptionally long shank of An 6 (2.565 m) has yielded a maximum figure of 14.15 l. The actual volume of An 2 very probably lay somewhere between these two figures.

An 9 was roughly identical with An 8 in all respects save the length of the shank and the size of the ring. If we assume that these anchors were indeed identical in all but these respects, we get a volume estimate for An 9 of 15.22 l. This volume must, of course, be considered a very rough estimate.

The well-preserved concretion shells that had formed around stocks St 1 and St 2 were in each case either broken into pieces or partially opened up at fairly regular intervals so that a substantial number of carefully measured sections could be made. The approximate volume of St 1 was mathematically calculated; the approximate volume of St 2 was determined by making a full-scale clay model. It was in this way possible to make a very close determination of the original volume of iron in each stock. The volume of St 1 complete with ring was approximately 4.035 l. The stock's approximate center of gravity with the ring is indicated on the detailed drawing of the stock (Fig. 6-24) by the point labeled CG. The volume of St 2 as restored and without a ring was approximately 1.791 l. Remember, however, that the small section missing from the middle part of St 2 may have been anywhere from 5 to 11 cm long. This uncertainty means that the volume estimate for St 2 without a ring becomes $1.791 \pm 0.026$ l.

An iron sample taken from An 1 has proven to be a wrought iron of high purity with a density of 7.807 g/cm$^3$ (see appendix B). Deposits of unoxidized iron belonging to other anchors and to the stocks were not detected; consequently we have no direct evidence of their densities. Thus, while it is possible that the density of iron in the anchors and stocks did vary somewhat (it is possible, for example, that the unoxidized iron in An 1 had a lower than normal carbon content and remained in an unoxidized state partly for this reason), the soundest approach in calculating the weight of all the anchors and stocks would appear to be the employment of a density factor of 7.807 g/cm$^3$ in each case. In doing so, we get an estimated weight of 31.47 kg for St 1 complete with its ring, 79.55 kg for the light anchors, and 139.12 kg for the heavy anchors; an estimated maximum weight of 14.19

kg for St 2 without a ring; a weight of between 104.07 kg and 110.47 kg for An 2; and a very approximate weight of 118.82 kg for An 9.

The practice of making anchors in an arithmetic progression of weights based on a common weight unit can be documented within the Mediterranean world from the present back to the thirteenth century when the weights of iron anchors at Genoa were multiples of one-quarter hundredweight,[10] and it very well may be that the Byzantine ship's anchors and stocks also came in a series of weights belonging to an arithmetic weight progression. The bronze steelyards recovered from the wreck were calibrated for a 315-g pound (see chapter 10). If we express the estimated weights of St 1 and of the light and heavy anchors (excluding the rather uncertain weights of St 2, An 2, and An 9) in terms of a 315-g pound, we get 100, 253, and 442. These figures are remarkably close to 100, 250, and 450.

Thus, it is possible that the anchors and stocks did come in a series of weights based on 50-unit multiples of a 315-g pound. If this was the case, St 1 would have weighed 31.5 kg, the light anchors 78.75 kg, and the heavy anchors 141.75 kg. An 2 would have weighed 350 of the 315-g pounds, or 110.25 kg. An 9's very approxi-

mate weight of 118.82 kg equals 377.2 of the 315-g pounds. In estimating this anchor's weight we assumed that the shank of An 9 had the same cross-sectional dimensions as that of An 8 and that the volumes of the arms of the two anchors were identical. Yet a comparison of the four measured cross-sections of An 8's shank with the one measured cross-section of An 9's shank will show that the shank of An 9 may well have been slightly thinner than that of An 8, and the span of An 8's arms was very probably a few centimeters greater than that of An 9's arms. Thus, it is more likely that the weight of An 9 was overestimated than underestimated, and it may have been closer to the weight of An 2. Finally, it is possible that St 2 originally had a ring and had then weighed 50 of the 315-g pounds, or 15.75 kg.[11]

It should be emphasized that a weight progression based on a 315-g pound must be considered as no more than a distinct possibility, as the case for this supposition is based on very close estimates of volumes and density rather than on precise weights. To be sure, the density of one small portion of An 1 is known precisely, but we must assume that slight variances from this density did occur throughout the anchors and stocks.

## Stowage

In considering how the anchors and stocks were stowed, we may best begin with An 1 and An 3, for we have more direct evidence for the exact locations of these anchors on the ship at the time of her sinking than we do for the other anchors. The final position on the seabed of the deck's juncture with the ship's port side after the hull had been flattened out is represented by a broken line along the port edge of the wreck on Wreck Plan III. This line can be extended with precision in the direction of the ship's bow as far as An 1's crown and falls about 10 cm to starboard of this anchor's shank. The restored hull further indicates that this line of juncture would have run roughly parallel to the shanks of both An 1 and An 3 about 10 cm closer to the keel. If the seabed in this area had been fairly flat, it would have been reasonable to conclude that An 1 and An 3 had been stowed on the

port bulwark in such a way that the shanks were at a level about 10 cm above the deck. There are further complicating factors, however, in that the seabed rises steeply away from the wreck in this area because of the presence of bedrock outcroppings. The actual distance between the anchor shanks and the line of juncture consequently was several tens of centimeters. Moreover, there probably was some settling of the port bulwark and of the anchors as well down and in toward the keel, causing, among other things, a doubling over of the remnant of planking strake 19. In any case, it is clear that An 1 and An 3 were bower anchors and had been secured to the port bulwark at a level above the deck that cannot be closely determined on the basis of the final position of the anchors on the seabed.

The locations on the wreck of An 2 and An 4 indicate that they, too, were bower anchors and had been secured to the starboard bulwark with An 2 placed opposite An 1 and An 4 placed opposite An 3. One sup-

---

[10] Among the extant contracts concerned with the chartering and construction of ships for the Seventh and Eighth Crusades by representatives of Louis IX at Genoa are thirteen that stipulate the weights of anchors to be carried (M. Champollion-Figeac, *Documents historiques inédits tirés des collections manuscrites de la Bibliothèque Royale et des archives ou des bibliothèques des departements*, vol. 1, XXII, nos. I, XIII–XIX, XXI–XXII, and XXIVg; vol. 2, B, XXIX, nos. II and III). The anchor weights mentioned are 4½, 4¾, 5, from 5 to 6, 6, 6½, 8, and 10 *cantaria* (hundredweights).

[11] A preliminary figure for the density of the iron from An 1 of 7.22 g/cm³ yielded lighter estimated weights for the anchors and raised the possibility, now to be rejected, that their weights had been based on a Roman pound of 290 g (G. F. Bass, ed., *A History of Seafaring Based on Underwater Archaeology*, p. 140).

poses that the crowns of An 4 and An 2 had faced fore and aft, respectively, thereby paralleling the arrangement of the starboard bowers. If An 2 and An 4 had fallen absolutely vertically from these positions as the hull collapsed, they would have come to rest about 1 m away from the keel on the starboard side and about 1.2 m aft of the final positions of An 1 and An 3, respectively, because of the attitude of the ship on the seabed. In the actual case of An 2, however, the presence of small hull fragments concreted to the side of the anchor which faced upward as it lay on the seabed and of three amphoras resting upon it clearly showed that it had fallen to the outside of the hull on the starboard side and that the hull had then collapsed on it. This explains why the anchor came to rest not 1 m but 2 m distant from the keel on the starboard side. It did come to rest, on the other hand, about 2 m aft of the position of An 1, this being within 1 m of the "ideal" position of 1.2 m aft of An 1 mentioned above. An 4 fell to the inside of the starboard bulwark and consequently came ultimately to rest on top of some amphoras and a preserved portion of one of the starboard ceiling strakes. It lay about 1 m away from the keel on the starboard side but 1.3 m farther downslope than the "ideal" position of 1.2 m aft of An 3. However, some amount of additional movement downslope could easily have occurred after An 4 came to rest on the amphoras, since the latter were not in a compact pile and were resting on a rather steep slope.

Some slight evidence coupled with practical considerations has led us to conclude that the bower anchors probably had been stowed on the bulwarks with their arms in a horizontal position; each anchor had its stock and one arm outboard and its other arm inboard (Fig. 4-5). It would have been possible to stow the anchors with their arms vertical and outboard, but An 1, at least, does not appear to have been so stowed, since its starboard arm came to rest upon, not beneath, some fragmentary remains of the hull's port side. In my preliminary study of the anchors I concluded that the arms of the bower anchors when stowed probably had been vertical but inboard.[12] However, there are a number of objections to this concept. Bringing the anchors so completely inboard would have needlessly added to the work of casting and shipping them. Furthermore, we would then have to hypothesize either exceptionally high bulwarks or thick pads on the rails beneath the anchors to keep the downward arms free of the deck. Finally, it is somewhat unlikely that An 2 would have fallen outboard had it been so stowed.

The seven anchors in the concreted anchor pile had been stacked neatly on the deck forward of midships with their shanks perpendicular to the longitudinal axis of the ship. Reference to Wreck Plan III will show that two stacks of anchors were involved, one placed just forward of the other. In the forward group, An 10, An 8, and An 5 were stacked one above the other in that order with their crowns facing to starboard. In the after group, An 11, An 9, An 7, and An 6 were similarly stacked with their crowns facing to port.

That the two piles originally had been set very closely together on the deck is suggested particularly by the overlapping of An 5 and An 6 in the concretion pile with An 5's shank resting on that of An 6 and An 6's head resting on An 5's after arm. A compact and stable arrangement which took up a minimal amount of space and made it easy to lash the anchors securely to the deck would, of course, have been very desirable, and experimentation revealed that the order in which the anchors had been stacked would have permitted the maximum degree of stability and compactness for the anchor pile that was possible.

We believe that the original arrangement of the seven anchors on the deck must have been much like that shown by Figs. 4-5 and 6-25. The find spots of St 1 and St 2 suggest that they had been stowed on the forward side of the anchor pile. It is interesting to note that the positional relationship between the two stacks of anchors is close to that of a pair of anchors brought to light on a shipwreck dating to about the ninth century discovered off the southern coast of France at Agay.[13] These anchors were also stowed on the deck with their shanks perpendicular to the ship's longitudinal axis. (A third anchor found on the Agay wreck may have been a bower.) Four anchors, of similar design to ours, had been stacked in one pile with all their crowns facing the same way on the deck of the small (about 12 × 5 m) Dramont F ship.[14]

We must now turn to the problem of the anchor pile's location on the deck of the ship. It will be seen by referring to Wreck Plan III that the anchor pile's port end came to rest on the seabed along the line of the deck's juncture with the port bulwark. The anchors apparently had broken free of their lashings and had slid across the deck to the port bulwark before the deck's collapse. Due to the slope on which the ship had come to rest, there must have been some movement of the anchors aft as well as to port when this happened. However, this shift in the anchors' position may not have

[12] F. H. van Doorninck, Jr., "The Seventh-Century Byzantine Ship at Yassi Ada: Some Contributions to the History of Naval Architecture" (Ph.D. diss., University of Pennsylvania, 1967), p. 255.

[13] A. Visquis, "Premier inventaire du mobilier de l'épave dite 'des jarres' à Agay," *CahArchSub* 2 (1973): 158 and pl. VI.

[14] J.-P. Joncheray, "Une Épave du Bas Empire: Dramont F," *CahArchSub* 4 (1975): 116–120 and wreck plan dated June, 1973.

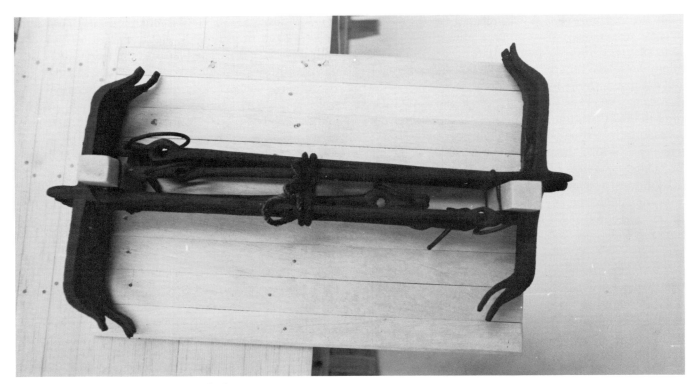

FIG. 6-25. Anchor pile on the model deck.

FIG. 6-26. The port bower anchors on the bulwark of the model. *JRS*

been very violent or of any great magnitude, for the essential compactness and orientation of the anchor pile was retained. If the shift in position was minimal, then the anchor pile had been located on the deck perhaps no more than about 1 m forward of its final resting place.

We have concluded that the anchor pile most probably had been placed so that the heads of the anchors on the bulwarks were directly to starboard and port of it (Figs. 4-5 and 6-26). This would have been a highly efficient arrangement, for any of the bower anchors that were lost could have been replaced by anchors from the pile with a minimum of effort. We might note here that the anchor pile so located would have prevented stowage

of the bower anchors with their stocks in a horizontal position. The inboard ends of the stocks would in this case have made free movement along the deck past the pile impossible.

We have hypothesized the presence of a through-beam set between frames 41 and 42A directly underneath the anchor pile and the heads of the bower anchors. An exceptionally strong deck beam was, of course, needed here to support the great weight of the anchors on the deck, but work on the model also indicated that a through-beam was desirable at about this point.

## Number and Use

No other anchors (other than the grapnel described in the next section) were found on the shipwreck, nor is there reason to suppose that the ship was carrying others just before her sinking. The thought might occur that there may have been additional anchors stowed farther aft and that these had been cast in an effort to keep the ship off the reef just before she ran aground. However, Fig. 4-5 shows that there were no suitable places farther aft on this small ship for stowage of either additional bowers or spare anchors on the deck. Apparently, then, the captain found it both advisable and sufficient to carry four bowers of the weight he used, and all four were still shipped when the vessel went down.

As we have seen, three of the bowers, An 1, An 3, and An 4, may have weighed 250 of the 315-g pounds; the other bower, An 2, may have weighed 350 of these pounds. Thus, An 2 served as either best bower or ready-sheet, as circumstances dictated. An 5–An 7 were spares for the three standard bowers, and An 9 was a spare for the best bower. These anchors were uppermost in the anchor pile. At the bottom of the pile were the heaviest anchors on board, An 8, An 10, and An 11, each weighing perhaps 450 of the 315-g pounds. These were sheet anchors, and they were to be used as a last resort in an emergency situation.[15]

The ship, then, was carrying a full set of spare bowers and enough sheet anchors to replace the standard bowers in an emergency. Our ship possibly had already sustained anchor loss during the voyage, but if her port of departure was somewhere near Constantinople (see chapter 14), she may not have been at sea for more than four days.[16] Thus, there is an excellent chance that

she had begun her last voyage with just eleven anchors on board.

It would appear that wooden stocks were regularly used with the anchors. The bower anchors clearly point to this conclusion. The port bowers came to rest on the seabed retaining a perfect alignment with the port bulwark; they had not undergone any significant dislocation as the hull flattened out. Certainly had these bowers been equipped with iron stocks when the ship sank, concreted remains of the stocks would have been found either still in place or in close proximity to the anchors.[17] The rising slope of the seabed immediately to port of the wreck would have prevented the stocks from making their way any appreciable distance in that direction. The anchors and the area immediately around them became well buried in sand; it is scarcely possible that the remains of iron stocks there would have been visible to and removed by some modern-day visitor. Yet despite the fact that the area around the two anchors was well excavated, remnants of iron stocks were not found. Nor were iron stock remnants found with the starboard bowers. However, these bowers had undergone considerable dislocation as the hull broke up, and the stocks could have become somewhat separated from them. St 3, found on the surface of the wreck and on the line of the deck's juncture with the port bulwark, apparently had come to rest on the deck up against the port bulwark. Perhaps it had belonged to the forward starboard bower, An 4, which had fallen inboard during the process of wreck formation. No iron stock remnants were found, on the other hand, that can be associated with An 2.

We must not suppose, as I did in my original study

[15] Such anchors were called "sacred" in the Greco-Roman period (L. Casson, *Ships and Seamanship in the Ancient World*, p. 252).

[16] Merchantmen in antiquity normally made the Constantinople-to-Rhodes coastal run under prevailing winds in five days (ibid., p. 288).

[17] Three iron bower anchors, two carried on the port bow and one on the starboard bow, were found with their iron stocks still in place on the Dramont D wreck (J.-P. Joncheray, "Étude de l'épave Dramont D: IV, les objets métalliques," *CahArchSub* 4 [1975]: 13–16 and wreck plan).

of the anchors, that the bowers were not equipped with stocks at all times. It would be a foolish captain indeed who did not have his bowers always ready for instant use. Thus, we have concluded that very probably both port bowers and at least one starboard bower had wooden stocks when the ship sank. The forward starboard bower, on the other hand, may have been equipped with an iron stock.

The thought may still persist that some of the iron stocks carried by the ship simply were not found. One might suppose that some of the iron stocks had been swept away when the ship sank or had come to rest outside the well-excavated area of the shipwreck, that the remnants of some iron stocks were so poorly preserved that they escaped notice, or that some stock concretions already had been removed from the wreck site before our excavation. Such explanations are, however, far from convincing.

Surely any iron stocks on board would have been either mounted on bowers or secured with lashings to the deck. It is difficult to see how any of them would have been lost overboard, particularly in view of the fact that the ship had sunk on an even keel. She had struck the seabed keel first, nothing belonging to the ship was found on the seabed anywhere beyond the confines of the wreck proper, and the rather compact distributions of various categories of objects found on the wreck indicate that the objects had not been flung violently about as the ship sank. Any stocks that were on the deck or mounted on the bowers when the ship began to break up would have come to rest within the well-excavated area of the wreck. Nothing belonging to the ship was found at any appreciable distance to port apart from the rest of the wreck. A concretion shell would have formed around an iron bar the size of an anchor stock whether it lay buried in the sand or not. For example, An 2 and the top part of the anchor pile were not covered with bottom sediments either before excavation or during the period in which the concretion shells were formed, and the concretions that formed around them are relatively thin and markedly even, fine-textured, and free of large-grained sand and shell. Deeply buried An 3 and An 4, in contrast, have markedly rough and conglomeratelike concretion shells containing great amounts of shell and large-grained sand. Broken concretion shells may erode greatly, however, and portions may become so badly broken up that they may be overlooked by the excavator, as may have happened to the missing portions of the concretion shell that had formed around St 3. Even so, the possibility that the entire shell of one or more iron stocks escaped detection in this way is rather remote.

Apparently no iron concretions were removed surreptitiously from the wreck after 1958, for Frost's plan of the shipwreck (Fig. 1-4), begun in 1958 and completed in 1959, shows exactly the same number of iron concretions that were visible on the wreck when the excavation was started in 1961. Nor is there reason to believe that anyone other than sponge divers visited the wreck before 1958. If any iron concretions were removed from the wreck, then, it almost certainly was done before 1958 either by a sponge diver or by nets dragging over the wreck. A sponge diver would not, of course, have wasted his time collecting pieces of broken iron concretions, although an intact iron stock concretion might have appeared to be of potential value. The removal of such a concretion is not a casual project because of its great weight, and an easy test of its value is readily at hand: if it contains no unoxidized metal, it can easily be broken with only slight effort. Indeed, a concretion shell of such a weight and length will often break under its own weight when lifted from the seabed. For example, while preparing to raise the concretion for the bottom half of An 2, I managed with great effort to lift it off the seabed. It immediately broke into three pieces under its own weight. Also note that the concretion shells which had formed around the shanks of An 2 and An 4 and around a large iron bar belonging to the galley hearth all broke into several pieces during the process of wreck formation.

It is quite likely, then, that the ship was carrying only a few iron stocks when she sank. These stocks probably were on hand with a specific and limited use in mind: facilitating the setting of anchors on a relatively short cable, as when kedging, by increasing the anchor's weight at the shank head. We have noted that the forward starboard bower may have been equipped with St 3. Perhaps it regularly served as a kedge anchor.

The spare iron stocks (St 1 and St 2) were apparently to be used with certain standard bowers as well. St 1 had a poorly developed shoulder which began 79 cm from the heavy end and which attained, 7 cm nearer that end, maximum elliptical dimensions of 6.3 × 5.6 cm. St 2 had a well-developed shoulder which began 43.8 cm from the heavy end and attained, just 1.4 cm nearer that end, maximum elliptical dimensions of 6.3 × 5.5 cm. A comparison of these maximum dimensions with those given in the anchor catalog for the stock apertures in the anchor shanks shows that the stocks probably were too small for use with the two best bowers (An 2 and An 9) and three sheets anchors (An 8, An 10, and An 11). Since the stock aperture dimensions given for An 5 through An 11 may be as much as a centimeter in error, there admittedly is some doubt on this point in the case of An 11; even so, it remains clear that the two stocks were not designed for general use with the larger anchors.

Turning to the bowers, we find that the stocks also were too small for use with An 3 and An 4 but that they would have seated at the shoulder when used with the remaining anchors (An 1 and An 5–An 7). It is possible that St 1 could not have been used with one or more of the spare standard bowers (An 5–An 7), for the stock probably could not have passed through any aperture with dimensions of less than 6.0 × 5.5 cm beyond the point marked by section D in Fig. 6-24, which shows the outline of an aperture with these minimal elliptical dimensions.

St 3's vital dimensions are unknown, but some general observations concerning its size can be made. The preserved section of its concretion shell is 88 cm long and has a more or less uniform interior diameter of 5.5 cm. There is a band 2 cm wide located 30 cm in from one of the concretion's broken ends within which the interior diameter of the shell increases from 5.5 cm to about 8 cm. In my original study of the anchors I suggested that this anomaly might have to do with a slight ridge running around the stock to seat at this point in the apertures of all eleven anchors.[18] This idea supposes, however, a radical departure in design from that of St 1 and St 2. Furthermore, the anomaly is of a kind often produced when a concretion shell has undergone a partial erosion, so a uniform diameter of about 5.5 cm for the preserved section of shell may be accepted. St 3's dimensions closely approximate those of the more slender part of St 1. However, the shell length does exceed that of St 1's slender part by a few centimeters, indicating that St 3 probably was either the same general size and weight as St 1 or was of a greater size and weight. Thus, it is possible that the stock could have been used with the larger anchors.

Certain peculiarities in the design of St 1 and of St 2 have led us to conclude that they must have been sheathed in wood when used. First, there is the problem of how these stocks had been fixed in place. Every extant Roman movable stock known to me has a small hole through it at the point where the lighter end of the seated stock emerged from the stock aperture. This hole was for a pin which secured the stock in place.[19] A thorough search was made for traces of such a hole on the interior surfaces of the concretion shells of both stocks. A rod of concretion bridging the interior hollow of the

shell would have formed wherever a hole might have been, yet no anomalies that remotely suggested the presence of holes were found despite the excellent state of preservation of both shells within the general area where the stocks would have seated. Thus, we can be certain that neither stock had been secured in place by a pin. I initially supposed that the stocks had been lashed in place.[20] However, attempts to lash a stock to a model anchor were not very successful, for the stock could not be maintained in a position rigidly perpendicular to the shank, and the ends wobbled a good deal. An anchor's canting efficiency would be significantly reduced under such circumstances.

It is particularly difficult to see how St 2 could have been used without an outer sheath of wood. When seated, the light end of this stock would have projected out from a shank more than twice as far as the heavy end, and the projecting length of the heavy end would have been only slightly over half the length of an arm of one of the anchors carried by the ship. A stock so far off center and with one end so short simply would not have functioned properly. J. Richard Steffy has experimented with a small model anchor equipped with a stock having St 2's proportions. He has found that the anchor will not cant when the stock's short end is down, and when the long end is down, the anchor has a tendency to flip completely over, bringing the short end into the downward position. Furthermore, reference to Fig. 6-24 will show that the stock's light end terminated in a rather sharp edge. If this end had not been sheathed, it would have readily tended to dig into the seabed, thereby decreasing canting efficiency.

Two-piece wooden stocks with an overall length slightly in excess of that of St 1 were fabricated for the model by Steffy (Fig. 6-27). A notch was cut on the inner side of each piece at the center point in its length so that the two pieces would fit snugly over the swelling in the anchor shanks where the stock apertures were located. The pieces for the all-wood stocks were otherwise made solid. The sheathing pieces for the iron stocks, on the other hand, were further hollowed out so that they could completely and tightly enclose the iron stocks after they had been seated in a stock aperture. The two pieces were secured in place with lashings.

Note here that the hole in the heavy end of St 2 would not have been located anywhere near the end of its outer wooden sheath. It is probably for this reason that no ring was found in the hole. However, the hole could have been used to receive an iron pin to bind the

---

[18] van Doorninck, "Seventh-Century Byzantine Ship," p. 237.

[19] The hole and pin are well illustrated by the Lake Nemi iron anchor (Frost, *Under the Mediterranean*, fig. 14).

[20] van Doorninck, "Seventh-Century Byzantine Ship," p. 235.

FIG. 6-27. Hypothesized stocks assembled on the model's bower anchors. *JRS*

stock and outer sheathing together. The overall configuration of this iron stock is indeed puzzling. Perhaps the bar originally had some other function and had been reworked to serve as a makeshift iron stock.

## *The Grapnel*

The seventh-century Byzantine ship was also carrying a small grapnel (Figs. 6-28 and 6-29). Its concretion shell had been very badly broken up, but the fragments recovered were all found in one small area at the stern end of the wreck (Wreck Plan *Ve*). The find spot suggests that the grapnel had been stowed in a boatswain's locker aft of the galley, and it was probably used as an anchor for the ship's boat (see p. 96).

The bottom of the grapnel shank had been subdivided into five segments in roughly the following manner: ⊕ . The four outer segments were then forged into the grapnel's four arms, while a hole was made in the remaining segment for a ring which has an outer diameter of 9–10 cm. The arms are circular in cross-section and gradually taper to points without flukes. The maximum diameter of the arms at their juncture with the shank is about 2.8 cm. The span between opposing arms was roughly 40–42 cm. The length of the shank is not known, since the top portion is missing. The preserved portions add up to a total length of about 46 cm. The

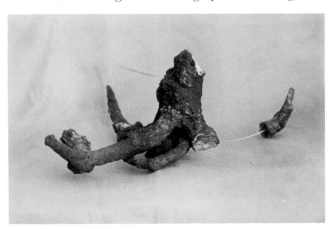

FIG. 6-28. Polysulfide replica of grapnel: side view.

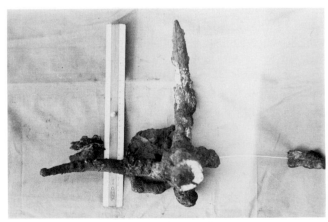

FIG. 6-29. Polysulfide replica of grapnel: top view.

shank is circular in cross-section, with a diameter of 3.6 cm for most of its preserved length, but it thickens to a diameter of about 5.6 cm just above the point where it divides into the arms.

Although it is very likely that grapnel anchors were

already being used in the Greco-Roman period, this grapnel is perhaps the earliest example we have of a Mediterranean grapnel anchor. Even so, it is of a type which may still be seen in the Mediterranean world today.

## History of the Anchor Type

Our study of the anchors has been somewhat lengthy and detailed, but not without reason, for although anchors of this design were probably in common use aboard Mediterranean ships for at least eight or nine hundred years, almost nothing was known about them and how they were stowed until quite recently. Furthermore, the earliest period for which we get a clear idea of the number and weight of iron anchors carried by a ship of a certain size is the thirteenth century, by which time anchors of the type under discussion may no longer have been widely used.

The earliest datable examples of this anchor type known to me are the four anchors that had been stacked on the deck of the Dramont F ship, which has been dated to the middle or second half of the fourth century.[21] No traces of stocks were found with the anchors, and they do not differ greatly in design from the Yassi Ada anchors, the most notable difference being that their shanks and arms are rectangular in section. The Dramont F anchors range from 1.36 m to about 1.8 m in length and from 64 cm to 86 cm in width. The ship had been very small, as mentioned earlier, having overall dimensions of no more than 12 × 5 m.

Eight iron anchors found in a chandlery storeroom at the Black Sea port of Tomis (Constanţa, Rumania) are probably slightly earlier in date.[22] They are very close to the Yassi Ada anchors in design and proportions, although they are smaller in size. All eight have overall lengths of about 1.5 m. No remains of accompanying stocks appear to have been uncovered. The anchors probably date from the sixth-century destruction of the chandlery.

An anchor of our type appears in a painting of Christ flanked by doctors of the Greek and Latin churches in the Church of Santa Maria Antiqua at Rome. Immediately to the right of Christ stands St. Clement, holding in his right hand the anchor, the instrument of his martyrdom. His hand obscures the shank's upper part, but the crown and one of the arms are clearly visible. The

crown projects below the base of the arms, while the arms are set perpendicular to the shank and curve up and out at the extremities in precisely the same way that the arms of the Yassi Ada anchors do. The painting is thought to have been done during the papacy of Paul I (757–767) by an artist strongly influenced by the Byzantine art of the time.[23]

An anchor of the same type was found at Corinth within one of the vaulted west shops in the agora.[24] No accompanying stock was found. One of the flukes is broken off; the other is badly corroded. Even so, it is clear that the arms terminated in the same way that the arms of the Yassi Ada anchors do. The shops apparently went out of use in the eleventh or twelfth century. Although it is impossible to say how long the anchor had stood in the shop before the shop was abandoned, it was of such a small size that it could have been transported and used at any time without undue difficulty even though the agora at Corinth is about 3 km from the sea. The anchor's present weight is approximately 40 kg, and judging by its overall length of 1.33 m and preserved arm span of 81 cm, its original weight was probably very close to that.

A number of other anchors of this same type have been recovered from the waters of Sicily,[25] two examples have been recovered off the island of Melita on the Dalmatian coast,[26] and some remains of anchors that may have been so designed have been found off Cape Andreas, Cyprus.[27] Two or three such anchors recently recovered from an anchorage site at Serçe Liman on the southern Turkish coast opposite Rhodes have not yet been published. As far as I know, none of these anchors were found in datable contexts.

Radius arms and rectangular stock apertures were

[21]Joncheray, CahArchSub 4 (1975): 116–120, 131–132.

[22]V. Canarache, The Archaeological Museum of Constantza, p. 85; and V. Canarache, The Mosaic-Floored Edifice of Tomi, pp. 7, 30.

[23]P. Romanelli and P. Nordhagen, S. Maria Antiqua, pl. 42.

[24]O. Broneer, "Excavations in Corinth, 1934," AJA 39 (1935): 74–75, fig. 20; and G. R. Davidson, Corinth, vol. XII, The Minor Objects, p. 193, no. 1446 (3807), pl. 87.

[25]P. Gargallo, "Anchors of Antiquity," Archaeology 14, no. 1 (1961): 34, type 5, fig. 11.

[26]D. Vrsalović, Istraživanja i Zaštita Podmorskih Arheoloških Spomenika u SR Hrvatskoj, p. 138, figs. 82 and 83.

[27]J. Green, "An Underwater Archaeological Survey of Cape Andreas, Cyprus, 1969–70," in Marine Archaeology, ed. D. J. Blackman, fig. 29, anchors 001, 008, and 013.

standard design for iron anchors during the early Empire.[28] Some cruciform iron anchors with rectangular stock apertures have also been found in the Mediterranean but in undatable contexts. Kapitän[29] has cited as examples an anchor found near Haifa and another found off the Spanish coast. Yet another such anchor, from Pisa, has flukes with well-developed palms.[30] Well-developed palms apparently did not make their first appearance until the third century, and only rarely then.[31] The earliest example known to me of an iron anchor with an elliptically shaped stock aperture (but not cruciform) was found on a shipwreck dating perhaps as early as the late first or early second century.[32] It would appear quite likely, then, that anchors of the type carried by our By-

zantine ship did not come into being until late Imperial times, but they were certainly in use by the latter half of the fourth century, as the Dramont F anchors have revealed. Perhaps the cruciform shape was first widely adopted in the wake of Christianity's triumph.

The Corinth anchor, found in an eleventh- or twelfth-century context, need not be regarded as a relic from an earlier era.[33] It may be that the geographical and temporal limits of the anchor type are closely tied to those of the Byzantine Empire. Before such a hypothesis can be tested, however, we will first have to determine what kinds of anchors were being used in all areas of the Mediterranean during those times.

# ANCHOR DESIGN

## J. RICHARD STEFFY

Half-scale models of our Byzantine anchors and of eighteenth-century anchors of like weight were made for comparative testing under various conditions.[34] The eighteenth-century anchors, with their radius arms and broad flukes, set more efficiently and held twice as well on soft bottoms. On harder ground, on the other hand, the Byzantine chisel-shaped flukes seemed to dig in better than did the eighteenth-century spaded flukes, and both designs did a comparable job of holding as long as sea and weather conditions remained tolerable. However, the Byzantine anchors had a tendency to unseat considerably faster when there was a swell running or a fresh breeze blowing. Although the spaded flukes did possess a superior holding power, the greater setting efficiency of the chisel-shaped flukes on a hard bottom would have been a more important factor for anchors as thin and light as the Byzantine anchors were. On a variety of rocky bottoms, the Byzantine anchors had a much greater tendency to wedge themselves fast. Their

S-curved arms, partly designed to set the narrow flukes, were undoubtedly also designed to help keep the arms from dropping into narrow rock crevices, but they still caught easily when dragged across a crevice that was nearly parallel to the arms. The Byzantine anchors also set more easily in heavy marine growth. Did Byzantine mariners tend to anchor mostly in hard ground or weeds? A check of ancient harbors is inconclusive, since dredging, silting, and coastline erosion have changed so many of these bottoms. Marine biologists tell us, however, that marine growth may have been much more heavily concentrated inshore in the Mediterranean during ancient times.

Precise mathematical analogies could be developed between our Byzantine anchors and modern ones, but such an elaborate procedure would be worthless. The Byzantine anchors were associated with different stocks, different cables, different hulls, and different tackle. Later anchors, designed for comparatively heavy ocean-going hulls using good cables or chain in estuaries and roadsteads, cannot be likened to those used on light ships that sailed the Mediterranean in fair-weather seasons and called in coves and harbors. Suffice it to say that the tests have convinced me that two Byzantine anchors should normally be set for one eighteenth-century anchor of comparable weight, all other things being equal. The employment of four bowers on the Byzantine ship is quite understandable in this light when one considers the anchor weights involved.

[28] Casson, *Ships and Seamanship*, p. 253, n. 114.

[29] G. Kapitän, "Greco-Roman Anchors and the Evidence for the One-Armed Wooden Anchor in Antiquity," in *Marine Archaeology*, ed. D. J. Blackman, p. 385.

[30] A. Neppi-Mòdona, "Ancora antica," *NSc*, 1932, pp. 434–436, figs. 1 and 2.

[31] Casson, *Ships and Seamanship*, p. 253, n. 116.

[32] F. Benoît, "Nouvelles épaves de Provence (II)," *Gallia* 18 (1960): 49, fig. 16. Benoît illustrates a few necks and bottoms of amphoras taken from the wreck (p. 48, fig. 15). He describes the amphoras as being "du Bas-Empire" but notes the closeness of the necks to Pelichet type 20a and of the bottoms to Dressel 17/27. Pelichet dates his type 20a to between A.D. 50 and 120 (E. Pelichet, "A Propos des amphores romaines trouvées à Nyon," *ZSchwAKg* 8 [1946]: 192). These dates probably should be regarded as too precise (M. H. Callender, *Roman Amphorae*, pp. 6–7).

[33] A possibility suggested by Broneer, *AJA* 39 (1935): 74–75.

[34] The tests were conducted from a twelve-foot motorboat on Chesapeake Bay.

Breakage and loss undoubtedly were the prime reasons for the full set of spare bowers on board our ship. While the ship's anchors were made of a good grade of iron, the cross-sections of their arms and shanks were only half those of eighteenth-century anchors of comparable weight. Once set deeply in hard-packed bottoms or rock, their thin arms and shanks were highly susceptible to breakage if they were tripped sharply. Without charts and marked anchorages, Byzantine seamen must have been greatly concerned with rocky bottoms when they anchored.

It seems unlikely that the idea of thicker arms and shanks never occurred to either mariner or forger in this period. The thinness of arms and shanks was probably quite deliberate. Anchors of the same weight but with arms and shank twice as thick would have been much reduced in size. A smaller anchor would have wedged between rocks more readily, and shorter arms would not have bitten as deeply into the bottom for good holding. Where good holding was possible with little bite, a shorter shank would not have provided as much leverage for tripping. The anchor as designed, on the other hand, covers more bottom area, occasionally an important factor in setting. It also is more easily boarded and handled, since more hands can get to it, and its weight can be more widely distributed, thus making possible a reduction in the scantling of the bulwarks and deck that support it.

The light weight of the anchors possibly reflects in part the limitations of technology at that time, but there probably were other factors of greater moment involved, the most important of which may have been the cables used. We need only consult a table to determine the size of hemp rope used with various nineteenth-century anchors, but who is to say what the tensile strength of 8-inch rope was in the seventh century? A 750-lb anchor cable in the earlier period may have been of such bulk that its handling and storage would have been impractical on a ship the size of ours. Three 250-lb anchors, however difficult to set and ride from, may have been more tolerable. Then, too, the holding power of the anchors was relatively poor. An increase in the number of anchors, and thus the odds of a holding anchor, may have more than offset the corresponding decrease in individual anchor weight. In addition, lighter anchors would have required a smaller foredeck crew and more modest ground tackle and would also have contributed to making possible lighter topside construction. And if spares were as necessary as we surmise, the economy of replacing lighter anchors needs no explanation. Thus, the weight of our anchors was probably dictated in the main by the size and efficiency of available anchor cable, a desire to increase the probability of holding by increasing the number of flukes on the bottom at any given time, and the economics of crew size, ground tackle, hull construction, and anchor replacement.

Little can be added to what has already been said concerning the stocks for the Byzantine anchors. Note only that the models dictated that the stocks have a minimum length equal to that of the arms. The setting ability of these anchors with a stock of any shorter length was seriously reduced. As with the eighteenth-century anchors, equal shank and stock lengths seemed the most efficient.

TABLE 7-1. Copper Coins of the Seventh-Century Byzantine Shipwreck at Yassi Ada.

| Emperor | Year of Reign | A.D. | Mint | | | | | | Total |
|---|---|---|---|---|---|---|---|---|---|
| | | | Constantinople | Thessalonica | Nicomedia | Cyzicus | Alexandretta ad Issum | Uncertain | |
| Maurice Tiberius | yr. 5 | 586/587 | 1 | | | | | | 1 |
| Interregnum | Ind. 13 or 14 | 609–610 | | | | | 1 | | 1 |
| Heraclius | | | | | | | | | |
| Class 1 | yr. 1 | 610/611 | 2 | | 1 | 1 | | | 4 |
| | yr. 2 | 611/612 | 1 | | 1 | 1 | | | 3 |
| | yr. 3 | 612/613 | 2 | | | 2 | | | 4 |
| Class 2 | yr. 3 | 613 | 7 | | 2 | | | | 9 |
| | yr. 4 | 613/614 | 7 | | 1 | | | | 8 |
| | yr. 5 | 614/615 | 2 | 2 | | | | | 4 |
| | ? | 613–616 | 5 | 1 | | | | 2 | 8 |
| Class 3 | yr. 6 | 615/616 | 2 | | | | | | 2 |
| | yr. 7 | 616/617 | 1 | | | | | | 1 |
| | yr. 8 | 617/618 | | | 1 | | | | 1 |
| | ? | 615–624 | 1 | | | | | | 1 |
| Class 4 | yr. 16 | 625/626 | 1 | | | | | | 1 |
| Uncertain | | | | | | | | 6 | 6 |
| Total | | | 32 | 3 | 6 | 4 | 1 | 8 | 54 |

TABLE 7-2. Eastern Site Finds and Hoards of Coins of the Interregnum and Heraclius.

| | Mint | | | | | | | | | | |
|---|---|---|---|---|---|---|---|---|---|---|---|
| | Constantinople | Thessalonica | Nicomedia | Cyzicus | Seleucia Isauriae | Alexandretta ad Issum | Cyprus | Alexandria, Egypt | Western | Barbaric | Uncertain |
| *Excavations* | | | | | | | | | | | |
| Athens* | 157 | 41 | 18 | 3 | | | | 2 | 2 | | 9 |
| Corinth† | 6 | 2 | 1 | | | | | | | | |
| Sardis I‡ | 22 | | 1 | 3 | | | | | | | |
| Sardis II§ | 122 | 2 | 26 | 14 | | | | | | | 16 |
| Antioch‖ | 39 | 1 | 6 | 2 | | | 2 | | | | 5 |
| Curium# | 29 | | 4 | 1 | | | 1 | 1 | | | |
| *Hoards* | | | | | | | | | | | |
| Sardis‡ | 114 | | 48 | 41 | | | | | | | |
| Izmir** | 11 | | 5 | 2 | | | | | | | |
| Yassi Ada | 31 | 3 | 6 | 4 | | 1 | | | | | |
| Syria†† | 226 | 6 | 60 | 34 | 1 | | 2 | | | 3 | |
| Coelesyria‡‡ | 59 | 2 | 17 | 7 | 1 | | 1 | | | | |
| Cyprus§§ | 65 | 3 | 16 | 7 | 2 | | | | | 2 | |

*M. Thompson, *The Athenian Agora*, vol. II, *Coins from the Roman through the Venetian Period*.

†K. M. Edwards, *Corinth*, vol. VI, *Coins, 1896–1929*. The subsequent reports on Corinth in *Hesperia* 6: 241–256, and 10: 143–162, give only the total number of coins of Heraclius.

‡H. W. Bell, *Sardis*, vol. XI, *Coins, 1910–1914*.

§G. E. Bates, *Archaeological Exploration of Sardis*, vol. I, *Byzantine Coins, 1958–1968*.

‖D. B. Waagé, *Antioch-on-the-Orontes*, vol. IV, part 2, *Greek, Roman, Byzantine and Crusaders' Coins*.

#D. H. Cox, *Coins from the Excavations at Curium, 1932–1953*.

**R. N. Bridge and P. D. Whitting, "A Hoard of Early Heraclius Folles," *NumCirc* 74, no. 5 (May, 1966): 131–132.

††E. Leuthold, "Monete bizantine rinvenute in Siria," *RIN*, 5th ser., 54–55 (1952–1953): 31–49.

‡‡G. E. Bates, "A Byzantine Hoard from Coelesyria," *ANSMN* 14 (1968): 67–109.

§§P. J. Donald and P. D. Whitting, "A VIIth Century Hoard from Cyprus," *NumCirc* 75, no. 6 (June, 1967): 162–165.

# VII

## THE COINS

### JOAN M. FAGERLIE

THE chief importance of the coins found on the seventh-century wreck is that they provided information regarding the date of the ship and the area of its activities. In both matters the copper coins, not the gold, afford the more specific information, since the copper coins are dated by regnal year and bear a mint mark on the reverse.

Fifty-four copper coins, of which only forty-eight could be identified, and sixteen gold coins (nine semisses and seven tremisses) were recovered from the wreck. The copper coins (Table 7-1) are all folles—40-nummi pieces—denoted by the reverse mark of $M$, which is the highest copper denomination and also the most common. The bulk of the copper coins—thirty-two—are from the mint of Constantinople, six are from Nicomedia, four are from Cyzicus, three are from Thessalonica, one is from Alexandretta ad Issum, and the remainder are of undetermined origin.

The earliest coin is a follis of Maurice Tiberius dated year 5 (586/587), the coin struck at Alexandretta ad Issum is from the period of the revolt against Phocas (608–610), and the remaining identified pieces are of Heraclius. The last group represents the first eight years of Heraclius' reign (610–618), followed by a gap of eight years, and the latest datable coin is of year 16 (625/626).

These data can be interpreted correctly only when set within the general framework of the coinage of Heraclius. And in this regard it is apparent that the shipwreck coins are a representative cross-section of material and thus a reliable index for dating purposes.

The great majority of the coins are from mints located on the Sea of Marmara: Constantinople, Nicomedia, and Cyzicus. This fact has little significance in itself, since these were the most common mints of Heraclius,

and their issues predominate in all site finds and hoards of an eastern locale in about the same proportions as those represented in this find, with Constantinople leading all other mints (Table 7-2).

The dates of the various mint issues also reflect the known pattern of the coinage as a whole.[1] The latest coin of Nicomedia in the shipwreck is from year 8, the year in which the mint activity at Nicomedia was interrupted, perhaps because of Persian occupation. It did not resume again until year 16, and then only for two years. The latest coins of Cyzicus in the wreck are of year 3; this mint was closed down in year 4 of Heraclius, also probably because of Persian occupation. Cyzicus was re-opened in year 16, and its latest known coins are of year 19. No coins from these later periods either at Nicomedia or Cyzicus are represented in the shipwreck find.

Thessalonica is represented by only three coins, yet this mint seems to have been active throughout the period (at least to 630) and was not endangered by Persian occupation as were Nicomedia and Cyzicus. Still, the size of its output seems to have been very limited, judging from its representation in other finds and in various collections (Table 7-2). One would expect to find a larger representation proportionately in finds from mainland Greece and a lower representation the further one gets from Thessalonica.[2] This is in contrast to the issues of Constantinople, which are by far the most common at any eastern site, and of Nicomedia and Cyzicus, also amply represented in all eastern finds for the period of their activity.

---

[1] Mint operations are summarized by Philip Grierson in *DOC* II, 219ff.

[2] Only at Athens and Corinth, for example, are coins of Thessalonica more numerous than those of Nicomedia and Cyzicus.

The series represented by the follis of Alexandretta ad Issum was issued during the revolt against Phocas by Heraclius Senior and his son, the future emperor Heraclius. It was a very limited issue, and in all likelihood its circulation was restricted to the near area. A single coin, however, can turn up anywhere, and its significance is difficult to assess.[3]

Constantinople was the chief mint for all metals during the reign of Heraclius. After the coinage reform in 630, it was the only eastern mint striking copper with the exception of Alexandria. The gap represented in the shipwreck coins from years 8 to 16 of Heraclius was at first not readily understood, yet within the general framework of the coinage as a whole, this gap is not only understandable but predictable, since the production of copper coinage was greatly reduced in years 7 to 15.[4] Why it was reduced is not known, but there are comparable gaps in other finds of the same period, and the rarity of coins from these years is also evident in the major coin collections.

Four other eastern mints known to have struck copper for Heraclius are not represented in the shipwreck coins: Cherson, Seleucia Isauriae, Isaura, and Cyprus. (The mint of Alexandria is also eastern, but its coinage was on a different denominational system and circulated almost exclusively in Egypt.) Cherson, in the Black Sea region, has an extremely rare issue dated to the period before the decline of the follis in the 620's. Only one specimen is listed in the catalog of the Dumbarton Oaks Collection, and its absence in the shipwreck is not surprising because of both its rarity and its late date. Seleucia Isauriae and Isaura in southern Anatolia operated briefly during the Persian campaigns: Seleucia in years 6–7 (615/616–616/617) and Isaura the following year (617/618). These coins also are very rare. A fourth mint on Cyprus operated only in the late 620's on a limited scale and after the date of our latest coin.

Also not represented in this find are copper coins of Phocas, although there is one gold coin of that period. The curious phenomenon of overstriking to which the Byzantines seem to have been particularly addicted accounts for this lack. The coins in circulation form the basis of material overstruck, and it is the most recent coins that make up the larger part of the circulating currency. Phocas was the immediate predecessor of Heraclius, under whom overstriking was extensively practiced, and it is Phocas' coins that most often are identi-

fied as undertypes of Heraclian issues.[5] Among the shipwreck coins, twenty have identifiable undertypes, of which eighteen are of Phocas and two are of Maurice Tiberius.

At any rate, what at first glance might appear to be a somewhat erratic distribution is in fact a closely dated chronological group, representative of eastern mints for the periods of their production and thus a valid body of material for dating purposes. The latest coin, and thus the *terminus post quem* for the date of the wreck, is of year 16 (625/626). No estimates of degree of wear of the coin are possible because of its corroded condition, but it is reasonable to suppose that the shipwreck must have occurred within a few years after that date.

The area of activity of the ship is indicated to be Asia Minor, a fact which might be guessed from the location of the wreck itself, although that alone would not rule out the possibility of a ship originating in a western port. The coins rule out such a possibility.

Compared with the composition of other hoards and site finds listed in Table 7-2, the mint of Thessalonica has a proportionately high representation of coins in the shipwreck and may suggest an area of activity to the north. At the same time, the single coin of Alexandretta, for what a single coin is worth, suggests contact with southern Asia Minor–North Syria, but such contact must have been contemporaneous with the issue in 609–610. The latest coins are of the northern mints. Moreover, most of the finds of the same period from Syria and Cyprus contain one or more coins from the mints of Seleucia and Cyprus (the latter not in operation until the late 620's, however) which are lacking in this find.

The gold coins add nothing to these conclusions. They were struck at Constantinople, the only mint in the East that issued fractional gold, and they are not dated except for an approximate estimation of the date of the change that occurred in the obverse legend. The solidus, on the other hand, underwent several type changes that can be more closely dated. It is remarkable that no solidi were found, since they are more common than the fractional issues. However, this group of coins can represent only a minor portion of the money that must have been on board the ship before it sank. The

---

[3] Of the finds listed in Table 7-2, the only coin of this mint recorded is from the Yassi Ada shipwreck.

[4] Grierson, *DOC* II, 227.

[5] Further, late issues of Heraclius are most often overstruck on his own early issues (see *DOC* II, Classes 5 and 6). This would seem to nullify the attribution of political significance to the overstriking of Phocas' coins as suggested by R. N. Bridge and P. D. Whitting, "A Hoard of Early Heraclius Folles," *NumCirc* 74, no. 5 (May, 1966): 131; and by P. J. Donald and P. D. Whitting, "A VIIth Century Hoard from Cyprus," *NumCirc* 75, no. 6 (June, 1967): 162.

total value of the gold and copper coins is about 7 solidi, the gold coins worth just less than 7 solidi and the fifty-four copper pieces a fraction of a solidus.[6] This is not a great sum for even a single traveller to be carrying.

The following data give some indication of the value of 7 solidi.[7] Most of the information on prices comes from papyri and pertains to Egypt, where conditions might have differed from those of other parts of the empire. Also, a poor harvest of wheat, for example, could double the price over that of normal times, and wherever transport by land was necessary, the price was much higher. The average price of wheat, however, when not inflated by famine or other causes, was about 1 solidus for 30 *modii*. It is estimated that the annual ration of wheat for a soldier in the sixth century was about 45 *modii*. His entire allotment for bread, meat, wine, and oil was reckoned at between 4 and 5 solidi a year. This amount is somewhat higher than that allotted an ordinary laborer, which could be as little as 2 solidi a year.

Clothing was relatively expensive. A monk in the seventh century paid 3 solidi for a new cloak; a second-hand one could be purchased for 1 solidus, as could an Antiochene cloak of inferior quality. The military *chlamys* also went for about 1 solidus, and cheap blankets could be had at the rate of four for a solidus in Alexandria.

Slaves under Justinian I were sold at 10 solidi for a child under ten years of age, 20 solidi for an unskilled worker, man or woman, 30 solidi for a skilled worker, 50 solidi for a trained clerk, and 60 solidi for a doctor. Seventh-century prices seem comparable, for there is a record of the sale of an African customs collector to a Jerusalem silversmith for 30 solidi.[8]

The data on business transactions are more instructive, I believe, in assessing the significance of this find.[9] A seventh-century document records a business venture in which a Constantinopolitan dealer entrusted an agent with clothing valued at 144 solidi and booked him passage on a ship bound for Carthage and perhaps Gaul with instructions to sell the goods at ports on the way. His pay for this service was to be 15 solidi a year.

In a typical business venture a merchant invested 360 solidi of his own and borrowed an equivalent amount for a total of 10 pounds of gold to be invested. Another case records a sum of 50 pounds of gold (3,600 solidi) to launch a merchant on a career. Fortunes of 70 and 275 pounds of gold are known for successful merchants; nevertheless, they are small when compared to those of the landowners, who had annual incomes of 1,500 to 4,000 pounds of gold.

In short, this group of coins cannot represent the total wealth on board the ship before it sank or give any indication of the size or nature of the ventures undertaken by this merchant vessel.[10]

In the following catalog the gold coins are described first, followed by the copper coins. All sixteen gold coins are from the mint of Constantinople, and they are listed chronologically. The copper folles are arranged by mint in the following order: Constantinople, Thessalonica, Nicomedia, Cyzicus, Alexandretta ad Issum, and uncertain mint. The chronological scheme of the copper folles is shown in Table 7-1.

A general description of each type or class precedes detailed descriptions of the individual coins of that type or class. Where appropriate, and when the data are available, the following information is given for each coin: variations in type or legend; year of issue; officina; metal, whether gold (A') or copper (Æ); die position as indicated by the arrow; weight in grams; diameter in millimeters; inventory and museum numbers; and references in *BMC* and *DOC*. Overstruck coins are also noted in the description. The dates and classifications used in this catalog are according to Alfred Bellinger and Philip Grierson in *DOC* I and II, and all Byzantine Greek characters and symbols used are reproduced from *DOC* II by permission of the Dumbarton Oaks Library and Collection. All references to *DOC* are to Vol. II except as noted.

All the gold coins are illustrated in Fig. 7-1 by their catalog numbers. Representative folles from the group are shown in Fig. 7-2.

[6]The solidus was revalued from 210 to 180 folles under Justinian I. By the time of Heraclius, it was worth even more, since the weight of the follis had declined. See P. Grierson, "The *Tablettes Albertini* and the Value of the *Solidus* in the Fifth and Sixth Centuries A.D.," *JRS* 49 (1959): 75.
[7]A. H. M. Jones, *The Later Roman Empire, 284–602*, I, 445–448, gives data on prices of food and clothing.
[8]Ibid., II, 852.
[9]Ibid., II, 867–871; for landowners, see also I, 554–555.

[10]Professor Tom B. Jones, who kindly read this paper, pointed out the fear of death by drowning held by the people of the ancient world. Passengers in imminent danger of shipwreck fastened "bags of money or objects of jewelry about their necks so that Charon's fee would be provided for anyone who found their bodies washed up on shore and thus ensure for them a decent burial" (*In the Twilight of Antiquity: The R. S. Hoyt Memorial Lectures* [1973], p. 105). This custom, plus the natural instinct to save one's valuables when possible, would explain the scarcity of currency aboard the ship when it went down.

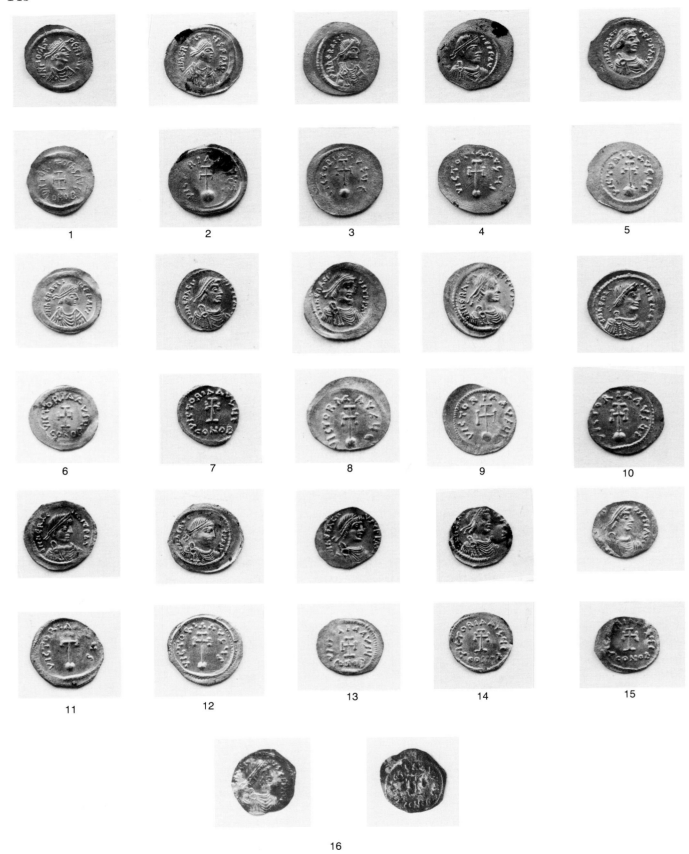

FIG. 7-1. The gold coins (semisses and tremisses). *MK*

FIG. 7-2. Examples of the fifty-four copper coins. *MK*

## Gold Coins

### CONSTANTINOPLE
#### Phocas (A.D. 602–610)

*Tremissis*—607(?)–610

| *Obverse* | *Reverse* |
|---|---|
| ♂NFOCAS PERPAVI | VICTORIFOCASAVϚ |
| Bust r., beardless, diademed, draped and cuirassed | Cross potent on base; CONOB in *ex*. |
| *BMC* 30 ff.; *DOC* 19 | |

1. A͵ ✓ 1.55 g; 19 mm. Inv. No. W3-245; Bodrum Museum 518.

#### Heraclius (A.D. 610–641)

*Semissis*—Class I, 610–613(?)

| *Obverse* | *Reverse* |
|---|---|
| ♂NhERACLI ϞSPPAVI | VICTORIAAVϚϞ |
| Bust r., beardless, diademed, draped and cuirassed | Cross potent on globe |
| *BMC* 81 ff.; *DOC* 51 | |

2. Off. E
   A͵ ✓ 2.3 g; 19 mm. Inv. No. W3-51; Bodrum Museum 418.
   *BMC* 82–83; *DOC* 51*b*

3. As above but cross separated from globe
   A͵ ↘ 2.3 g; 19 mm. Inv. No. W3-237; Bodrum Museum 517.
   *BMC* 82–83; *DOC* 51*b*

4. Obv. ends PPAV; off. S (?)
   A͵ ↓ 2.2 g; 19 mm. Inv. No. W3-53; Bodrum Museum 415.
   *BMC* —; *DOC* —

5. Off. S (?)
   A͵ ↓ 2.4 g; 19 mm. Inv. No. W3-194; Bodrum Museum 422.
   *BMC* —; *DOC* —

*Tremissis*—Class I, 610–613(?)

| *Obverse* | *Reverse* |
|---|---|
| As above | VICTORIAAVϚϞ |
| *BMC* 91 ff.; *DOC* 53 | Cross potent on base; CONOB in *ex*. |

6. Off. —
   A͵ ✓ 1.5 g; 16 mm. Inv. No. W3-192; Bodrum Museum 420. Of good style.
   *BMC* 91; *DOC* 53*d*

7. Off. S
   A͵ ✓ 1.5 g; 18 mm. Inv. No. W3-241; Bodrum Museum 515.

*BMC* 93–94; *DOC* 53*b*

*Semissis*—Class II, 613(?)–641

| *Obverse* | *Reverse* |
|---|---|
| ♂NhERACLI ϞSϹPPAVI | VICTORIAAVϚϞ |
| Bust r., as above | Cross potent on globe |
| *BMC* 85 ff.; *DOC* 52 | |

8. Off. E
   A͵ ✓ 2.4 g; 20 mm. Inv. No. W3-243; Bodrum Museum 519.
   *BMC* 85; *DOC* 52*a*

9. Off. S
   A͵ ✓ 2.5 g; 18 mm. Inv. No. W3-244; Bodrum Museum 516.
   *BMC* 86–90; *DOC* 52*b*

10. Obv.: C–LI; off. S
    A͵ ↓ 2.3 g; 19 mm. Inv. No. W3-52; Bodrum Museum 417.
    *BMC* 86–90; *DOC* 52*b*

11. Obv.: C–LIϞSϹPAV; off. S
    A͵ ↓ 2.4 g; 18 mm. Inv. No. W3-193; Bodrum Museum 424.
    *BMC* 86–90; *DOC* 52*b*

12. Obv.: C–LI; off. S
    A͵ ✓ 2.25 g; 18 mm. Inv. No. W3-197; Bodrum Museum 423.
    *BMC* 86–90; *DOC* 52*b*

*Tremissis*—Class II, 613(?)–641

| *Obverse* | *Reverse* |
|---|---|
| ♂NhERACLI ϞSϹPPAVI | VICTORIAAVϚϞ |
| Bust r. as above | Cross potent on base; CONOB in *ex*. |
| *BMC* 95; *DOC* 54 | |

13. Off. —
    A͵ ↓ 1.5 g; 16 mm. Inv. No. W3-195; Bodrum Museum 421.
    *BMC* —; *DOC* —

14. Off. S
    A͵ ↓ 1.6 g; 16 mm. Inv. No. W3-88; Bodrum Museum 416.
    *BMC* 95; *DOC* 54

15. As above
    A͵ ↓ 1.5 g; 16 mm. Inv. No. W3-196; Bodrum Museum 419.
    *BMC* 95; *DOC* 54

16. As above
    A͵ ↓ 1.3 g; 17 mm. Inv. No. W3-328; Bodrum Museum 940.
    *BMC* 95; *DOC* 54

## Copper Coins

CONSTANTINOPLE
### Maurice Tiberius (A.D. 582–602)

| Obverse | Reverse |
|---|---|

**DNΜAVRC TIbERPPAVC**
Bust facing, in cuirass and
helmet with plume;
globus cruciger in r. hand;
shield at l. shoulder
*BMC* 26 ff.; *DOC* I, 20 ff.

Below, officina
To right, year

A N N O †M CON

17.] VRIC TIbERPPAV
    Year Ч = 586/587; off. Є
    Æ ✓ 10.65 g; 31 mm. Inv. No. W3-260; Bodrum
Museum 522.
    *BMC* 41; *DOC* I, 28*e*

### Heraclius (A.D. 610–641)
Class 1, Heraclius alone

| Obverse | Reverse |
|---|---|

**ठNhRACLI ЧSPERPAVI**
Bust facing, bearded, in
cuirass and helmet with
plume or cross; globus
cruciger in r. hand; shield
at l. shoulder
*BMC* 109 ff.; *DOC* 69 ff.

Below, officina
To right, year

A N N O †M CON

18. ] NhRACLI PERPAV; plume on helmet
    Year I = 610/611; off. A
    Æ ✓ 11.00 g; 30 mm. Inv. No. W3-256; Bodrum
Museum 523.
    *BMC* —; *DOC* 69*a*

19. ] hRACLI P[ ; plume on helmet
    Year I = 610/611; off. Є
    Æ ↓ 10.65 g; 30 mm. Inv. No. W3-286; Bodrum
Museum 286.
    Overstruck.
    *BMC* —; *DOC* —

20. ] ACLI PERPA[ ; cross on helmet
    Year II = 611/612; off. Δ
    Æ ↑ 10.15 g; 33 mm. Inv. No. W3-267; Bodrum
Museum 267.
    Overstruck.
    *BMC* 111; *DOC* 70*c*

21. ठNhRACL PERPAVI ; cross on helmet
    II
    Year I = 612/613; off. Γ
    Æ ↗ 10.90 g; 31 mm. Inv. No. W3-283; Bodrum
Museum 525.
    *BMC* 113; *DOC* 71*b*

22. ठIRACL[ ] AVⱾ ; cross on helmet
    II
    Year I = 612/613; off. Є
    Æ ✓ 12.50 g; 35 mm. Inv. No. W3-275; Bodrum
Museum 275.

Overstruck on a follis of Phocas.
*BMC* 115; *DOC* 71*d*

Class 2, Heraclius, Heraclius Constantine

| Obverse | Reverse |
|---|---|

**ddNNhERACLI ЧSEᲜhERA CONSᲜPAV**
Two standing figures,
robed; Heraclius bearded
on l.; Heraclius Con-
stantine on r.; each has
crown with cross and
holds globus cruciger in r.
hand; between heads,
cross
*BMC* 116 ff.; *DOC* 76 ff.

Below, officina
To right, year

A N N O ⚹M CON

23. **ddNNhRAC[ ]EᲜ[**
    II
    Year I = 613; off. A
    Æ ↓ 10.80 g; 31 mm. Inv. No. W3-274; Bodrum
Museum 274.
    Overstruck on a follis of Phocas.
    *BMC* 116–117; *DOC* 76*a*

24. Inscription illegible; surface badly corroded
    II
    Year I = 613; off. Γ (cut over A )
    Æ ✓ 8.30 g; 30 mm. Inv. No. W3-299; Bodrum Mu-
seum 299.
    *BMC* 122; *DOC* 76*c*

25. Inscription illegible
    II
    Year I = 613; off. Δ
    Æ ↗ 30 mm. Inv. No. W3-292; Bodrum Mu-
seum 263.
    Overstruck on a follis of Phocas over another coin.
    *BMC* 123–124; *DOC* 76*d*

26. ] ACONSᲜP
    II
    Year I = 613; off. Δ
    Æ ↓ 34 mm. Inv. No. W3-270; Bodrum Mu-
seum 532.
    Overstruck on a follis of Maurice Tiberius, year 20.
    *BMC* 123–124; *DOC* 76*d*

27. Inscription illegible
    II
    Year I = 613; off. Δ
    Æ ↗ 3.60 g; 30 mm. Inv. No. W3-601; Bodrum Mu-
seum 293.
    *BMC* 123–124; *DOC* 76*d*

28. ] dNNh[
    II
    Year I = 613; off. Є
    Æ ↑ 9.30 g; 29 mm. Inv. No. W3-273; Bodrum Mu-
seum 526.

*BMC* 125–126; *DOC* 76*e*

29. Inscription illegible

||

Year | = 613; off. ?

Æ ↙ 7.85 g; 32 mm. Inv. No. W3-277; Bodrum Museum 277.

Overstruck on a follis of Phocas.

30. ]NSƮ[

||

Year || = 613/614; off. A or Δ

Æ ↙ 9.75 g; 32 mm. Inv. No. W3-301; Bodrum Museum 292.

31. Inscription illegible

||

Year || = 613/614; off. B

Æ ↗ 6.00 g; 27 mm. Inv. No. W3-600; Bodrum Museum 297.

*BMC* —; *DOC* 79*b*

32. ]dNNhE[          ]ƮhERACON

||

Year || = 613/614; off. Γ

Æ ↗ 11.40 g; 31 mm. Inv. No. W3-259; Bodrum Museum 531.

Overstruck on a follis of Phocas of Nicomedia.

*BMC* 127–131; *DOC* 79*c*

33. Inscription illegible

||

Year || = 613/614; off. Δ

Æ ↗ 4.70 g; 26 mm. Inv. No. W3-294; Bodrum Museum 294.

Overstruck on a follis of Phocas from Cyzicus.

*BMC* 132; *DOC* 79*d*

34. ]dNNh[          ]EƮhE[

||

Year || = 613/614; off. Δ

Æ ↑ 10.25 g; 34 mm. Inv. No. W3-265; Bodrum Museum 265.

Overstruck on a follis of Phocas from Constantinople.

*BMC* 132; *DOC* 79*d*

35. ddNNh[

||

Year || = 613/614; off. E

Æ ↙ 9.40 g; 34 mm. Inv. No. W3-295; Bodrum Museum 295.

Overstruck on a coin of Phocas from Constantinople over a coin of Justinian I.

*BMC* 133; *DOC* 79*e*

36. Inscription illegible

||

Year || = 613/614; off. E

Æ ↙ 8.90 g; 30 mm. Inv. No. W3-287; Bodrum Museum 287.

Overstruck on a follis of Phocas and Leontia from Antioch.

*BMC* 133; *DOC* 79*e*

37. ]CONSƮ[ ; + instead of ⚹ on rev.

Year Ч = 614/615; off. Γ

Æ ↙ 8.95 g; 27 mm. Inv. No. W3-281; Bodrum Museum 281.

Overstruck on a follis from Nicomedia.

*BMC* 136–137; *DOC* 80*c*

38. ddNNhER[          ]ƮhERACO[ ; + instead of ⚹ on rev.

Year Ч = 614/615; off. E

Æ ↙ 8.30 g; 30 mm. Inv. No. W3-272; Bodrum Museum 272.

Overstruck on a follis of Phocas.

*BMC* 139; *DOC* 80*e*

39. Inscription illegible

Year ? 613–616; off. A

Æ ↙ 6.00 g; 29 mm. Inv. No. W3-297; Bodrum Museum 300.

Overstruck.

40. ddNNhE[          ]CON ; mint mark illegible, but off. Γ and ⚹ above M indicate Constantinople

Year ? 613–616; off. Γ

Æ ↙ 10.50 g; 30 mm. Inv. No. W3-271; Bodrum Museum 271.

Overstruck on a follis of Maurice Tiberius from Constantinople, year 14.

41. ]ACO[

Year ? 613–616; off. Δ

Æ ↗ 10.60 g; 33 mm. Inv. No. W3-261; Bodrum Museum 261.

Overstruck on a follis of Phocas from Constantinople.

42. ddNNh[

Year ? 613–616; off. E

Æ ↓ 10.30 g; 31 mm. Inv. No. W3-268; Bodrum Museum 268.

Overstruck on a follis of Phocas from Cyzicus.

43. Inscription illegible

Year ? 613–616; off. ?

Æ ↗          27 mm. Inv. No. W3-290; Bodrum Museum 290.

Class 3, Heraclius, Heraclius Constantine, Martina

| *Obverse* | *Reverse* |
|---|---|

No inscription. Three standing figures, robed; Heraclius, center; Heraclius Constantine to r.; Martina to l.; each has crown with cross and

Below, officina To right, year

ANNO + M CON

holds globus cruciger in
r. hand; between heads,
crosses
*BMC* 170 ff.; *DOC* 89 ff.
44. Year **ꟼ** = 615/616; off. **A**
    Æ ↓ 11.50 g; 34 mm. Inv. No. W3-269; Bodrum
    Museum 533.
    Overstruck on a follis of Phocas from Constan-
    tinople.
    *BMC* —; *DOC* —
45. Year **ꟼ** = 615/616; off. **Γ**
    Æ ↗ 8.10 g; 27 mm. Inv. No. W3-257; Bodrum Mu-
    seum 528.
    *BMC* —; *DOC* 89*b*
46. Year **ꟼI** = 616/617; off. ?
    Æ ↙ 9.15 g; 28 mm. Inv. No. W3-280; Bodrum Mu-
    seum 280.
    Overstruck.
47. Year ? 615–624; off. ?
    Æ ↙ 5.30 g; 27 mm. Inv. No. W3-302; Bodrum Mu-
    seum 302.

Class 4, Heraclius, Heraclius Constantine, Martina

| Obverse | Reverse |
|---|---|
| As above | ANNO Below, officina |
| *BMC* 181 ff.; *DOC* 99 ff. | ᴿ M̶ To right, year |
| X | CON |

48. Year **ꟼ** = 625/626; off. **Γ**
    Æ ↙ 4.30 g; 23 mm. Inv. No. W3-300.
    *BMC* 183; *DOC* 100*c*

### THESSALONICA
#### Heraclius (A.D. 610–641)
Class 2, Heraclius, Heraclius Constantine

| Obverse | Reverse |
|---|---|
| **dNhERAC LIꟼSPPAVC** | Below, officina |
| Two standing figures, | ᴬⁿⁿᵒ M̶ To right, year |
| robed; Heraclius bearded | ΘEC |
| to l.; Heraclius Con- | |
| stantine to r.; each has | |
| crown with cross and | |
| holds globus cruciger in | |
| r. hand; between heads, | |
| cross | |

*BMC* 213 ff.; *DOC* 134 ff.
49. **]PAVC**
    Year **ꟼ** = 614/615; off. **B**
    Æ ↓ 10.80 g; 32 mm. Inv. No. W3-258; Bodrum
    Museum 534.
    Overstruck on a follis of Phocas, year 7.
    *BMC* 213–216; *DOC* 135*a*
50. Inscription illegible

Year **ꟼ** = 614/615; off. **B**
    Æ ↓ 8.30 g; 32 mm. Inv. No. W3-284; Bodrum Mu-
    seum 527.
    Overstruck on a follis of Phocas over a coin of
    Maurice Tiberius.
    *BMC* 213–216; *DOC* 135*a*
51. Inscription illegible
    Year ? 613–618; off. **B**
    Æ ↘ 9.75 g; 29 mm. Inv. No. W3-289; Bodrum Mu-
    seum 301.
    Overstruck on a follis of Phocas from Nicomedia,
    year 4.

### NICOMEDIA
#### Heraclius (A.D. 610–641)
Class 1, Heraclius alone

| Obverse | Reverse |
|---|---|
| **DNhERACL IꟼSPPAVC** | Below, officina |
| Bust facing, bearded, | ᴬⁿⁿᵒ M̶ To right, year |
| wearing paludamentum | NIKO |
| and helmet with cross; | |
| globus cruciger in r. hand | |
| *BMC* 229 ff.; *DOC* 153 ff. | |

52. Inscription illegible; with cuirass and shield at l.
    shoulder
    Year I (?) = 610/611; off. **A**
    Æ ↘ 9.50 g; 29 mm. Inv. No. W3-278; Bodrum
    Museum 524.
    *BMC* 229–230; *DOC* 153*a*
53. Inscription illegible; surface badly corroded
    Year II = 611/612; off. **A**
    Æ ↗ 7.50 g; 28 mm. Inv. No. W3-291; Bodrum Mu-
    seum 562.
    *BMC* 231; *DOC* 154*a*

Class 2, Heraclius, Heraclius Constantine

| Obverse | Reverse |
|---|---|
| | Below, officina |
| Fragmentary inscription. | ᴬⁿⁿᵒ M̶ To right, year |
| Two standing figures, | NIKO |
| robed; Heraclius bearded | |
| to l.; Heraclius Con- | |
| stantine to r.; each has | |
| crown with cross and | |
| holds globus cruciger in | |
| r. hand; between heads, | |
| cross | |
| *BMC* 234 ff.; *DOC* 158 ff. | |

54. **DNh[    ]Ch[**
    **II**
    Year I = 613; off. **A**
    Æ ↓ 10.70 g; 33 mm. Inv. No. W3-285; Bodrum

Museum 285.
Overstruck.
*BMC* 234–236; *DOC* 158*a*

55. ]ONSƵPPAV

        ‖
Year ‖ = 613; off. **A**
Æ ↙ 12.65 g; 33 mm. Inv. No. W3-279; Bodrum
Museum 279.
Overstruck.
*BMC* 234–236; *DOC* 158*a*

56. Inscription illegible

        ‖
Year ‖ = 613/614; off. **A**
Æ ↙ 11.65 g; 29 mm. Inv. No. W3-266; Bodrum
Museum 529.
Overstruck.
*BMC* 240–241; *DOC* 159*a*

Class 3, Heraclius, Heraclius Constantine, Martina

| *Obverse* | *Reverse* |
|---|---|
| No inscription. Three standing figures, robed; Heraclius, center; Heraclius Constantine to r.; Martina to l.; each has crown with cross and holds globus cruciger in r. hand; between heads, crosses | Below, officina To right, year |

A
N ☩
N M
O
    NIKO

*BMC* 244 ff.; *DOC* 162 ff.

                                    I G
57. Year I = 617/618; off. **A**
Æ ↓ 5.60 g; 27 mm. Inv. No. W3-296; Bodrum Museum 296.
Overstruck.
*BMC* —; *DOC* —

### CYZICUS
#### Heraclius (A.D. 610–641)

Class 1, Heraclius alone

| *Obverse* | *Reverse* |
|---|---|
| ẟNhRACLI PERPAVC | Below, officina |
| Bust facing, bearded, in cuirass and helmet with plume; globus cruciger in r. hand; shield at l. shoulder | To right, year |

A
N ☩
N M
O
    KYZ

*BMC* 250 ff.; *DOC* 167 ff.

58. ]hRACL[ ] PERPAVC
Year I = 610/611; off. **A**
Æ ↓ 11.30 g; 31 mm. Inv. No. W3-262; Bodrum
Museum 520.
Overstruck.
*BMC* 250; *DOC* 167*a*

59. ẟNhRACLI PERPAVC
Year ‖ = 611/612; off. ?
Æ ↙ 6.25 g; 30 mm. Inv. No. W3-276; Bodrum Museum 276.

60. ]RACLI [ ]R[
Year ‖‖ = 612/613; off. **A**
Æ ↓ 8.50 g; 31 mm. Inv. No. W3-264; Bodrum Museum 264.
Overstruck on a follis of Phocas, year 4.
*BMC* 256–259; *DOC* 169*a*

61. ]RACLI [
Year ‖‖ = 612/613; off. **B**
Æ ↑ 11.70 g; 34 mm. Inv. No. W3-255; Bodrum Museum 521.
Overstruck.
*BMC* 260; *DOC* 169*b*

### ALEXANDRETTA AD ISSUM
#### Interregnum (A.D. 608–610)

| *Obverse* | *Reverse* |
|---|---|
| ẟⱮNЄRACLIOCONSULII | Below, officina |
| Busts of Heraclius on l. and his father on r., facing; both bearded and bareheaded, wearing consular robes; between heads, cross | To right, indiction |

A
N ☩
N M
O
    ΛΛЄXΛNΔ

*BMC* —; *DOC* 15–16

62. ]ⱮNЄRACLIOCONSULII

        X   X
Ind. ‖‖ or ‖‖‖ = 609–610;[11] off. **A**
Æ ↙ 8.10 g; 28 mm. Inv. No. W3-282; Bodrum Museum 530.
*BMC* —; *DOC* 15–16

### UNCERTAIN MINT
#### Heraclius (A.D. 610–641)

Class 2, Heraclius, Heraclius Constantine

63. ]hЄRA
Year ?; off. **A**
Æ ↙ 8.10 g; 30 mm. Inv. No. W3-288; Bodrum Museum 288.
Overstruck on a follis of Phocas.

64. Inscription illegible
Year ?; off. ?
Æ ↗          30 mm. Inv. No. W3-293; Bodrum Museum 291.
Overstruck.

#### Emperor (?)

Six unidentifiable fragments, four with facing bust

[11] These issues of the Interregnum were dated by indiction. See Grierson's introduction in *DOC* II, part I, pp. 207ff.

# VIII

## THE POTTERY

GEORGE F. BASS

### Cargo Amphoras

The ship's cargo comprised between 850 and 900 amphoras. A representative sample of slightly more than 100 of them was raised to the surface and cataloged; the remainder were simply removed from the wreck and placed on either side of the excavation site, where they remain. The cargo amphoras (CA) are of two basic shapes, designated type 1 and type 2.

#### TYPE 1 AMPHORAS

Thirty of this type were cataloged, but as the type is relatively light and easily moved under water, that number is a misleadingly high indication of their proportion of the total cargo (see below). Amphoras of type 1 have nearly cylindrical bodies tapering slightly to plain round bases and are usually pinched slightly at the waist to give an "hour-glass" shape (Fig. 8-1). Handles are attached asymmetrically, as seen from above (Fig. 8-2). The orange brown fabric is fairly coarse, often with white grit and, in at least one case, with some black grit as well.

Sizes are by no means standard, the averages of those cataloged being 45.3 cm in height, 22.1 cm in diameter at the broadest point, and 8.2 cm in diameter at the mouth (mouths are oval, not round, however, and average 8.5 × 7.9 cm). The greatest height recorded is 50.5 cm, the greatest maximum diameter 27 cm, and the largest mouth diameter 9.7 cm; none of these figures were taken from the same amphora, which shows that proportions as well as sizes vary, although one amphora does show unusually large overall dimensions. The shortest type 1 amphora is 41.1 cm high, and there are a number only 19.5 cm in diameter at their shoulders and 7 cm in diameter at their mouths; again, shortness is not

necessarily an indication of a small mouth or a narrow shoulder. Nor are volumes standard, ranging between 6 and nearly 10 l among those measured, with an average capacity of 8.2 l.

Surface decorations on the bodies of type 1 amphoras vary as greatly as do their sizes: some are lightly grooved horizontally from bottom to top, while others have bands of grooves that are often separated by pronounced and more widely spaced ridges, or flat planes that are often oblique to the horizontal grooves. Although necks seem always to be plain, bases can be either plain or grooved with concentric circles. None of the grooves usually rise above the lower handle attachments, but in some few cases they cover the shoulders.

In spite of these differences, most examples of type 1 are so similar that it would be repetitive to catalog completely here more than a few representative examples. The basic variations in shape and decoration are seen in the first five. Dimensions in the catalogs are given in meters.

CA 1. Figs. 8-2 and 8-3. H. 0.485; max. diam. 0.213; oval mouth diam. approx. 0.088, mostly covered with encrustation. Lip slightly chipped.

Orange to orange brown ware. Rounded bottom reaches diameter of 0.195 at height of 0.095, followed by long reverse curve to max. diam. at about three-fifths total height. Rounded shoulder joined to neck, which tapers slightly to splayed rim; well-defined ridge below rim at height of handle tops. About one dozen grooves closely spaced around the lower part of the rounded bottom to a height of 0.06. Second band of eleven

FIG. 8-1. Typical cargo amphoras of type 1.

fairly evenly spaced grooves, 0.055 wide, rises from height of 0.10. In center of body are four slightly oblique ridges, angular in section. Another band of thirteen grooves, closely spaced, rises 0.065 above the center section to the bottom of the handles. Handles are "stepped" on opposite sides with finger-made grooves.

CA 2. Fig. 8-3. H. 0.435; max. diam. 0.212; mouth diam. approx. 0.087.
Partly encrusted; piece of bottom missing.

Fairly coarse, orange brown ware. Shape similar to that of CA 1. Handles, round in section beneath, are ridged on top as if smoothed by thumb and two fingers. Band of six closely spaced ridges

extends downward 0.06 from junction of handles with body; seven more ridges, about 0.025 apart, extend downward to top of hemispherical base. Neck nearly cylindrical.

CA 3. Fig. 8-3. Not described, probably being one of the amphoras which crumbled and fell apart on drying. The illustration, however, shows that its broader shoulders force the neck to taper more than those of the previous two examples. Central decoration is a series of broad planes stepping downwards instead of simple ridges.

CA 4. Fig. 8-3. H. 0.44; max. diam. 0.195; mouth diam. approx. 0.078. Coarse, orange brown fabric with white grit. Shape is slimmer than those above,

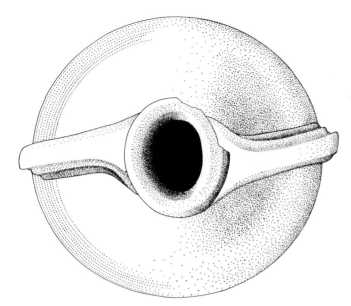

FIG. 8-2. Top view of cargo amphora CA 1, showing asymmetry of the handles. *SWK*

but neck tapers more like that of CA 3. Handles ridged as if by thumb and index finger. Horizontal ridges, spaced from 0.015 to 0.02 apart, extend from rounded bottom to lower handle attachments.

CA 5. Fig. 8-3. H. 0.484; max. diam. 0.246; mouth diam. 0.082. The shape differs from those of most examples in that the maximum diameter is reached at closer to one-half than to three-fifths of total body height; further, the relatively slim bottom gives the amphora a uniquely piriform shape. Horizontal grooves continue above handles onto shoulder.

A number of additional amphoras of type 1 (CA 6–CA 12) may be mentioned for special features; they are otherwise similar in size, shape, fabric, and decoration to those above and will not be described completely.

CA 6. Contained round sherd stopper (see a later section for stoppers, generally found loose in the wreck; only one other cataloged type 1 amphora was found to contain a stopper); well-defined ridges inside neck.

CA 7–CA 10. Five to eight grooves form concentric circles on bottom of each amphora (eight circles on CA 8).

CA 11–CA 12. Little narrowing at waist, making these amphoras quite fat.

### TYPE 2 AMPHORAS

Eighty larger, nearly globular amphoras (Fig. 8-4) were raised from the wreck and cataloged. The bottom of each is again plain and rounded, and the maximum diameter is found at the shoulder, usually at three-fifths of the total height. Crudely made handles, somewhat oval in section, rise from the center of the shoulder to the neck just below the lip; the neck tapers upward to a slightly splaying rim. Handles are asymmetrically placed, sometimes twisted slightly, as on amphoras of type 1. The fabric differs from that of type 1, being dark brown or reddish brown in most cases, usually without noticeable grit.

Globular amphoras may be divided into two subtypes on the basis of body decoration. In subtype 2*a*, the body of the amphora is decorated by one continuous band of narrow, sometimes wavy grooves. Fifty of the eighty type 2 amphoras cataloged are of this subtype. In general, they are slightly larger than amphoras of subtype 2*b*, averaging 54.5 cm in height, 42.3 cm in diameter, and 9.5 cm in diameter at the mouth. The following are typical examples of subtype 2*a*:

CA 13. Fig. 8-5. H. 0.56; max. diam. 0.438; mouth diam. 0.092. Band of thirty closely spaced

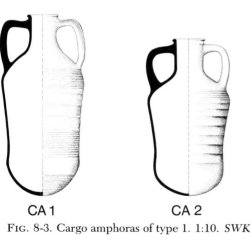
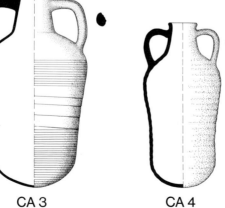
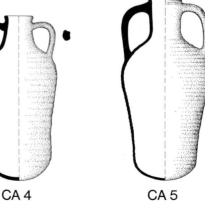

CA 1          CA 2          CA 3          CA 4          CA 5

FIG. 8-3. Cargo amphoras of type 1. 1:10. *SWK*

FIG. 8-4. Typical cargo amphoras of type 2.

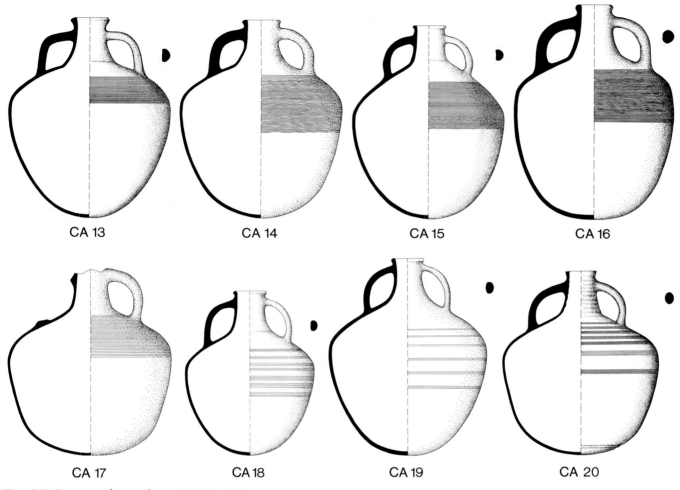

CA 13  CA 14  CA 15  CA 16

CA 17  CA 18  CA 19  CA 20

FIG. 8-5. Cargo amphoras of type 2. 1:10. *SWK*

grooves extends downward 0.103 from below junction of handle and shoulder. Two wider grooves (not shown in drawing) form ring around bottom. Seven finger grooves around neck.

CA 14. Fig. 8-5. Band of thirty-five narrowly spaced, wavy grooves extends 0.115 downward from below junction of handle and shoulder. Two wider grooves (not shown in drawing) form ring around the bottom. Handles slightly ridged in center. Neck has six finger grooves.

CA 15. Fig. 8-5. H. 0.54; max. diam. 0.408; mouth diam. 0.088. Band of forty-two closely spaced grooves extends 0.14 downward from below junction of handle and shoulder; lower grooves slightly wavy. Neck has at least five finger grooves.

CA 16. Fig. 8-5. H. 0.585; max. diam. 0.43; mouth diam. 0.107. Band of fifty-nine to sixty closely spaced grooves extends 0.175 downward from

just below junction of handle and shoulder. Ring of three more widely spaced grooves on bottom. Five or six finger grooves around neck.

CA 17. Fig. 8-5. Pres. h. 0.51; max. diam. 0.43. Lip and one handle missing. About thirty grooves in band.

Among the subtype 2*b* amphoras, the body is decorated by several separate bands of narrow grooves. Although the largest of these amphoras is nearly the size of the largest of subtype 2*a* (height 57.1 cm; max. diam. 45.1 cm; mouth diam. 10.3 cm), and the smallest (height 41 cm; diam. 32 cm; mouth diam. 9.2 cm) not so small as the smallest of subtype 2*a*, the average size of the subtype 2*b* amphoras is smaller, nearly half being only 44–47 cm high, with a maximum diameter of 35 cm.

CA 18. Fig. 8-5. Eight bands of narrowly spaced grooves (three to five grooves in a band); top band incomplete. Four finger grooves around neck.

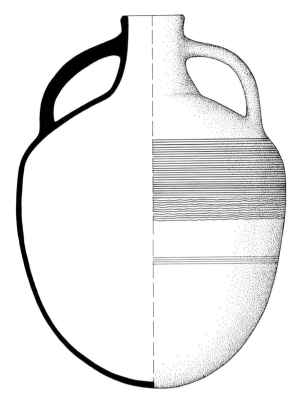

FIG. 8-6. Cargo amphora CA 21, showing features of both subtypes 2*a* and 2*b*. *SWK*

CA 19. Fig. 8-5. H. 0.536; max. diam. 0.417; mouth
        diam. 0.085.
        Bands of two, three, and four grooves.
CA 20. Fig. 8-5. H. 0.505; max. diam. 0.415; mouth
        diam. 0.08.
        Bands of three to five grooves. Pronounced fin-
        ger grooves around neck, and ring of three
        grooves around base.
    A combination of subtypes 2*a* and 2*b* may be seen
in CA 21.
CA 21. Fig. 8-6. H. 0.568; max. diam. 0.431; mouth
        diam. 0.102.
        Band of thirty-seven closely spaced grooves ex-
        tends downward 0.135 below junction of handle
        and shoulder; 0.055 below the wide band, a nar-
        row (0.01) band of three grooves circles the
        amphora. Two wide grooves form ring around
        bottom. Four finger grooves around neck.

### STOPPERS

Roughly rounded amphora sherds served as amphora
stoppers, their convex sides often grooved and their concave sides often bearing remnants of resin that coated
the interiors of amphoras from which they were broken

FIG. 8-7. Amphora sherds used as amphora stoppers. 1:2. *SWK*

(Fig. 8-7). Shaped to fit loosely into the amphoras'
mouths, they must have been held in place with un-
baked clay or some similar substance that has left no

trace.[1] They average about 6 cm in diameter, the largest cataloged being 9.7 cm and the smallest 4 cm, but few are smaller than 5 cm or larger than 7 cm in diameter; thickness varies between 5 mm and 17 mm but is usually between 7 mm and 8 mm.

About 165 stoppers were found on the wreck, mostly within areas 4A–4C through 7A–7C and fully half within step-frames 5 and 6. Most of them had filtered down through the cargo and had come to rest on or just above wooden hull remains. Although some or many probably were overlooked and accidentally discarded by excavators as simple sherds, and others may remain inside amphoras left on the seabed, neither explanation can account for the large discrepancy between the number of stoppers and the number of cargo amphoras: divers learned quickly to recognize and collect round sherds on the site, and very few stoppers were found inside the 110 amphoras raised and cleaned for cataloging. The small number of sherd stoppers suggests either that some perishable material was used for stoppers in the majority of amphoras or that, less likely, many of the amphoras on board were empty during the ship's final voyage.[2]

## GRAFFITI

In 1980, during cleaning of the Bodrum Museum storeroom, which had housed most of the Yassi Ada amphoras since the time of their excavation, archaeology students from Istanbul University noticed graffiti on the shoulders of several type 2 amphoras. Van Doorninck then examined and in some cases partially cleaned more amphoras, revealing that graffiti scratched into the clay before it was fired were not uncommon, although they seemingly were restricted to the largest type 2 amphoras. Although the angle of sunlight was important for the discovery of the graffiti, it remains perplexing and embarrassing that they had never before been noticed on amphoras so frequently handled and examined for catalogs, drawings, and photographs.

Netia Piercy's drawings of the graffiti were completed only weeks before these pages went to the printer. Rather than delay publication of the book for hasty or partial interpretations of the graffiti, we have decided it best to publish their illustration without further comment (Fig. 8-8. These amphoras were lettered arbitrarily by the artist; the letters do not correspond to any of the amphoras otherwise cataloged or mentioned here.). One amphora raised from the wreck in 1980 and found to contain grape seeds (Fig. 8-4, upper left), bears a graffito which seems to read ICIΛN (ISIAN). Any future thoughts on the graffiti will be submitted to the *International Journal of Nautical Archaeology*. About one-fifth of sixty globular amphoras raised from the amphora dump in 1981 bore graffiti which have not yet been drawn, and we may later raise all remaining amphoras from the seabed.

## CAPACITY AND WEIGHT OF AMPHORAS

Most amphoras appear on Wreck Plan III, with their positions carefully plotted. Their total number, however, is based on the number of amphora necks recorded. An otherwise complete amphora, if missing its neck, has not been included in the total, nor has less than half a neck.

Not all amphoras, therefore, can be identified by type. Excavators, in collecting and discarding unplotted sherds, noted the necks among them but not always their types. In other cases, the type cannot be distinguished in the photographs and drawings from which our plans were made, and the amphora or amphora neck was removed from the site without its type being recorded. Nevertheless, an accurate account of most amphoras has been made by van Doorninck, who made a thorough review of all graphic records and notebooks and also inspected the pottery discard piles on the seabed.

In his accounting, van Doorninck divided globular type 2 amphoras into two groups based on size, with large globular amphoras having approximately twice the capacity of small globular amphoras. These groups, as seen below, bear no relation to the subtypes 2a and 2b, which are based on surface decoration.

| | |
|---|---:|
| Number of plotted amphoras of unknown type | 20 |
| Number of unplotted amphoras of unknown type | 9 |
| Number of plotted type 1 amphoras | 97 |
| Number of unplotted type 1 amphoras | 2 |
| Number of plotted large type 2 amphoras | 579 |
| Number of unplotted large type 2 amphoras | 40 |
| Number of plotted small type 2 amphoras | 72 |
| Number of unplotted small type 2 amphoras | 3 |
| Total number of recorded amphoras | 822 |

If the amphoras of unknown type are assigned proportionally to the three categories, the result is:

---

[1] H. E. Winlock and W. E. Crum, *The Monastery of Epiphanius at Thebes*, I, 79–80, with pl. XXIX, describes how similar ribbed amphoras of wine were hermetically sealed with stoppers of black earth and straw molded over wads of vine leaves stuffed into amphora necks. Byzantine amphoras now in the Archaeological Museum of Constanţa were sometimes stopped with stones, and these, too, must have required a sealing substance.

[2] There is evidence that the Kyrenia ship was laden with full amphoras when she sank, yet no stoppers were found in the wreck (personal communication from J. R. Steffy). Thus, the absence of stoppers on the Byzantine wreck would be unimportant had not about 165 been found.

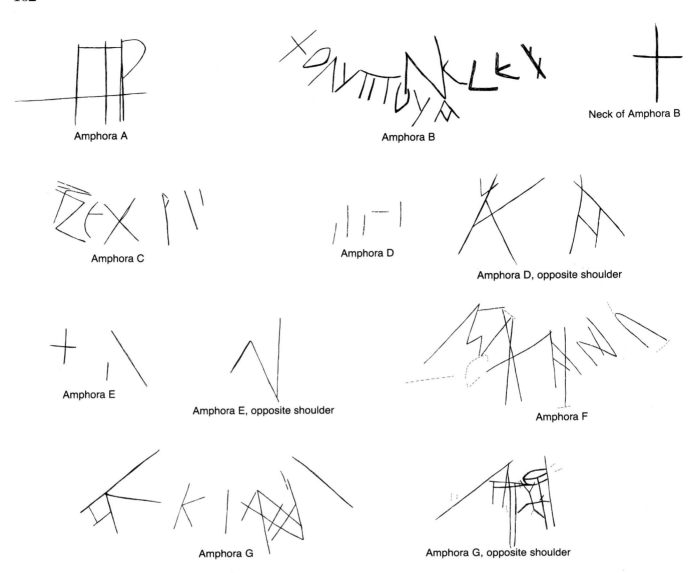

FIG. 8-8. Graffiti on shoulders of type 2 amphoras. *NP*

| Type 1 amphoras | 103 |
|---|---|
| Large type 2 amphoras | 641 |
| Small type 2 amphoras | 78 |
| Total | 822 |

We must also allow for neck fragments removed from the wreck without being recorded, amphoras smashed beyond accounting, and amphoras taken away by divers before the excavation began in 1961. This adjustment would surely have brought the total to something between 850 and 900 amphoras. In the calculations which follow, van Doorninck has simply opted for the round figure of 900 and has again allotted the amphoras of unknown type proportionally among the three categories:

| Estimated total number of type 1 amphoras | 113 |
|---|---|
| Estimated total number of large type 2 amphoras | 702 |

| Estimated total number of small type 2 amphoras | 85 |
|---|---|
| Estimated total number of amphoras | 900 |

Next, in order to calculate the total weight of the ship's cargo, van Doorninck obtained average capacities and weights by measuring a number of complete amphoras and weighing them when empty.[3] The following are the capacities and weights of ten type 1 amphoras:[4]

---

[3] For a study of the capacities of similar, but slightly earlier, type 2 amphoras inscribed with marks of capacity, see A. V. Radulescu, "Amfore cu inscriptii de la edificiul roman cu mozaic," *Pontica* 6 (1973): 193ff.

[4] None of the amphoras used in van Doorninck's calculations are among those cataloged in this book. Their excavation labels are, in the same order as listed, PF, CJ, ACP, 153, 152, KQB, KKP, KJO, AAV, and KMY.

| Capacity (l) | Weight Empty (kg) |
|---|---|
| 9.75 | — |
| 6.00 | 3.5 |
| 6.85 | 3.0 |
| 8.05 | 5.0 |
| 8.65 | 5.0 |
| 8.90 | 4.0 |
| 6.90 | 5.0 |
| 8.65 | — |
| 9.55 | — |
| 8.65 | — |
| Average 8.2 | 4.3 |

If we assume that the amphoras contained wine, and if we use a conservatively chosen specific gravity of 1.000, as suggested by vitaculturalists, we achieve the following estimates:

Capacity of 113 type 1 amphoras                927 l = 927 kg
Weight of 113 empty type 1 amphoras                      486 kg
    Total weight of 113 full type 1 amphoras      1,413 kg

In the same way we can measure the capacities and weights of twelve large type 2 amphoras.[5]

| Capacity (l) | Weight Empty (kg) |
|---|---|
| 37.15 | 11.25 |
| 36.50 | — |
| 35.50 | — |
| 43.05 | — |
| 42.50 | — |
| 30.75 | 9.8 |
| 40.50 | 11.0 |
| 32.55 | 10.5 |
| 34.75 | 11.0 |
| 33.75 | 7.5 |
| 37.00 | 10.5 |
| 29.85 | 11.5 |
| Average 36.2 | 10.4 |

Again using a specific gravity of 1.000, we achieve the following estimates:
Capacity of 702 large type 2
amphoras                25,412 l = 25,412 kg
Weight of 702 empty large type 2
amphoras                              7,301 kg
    Total weight of 702 full type 2
      (large) amphoras                32,713 kg

Finally, the capacities and weights of seven small type 2 amphoras can be measured.[6]

| Capacity (l) | Weight Empty (kg) |
|---|---|
| 17.45 | 4.9 |
| 16.05 | 5.0 |
| 13.30 | 4.5 |
| 10.25 | 3.5 |
| 14.10 | 5.0 |
| 20.05 | 4.5 |
| 15.60 | 5.5 |
| Average 15.3 | 4.7 |

Once again based on a specific gravity for the contents of 1.000, the following estimates can be made:
Capacity of eighty-five small
    type 2 amphoras                1,301 l = 1,301 kg
Weight of eighty-five empty small
    type 2 amphoras                              400 kg
    Total weight of eighty-five full
      type 2 (small) amphoras          1,701 kg

The total estimated weight of a cargo of full wine amphoras is thus the combined total weight for the three types: 32,713 kg + 1,701 kg + 1,413 kg = 35,827 kg (= 78,819 lb = 39.4 tons).

## ORIGINS AND CONTENTS OF AMPHORAS

Although amphoras of type 1 are of a common sixth- and seventh-century shape that occurs over a wide geographical area,[7] they are especially plentiful along the eastern coast of the Black Sea.[8] Further, although a few random amphoras of type 2 are found elsewhere (Thasos,[9] Chios,[10] and Constantinople[11]), their closest and most numerous parallels are found in the same region.[12]

[5] Field identification labels of the amphoras measured are, in order, 78, 173, 184, 17, 171, 129, KKW, 157, 185, KJL, KKO, and KFZ.
[6] Field identification labels are, in order, KQX, EY, KMR, QQW (?), no label, KQR, and KCP.

[7] H. S. Robinson, *The Athenian Agora*, vol. V, *Pottery of the Roman Period: Chronology*, p. 115 (M333), with pl. 32, is an early sixth-century example with much straighter sides than most of those at Yassi Ada; there were at least two similarly straight-sided type 1 amphoras at Yassi Ada (CA 11 and CA 12), unfortunately not illustrated. Hayes (personal communication, April 20, 1970) compares our CA 1 to the "very common British type B(ii) = Ballana type 6 (the commonest type in the seventh-century group at Saraçhane)." See J. W. Hayes, "Excavations at Saraçhane in Istanbul: A Seventh-Century Pottery Group," *DOP* 22 (1968): 215 with n. 33. See also W. B. Emery and L. P. Kirwan, *The Royal Tombs of Ballana and Qustul: Mission Archéologique de Nubie, 1929–34*, II, pl. III ff.
[8] The best parallels I have found are unpublished examples in the storerooms of the Archaeological Museum of Constanţa. See also C. Scorpan, "Sapaturile arheologice de la Sacidava," *Pontica* 6 (1973): fig. 34 on p. 310; R. Vulpe and I. Barnea, *Din Istoria Dobrogei*, vol. II, *Romanii la Dunărea de Jos*, p. 536, whereon fig. 47, no. 4 (sixth century from Dinogetia), is like our CA 1 except that its sides are straighter. Similar amphoras from Sucidava (D. Tudor, *Oltenia Romana*, p. 462, fig. 143, no. 3) are in yellowish clay, 40–51 cm high (D. Tudor, "Sucidava II," *Dacia*, 1st ser., 7–8 [1937–1940]: 384, no. 16, with fig. 15e on p. 383); they are the most common pottery type in all levels of the city except for the prehistoric level. J. Čangova, "Amphores du Moyen Age en Bulgarie," *BIABulg* 22 (1959): 249, 261, with figs. 1, no. 8, and 3, describes their frequency in the Black Sea region. See also A. L. Iacobsen, "Srednevekovye amfory severnogo prichernomor'ya," *SovArch* 15 (1951): 329, fig. 4 (with ledges protruding on up-

After seeking parallels in museums in Turkey, Cyprus, Greece, Lebanon, and Syria, and after comparing published and unpublished photographs of body sherds, handles, and necks from these countries as well as from Italy, Egypt, and the British Isles, I found at best similarities of shape and decoration. The basement storerooms of the Archaeological Museum of Constanţa, Rumania, however, hold numerous amphoras identical to those found at Yassi Ada.

The Constanţa collection contains exact duplicates of the Yassi Ada types and their variations. Type 1 amphoras are of the same yellow brown or orange brown fabric, with the same horizontal banding. Both subtypes 2a and 2b occur there in the darker reddish brown fabric found at Yassi Ada, with the same variations of wavy and straight grooves in wide and narrow bands. Much of the Constanţa material is as yet unpublished, but I understand that most of it was found along the coast.

Visual inspection convinces me that these amphoras in the Black Sea region came from the same production center as those found on the Yassi Ada shipwreck. This comparison offers no clue about their place of origin, however, for type 2 amphoras, at least, are considered imports into the Black Sea. A tentatively hypothesized Aegean manufacture is based on little evidence.[13] Thus, unless the source of their clay can be identified by analysis, or until their production center is found and excavated, we can surmise little more about where they were made.[14]

The greatest concentration of type 2 amphoras outside the Yassi Ada shipwreck, about 120 examples, was found in the vaulted rooms of the great Mosaic-Floored Edifice of the ancient port of Tomis (modern Constanţa).[15] Although these examples are somewhat earlier than the Yassi Ada amphoras, being probably from the sixth century, and therefore not their closest parallels, a study of their contents reveals a great deal about the mechanics of amphora trade.

The vaulted rooms of the Mosaic-Floored Edifice, containing iron anchors, lamps, weights, and amphoras filled with pigments, resins, and iron nails, seem to have been a chandlery. The amphoras suggest a cargo of materials shipped to Tomis in containers manufactured neither in Tomis nor in the places from which their contents were brought. It is, of course, possible that the contents were brought to Tomis in bulk and put into amphoras there for storage, sale, or shipment, but it is unreasonable to believe that those amphoras containing olibanum (frankincense) from Somalia were fired in Somalia, those containing myrrh from Arabia were manufactured in Arabia, those containing mastic from Chios were made there, and so on.[16] The frequent reuse of these amphoras, as indicated by inscriptions painted on them,[17] further shows that they were not made near various vineyards for one-way traffic in wine, but served as valuable commodities themselves. How were they dealt with?

Cargoes of new, empty storage jars may still be seen being shipped for sale in Aegean boats, and the fact that relatively simple terra-cotta objects were shipped for their own value in the past is indicated by the large number of sunken cargoes of roof tiles.[18] Other lost cargoes of plates, cups, and open bowls are too numerous to mention. Thus, a shipment of empty Byzantine amphoras would not have been surprising. Nevertheless, I doubt that a Byzantine merchant would have carried a load of empty amphoras for any long distance simply to be filled before the return voyage. It would have made better economic sense if the merchant were to have carried amphoras already filled with some material on the outward leg of his voyage, either selling the material en route or at his farthest destination. In either case the amphoras could have been emptied and refilled during the voyage and for some undetermined period of time could have been empty.

The interior coating of resin found in most amphoras of both type 1 and type 2 at Yassi Ada suggests that they contained liquid at some time, for similar resinous

per instead of lower sides), for another more straight-sided example.

[9] G. Daux, "Chronique des fouilles 1964, Thasos," *BCH* 89 (1965): 947, with fig. 22. This late sixth- or early seventh-century example is much more elongated than ours, and its upper neck and mouth are quite dissimilar.

[10] I wish to thank John Boardman for providing me with many photographs of unpublished finds from seventh-century Emporio on Chios mentioned here and below.

[11] Hayes, *DOP* 22 (1968): 215, type 8.

[12] The best published parallel is from Histria (*MCA* 7: 240, fig. 11, bottom right); Joan du Plat Taylor brought this to my attention, ending a long and fruitless search. Published sixth-century examples from the Black Sea region are numerous, but usually have a funnel-shaped mouth (Scorpan, *Pontica* 6 [1973]: fig. 36, no. 3, on p. 314 [Sacidava], and fig. 7 on p. 199 [Tomis]; I. Barnea, "L'Incendie de la cité de Dinogetia au VIᵉ siècle," *Dacia*, n.s. 10 [1966]: fig. 5, no. 7, on p. 242, and fig. 12, no. 7 on p. 251 [Dinogetia]).

[13] Radulescu, *Pontica* 6 (1973): 205, 207.

[14] Such identification by analysis has been done with Bronze Age pottery (H. W. Catling, "Minoan and Mycenaean Pottery: Composition and Provenance," *Archaeometry* 6 [1963]; H. W. Catling et al., "Correlations between Composition and Provenance of Mycenaean and Minoan Pottery," *BSA* 58 [1963]).

[15] Radulescu, *Pontica* 6 (1973): 193ff.; V. Canarache, *The Mosaic-Floored Edifice of Tomi*; and V. Canarache, *The Archaeological Museum of Constantza* (the Canarache titles are guidebooks published by the Regional Archaeological Museum of Dobrudga).

[16] Radulescu, *Pontica* 6 (1973): 197–198, gives the contents.

[17] Ibid., pp. 201–205.

[18] G. Bass, "Turkey: Survey for Shipwrecks, 1973," *IJNA* 3 (1974): 335, 337; H. Frost, *Under the Mediterranean*, pp. 214–221, pl. 28; and J. N. Green, "Cape Andreas," *IJNA* 1 (1972): 190.

linings have been found elsewhere in amphoras which carried wine or olive oil; such a lining is found also in oinochoai from the ship's galley.[19] In estimating the total weight of the cargo of the Yassi Ada ship, we assumed that all of the amphoras were full of wine during the ship's final voyage, an assumption strengthened by the discovery that nine of sixteen type 2 amphoras raised and inspected in 1980 contained grape seeds (see p. 29 and Appendix E); regrettably, no type 1 amphoras were found remaining on the seabed, and thus their contents can not now be guessed. Because almost no other ancient amphoras had yielded grape seeds, the sole exception known to me being a single amphora from the Roman wreck at Giens, we initially questioned the Yassi Ada seeds as evidence of wine, thinking they might instead be remains of raisins. The lack of grape seeds from amphoras excavated earlier, however, now seems due to the lack of close inspection of amphora contents by archaeologists; we recently have found grape seeds in Knidian wine amphoras raised from a Hellenistic shipwreck at Serçe Liman, Turkey; from Byzantine amphoras excavated on an eleventh-century wreck at Serçe Liman; and from single amphoras raised from two other Byzantine shipwrecks during a survey in 1980. Clearly we need to know more about ancient vintages and shipping to understand the large number of seeds presumably present in most ancient wine, at least during its transport.

There is, on the other hand, some slight evidence —the paucity of stoppers—that not all of the Yassi Ada amphoras were full when the ship sank. From such in-

complete evidence several suggestions for the nature of the Yassi Ada cargo may be presented:

1. The ship carried a cargo of wine from one or more undetermined vineyards, using amphoras from an unknown center, and the entire cargo was lost on the reef at Yassi Ada.

2. The ship carried a cargo of wine from one or more undetermined vineyards, and this wine was sold at ports along the route, with empty amphoras being kept on board.

3. The ship carried a cargo of empty amphoras from an undetermined port; most or all of the amphoras had been used previously for wine, and they had not been cleaned thoroughly of dregs.

Because other data from the voyage must be considered, the first possibility is most acceptable; the amount of money on board was not large enough to have purchased a cargo, suggesting that the merchant had not yet sold a great deal. At the same time, we must consider the possibility that the merchant escaped from the sinking ship with most of his profits, making the second and third possibilities more reasonable.

In conclusion, we must state that at this moment it is impossible to guess the place of origin of the amphoras or of their contents. As will be seen from other evidence, the ship seems to have sailed from north to south on its last voyage, making a northern provenance probable for any wine involved. But this deduction does not necessarily point to a northern origin for the amphoras.

## Galley Wares

With the exception of a pitcher (P 17) found far forward in the cargo, where it had either floated or had been left by a crew member, all of the cooking, eating, and pantry wares were found in the galley area of the wreck.

### GLAZED WARES

P 1.   Bowl.                                        Inv. No. W3-43.
       Figs. 8-9 and 8-11; Wreck Plan V*d*.        EW (6A).
       Max. h. 0.056; max. diam. 0.101; base diam. 0.045.
       Complete. Medium fine, reddish brown fabric. Interior and top of rim (a flange cut to form two sets of three petallike protrusions) coated with or-

ange to grey green crackled glaze through which numerous small pits in the fabric are visible. Tops of flange segments incised with "thumbnail" impressions, all pointing in the same direction and circumscribing rim in two rows.

A similar bowl, with cutaway flange and orange brown glaze, is represented by a fragment from the seventh-century deposit at Saraçhane in Istanbul.[20]

P 2.   Two-handled bowl.                            Inv. No. W3-235.
       Figs. 8-9 and 8-11; Wreck Plan V*d*.        PI (8B).
       H. 0.104; max. diam. 0.135; oval mouth diams. 0.109 × 0.095.
       Complete. Fairly fine, brownish buff fabric with

---

[19] No sample of the resin was removed for analysis and identification; it would be interesting to learn which, if any, of the resins stored in the Mosaic-Floored Edifice of Tomis were meant for the aromatic lining of amphoras and wine pitchers. Resin was heated in a crude cooking pot (P 56, discussed below) for some shipboard use. That reused amphoras received new resin coatings from time to time is known (Winlock and Crum, *Monastery of Epiphanius*, I, 79).

[20] Hayes, *DOP* 22 (1968): 205, no. 8, with fig. on p. 204. Hayes notes: "Cf. Robert B. K. Stevenson, *The Great Palace of the Byzantine Emperors* I (Oxford 1947) pl. 15.31 (with ref. [p. 34] to similar example in Stage I)."

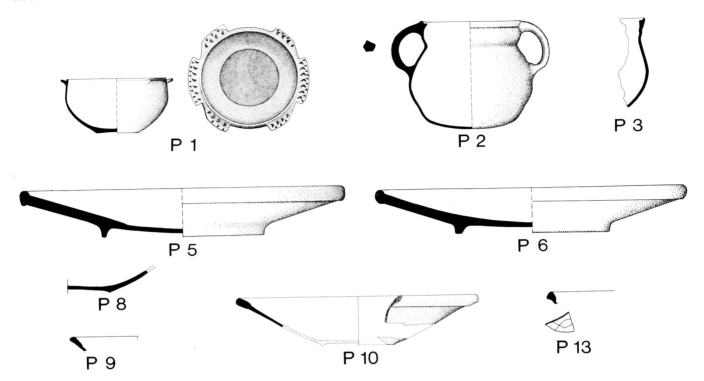

FIG. 8-9. Glazed bowls, plates, and dishes. approx. 1:4. *SWK*

browner, poorly fired surface crackling in spots.

Interior coated with crackled green brown glaze. Wheel marks form rough spiral in center of interior and are visible on exterior. Round base slightly set off by bulge at lower part of body. Shallow groove just below lip, which is attached to neck in a way that leaves a ledge inside. Handles, from just above maximum body diameter to rim, are irregular in section: one is almost oval, with central rib, the other being nearly trapezoidal.

This type of bowl is represented by many fragments at Saraçhane from the seventh century,[21] and it occurred also in stage I of the excavation of the Great Palace in Istanbul.[22]

P 3.   Bowl or jar.        Inv. Nos. W3-507 and W3-518.
Fig. 8-9; Wreck Plan V*d*.    NI (9B) and EM (7C).
Pres. h. 0.09; est. mouth diam. approx. 0.08.
Six sherds, of which only one (NI) appears in Fig. 8-9, possibly from the same bowl with internally ledged rim, on the basis of similarity of fabric and brown to golden honey yellow crackled glaze, with traces of green, on their interior; none of the sherds join.

Wheel marks appear as a raised spiral on the interior center of the plain rounded base (EM) and as an incised spiral on the exterior. No traces

of handles are preserved, but the vessel may have had one or two, since it closely resembles P 2 and even more closely resembles a Saraçhane piece in profile.[23]

P 4.   Bowl or jar.                    Inv. No. W3-519.
Not illustrated; Wreck Plan V*d*.        MCK (9B).
Seven sherds, not joining, with hazel (greenish brown) glaze on interior surfaces. Base (fragment MCK) like that of P 3.

These four or possibly five or even more vessels (the sherds of P 3 and P 4 represent a minimum of two bowls, by base fragments, but may, in fact, represent more) may offer the earliest well-dated examples of Byzantine lead-glazed pottery, perhaps manufactured in Constantinople.[24]

There was an additional glazed sherd (inventoried as MBP, no. W3-510) on the wreck, but its bright green, somewhat iridescent crackled glaze disturbed us at the time of its discovery; we were virtually certain that it was not Byzantine. In 1967, during the excavation of the neighboring fourth-century Roman wreck,[25] we found joining fragments from what proved to be an open bowl. From its position on that wreck we are certain that all of the pieces came from a late-sixteenth-century

[21] Hayes, *DOP* 22 (1968): 203–205, no. 1, with fig. on p. 204.
[22] Stevenson, *Great Palace* I, 34–35, pl. 15.5. Stage I is dated by two seventh-century coins.

[23] Hayes, *DOP* 22 (1968): 203–205, no. 1, with fig. on p. 204.
[24] Ibid., p. 216. For a full discussion of the origins of medieval glazed pottery, see D. Whitehouse, "The Medieval Glazed Pottery of Lazio," *BSR* 35 (1967): 42–48.
[25] G. F. Bass and F. H. van Doorninck, Jr., "A Fourth-Century

wreck lying between the Byzantine and Roman ships and partly over the Roman ship; that latest wreck was dated by a coin of Philip II of Spain (1556–1598). This overlapping shows the possibility of instrusive material entering even such closed deposits as those offered by shipwrecks; yet the amount of contamination on the Byzantine wreck must be considered exceedingly small, for almost all its artifacts, with the exception of the cargo and the ship's fittings, were found in the galley area; artifacts found outside that restricted area are more suspect.

## PLATES AND DISHES

P 5.   Plate.                              Inv. No. W3-60.
Figs. 8-9 and 8-11; Wreck Plan V*a*.        PK (7A).
Diam. 0.33; base diam. 0.168; h. 0.05.
Complete. Reddish ochre fabric with some red and white grit, probably slipped originally with dark red.

The bottom of the interior is stepped down slightly from the sides, giving a profile similar to that of Hayes's African Red Slip Ware, form 105[26] (= Late Roman B Ware, Antioch 802),[27] which he dates from about 580 to some time after 660. The rim, however, is more like the rims of Antioch 805, rounded above and below;[28] these rims, also in Late Roman B Ware, are more usually found on deeper dishes.

P 6.   Plate.                              Inv. No. W3-61.
Fig. 8-9; Wreck Plan V*a*.                 QR (7/8A).
Diam. 0.317; base diam. 0.157; h. 0.052.
Complete. Reddish ochre fabric, with part of original dark red slip preserved.

The interior of the plate, from rim to rim, is a continuous curve, unlike P 5; the ring base is the same height as that of P 5 (0.015) but is a bit thicker. The rim does not extend downward as much as that of P 5.

P 7.   Plate.                              Not inventoried.
Not illustrated; Wreck Plan V*a*. QA(?) + FW (7A).
Diam. 0.323; base diam. 0.162; h. 0.048.
Two joining fragments. Reddish ochre fabric with dark red slip.

P 8.   Plate.                              Inv. No. W3-498.
Fig. 8-9.                                  (?).
Sherd of base of a Red Ware plate.

P 9.   Dish.                               Inv. No. W3-494.
Fig. 8-9.                                  VI (8B).
Est. diam. approx. 0.22; est. base diam. 0.10.
Two sherds, the fragments of a rim and base of similar red ware, very possibly from the same deep dish or bowl.

This was most probably a Late Roman C Ware dish with flat, elongated rim (= Antioch 949*y*)[29] of the type which Hayes states was relatively uncommon at Saraçhane (only thirty to forty examples from more than thirteen hundred sherds); he dates the form to between about 550 and 600–620 for the most part.[30] The Yassi Ada example has a slight ring base.

P 10.  Dish.                              Inv. No. W3-497.
Fig. 8-9; Wreck Plan V*a*. EO (8A) and MBM (9B).
Est. diam. 0.23; est. base diam. 0.10.
Two rim fragments and one base fragment, not joining but of same red fabric; a number of much darker sherds probably also belong but have been badly discolored by large amounts of iron adhering to them.

Same type as P 9. The same type appears at Histria from about the same period.[31]

P 11.  Dish.                              Inv. No. W3-495.
Not illustrated.                           (?).
Est. diam. 0.26.
Rim fragment. Much thicker than P 9 and P 10, but with profile like that of P 10.

P 12.  Dish.                              Inv. No. W3-493.
Not illustrated; Wreck Plan V*a*.
                          BI (7B) and AO (7B).
Est. diam. 0.25.
Two fragments of rim similar to that of P 9.

P 13.  Dish.                              Inv. No. W3-499.
Fig. 8-9. WO (6B′), ZO (6C′), and DD (air-lifted).
Est. diam. 0.26; est. base diam. 0.10.
Several sherds of similar red fabric except for rim, which is fired yellow.

The heavy rim and more substantial ring base than that of P 9 suggest that this was a dish or bowl of a Late Roman C Ware type found commonly at Saraçhane[32] (= Antioch 947, 949*a-k*).[33] The thickened rim extends farther into the interior than onto the exterior, however—more like that of P 9. One body sherd is incised with a fish(?) pattern.

---

Shipwreck at Yassi Ada," *AJA* 75 (1971): 37; uncleaned coin misdated.

[26] J. W. Hayes, *Late Roman Pottery*, pp. 167, 169, lists the Yassi Ada plate as no. 14; Hayes, *DOP* 22 (1968): 208, no. 40, with fig. E on p. 209.

[27] F. O. Waagé, *Antioch-on-the-Orontes*, vol. IV, part 1, *Ceramics and Islamic Coins*, p. 47, no. 802, with pls. VII, 802*f* and VIII, 802*k*, especially for step-down floor.

[28] Ibid., p. 47, no. 805, with pl. VIII, 805*k*.

[29] Ibid., p. 53, with pl. XI, 949*y*.

[30] Hayes, *DOP* 22 (1968): 208–211, esp. nos. 62–64, with figs. on p. 210.

[31] An example was shown to me by Dr. Alex. Suceveanu during my visit to the Histria excavations.

[32] Hayes, *DOP* 22 (1968): 208, no. 59, with fig. on p. 209.

[33] Waagé, *Antioch* IV, part 1, 53, with pl. XI.

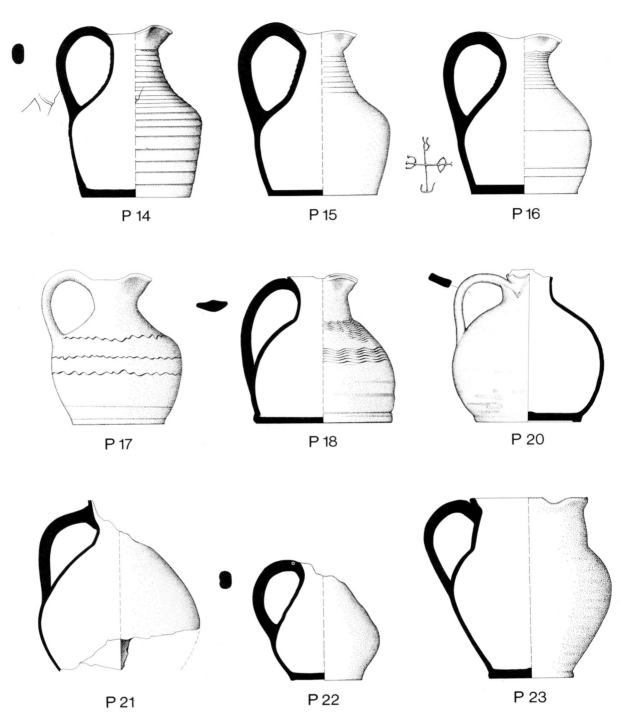

FIG. 8-10. Pitchers. approx. 1:4. *SWK*

## PITCHERS

P 14. Oinochoe.                          Inv. No. W3-44.
      Figs. 8-10 and 8-11; Wreck Plan V*d*.        PU (7B).
      Max. h. 0.204; max. diam. 0.152; base diam. 0.127.
      Complete. Orange ochre, somewhat coarse and
      sandy fabric, partly encrusted on exterior. Interior
      coated with resin.

      Body swells upward from flat base to maximum

diameter at shoulder. Handle, oval in section, and
with ridge down center, between shoulder and
trefoil pinched lip. Body and neck decorated by
nineteen incised horizontal lines which become
more closely spaced and form a "stepped" surface
on shoulder and neck. Scratched lines on shoulder
may be accidental; opposite side of shoulder too

badly encrusted to be cleaned without endangering surface.

This oinochoe resembles in shape an early-seventh-century example from the Athenian Agora, but the two are not really parallels.[34]

P 15. Oinochoe.　　　　　　　Inv. No. W3-305.
Fig. 8-10; Wreck Plan V*d*.　　　MBU (9B).
Max h. 0.21; max. diam. 0.156; base diam. 0.124.
Complete. Brownish fabric. Resin coating inside.

Very similar to P 14 except for fabric and undecorated body and shoulder.

P 16. Oinochoe.　　　　　　　Inv. No. W3-306.
Figs. 8-10 and 8-11; Wreck Plan V*d*.　　MBV (9B).
H. 0.19; max. diam. 0.154; base diam. 0.125.
Complete. Brown fabric, darkened over most of surface. Resin coating in bottom half.

Similar to P 15 except for squatter body, with shoulder less pronounced and lower and grooves on neck that are more numerous and closer together. Removal of concretion for photography in 1981 revealed a monogram incised on the shoulder. Capacity to point of minimum diameter on the neck is 1.30 l; capacity to base of flaring mouth is 1.34 l.

P 17. Oinochoe.　　　　　　　Inv. No. W3-154.
Figs. 8-10 and 8-11; Wreck Plan V*d*. KMN (4A/B).
Max. h. 0.195; max. diam. 0.15; base diam. 0.104.
Complete. Orangish fabric, with most of original surface missing. Resin coating inside neck and body.

Squatter body than that of P 15 (its high-swung handle alone makes their heights similar), with slightly concave base. Three widely spaced horizontal wavy lines incised just above and below shoulder, and two straight lines above base.

P 18. Oinochoe.　　　　　　　Inv. No. W3-230.
Figs. 8-10 and 8-11; Wreck Plan V*d*.　　OI (7B/C).
H. 0.178; base diam. 0.158.
Complete. Orange brown, slightly micaceous fabric with white grit; surface brown. Interior coated with resin, which has spilled over top of handle near lip.

Flat base, 0.01 thick, set off from body by rough groove. Body curves out slightly from this groove and then curves back gently to neck. Top of neck flares out, but is separated from overhanging rim by very shallow groove, 0.0025 wide, which rises more vertically than neck. Wide strap handle runs from maximum body diameter to top of neck but does not rise above rim; rounded ridge runs down its center. Handle is not well smoothed at either point of attachment. Two irregular combed patterns, each approx. 0.025 wide, on shoulder; where comb has been lifted and put back down, lines cross and make the band much wider in places.

A very similar pitcher of light-colored fabric, missing all of its mouth and the top of its handle, is from seventh-century Emporio on Chios;[35] the minor differences are that it has a third band of wavy lines lower down on its body, the lower handle attachment is slightly higher, and the base is smaller in relation to the rest of the body and is not set off. Although the upper handle attachment is not preserved, it should be noted that other handles on oinochoai at Emporio do not seem to rise above the rims, as on P 18.

P 19. Oinochoe.　　　　　　　Not inventoried.
Not illustrated.　　　　　　　　　　(?).
Three fragments (two joining) of a pitcher almost identical to P 18 in size, decoration, and fabric.

P 20. Pitcher.　　　　　　　　In Izmir Museum.
Figs. 8-10 and 8-11.　　Raised before excavation.[36]
Pres. h. 0.182; max. diam. 0.172; base diam. 0.118.
Mouth missing. Brown to dark purplish brown fabric. Possible traces of resin inside, but interior is not completely coated.

This pitcher differs from those previously described in that it has a low ring base and an upper handle attachment on the neck instead of the rim; further, its decoration is dissimilar. The curve of its body is more similar to that of the pitcher from Emporio, just described, than is that of P 18.

P 21. Pitcher.　　　　　　　　Inv. No. W3-338.
Figs. 8-10 and 8-11; Wreck Plan V*d*.　　MCI (9B).
Pres. h. 0.21; max. diam. 0.183.
All of base and mouth missing. Brown fabric with white grit. No trace of resin inside.

P 22. Pitcher.　　　　　　　　Inv. No. W3-62.
Figs. 8-10 and 8-11; Wreck Plan V*d*.　　NS (7B).
Pres. h. 0.145; base diam. 0.079.
Most of mouth missing. Pinkish (at bottom) to yellowish buff, somewhat coarse fabric with some brick red and white grit; partly encrusted outside and inside. Coated with resin up to neck.

Minimal ring base. Very low shoulder, from which handle (oval in section) rises to mouth.

P 23. Oinochoe.　　　　　　　Inv. No. W3-115.
Figs. 8-10 and 8-11; Wreck Plan V*d*. XM (7B/C).
H. 0.215; max. diam. 0.191; base diam. 0.095.
Complete, but badly eroded by sea organisms.

[34] Robinson, *Athenian Agora* V, 122, no. N7, with pl. 35.

[35] Boardman, supra n. 10.
[36] Frost, *Under the Mediterranean*, p. 173.

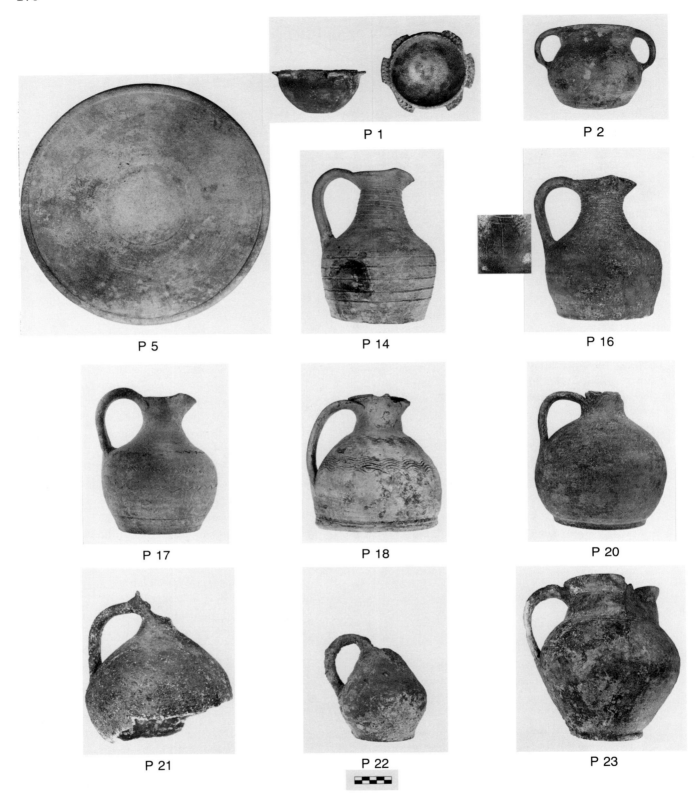

P 1

P 2

P 5

P 14

P 16

P 17

P 18

P 20

P 21

P 22

P 23

FIG. 8-11. Glazed bowls, plate, dishes, and pitchers.

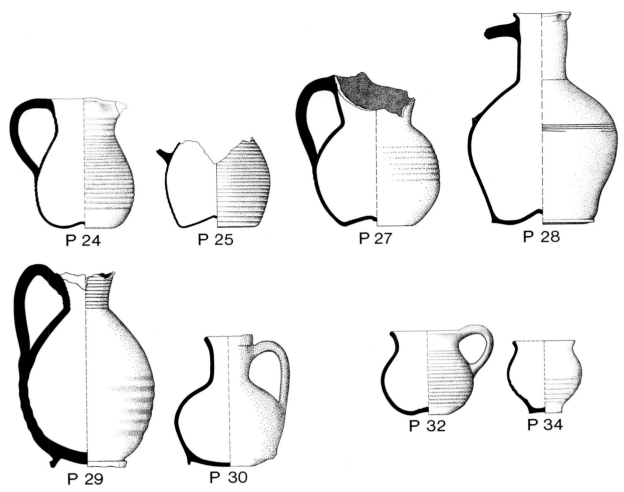

Fig. 8-12. Pitchers and cups. 1:4. *SWK*

Coarse, sandy fabric, not well fired; yellowish brown, with nearly pink core, darkened to grey over most of surface. No traces of resin. (This item was inadvertently inventoried twice, the second time with inventory no. W3-326.)

This is unusually fat for an oinochoe, with a mouth almost as large as the vessel's body. The very slightly concave base is set off from the rest of the body. Wide handle, with shallow central groove, runs from just below shoulder to a point on the wide neck just below mouth.

This piece slightly resembles an example from the Athenian Agora that has been restored with a round rather than trefoil mouth,[37] but the upper handle attachment, base, and fabric all differ.

[37] Robinson, *Athenian Agora* V, 122, no. N3, with pl. 35.

P 24.  Oinochoe.                    Inv. No. W3-307.
Figs. 8-12 and 8-14.                    MBI (8A).
H. 0.147; max. diam. 0.11.
Almost half of mouth and part of body missing. Brownish fabric with grey core.

Concave base with crude button in center. Egg-shaped body, with no neck, flares out to form trefoil mouth. Flat handle from lip to just above maximum body diameter. Rounded horizontal ridges around body from just above base to point at which mouth is pinched.

This piece is similar to examples from Chios[38] and Samos,[39] but they are not perfect parallels.

[38] Boardman, supra n. 10.
[39] H. P. Isler, "Heraion von Samos: Eine frühbyzantinische Zisterne," *AthMitt* 84 (1969): 207 (K3810), with pl. 89, no. 2.

P 25. Oinochoe (?). Inv. No. W3-504.
Fig. 8-12. (?).
Pres. h. 0.10; base diam. 0.09.
Upper part of handle and body, including all of mouth, missing. Crumbling and flaky light brown buff fabric.

Concave base with button in center. Horizontal ribbing begins just at base. It is not certain that this is part of a pitcher, but it may well have been broken from an oinochoe similar in type to P 24.

P 26. Oinochoe (?). Inv. No. W3-513.
Not illustrated. (?).
Pres. h. 0.104.
Fragments of body and one handle attachment preserved. Orange brown fabric.

Seems to be part of a vessel similar to P 24 and P 25.

P 27. Oinochoe. Inv. No. W3-209.
Figs. 8-12 and 8-14; Wreck Plan V*d*. DO (7C).
Pres. h. 0.18; max. diam. 0.14; base diam. 0.085.
Part of neck and most of mouth missing. Coarse, dark brown fabric with white grit; surface pitted and flaking off in places, half covered with concretion. No traces of resin.

Concave base with button in center. Handle, oval in section, from center of globular body to just beneath lip. Preserved part of upper neck shows pinching, probably the start of a trefoil mouth. Seven horizontal grooves in band around center of body, and four or five similar grooves on neck; the latter appear inside as well.

This slightly resembles an oinochoe from the seventh-century level at Emporio on Chios.[40]

P 28. Oinochoe. Inv. No. W3-323.
Figs. 8-12 and 8-14; Wreck Plan V*d*. (8/9B).
H. 0.236; max. diam. 0.163; base diam. 0.115.
Most of handle and parts of neck missing. Light yellowish brown fabric. Traces of resin inside at bottom.

Concave base with raised button in center; body wall extends down over base, forming a slight ridge. Just below lower handle attachment on round shoulder, two to four lines incised roughly around vessel. Neck is unusually tall and cylindrical, flaring out slightly to form pinched trefoil mouth. Handle is oval in section, with large central groove.

P 29. Pitcher. Inv. No. W3-221.
Figs. 8-12 and 8-14; Wreck Plan V*d*. KGL (8B).

Max. pres. h. (to handle top) 0.228; max. diam. 0.151.
All of mouth missing. Light brown fabric, loaded with fine mica particles and with a soapy surface. Light coating of resin inside bottom half.

Oval body extends into ring base. Broad, low wheel marks on body become horizontal grooves on neck.

This item is similar to a pitcher from Histria, dated to the sixth century; on that, however, the maximum diameter is lower on the body.[41] John Hayes has suggested to me that the Yassi Ada example may be from the Ephesus region,[42] and he compares it to a jug in Vienna (Kunsthist. Mus. IV.3065) also with lower maximum diameter; the Vienna pitcher further has a higher ring base. Fabric seems to be identical on both pieces. A pitcher of the same family, but with a different base, comes from a Byzantine cistern on Samos.[43]

P 30. Jug. Inv. No. W3-92.
Figs. 8-12 and 8-14; Wreck Plan V*d*. RM (7B).
H. 0.155; max. diam. 0.125; base diam. 0.10.
Complete. Yellow ochre, coarse fabric blackened over most of surface and discolored by encrustation. No trace of resin.

Convex bottom with ridge which is not high enough to serve as an effective ring base. Neck tapers outward slightly from piriform body to form a plain round mouth. Handle, oblong in section, between shoulder and neck.

P 31. Oinochoe. Inv. No. W3-121.
Fig. 8-14; Wreck Plan V*d*. EH (8B).
Max. pres. h. 0.097; w. of mouth 0.084.
Only trefoil mouth, more tightly pinched than on other examples, preserved. Reddish brown fabric, heavily concreted.

### CUPS

P 32. One-handled cup. Inv. No. W3-84.
Figs. 8-12 and 8-14; Wreck Plan V*a*. ABR (6A).
H. 0.09; max. diam. 0.103; mouth diam. 0.083.
Complete. Medium fine, orange buff to grey fabric, with traces of redder surface surviving.

Concave bottom. Globular body, with short lip. Handle, nearly circular in section, rises above mouth from mid-body height and then curves down to join lip. Body decorated with sixteen horizontal ribs.

---

[40] Boardman, supra n. 10.

[41] *Histria* I, 460, and fig. 392 on p. 463.
[42] Personal communication of April 20, 1970.
[43] Isler, *AthMitt* 84 (1969): 207 (K3811), with pl. 90, no. 1.

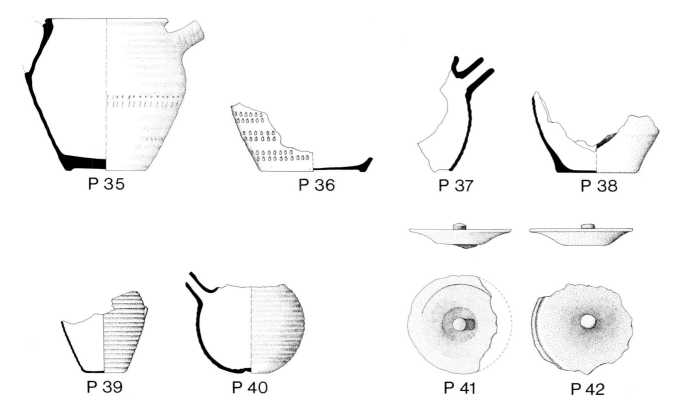

FIG. 8-13. Tube-spouted jars and lids. approx. 1:4. *SWK*

P 33. Cup fragment. Inv. No. W3-514.
Not illustrated; Wreck Plan V*a*. JI (8B).
Pres. h. 0.07.

Part of lip, shoulder, and lower handle attachment, in brownish fabric, from vessel similar and perhaps identical to P 32 in shape. (This item was found in a pile of sand swept from farther upslope on the wreck, and it may have been displaced.)

P 34. Cup fragments. Not inventoried.
Figs. 8-12 and 8-14; Wreck Plan V*a*. OB (9A).
H. 0.084; max. diam. 0.082; mouth diam. 0.07; base diam. 0.036.

Of two fragments, one (OB) includes entire base; other, discovered in sherd box in 1977, includes one-quarter of rim. The fragments do not join, but their profiles have an overlap of 0.025, which includes top three of six horizontal grooves on outer surface. It is not known if the cup had one or more handles, but a very similar example in the Bodrum Museum (not from the shipwreck) does not have handles.

### TUBE-SPOUTED JARS

P 35. Spouted jar. Inv. No. W3-81.
Figs. 8-13 and 8-14; Wreck Plan V*a*. HW (7B).

H. 0.162; max. diam. 0.172; mouth diam. 0.128; base diam. 0.083.

Mended from several fragments; parts of body and most of handle missing. Somewhat coarse, orange ochre fabric.

Low ring base. Hole cut through shoulder wall, and tubular spout (0.025 in diam.) attached in it, but not perfectly centered, at an upward angle of about 45° from the vertical. Opposite spout was a wide handle. Small ledge inside mouth. Body covered with shallow horizontal grooves, perhaps intentionally. Two incised lines, the highest about 0.07 from the bottom, are crossed by short, vertical incisions with points above the upper line.

This jar may be based on metal prototypes, such as the silver spouted cup from Room 1 of Tomb 14 at Ballana.[44] It finds its closest ceramic parallels at Emporio on Chios, but the fabric does not appear in photographs to be similar.[45] Although there is an example from Emporio with the vertical handle opposite the spout, as at Yassi

[44] Emery and Kirwan, *Royal Tombs* I, 277, no. 421; II, pl. 64*E* and *F*; W. B. Emery, *Nubian Treasure: An Account of the Discoveries at Ballana and Qustul*, pl. 24*b*.
[45] Boardman, supra n. 10.

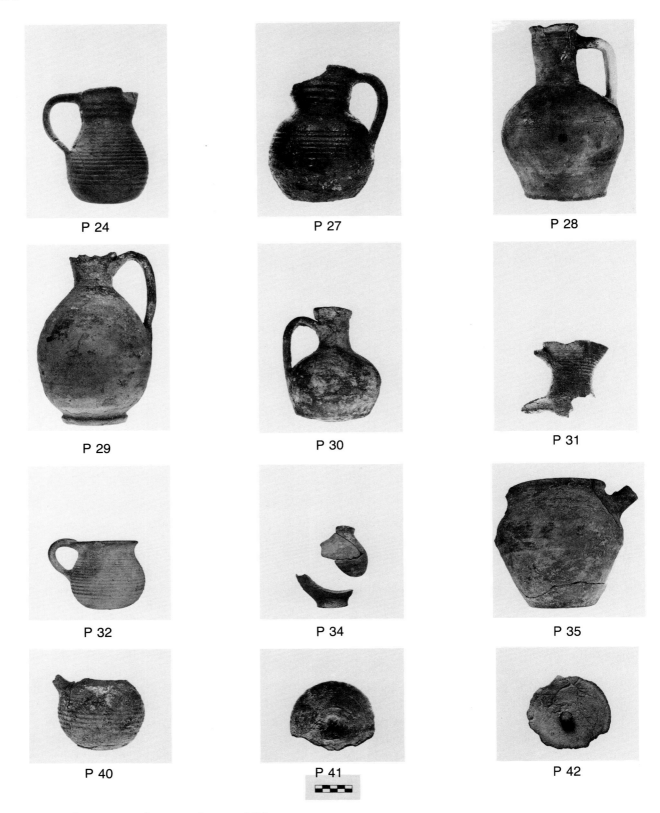

FIG. 8-14. Pitchers, cups, tube-spouted jars, and lids.

Ada, the example whose body, rim, and spout are most similar has handles perpendicular to the spout on opposite sides of the jar. Even less similar, but worth mentioning, is the later spouted jar from the excavations of the Great Palace in Istanbul.[46] The same family of tubular spouted jars is represented on Samos.[47]

P 36. Base fragment.      Inv. No. W3-517.
Fig. 8-13.      KO (8A or 8B).
Pres. h. 0.067; base diam. 0.11.
Brown fabric.

Low ring base with rouletting in three horizontal double rows on preserved portion of lower body. Seems very similar to the bottom of P 35 and may well be from another spouted jar.

P 37. Tube-spouted jar fragment.    Not inventoried.
Fig. 8-13; Wreck Plan V*a*.    MBR (9B).
This was one of a few fragments from the excavation that were drawn but could not later be located in the sherd boxes. Thus, its fabric was not recorded, and its dimensions are known only from the scale drawing. It was obviously quite similar to P 35.

P 38. Base fragment.      Inv. No. W3-360.
Fig. 8-13; Wreck Plan V*a*.    MCV (8B).
Max. pres. h. 0.084; base diam. 0.085.
Part of base and lower body only. Very flaky, fine fabric with light grey core and pinkish buff surface.

Most of center of base missing, but it seems to have been from a flat-bottomed vessel with shallow horizontal grooves starting about 0.05 above base. It is far from certain that this is part of a tube-spouted jar, but it bears some resemblance to P 35.

P 39. Jar fragment.      Inv. No. W3-501.
Fig. 8-13; Wreck Plan V*a*.    NO (7B).
Pres. h. 0.088; base diam. 0.045.
Base, body, lower handle attachment, and part of shoulder only. Flaking, reddish brown ware.

Again, it is not certain that this fragment is from a spouted jar, but its shape suggests that it is; the fabric and ribbing, however, more closely resemble those of tube-spouted jar P 40, which has quite a different shape.

P 40. Tube-spouted jar.      Inv. No. W3-19.
Figs. 8-13 and 8-14; Wreck Plan V*a*.    AM (7B).
Max. pres. h. (to top of spout) 0.11; max. diam. 0.11.

Mouth missing. Rather fine, red orange fabric with little or no grit.

Globular body with concave base forming a whorl of grooves. Approximately fifteen well-defined ridges, more closely spaced near the top. Spout, heavily encrusted, protrudes upwards at about a 45° angle from vertical.

No complete example of this shape was found, but its globular body, slight ridging, base, spout, and, possibly fabric all resemble those of the slightly larger spouted jugs with "double" handles found at Saraçhane in Istanbul;[48] there is no trace of the handle on the Yassi Ada fragment, and no evidence of any "double" handles was noted on the shipwreck.

## LIDS

P 41. Jar lid.      Inv. No. W3-82.
Figs. 8-13 and 8-14.      (?).
Diam. 0.106.
One side missing. Orangish fabric with some fine white surface grit plus a little brick red grit; mostly darkened and discolored by encrustation.

This is like Hayes's "concave saucer-shaped lid with knob at center; rim marked off by a slight groove. Wheel made, with wire drawn base."[49] It fits the mouth of tube-spouted jar P 35 and may very well have belonged to it.

P 42. Jar lid.      Inv. No. W3-176.
Figs. 8-13 and 8-14; Wreck Plan V*a*.    KNH (6A).
Est. original diam. 0.12.
Most of rim missing. Orange brown fabric.

Similar to P 41 except that incised line on upper surface is closer to the outer edge.

## COOKING POTS AND BASIN

P 43. Two-handled pot.      Inv. No. W3-65.
Figs. 8-15 and 8-17; Wreck Plan V*a*.    DM (6A).
H. 0.178; max. diam. 0.197.
Complete. Somewhat coarse, brownish red fabric, partly blackened and encrusted.

Rounded base set off from body by slight ridge. Two handles, almost round in section but with central ribs, from just below maximum body diameter to top of shoulder; they are not absolutely vertical or symmetrically positioned. Rim slightly stepped out from body on exterior, with prominent ledge on interior.

---

[46] Stevenson, *Great Palace* I, pl. 15, no. 46.
[47] Isler, *AthMitt* 84 (1969): 207 (K3809), with pl. 89, nos. 1 and 3.

[48] Hayes, *DOP* 22 (1968): 206, no. 26, with fig. on p. 207. I should point out that Hayes (personal communication, April 20, 1970) does not agree on the close similarity.
[49] Hayes, *DOP* 22 (1968): 206, no. 31, with fig. on p. 207.

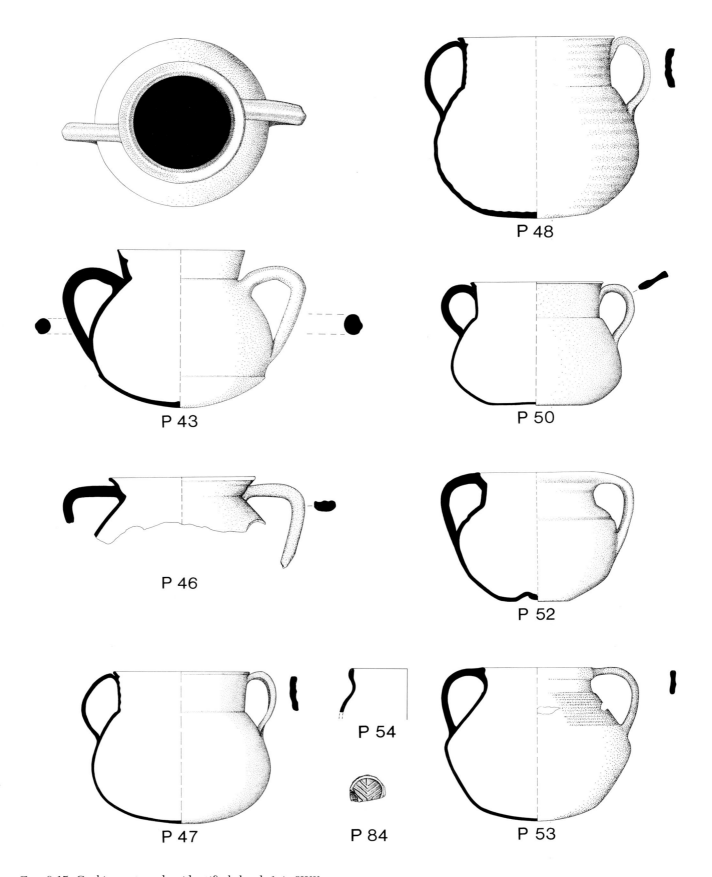

Fig. 8-15. Cooking pots and unidentified sherd. 1:4. *SWK*

John Hayes states that this is the commonest type at Saraçhane,[50] and his illustration of one offers a nearly identical piece of "intense grey ware of gritty texture. . . ."[51] Another excellent parallel, also cited by Hayes, is from Histria; only its twisted handles differ from ours.[52]

P 44. Two-handled pot. Inv. No. W3-66.
Fig. 8-14; Wreck Plan V*a*. PC (7B).
H. 0.17; max. diam. 0.216.
Rim chipped slightly in two places and bottom cracked. Somewhat coarse, brown fabric blackened over much of surface.
Nearly identical in shape to P 43.

P 45. Two-handled pot fragment. Inv. No. W3-515.
Not illustrated; Wreck Plan V*a*.
KRZ (9B) and MBY (8C).
Pres. h. 0.13; mouth diam. 0.15.
Rim, shoulder, and handles (one, MBY, not actually joining) preserved. Brown fabric.
Same shape as P 43 and P 44.

P 46. Two-handled pot fragment. Inv. No. W3-511.
Fig. 8-15; Wreck Plan V*a*. GM (7A).
Mouth diam. 0.159.
Parts of rim, shoulder, and both handles preserved. Brown fabric, fire-blackened over all of exterior including handles.
Handles rise nearly vertically from body and then turn in sharply to join pot on base of rim. Lip flares out, then up sharply, then out again more sharply than before to form an interior ledge.

P 47. Two-handled pot. Inv. No. W3-64.
Figs. 8-15 and 8-17; Wreck Plan V*a*. PQ (7B).
H. 0.173; max. diam. 0.198.
Complete except for small hole and several cracks. Somewhat coarse, brown fabric.
Round body and base with broad, vertical neck which flares out to form a short lip with interior ledge. Two broad, nearly flat handles, with shallow grooves, from shoulder to bottom of lip. Wheel marks prominent inside neck.
This piece is quite like a pot from the grave by the church at Misokampos, Samos, although that one lacks a ledge.[53]

P 48. Two-handled pot. Inv. No. W3-63.
Figs. 8-15 and 8-17; Wreck Plan V*a*. TJ (7A).
H. 0.20; max. diam. 0.216.

Complete. Somewhat coarse, brownish black fabric.
Except for larger size and lightly grooved body, this item is nearly identical to P 47.

P 49. Pot handle. Inv. No. W3-520.
Not illustrated. OA (9B).
Single dark, reddish brown handle from pot like P 47 and P 48.

P 50. Two-handled pot. Inv. No. W3-330.
Figs. 8-15 and 8-17; Wreck Plan V*a*. MCB (9B).
H. 0.132; max. diam. 0.178; mouth diam. 0.131.
Almost one-third missing. Coarse brown fabric.
Flat base and squat body, with neck set in from shoulder. Traces of rough groove inside short, splaying lip, which served to hold lid. Nearly flat handles from shoulder to middle of neck.

P 51. Pot rim. Inv. No. W3-524.
Not illustrated. Probably GO (8B).
Mouth diam. 0.082.
Rim and handle fragment.

P 52. Two-handled pot. Inv. No. W3-249.
Figs. 8-15 and 8-17; Wreck Plan V*a*. ZI (8A).
H. 0.147; max. diam. 0.175; mouth diam. 0.13.
Complete. Nearly black surface with dark grey core.
Concave base with raised button in center. Pair of shallow horizontal grooves on shoulder. Pair of flat handles, each with three shallow vertical grooves, swing out slightly from maximum body diameter and then return to join rim. No ledge inside, but lip is formed so that it can hold a lid.
An excellent parallel is from Lake Razeln, Rumania (Archaeological Museum of Constanţa No. 5423), dated to the sixth century; it is of soft, grey fabric, with the same shoulder and a concave base with "button." According to one of the excavators at Histria with whom I spoke during my brief visit to that site, the concave base with "button" is common there from the seventh century.

P 53. Two-handled pot. Inv. No. W3-116.
Figs. 8-15 and 8-17; Wreck Plan V*a*. AW (7A/B).
H. 0.172; max. diam. 0.195; mouth diam. 0.115.
Missing pieces, but profile complete. Purplish ochre fabric.
Round base below body, which is nearly in form of two truncated cones with joining bases. Slightly concave shoulder encircled by band of nine raised ridges, irregularly spaced. Plain loop handles, nearly flat in section, from shoulder to rim.[54]

---

[50] Personal communication on May 27, 1968.
[51] Hayes, *DOP* 22 (1968): 214, no. 108, with fig. H.
[52] *Histria* I, 462, with fig. 393 on p. 463, dated to the sixth century.
[53] A. M. Schneider, "Samos in frühchristlicher und byzantinischer Zeit," *AthMitt* 54 (1929): 76, 128, no. 10, with fig. 21, no. 2.

[54] Barnea, *Dacia*, n.s. 10 (1966): 253, and fig. 14, no. 1, on p. 255, illustrates a somewhat similar pot, but it is difficult to compare its pro-

P 54.  Pot fragment.                    Inv. No. W3-523.
       Fig. 8-15.                                  JO (8A).
       Pres. h. 0.048; est. mouth diam. 0.12.
       Rim fragment, similar in fabric to P 53. (From pile
       of sand swept from up slope on wreck and possibly
       not *in situ*.)

P 55.  Two-handled pot.                 Inv. No. W3-361.
       Figs. 8-16 and 8-17; Wreck Plan V*a*.      FM (7A).
       Pres. h. 0.168; max. diam. 0.23; mouth diam.
       0.155.
       Mended from many sherds; all of bottom missing.
       Purplish brown fabric.

       Depressed globular shape, perhaps like that of
       P 53. Shoulder banded by ridges. Thick handles
       between maximum diameter and rim.[55]

P 56.  Two-handled pot for heating resin.
                                        Inv. No. W3-114.
       Figs. 8-16 and 8-17; Wreck Plan V*a*.      XW (7B).
       H. 0.142; max. diam. 0.192; mouth diam. 0.172.
       Part of rim missing. Extremely coarse, dark
       brown fabric with large white grit. Mass of resin
       several centimeters thick has congealed in bottom
       and over much of interior, especially on the side
       from which it seems to have been poured.

       Flat bottom flares out in almost straight line to
       rounded shoulder which, with a reverse curve,
       forms thick, plain lip. Two and sometimes three
       incised bands visible in curve below lip. Loop
       handles rise from maximum body diameter to rim
       with shallow central grooves.

P 57.  One-handled pot.                 Inv. No. W3-21.
       Figs. 8-16 and 8-17; Wreck Plan V*a*.      CW (7A).
       H. 0.10; max. diam. 0.179; mouth diam. 0.19.
       Handle missing. Very coarse, poorly fired and
       gritty fabric; dark orange brown, fire-blackened
       over most of exterior. Flat base. Traces of single
       handle from bottom of shoulder to plain, irregu-
       lar, splaying lip.

P 58.  Two-handled pot.                 In Izmir Museum.
       Figs. 8-16 and 8-17.      Raised before excavation.
       H. 0.123; mouth diam. 0.175; base diam. 0.18.
       Dark brown fabric with orangish core.

       Round base, nearly vertical sides, and nearly
       vertical rim set out slightly from body to leave in-
       terior ledge for lid. Pair of loop handles on body.

       This pot was raised by Throckmorton and Frost

during the preliminary inspection of the wreck
before excavation, but Frost has noted its location
in the wreck on her published sketch plan (Fig.
1-4, no. 15).[56]

P 59.  Pot.                             Inv. No. W3-502.
       Fig. 8-16; Wreck Plan V*a*.               DI (7A).
       Pres. h. 0.127; est. max. diam. 0.247.
       More than half missing. Very sandy brown fabric
       with much white grit; interior completely black-
       ened.

       Round base with straight sides tapering inward
       to splaying rim; secondary rim rises nearly ver-
       tically to form an exterior ledge (for a cover?).

       John Hayes states that this shape, in a gritty in-
       tense grey fabric, is extremely common among
       the unpublished cooking wares from the seventh-
       century group at Saraçhane.[57]

P 60.  Two-handled pot.                 Inv. No. W3-503.
       Fig. 8-16; Wreck Plan V*a*.               LM (7B).
       Pres. h. 0.185; mouth diam. 0.158.
       Most of mouth, both handles, and about half of
       body preserved. Brown, gritty fabric.

       Tall, rounded body with at least three horizon-
       tal grooves just above base. Slight ledge inside
       plain, splaying lip. Pair of vertical loop handles
       from center of gently sloping shoulder to bottom
       of lip.

P 61.  Pot base.                        Inv. No. W3-355.
       Not illustrated; Wreck Plan V*a*.       MCN (10B).
       Diam. 0.122.
       Plain flat base of brown, gritty fabric.

P 62.  Basin fragment.                  Inv. No. W3-516.
       Fig. 8-16; Wreck Plan V*a*.               NW (8A).
       Pres. h. 0.095; mouth diam. 0.243.
       Half of upper half of body preserved, with other
       handle found but not joining. Coarse orangish
       ochre fabric.

       Shallow basin splays widely from unknown base
       to shoulder. Plain, nearly horizontal rim. Hori-
       zontal handles attached to shoulder rise at such an
       angle (about 45°) that they are also attached to un-
       derside of rim, leaving only a very tiny opening
       visible.

P 63.  Basin or pot handle.             Inv. No. W3-522.
       Not illustrated.                          YO (5B').
       Horizontal loop handle, tilted up at about 45°
       angle.

P 64.  Pot handle.                      Inv. No. W3-521.
       Not illustrated.                               (?).

---

file because the photograph has been cut out and mounted. See also
H. W. Catling, "An Early Byzantine Pottery Factory at Dhiorios in
Cyprus," *Levant* 4 (1972): 45, fig. 27, P185.

[55] Cf. Catling, *Levant* 4 (1972): 45, fig. 27, for Cypriot examples
from the same "family."

[56] Frost, *Under the Mediterranean*, pp. 166–167, figs. 33 and 34,
no. 15.

[57] Personal communication of April 20, 1970.

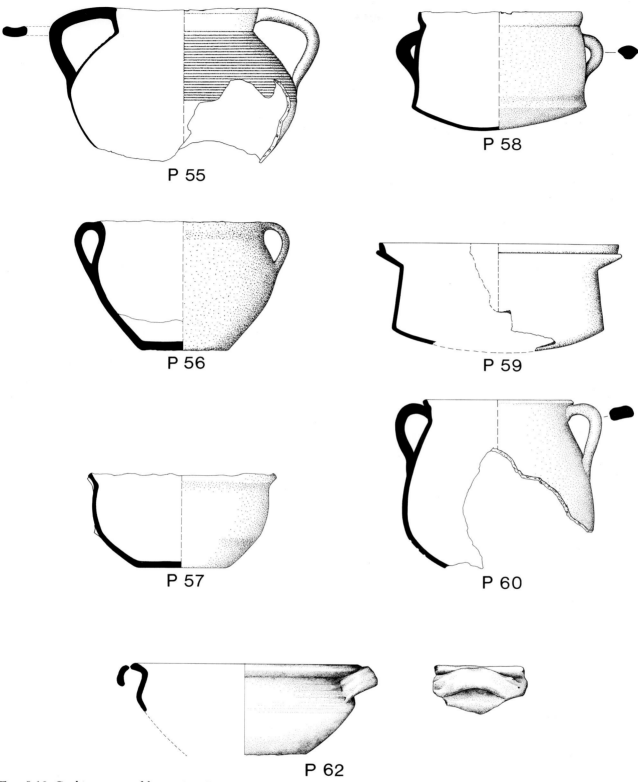

P 55

P 58

P 56

P 59

P 57

P 60

P 62

FIG. 8-16. Cooking pots and basin. 1:4. *SWK*; P 62, *GG*

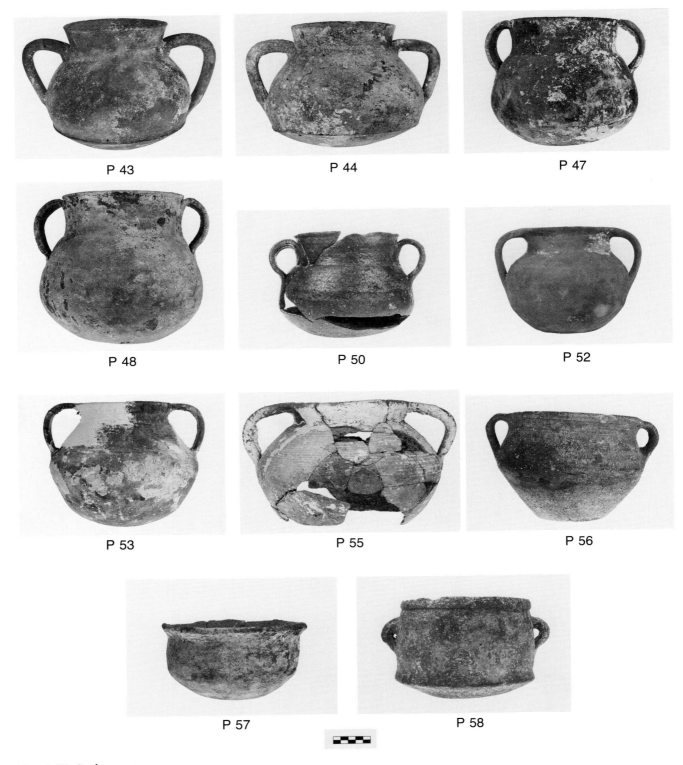

FIG. 8-17. Cooking pots.

Horizontal loop handle of brown buff, flaky fabric.

### WINE THIEF

P 65.   Wine thief.                             Inv. No. W3-67.
Figs. 8-18 and 8-22; Wreck Plan V*f*.      KW (8C).
Pres. h. 0.41; max. diam. 0.145.
Bottom of tube missing. Somewhat coarse, brownish fabric.

Globular body with tubes above and below; lower, longer tube (pres. l. 0.189) tapers to an unknown end; upper, shorter tube forms neck to plain, thickened rim of small diameter. Single vertical handle, flat inside and rounded outside, runs between shoulder and top of neck.

This item is just like the modern wine thief, or pipette, used for drawing liquid from a closed container. The lower tube is thrust into a barrel (or amphora) of wine, and the user's thumb is placed over the wine thief's small mouth to create a vacuum and hold wine in the lower tube when it is withdrawn from the container; removing the thumb from the small mouth allows the liquid to flow out of the bottom into a pitcher or other vessel. To fill the globular body, either the amphoras were tipped onto their sides or the user sucked wine up into the pipette before placing his thumb over the top. Similar pipettes may be seen used by lemonade vendors in Turkey today. The only parallels from antiquity of which I am aware are from shipwrecks—one from the sixth-century Marzamemi Church Wreck off Sicily[58] and the other netted on a shipwreck of unknown date by a sponge dragger (now Bodrum Museum No. 398). It is possible that the use of such pipettes on ancient ships allowed the use of globular amphoras which, lacking bases or knobs, are extremely unwieldy to handle and pour from.

The wine thief's present capacity is 1.24 l. If we assume that the original capacity was the same as that of P 16, we must restore approximately 5 to 10 cm additional length to the broken lower end. It would then compare favorably with the dimensions of the nearly identical Bodrum Museum No. 398.

### PANTRY WARES (STORAGE JARS)

P 66.   Amphora.                              Inv. No. W3-70.

Figs. 8-18 and 8-22; Wreck Plan V*d*.     AFQ (6C).
H. 0.43; max. diam. 0.08; mouth diam. 0.06.
Complete. Somewhat coarse, reddish brown fabric partly blackened by lime deposits.

Long, cylindrical body with pointed base and slight tapering shoulders. Small handles between shoulder and heavy lip.

Although the Yassi Ada example is comparatively small, similar "carrot-shaped" amphoras appear in late-sixth-century and seventh-century deposits at Saraçhane,[59] Histria,[60] and Emporio (where one was also netted in the sea).[61]

P 67.   Alabastron.                        In Izmir Museum.
Figs. 8-18 and 8-22      Raised before excavation.
H. 0.448; max. diam. 0.083.
Complete. Reddish brown to yellow buff fabric, somewhat coarser than that of P 66.

Except for lack of handles, this jar is identical to P 66. It was raised from the shipwreck during the earlier investigations by Throckmorton and Frost, and its position is noted on Frost's sketch plan (Fig. 1-4, no. 11).[62]

P 68.   Pointed amphora or alabastron base.
                                      Inv. No. W3-505.
Fig. 8-18.                            RI (4C').
Pres. h. 0.081.
Base of a container, in light brown buff fabric, similar to those of P 66 and P 67.

P 69.   Small pointed amphora base.    Inv. No. W3-506.
Fig. 8-18; Wreck Plan V*d*.           ZW or MZ (6A).
Pres. h. 0.056.
Base, in brown buff fabric, of a small container of unknown shape; wheel marks distinct inside.

P 70.   Flat-bottomed amphora.         Inv. No. W3-68.
Figs. 8-18 and 8-22; Wreck Plan V*d*.     LW (7A).
H. 0.22; max. diam. 0.142; base diam. 0.07.
Complete except for small cracks and holes; surface badly eroded. Somewhat coarse fabric, orange buff to gray and brown. No resin inside.

Flat base, with trace of ring. Body in shape of inverted truncated cone, with hemispherical shoulder above. Handles, centrally ribbed, rise from bottom of shoulder to bottom of funnel-shaped mouth with ledge inside.

I do not know of perfect parallels, but this item is similar in shape to a type commonly found in

---

[58] G. Kapitän, "The Church Wreck off Marzamemi," *Archaeology* 22 (1969): 132; G. F. Bass, ed. *A History of Seafaring Based on Underwater Archaeology*, p. 152, pl. 11. An excellent photograph of a glass pipette of the same shape being used appears on p. 1149 of *Country Life* for November 8, 1962.

[59] Hayes, *DOP* 22 (1968): 215, type 7.
[60] *Histria* I, 460, type 7*b* amphora, with fig. 388 on p. 461, dated to the end of the sixth century.
[61] Boardman, supra n. 10.
[62] Frost, *Under the Mediterranean*, pp. 166–167, figs. 33 and 34, no. 11.

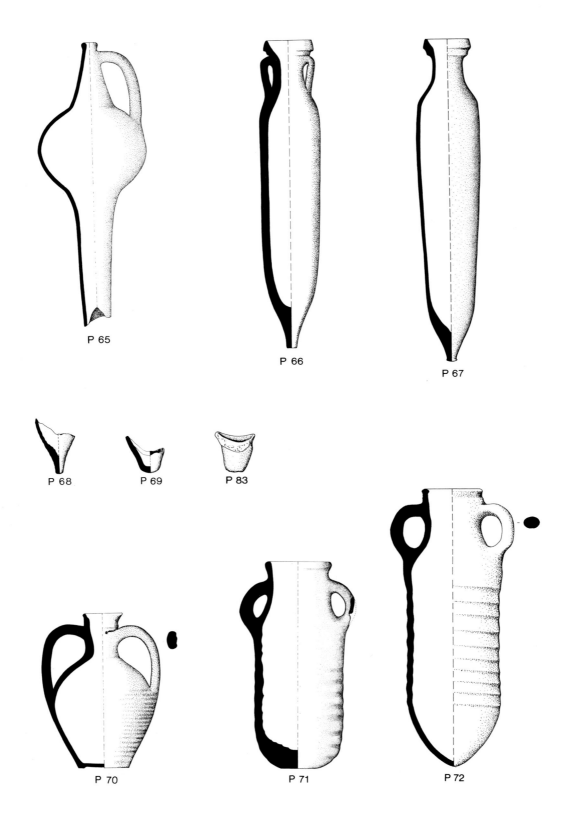

Fig. 8-18. Wine thief and pantry wares. 1:5. *SWK*

the Byzantine layers of Sucidava[63] and in sixth-century Dinogetia;[64] a somewhat less similar example of the same general type was found in seventh-century Emporio.[65]

P 71. Amphora.                    Inv. No. W3-69.
Figs. 8-18 and 8-22; Wreck Plan V*d*.    NN (7B).
H. 0.29; max. diam. 0.123; mouth diam. 0.084.
Chipped slightly. Reddish brown fabric, poorly fired.

Squat, cylindrical body with rounded base, flattened on bottom. Neck and slightly splaying plain lip almost as broad as body. Handles, almost round in section, between shoulder and middle of neck. Shallow horizontal grooves on lower part of body.

P 72. Amphora.                    Inv. No. W3-329.
Figs. 8-18 and 8-22; Wreck Plan V*d*.    MBX (8B).
H. 0.38; max. diam. 0.125; mouth diam. 0.082.
Complete. Very poorly made; orangish ochre fabric containing brick red and grey pebbles and grit. Surface has turned to powder.

Roughly rounded, slightly pointed base below cylindrical body with crude handles, oval in section, between shoulder and high on neck. Vertical rim thickened inside and out. A shallow finger groove spirals around body.

The same general shape, but with a more pointed base with a "button" on the bottom, is known at sixth-century Dinogetia.[66]

P 73. Pointed amphora base.        Inv. No. W3-500.
Figs. 8-19 and 8-22; Wreck Plan V*d*.    BT (7B).
Pres. h. 0.59; max. diam. 0.24.
Base and lower body only. Ochre fabric, darkened and flaking on part of exterior.

Pointed base (flattened on very bottom); nearly cylindrical body beginning to curve inwards at break. Above base, three horizontal finger grooves, then about nine closely spaced ridges, and then four or five more shallow grooves; grooves are visible, in reverse, on interior surface.

This item is almost surely the bottom of an amphora of Histria Type 7*c*, from the end of the sixth century and the seventh century,[67] that appears commonly from at least the northern Black

Sea coast[68] to Tarsus[69] and Ashdod[70] in the eastern Mediterranean. Amphoras of this type at Tomis were used for shipping or storing iron nails and spikes.[71]

P 74. Knobbed jar or amphora base.  Inv. No. W3-509.
Fig. 8-19; Wreck Plan V*d*.          YW (6C).
Pres. h. 0.33; est. max. diam. 0.18.
Base and lower part of body only. Brown micaceous fabric.

Nearly cylindrical, but swollen body with wide and shallow horizontal grooves. Bottom tapers to a hollow-knob base, almost closed.

This shape is found at Dinogetia.[72] Hayes has pointed out to me[73] that the fragment is part of a very late example of the well-known "thin-walled brown micaceous jars" found earlier in the Athenian Agora and elsewhere;[74] we have, in fact, found a complete example of similar size and fabric on the neighboring fourth-century A.D. shipwreck at Yassi Ada.[75] Jean-Pierre Sodini[76] has brought to my attention an example from Thasos[77] and has suggested a possible origin for the type on Thasos, based on the micaceous fabric.

P 75. Knobbed jar or amphora base.  Inv. No. W3-122.
Fig. 8-22; Wreck Plan V*d*.          WH (7B).
Pres. h. 0.30; max. pres. diam. 0.14.
Base and lower part of body only. Brownish buff, fairly fine, micaceous fabric.

Stem hollow from inside, but knob closed on bottom. This base also differs from P 74 in that horizontal ridges and grooves from the wheel are evident on both exterior and interior.

P 76. Amphora(?) base.              Inv. No. W3-118.
Fig. 8-20; Wreck Plan V*d*.          JAP (7C).
Pres. h. 0.057.

[68] N. I. Sokol'skii, "Gorodishche Il'ichevskoye," *SovArch*, 1966, pt. 4, p. 131, amphora type 3 in fig. 4.
[69] H. Goldman et al., *Excavations at Gözlü Kule, Tarsus*, vol. I, *The Hellenistic and Roman Periods*, p. 278, no. 835, fig. 167.
[70] *Ashdod I* (='Atiquot, English series, VII [1967]), fig. 14.1, pl. XI.4.
[71] Radulescu, *Pontica* 6 (1973): 194, with fig. 5 on p. 197.
[72] Vulpe and Barnea, *Din Istoria Dobrogei* II, 537, no. 5, fig. 48 (sixth century).
[73] Personal communication of April 20, 1970.
[74] Robinson, *Athenian Agora* V, 17, no. F65, contains a discussion of shape evolution and the wide spread of type. The base is most like that of Robinson's M373 (late sixth century), p. 119 and pl. 41. The latest example I have found is from the Arab building K11:1, built around A.D. 700, at Khirbat al-Karak; see P. Delougaz and R. C. Haines, *A Byzantine Church at Khirbat al-Karak*, pl. 38, no. 10 (= pl. 54:18).
[75] Bass and van Doorninck, *AJA* 75 (1971): 35, with pl. 2, no. 25.
[76] Personal communication of September 7, 1973.
[77] *BCH* 96 (1972): 948, fig. 46.

[63] Tudor, *Dacia*, 1st ser., 7–8 (1937–1940): 383, no. 8, with fig. 15c.
[64] Barnea, *Dacia*, n.s. 10 (1966): 246, fig. 8, no. 4.
[65] Boardman, supra n. 10.
[66] Barnea, *Dacia*, n.s. 10 (1966): 248, fig. 10, no. 1.
[67] *Histria* I, 460, with fig. 389 on p. 461 (end of sixth century); *MCA* 7: 240, fig. 11, top center (sixth–seventh centuries).

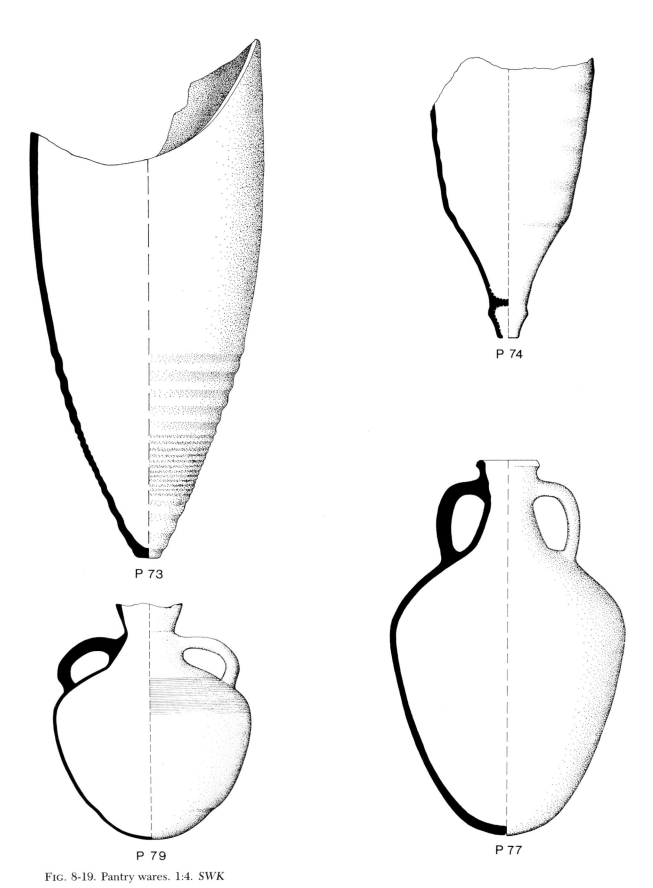

Fig. 8-19. Pantry wares. 1:4. *SWK*

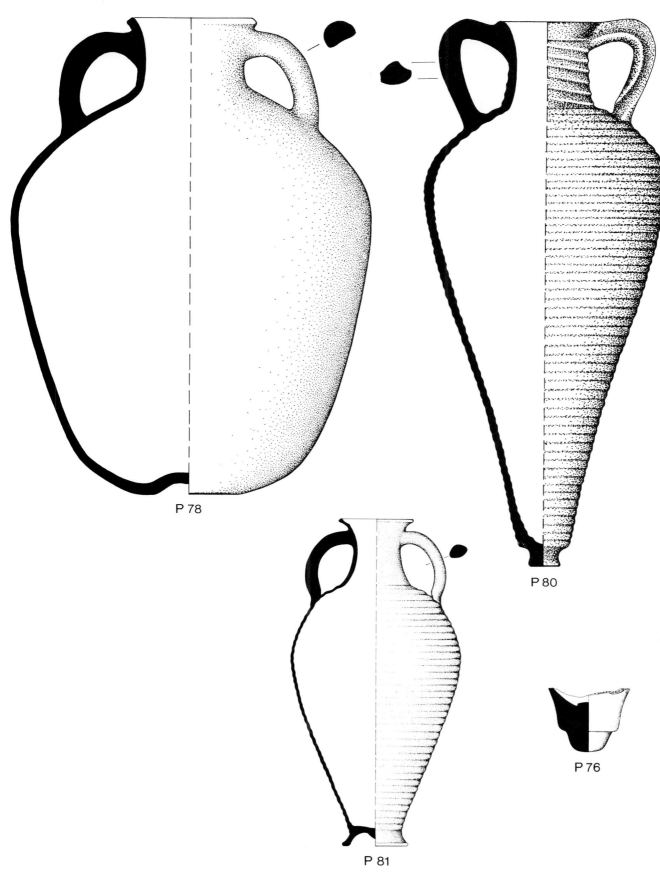

P 78

P 80

P 81

P 76

Fig. 8-20. Pantry wares. 1:4. *SWK*

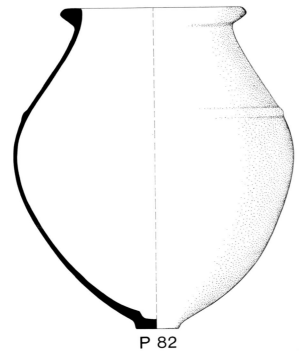

**P 82**

FIG. 8-21. Ship's water jar. 1:8. *SWK*

Coarse orange red fabric with large black grit.

A plug of clay has been thrust through the flat bottom of an amphora(?) with a tapering body; the knob which protrudes is a small dome 0.020 high and 0.045 in diam. at its base.

P 77. Amphora.                          Inv. No. W3-303.
Figs. 8-19 and 8-22.                          MBL (8A).
H. 0.41; max. diam. 0.24; mouth diam. 0.065.
Complete. Brick red fabric.

Piriform amphora with round bottom. Slight traces of finger grooves are the only surface marks.

P 78. Amphora.                          Not inventoried.
Fig. 8-20.     Found in excavation amphora dump.
H. 0.52.
Complete. Fabric not recorded at time of drawing, and piece could not be located in museum's storerooms at later date; measurement taken from drawing. This amphora is vaguely similar to the globular amphoras of the cargo, but it has a more elongated, plain body with a concave base.

P 79. Globular amphora.          Inv. No. W3-324.
Fig. 8-19.                                    (8/9B).
H. 0.275; max. diam. 0.216; mouth diam. 0.072.
Rim chipped. Brick red fabric.

A small, globular amphora from the galley almost identical to some of the larger amphoras of the cargo; there are other differences than the fabric, however: the rounded base is curiously set

off, the handles are placed lower on the neck and shoulder (giving them a different angle), and the flaring rim is much taller and funnel-shaped.

Except for its base and its small size, the amphora is quite similar to sixth-century examples from Histria,[78] Tomis,[79] Sacidava,[80] and Dinogetia.[81] I have not found seventh-century parallels, and one must wonder if the amphora from the shipwreck was an antique on board.

P 80. Conical amphora.                In Izmir Museum.
Figs. 8-20 and 8-22.     Raised before excavation.
This was one of the objects raised from the wreck before 1961. It does not appear on Frost's plan or among her object drawings in *Under the Mediterranean*, but it is labeled in the Izmir Museum as being from the Yassi Ada wreck. I have not seen the actual piece, but Susan Womer Katzev drew it in the storerooms of the museum. Measurements taken from the drawing give its height as 0.60. It is of the same general type as an early-sixth-century piece from the Athenian Agora.[82]

P 81. Amphora.                          In Izmir Museum.
Figs. 8-20 and 8-22.     Raised before excavation.
H. 0.355; max. diam. 0.175; base diam. 0.069; mouth diam. 0.071.
Grey exterior, reddish brown interior.

Piriform amphora with slightly splaying ring stand; pointed base of amphora body appears in concavity of base. Handles from shoulder to top of neck, which flares out to form lip with slight ledge inside. Body and shoulder ridged horizontally. This piece was raised before the excavation of the wreck, and I have not seen it; it was drawn and studied for me by Susan Womer Katzev in the Izmir Museum.[83] It is no. 16 in Fig. 1-4.

This amphora is similar to an example from Dinogetia[84] and bears a slight family resemblance to a sixth-century amphora from Histria.[85]

P 82. Water pithos.                     Inv. No. W3-127.
Figs. 8-21 and 8-22; Wreck Plan V*d*.     ER (7B).
H. 0.71; max. diam. 0.585; th. 0.011.
Largely mended from fragments. Brownish buff fabric.

Pithos with small, flat base, egg-shaped body,

[78] *Histria* I, 459, fig. 384.
[79] Radulescu, *Pontica* 6 (1973): 199, fig. 7.
[80] Scorpan, *Pontica* 6 (1973): 314, fig. 36.3.
[81] Barnea, *Dacia*, n.s. 10 (1966): 242, fig. 5.7, and 251, fig. 12.7.
[82] Robinson, *Athenian Agora* V, 115, no. M334, with pl. 33.
[83] Frost, *Under the Mediterranean*, 166–167, figs. 33–34, no. 16.
[84] Gh. Stefan, "Dinogetia I," *Dacia*, 1st ser., 7–8 (1937–1940): 414, fig. 17, no. 2.
[85] *Histria* I, 457, fig. 381; cf. also Iacobsen, *SovArch* 15 (1951): 325.

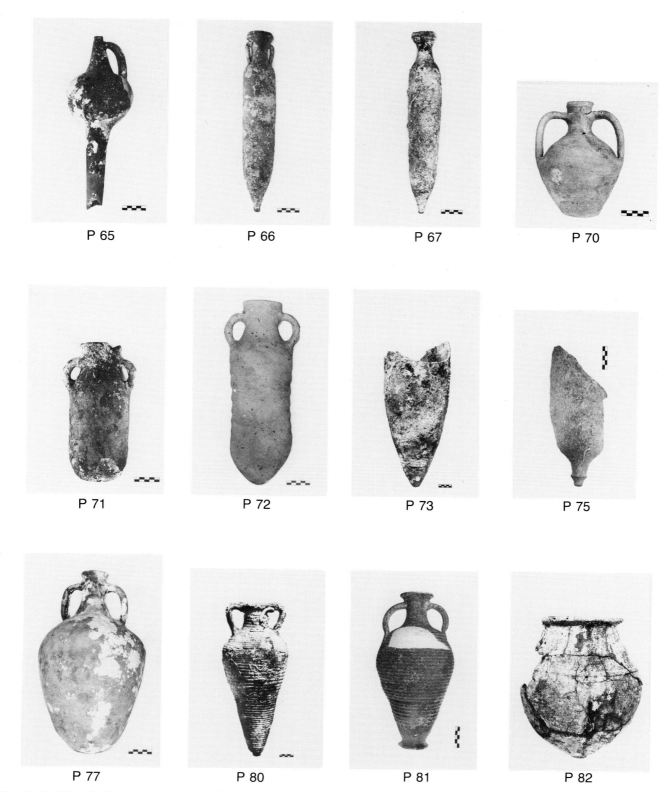

P 65          P 66          P 67          P 70

P 71          P 72          P 73          P 75

P 77          P 80          P 81          P 82

FIG. 8-22. Wine thief, pantry wares, and ship's water jar.

and thick, horizontal rim. Decorated by a solid raised band low on shoulder.

This was surely the ship's water jar, and it was probably covered with a wooden lid, as are those on modern vessels in the same region.

P 83. Knobbed amphora base.          Not inventoried.
          Fig. 8-19.                              MBC (7A').

My only knowledge of this fragment is from a drawing made at the time it was raised. It is in-cluded in this catalog as evidence of an otherwise unknown pantry vessel.

### MISCELLANEOUS

P 84. Molded fragment.                  Not inventoried.
          Fig. 8-15; Wreck Plan V*f*.          SI (7C).

The only record of this fragment is the drawing, published here, made at the time it was raised.

## Conclusions

A reasonably accurate inventory of the ship's galley wares comprises four glazed bowls, four plates, five smaller dishes, three cups, eighteen pitchers, six tube-spouted jars, two lids, twenty-one cooking pots, one or two basins, one wine thief, seventeen storage jars, and a large water pithos. To these should be added the copper ware described in chapter 12.

The finer tableware (glazed bowls, plates, and dishes) may represent four, or possibly five, table set-tings for officers or important passengers, but the quan-tity of cooking pots (at least one-third of them still black-ened from use) suggests a far larger shipboard roster; the equally large number of pitchers, half of them still coated inside with resin, supports the suggestion of a crowded deck, unless a small "wine festival" was held in ports where wine was sold.

With the exception of the plates, of possible African origin, most of the galley wares are of types found almost exclusively north of Yassi Ada, from the western coast of the Black Sea, Constantinople, and the islands of Chios and Samos. I do not mean to suggest any of those places as the sources of the pottery, but the availability of the pottery types there does point logically to a southbound shipment for the Byzantine ship's last voyage.

# IX

## THE LAMPS

### Karen D. Vitelli

Twenty-four unglazed terra-cotta lamps and lamp fragments were recovered from the wreck, all from the general area of the galley (see Wreck Plan V*b*). Two lamps were found somewhat forward of the galley and may have been in a hypothetical dining area, but all of them could well have been inside the galley when the ship went down and may have reached their find spots by drifting and settling. It is certain, in any case, that the bulk of the lamps were stored in or near the galley, either as items of the ship's cargo or waiting to be filled with oil for use on board.

Eight of the lamps still show traces of charring and smoke on their nozzles, indicating conclusively that they had been used. The others, although uncharred, may still have seen use, since the porosity of the clay, the circumstances of preservation, and the possibility that they were cleaned just before the ship sank could all have prevented the existence of a black residue on them when they were recovered.[1] Thus, we cannot say with certainty that the lamps were part of the ship's equipment or that they were items intended for trade. It is likely that lamps were an inexpensive and useful commodity that were purchased when a ship was in port for use on board, as souvenir items with potential trade value (there seem to have been hardly enough lamps on board both to supply the ship and to constitute one of the main items of trade), and to have on hand for dedication at shrines along the way. This last possibility is suggested by the thousands of lamps found on Delos, in the Vari Cave, in the Cave of Pan, and at the Fountain of the Lamps at Corinth, often as dedications at Christian shrines. At Delos, for example, there seems to have

been no local manufacture of lamps on the island.[2] Perhaps sailors were among those who stopped at shrines, leaving lamps and prayers for a safe voyage.

A quick comparison of the seventh-century Yassi Ada lamps with other ancient lamps shows clearly that they are related to the long line of molded Hellenistic and Roman lamps that precedes them instead of the Byzantine wheel-made, glazed lamps which begin somewhat later. If they had not come from a closed deposit, it would have been tempting to arrange the twenty-four lamps stylistically to cover a long period of gradual development. But they are contemporaries, with presumably little chronological variation, and they show us that in the early seventh century there was no single lamp type (Fig. 9-1). Lug, loop, or large decorative handle; round, curvaceous, or streamlined body; decorated shoulder or decorated discus; channel or no channel—all styles are represented in this small collection of lamps. The differences apparently reflect local fashions rooted in the previous centuries. They are not decadent fashions, for the lamps are well made, of fine clay that is fired hard. Several have emerged from hundreds of years in salt water still in factory-fresh condition.

In the catalog which follows, three measurements are usually given for each lamp. The length (l.) includes the nozzle but not the handle. The width (w.) is measured across the lamp at the widest point. The height (h.) is the distance from bottom to top, excluding the handle unless it is specifically noted. The names of parts of lamps are, I think, quite clear and in common use. The large hole in the discus is the oil hole; the hole at the end of the nozzle is the wick hole.

[1] My thanks to Dr. Fred Matson of Pennsylvania State University for this information.

[2] P. Bruneau, *Exploration archéologique de Délos*, vol. XXVI, *Les Lampes*, p. 14.

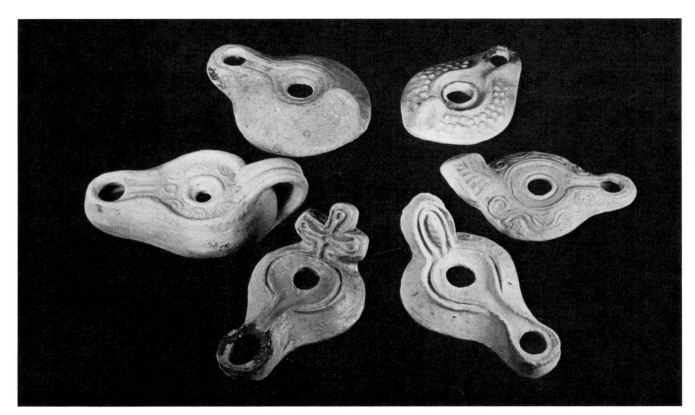

FIG. 9-1. Selection of lamps. *DAF*

The most similar pieces from other sites are listed in footnotes below the catalog description of each lamp, with other closely related examples being mentioned in the discussion of each lamp type.

## *Byzantine Asia Minor Type*

This group, numbering twelve lamps (including several mold brothers), is the most numerous group among the Yassi Ada examples. The Asia Minor lamps were so named by Miltner on the basis of the numerous lamps of this type, dated from the fourth to the sixth centuries, that were found at Ephesus.[3] Their general characteristics are a raised edge around the wick hole, sloping shoulders, a handle ending in an "anchor" or "fishtail," double grooves setting off the underside of the nozzle, loops or tongues between the nozzle and the discus, and a *planta pedis* on the base. Only the last two characteristics are not found on any of this group of Yassi Ada lamps. The otherwise close similarity to the Asia Minor type and the number of close parallels from Ephesus and Miletus suggest that these Yassi Ada lamps are later members of the same family.

Both the hollow molded palmette handle and the solid vertical lug handle are used on these lamps.

[3] F. Miltner, *Forschungen in Ephesos*, vol. IV, part 2, *Das Coemetarium der sieben Schläfer*, p. 100.

L 1.    Lamp.                              Inv. No. W3-191.
        Figs. 9-2 and 9-4; Wreck Plan V*b*.        AI (6B').
        L. 0.106; w. 0.065; h.0.022; h. with handle 0.041.
        Intact. Fish nibbles.[4] Orange buff terra-cotta.

Round body, U-shaped nozzle, triangular handle, inset flat discus, raised rim around oil hole, and channel to wick hole. Discus, channel, and wick hole outlined by double raised ridge. Stylized vines and grapes in relief on shoulders. Impressed palmette handle.

Reverse: Double concentric circles incised around slightly inset, flat base. Triple incised lines either side of nozzle and handle. Incised line bisects nozzle and handle.

[4] Fish nibbles are small curved lines, generally in clusters, which may be fingernail impressions in some cases, as when they appear at a joint between the upper and lower parts of a mold. In most instances, however, they occur randomly on the surface of the lamps and on pottery from this and other wrecks and may best be interpreted as fish nibbles. Divers have observed fish, mostly parrot fish, making these marks on pottery with their mouths.

Cf. Miltner, *Ephesos* IV, part 2, pl. X, nos. 1887 and 1888 (Byz. type IV, sixth century); A. M. Schneider, "Samos in frühchristlicher und byzantinischer Zeit," *AthMitt* 54 (1929): 133, no. 36, with fig. 30, 3 (lower half) and 4, on p. 134 (Samos, fourth–sixth centuries); and O. Wulff, *Königliche Museen zu Berlin*, vol. III, part 1, *Altchristliche und mittelalterliche byzantinische und italienische Bildwerke*, pl. LXII, no. 1267 (Fayum, fifth–sixth centuries).

L 2. Lamp. Inv. No. W3-252.
Figs. 9-2 and 9-4; Wreck Plan V*b*. UO (6B').
L. 0.102; w. 0.064; h. with handle 0.040.
Intact. Fish nibbles. Orange buff terra-cotta.

Round body, U-shaped nozzle, triangular handle, concave discus, and raised rim around oil hole. Channel to wick hole has incised line down center, with three dots in a perpendicular line in front of oil hole. Discus, channel, and wick hole outlined by raised ridge, worn smooth at nozzle. Scroll pattern in relief on shoulders. Impressed palmette handle.

Reverse: Double concentric circles around flat base. Triple incised lines either side of nozzle. Relief crescents (fishtail) on either side of handle, which is bisected by incised line.

Cf. parallels given for L 1, above.

L 3. Lamp. Inv. No. W3-304.
Figs. 9-2 and 9-4; Wreck Plan V*b*. MBW (9B).
L. 0.100; w. 0.067; h. with handle 0.040.
Intact. Brownish ochre terra-cotta.

Round body, U-shaped nozzle, triangular handle, slightly concave discus, and raised rim around oil hole. Channel to wick hole with two lightly incised lines running into wick hole; two stronger lines across nozzle connecting opposite sides of discus. Discus, channel, and wick hole outlined by raised rim. Relief loops on shoulders. Impressed palmette handle.

Reverse: Double concentric circles around flat base, with small incised circle at center. Triple incised lines either side of nozzle. Relief crescents (fishtail) on either side of handle.

Cf. Miltner, *Ephesos* IV, part 2, pl. X, no. 1877, and pl. XIV, no. 327 (both Byz. type II, sixth century); and J. Brants, *Antieke Terra-Cotta Lampen uit het Rijksmuseum van Oudheden te Leiden*, pl. VIII, no. 1118 (type XXVIII, Troad, third–fourth centuries). A similar, unpublished handle was found in the Mosaic-Floored Edifice at Constanţa.[5]

L 4. Lamp. Inv. No. W3-85.
Figs. 9-2 and 9-4; Wreck Plan V*b*. NM (6A).
L. 0.098; w. 0.068; h. 0.022; h. with handle 0.043.
Intact, but original surface almost entirely flaked away. Fine-grained buff terra-cotta with grey and ochre shadows due to encrustation.

Round body, U-shaped nozzle, triangular handle, inset discus, raised rim around oil hole, and channel to wick hole. Discus, nozzle, and wick hole outlined by raised rim. Surface too badly worn to recognize any decoration. Impressed palmette handle.

Reverse: Traces of single circular rim around flat base. Incised line bisects handle. Traces of crescent (fishtail) and triple incised lines on one side of handle and nozzle.

Cf. Archaeological Museum of Constanţa no. 13201 (unpublished; excavated in the Mosaic-Floored Edifice in 1960).[6]

L 5. Lamp. Inv. No. W3-190.
Figs. 9-2 and 9-4; Wreck Plan V*b*. YM (7C).
L. 0.110; w. 0.083; h. 0.025; h. with handle 0.038.
Intact. Fish nibbles. Orange buff terra-cotta.

Round body, U-shaped nozzle, vertical lug handle, inset discus, and raised rim around oil hole. Channel to wick hole with impressed dot rosette in front of oil hole. Discus and channel outlined by double raised rim. Single raised rim around wick hole. Between handle and oil hole, and on the raised rims, are faint impressions of rows of dots. Relief guilloche pattern with dot rosette in center of each loop on shoulders.

Reverse: Double raised concentric circles around slightly inset flat base. Incised line bisects handle and nozzle. On nozzle, line ends in small circle with dot in center. Double incised lines either side of nozzle. Fishtail crescents below handle.

Cf. Menzel, *Antike Lampen in Römisch-Germanischen Zentralmuseum zu Mainz*, p. 99, no. 643, with fig. 81, 1 (Miletus); and Miltner, *Ephesos* IV, part 2, pl. XIV no. 347 (both Byz. type IV, sixth century); also, for discus treatment, cf. Bruneau, *Délos* XXVI, pl. 34, no. 4714.

L 6. Lamp. Inv. No. W3-208.
Figs. 9-2 and 9-4; Wreck Plan V*b*. WZ (6B').

---

[5] Although I have not seen this parallel at the Archaeological Mu- seum of Constanţa, it was noted by George Bass through the kindness of A. Radulescu, museum director, and M. Bucovala. Publication of the Mosaic-Floored Edifice of Tomis has been delayed by the untimely death of its excavator, V. Canarache; guide books are available in a number of languages.
[6] Ibid.

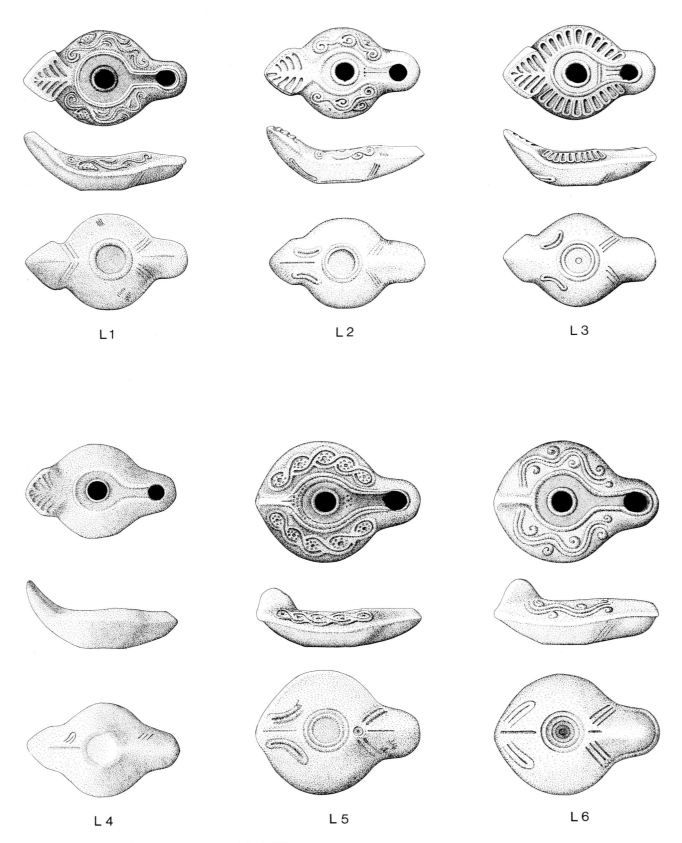

L 1                          L 2                          L 3

L 4                          L 5                          L 6

FIG. 9-2. Lamps of the Asia Minor type. 2:5. *SWK*

L. 0.112; w. 0.082; h. 0.033; h. with handle 0.045. Small fragment of base missing. Discus badly damaged by iron fragment which was corroded to top of lamp. Orange buff terra-cotta.

Round body, U-shaped nozzle, vertical lug handle, inset discus, raised rim around oil hole, and channel to wick hole. Discus, nozzle, and wick hole outlined by raised rim. Scroll pattern in relief on shoulders.

Reverse: Base formed by six raised concentric circles; outer three circles are higher relief and form the foot. Central longitudinal incised lines. Triple incised lines on either side of nozzle. Fishtail crescents below handle. Same mold as L 7.

Cf. Miltner, *Ephesos* IV, part 2, pl. XIV, nos. 345 and 347 (Byz. type IV, sixth century).

L 7. Lamp.                          Inv. No. W3-253.
Fig. 9-4; Wreck Plan V*b*.          RO (7B').
L. 0.111; w. 0.082; h. 0.033; h. with handle 0.043. Intact; surface very worn. Orange buff terra-cotta.
Same mold as L 6.

L 8. Lamp.                          Inv. No. W3-309.
Fig. 9-4.                           VO (6B').
L. 0.110; w. 0.082; h. 0.030; h. with handle 0.040. Intact. Fish nibbles on nozzle and shoulder decoration. Fine-grained orange buff terra-cotta.

Round body, slightly angular nozzle, vertical lug handle with central groove, and inset discus. Raised rim around oil hole with small incisions producing beaded appearance. Channel to wick hole. Double raised rim around discus and nozzle; single rim around wick hole. Pair of facing fish in relief on either side of shoulder; punched depressions mark eyes, mouths, scales, and tails.

Reverse: Raised circular band with extension at back around flat base in which a cross is inscribed. Triple incised lines on either side of nozzle. Lopsided relief fishtail below handle. Same mold as L 9 and L 10.

Cf. Corinth Springhouse Basin no. 3007 (unpublished; 1933, notebook 136, p. 162).[7]

L 9. Lamp.                          Inv. No. W3-254.
Fig. 9-4; Wreck Plan V*b*.          TI (6C).
L. 0.110; w. 0.083; h. 0.030; h. with handle 0.040. Intact, but surface badly worn. Fine-grained orange buff terra-cotta.
Same mold as L 8 and L 10. Lacks inscribed cross in base ring.

L 10. Lamp.                         Inv. No. W3-343.

Fig. 9-4; Wreck Plan V*b*.          MCL (8B').
L. 0.110; w. 0.083; h. 0.030; h. with handle 0.040. Intact, with small chip at oil hole. Surface badly worn. Fine-grained orange buff terra-cotta.
Same mold as L 8 and L 9. Lacks inscribed cross in base ring.

L 11. Lamp.                         Inv. No. W3-56.
Figs. 9-3 and 9-4; Wreck Plan V*b*.  KM (7A).
L. 0.105; w. 0.075; h. 0.024; h. with handle 0.040. Complete profile preserved; a number of body fragments missing. At present, disintegrated into a number of barely distinguishable pieces. Charred nozzle. Fine-grained buff terra-cotta.

Round body, U-shaped nozzle, triangular handle with impressed palmette, inset discus, raised rim around oil hole, and channel to wick hole. Double raised rim around discus and channel; single rim around wick hole. Relief scroll pattern on shoulders.

Reverse: Raised circular rim around flat base. Profile from base to nozzle is concave-convex curve, unlike simple convex curve of other examples.

Cf. Miltner, *Ephesos* IV, part 2, pl. X, no. 1888 (Byz. type IV, sixth century); also Wulff, *Königliche Museen* III, part 1, pl. LXII, no. 1267 (Fayum, fifth–sixth centuries).

L 12. Lamp.                         Inv. No. W3-98.
Figs. 9-3 and 9-4; Wreck Plan V*b*.  QW (7B).
L. 0.090; w. 0.060; h. 0.030; h. with handle 0.040. Intact. Traces of bronze encrustation on right side of nozzle. Charred nozzle. Fine-grained buff terra-cotta.

Pear-shaped body and nozzle in a continuous curve, vertical lug handle, inset discus, pronounced rim at oil hole, and channel to wick hole. Pronounced rim around discus, channel, and wick hole. Triple row of relief beads on shoulders.

Reverse: Two concentric circles around flat base. Two incised lines either side of nozzle. Two relief arrows from base rings toward handle—a stylized fishtail.

Cf. Brants, *Antieke Terra-Cotta Lampen*, pl. VIII, no. 1120 (type XXVIII, Smyrna, third–fourth centuries); Miltner, *Ephesos* IV, part 2, pl. IX, nos. 1834 and 1783 (Asia Minor type XI, fifth–sixth centuries); J. Perlzweig, *The Athenian Agora*, vol. VII, *Lamps of the Roman Period*, p. 192, pls. 44, 50, nos. 2807–2817 (second half of sixth century); D. T. Rice, in *Second Report upon the Excavations Carried Out in and near the Hippodrome of Constantinople*, fig. 40, top left cor-

---

[7]My thanks go to C. K. Williams, director of the American excavations at Corinth, for permission to mention this lamp.

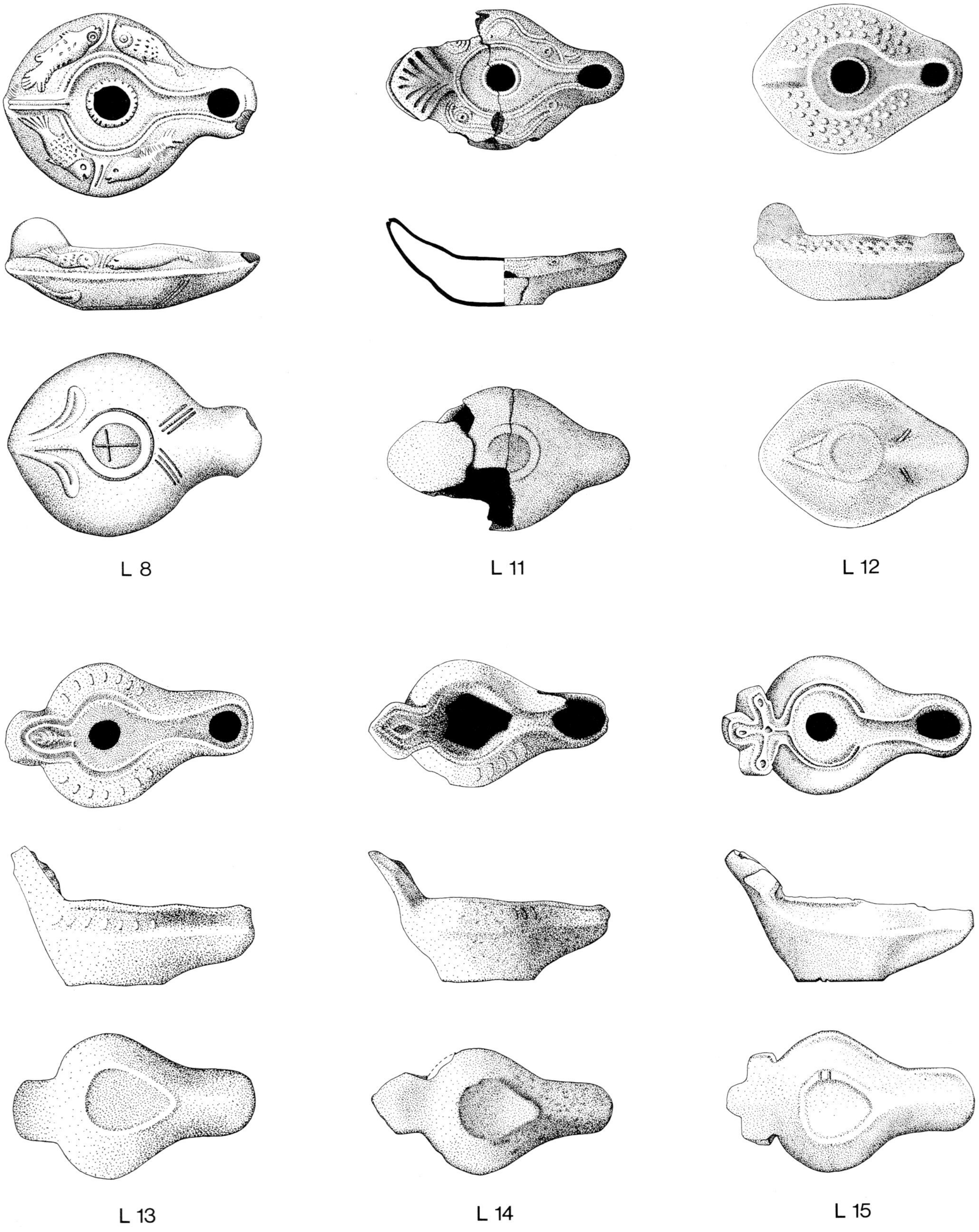

L 8                          L 11                          L 12

L 13                         L 14                         L 15

Fig. 9-3. Lamps of Asia Minor and Balkan types. 2:5. *SWK*

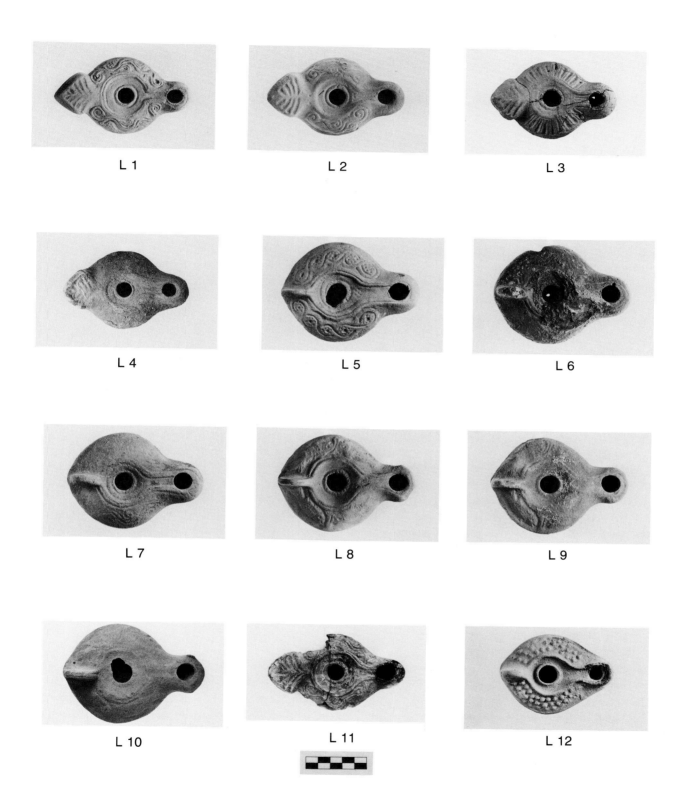

FIG. 9-4. Lamps L 1–L 12.

ner; D. Tudor, "Sucidava III," *Dacia*, 1st ser., 11–12 (1945–1947): 169, with fig. 20, no. 4 (Sucidava, sixth century); Bruneau, *Délos* XXVI, pl. 33, nos. 4706–4709 (transitional fifth–sixth centuries); C. Iconomu, *Opaiţe greco-romane*, p. 136, no. 703, with fig. 50 on p. 26 (Constanţa [Tomis], fifth–sixth centuries); D. P. Dimitrov et al., "Archeologicheskie raskopki v vostochnom sektore nove v 1965 g," *BIABulg* 30 (1967): 98, fig. 30 (Novae); C. H. Kraeling, *Ptolemais, City of the Libyan Pentapolis*, pl. LXII*D*, and p. 270; C. Blinkenberg, *Lindos*, vol. I, *Les Petits Objets*, pl. 151, no. 3207 ("*bas empire*"); and Byzantine Museum, Athens, No. 806 (unpublished).

The best parallels for the Yassi Ada lamps with palmette handles are those from Samos, Ephesus,[8] Smyrna, and Troy. These lamps are so close to the Yassi Ada examples that they, too, should probably be dated in the early seventh century. Other examples from Ephesus,[9] Miletus, Lindos, and the Fayum are earlier relatives of the Yassi Ada group but should belong at least to the sixth century.

The lamps with vertical lug handles find their parallels in the same geographical area. Very close examples are published from Ephesus,[10] the Heraion at Samos, Miletus, and Delos, and these should likewise be dated to the late sixth–early seventh centuries. Lamps very similar to these have also been found in the seventh-century destruction level of the fortress at Emporio, Chios.[11]

Variations on the shoulder designs of vines, scrolls, guilloche, and loops found on the Yassi Ada lamps are frequent on lamps from Hellenistic times through the sixth century. More indicative of the late date and provenance of the lamps is the treatment of the reverse. The true Asia Minor fishtail[12] has, by the seventh century,

become little more than a pair of crescents or even a few sketchy oblique lines. Below the nozzle is a pair of two, three, or more oblique lines; the base consists of one to six concentric rings; the *planta pedis* no longer occurs. None of these markings appear on any of the other non–Asia Minor lamp types from this excavation.

In spite of the closeness of the lamps within the group, there are some peculiarities that merit special mention. The three mold brothers with the facing fish on the shoulders (L 8–L 10) stand out as the finest pieces. The nozzles are slightly more angular, the lug handle has a very careful groove down the center, the rim around the oil hole is beaded, and the fishtail is rather elaborate. Most unusual is the figured decoration. The only similar example that I know of is an unpublished lamp from the Springhouse Basin at Corinth. It also has four strange animals in relief on the shoulders, with details added by a punch tool, and a variation of the Asia Minor base.

Yassi Ada L 11 has the general characteristics of the Asia Minor group, but the fabric and general impression are somehow different. The profile of the underside of the nozzle is reminiscent of the Balkan group (described below), and this lamp may well be a Balkan imitation of the Asia Minor type.

The same is perhaps true of L 12. This little lamp, with its knobby decoration, is a ubiquitous type, finding vague parallels from fourth-century Smyrna, slightly later ones at Ephesus and Delos, and others from the late sixth century at Athens. Closer parallels come from Constanţa (ancient Tomis), Novae, and the Hippodrome at Constantinople. Tudor says that this lamp style is specifically Byzantine, common in the lower Danube, and he thinks his examples are probably imported from Scythia Minor.[13] It is likely that the Yassi Ada lamp is also a Balkan imitation of the Asia Minor type.

## *Balkan Type*

Seven of the Yassi Ada lamps are of this type. Similar lamps are a fairly common find in excavations in Bulgaria, Rumania, Thrace, and Constantinople. Iconomu suggests that the type is a local imitation of North Af-

rican lamps.[14] There are some similarities, and the connection is not unlikely, since they begin to appear about the time of Justinian's conquest of North Africa, but to my knowledge close parallels to this kind of lamp have not been found in North Africa. A stronger influence seems to come from bronze lamps,[15] of which there are

---

[8] Miltner, *Ephesos* IV, part 2, pl. X, no. 1877 (Byz. type II, sixth century); pl. XIV, no. 327 (Byz. type II, sixth century); and pl. X, nos. 1887 and 1888 (Byz. type IV, sixth century).

[9] Ibid., pl. IX, no. 1614 (Asia Minor type X, fifth century).

[10] Ibid., pl. XIV, nos. 345 and 347 (Byz. type IV, sixth century).

[11] My thanks go to John Boardman for his offer of photographs and permission to mention this material from the British excavations at Chios.

[12] For example, see Miltner, *Ephesos* IV, part 2, pl. X.

[13] D. Tudor, "Sucidava III," *Dacia*, 1st ser., 11–12 (1945–1947): 168, no. 6.

[14] C. Iconomu, *Opaiţe greco-romane*, p. 28.

[15] O. Wulff, *Königliche Museen zu Berlin*, vol. III, part 1, *Altchristliche und mittelalterliche byzantinische und italienische Bildwerke*, p. 243.

some examples quite close to the Yassi Ada lamps dated to the fifth to eighth centuries.[16]

A cross, oval, and diamond adorn the Yassi Ada lamps. Other Balkan examples include rams' heads, human heads, and various palmettes.[17] Almost always there are small relief rays on the steeply sloping shoulders. A double raised ridge starts at the handle and outlines the discus. The profile is quite high; on the reverse is a simple egg-shaped base.

L 13. Lamp.                               Inv. No. W3-90.
Figs. 9-3 and 9-6; Wreck Plan V*b*.          YM (6B).
L. 0.105; w. 0.066; h. 0.032; h. with handle 0.052.
Intact, perfect condition. Fine-grained red ochre terra-cotta.

Shoe-shaped carinated body, elongated nozzle, solid oval handle with branch in relief, inset discus, and channel to wick hole. Double relief line around handle and continuing around discus; single relief line around channel and wick hole. Row of relief rays on shoulders.

Reverse: Egg-shaped raised rim around inset base.

Cf. Iconomu, *Opaiţe greco-romane*, p. 148, no. 772, with fig. 183 on p. 150 (Constanţa, sixth century); Saraçhane (Constantinople) lamp no. 56 and, for handle only, lamp no. 10.[18] Also, Archaeological Museum of Constanţa no. 13456, without rays on shoulder, from the Mosaic-Floored Edifice (unpublished).[19]

L 14. Lamp.                               Inv. No. W3-58.
Figs. 9-3 and 9-6; Wreck Plan V*b*.          BM (7B).
L. 0.102; w. 0.060; h. 0.039; h. with handle 0.063.
Fragment of right shoulder missing. Oil hole and wick hole enlarged by breakage. Coarse red ochre terra-cotta, with grey core.

Shoe-shaped carinated body, elongated nozzle, solid diamond-shaped handle with relief outline of diamond in center, inset discus, and channel to wick hole. Handle, discus, channel, and wick hole outlined by raised ridge. Traces of relief rays on shoulders.

Reverse: Egg-shaped raised rim around inset base.

Cf. Wulff, *Königliche Museen* III, part 1, pl.

LXII, no. 1272 (Constantinople, fifth–sixth centuries); Saraçhane (Constantinople) lamp no. 64.[20]

L 15. Lamp.                               Inv. No. W3-240.
Figs. 9-3 and 9-6; Wreck Plan V*b*.          QO (6B).
L. 0.104; w. 0.060; h. with handle 0.060.
Intact, surface crackly and flaking. Heavily charred nozzle. Brown ochre terra-cotta.

Shoe-shaped carinated body, elongated nozzle, and solid cross-shaped handle outlined by relief line which continues down and around discus. Handle area decorated by relief cross with circles at ends of top three bars and at center of cross; lowest bar splits at discus and circles it. Double relief line around inset discus; single ridge around channel and wick hole. No trace of shoulder decoration.

Reverse: Egg-shaped rim around inset base. Two grooves cut through rim on one side—perhaps a potter's mark.

Cf. Iconomu, *Opaiţe greco-romane*, p. 148, no. 770, with fig. 58 on p. 29 (type XXXIII, Constanţa [Tomis] sixth century); Wulff, *Königliche Museen* III, part 1, pl. LXII, no. 1273 (Constantinople, fifth–sixth centuries); and Saraçhane (Constantinople) lamp no. 22.[21]

L 16. Lamp.                               Inv. No. W3-236.
Figs. 9-5 and 9-6; Wreck Plan V*b*.          PO (8B).
L. 0.104; w. 0.065; h. with handle 0.063.
Intact; pitted surface. Nozzle charred back to oil hole. Coarse orange buff terra-cotta.

Shoe-shaped carinated body, elongated nozzle, solid cross-shaped handle outlined by relief line which continues down and completely around inset discus, and no channel. Handle area has relief cross whose bottom bar ends in a loop at edge of oil hole. Inset ring around wick hole. Uneven relief rays on shoulders.

Reverse: Egg-shaped raised rim around inset base. Same mold as L 17.

Cf. Wulff, *Königliche Museen* III, part 1, pl. LXII, no. 1274 (Constantinople, fifth–sixth centuries); D. Tudor, *Sucidava: Une Cité daco-romaine et byzantine en Dacie*, p. 113, fig. 29, no. 6 (late sixth century); and Saraçhane (Constantinople) lamps nos. 69 and 41.[22] Also, R. Vulpe and I. Barnea, *Din Istoria Dobrogei*, vol. II, *Romanii la Dunărea de Jos*, p. 539, fig. 50, no. 5 (Constanţa [Tomis], sixth century); and D. Tudor, *Oltenia Ro-*

---

[16] H. Menzel, *Antike Lampen in Römisch-Germanischen Zentralmuseum zu Mainz*, pl. 92; J. Perlzweig, *The Athenian Agora*, vol. VII, *Lamps of the Roman Period*, p. 48; and J. Strzygowski, *Koptische Kunst*, pl. 33.

[17] Iconomu, *Opaiţe greco-romane*, p. 150, figs. 179–188.

[18] Thanks to Martin Harrison for permission to mention this parallel from Saraçhane before its publication.

[19] Supra n. 5.

[20] Supra n. 18.

[21] Ibid.

[22] Ibid.

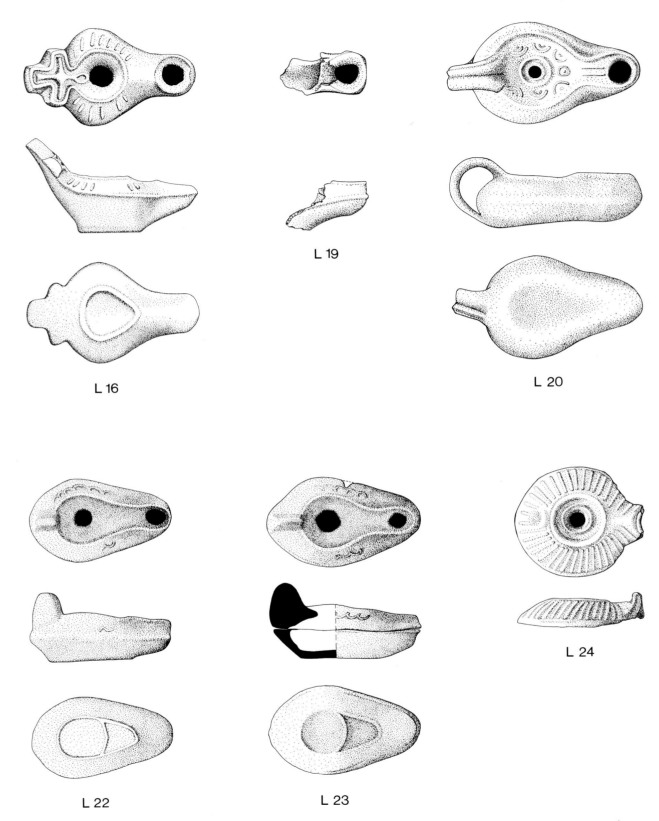

L 19

L 16

L 20

L 22

L 23

L 24

FIG. 9-5. Lamps of Balkan and various other types. 2:5. *SWK*

*mana*, figs. 147 and 20 (Sucidava). Archaeological Museum of Constanța no. 13361, from the Mosaic-Floored Edifice,[23] is very close but has extra line around sunken discus.

L 17. Lamp.                           Inv. No. W3-239.
Fig. 9-6; Wreck Plan V*b*.                 QI (6B).
L. 0.108; w. 0.060; h. with handle 0.067.
Intact, but surface worn nearly smooth. Coarse orange ochre terra-cotta.
    Same mold as L 16.

L 18. Lamp bottom.                    Inv. No. W3-311.
Fig. 9-6; Wreck Plan V*b*.                 XI (6B′).
L. 0.087; w. 0.058; pres. h. 0.026.
Bottom half of lamp like L 16. Underside of nozzle charred. Coarse orange buff terra-cotta.

L 19. Lamp nozzle.                    Inv. No. W3-508.
Figs. 9-5 and 9-6; Wreck Plan V*b*.        HI (8B).
Pres. l. 0.060.
Fragment of nozzle. Charred. Orange buff crumbly terra-cotta.
    Elongated nozzle with inset ring around wick hole and profile similar to that of L 16.

Previously, lamps of this type have been dated from the fourth to the sixth centuries. In view of the Yassi Ada lamps, they might better be considered as of the late sixth and seventh centuries. As more lamps from this area are excavated and published, the sequence should be easier to establish. If it follows the pattern of Hellenistic and Roman lamps, then those with decoration in the discus, a great many small relief rays on the shoulders, and the relief line of the discus ending in a volute at the nozzle are somewhat earlier than the simpler lamps found at Yassi Ada.

At Sucidava a number of lamps were found in the basilica, which was destroyed, on the evidence of coins of Maurice Tiberius (582–602), at the end of the sixth century.[24] Several of the lamps from the basilica[25] have relief decoration in the discus. Lamps from the excavations at Novae[26] are similar, with decoration in the discus. These belong in Iconomu's type XXXII,[27] somewhat earlier than the Yassi Ada lamps but still well into the sixth century. The Yassi Ada lamps fit most comfortably into Iconomu's Byzantine type XXXIII. Other examples have been found at Tomis[28] and from Thrace.[29]

The best parallels to the Yassi Ada lamps, however, are from Constantinople: those excavated at Saraçhane and those illustrated by Wulff.[30] The fact that such lamps do not appear south of the city, however, may suggest that they were imports, perhaps by way of the Black Sea, or that they were made largely for a northern trade.

### Various Types

I group the following five lamps together without title because they do not fit with the two main groups, do not fit clearly into any previously published groups, and are too few in number to create new groups.

L 20. Lamp.                           Inv. No. W3-54.
Figs. 9-5 and 9-6; Wreck Plan V*b*.        MK (7A).
L. 0.110; l. with handle 0.130; w. 0.075; h. 0.032; h. with handle 0.045.
Intact. Yellow buff terra-cotta.
    Egg-shaped body, long nozzle in continuous curve with body, and centrally grooved vertical strap handle from discus to base. Discus, channel, and wick hole all inset and outlined by raised rim, on exterior of which is a barely visible incised scalloped pattern. Oil hole outlined by two raised rims, the second of which has traces of an incised zigzag pattern. Discus decorated with three double semicircles in relief on each side (one of which is turned in the opposite direction from the others). A full circle with dot in center lies in the longitudinal axis. Two longitudinal lines in the channel.
    Reverse: Flat bottom without decoration.
    Cf. Rice in *Hippodrome of Constantinople*, fig. 40, row 2, no. 1, and row 3, no. 4; Saraçhane (Constantinople) lamp nos. 14 and 18.[31]

L 21. Lamp.                           Inv. No. W3-55.
Fig. 9-6.                                  Air-lifted.

[24] D. Tudor, *Sucidava: Une Cité daco-romaine et byzantine en Dacie*, p. 114.

[25] Ibid., p. 112, fig. 29, no. 4, and pl. V, no. 2.

[26] D. P. Dimitrov et al., "Archeologicheskie raskopi v vostochnom sektore nove v 1962 gody," *BIABulg* 27 (1964): 230, no. 3, fig. 18; D. P. Dimitrov et al., "Archeologicheskie raskopi v zapadnom sektore nove v 1965 g," *BIABulg* 30 (1967): 64, fig. 6.

[27] Iconomu, *Opaițe greco-romane*, pp. 146–147.

[28] I. Stoian, "La città pontica di Tomis," *Dacia*, n.s. 5 (1961): 237, fig. 3; G. Severeanu, "Lampes en terre-cuite appartenant aux collections du Musée Municipal de Bucarest et du Dr. Severeanu," *Bucurestii* 2, nos. 1–2 (1936): 84.

[29] M.-L. Bernhard, *Lampki starozytne*, pl. XCVI, no. 340, and pl. XCV, nos. 338, 339.

[30] Wulff, *Königliche Museen* III, part 1, pl. LXII, with pp. 251–252.

[31] Supra n. 18.

[23] Supra n. 5.

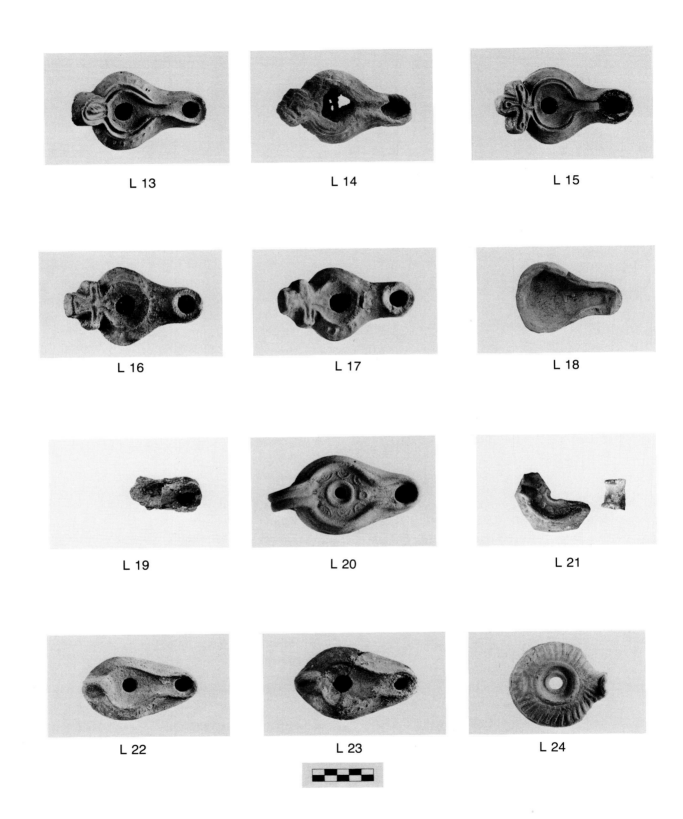

FIG. 9-6. Lamps L 13–L 24.

Discus fragment pres. l. 0.055; w. 0.035; h. 0.018. Nozzle fragment pres. w. 0.026; h. 0.021.

Two fragments of a lamp; one includes part of discus, body, and handle, and other is possibly part of a nozzle. Grey buff terra-cotta.

Relief ridge circles discus and breaks off at point where channel might have been. Beginning of centrally grooved vertical strap handle at edge of discus. Incised scalloped pattern barely visible around oil hole, within discus. On exterior of relief ridge is incised frieze of circles with dots in centers.

Generally, much like L 20.

Both L 20 and L 21 have a large, flat discus which carries the major decoration. An example from Novae in Bulgaria seems, from a poor photograph, to be the closest published parallel to the two Yassi Ada lamps.[32] Better parallels, unpublished, have been found in Constantinople in the excavations at the Hippodrome and at Saraçhane.

L 22. Lamp.                                Inv. No. W3-93.
Figs. 9-5 and 9-6; Wreck Plan V*b*.         SM (7B).
L. 0.095; w. 0.053; h. 0.028; h. with handle 0.042. Intact, but surface worn and crumbling. Charred nozzle. Fine-grained orange ochre terra-cotta.

Egg-shaped body, nozzle in continuous line with body, and tall vertical lug handle. Discus, channel, and wick hole deeply inset and encircled by raised rim. Wave pattern in relief on shoulders.

Reverse: Raised egg-shaped rim with relief bar across it.

L 23. Lamp.                                Inv. No. W3-57.
Figs. 9-5 and 9-6; Wreck Plan V*b*.         ML (7A).
L. 0.097; w. 0.060; h. 0.032; h. with handle 0.050. Complete (four mended fragments). Nozzle heavily encrusted, probably from burning. Orange buff terra-cotta.

Lamp like L 22.

Lamps L 22 and L 23 do not find exact parallels among published material. The rather distinctive base may be the clue, but it has not always been the practice to publish illustrations or careful descriptions of the reverses of lamps. Lamps of similar shape were found in

the Athenian Agora and published as seventh-century Attic.[33] In Italy there are some local products of approximately fifth-century date[34] that are generally similar. The two lamps have some slight affinities with Miltner's Asia Minor type IX;[35] Iconomu's type XXX,[36] from in and around Constanța, matches the Yassi Ada lamps as well as any. It seems wiser not to assign these lamps to any particular locale until closer parallels are known.

L 24. Lamp.                                Inv. No. W3-59.
Figs. 9-5 and 9-6; Wreck Plan V*b*.         BW (7A).
Pres. l. 0.085; w. 0.074; pres. h. 0.020. Fragment of upper part of lamp, missing handle and part of nozzle. Fine-grained yellow buff terra-cotta with greenish tinges.

Round body with small circular flat scar from attachment of handle. Decoration continued under handle. Inset discus with framing ring around oil hole and another around discus. No channel. High rim encircles wick hole. Shoulders and nozzle decorated with relief rays.

The examples closest to L 24 are from Miletus[37] and Ephesus,[38] where, in particular, the treatment of the discus, the high rim around the nozzle, and the sloping shoulders are similar, although still a long way from being exactly parallel. It is unfortunate that we do not have the reverse of this lamp to tell whether or not this is a true Asia Minor type, although that does seem the most likely possibility.

Lamps are common finds on most excavations, but at present few early Byzantine sites provide the firmly dated context necessary to establish useful typologies. The Yassi Ada wreck provides a variety of early Byzantine lamp types from a firmly dated closed deposit. Beyond suggesting a northern port of call for our ship, the lamps should be useful in sorting out and solidifying the chronologies of a number of other Byzantine and Late Roman excavations.

[32] Dimitrov, *BIABulg* 27 (1964): 230, no. 4, middle row, right.

[33] Perlzweig, *Athenian Agora* VII, pl. 12, 50, no. 2933, and pl. 46, no. 2935.
[34] G. Libertini, *Il Museo Biscari*, pl. CXXX, no. 1479.
[35] Miltner, *Ephesos* IV, part 2, pl. VIII.
[36] Iconomu, *Opaițe greco-romane*, pp. 139ff.
[37] Menzel, *Antike Lampen*, pl. 81, 13, no. 638.
[38] Miltner, *Ephesos* IV, part 2, pl. III, nos. 300–302 (Asia Minor type, late fourth century).

# X

## THE WEIGHING IMPLEMENTS

### G. KENNETH SAMS

No merchantman would have been properly outfitted without the necessary implements for weighing commodities of varying kind and bulk. The Yassi Ada Byzantine ship carried eight bronze weights forming a graded set (W 1–W 8), a glass pendant weight (W 9), and at least three steelyards (B 1–B 3). With these metrological tools the ship had available the means for weighing amounts from a small fraction of an ounce up to at least four hundred Roman pounds.

## *Weights*

W 1.   Bronze weight.                     Inv. No. W3-89*A*.
Figs. 10-1 and 10-2; Wreck Plan V*c*.        (7B).
Diam. 0.058; th. 0.013; weight 284 g.
A bit of the silver inlay appears to be missing; otherwise well preserved.

   Both surfaces flat, with slightly raised edges around the peripheries. The edge has a wide, rounded, medial ridge with single grooves on either side.

   Reverse plain. Obverse framed, near periphery, by a simple wreath consisting of an outer, solid groove and an inner row of tiny, obliquely incised dashes. At top center is an incised Greek cross containing a smaller plain cross with silver inlay. Below are the designations ↑ and A, both inlaid with silver.

W 2.   Bronze weight.                     Inv. No. W3-89*B*.
Figs. 10-1 and 10-2; Wreck Plan V*c*.        (7B).
Diam. 0.047; th. 0.010; weight 124.0 g.
Excellent condition; in fact, the best-preserved piece in the set.

   Surfaces and edge like those of W 1; tiny circular indentation at center.

   Reverse plain. Obverse has same wreath and cross as on W 1, although here the inlaid cross is proportionately smaller. Beneath the crosses are the incised designations Γ and S; in this case there are smaller inlaid letters within the larger incised ones. The silver inlay rises above the weight's surface.

W 3.   Bronze weight.                     Inv. No. W3-89*C*.
Figs. 10-1 and 10-2; Wreck Plan V*c*.        (7B).
Diam. 0.033; th. 0.007; weight 59.255 g.
Surfaces and edge more worn than those of W 1 and W 2.

   Flat surfaces. Edge now rounded, although it may have been grooved originally; same circular indentation at center as seen on W 2.

   Reverse plain. Obverse has same type of encircling wreath as seen on W 1 and W 2. At top center a cross with only part of its silver inlay is preserved. Below are two incised letters, ΓΓ, with silver inlay partially intact. Engulfing the gamma on the right is a large incised Greek cross such as that found at top center on W 1 and W 2.

W 4.   Bronze weight.                     Inv. No. W3-89*D*.
Figs. 10-1 and 10-2; Wreck Plan V*c*.        (6/7B).
Diam. 0.029; th. 0.008; weight 44.075 g.
Well preserved. Parts of silver inlay missing. On the reverse is a white encrustation.

   Surfaces and edge very similar to those of W 1 and W 2; central circular indentation.

FIG. 10-1. Bronze weights W 1–W 8.

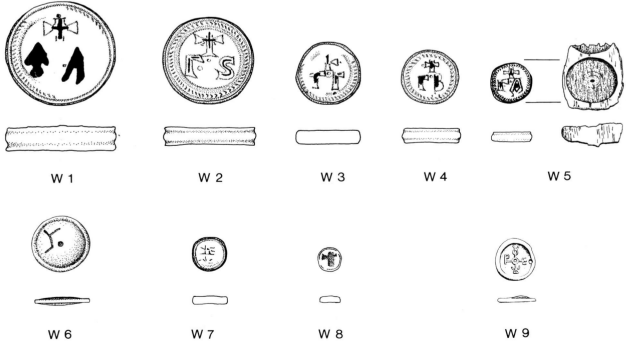

FIG. 10-2. Bronze weights W 1–W 8 and glass weight W 9. 1:2. *NP*

204 YASSI ADA

Reverse plain. Obverse has wreath as on W 1–
W 3. Small incised Greek cross at top center;
only the vertical bar of the smaller inlaid cross
within is preserved. Below, ΓΒ, each with silver
inlay.

W 5.  Bronze weight.  Inv. No. W3-322.
Figs. 10-1 and 10-2.  (7A′).
Diam. 0.022; th. 0.006; weight 19.2 g.
Surface is worn. Only parts of the silver inlay are
intact.

Surfaces and edge like those of W 1, W 2, and
W 4; central circular indentation.

Reverse plain. Obverse has a row of incised
chevrons near periphery. At top center is a
Greek cross. Below are the letters ΓΑ.

W 6.  Bronze weight.  Inv. No. W3-202.
Figs. 10-1 and 10-2; Wreck Plan Vc.  KAE (7B).
Diam. 0.029; th. 0.005; weight 17.5 g.
Well preserved. Part of ligature either worn or
never completed.

Convex on both sides; rim narrow, shallowly
concave; edge plain. Circular indentation 0.003
in diam. in center of each face.

Reverse plain. Obverse preserves about half of
what is here restored as the ligature ⚮ .

W 7.  Bronze weight.  Inv. No. W3-89E.
Figs. 10-1 and 10-2.  Air-lifted.
Diam. 0.017; th. 0.004; weight 8.906 g.
Worn.

Flat surfaces; edge plain.

On obverse, simple grooving at periphery; at
top center, perhaps ΙΒ.

W 8.  Bronze weight.  Inv. No. W3-89F.
Figs. 10-1 and 10-2.  Air-lifted.
Diam. 0.012; th. 0.002; weight 2.95 g.
Worn.

Surfaces flat; edge plain.

Only the ghost of a cross can be seen filling
most of the obverse field.

W 9.  Glass weight.  Inv. No. W3-87.
Figs. 10-2 and 10-3.  Air-lifted.
Diam. 0.0232; weight 1.7 g.
Well preserved. Molded yellow glass.

Reverse flat. Obverse irregularly convex with
thick rounded border. Tiny suspension hole near
edge.

Reverse plain. Obverse with raised, mold-
formed monogram of cruciform type giving the
name Theodoros in the genitive: ΘΕΟΔΩΡΟΥ.
The hole is so placed that the monogram would
have been turned 90° to the left of its proper orientation when the weight was suspended.

FIG. 10-3. Glass weight W 9.

W 10.  Lead weight.  Inv. No. W3-179.
Figs. 10-4 and 10-5; Wreck Plan Vc.  KNE (6B).
H. 0.053; diam. 0.051–0.053; weight 541 g.
Broken away around hole openings at both ends;
lead oxide over much of surface.

Piriform. Square hole through longitudinal
axis.

This weight was found close to the steelyards
and their counterweights and may have contained a bronze rod with a ring at one end (cf.
B 2.d.1, p. 220).

W 11.  Lead weight.  Inv. No. W3-444.
Figs. 10-4 and 10-6; Wreck Plan Vc.  KTB (8B).
L. 0.078; w. 0.072; h. without handle 0.037; h.
with handle 0.067; weight 933 g.
Whole. Iron handle restored (cast with Smooth-
On; see pp. 231–233).

Ellipsoidal, bun-shaped weight with flat bottom, convex sides, and a slightly sloping top. In
top there is the impression of a tack with l. 0.034
and diam. of head 0.019 and a roughly round depression with max. diam. 0.027 and max. depth
0.008. An iron disc with diam. 0.023 and th. 0.011
(cast with Smooth-On) was imbedded in the top.
An iron basket handle, roughly rectangular in section, was set into the top but not centered. The
tack impression, round depression, and iron disc
suggested to M. L. Katzev, when he studied the
piece with other iron objects, that adjustments
were made to the weight in order to satisfy a
standard.

## THE BRONZE WEIGHTS

Of the eight bronze weights retrieved from the ship, five
pieces, W 1–W 5, came from the area of the galley and
were, in fact, scattered around and near the two steelyards B 1 and B 2 (sector 7B); W 6 came from the same
grid square but was farther removed from this concentration of metrological equipment, and W 5 was
found in overlapping sector 7A′. The remaining two
weights, W 7 and W 8, presumably had the same provenance but were retrieved by the air lift. This assumption
is strengthened by the fact that W 5 was discovered

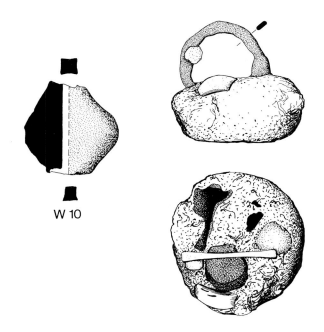

W 10

W 11

FIG. 10-4. Lead weights W 10 and W 11. 1:2. *SWK*

FIG. 10-5. Lead weight W 10.

FIG. 10-6. Lead weight W 11.

within a fragment of the custom-made wooden case which most likely held most, if not all, the pieces (Fig. 10-2). The case would have been very similar to those used today for weights, with circular housings cut to the size of each piece. The fragment preserves one complete housing, that for W 5, and part of a second for a larger weight, presumably W 4, the next largest in the set. A bronze pan (B 4, below) may be the sole remains of the equal-armed balance or pan scale with which such weights would have been used.[1]

Circular or disc weights were one of the two most common weight types employed during the Byzantine period. The other and perhaps more frequent type was the square or rectangular weight.[2] The combination of a cross over the weight designation within a wreath is a common pattern on both circular and rectangular forms.[3] The weights from the Yassi Ada ship are somewhat unusual for the simplicity of their decoration; their incised wreaths are relatively plain, and they lack the accessory ridges and other embellishments found on many circular weights of this period. Likewise, none of them seem to have possessed the central boss or hub which often appears on similar weights.[4] W 2 to W 6, however, each possess a shallow indentation in the center, perhaps the result of having been finished on a

[1] Cf. G. R. Davidson, *Corinth*, vol. XII, *The Minor Objects*, p. 216, no. 1672, and pl. 99.

[2] K. Pink, *Römische und byzantinische Gewichte in österreichischen Sammlungen*, p. 18; M. C. Ross, *Catalogue of the Byzantine and Early Mediaeval Antiquities in the Dumbarton Oaks Collection*, pp. 66–67; and H. Chantraine, "Uncia," *RE* 9, A, 1: 627–628, wherein only fourteen of his ninety examples of Period III weights are discs. In the Corinth collection, however, circular weights predominate (Davidson, *Corinth* XII).

[3] Cf. Ross, *Catalogue of the Antiquities*, pl. 46, nos. 77, 79–81; Davidson, *Corinth* XII, pl. 94, nos. 1599–1601; and W. Deonna, *Exploration archéologique de Délos*, vol. XVIII, *Le Mobilier délien*, p. 148, no. B712.

[4] I am grateful to Dr. Avraham Eran of Jerusalem for bringing to my attention the central boss or hub which is lacking on the Yassi Ada weights.

lathe.[5] In its basic form, double convex with a rim instead of disc-shaped, W 6 differs from the other weights found on board the ship. As will be seen below, it was probably a replacement piece.

The use of silver inlay is a common feature of Byzantine weights; one wonders, in fact, how closely the silver's own weight was taken into account during the manufacture.[6]

The weight designations preserved on some pieces in the set are the ones most commonly employed in Byzantine times.[7] On W 1 the upright arrow is the standard symbol for pound (Latin *libra*, Greek λίτρα), while the alpha, A, is the Greek alphabetic sign for one—thus, 1 pound. The Γ which appears on W 2–W 5 is a standard Greek designation for ounce (Latin *uncia*, Greek οὐγγία). The alphabetic numerals following denote the number of ounces. Thus, W 2 with ΓS is 6 ounces,[8] the ΓΓ of W 3 indicates 3 ounces, ΓB of W 4 indicates 2 ounces, and W 5, with its ΓA, is the 1-ounce piece. W 6, however, preserves about half of what is here restored as the common ligature for ounce, ☧ , a form which combines the omicron and the upsilon of the Greek word.

[5]The shallow indentations appear to be similar to that shown in Ross, *Catalogue of the Antiquities*, pl. 46, no. 80.

[6]O. M. Dalton, *A Guide to the Early Christian and Byzantine Antiquities*, p. 68. Deonna, *Délos* XVIII, 148, no. B712, is likewise inlaid with silver. Cf. also Pink, *Römische und byzantinische Gewichte*, p. 21. Little is written on the production of bronze weights. For disc and rectangular forms, the molten bronze could have been poured into an open mold. For discs with more undulating surfaces, such as W 6 from the ship's set, there are at least two techniques that could have been used: the pieces could have been cast in closed molds, or else in open molds as blank discs which were then turned on a lathe. The indentations noted on several pieces could have resulted from such a turning process. The incision on the surfaces would have been done after the bronze had cooled, although the bedding trenches for silver or gold inlay could have been formed in the casting.

In any case, it was essential that the manufacturer adhere as closely as possible to the official weight standards of his time or region. Either the bronze was weighed before melting, or the master mold was designed to hold only a certain amount of molten bronze. Still, the specific gravity of the bronze would have fluctuated a little according to its admixture of copper and tin. Surface engraving could also have had a slight effect on the weight of a piece, as could the application of inlay. The fluctuation in specific gram weight of Byzantine weights suggests that manufacturers may not have taken all these factors into consideration. It is equally possible that officialdom did not always enforce strict standards, thereby allowing the production of weights to become an approximate rather than an exact enterprise. The close interrelations of the weights from the Yassi Ada ship suggest a high degree of exactitude.

[7]For a concise explanation of these symbols, see Pink, *Römische und byzantinische Gewichte*, pp. 33ff. A convenient table showing the normal divisions of the Roman pound and their ideal gram equivalents is found in Chantraine, *RE* 9, A, 1: 620. See also the last column in Table 10-1, below.

[8]The S of W 2 represents the Greek alphabetic numeral six, digamma, whose form at this time is often difficult to distinguish from the lowercase sigma, ς, and from the Latin S, which is often used on weights to denote *semis*, or half.

Thus, in appearance there is nothing particularly unusual or remarkable about the eight weights from the ship: form, decoration, and designations are all well paralleled in numerous other examples. What does make them extraordinary is the fact that together they make up at least a partial set of Byzantine weights, to my knowledge the only one in existence. There seems no doubt that this is the case: they form a series graduated in size and weight; they were found in a single, closed deposit, wherein at least four were close together in the galley area; they exhibit an overall consistency in form and decoration (with the exception of W 6); a fragment of their custom-made case was discovered; and, not least, the close interrelationships of their specific weights, to be discussed below, indicate that they were made and used as a set based on a single standard.

The well-preserved quantitative designations of five of the weights leave no doubt about their values: W 1 through W 5 were respectively the 1-pound, 6-ounce, 3-ounce, 2-ounce and 1-ounce pieces. W 7 was not seen by this author after it was electrolytically cleaned in 1979–1980. Markings indicated at that time by the drawer of the figure here illustrated suggest a possible restoration of IB, iota beta, for twelve scripula, a common designation of a 3-nomisma weight, ordinarily half an ounce. The smallest piece, W 8, preserves no indications of weight but seems a safe candidate for the set's 1-nomisma piece. At 2.95 g, W 8 is almost exactly one-third the weight of W 7, which is 8.906 g. Other interrelationships of these two smallest pieces with certain of the larger ones will be examined shortly.

W 6 requires somewhat more in the way of discussion. With its weight of 17.5 g it is almost exactly six times as heavy as W 8, the 1-nomisma piece, and twice as heavy as the 3-nomisma piece, W 7. Thus, a value of 6 nomismata is indicated for W 6. Normally such a value would be the equivalent of 1 ounce, and in fact if the designation on its surface is the ligature for ounce, this is exactly what the piece is. However, there is already a 1-ounce piece, W 5, clearly designated as such by ΓA yet weighing nearly 2 g more than W 6. A possible explanation for this discrepancy must await further examination of the weights and their standard. For the moment, suffice it to say that W 6 appears to be a lighter 1-ounce piece that was added as a supplementary or replacement piece for the set. As noted above, its profile is entirely different from that of other pieces in the set. Likewise, it is greater in diameter than W 5, even though it weighs less, and it employs a ligature designation for ounce rather than the Γ of the heavier pieces.

The values of the weights are summarized in Table 10-1. It is doubtful that the set is complete, since as it is

TABLE 10-1. Gram Weights and Derived Ounces of the Eight Bronze Weights.

| | Value | Gram Weight | Derived Ounces in Grams | Mommsen's Roman Norm Equivalents in Grams |
|---|---|---|---|---|
| W 1 | 1 pound | 284.0 | 20.286* | 327.45 |
| W 2 | 6 ounces | 124.0 | 20.667 | 163.728 |
| W 3 | 3 ounces | 59.255 | 19.752 | 81.864 |
| W 4 | 2 ounces | 44.075 | 22.037 | 54.576 |
| W 5 | 1 ounce (7 nomismata) | 19.2 | 19.2 | 27.288 |
| W 6 | 1 ounce (6 nomismata) | 17.5 | 20.417[†] | 27.288 |
| W 7 | 3 nomismata | 8.906 | 20.781[†] | 13.644 |
| W 8 | 1 nomisma | 2.95 | 20.65[†] | 4.548 |

*Based on 14 ounces to the pound.

[†] Based on 7 nomismata to the ounce.

now preserved, certain amounts could not have been weighed. Of this more will be said later.

In order to discuss the weights and the standard upon which they were based, it will prove useful to review some basic principles of Roman and Byzantine metrology. The Byzantine pound is directly descended from that of the Roman Empire. On the basis of coin weights, Theodore Mommsen long ago established the theoretical weight of the Roman pound at 327.45 g, with its twelfth part, the ounce, at 27.288 g.[9] From the time of Constantine I, the ounce was normally divided into six smaller units, the nomismata. As its name implies, the nomisma was a unit connected with coinage weights; the solidus, its numismatic equivalent, became the coin of the Byzantine realm, supplanting the old denarius of the Empire. The nomisma was one seventy-second of a pound, and, using Mommsen's computation for the pound, 1 nomisma has a theoretical weight of 4.548 g. There were still smaller divisions of weight: the scripulum or scruple (one-fourth of a nomisma) and the siliqua (one-sixth of a scripulum). Throughout the Byzantine period there was a tendency for the weight of the pound, and thereby its constituent units, to decrease. This trend is evident from the downward fluctuation of the coin weights which apparently governed weight standards in general.[10]

From the pound of the set's standard it is readily apparent that the 284-g weight of W 1 falls far below Mommsen's theoretical 327.45 g; it is as well substantially lighter than the sixth-century–seventh-century

range of 313–322 g given by Erich Schilbach in his study of Byzantine metrology.[11] Since the piece is very well preserved, excessive weight loss cannot be assumed. Rather, W 1 must represent a considerably lightened pound that was current in the time of Heraclius. Important in this connection is the fact noted by Schilbach that the pounds of the provinces, as reckoned on the basis of the weights of provincial coin issues, were considerably lighter than the pound current in Constantinople during the seventh to ninth centuries. For the provinces a pound of about 285 g seems to have been fairly normal.[12] Thus, W 1 may well represent a provincial pound unit, one that was not in accord with the heavier standards current in the mainstreams of the Constantinopolitan administrative sphere.

Provincialism alone, however, cannot explain certain other peculiarities of the set's standard—namely, deviations from what are accepted as the normal interior divisions of both the pound and the ounce units: the pound consists of 14 ounces instead of the regular 12 ounces, while the ounce, normally containing 6 nomismata, was divided into 7 nomismata instead. Evidence of these irregularities follows. Throughout the discussion one should note that the close interrelation of specific weights among the pieces is a strong argument against the possibilities of extreme weight loss since antiquity.

W 2 provides firm ground from which to begin an examination of the pound's division (see Table 10-1). At 6 ounces, its doubled weight should ordinarily yield the full pound unit of 12 ounces. Yet the 248-g sum which results is 36 g lighter than the weight of the pound

[9]T. Mommsen, *Geschichte des Römischer Münzwesens*, p. xix. See also Chantraine, *RE* 9, A, 1.

[10]E. Schilbach, *Byzantinische Metrologie: Handbuch der Altertumswissenschaft*, XII, 166.

[11]Ibid.

[12]Ibid., pp. 167–168.

piece, W 1. Weight loss cannot account for the difference, for W 1 and W 2 are among the best-preserved pieces in the set. For example, one may not assume that W 2 originally weighed about 142 g and has lost 18 g, or over 12 percent of its original weight (a mass, incidentally, that is roughly equal to W 6). One-sixth of W 2— that is, its derived ounce—is 20.667 g. W 1, the pound piece, has a derived ounce of 23.667 g if it is reckoned in twelfths; yet if its weight is divided by fourteen, the resultant derived ounce of 20.286 g is less than 0.4 g lighter than that of W 2. W 3 and W 5 further support this division into fourteenths, for their derived ounces of 19.752 g and 19.2 g, respectively, come much closer to being fourteenth parts of the pound unit than they do to being twelfths. W 5 has the lowest derived ounce weight because of its missing silver inlay. W 4, on the other hand, has the highest of the derived ounces (22.037 g) because of an encrustation on its surface.

We shall now focus on the smaller units of weight. What is assumed to be the 1-nomisma piece, W 8, has a weight of 2.95 g, almost exactly one-third of the weight of W 7, thus suggesting that the latter is the 3-nomisma weight. Because of the very close correspondence of specific weight, we can also assume that neither of these pieces has suffered a significant loss of weight. Yet W 8 is about 0.5 g lighter than the sixth part of the derived ounces of W 1 and W 2. The 3-nomisma weight, W 7, should be the equivalent of half an ounce of 6 nomismata, yet its doubled weight (17.812 g) is 2.85 g lighter than the derived ounce of the best-preserved piece, W 2. In other words, there is room for an additional unit nearly equal in weight to W 8 (2.95 g), thus suggesting that the ounce of this set's standard contained 7 nomismata instead of the normal 6. This fact is also indicated by the close correlation of the 6-ounce weight, W 2, and the 1-nomisma piece, W 8. With 7 nomismata to the ounce, W 2 would be equivalent to 42 nomismata, and it is in fact only 0.1 g heavier than forty-two times the weight of W 8. Furthermore, the derived ounces of W 7 and W 8, if a 7-nomisma ounce is assumed, approximate within fractions of a gram the derived ounces of W 1 and W 2 (Table 10-1); this correspondence provides at the same time additional corroboration for an ounce that is a fourteenth part of the pound unit.

Some additional evidence of this extraordinary division of the ounce can be gained from the presumed latecomer to the set, W 6. Its weight of 17.5 g is only fractionally lighter than the doubled weight of W 7, the 3-nomisma piece, and is even closer to being six times the weight of W 8, the nomisma. Clearly, W 6 is a 6-nomisma weight, yet it is at the same time about 3 g lighter than the 20–21-g ounce suggested by the derived

ounces of W 1, W 2, W 7, and W 8. The difference is approximately equal to the weight of the 1-nomisma piece (2.95 g), thereby indicating that W 6 is a 6-nomisma piece in a system based on 7 nomismata to the ounce. The full 7-nomisma ounce would have been represented by W 5, which has unfortunately lost at least 1–1.25 g of its original weight. The derived (7-nomisma) ounce of W 6, 20.417 g, falls well within the 20–21-g range of other pieces (Table 10-1).

If the reading of the ounce ligature, ४ , on W 6 is correct, yet another abnormality is introduced in the suggestion that this piece was an ounce weight in a still lighter standard of 6 nomismata to the ounce. If such is the case, the ounce system which W 6 represents would have been closely tied to that of the ship's set: its lighter ounce was six-sevenths of the heavier ounce, while the heavier 20–21-g ounce was one and one-sixth times the weight of the lighter. Thus, W 6, an ounce in its own right, was able to serve as a useful addition or replacement within the ship's set because of its relation to the standard. A distant analogy might be that of the guinea and the pound sterling.

It is very doubtful that all the pieces of the original set are preserved, for as it now exists, it would have been incapable of weighing certain amounts. With the addition of a 2-nomisma piece and a second 1- or 2-ounce piece, the set could have weighed any even amount from 1 nomisma to 2 pounds.

The standard represented by the set of weights from the ship is remarkable, because it combines three separate abnormalities within its composition: a considerably lightened pound, perhaps provincial; a 14-ounce pound; and a 7-nomisma ounce. All in all, these irregularities constitute a threefold reduction in weight from what are considered normal contemporary systems. The least unusual feature is the lightened pound of about 284 g, for which there exists some substantiating evidence. The divisions of pound and ounce, however, are less easily reconciled, for they are without precise parallel. Nevertheless, some analogies and precedents do exist, especially for the division of the ounce into sevenths.

The more cogent of these precedents is the phenomenon of the Byzantine lightweight solidus minted from the time of Justinian until the late seventh century. These solidi may be as light as 20–21 siliquae, thereby making them one-sixth to one-eighth lighter than the normal solidus of 24 siliquae. Thus, a normal pound would have contained approximately eighty-four such lightened solidi, while a normal ounce would have been composed of roughly seven instead of the normal six.[13]

---

[13] For a general explanation of these light issues, see H. L. Adel-

A

B

C

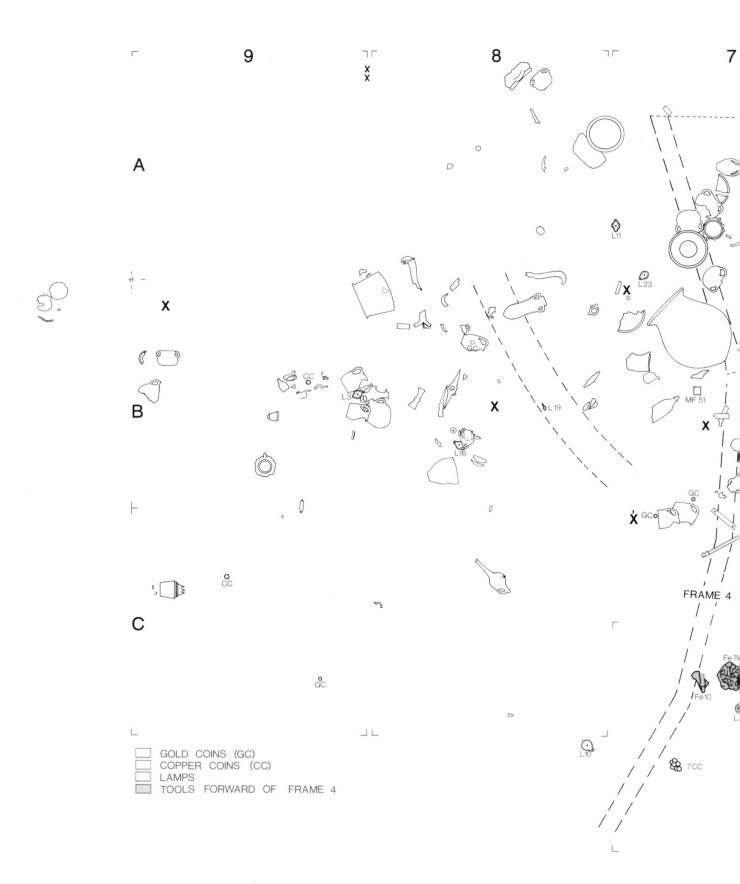

9    8    7

A

X
X

X

B

CC

L3

X

L19

X

L11

L23

X

MF 51

X

C

CC

GC

L16

GC

X
X GC

GC

FRAME 4

Fe 7

Fe10

L10

7CC

☐ GOLD COINS (GC)
☐ COPPER COINS (CC)
☐ LAMPS
▨ TOOLS FORWARD OF FRAME 4

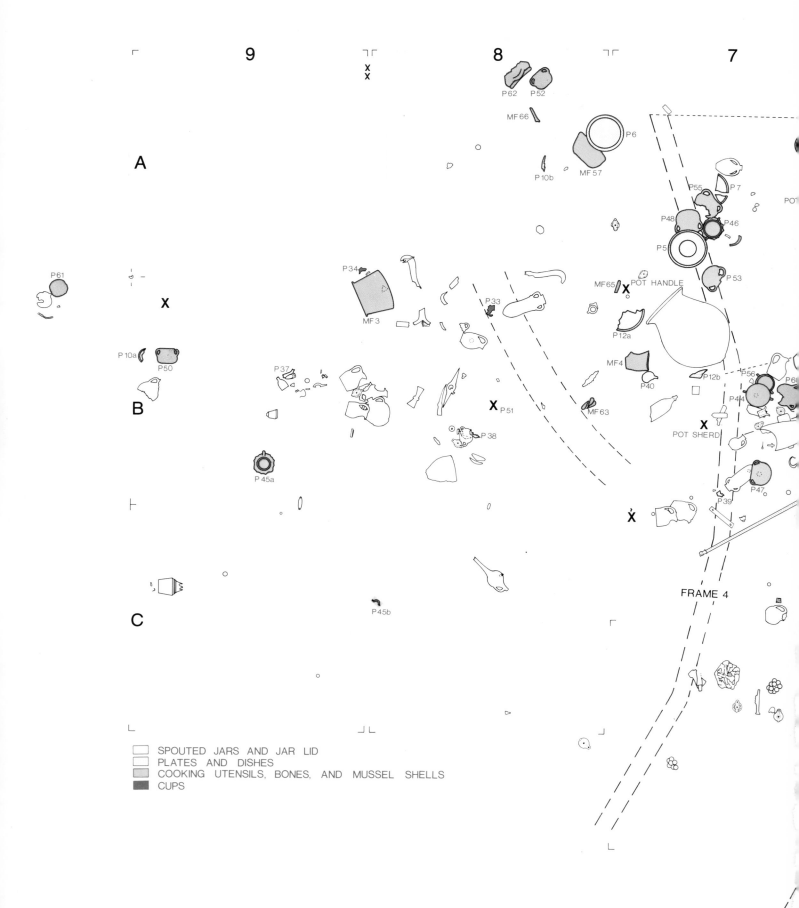

9 8 7

A

P62 P52

MF66

P6

MF57

P10b

P61

P55 P7

P48 P46

P5

X

P34 POT

MF65 X POT HANDLE P53

P33

P10a MF3 P12a

P50 MF4

B P37 P40 P12b P56

P51 P44

P38 MF63 X

POT SHERD

P45a

Ẋ P47

P39

FRAME 4

C

P45b

SPOUTED JARS AND JAR LID
PLATES AND DISHES
COOKING UTENSILS, BONES, AND MUSSEL SHELLS
CUPS

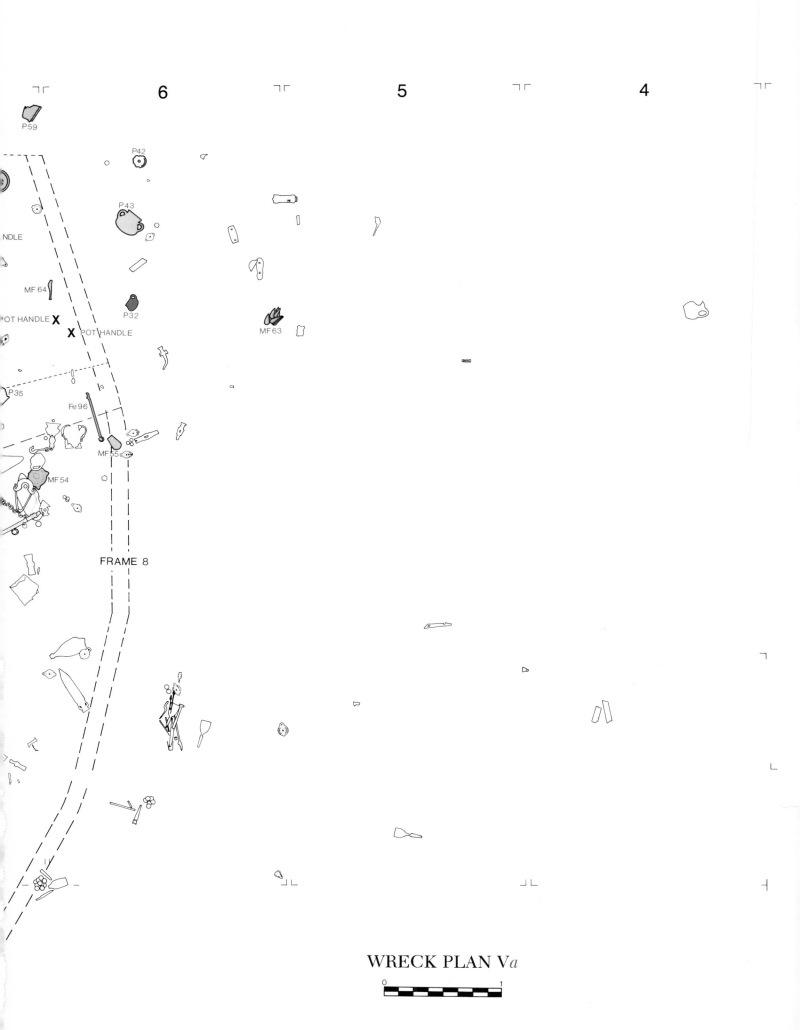

6    5    4

P59

P42

P43

NDLE

MF 64

POT HANDLE  X

X  POT HANDLE

P32

MF 63

P35

Fe 96

MF 55

MF 54

FRAME 8

WRECK PLAN V*a*

0    1

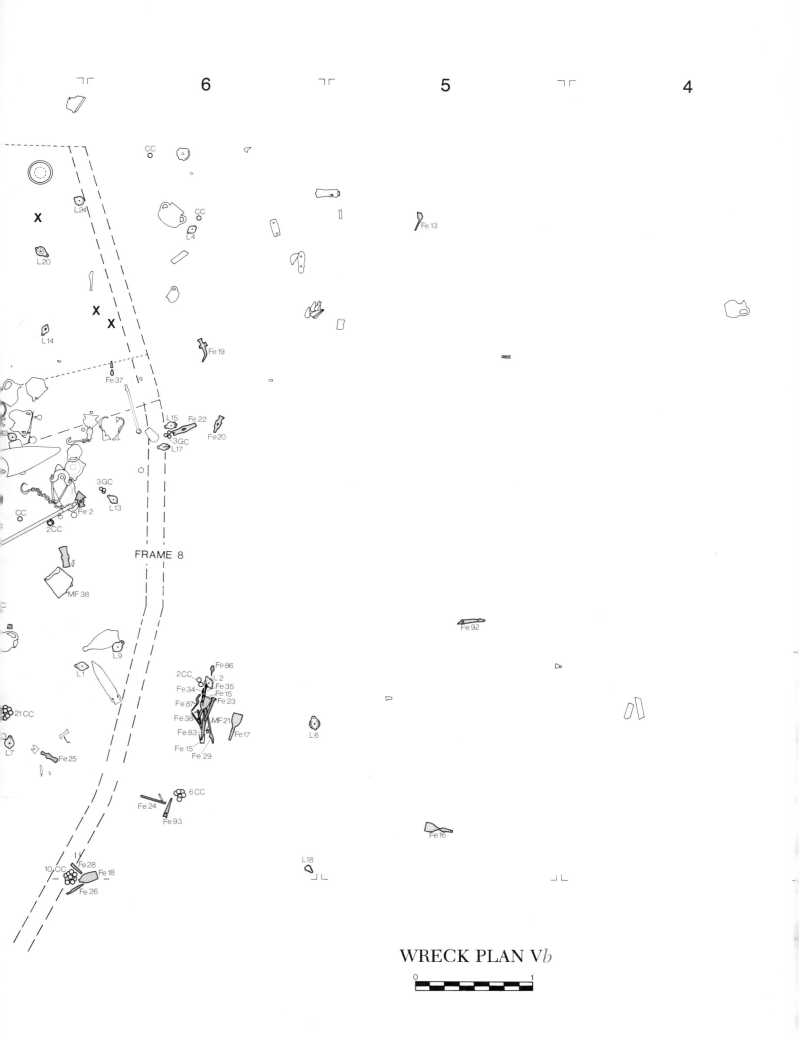

WRECK PLAN V*b*

3　　　　　⌐⌐　　　　　2　　　　　⌐⌐　　　　　1　　　　　⌐

A

⊣

B

⊣

C

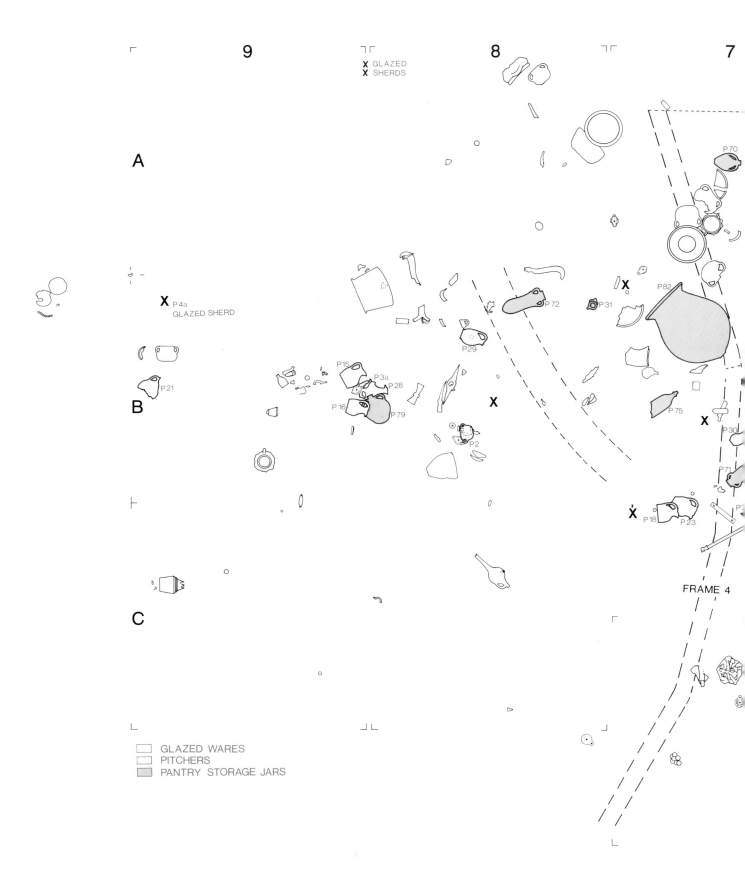

9      8      7

**X** GLAZED
**X** SHERDS

A

**X** P 4a
GLAZED SHERD

B

P 21

P 15
P 3a
P 28
P 16   P 79

P 29

**X**

P 72
P 31

**X** P82
P 75

**X** P30

P 71

P 2

**X** P 18   P 23

FRAME 4

C

☐ GLAZED WARES
☐ PITCHERS
▨ PANTRY STORAGE JARS

3        2        1

A

B

C

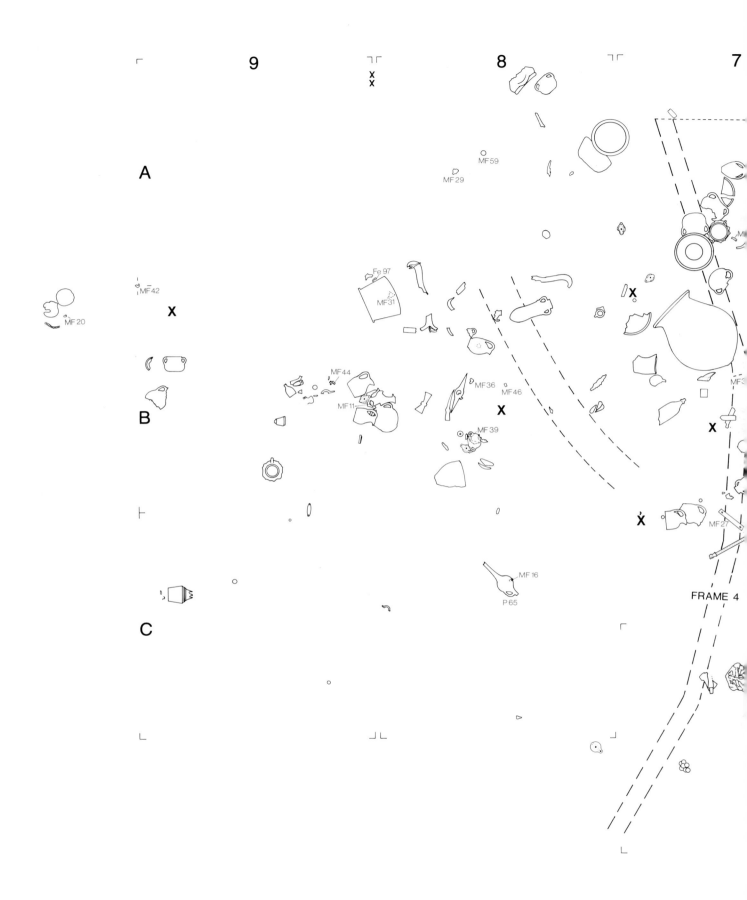

9       8       7

A

MF 59

MF 29

MF 42

X

MF 20

Fe 97

MF 31

X

B

MF 44

MF 36

MF 46

MF 11

X

MF 39

X

MF 27

X

MF 16

P 65

FRAME 4

C

3      2      1

A

MF 40

B

MF 50

C

MF 53

TOOLS AFT OF FRAME 4
LEAD WEIGHTS AND FISHING GEAR

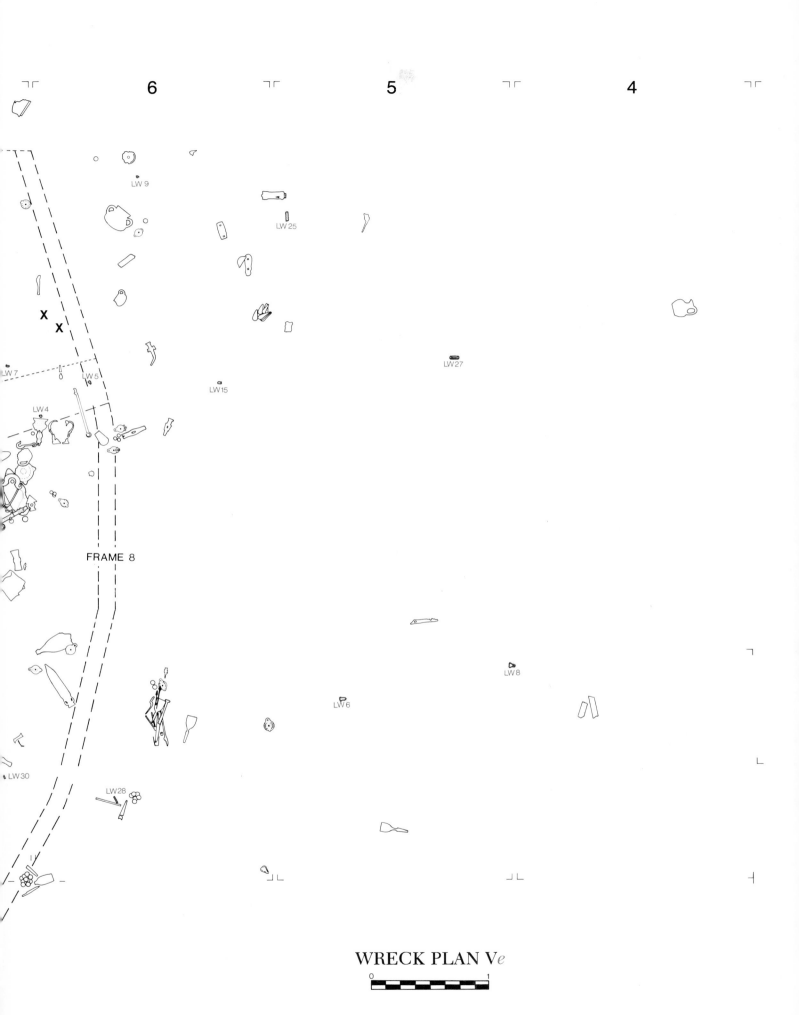

6       5       4

LW 9

LW 25

X
X

LW 7     LW 5

LW 4

LW 27

LW 15

FRAME 8

LW 8

LW 6

LW 30

LW 28

WRECK PLAN V*e*

0       1

X

X
 X

60

MF 37
MF 52

MF 25

MF 26

MF 56

MF 28

S 3

13

FRAME 8

P 84

Fe 99  Fe 98

WRECK PLAN V*f*. Miscellaneous Finds and Other Articles

0                  1

These coins were heavily circulated in the West, where, by the mid–sixth century, they seem to have given impetus to a barbarian series, the so-called Frankish solidus; minted at 21 siliquae, these Frankish coins would again have at least approximated one-seventh of an ounce.[14] A considerably earlier precedent for a division into sevenths is to be found in the early Roman Empire, where, until the time of Nero, the denarius was minted at one-seventh of an ounce.[15]

Although ounces of seven parts are thus not unprecedented, there is no ready parallel for the lightening of the ounce by one-seventh by making it a fourteenth instead of a twelfth part of the pound. Thus, the lightweight solidus, at approximately seven to the ounce in its lightest category, is one eighty-fourth of the 12-ounce pound, whereas the nomisma of the set's standard is one ninety-eighth due to the increased number of ounces. References to pounds of more than 12 ounces are known, but these involve pounds made heavier by additional ounces instead of pounds whose constituent units are increased in number and thus lightened. Furthermore, such pounds appear as units of account rather than actual weight standards. One such example is found in a law of Valentinian I dated to A.D. 367 and preserved in the Theodosian Code (V.19.4).[16] The law is connected singularly with gold mining, and it stipulates that mine operators must pay to the state a 14-ounce pound of gold in exchange for mining rights. It does not prescribe a lighter ounce, but rather a pound of two additional ounces—that is, one-sixth heavier than the normal.[17] What is probably a similar situation can be seen in the ἀργυρική λίτρα, a silver pound of 12½ ounces. Again, the pound is heavier than normal, this time by 0.5 ounce.[18]

Despite the lack of historical evidence for the division of the Yassi Ada set's pound, there are a few examples of single weights which suggest that the 14-ounce pound seen here was not unique. Of particular interest is a 1-ounce weight in the Naville Collection in Geneva which weighs 20.43 g.[19] Excellently preserved, it is only

0.01 g heavier than the derived ounce of W 6, and it is within the 0.5-g range of the derived ounces of four other weights from the ship. If it were the twelfth part of a pound, that pound unit would have had the very low weight of about 245 g, whereas a pound of 14 ounces would be 286.02—that is, only a couple of grams heavier than W 1 and at the same time corresponding closely to Schilbach's 285-g provincial pound.[20] Note that the Naville piece could not have belonged to precisely the same standard as that of the ship's set, for its value is clearly designated as 6 solidi; in other words, it was an ounce possessing the regular number of nomismata.

Long ago, E. Pernice published a 1-ounce piece in Athens, apparently in mint condition, with a weight of 21.04 g.[21] A pound of twelve such ounces would weigh a very light 252.48 g, whereas a pound of fourteen of these ounces is a more plausible 294.56 g.

It has already been noted that a light pound of about 285 g is not exceptional for the Byzantine period, especially among the provincial standards of the empire. Were such lightened standards established in an arbitrary manner, with no reference to the heavier weights of Byzantine officialdom, or were they somehow based upon a traditional, widely accepted or known standard against which they could be checked and controlled? The weights from Yassi Ada provide evidence in support of the latter possibility, since the standard they represent appears to be based on a pound very close to Mommsen's theoretical Roman norm of 327.45 g. Mommsen's figure is the close approximate of sixteen of the set's lighter ounces: its own sixteenth part, 20.465 g, is well within the 20–21-g range of five of the derived ounces in the set. Thus, the pound of the set's standard is equivalent to fourteen-sixteenths or seven-eighths of a figure very close to the theoretical 327.45 g. Seven-eighths of that norm, 286.51 g, is less than 3 g heavier than the ship's pound piece, W 1, and, it might be added, less than 0.5 g heavier than the derived 14-ounce pound of the weight in the Naville Collection discussed above. In turn, the ounce, being the fourteenth part of this lightened pound, is equal to three-fourths of the norm of about 27.288 g.

With this kind of relationship, it would have been possible to check and/or regulate the lighter standard against the heavier. Whether conversion from one standard to the other was ever an important issue is unclear, especially since the working pound units of the period tend to be lighter than Mommsen's norm. Even the derived pounds of the best-preserved gold solidi are more

son, *Light Weight Solidi and Byzantine Trade During the Sixth and Seventh Centuries*, ANSNNM, no. 138; and P. Grierson, *DOC* II, 11–17. Assuming a theoretical ounce of 27.288 g, solidi of 20.5 siliquae or 3.87 g result in an ounce of 7.05 solidi.

[14] Adelson, *Light Weight Solidi*, pp. 11–12, n. 22, and pp. 129–130.

[15] Schilbach, *Byzantinische Metrologie*, p. 184.

[16] T. Mommsen and P. M. Meyer, *Codex Theodosianus*, I, part 2, 558.

[17] Adelson, *Light Weight Solidi*, pp. 12–13.

[18] Schilbach, *Byzantinische Metrologie*, p. 175.

[19] N. Dürr, "Catalogue de la Collection Lucien Naville au Cabinet de Numismatique du Musée d'Art et d'Histoire de Genève," *Genava* 12 (1964): no. 268.

[20] Schilbach, *Byzantinische Metrologie*, pp. 167–168.

[21] E. Pernice, *Griechische Gewichte*, p. 203, no. 855.

than 3 g lighter.[22] Nevertheless, conversion, at least in theory, would have been relatively simple in the case of ounces, where a workable 3:4 ratio existed between the heavier and the lighter standards: 7 heavy ounces equal 9⅓ light ounces, or 9 ounces, 2 nomismata, and 8 siliquae; 7 light ounces are the equivalent of 5¼ heavy ounces, or 5 ounces, 1 nomisma, and 2 scripula (12 siliquae). Conversion of whole pounds would also have been possible: 5 heavy pounds represent 5 pounds and 10 ounces on the light scale; 5 light pounds equal 4 pounds, 4½ ounces on the heavy scale. It is likely that conversion tables existed to facilitate the reckoning.

While the ounces and pounds of the two standards present manageable ratios for conversion, such is not the case with the nomismata. At 1/112 of the 327.45-g norm, the nomisma of the lightened standard would have had a theoretical weight of 2.924 g (W 8 weighs 2.95 g)—in other words, a grotesque 9/14 of Mommsen's 4.548-g norm for the nomisma. In a relationship where 4 of the light nomismata equal 2.57 of the heavy ones (a figure understandable in decimal form but representative of no even amount in scripula or siliquae), the extreme difficulties of conversion are readily apparent. Had the lightened ounce been divided into sixths, however, the light nomisma would have been 1/96 (3.41 g) of Mommsen's norm, with the result that heavy and light nomismata would have been in the same 3:4 ratio that allows easy conversion of the ounces (for example, 5 light nomismata would have equaled 3¾ heavy nomismata, or 3 nomismata and 3 scripula). With the precedent of the lightweight solidus, in which the intentional reduction of weight resulted in an ounce of approximately 7 solidi instead of 6 (in the case of a solidus of 20–21 siliquae), the possibility of a similar reckoning in the Yassi Ada standard should at least be considered. It is, in other words, conceivable that the division into nomismata was reckoned at six, whereas in fact there were seven per ounce. The difference in weight, as in the case of lightweight solidi, would have been minimal (about 0.5 g) yet perhaps significant enough to make a real difference in the weighing out of such precious materials as gold and silver.

It is likewise possible that the lightening of weight was structured along lines similar to that of the lightweight solidus. Had the lightened ounce been divided into sixths, the theoretical weight of its nomisma, at 1/96 of Mommsen's 327.45-g norm, would have been 3.41 g, while 1/24, the siliqua, would have been 0.142 g. Twenty and one-half such siliquae equal 2.911 g; twenty-one equal 2.982 g. These figures bracket closely both the

2.924-g nomisma, which is 1/112 of Mommsen's norm, and the 2.95-g weight of W 8 in the ship's set. Continuing this line of speculation, one can perhaps see W 6 in a different light, as a piece representing an ounce of six of these lightweight nomismata. This concept would explain both the ounce designation on its surface and also the fact that two separate ounce pieces, one of six nomismata and the other of seven, were used in the set. Here, however, the speculation must end; the why and the wherefore of such an intricate system remain entirely unclear.

Whatever rationale lay behind the standard of the Yassi Ada weights and its internal divisions, it does appear most certain that the system was based on a heavier Roman or Byzantine standard. The present discussion has tended to use Mommsen's convenient figure of 327.45 g but does not suggest that this was precisely the standard of reference for the lighter system. A slightly lighter pound, such as the 326.16-g pound proposed by Oxé,[23] is equally possible, but the 320-g unit which Schilbach considers a workable weight for the Byzantine pound is a little too light.[24] It is very likely that the provincial pounds of about 285 g cited by Schilbach also bespeak standards based on such a heavier unit of reference and represent seven-eighths of that heavier unit.[25]

At least one case of a still lighter pound based on a heavier unit of reference is known—the σουάλια λίτρα used for weighing wood and oil. According to Schilbach, the σουάλια λίτρα was not an arbitrary unit but was established at four-fifths the weight of the normal pound and was thus equal to nine and three-fifths normal ounces. Internal adjustments would have been made in order to give this lightened pound a normal complement of twelve ounces, each the equivalent of four-fifths of a normal ounce.[26] In certain ways, the σουάλια λίτρα provides interesting analogies for the standard of the Yassi Ada weights: like the ship's weights, this specialized pound could be checked and regulated with reference to a heavier unit; at the same time, its highly contrived and artificial internal division reflects much the same kind of elasticity regarding the structure of weight units that is

[22] Grierson, DOC II, 10.

[23] August Oxé, "Kor und Kab. antike Hohlmasse und Gewichte in neuer Beleuchtung," BonnJbb 147 (1942): 191.

[24] Schilbach, Byzantinische Metrologie, p. 174.

[25] Ibid., p. 168.

[26] Ibid., pp. 179–180. Since Schilbach uses 320 g as a working weight for the Byzantine pound (see his p. 174), his σουάλια λίτρα has a weight of 256 g and an ounce of 21.333 g, whereas Mommsen's norm would result in a pound of 261.96 g and an ounce of 21.83 g. Moreover, Schilbach assumes that Pernice's 21.04-g ounce weight belongs to this lightened standard, but unless the standard of the σουάλια λίτρα had other purposes, it is difficult to imagine these relatively light bronze weights being used for wood and oil.

seen in the standard of the ship's set. It is tempting to think that, like the σουάλια λίτρα, this lightened standard of 14 ounces or 98 nomismata was developed for a highly specialized purpose, but if such were the case, it would then leave the ship without a regular set of weights with which day-to-day transactions in a variety of materials would certainly have been made. A rather forced conclusion might be that the set did indeed exist for weighing a particular item, or a particular category of items, but because of its direct relationship to a heavier, more universal standard, it could be used for general purposes as well.

The discovery of the Yassi Ada weights in a closed context of the early seventh century has allowed the unprecedented opportunity for examining several Byzantine weights belonging to a single set and standard. The peculiarities in composition of that standard are no less remarkable than the existence of the set itself. Had only one or two of its pieces been retrieved, the latitude for analysis and commentary would have been severely restricted; in fact, the idiosyncracies of the standard would most likely have eluded modern investigation had there been anything less than several pieces. Although the standard itself is thus revealed, the problematical issues raised by it defy an easy interpretation. The motivation for such a divergent system of weight is totally unclear, as are its geographic, economic, and extended chronological implications. The standard could not possibly have been unique, for its very presence on a seagoing vessel reflects a widespread acquaintance with its purpose and system. Furthermore, it is doubtful that it was the only such divergent standard employed by the Byzantines. As the study of the metrology of this period progresses, the set of eight bronze weights from Yassi Ada may come to be seen in a clearer historical and economic perspective. For the time being, however, it must be classified as an enigma.

### THE GLASS WEIGHT

Glass pendant weights were common in the Balkans and eastern Mediterranean in the sixth and seventh centuries. Their place or places of origin are uncertain. Some scholars favor Egypt, where many have been found, while others see them as issuing from Constantinople.[27] The glass pendant from the ship (W 9) belongs to a large class of such weights which contain only a cruciform monogram whose letters and bars usually incorporate all or most of the letters of a Christian name. In the case of the Theodoros of the ship's example (actu-

ally the genitive or possessive form ΘΕΟΔΩΡΟΥ), all letters are somehow included; what may not be apparent at first glance are the theta in the center of the monogram, its cross-bar formed by the horizontal arm of the cross, and the omega, which perches atop the delta at the bottom. Other types of glass weights may combine a bust or monogram with the name and title of an official, often an eparch.[28] Presumably those possessing only a monogram were made in the name of important officials as well, although the nature of the evidence does not warrant a categorical assumption. The name Theodoros recurs occasionally on other examples, although it is impossible to know whether all represent the same Theodoros, a fairly common name.[29]

The purpose most often proposed for these glass pieces is a use as coin weights—that is, a handy means of checking the actual weight and thus value of a gold coin. With such a function it is understandable that the pendant's own weight would have been carefully regulated and guaranteed by a government official or agency. While many glass weights undoubtedly served this purpose, there are others, including that from the ship, whose weights do not correspond to any known coin type.[30]

The 1.7-g weight of the example from the ship finds close correspondence in a few other glass weights. In 1898, Mordtmann published a weight of the Eparch Flavius Gerontius (559/560) which also weighs 1.7 g. Mordtmann considered this to be the weight of the half-solidus coin or semissis, a common Byzantine issue during the sixth and seventh centuries. Ross, however, in his publication of a 1.75-g glass weight in Dumbarton Oaks, notes Grierson's observation that the weight does not correspond to that of any known coin type. The weight is in fact too light to represent one-half a normal solidus, which, in the time of Heraclius, averaged between 4.45 and 4.50 g. The weight is also too light to represent one-half a lightweight solidus; even those of the lightest twenty-siliqua category ideally weigh 3.7 to 3.75 g.[31]

---

[27] Cf. Ross, *Catalogue of the Antiquities*, pp. 83–84, and the bibliography under his no. 98.

[28] For a useful discussion of monogram types, see Grierson, *DOC* II, 107–111. See also G. Schlumberger, "Poids de verre étalons monétiformes d'origine byzantine," *REG* 8 (1895): 59–76, where four types of glass weights are isolated; Schlumberger's third type is composed of those examples with monogram only.

[29] Ross, *Catalogue of the Antiquities*, pp. 83–84, no. 98, has been read by Grierson as θ[E]ΟΔΟΡΟΥ. Two weights published by Schlumberger provide the same name. One, no. 9, combines a bust with the inscription of the Eparch Theodoros. The other, no. 30, provides essentially the same monogram form that is seen on the ship's weight, although enclosed in a wreath.

[30] Cf. Ross, *Catalogue of the Antiquities*, pp. 84–85.

[31] Dr. Mordtmann, "Byzantinische Glasstempel," *BZ* 7 (1898): 605, no. 5; Ross, *Catalogue of the Antiquities*, p. 84, no. 99; Grierson, *DOC* II, 10.

Although no close correspondence with the weight of a coin type is forthcoming for the ship's glass pendant, its 1.7-g weight does seem to represent a recognizable fraction of the ounce. From the time of Nero, the denarius, the coin of the realm of the Roman Empire, was set at one-eighth of an ounce, or 3.41 g if Mommsen's ideal 27.288-g ounce is used. During the Roman Empire the older Greek coin, the drachma, was equivalent in weight to the denarius. After 307, when Constantine I introduced the gold solidus at one seventy-second of the Roman pound, the denarius eventually ceased to be minted, but its equivalent, the drachma, continued in use, more as a unit of weight at one-eighth of an ounce than as a coin type, through the Byzantine period.[32] The glass weight from the ship is precisely one-half the theoretical 3.41-g weight of this drachma unit, or one-sixteenth of Mommsen's norm for the Roman ounce, 27.288 g. In Greek parlance, the pendant has a weight of 3 *obols*. It will be recalled that the standard of the eight bronze weights from the ship is directly related to a pound at or very close to Mommsen's 327.45-g norm. Thus, it should not be surprising to find contemporary

units, such as the glass pendant, whose weight is also in close relationship to such a norm, even though other evidence indicates the gradual lightening of working standards of weight during the Byzantine era. Since the glass weight is directly related to this norm, it is also directly related to the lightened standard of the set of bronze weights in being one-twelfth the hypothetical ounce of that system, 20.465 g (one-sixteenth Mommsen's norm for the pound). In other words, had this light ounce been divided into the normal 6 nomismata instead of 7, the glass pendant would represent one-half a nomisma or 2 scripula or 12 siliquae. This aspect is particularly interesting in light of the possibility ventured above that the ounce of the bronze weights may have been reckoned at 6 nomismata rather than at the actual 7 nomismata which it contained. If this were so, the glass pendant would then become a reminder of the more normal ounce division.

Despite these close correspondences, the purpose of the glass weight remains unclear. It is at any rate very doubtful that it served as a check against the weight and value of a particular coin type.

## Balances and Accessories

B 1. Bronze steelyard and accessories.
                Inv. No. W3-112.
    Figs. 10-7–10-18; Wreck Plan V*c*.
                (spanning 7B/C).
  *a.* Steelyard bar and attached suspension hooks.
    Figs. 10-7 and 10-8.
    L. 1.46; max. th. 0.04; weight with attached fulcrum hook 7,750 g.
    Bar intact but pitted, chipped, and corroded in places; one of the two suspension fixtures missing. Solid bronze, presumably cast as a single piece.

    The length of the bar is divided into the following seven sections, from right to left in Figs. 10-7 and 10-8:
  1. Boar's head terminal at right end.
    Figs. 10-7, 10-8, and 10-10.
    L. 0.07.
      The head's snout and underside are wide and flattened. The eyes are oval, outlined with incision, and have a punched dot for the iris. Short, pointed ears protrude from the rear of the head, while on top, between the eyes, is a rounded knob. Facial bristles

and eyelashes are incised and were perhaps originally filled with a white substance. Low and towards the front of the snout is a small transverse hole, either drilled or formed during the casting. Immediately behind the head is the weighing collar.
  2. Weighing collar.
    Fig. 10-10.
    L. 0.034.
      Round in section; deeply grooved all around in order to house the yoke support for the load hooks and their chains (B 1*c*, below). Behind the collar is a short decorated segment.
  3. Short decorated segment.
    Fig. 10-11.
    L. 0.055.
      Rectangular in section. On both broader faces are incised floral-leaf designs. The incision may have been emphasized by a white filling substance, although what remains could also be a later deposit. A low, narrow band bearing an incised herringbone pattern separates this segment from the fulcrum bar.
  4. Fulcrum bar.
    L. 0.178.

---

[32] Schilbach, *Byzantinische Metrologie*, pp. 160, 184.

FIG. 10-7. Bronze steelyard B 1 and accessories, with fulcrum hook B 1*b* located incorrectly on the suspension apparatus (see Fig. 10-8).

Continues the rectangular section of the decorated segment. Of the two fulcrum fixtures, only that nearer the weighing collar (0.105 distant) is preserved intact and attached; its use corresponds to an upright position for the boar's-head terminal at the right (Position B, discussed on pp. 228–229). This point of suspension has been pierced transversely by a hole placed within a low, convex rise in the segment's profile. Into the hole has been inserted a bronze pin which protrudes sufficiently at either side to allow for the attachment of a U-shaped swivel with two eyelets. The swivel is held in place by hemispherical heads attached to the pin. A solid ring, oval in section and 0.053 in diam., connects the swivel to the suspension hook. The hook itself is roughly square in section, with a max. dimension of 0.158. Its lower end is bent double to enclose the ring, while the upper end terminates in a thickened conical knob. The second fulcrum, 0.127 from the first and 0.232 from the weighing collar, is placed within a low rise on the opposite edge of this section; only the hole is preserved, now clogged with

what may be the remains of the inserted pin. Its use would have seen the boar's-head terminal in an inverted position (Position A, discussed on pp. 225–228). A detached hook (B 1*b*, below), by reason of its similarity to the hook of the intact fixture, may be associated with this second fulcrum. Between the two fulcra, on the broad side of this section which would have faced the user when the boar's head was upright (Position B), is a two-line statement of ownership rendered in punched dots (Fig. 10-12) which reads:

ΓΕΟΡΓΙΟΥ ΠΡΕΣΒΥ / ΤΕΡΟΥ
ΝΑΥΚΛΕΡΟΥ

A low, narrow band separates this section of the steelyard bar from the beam scale.

5. Beam scale or graduated segment.
Figs. 10-9 and 10-13.
L. 1.01.

Lozenge-shaped in section, this portion of the bar is so oriented that its 0.023-wide faces would be at roughly 45° angles as the instrument was suspended from one or the other fulcrum hook. With fulcra and boar's head on the right, one of the two graduated faces appears on an upper sloping surface:

FIG. 10-8. Bronze steelyard B 1 and accessories. *SWK, GKS, and FM*

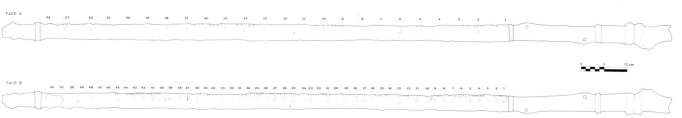

FIG. 10-9. Calibrated faces of B 1 beam scale. *GKS and FM*

FIG. 10-10. Boar's head terminal of B 1. *GFB*

FIG. 10-11. Incised floral segment of B 1. *GFB*

FIG. 10-13. Detail of Face B, first three calibrations, of B 1.

FIG. 10-12. Inscription of B 1. *GKS*

FIG. 10-14. Small animal-head terminal of B 1. *GFB*

Face B when the fulcrum nearer the weighing collar is used (Position B), and Face A with the second fulcrum (Position A). The calibrations extend from right to left (retrograde) along these two faces. They consist of Greek alphabetic numerals rendered in punched dots, with four short, vertical lines between each pair of letters. On both faces the letters average 0.019 in height, while widths vary considerably depending upon the letter. On Face A, the letters are spaced 0.04 to 0.045 apart, while those of Face B are normally spaced between 0.016 and 0.022 apart. Towards the end (left) on both faces the letters are illegible because of extensive wear and corrosion. Separated from the beam scale by a low convex band is a short, plain segment.

6. Short, plain segment.
    L. 0.04.
    Oval in section, this segment tapers towards another low offsetting band, beyond which is an animal-head terminal.

7. Animal-head terminal at left end.
    Figs. 10-7, 10-8, and 10-14.
    L. 0.033.
    Although very worn, the head, with its compact muzzle and short, perky ears, appears to be that of either a feline or a dog.

The head is pierced by two holes which meet to form a **T**: one is placed transversely through the muzzle, and the other runs lengthwise from the flattened end.

b. Large hook with attached ring.
    Fig. 10-15.
    Max dimension 0.153; max. th. 0.015.
    Probably for use with the fulcrum farther from the weighing collar. Square in section; similar in form to the fulcrum suspension hook in place on the steelyard. The connecting ring, 0.033 in diam., is thinner than the one still attached to the intact fixture.

c. Bronze suspension apparatus, all found together and connected.
    Figs. 10-7, 10-8, and 10-15.
    Weight 3,308 g.
    The load suspension apparatus is made up of the following four parts:

1. Yoke.
    Fig. 10-15.
    Max h. 0.120; max. w. 0.180.
    Shaped like a broad, flattened horseshoe, the yoke is designed to slip over and rest directly on the weighing collar. The long, tapered ends are bent back double, but only after having been slipped through the eyelets of a **V**-shaped swing.

2. **V**-shaped swing.

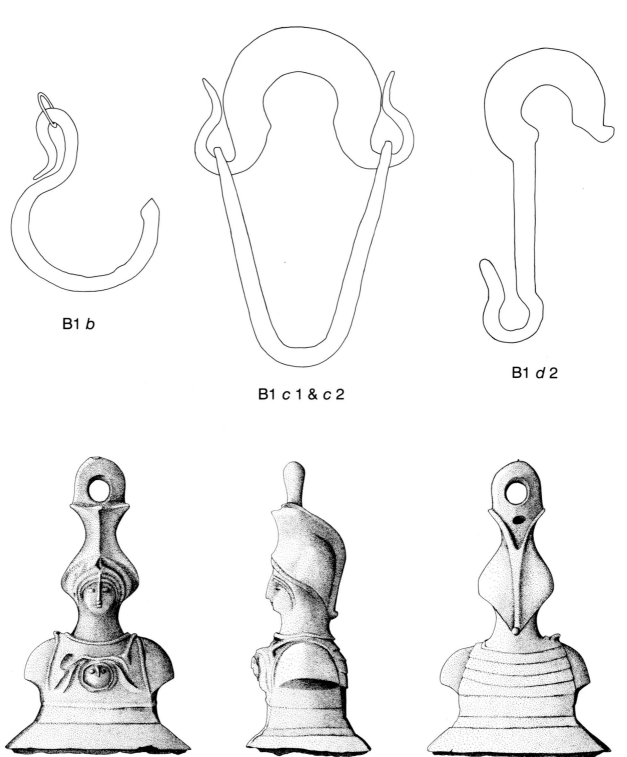

B1 *b*

B1 *c* 1 & *c* 2

B1 *d* 2

B1 *d* 1

FIG. 10-15. Steelyard B 1 accessories: B 1*b*, detached fulcrum hook with ring; B 1*c*1 and B 1*c*2, yoke and swing for weighing collar; B 1*d*2, counterweight hook; and B 1*d*1, Athena bust counterweight. 1:3 *SWK*

FIG. 10-17. Views of the Athena bust counterweight.

FIG. 10–16. Athena bust counterweight B 1*d*1 as it was raised from the sea. *Robert B. Goodman,* © National Geographic Society.

Fig. 10-15.

H. 0.185; max. w. 0.143.

Approximately square in section. Found attached to the swing were two lengths of chain.

3. Two lengths of chain.

    *a.* 17 twisted links; l. 0.675.

    *b.* 13 twisted links; l. 0.480.

Attached to the ends of the chains were load hooks.

4. Two load hooks.

Max. dimensions of each 0.13.

Practically identical, the hooks are square in section and have sharply outwardly bent, pointed ends.

*d.* Counterweight and suspension hook, found together but separated.

Total weight 8,632.50 g.

1. Athena bust counterweight.

Figs. 10-15–10-17.

H. 0.250; max. w. 0.150; weight 7,970.0 g.

Surface pitted; small chips of bronze missing along lower edge; seemingly small amount of the lead filling missing. Hollow cast bronze, open at bottom and filled with lead.

Above a spreading, rectangular base the upper torso and head of Athena appear in bust form. Over an undergarment that is suggested only by the intentionally armless short sleeves she wears her protective cloak or *aegis*. Of basically cuirass form, with narrow shoulder straps, the *aegis* is flounced on the back in suggestion of leatherworking; centered on the front is the *gorgoneion*, or head of Medusa. The gorgon's head is a projecting circle within which eyes, nose, and broadly grinning mouth are cursorily rendered. What appear to be casual folds around the head are more likely to be interpreted as the snakes which form Medusa's hair, but here they are apparently unattached. In frontal view, Athena's head appears diminutive in relation to her torso and thick neck, although in profile the distinctive lines of nose, mouth, and chin reveal a more plausible proportioning. The face is framed by thickened strands of hair that extend outward from center forehead and down along the sides of the face in shallow arcs. A solid mass of hair is revealed beneath the rim of her helmet. This piece of headgear seems to perch lightly atop her head instead of resting securely upon it. Its rim rises high in front as a shallow, inverted V, and in gentle, double curves angles sharply downward to define a tapered and peaked neck guard behind. A medial crest begins at this lower point, punctuated by a small rounded knob, and rises along the rear of the helmet, gaining height, until it splits to form the petals of a large lotus-flower finial. From this bloom atop the helmet rises the ring by which the counterweight was attached to its suspension hook.

2. Suspension hook.
   Figs. 10-15 and 10-18.
   L. 0.217; w. 0.095; th. 0.010; weight 662.5 g.

This piece consists of two hooks of unequal size: a smaller one for attachment to the counterweight and, at the other end of a long bar, the hook which was slipped over the beam scale. The latter hook is broad and flattened and, to facilitate reading, is thinned to about one-half centimeter where it rests on the beam scale. Two small notches or grooves cut into the inner edge of this hook serve to help guide the hook along the scale.

FIG. 10-18. Counterweight suspension hook B 1*d2*.

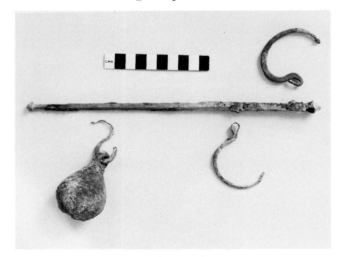

FIG. 10-19. Bronze steelyard B 2 and accessories.

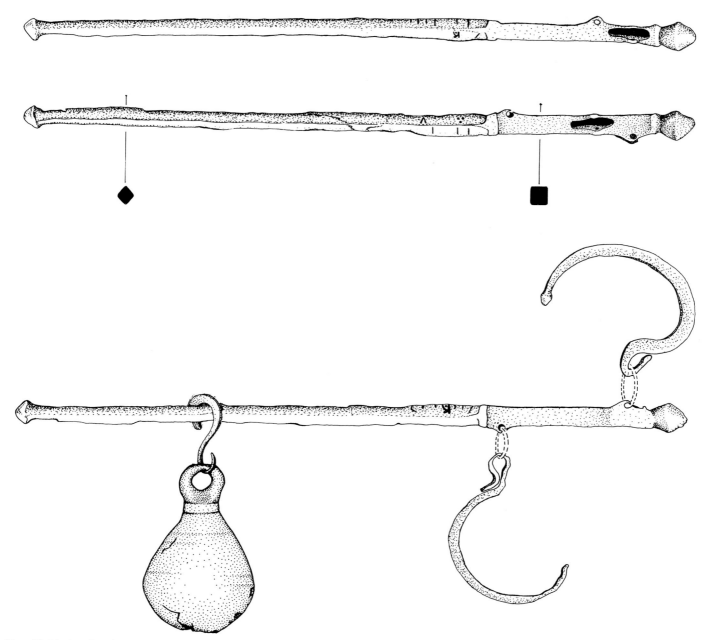

FIG. 10-20. Steelyard B 2, showing, *top to bottom*, Face B, Face A, and Face C. 2:3. *SWK*

B 2. Small bronze steelyard and accessories.

Inv. No. W3-113.
Figs. 10-19 and 10-20; Wreck Plan V*c*.

(Found near B 1 in 7B).

*a*. Steelyard bar.

L. 0.278; max. th. 0.007; weight 85 g.

Bar intact but chipped and worn. Like B 1, formed in a single piece.

Behind a thickened, biconical finial at the right is the weighing collar, here little more than an articulated, grooved constriction circular in section; the weighing apparatus which

would have been suspended from this collar (cf. B 1*c*, above) was not found. The fulcrum bar directly behind is square in section and 0.07 long. Three fulcrum points are located on three different sides of the bar at distances of 0.0095, 0.0265, and 0.063 from the groove of the weighing collar (Positions C, B, and A, respectively, shown from right to left in Fig. 10-20). Each point is formed by a pair of almost triangular flanges rising flush with the adjacent sides; the flanges are pierced by holes about 0.002 in diameter, presumably for the insertion of a pin;

the surface of the bar between each pair of flanges is hollowed out, probably in order to allow for a ring which would have linked the pin and the suspension hook together.[33] Beyond a low and poorly defined band is the beam scale, 0.185 long, lozenge-shaped in section, and oriented so that each face is at an angle with respect to the fulcrum bar. As with B 1, each of the graduated faces would have been on an upper sloping surface when its corresponding fulcrum at the right was in use. Due to wear, the calibrations are not preserved beyond the first third of the scale's length: on Face A (corresponding to Position A) only two calibrations are discernible; these are spaced 0.016 apart. Face B, the best preserved, has calibrations spaced between 0.003 and 0.004 apart. Face C has visible marks at intervals of 0.005. Most of the legible calibrations are vertical lines, although a few Greek alphabetic numerals can be detected. The steelyard bar terminates at the left in a thickened, conical knob.

*b*. Bronze fulcrum hook.
Fig. 10-20, attached for use at Position C.
                                                              VW (7B).
Max. dimension 0.064; max. th. 0.005.

Square in section. Hook tapers and terminates in a small, conical knob; other end tapered and doubled back, probably for a connecting ring similar to that seen on B 1.

*c*. Bronze fulcrum hook.
Fig. 10-20, attached for use at Position A.
                                                              VM (7B).
Max. dimension 0.051; max. th. 0.005.
Corroded at ends.

Rectangular in section (0.003 × 0.005); tapered towards hook end; other end thinned and doubled back in an S-curve.

*d*. Counterweight and hook.
Combined weight 547 g.
1. Counterweight.
    H. 0.073; max. diam. 0.057.

    Lead weight, piriform in shape. A bronze rod, 0.004 in diam., passes through the entire length of the weight; one end is visible at the bottom, while the other terminates in a ring. The juncture between ring and weight has been smoothed over with lead.
2. Bronze suspension hook.
    L. 0.041; max. th. 0.004.

[33]Cf. Ross, *Catalogue of the Antiquities*, no. 73.

Rectangular in section and S-shaped. Hooked ends of unequal size: smaller for attachment to weight; larger, thinned to less than 0.001, slid along the beam scale.

B 3. Bronze steelyard bar.                    Inv. No. W3-233.
Figs. 10-21 and 10-25. (Found very near B 1 in 7B).
L. 0.253; th. 0.003–0.009.
Badly corroded; bent at what is now thinnest point to about 40° angle. Neither divisions of the bar nor calibrations are discernible.

Both ends terminate in a thickened, conical knob, as seen in B 2 above. End at the left in the illustrations is the larger; on the analogy of B 2, the weighing collar may have been directly behind that end. Where best preserved, the rod is square or lozenge-shaped in section, again reminiscent of B 2.

For accessories which may possibly be associated with this steelyard, see B 5, B 7, and B 8–B 9 below and pp. 229–230.

B 4. Fragmentary bronze pan.                  Inv. No. W3-354.
Fig. 10-25; Wreck Plan V*c*.                  MCO (10B).
Est. diam. 0.15; max. th. 0.005.
Worn, encrusted and broken; most of rim missing.
Shallowly concave pan with low, turned-up rim. Two holes near periphery.

Found with the pan were ten links of bronze chain having a total length of 0.20; the links are of the same S-shaped, twisted variety as that found connected to B 6 below.

B 5. Lead weight with copper sheathing.
                                              Inv. No. W3-207.
Figs. 10-22 and 10-25; Wreck Plan V*c*.       FO (8A).
H. 0.071; max. diam. 0.056; weight 1,230 g.
Intact but worn.
Oval in shape, circular in section. Upper half covered with paper-thin copper sheathing which terminates along an uneven line at midway. Immediately below this line, on the lead surface, is a row of very closely spaced, punched dots, perhaps connected with the securing of the copper leaf (now missing or removed at this point) to the weight. Into the top a roughly rectangular hole has been cut that pierces the weight along its main axis to a depth of at least 0.018; traces of iron were found in and around the hole, suggesting that an iron rod or pin had been inserted. The area around the mouth of the hole is rough and jagged, perhaps the result of an eyelet or ring that has broken away or disintegrated (compare the counterweight of B 2).

B 6. Bronze hook and link of chain.  Inv. No. W3-331.
Fig. 10-25; Wreck Plan V*c*.                  MCD (9B).

FIG. 10-21. Bronze steelyard bar B 3.

FIG. 10-22. Lead weight with copper sheathing B 5.

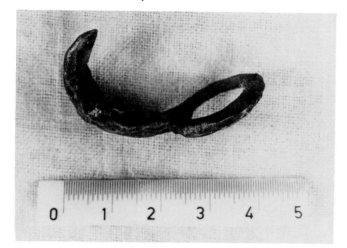

FIG. 10-23. Bronze ring with hook B 8.

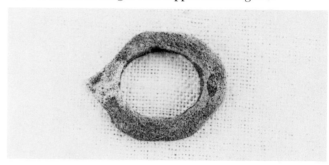

FIG. 10-24. Bronze ring B 9.

Max. dimension of hook 0.072; max. th. of hook 0.004; l. of chain 0.02.

Hook extremely thinned from corrosion at outer bend.

Hook rectangular in section; thicker central portion forms a broad oval. Both ends bent out sharply at an angle. Outer end thickened and tapered to a point; other end flattened and formed into a small eyelet for attachment to chain. Chain link found attached to hook is **S**-shaped and twisted.

B 7. Bronze hook.      Inv. No. W3-353.
Fig. 10-25; Wreck Plan V*c*.      MCY (9C).
Max. dimension 0.078; max. th. 0.003.

Outer end terminates in a small, thickened knob. Other end, bent outward from bow of hook, is of irregular line, suggesting perhaps that it was originally bent double and then partially straightened out in antiquity.

B 8. Bronze ring with hook.      Inv. No. W3-95.
Fig. 10-23.      (7B).
L. 0.039; diam. of ring 0.020; max. th. 0.005.

Flattened ring formed of one piece together with a plain, open hook; hook circular in section and set at a right angle to the ring.

B 9. Bronze ring.      Not inventoried.
Fig. 10-24; Wreck Plan V*c*.      (7B).
Diam. 0.019.

Close in form and size to the ring of B 8; pro-

tuberance suggests possibility of similar hook as well.

Bronze weights W 1 to W 8 would have been used with an equal-armed or pan balance for weighing relatively light quantities of up to about two pounds. For heavier payloads, however, the equal-armed balance was cumbersome, for it necessitated having on hand weights equal to the amount being weighed, be it four or four hundred pounds.[34] A much more versatile scale was the steelyard, of which no fewer than three were carried on the ship (B 1–B 3).

An ingenious yet simple machine, the steelyard was essentially a lever divided by a fulcrum into two unequal arms. The longer arm was graduated, the shorter arm supported the payload near its end, and the whole turned on a fulcrum which was the point of suspension for the beam. When goods were hung from a weighing collar on the shorter arm, a counterweight or counterpoise was moved back and forth along the graduated arm

---

[34] Despite its inefficiency, the equal-armed balance, in varying sizes for varying payloads, is the only means of practical and accurate weighing attested in Near Eastern and Classical antiquity before the Hellenistic Age; see B. Kisch, *Scales and Weights: A Historical Outline*, figs. 3–6, and this work, below, p. 223.

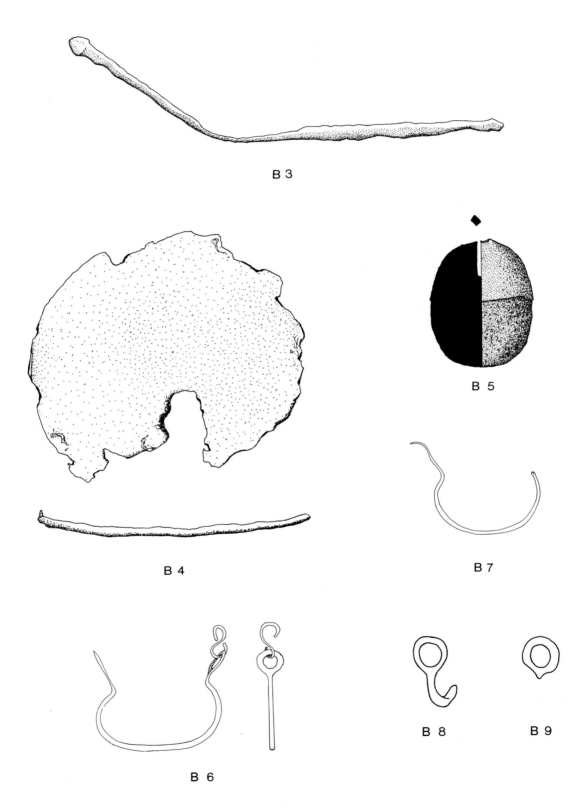

FIG. 10-25. Small steelyard bar B 3, balance pan (?) fragment
B 4, copper-sheathed lead weight B 5, and hooks B 6 and B 7.
1:2. SWK

until the beam was horizontal. This state of equilibrium meant that the counterweight had compensated through its distance from the fulcrum for the weight suspended from the other end and that the turning moments to either side of the fulcrum, taking into account as well the weight of the beam and its center of gravity, were of equal magnitude. The weight of the goods was then indicated by the position of the counterweight on the graduated scale.[35]

The method of the steelyard's use is a direct reflection of its manufacture, for each was calibrated empirically with known, probably official weights and with the counterweight that was to be used with the machine. Since the counterweight itself was one of the constant factors in the mechanics of the instrument, it was essential that one counterweight not be substituted for another unless exact duplication of weight could be maintained.

In order to maximize their efficiency, most steelyards possess two or three fulcra with suspension hooks, each placed on a different side of the beam at varying distances from the weighing collar. The fulcrum farthest from the collar served for the lightest amounts the machine could weigh; that closest, for the heaviest. Each fulcrum corresponded to a separate calibrated face on the longer arm or beam scale which would have been brought into convenient view when the new fulcrum was used. Since the distance of the increments of calibration varies from one face to another because of the changing point of the fulcrum, each face had to be graduated individually.

It would not have been necessary to set every calibration against a known weight, for the increments of pounds (single pounds, fives of pounds, tens of pounds, and so on) would have been of equal distance along the length of the scale on any one weighing face. Theoretically, only two tested marks needed to be made to establish the intervals. For example, once the distance for an increment of 5 pounds was derived through tested weights (say the interval between 50 and 55 pounds), twice this distance became the 10-pound interval and one-fifth the distance, the 1-pound interval; such could have been measured and marked off with the aid of calipers, as is done today. Inconsistencies in spacing would have affected the accuracy of the instrument.

When and where the principles of the lever came to be applied to a weighing machine are unclear. Simplicius, a sixth-century commentator on Aristotle, attributed

the steelyard's invention to Archimedes (in *Aristotelis Physica commentaria* 7.5), although no such instruments are attested as early as the third century B.C., the floruit of the great Syracusan inventor. It is likely, however, that the mechanical principles which govern the steelyard were beginning to be understood during the Hellenistic Age. The important *Liber Karastonis*, or *Book on the Roman Balance*, edited by the ninth-century mathematician Thabit ibn Qurra, very probably had its origin in Hellenistic scholarship of the last centuries before Christ. At any rate, by A.D. 79 the steelyard had become well established at least in Campania, as many examples discovered at Pompeii attest.[36]

The instrument became a mainstay of ancient commerce since it was able to perform many tasks of weighing with greater ease and less paraphernalia than the equal-armed balance. Numerous steelyards of Roman and Mediaeval date are known from one end of the Mediterranean to the other. Most are of bronze and, because of necessary compliance with the principles of physics which govern them, are very similar in basic appearance. Most variables are decorative in nature and include the form of the beam's terminals and the use of incised decoration, usually on the fulcrum bar. The shape of the counterweight also varies from simple geometric forms to elaborate sculptured heads and busts. While these will undoubtedly prove to be valuable criteria when and if a comprehensive study of ancient steelyards is ever made, analysis of beams and counterweights will unfortunately have to be made largely along separate lines of investigation, since only rarely are the two found together in secure association. In fact, the integrity of allegedly complete sets of undocumented origin or context should be automatically suspect.[37]

A distinguishing factor of a different nature, and one with historical and distributive implications, is the system of graduation employed on the beam scale. The system used allows a division of ancient Mediterranean steelyards into two broad categories: those gauged with Roman numerals and those employing the Greek system of alphabetic numerals. The evidence of distribution indicates that the Roman type knew no bounds, being

[35] See D. K. Hill, "When Romans Went Shopping," *Archaeology* 5 (1952): 51–55, for a helpful examination of the principles of the steelyard and the modern application of them.

[36] For the *Liber Karastonis* and other early treatises dealing with related mechanical principles, see E. A. Moody and M. Clagett, *The Medieval Science of Weights*. Pompeiian steelyards are shown in Kisch, *Scales and Weights*, figs. 16 and 24.

[37] For ancient steelyards in general, see the bibliography at the end of Hill, *Archaeology* 5 (1952): 55; C. Daremberg and E. Saglio, *Dictionnaire des antiquités grecques et romaines*, III, part 2, 1227–1228; E. Nowotny, "Zur Mechanik der antiken Wage," *JOAIBeibl* 16 (1913): 5–36; and M. Lazzarini, "Le Bilance romane del Museo Nazionale e dell' Antiquarium Communale di Roma," *RendLinc*, 8th ser., 3 (1948): 221–254.

found throughout the Mediterranean basin. Those graduated in Greek, on the other hand, were seemingly restricted to the eastern Mediterranean, the Greek mainland itself probably representing the westernmost extent of their distribution.[38]

Evidence for the chronology of either type is currently weak, although it is presumed that the Roman steelyard had considerable priority and was in fact the original type and that the Greek variety was a later development from it. Available data suggest the likelihood that the latter did not come into existence until sometime after the imperial residence was moved to Constantinople in 330—i.e., that it developed in Late Antiquity. The Roman type continued to be used in the eastern Mediterranean into Byzantine times, but for how long and in what proportion to the Greek is uncertain.[39] The earliest Greek steelyards from a closely datable and documented context may well be the two instruments B 1 and B 2 from our early-seventh-century Yassi Ada merchantman.

### STEELYARD B 1

The large steelyard B 1, with a length of 1.46 m, may be the largest steelyard preserved from antiquity. With a maximum weighing capacity of about 400 Roman pounds, it would have been used for heavy cargo, either for selling and buying or for appraising shipping fees.[40]

In form and detail, little is exceptional about B 1. The animal-head terminals are standard devices, especially on large steelyards.[41] The holes pierced through them probably had something to do with securing the instrument when it was suspended. Both suspension and load hooks are of common form, as is the yoke and swing apparatus which supported the weighing chains.[42] The

incised floral segment between the weighing collar and the first fulcrum is, however, without close parallel in published examples. The statement of ownership placed between the two fulcra adds another example to many in Greek that are known. The terms *presbyteros* and *naukleros* found in the inscription are discussed in the summary chapter (pp. 313–314). The crosses which flank the inscription need not have any religious significance; rather, they could simply be indicators that what lies between them is worthy of note.[43] The calibrations of the beam scale will be examined below. It can be noted here, however, that the diamond-shaped section of the scale is ordinary, as is the slanting orientation of its faces in relation to the fulcrum bar and the angle of suspension.

Except for its specific weight, the Athena counterweight is primarily a concern of sculptural interests. Busts and heads, both mythological and portrait, were popular counterweight types as early as the first century A.D.[44] Those depicting Athena began sometime during the Roman Empire and, despite their pagan associations, continued well into the Byzantine era. The Athena from the ship belongs to a group of such weights classified by C. W. J. Eliot as the Sofia Type, characterized by "its large size, the aegis worn frontally, and the spreading base."[45] The majority of the examples are dated by Eliot to the fifth and sixth centuries. The Yassi Ada example, by reason of both its dated context and its style in relation to the others of the group, belongs at the very end of the series.[46]

The calibrations on the two faces of B 1's beam scale, insofar as they are preserved and legible, seem to conform well to the system of graduations known from other steelyards of the Greek type.[47] In this alphabetic

---

[38] Published examples of Greek steelyards include Davidson, *Corinth* XII, nos. 1663–1664; Ross, *Catalogue of the Antiquities*, nos. 71, 73–74; H. B. Walters, *Catalogue of the Bronzes, Greek, Roman, and Etruscan, in the Department of Greek and Roman Antiquities, British Museum*, no. 2992; and Daremberg and Saglio, *Dictionnaire des antiquités* III, part 2, 1228, for an example from Laodicaea in Syria. Many steelyards are published summarily, without reference to the calibration system employed.

[39] Davidson, *Corinth* XII, no. 1661, has Roman numerals and a Christian Greek statement of ownership; Davidson's nos. 1662 and 1665, also of Roman type, were found in Byzantine contexts at Corinth.

[40] In Walters, *Catalogue of the Bronzes*, no. 2986 has a length of 1.05 m. An example which appeared recently on the antiquities market is 1.06 m long (Palladion, *Antike Kunst, Katalog 1976*, no. 113). The statutes of Venice required a shipowner to have a balance on board his vessel for weighing cargo (W. Ashburner, *The Rhodian Sea-Law*, p. clxxxviii).

[41] Walters, *Catalogue of the Bronzes*, no. 2986; Palladion, *Antike Kunst*, no. 113.

[42] Cf., among others, Ross, *Catalogue of the Antiquities*, no. 71, and Palladion, *Antike Kunst*, no. 113.

[43] The standard citation for such inscriptions is Daremberg and Saglio, *Dictionnaire des antiquités* III, part 2, 1228. See also Walters, *Catalogue of the Bronzes*, nos. 2990 and 2992; Davidson, *Corinth* XII, no. 1661; and Ross, *Catalogue of the Antiquities*, nos. 71 and 73. I am grateful to John Nesbitt of Dumbarton Oaks for the information on the significance of the crosses.

[44] F. O. Waagé, "Bronze Objects from Old Corinth, Greece," *AJA* 39 (1935): 80–81, with bibliography in notes. For varied counterweight types from Pompeii, to be dated no later than A.D. 79, see Kisch, *Scales and Weights*, figs. 16 and 24.

[45] C. W. J. Eliot, "A Bronze Counterpoise of Athena," *Hesperia* 45 (1976): 166, cites seven examples of the Athena type known to him, including the Yassi Ada example and the featured Athena, a counterweight discovered at Anemurium on the southern Turkish coast. To his list may be added the Palladion example (supra n. 40, no. 113); although dated by the dealer to the Roman Empire, it is surely Byzantine. For a Byzantine Athena weight of markedly different form, see D. G. Mitten and S. F. Doeringer, *Master Bronzes from the Classical World*, no. 315.

[46] Eliot, *Hesperia* 45 (1976): 167.

[47] Cf. Ross, *Catalogue of the Antiquities*, nos. 71, 73–74; Davidson, *Corinth* XII, nos. 1663–1664. Walters, *Catalogue of the Bronzes*, no. 2992, is likewise on the Greek system, although its graduated faces

scale the major increments occur at 5-pound intervals. The even tens are represented by the appropriate Greek letter for that number, I, iota, for ten to P, rho, for one hundred. Ninety was indicated by the otherwise little used ϙ, koppa. Intermediate fives are designated by E, epsilon, the Greek five. Thus, the major calibrations from one, A, to one hundred would appear as follows:

| A | E | I | E | K | E | Λ | E | M | E | N |
|---|---|---|---|---|---|---|---|---|---|---|
| 1 | 5 | 10 | 15 | 20 | 25 | 30 | 35 | 40 | 45 | 50 |

| E | Ξ | E | O | E | Π | E | ϙ | E | P |
|---|---|---|---|---|---|---|---|---|---|
| 55 | 60 | 65 | 70 | 75 | 80 | 85 | 90 | 95 | 100 |

In excess of 100 pounds, the system is repeated (P E I E K E . . .). One-pound increments are usually indicated by plain vertical lines between the major calibrations. Still smaller divisions may occur, especially on lighter weighing faces where the major increments are necessarily widely spaced.[48] Since the weighing collar and fulcra were on the right when the steelyard was being used, the scale is calibrated from right to left, or retrograde. Because retrograde writing was already a thing of the distant past, it is perhaps understandable that the directions of letters vary from one example to another and even within a single instrument. On some steelyards all letters face right; on others, all face left. On still others, the epsilons face left in sympathy with the retrograde reading of the scale, while other nonsymmetrical letters face right.[49] B 1 appears to follow the last system, insofar as the nonsymmetrical letters are preserved.

Fig. 10-9 illustrates the calibrations still visible on the two scale faces of B 1; Faces A and B correspond to Positions A and B, respectively. Position A uses the fulcrum farther from the weighing collar and thus employs the lighter of the two weighing scales. For this reason, its calibrations are spaced about twice as far apart as those of the heavier scale of Face B. Both faces have undergone wear and corrosion to the extent that many calibrations are only partially preserved and others have disappeared completely. Nevertheless, the presumed regularity of the Greek alphabetic system plus the fact that the calibrations on a face will be spaced at more-or-less equal intervals allow restoration of the two graduated faces as presented in Table 10-2.

The key to fixing Face A's sequence is provided by the ninth letter—O for seventy, the only unambiguous calibration for an even 10-pound increment on the scale. Working in either direction from this mark, it becomes possible to restore the initial calibration as Λ for thirty and the last as an E for forty-five, having passed what should be a hundred-pound indicator, letter number 15 in Table 10-2, Face A. Some partially preserved or ambiguous letters now come into sharper focus. For example, letter number 17, which as a single vertical could have been one of several letters, is now seen to be a completely preserved I, or iota, for ten, while the penultimate letter number 23, preserving a diagonal line and circle, becomes a mu for forty and as such compares very favorably with the well-preserved letter number 40 on Face B. Calculations will show that the scale on Face A began at 30 pounds and terminated with 145 pounds.

By reason of their better state of preservation, the calibrations of Face B provide more fixes on the sequence and in so doing help to confirm the mostly restored sequence of Face A. Several marks for even 10-pound increments on Face B are preserved, all falling as they should in the Greek numerical order (letters numbers 2, 4, 18, 26, 28, 38, 40, and 42 in Table 10-2). Of note are the apparently calligraphic forms of mu (letter number 40) and xi (letter number 4).[50] No complete examples of K, ϙ, or P are preserved. The initial E, followed by N, or nu, for fifty, becomes forty-five. The series of graduations carries twice through the hundred-pound mark P (letters numbers 12 and 32), beyond which the last preserved letter (number 49) is an E for eighty-five. Thereafter, space allows three more letters at the normal interval, the last (number 52) restored as a third P. The calculations to be discussed below reveal that B 1's Face B was gauged to weigh amounts from 145 pounds to 400 pounds, a range which provided neither gap nor overlap with Face A.

Since the counterweight and other key components of B 1 are preserved, it becomes possible to ascertain in metric terms approximately how much was being weighed at any given calibration. Division of the gram results by the stated weights on the scale yields derived pounds, the units crucial for assessing the standard upon which the machine was based. The procedure relies upon the physical principles inherent in the machine's operation—namely, the relationships which ensue when the steelyard is in a state of equilibrium. These relationships may be expressed by the equation $CD + RD' =$

---

are not illustrated; I am grateful to D. M. Bailey for drawings of the beam scale and other helpful information.

[48] On no. 73 in Ross, *Catalogue of the Antiquities*, the pounds of the lightest weighing face (which begins with 1 pound, A) are divided into halves by dots; each half-pound division, in turn, is divided by five short dashes into ounces. The smallest division of the next heaviest weighing face, where the pound increments are about twice as close together, is the quarter-pound, or 3 ounces.

[49] Right-facing: Walters, *Catalogue of the Bronzes*, no. 2992; Ross, *Catalogue of the Antiquities*, no. 74. Left-facing: Ross, *Catalogue of the Antiquities*, no. 73. Mixed: Davidson, *Corinth* XII, no.

1663; Ross, *Catalogue of the Antiquities*, no. 71. The Davidson example, incidentally, is published upside-down; one of its two preserved kappas faces left (cf. Davidson, *Corinth* XII, 215, fig. 36).

[50] Cf. the more deftly rendered forms of these letters on Ross, *Catalogue of the Antiquities*, no. 71.

TABLE 10-2. Calibrations and Their Derived Pounds of Steelyard B 1.

*Face A*

| Calibration | Distrance from Fulcrum (cm) | Value in Pounds | Derived Pounds in Grams with Hypothetical *RD′* Value of 242,575 g-cm | | |
| | | | Minimum Shift | Hook Centered | Maximum Shift |
|---|---|---|---|---|---|
| 1. [Λ] | — | 30 | — | — | — |
| 2. E | 10.5 | 35 | 313.19 | 315.85 | 318.51 |
| 3. [M] | — | 40 | — | — | — |
| 4. [E] | — | 45 | — | — | — |
| 5. Ṇ | 23.2 | 50 | 313.74 | 315.60 | 317.47 |
| 6. Ẹ | 27.4 | 55 | 313.64 | 315.33 | 317.02 |
| 7. [Ξ] (Ξ) | — | 60 | — | — | — |
| 8. Ẹ | 35.9 | 65 | 314.04 | 315.47 | 316.91 |
| 9. O | 40.0 | 70 | 313.40 | 314.73 | 316.06 |
| 10. E | 44.2 | 75 | 313.35 | 314.59 | 315.83 |
| 11. [Π] | — | 80 | — | — | — |
| 12. [E] | — | 85 | — | — | — |
| 13. Ϙ | 56.9 | 90 | 313.63 | 314.66 | 315.69 |
| 14. E | 61.2 | 95 | 313.96 | 314.94 | 315.92 |
| 15. Ṛ | 65.6 | 100 | 314.64 | 315.57 | 316.50 |
| 16. E | 69.8 | 105 | 314.54 | 315.43 | 316.32 |
| 17. I | 74.0 | 110 | 314.45 | 315.29 | 316.13 |
| 18. Ẹ | 78.2 | 115 | 314.37 | 315.18 | 315.99 |
| 19. Ḳ | 82.5 | 120 | 314.60 | 315.38 | 316.16 |
| 20. [E] | — | 125 | — | — | — |
| 21. [Λ] | — | 130 | — | — | — |
| 22. Ẹ | 94.6 | 135 | 313.00 | 313.68 | 314.36 |
| 23. Ṃ | 99.6 | 140 | 315.11 | 315.77 | 316.43 |
| 24. [E] | — | 145 | — | — | — |

*Face B*

| Calibration | Distrance from Fulcrum (cm) | Value in Pounds | Derived Pounds in Grams with Hypothetical *RD′* Value of 365,800 g-cm | | |
| | | | Minimum Shift | Hook Centered | Maximum Shift |
|---|---|---|---|---|---|
| 1. E | 17.6 | 145 | 315.82 | 317.24 | 318.66 |
| 2. N | 19.5 | 150 | 315.71 | 317.08 | 318.45 |
| 3. Ẹ | 21.1 | 155 | 314.01 | 315.34 | 316.67 |
| 4. Ξ̣ (Ξ) | 23.0 | 160 | 313.96 | 315.25 | 316.54 |
| 5. Ẹ | 24.8 | 165 | 313.42 | 314.66 | 315.90 |
| 6. Ọ | 26.9 | 170 | 314.35 | 315.56 | 316.77 |
| 7. E | 28.6 | 175 | 313.36 | 314.53 | 315.70 |
| 8. Π | 30.8 | 180 | 314.70 | 315.84 | 316.98 |
| 9. E | 32.6 | 185 | 314.20 | 315.31 | 316.42 |
| 10. Ϙ | 34.5 | 190 | 314.15 | 315.23 | 316.31 |
| 11. Ẹ | 36.5 | 195 | 314.53 | 315.58 | 316.63 |
| 12. P | 38.4 | 200 | 314.47 | 315.57 | 316.67 |
| 13. E | 40.2 | 205 | 314.02 | 315.02 | 316.02 |
| 14. [I] | — | 210 | — | — | — |
| 15. E | 44.1 | 215 | 314.33 | 315.29 | 316.25 |
| 16. Ḳ | 46.0 | 220 | 314.29 | 315.22 | 316.15 |
| 17. E | 47.9 | 225 | 314.24 | 315.16 | 316.08 |
| 18. Λ | — | 230 | — | — | — |
| 19. Ẹ | 51.8 | 235 | 314.52 | 315.39 | 316.26 |
| 20. [M] | — | 240 | — | — | — |
| 21. E | 55.7 | 245 | 314.77 | 315.60 | 316.43 |
| 22. [N] | — | 250 | — | — | — |
| 23. Ẹ | 59.4 | 255 | 314.35 | 315.16 | 315.97 |

*Face B*

| Calibration | Distrance from Fulcrum (cm) | Value in Pounds | Derived Pounds in Grams with Hypothetical RD' Value of 365,800 g-cm | | |
| | | | Minimum Shift | Hook Centered | Maximum Shift |
|---|---|---|---|---|---|
| 24. Ϙ | — | 260 | — | — | — |
| 25. E | 63.2 | 265 | 314.28 | 315.05 | 315.82 |
| 26. O | — | 270 | — | — | — |
| 27. E | 67.1 | 275 | 314.51 | 315.26 | 316.01 |
| 28. Π | — | 280 | — | — | — |
| 29. E | 71.0 | 285 | 314.72 | 315.45 | 316.18 |
| 30. Ϙ | 72.9 | 290 | 314.68 | 315.39 | 316.10 |
| 31. E | 74.8 | 295 | 314.65 | 315.34 | 316.03 |
| 32. Ṛ | 76.5 | 300 | 314.06 | 314.75 | 315.44 |
| 33. Ẹ | 78.5 | 305 | 314.30 | 314.98 | 315.66 |
| 34. [I] | — | 310 | — | — | — |
| 35. E | 82.2 | 315 | 313.98 | 314.63 | 315.28 |
| 36. Ḳ | 84.1 | 320 | 313.96 | 314.60 | 315.24 |
| 37. Ẹ | 86.1 | 325 | 314.19 | 314.82 | 315.45 |
| 38. Λ | — | 330 | — | — | — |
| 39. E | 89.9 | 335 | 314.13 | 314.75 | 315.37 |
| 40. M | — | 340 | — | — | — |
| 41. E | 93.7 | 345 | 314.08 | 314.68 | 315.28 |
| 42. N | — | 350 | — | — | — |
| 43. Ẹ | 97.6 | 355 | 314.27 | 314.85 | 315.43 |
| 44. [Ϙ] | — | 360 | — | — | — |
| 45. Ẹ | 101.3 | 365 | 313.99 | 314.56 | 315.13 |
| 46. [O] | — | 370 | — | — | — |
| 47. Ẹ | 105.1 | 375 | 313.95 | 314.50 | 315.05 |
| 48. Π | — | 380 | — | — | — |
| 49. Ẹ | — | 385 | — | — | — |
| 50. [Ϙ] | — | 390 | — | — | — |
| 51. [E] | — | 395 | — | — | — |
| 52. [P] | — | 400 | — | — | — |

*XD''*, where *C* is the weight of the counterweight, *D* is the distance from the counterweight to the fulcrum, *R* is the weight of the beam, *D'* is the distance from the beam's center of gravity to the fulcrum, *X* is the payload, and *D''* is the distance from the weighing collar to the fulcrum.[51] Knowing the other factors, we can determine the value of *X* by simple manipulation of the equation: $(CD + RD') \div D'' = X$. In itself, *X* is a raw gram figure which achieves meaning only when divided by the scale's stated weight at distance *D* from the fulcrum, for this yields the derived pound. Before this, however, the raw figure of *X* must be reduced by the weight of the suspension apparatus (in the case of B 1, a weight of 3,308 g); this weight is an amount which the scale's

stated value does not include but which does figure in calculation.[52]

Another factor to consider stems from modern ignorance, for it is not known whether the counterweight's hook was to be centered over a calibration or whether its right or left margin indicated the weight; the position affects the value of *D* and thus the results. In order to allow for this ambiguity, three computations for each cal-

[51] *RD'* may be ignored if the fulcrum is at the same time the bar's center of gravity (cf. Hill, *Archaeology* 5 [1952]: 52–53).

[52] When the manufacturer gauged the instrument, he would ideally have used the apparatus so that the tested marks would reflect both its weight and that of the known weights; otherwise, the scale would not provide accurate readings. The weight of the apparatus can, however, be ignored on scale faces which begin at zero, for presumably the counterweight at this position would have balanced against the empty suspension apparatus. In some cases it may also be possible to include the apparatus's weight under *R* of *RD'*; the center of gravity will naturally be affected, and its new position must be found.

ibration become necessary: one for left-margin reading or minimum shift of the hook, another for the hook centered directly over the calibration, and a third for maximum shift, with reading along the hook's right margin. In the case of B 1, these adjustments amount to a shift of about 2.5 mm to either side of a calibration's exact position. As will be seen, the differences in results are slight.

A further consideration is that the equation given above assumes the original state of the instrument, when it would have been operational and perhaps even subject to official inspection; anything other than the original conditions will in fact produce aberrant results. In the case of B 1 there are two alterations for which some compensation must be made. A minimal loss of weight suffered by Athena will affect the value of $CD$, but more serious is a change in the bar's weight, which affects as well its center of gravity. With the attached Fulcrum B hook, the weight of the bar is about 7,750 g, the center of gravity falling at a point 52 cm from the weighing collar and 28.8 cm from Fulcrum A (the fulcrum to which this center of gravity applies). Since the outer end of the beam scale is very worn and moreover exhibits a large, deep gash, the original weight would have been greater and the center of gravity farther removed from the fulcrum and weighing collar, as is reflected in calculations made on Face A of the machine using the preserved weight and center of gravity.

The gram weights computed for the calibrations, taken in their sequence, yielded derived pounds which presented no consistency but rather an ascending range extending from about 290 g to about 310 g. In order to attempt an approximation of the original conditions under which the machine operated, it therefore becomes necessary to find a figure for $RD'$ of the equation which will result in derived pounds of some consistency. Figures considerably less than the original product will yield a markedly ascending series of derived pounds, as seen in the experiment using present conditions, whereas a product greater than the original will result in a markedly descending series. The best results were obtained with a product $RD'$ of 242,575 g-cm, equivalent to a force of about 10.4 kg against the payload. This figure represents a combined compensation for the bar's loss of weight and its consequently shifted center of gravity, although neither $R$ nor $D'$ can be restored with any accuracy. The center of gravity for Position A would have been somewhere between its present point and about 31.3 cm from Fulcrum A, while the original weight of the bar, with one fulcrum hook, lay somewhere between the preserved 7,750 g and about 8,420 g. The procedure automatically compensates as well for the other altered condition, Athena's weight loss, since what is being ad-

justed in order to find a consistency of derived pounds is the total force acting against the value of $XD''$. The results yielded by this method for the fifteen legible or measurable calibrations of Face A are presented in Table 10-2 for Face A and may be summarized as follows:[53]

Minimum shift: derived pounds between 313.00 g and 315.11 g; average of 313.98 g

Hook centered: derived pounds between 313.68 g and 315.85 g; average of 315.16 g

Maximum shift: derived pounds between 314.36 g and 318.51 g, average of 316.35 g

For Position B the same method can be employed once a workable product for $RD'$ is found. The value of $R$, the bar's weight, is assumed to have been practically the same for this position as it was in Position A, the difference being that it would have included the weight of the once inverted and dangling fulcrum hook for Position A (hook B 1$b$), plus its attachment device, instead of that for Position B. Since the hook for Position A is attached farther from the boar's-head end, the center of gravity for Position B will not be the same as that for Position A, but farther out towards the center of the bar. Results that were consistent in terms of derived pounds, and at the same time commensurate with those gained for Face A, come with a product for $RD'$ of about 365,800 g-cm, a force of approximately 34.5 kg against the value of $XD''$. Of the fifty-two calibrations on the scale, the thirty-four that could be computed yielded the results seen in Table 10-2 for Face B, summarized as follows:

Minimum shift: derived pounds between 313.36 g and 314.77 g; average of 314.23 g

Hook centered: derived pounds between 314.5 g and 315.84 g; average of 315.10 g

Maximum shift: derived pounds between 315.05 g and 316.98 g; average of 315.98 g

The first two calibrations of Face B, for 145 pounds and 150 pounds, have been omitted from these summarized results. As Table 10-2 shows for Face B, those two calibrations are the most extreme high pounds, falling noticeably outside the majority range. These discrepancies are apparently the result of limited foresight: the man-

---

[53]The exact procedure may be illustrated with calibration 9 on Face A, which is marked O, or omicron, for seventy. This calibration mark is 40.00 cm from the fulcrum. We can calculate the calibrated weight by using the equation $(CD + RD') \div D'' = X$, where $C = 8,632.5$ g, $D = 40$ cm, $RD' = 242,575$ g-cm, and $D'' = 23.2$ cm. Thus, $X = [(8,632.5 \text{ g} \times 40 \text{ cm}) + 242,575 \text{ g-cm}] \div 23.2 \text{ cm} = 25,339.44$ g. When the weight of the suspension apparatus, 3,308 g, is subtracted from $X$, the result is 22,031.44 g; this figure divided by the calibration's stated value, 70, then yields the derived pound of 314.73 g. In order to compute minimum and maximum shift readings, half the hook's width at the top, 0.25 cm, is respectively subtracted from or added to the 40-cm measurement for $D$.

ufacturer, gauging this face by working in the direction of the fulcrum, did not have enough room at this end to give the N and the E their proper spacings.

The derived pounds for Face B are closely bracketed by the high and low results obtained for Face A. These broadest limits indicate a pound that fell somewhere between 313 g and 318.5 g. Since the method employed to achieve these figures is approximate to begin with, and since minor inaccuracies in gauging cause uncontrollable inconsistencies in the derived figures, further narrowing of the range does not seem warranted. Uncertainty about the hook's position likewise cautions against more refined limits.

Even with its 8.5-g leeway, the standard indicated by B 1 is consistent with what is known of weight systems for the period, for a pound of between 313 g and 322 g appears to have been normal for the sixth and seventh centuries.[54] Whereas the bronze weights W 1–W 8 may reflect a provincial system, the steelyard most likely represents a more widely held standard of weight—one that was employed for routine commercial transactions in the world known to the ship. Some confirmation of this idea may be seen in components of B 1 itself, for they seem to have been manufactured at predetermined weights of a similar standard, no doubt as an index for cost. The Athena bust becomes roughly 25 pounds of bronze and lead, its hook a little over 2 pounds.[55] The suspension apparatus is close to 10½ pounds; the bar itself may well have been cast from an amount of bronze set at between 20 and 25 pounds. It may be added that the counterweight of the smaller B 2 is very close to being 1¾ of B 1's pounds. Further evidence of this pound as a standard which saw common use is provided by van Doorninck's independent computation of the weight of the iron anchor stock St 1 (p. 133). His figure of 31.47 kg (though an estimate based on the concretion casting) falls too comfortably within B 1's range to be intepreted as anything other than a 100-pound unit.

## B 2 AND B 3

B 2 was found together with its accessories close to B 1 in the galley area. The suspension apparatus and a fulcrum hook are missing, as are the pins and rings which would have connected the hooks to the fulcra. Much less elaborate than B 1, the machine terminates in conical knobs and has a plain piriform counterweight of lead, both common and unexceptional features.[56] B 2

differs as well from B 1 in having three instead of two fulcra, which meant three corresponding graduated faces of the beam scale, each of which had to be gauged separately. The relation of beam scale to fulcrum bar remains the same, the graduated face for each position being on an upward-slanting surface of the lozenge-shaped beam with the fulcra on the right.

The three graduated faces of the beam scale are worn and corroded to the extent that only a relatively few calibrations, or parts of them, are preserved, all being at the beginning of the scales. The calibrations are too few to establish the sequences with any accuracy; at the same time, they are insufficient to provide the large series necessary in order to establish consistency patterns for derived pounds as was possible with B 1. Some observations can, however, be made on the three scales.

In Position A, which brings into view the lightest scale, two marks are preserved: a triangular grouping of three dots at 2 cm from the fulcrum and a letter that could be restored as A, for one, at a distance from the fulcrum of 3.6 cm. On the analogy of other steelyards, the dots most likely represent ½ pound, or 6 ounces.[57] On this assumption, extension of the interval between the dots and the restored A to the end of the bar indicates a weighing potential of a little over six pounds for the scale. If the sequence did begin at zero pounds, there was presumably a point close to the fulcrum, probably on the collar separating the fulcrum bar from the scale, where the counterweight and empty suspension apparatus would have balanced the rod. This being the case, the apparatus's weight would not be a factor were computation possible.

Position B, employing the middle scale, preserves two letters with several vertical lines between, these spaced at 3–4 mm intervals. The first letter, at 5.4 cm from the fulcrum, is clearly a retrograde E for some five. Ideally it was no more than five, for this amount would then have provided a slight overlap with the lightest scale. The other letter, at 9.6 cm from the fulcrum, is preserved as Λ; distance, however, argues against its being lambda for 30 pounds and suggests rather that it represents something considerably less. This is further indicated by the plain verticals, for their intervals, computed without consideration of the *RD'* factor, suggest increments that were fractions of pounds—in other words, ounces. (While computation without considering *RD'* cannot offer evidence for the derived pounds, it

[54] Schilbach, *Byzantinische Metrologie*, p. 166.

[55] The Athena and hook from Anemurium (Eliot, *Hesperia* 45 [1976]) together weigh 10.58 kg, or roughly 33½ of B 1's pounds.

[56] No. 73 in Ross, *Catalogue of the Antiquities*, is particularly close in the form of its rod, both the terminals, and the fulcrum hous-

ings. The same example now has a piriform counterweight. See also Davidson, *Corinth* XII, no. 1642.

[57] Davidson, *Corinth* XII, no. 1663, and Walters, *Catalogue of the Bronzes*, no. 2992, employ the same half-pound convention.

does establish a rough approximation of the increments, and so is not totally invalid.)

The heaviest scale, that of Position C, preserves towards its beginning, at 7.5 cm from the respective fulcrum, what may be a **K**. If so, the scale began at something less than twenty pounds. The few verticals to either side of the letter, at regular intervals of 5 mm, prove upon computation without *RD'* to represent increments of 1 pound. Assuming that what appears as **K** is indeed kappa for twenty, the maximum potential of the scale and the machine would have been about 55 pounds.

B 3, like B 1 and B 2, was found in the galley area. Bent and deteriorated to the extent that neither fulcrum points nor calibrations are discernible, it is nevertheless betrayed as a balance by its general similarity in form, particularly in the knobbed ends, and size to B 2. B 5, B 7, and B 8 or B 9 may well be associated with B 3, since any would duplicate or else be poorly matched with the accessories of B 2. B 5 seems very plausible as a counterweight, especially in view of the similar combining of two metals seen in the counterweight of B 2; furthermore, both are roughly commensurate in size, although B 5, at a preserved 1,230 g, is two and one-quarter times heavier. The copper sheathing of B 5, which seemingly covered the entire weight originally, may have been a protective device intended to prevent weight loss through wear.[58] B 8 or B 9 may well have been the hook by which B 5 was suspended from B 3.[59]

[58] So was a similarly clad counterweight found on the Russian pink *Eustaff* interpreted by R. Stenuit ("The Wreck of the Pink *Evstafii*," *IJNA* 5 [1976]: 228, fig. 7). Reference provided by F. H. van Doorninck, Jr.

[59] The form finds close parallels in suspension hooks for counterweights; cf., for example, Ross, *Catalogue of the Antiquities*, no. 71, pl. 45*c*.

B 7, if connected at all with a weighing instrument, seems most likely to have been a fulcrum hook. Since its form differs from that of the two preserved hooks of B 2, B 3 would again become the most probable association.

The close similarity in size between B 2 and B 3 suggests that both had a similar weighing range. What cannot be known is whether both were gauged on the same standard or whether the standard of one or both corresponded with that of B 1. The counterweight of B 2 would suggest that at least this instrument was of B 1's standard, for its weight approximates very closely 1¾ pounds in terms of the range revealed by the larger steelyard. If this is the case, the two balances together would have permitted the weighing of amounts on a single standard from a fraction of a pound up to 400 pounds. B 5 may too have been of a similar standard: its present weight, certainly less than what it was originally, is about 20–30 g short of being four of B 1's pounds.

## B 4 AND B 6

Two items whose associations remain ambiguous are B 4 and B 6. B 4 could be a balance pan from an equal-armed scale, in which case it would have been used with W 1 to W 8. On the other hand, it could have been substituted for load hooks on either B 2 or B 3.[60] The latter possibility receives some strength from the fact that only a single pan was found, whereas an equal-armed balance would have required two. The form of B 6, especially its sharply outward-bent and pointed extremity, suggests that it was a load hook rather than a fulcrum hook for a steelyard (compare the load hooks of B 1). As such, its association could be either of the two small steelyards, B 2 or B 3.

[60] Cf. ibid., no. 74.

# XI

## IRON OBJECTS

### Michael L. Katzev

When the Byzantine merchant ship sank, she carried to the bottom a broad assortment of contemporary smithy's products. Relatively fresh from the forge, these iron objects immediately began to corrode and decay. As they decomposed and became buried by the surrounding sediment, grains of sand and pieces of shell cemented together around them, forming encrustations which we called concretions. As sand and shell slowly built up, the concretions continued to retain roughly the shapes of the iron objects; inside, exact molds of the original implements were simultaneously being formed as the iron disintegrated.

In the four seasons of excavations more than 150 concretions of various sizes and shapes were recovered. Within one or possibly two of the anchors, which were our largest finds, bits of metallic iron were still preserved. On the other hand, when concretions of the smaller tools were sawed or broken open, no iron was found within them. Instead, only a sludge of iron oxides remained as residue within the molds. (See Appendix C for an analysis of an iron concretion.)

During the summer of 1962 Eric Ryan undertook to develop a means of iron replacement with materials readily at hand in Bodrum. After laboriously cutting a concretion in half with a hacksaw, he brushed out the residue of iron oxides to expose a perfect mold of the object. Setting a wire armature in the cavity, he then poured an excess of plaster into the two halves of the mold and fitted them together as the plaster began to set. When the plaster had hardened, the two pieces of the concretion easily separated, and an exact replica of the original iron object was revealed.[1] After several nails

were successfully cast, however, it was decided that the results were not totally satisfactory since the plaster's stark color and friable nature produced casts which were less than ideal for photography and exhibition.

Seeking an improved method of iron replacement, Laurence Joline and Frederick van Doorninck, Jr., subsequently investigated various commercial sawing and casting techniques in the United States. Fortunately they found equipment which would make the operation more efficient and materials which would yield more aesthetic replicas. Their findings were put into use during the summer of 1964.[2]

The first step in the new process was to cut each rock-hard concretion in half using a lapidary saw (Fig. 11-1). An electric rotary saw, a Frantom No. 810, with diamond-tipped abrasive saw blades 10 inches and 6 inches in diameter and 0.050, 0.032, or 0.020 inches thick was used in this operation. The equipment was purchased from Lapidabrade, Inc., of Havertown, Pennsylvania. Care had to be exercised constantly to supply the blade with sufficient lubricant, a mixture of kerosene and motor oil, to ease cutting and prevent overheating. When we sawed a concretion of more complicated shape or one in which several implements lay close together, a number of cuttings (Fig. 11-2) were needed to expose the

---

[1] A similar technique was used to cast iron objects salvaged from the Chrétienne A wreck of the first century B.C. (F. Benoît, "Jas d'ancre et pièces d'outillage des épaves de Provence," *RStLig* 21 [1955]: 126–128, figs. 10–11; L. Casson, "More Sea-Digging," *Archaeology* 10 [1957]: 254–255; G. Barnier, "Découvertes d'outils antiques au fond de la mer," in *Atti del II Congresso Internazionale di Archeologia Sottomarina, Albenga, 1958*, pp. 310–314, figs. 9–15; and H. Frost, *Under the Mediterranean*, pp. 20–21, pl. 2).

[2] Van Doorninck and I supervised the casting process, assisted by Susan Womer Katzev and Önder Seren. Eric Ryan helped with the anchor. Susan Katzev skillfully executed the drawings, and Donald Rosencrantz took the excellent photographs.

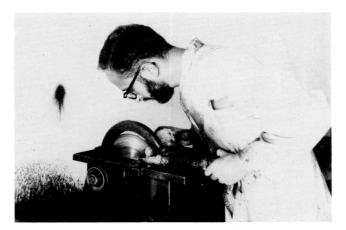

FIG. 11-1. Cutting a concretion with a lapidary saw.

FIG. 11-3. Cast replicas of twelve iron implements originally concreted together.

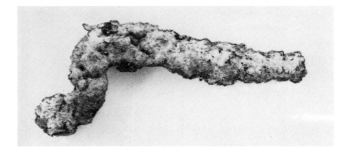

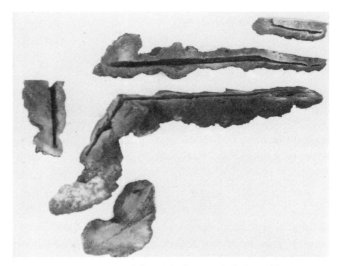

FIG. 11-2. Concretion (*above*) before and (*below*) after cutting.

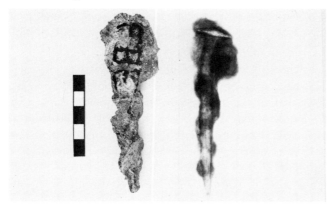

FIG. 11-4. Concretion of an iron nail and its X-ray radiograph.

form of the objects. This was particularly the case when we dealt with a box-shaped concretion that revealed twelve different implements (Fig. 11-3), all of which must have originally been contained in the carpenter's tool chest. Ideally, two-dimensional X-ray radiographs or stereo X-radiographs of these concretions should have been taken before this operation (Fig. 11-4). Such radiographs would have revealed the original shape of the iron objects before their concretions were partially destroyed and would have permitted a more rational approach in their destruction.[3] Unfortunately, such X-ray

equipment was not available in Bodrum and was too expensive for the expedition to purchase and transport there, and only a very few nail concretions could be removed from Turkey as samples for analysis and study.

After it was sawed, a concreted mold was thoroughly cleaned of its residue matter. Then a shim of heavy paper or thin cardboard was glued to its cut surfaces to compensate for the thickness of the saw blade. It was then ready for casting. (Before anchor An 2 was cast, an iron armature, made by the local blacksmith, was set in the mold to reinforce the casting; see Fig. 6-5.)

In the casting process we experimented with three different compounds: Silastic 589 RTV, a silicone rubber compound manufactured by Dow Corning Corporation of Englewood Cliffs, New Jersey, and Smooth-On Flexible Mold Compounds Nos. 100 and 300, polysulfide rubber compounds produced by Smooth-On Manufacturing Company of Jersey City, New Jersey. These liquid compounds, when mixed thoroughly with a catalyst, harden and fully cure to a rubbery solid within twenty-four hours. All of them readily penetrated the depressions and indentations of the molds. However, the Silas-

[3]M. Peterson, *History Under the Sea*, p. 61, pl. 20.

tic compound did not hold up under an extended period of storage in our less than favorable field conditions. The shelf life of Silastic 589 RTV is advertised as about six months under normal conditions, but after one year of storage, upon curing it had a greater tendency to form bubbles on the surface or within the casts than either of the Smooth-On compounds. Silastic, a red compound of low viscosity, flowed smoothly and set slowly—allowing a maximum of pouring time—and when cured had a high level of hardness and tensile strength.

Smooth-On No. 100, a tan compound of medium viscosity, flowed easily, and although it began to set immediately, there was adequate working time to fill a mold. When cured, it had a low level of hardness and tensile strength, which produced replicas slightly more flexible than was desired. Smooth-On No. 300, a black compound of high viscosity, quickly became tacky and set rapidly, allowing a minimum of working time. Therefore, it was found expedient to patiently mix small amounts of the compound and apply them with a probe and flat instrument. When Smooth-On No. 300 cured, it was tougher and less flexible than Smooth-On No. 100, being comparatively equal in these qualities to Silastic.

These synthetic rubber compounds were just as accurate as plaster in making casts from molds. Furthermore, a thin crust of iron oxides adhered to the surfaces of the casts made with the rubber compounds, so each replica took on a realistic rustlike coating. Because it is the darkest compound, Smooth-On No. 300 gave the most convincing appearance of rusted iron—a disguise not frequently detected by visitors before the glass cases of the Bodrum Museum. The two Smooth-On compounds also have the advantage of being adhesive to

FIG. 11-5. Polysulfide rubber cast of an iron billhook.

themselves as well as to each other, which is not true of Silastic. As a result, parts of an object could be cast with either Smooth-On No. 100 or No. 300, and the parts could then be joined together after the compounds had cured, or the Smooth-On compounds could be applied in layers alternated with layers of burlap mesh reinforcing material to conserve the compounds and to strengthen the casts of large objects. When objects were built up in this manner, a layer at a time, we were certain that the casts would be solid. Such techniques could not be employed with the Silastic compound. In general, then, we recommend from our experiences that the Smooth-On compounds be used in a process of iron replacement: Smooth-On No. 100 for small, narrow objects, and Smooth-On No. 300—or a combination of the two—for larger and more complex objects.

Once the rubber compounds had been poured into the molds, the halves of the concretions were fitted together and set aside to cure for twenty-four hours. The concretions were then carefully broken up and the shattered pieces peeled from the casts to reveal perfect replicas of the original objects (Fig. 11-5; see also Figs. 6-6–6-8).[4]

## Spade

Fe 1.   Spade.                         Inv. No. W3-396.
Figs. 11-6 and 11-8; Wreck Plan V*e*.
                   FBO+FCA+KTC (8B).
Max. pres. l. 0.254; max. pres. w. 0.232; max. pres. th. 0.016.
Edge poorly preserved; collar of socket missing. Smooth-On.

The spade was shaped like a heraldic shield. In the middle of its almost straight, flat top the handle's socket extended down into the blade in the form of an arrowhead-shaped cavity. Its curved sides and rounded bottom had dull knife edges.

The blade was very slightly dished.[5]

A spade would not have been much used on a ship. However, ashore a crew would have needed this implement to clear a freshwater spring, to cover a cook's fire, or to collect ballast.

[4] The preceding paragraphs are a revision of a paper I presented at the Second Conference on Underwater Archaeology, April 16, 1965, Royal Ontario Museum, Toronto, Canada, and of M. L. Katzev and F. H. van Doorninck, Jr., "Replicas of Iron Tools from a Byzantine Shipwreck," *Studies in Conservation* 11, no. 3 (1966): 133–142.

[5] A similar spade has been found at the Roman fort of Saalburg, Germany (Carl Blümlein, *Bilder aus dem römisch-germanischen Kulturleben*, p. 86, fig. 267.5; and K. D. White, *Agricultural Implements of the Roman World*, pp. 177–178, fig. 8).

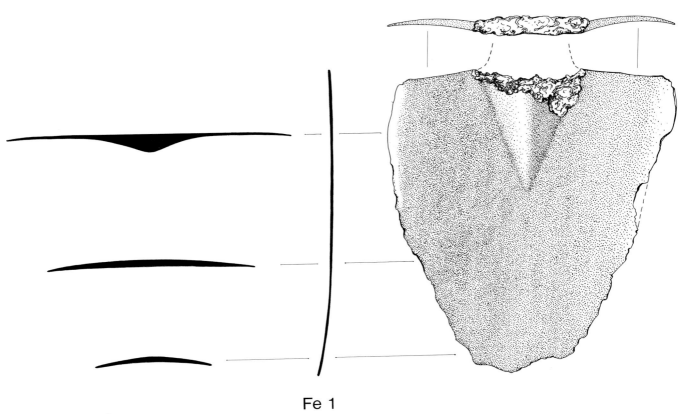

Fe 1

FIG. 11-6. Iron spade. 1:3. *SWK*

## Hoe

Fe 2.   Hoe-hammer.                    Inv. No. W3-460.
Figs. 11-7 and 11-8; Wreck Plan V*b*.  FCS (6/7B).
Max. pres. l. 0.142; max. pres. w. 0.119; max.
pres. th. of blade 0.005; socket eye diam. 0.035.
Most of hoe's blade missing; surface of concretion's mold disintegrated around portions of
socket and part of hammer's head. Smooth-On.

Probably triangular in outline, the hoe's blade
was slightly dished and curved back towards the
handle. Since the juncture of one top edge and
one side was preserved, the blade's original dimensions may be restored as l. 0.12 and w. 0.14.

The tool's socket had a round eye; in it a part of
the wood handle is preserved. Above the socket
the tool formed a hammer head with a curved
face. This head had unusual projections, front and
back, which curved down towards the socket.

Like a spade, a hoe would be employed ashore in
furrowing around a spring or grubbing for roots. But this
double-headed tool was also intended for hammering,
and the very peculiar projections of its hammerhead—
for which I can find no ancient or modern parallels—
could have been used for prying.

## Billhooks

Fe 3.   Billhook.                       Inv. No. W3-453.
Figs. 11-7 and 11-8; Wreck Plan V*e*.
                           FCT-A≡KZI (8A).
Overall pres. l. 0.339; max. w. of blade 0.071;
max. th. of blade 0.014.
Whole. Smooth-On.
The blade was crescent-shaped in outline,

curving back from the handle and then hooking
forward and tapering to a bluntly pointed bill. It
was triangular in section with a flat back and a
sharp cutting edge. The wraparound socket was
circular in section, and its edges met; part of the
tool's wood handle is preserved in it.

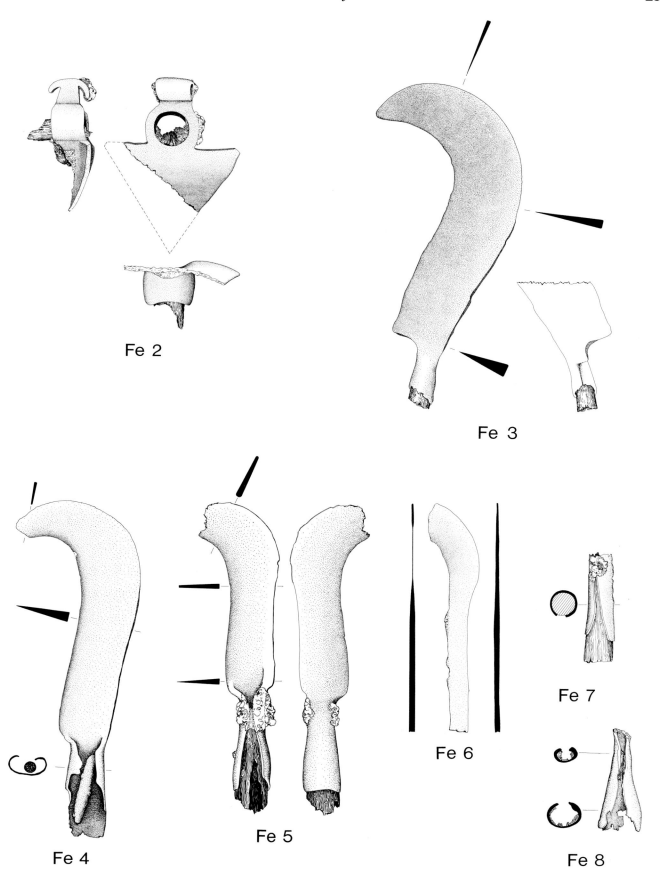

Fe 2

Fe 3

Fe 4

Fe 5

Fe 6

Fe 7

Fe 8

FIG. 11-7. Iron hoe and billhooks. approx. 1:4. *SWK*

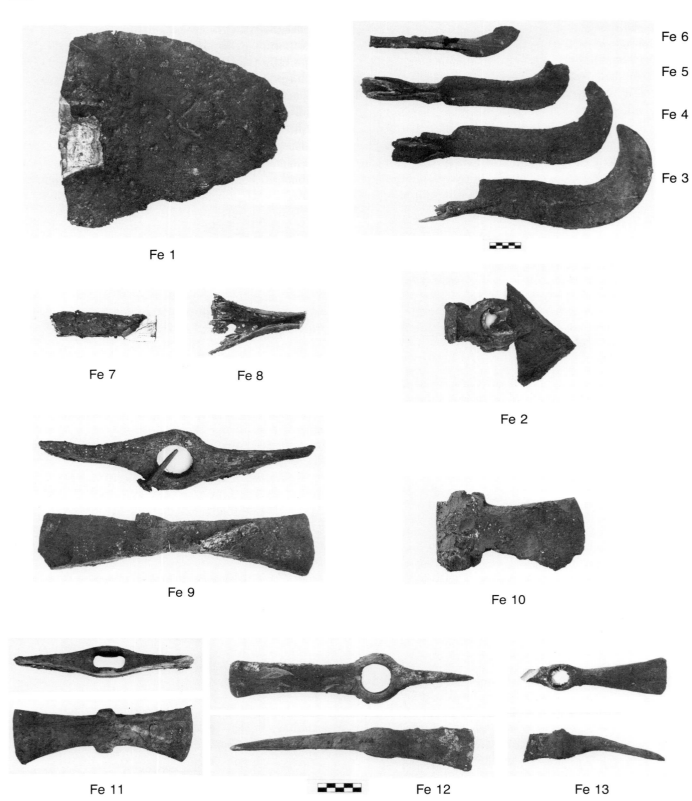

Fe 1

Fe 6
Fe 5
Fe 4
Fe 3

Fe 7          Fe 8

Fe 2

Fe 9

Fe 10

Fe 11                          Fe 12                    Fe 13

FIG. 11-8. Cast replicas of spade, hoe, billhooks, axes, and mattocks.

Fe 4. Billhook.                    Inv. No. W3-454.
Figs. 11-7 and 11-8; Wreck Plan V*e*.    FCU (8A).
Overall l. 0.354; max. w. of blade 0.062; max. th.
of blade 0.010.
Tip of bill missing; cutting edge nicked; parts of
the socket's edges disintegrated. Smooth-On.

The blade was similar to the preceding Fe 3.
The wraparound socket was elliptical in section,
and its edges, which clamped downward, did not
meet. An iron peg had been driven into the
blade end of the handle to hold it secure in the
socket; the peg was round in section, diam.
0.012, l. 0.075, and tapered to blunt points.

Fe 5. Billhook.                    Inv. No. W3-455.
Figs. 11-7 and 11-8.            FAO-C (5A).
Overall pres. l. 0.330; max. w. of blade 0.057;
max. th. of blade 0.006.
End of bill missing; socket at juncture with blade
decomposed. Smooth-On.

The blade was similar to the preceding Fe 3
and Fe 4, although the cutting edge had dulled
over part of its length. The wraparound socket
was elliptical in section, and its edges did not
meet; part of the tool's wood handle is preserved
in it.

Fe 6. Billhook.                    Inv. No. W3-456.
Figs. 11-7 and 11-8.                  (?).
Pres. l. 0.242; max. w. of blade 0.036; max. th. of
blade 0.006; pres. l. of shank 0.16; shank w.
0.019; shank th. 0.006.
End of bill missing; end of shank missing. Silastic.

The blade, though smaller, was similar in
shape to the preceding Fe 3–Fe 5. However,
unlike those billhooks, this tool had a long shank,
rectangular in section. There was no evidence
that the tool was socketed or tanged, and the
shank's length was already ample for a hand grip.

Fe 7. Billhook socket.              Inv. No. W3-415.
Figs. 11-7 and 11-8.            FBT (9C).
Overall pres. l. 0.118; pres. l. of socket 0.094.
Socket decomposed and broken near juncture
with blade. Smooth-On.

The wraparound socket was circular in section, but its edges did not meet. The socket narrowed slightly towards the blade. Part of the
tool's wood handle was preserved (cast with
Smooth-On). Since the socket was so similar to
those of Fe 3–Fe 5, it can most probably be
identified as part of a billhook.

Fe 8. Billhook socket.              Inv. No. W3-414.
Figs. 11-7 and 11-8.[6]           FBM-A (8A).
Pres. l. 0.110.
Socket broken near juncture to blade; handle
end poorly preserved. Smooth-On.

The wraparound socket was elliptical in section, and its edges did not meet. The socket narrowed considerably towards the blade. Fragments of the wood handle are preserved within
it.

The mold of part of another billhook, comparable in
size and shape to Fe 3–Fe 5, had to be destroyed during
the casting of axe Fe 10; the two objects were so concreted together that one mold had to be lost to save the
other (Wreck Plan V*b*, sector 7C).

It is remarkable that so many billhooks were carried
on the ship at the time of her sinking, but I am at a loss
to provide an explanation for the number.[7] This tool designed to cut by hacking would not find use on board a
ship except possibly in an emergency. Rather, it is a
landlubber's tool employed for pruning the vine,[8] trimming saplings, or shaping hedges. In the hands of a mariner certainly it could also be used to obtain brushwood
for the cargo's dunnage or to chop branches for the cook's
fire. Even so, the number found remains enigmatic.

*Axes*

Fe 9. Double-bladed axe.            Inv. No. W3-465.
Figs. 11-8 and 11-9; Wreck Plan V*e*.    KTZ (8B).
L. 0.309; w. at blade edge 0.074; th. at eye 0.070;
eye diam. 0.044.
Corner of one blade edge missing. Smooth-On.

The top plane of the axe was almost flat; the
bottom plane was concave. The blades tapered to
curved cutting edges, one of which was slightly
sharper than the other. The eye was round.[9] On
the top surface of the axe and over the eye there
was a nail; the end of its shank was missing. The

nail had probably been driven into the top of the

[6] Regrettably, the thin cast had splayed by the time it was
photographed.

[7] White, *Agricultural Implements*, pp. 85ff., presents a thorough
discussion of this type of tool and its functions and notes also "the large
number of surviving specimens."

[8] A mosaic datable to the mid-sixth century A.D. shows a vintner
holding a billhook in his right hand and a bunch of grapes in his left
(G. M. Fitzgerald, *A Sixth Century Monastery at Beth-Shan [Scy-
thopolis]*, p. 9, pl. XVI).

[9] A similar, but smaller (length 17 cm), double-bladed axe has
been found at Priene (T. Wiegand and H. Schrader, *Priene*, pp.
387–388, fig. 494.1).

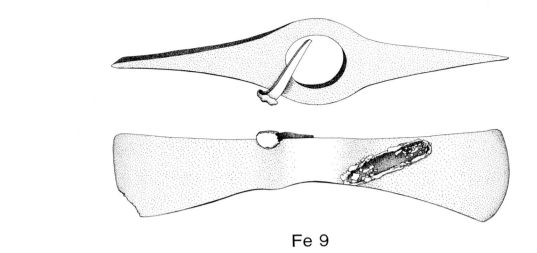

Fe 9

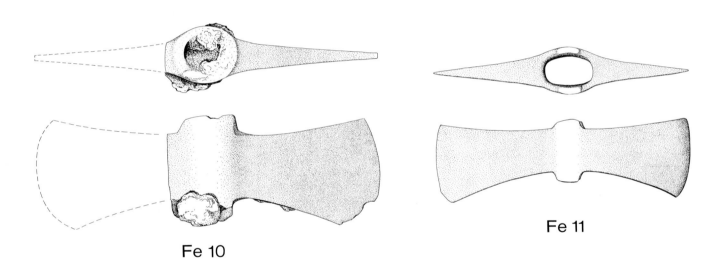

Fe 10                                          Fe 11

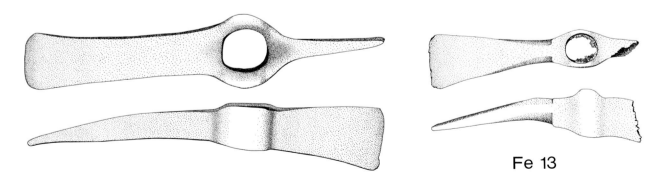

Fe 12                                          Fe 13

FIG. 11-9. Iron axes and mattocks. 1:3. *SWK*

axe's handle, acting as a wedge to hold the handle tightly in the eye. No trace of the handle was found. Adhering to a side surface of one blade is a long, ellipsoidal deposit of dark grey, crystalline material, the identity of which is not known.

Fe 10.  Double-bladed axe.              Inv. No. W3-466.
Figs. 11-8 and 11-9; Wreck Plan V*b*.

KAA ≡ KQP (7C).

Pres. l. 0.165; est. w. at blade edge 0.095; th. at eye 0.046; est. diam. of eye 0.032.

Corner of one blade edge missing; most of other blade missing; eye poorly preserved. Silastic.

The top and bottom planes of the axe's blades were concave. The preserved blade tapered to a blunt, curved cutting edge. The eye was round. At each side of the eye, top and bottom, there were lugs for holding the handle more securely in place.

Fe 11.  Double-bladed axe.         Inv. No. W3-464.
Figs. 11-8 and 11-9; Wreck Plan V*e*.     KTN (8B).
L. 0.199; w. at blade edge 0.064; th. at eye 0.039; eye l. 0.033; eye w. 0.023.

Corner of one blade edge chipped. Smooth-On.

The top plane of the axe's blades was slightly concave; the bottom plane was more concave. The blades tapered to curved cutting edges, one of which was very slightly sharper than the other. The eye was elliptic. At each side of the eye, top and bottom, there were sharply defined lugs.[10]

Another double-bladed axe concretion, l. approx. 0.18, was lost before a cast could be made. Its find spot in sector 7C is shown on Wreck Plan V*b*.

Double-bladed axes retain sharp cutting edges twice as long as their single-bladed counterparts. As one edge dulls, it is directed to rough work while the sharper edge is reserved for fine work. Whetstone MF 56 (pp. 289–292) would have been employed for sharpening the four axes and other bladed tools found on board the ship. The heavier axes, Fe 9 and Fe 10, might have been used for felling trees, lopping off branches, and chopping and splitting logs; the lighter axe, Fe 11, might have been selected for cutting and splitting boards.

## *Mattocks*

Fe 12.  Mattock.                    Inv. No. W3-462.
Figs. 11-8 and 11-9; Wreck Plan V*e*.     KTX (8B).
L. 0.280; w. of axe blade edge 0.050; w. of adze blade edge 0.046; th. at eye 0.059; eye diam. 0.036.

Whole except for nick in axe blade edge. Smooth-On.

The top plane of the axe blade was flat; the bottom plane was slightly concave. The blade tapered to a dull, very slightly curved cutting edge. The top plane of the adze blade was slightly convex; the bottom plane was very slightly concave. Hence, the blade curved downward slightly. Both sides of the adze blade were very slightly concave; this blade thinned to a dull, slightly curved cutting edge. The tool's eye was roughly round. At each side of the eye, top and bottom, there were low rising lugs. The length of the adze blade was almost twice that of the axe blade.[11]

Fe 13.  Mattock.                   Inv. No. W3-463.
Figs. 11-8 and 11-9; Wreck Plan V*b*.     FAF (5A).
Pres. l. 0.164; w. of adze blade edge 0.044; th. at eye 0.031; eye diam. 0.024.

Adze blade edge nicked; most of axe blade missing. Smooth-On.

The top and bottom planes, as well as the sides, of the adze blade were flat. The blade thinned and flared to a dull, straight cutting edge. For most of its length the blade was rectangular in section; nearer the socket the blade became rounder, and there the blade was bent so that it angled slightly downward. The juncture of the blade with the socket was sharply defined as the socket became rectangular in section. The eye through the socket was round. At each side of the eye, top and bottom, there were lugs.[12] In

---

[10] A similar axe was sculpted on the tombstone of Maecius Aprilis in the catacombs of Cyriaca in Rome (H. Gummerus, "Darstellungen aus dem Handwerk auf römischen Grab- und Votivsteinen in Italien," *JdI* 28 [1913]: 104–105, 122, no. 57, fig. 23).

[11] White, *Agricultural Implements*, pp. 36–68, identifies and illustrates various forms of this tool. A similar mattock was found in the Chrétienne A wreck (Benoît, *RStLig* 21 [1955]: 126–128, fig. 11; and Casson, *Archaeology* 10 [1957]: 254–255). Another similar mattock has been found in the Grand Ribaud A wreck of *ca*. 130 B.C. (F. Carrazé, "L'Épave 'Grand Ribaud A,'" *CahArchSub* 4 [1975]: 25–26, fig. 6).

[12] Three similar mattocks have been found at Priene (Wiegand and Schrader, *Priene*, fig. 494.2–4).

the eye a small part of the wood handle is pre-served.

These double-headed mattocks combined features of two tools. Their axe blades might have served for chopping and cutting, especially at roots, while the adze blades, probably used more like picks, could have served for digging and grubbing as well as cutting. These tools would have been particularly effective in clearing areas around freshwater springs.

## Adzes

Fe 14. Adze.					Inv. Nos. W3-407 and W3-446.
Figs. 11-10 and 11-13; Wreck Plan V*e*.
						MBS and MBR (9B).
Est. original l. 0.24; max. w. of blade 0.072; max. th. of blade 0.022.
The two pieces of the tool's concretion were found side by side; the badly worn, broken sur-faces could not be joined. The tool has been re-stored on paper. A part of its tongue is missing. Blade Silastic; tongue and collar Smooth-On.

The sloping-shouldered sides of the blade broadened to a maximum width before narrow-ing to the slightly curved cutting edge. The flat faces of the blade tapered to form this edge. Over most of its length the blade was rectangular in section, but near the juncture to the tongue it became round. The tongue was rectangular in section; its sides narrowed, and its faces tapered to a rounded, blunt end. The collar, which had held the blade to the handle, was found in place wrapped around the tongue. At this end the col-lar was squared in shape. The opposite end, which would have been jammed down around the handle, was rounded, and its lower edge was slanted outward. Maximum interior dimensions of the collar were l. 0.085 and w. 0.027; it was rectangular in section, h. 0.017 and th. 0.003.

Fe 15. Adze.				Inv. Nos. W3-406 and W3-397.
Figs. 11-10 and 11-13; Wreck Plan V*b*.
				KZP-12+KZP-7 (6C—tool chest).
L. 0.224; max. w. of blade 0.079; max. th. of blade 0.024.
Blade's cutting edge nicked; collar's rounded end missing. Smooth-On.

The blade was similar to that of Fe 14. Both blade and collar were found in the tool chest, and although the collar was not in position around the tongue, it no doubt would have been the one used to hold the blade to the handle. This collar was similar to that of Fe 14; however, its outer face was slightly beveled. Its preserved interior l. was 0.092, and its maximum interior w. was

0.029; it was rectangular in section, h. 0.016 and th. 0.003.

Fe 16. Adze.					Inv. No. W3-404.
Figs. 11-10 and 11-13; Wreck Plan V*b*.
						FDC (5B').
L. 0.240; max. w. of blade 0.073; max. th. of blade 0.023.
Corner of cutting edge nicked. Silastic.
The blade was similar to those of the preceding Fe 14 and Fe 15.

Fe 17. Adze.					Inv. No. W3-405.
Figs. 11-10 and 11-13; Wreck Plan V*b*.
						KZM-A (6C).
L. 0.237; max. w. of blade 0.081; max. th. of blade 0.020. Whole. Smooth-On.
The blade was similar to those of the preceding Fe 14–Fe 16.

Fe 18. Adze.					Inv. No. W3-408.
Figs. 11-10 and 11-13; Wreck Plan V*b*.
						FCZ-1 (6B'/C').
Pres. l. 0.178; max. w. of blade 0.083; max. th. of blade 0.024.
Corner of cutting edge missing; end of tongue missing. Smooth-On.
The blade was similar to those of the preceding Fe 14–Fe 17. It was found in contact with a thin piece of wood.

These five virtually identical tools were not axes, since the positioning of the collar around the tongue of Fe 14 indicates that the blade was set perpendicular to the handle.[13] Also, because the face of the blade bulged near its juncture with the tongue and the thick collar projected considerably beyond the tongue's face, the tools would not have been effective planes.[14] Rather,

[13] A tool whose blade is shaped like those of Fe 14–Fe 18 appears on a tombstone set up for P. Ferrarius Hermes; the tombstone is now in the Uffizi Gallery. Gummerus, *JdI* 28 (1913): 113, 124, no. 84, fig. 31, dated the tombstone to the early Roman Imperial period and identi-fied the tool as an axe.

[14] On the grave stele of P. Beitenos Hermes, a maker of couches, is a tool, the blade of which is somewhat similar to those of Fe 14–Fe 18, which has been identified as a plane; the stele, dating to the Roman period, is now in the Louvre, No. 934 (C. Daremberg and

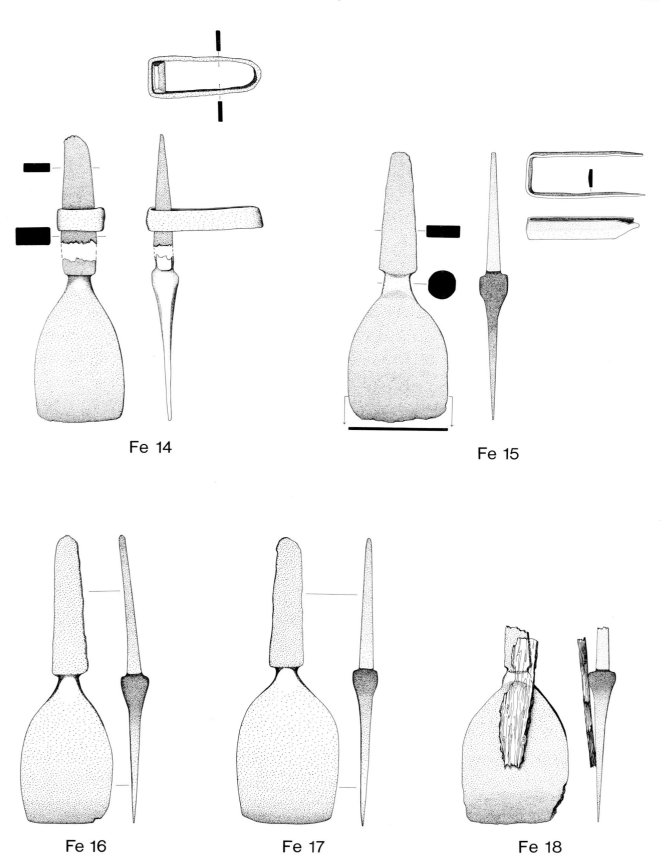

Fe 14

Fe 15

Fe 16

Fe 17

Fe 18

FIG. 11-10. Iron adzes. 1:3. *SWK*

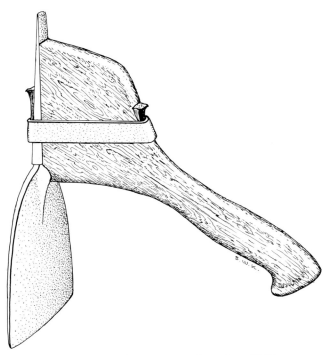

FIG. 11-11. Conjectural restoration of an adze. *SWK*

these tools were adzes of a type called a "slot adze" which has been in use from Ptolemaic to recent times.[15]

A typical handle for the adzes found in the ship can be conjectured (Fig. 11-11) from the configuration of the blade and collar of Fe 14. The handle's head would have been flat against the tongue and along its sides. At the back the handle would have been rounded and would have slanted out at an angle to match the inner face of the collar. Here, as well as between the collar and the front face of the tongue, wedges might have been inserted to prevent the collar from slipping up. The bottom of the handle's head would have been cut to fit around the bulge in the blade. The haft of the handle was probably curved so that the adze could be swung comfortably. With each strike the wedge-shaped tongue would have been pushed against the collar and the handle's head, keeping the blade tightly in place. However, the blade could have been easily removed for sharpening; a tap on the rounded end of the tongue would have released it.

The adze was the preeminent tool of the shipwright. With it he could strip surplus material from logs and roughly shape a keel, a plank, or a frame; he could level edges to yield flush joints, trim flat and curved faces to obtain tight fits and finish surfaces smoothly.[16] It was this tool that he would use most in building a ship, and, similarly, it was this tool that the Byzantine ship's carpenter would have found so versatile for making repairs.

## *Hammers*

Fe 19. Adze-hammer.                    Inv. No. W3-461.
    Figs. 11-12 and 11-13; Wreck Plan V*b*. MBE (6B).
    L. 0.209; th. at eye 0.041; eye diam. 0.029; hammerhead diam. 0.044.

Corner of adze's blade edge missing; surface of concretion's mold disintegrated around part of hammer's poll and face. Silastic.

The top and bottom planes of the adze's blade were flat. Both sides of the blade were concave. The blade thinned and flared to a straight cutting edge, est. w. 0.058. For most of its length the blade was rectangular in section. Near the socket the blade was bent so that it angled downward, and between the bend and the socket the blade was round in section. The juncture of the blade to the socket was sharply defined as the socket

E. Saglio, *Dictionnaire des antiquités grecques et romaines*, IV, 104, s.v. "norma," fig. 5328; W. Deonna, "Ex-voto déliens," *BCH* 56 [1932]: 442, fig. 7.1; P. Cloché, *Les Classes, les métiers, le trafic*, p. 61, pl. XXVII.3; G. M. A. Richter, *The Furniture of the Greeks, Etruscans, and Romans*, p. 127, fig. 612; A. Burford, *Craftsmen in Greek and Roman Society*, p. 182, pl. 8; J. Liversidge, "Woodwork," in *Roman Crafts*, ed. D. Strong and D. Brown, p. 163, pl. 271).

[15] For the term *slot adze*, see R. A. Salaman, *Dictionary of Tools*, p. 29, s.v. "Adze, Slot," fig. 22. For other names for these tools, see P. B. Kebabian and D. Witney, *American Woodworking Tools*, p. 40, fig. 26, right, a "strap adz"; and *Traditional Tools of the Carpenter and Other Craftsmen*, Christie's Sale No. CA794/5T, London, April 23–24, 1979, p. 10, nos. 41, 43, 45, pl. 2, "stirrup-adzes." An example of the slot adze was found at Abydos (W. M. F. Petrie, *Tools and Weapons*, p. 18, section 42, Z 132, pl. XVIII; and W. L. Goodman, *The History of Woodworking Tools*, pp. 25–27, fig. 38). Two other examples are said to come from Pompeii and date to the first century A.D. ("The Victor Merlo Collection," *Los Angeles Museum Bulletin*, July, 1932, pp. 19, 23, fig. 8); they are now in the University Museum, Philadelphia (University Museum Nos. 69-8-4 and 69-8-5). One from Connecticut is dated 1720 (E. Sloane, *A Museum of Early American Tools*, p. 29).

[16] In the Museo Nazionale, Ravenna, is the tombstone of P. Longidienus Camillus, dating to the late second or early third century A.D., which shows Longidienus, a shipwright, trimming a frame with an adze (H. Blümner, *Technologie und Terminologie der Gewerbe und Künste bei Griechen und Römern*, II, 341, fig. 55; Gummerus, *JdI* 28 [1913]: 91–93, 121, no. 38, figs. 14–15; S. Muratori, *Il R. Museo Nazionale di Ravenna*, pp. 9, 45, no. 64; L. Casson, *The Ancient Mariners*, pl. 15a; L. Casson, *Illustrated History of Ships and Boats*, p. 46, pl. 57; L. Casson, *Ships and Seamanship in the Ancient World*, p. 206 n. 24, pl. 163; Burford, *Craftsmen*, p. 182, pl. 9; and Liversidge, "Woodwork," pp. 164–165, pl. 273).

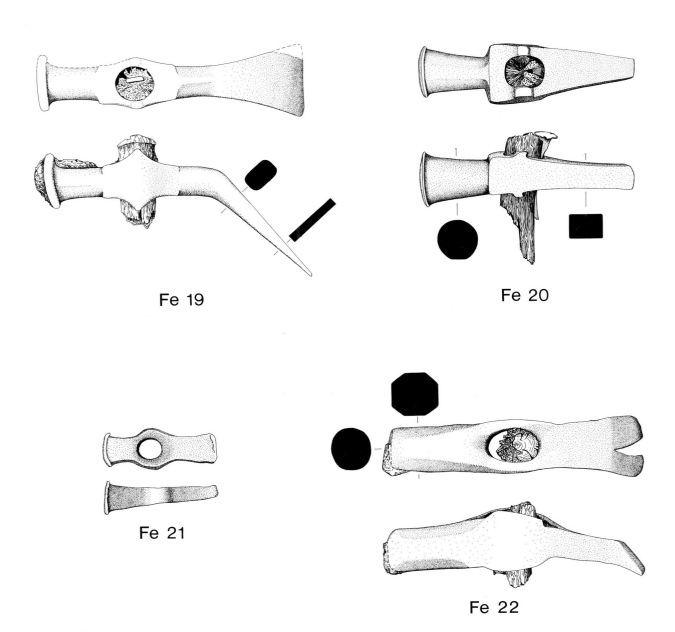

Fe 19

Fe 20

Fe 21

Fe 22

FIG. 11-12. Iron hammers. 1:3. *SWK*

became rectangular in section. The eye through the socket was round. At each side of the eye, top and bottom, there were bluntly pointed lugs. The juncture of the socket to the hammer's poll was again sharply defined as the tool went from rectangular to round in section. The poll flared to form a bulbous head whose face was slightly curved.[17] In the eye a part of the wood handle is

[17]Two comparable adze-hammers have been found in Compiègne, France (B. Champion, "Outils en fer du Musée de Saint-Germain," *RA*, 1916, no. 1, pp. 215–216, nos. 15860A and 28992, pl. II; and S. Reinach, *Catalogue illustré du Musée des Antiquités Nationales au Chateau de Saint-Germain-en-Laye*, pp. 260–262, nos. 15860A and

preserved. An iron pin, rectangular in section, w. 0.014 and th. 0.004, had been driven into the end of the handle; acting as a wedge, it would have helped to hold the handle tightly in the eye.

Fe 20.  Hammer.                               Inv. No. W3-458.
Figs. 11-12 and 11-13; Wreck Plan V*b*. KKK (6B). L. 0.168; th. at eye 0.044; eye l. 0.030; eye w. 0.025; round head diam. 0.046; rectangular head w. 0.020; rectangular head th. 0.015.
Whole. Smooth-On.

28992, fig. 272). Another has been found at Great Chesterford, Essex, England (Liversidge, "Woodwork," p. 161, pl. 270).

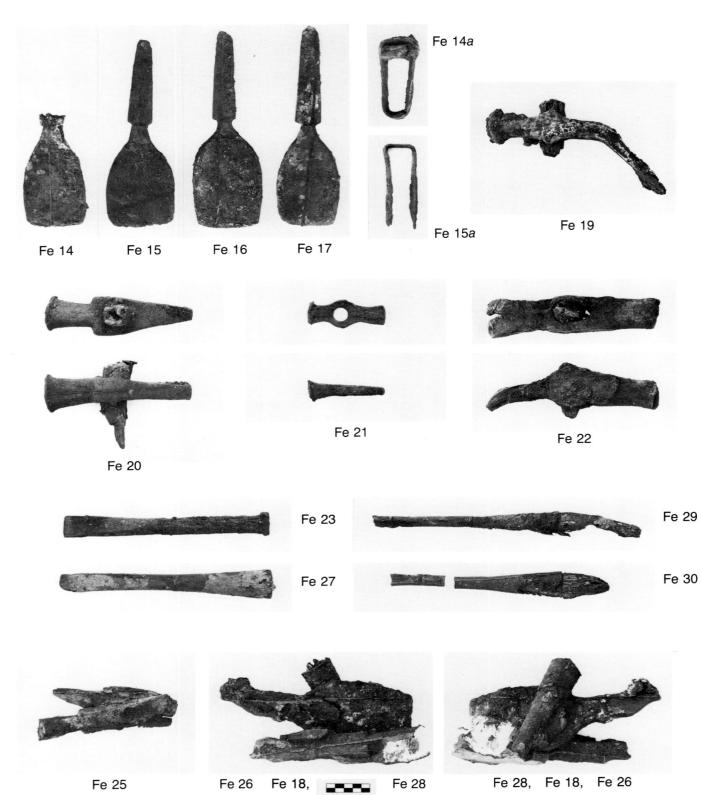

Fe 14a

Fe 14    Fe 15    Fe 16    Fe 17    Fe 15a    Fe 19

Fe 20    Fe 21    Fe 22

Fe 23    Fe 29

Fe 27    Fe 30

Fe 25    Fe 26    Fe 18,    Fe 28    Fe 28,   Fe 18,   Fe 26

FIG. 11-13. Cast replicas of adzes, hammers, chisels, and gouges.

Flaring out from its poll, one head of the hammer was round with a slightly curved face. The poll was virtually round in section and narrowed slightly towards the tool's socket. The juncture of this poll to the socket was sharply defined, as the socket was rectangular in section. The eye through the socket was elliptic. At each side of the eye, top and bottom, there were lugs shaped like shark's fins. From the socket to the other head the tool gradually tapered, retaining its rectangular section, until it terminated in a rectangular head with a flattish face. In the eye a part of the wood handle is preserved. A nail had been driven into the top of the handle, and the shank of the nail extended through the eye; the tip of the nail's shank was missing.

Fe 21.  Hammer.                    Inv. No. W3-459.
        Figs. 11-12 and 11-13.                  (?).
        L. 0.089; th. at eye 0.031; eye diam. 0.016; short head th. 0.027; short head w. 0.025; long head th. 0.008; long head w. 0.022.
        Whole. Smooth-On.

From the socket the top and bottom planes of the shorter head diverged, and the concave sides flared, to form a roughly rectangular head with a slightly curved face. The mushroomed edges of this face showed that the hammer had been extensively used. The eye of the socket was round. The top and bottom planes of the longer head converged slightly, and the concave sides spread to form a rectangular head with a very slightly curved face.[18]

Fe 22.  Claw hammer.               Inv. No. W3-457.
        Figs. 11-12 and 11-13; Wreck Plan V*b*.  KZO (6B).
        L. 0.201; th. at eye 0.044; eye l. 0.039; eye w. 0.028; elliptic head th. 0.035; elliptic head w. 0.031.
        Whole; surface of concretion's mold disintegrated around part of hammer's head. Smooth-On.

The hammer's poll was octagonal in section, ending in an elliptic head with a very slightly curved face. The eye through the socket was elliptic. At each side of the eye, top and bottom, there were long, low-rising lugs. From the sock-

et the peen of the hammer bent down slightly and was rectangular in section. Near its end the peen divided into claws, which were angled down more sharply.[19] In the eye a part of the wood handle is preserved.

We know the find spots for three (Fe 19, Fe 20, and Fe 22) of these four hammers. They came from 6B, and as well as being within reach of one another, they were also near the carpenter's tool chest in 6C. Perhaps all the hammers had been stowed with the tool chest.

Each of the hammers had a distinctly different shape, providing the carpenter with an ample choice for a variety of jobs. Fe 19 combined the functions of an adze and a hammer in a single well-balanced tool. Its bulbous hammerhead could have been suitable for working metal. However, since it was associated with an adze head, the ship's carpenter more probably employed this dual-purpose tool while working wood, and its hammer might have been used most often for hitting a chisel.

While doing work with a chisel, the ship's carpenter could as likely have used the round head of Fe 20. This head would also have been as suitable as the hammerhead of Fe 19 for beating metal sheeting. The counterbalancing head of Fe 20, however, seems out of context in either of these functions. Rather, this rectangular head would have served well for pounding treenails into predrilled holes. In such work the hammer could then have been turned around and its round head used for driving nails through the treenails. Pounding treenails and driving nails, in fact, might well have been the primary function of this tool.

A folded sheet of lead and some waste from lead castings were found in the ship (see chapter 12). The small hammer Fe 21 was most probably used to beat this lead into patches for sheathing leaky seams in the hull or to form lead fishing weights used on nets and lines (chapter 13). Although it could also have been used for hammering tacks, this tool was designed particularly for metalwork.

The head of the claw hammer Fe 22 was used for driving nails and spikes and its claw for pulling them out. It was especially well balanced and designed for these functions. But, like its modern descendants, the claw hammer might just as well have been used as an all-purpose striking or prying tool by a shipwright, carpenter, or general handyman.

---

[18] A hammer similar in shape and size (length 9 cm) was found at Heidenberg, Germany (L. Lindenschmit, "Ein Massenfund römischer Eisengeräte," in *Die Altertümer unserer heidnischen Vorzeit*, V, 259, no. 794, fig. 46; and Petrie, *Tools and Weapons*, p. 40, section 111, M 102, pl. XLV).

[19] A similar claw hammer has been found at Trier, Germany (A. Neuburger, *Die Technik des Altertums*, p. 51, fig. 56; and H. C. Mercer, *Ancient Carpenters' Tools*, pp. 265–266, fig. 222).

## Chisels

Fe 23. Chisel.                          Inv. No. W3-421.
Figs. 11-13 and 11-14; Wreck Plan V*b*.
                              KZP-2 (6C—tool chest).
L. 0.239; diam. of head 0.029; w. of cutting edge
0.027.
Whole. Smooth-On.

The chisel's head was round with a flat face.
The shank was round in section until it began to
taper; then it formed two flat faces and splayed
very slightly near the tip, ending in a straight
cutting edge.[20]

Fe 24. Chisel.                          Inv. No. W3-424.
Fig. 11-14; Wreck Plan V*b*.    FDK-B-1 (6B').
Pres. l. 0.234; max. pres. w. 0.015; max. pres. th.
0.010.
Head missing; surface of concretion's mold badly
disintegrated around cutting edge. Smooth-On.

The blade was rectangular in section; the
cross-sectional dimensions did not decrease significantly down its length. Only a small part of
the blade's tip was preserved. It appears that the
blade had not narrowed, but only thinned, and
that only one face had been sharply beveled to
form the cutting edge.

Fe 25. Chisel.                          Inv. No. W3-422.
Figs. 11-13 and 11-14; Wreck Plan V*b*. FDF (7C).
Pres. l. 0.150; max. pres. diam. of shank 0.026;
w. of cutting edge 0.043.
Head missing; cutting edge nicked. Silastic.

The shank was round in section, narrowing towards the blade. The juncture of the shank with
the blade was sharply defined, as the blade was
rectangular in section. The blade flared and
tapered to a slightly curved cutting edge.[21] It was
found in contact with a piece of wood.

Fe 26. Chisel.                          Inv. No. W3-423.
Figs. 11-13 and 11-14; Wreck Plan V*b*.
                              FCZ-3 (6B').
Pres. l. 0.196; max. pres. diam. of shank 0.025.
Head missing; cutting edge missing. Smooth-
On.

The shank was round in section, narrowing towards the blade. The juncture of the shank with
the blade was sharply defined, as the blade was
rectangular in section. The width of the blade

did not decrease appreciably, while its faces
tapered towards the cutting edge.[22]

Fe 27. Chisel.                          Inv. No. W3-420.
Figs. 11-13 and 11-14.                  FDM-A (6C).
L. of chisel 0.245; diam. of head 0.034; pres. w.
of cutting edge 0.020.
One side of chisel chipped near cutting edge.
Silastic.

The circular head had a socket of diam. 0.028.
One end of the tool's wood handle is found in the
socket and is preserved beyond the top of the
chisel's head for a length of 0.005. Based upon
the configuration of this end of the handle, the
socket would have been 0.033 deep. It would
have narrowed slightly for 0.019 of its depth,
contracted more sharply at this point, and then
continued to its bottom. Rising from the bottom
of the socket there would have been a roughly
rectangular tang, w. 0.008 and th. 0.005; thin-
ning and tapering very slightly to a blunt end,
the tang would have been 0.020 long. The
chisel's shank was round in section. For about
half of its length the shank gradually narrowed;
then, forming two flat faces, it began to taper and
to splay slightly near the tip, ending in a curved
cutting edge.[23]

Fe 28. Chisel.                          Inv. No. W3-416.
Fig. 11-13; Wreck Plan V*b*.        FCZ-4 (6B').
Pres. l. of chisel 0.129; diam. of head 0.033;
diam. of socket 0.029.
Lower half of shank missing. Smooth-On.

Since the preserved portion of this tool was
virtually identical in size and shape to the preceding Fe 27, it is identified as a socketed chisel.
A part of the tool's wood handle, preserved for a
length of 0.008 beyond the top of the chisel's
head, is found in the socket.

It is clear that Fe 23 had a forged iron head while
Fe 27 and Fe 28 had wood handles fitted in their sockets.
Since the tops of the shanks of Fe 24, Fe 25, and Fe 26
were not preserved, it is uncertain whether they had
iron heads or sockets for wood handles. Chisels with
metal heads are usually worked with a hammer, while
those with wood handles are better struck by a mallet or
worked by hand pressure.

---

[20] A similar chisel, but with a more mushroomed head, has been
found in Compiègne, France (Champion, *RA*, 1916, no. 1, pp. 212–213,
no. 15910, pl. I; and Reinach, *Catalogue illustré*, pp. 258–259, no.
15910, fig. 271).

[21] A similar socketed chisel was found at Pompeii (Petrie, *Tools
and Weapons*, p. 22, section 55, C 155, pl. XXIII).

[22] A similar socketed chisel has been found in Compiègne, France
(Champion, *RA*, 1916, no. 1, pp. 213–214, no. 28986A, pl. I; and Reinach, *Catalogue illustré*, pp. 259–260, no. 28986A, fig. 271).

[23] Two similar socketed chisels have been found at Silchester,
Hampshire, England (G. C. Boon, *Roman Silchester*, p. 183, fig. 35,
nos. 1–2).

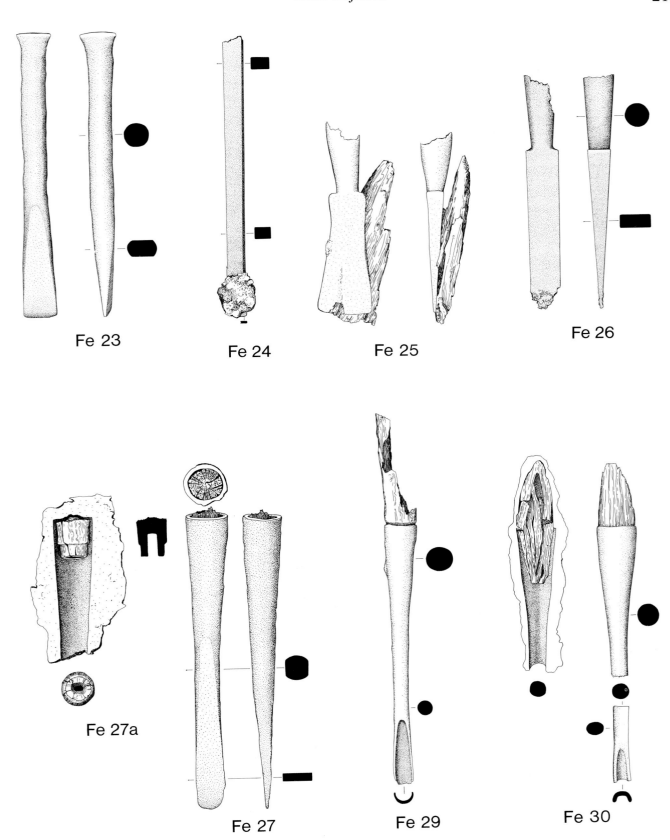

Fe 23

Fe 24

Fe 25

Fe 26

Fe 27a

Fe 27

Fe 29

Fe 30

FIG. 11-14. Iron chisels and gouges. 1:3. *SWK*

The combination of a socket and a tang fitting for the handle of chisel Fe 27 is most unusual, and it would have been difficult to forge. In fact, it is possible that the socket for this chisel was simply conical in shape, that the wood found in the socket was being reused, and that this handle had previously been fitted to a smaller chisel with a tang. These suppositions would explain why the handle contracts sharply, for around its narrowest section it would in its previous use have had a metal band—a ferrule—to prevent it from splitting as it was driven against a tang.

Of the chisels found in the ship, Fe 24 with its straight sides and single beveled face would have been the most effective in cutting mortises. The other chisels, which all have tapering faces, were more suitable for chipping, notching, edging, or smoothing where adzes could not reach. When planks needed to be replaced, these chisels could have wedged open seams and cut through tenons.

## Gouges

Fe 29. Gouge.                         Inv. No. W3-418.
    Figs. 11-13 and 11-14; Wreck Plan V*b*.
                            KZP-1 (6C—tool chest).
    Overall pres. l. 0.312; l. of gouge 0.213; diam. of head 0.028; diam. of socket 0.024; w. of cutting edge 0.015.
    Cutting edge nicked. Smooth-On.
    A part of the tool's wood handle (cast with Smooth-On) was found in the socket and was preserved beyond the top of the gouge's head for a length of 0.099. The shank was round in section; it gradually narrowed down its length. Near its end the tool became a crescent in section, ending in a cutting edge.[24]

Fe 30. Gouge.           Inv. Nos. W3-417 and W3-419.
    Figs. 11-13 and 11-14.          FAW and FAB (6B).
    Overall pres. l. of larger piece 0.179; pres. l. of smaller piece 0.064; diam. of head 0.033; diam. of socket 0.029.

Part of shank missing; end of cutting edge missing. Larger piece Smooth-On; smaller piece Silastic.
    The socket was conical in shape. A part of the tool's wood handle, found in the socket, is preserved beyond the top of the gouge's head for a length of 0.054. The shank was round in section; it gradually narrowed down its length. The larger shank piece had a diam. of 0.014 at its broken end. The smaller piece also had a diam. of 0.014 at its broken end. There seems little doubt that the two pieces, which were found near one another, had been part of the same gouge. Near its end the tool became a crescent in section; the max. pres. w. of the hollow was 0.015.

Gouges which cut channels and scoop holes would have been particularly needed on board ship to make blocks and deadeyes used in the rigging.

## Caulking Iron

Fe 31. Caulking iron.              Inv. No. W3-409.
    Figs. 11-15 and 11-16.              FCY-A (6A).
    Pres. l. 0.123; w. of blade edge 0.056; max. pres. th. 0.012.
    Head missing; blade edge nicked. Silastic.

The blade flared to a straight edge. It was rectangular in section, thickening towards its missing head.[25]

The ship's carpenter would have used the caulking iron with a mallet or hammer to pound tarred oakum or cotton into leaky seams in order to make the hull watertight.

[24] Similar socketed gouges have been found at Silchester (J. Evans, "On Some Iron Tools and Other Articles Formed of Iron Found at Silchester in the Year 1890," *Archaeologia* 54 [1894]: 150, fig. 16; and Boon, *Roman Silchester*, p. 183, fig. 35, nos. 5–6).

[25] A similar caulking iron with a mushroomed head was found at Pompeii (P. Gusman, *Pompei*, p. 269).

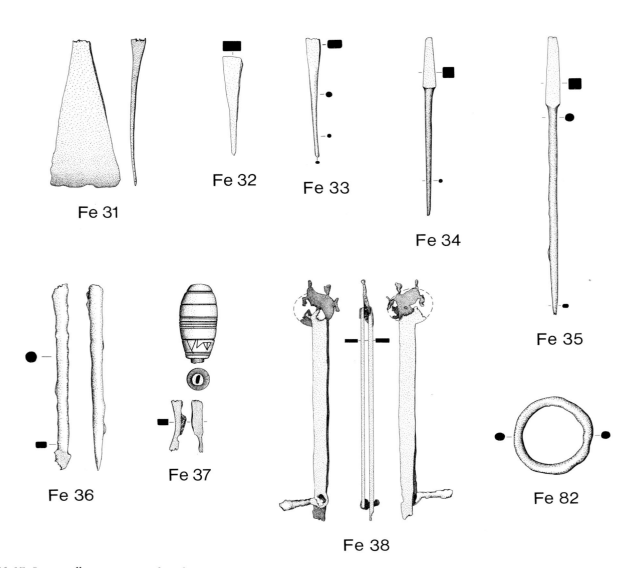

Fe 31

Fe 32

Fe 33

Fe 34

Fe 35

Fe 36

Fe 37

Fe 38

Fe 82

FIG. 11-15. Iron caulking iron, punches, bits, awl, carpenter's compass, and ring. 1:3. *SWK*

## Punches

Fe 32. Punch.                           Inv. No. W3-389.
Figs. 11-15 and 11-16.                        (?).
L. 0.083; head w. 0.015; head th. 0.009.
Whole. Silastic.

The head was flat and rectangular. The shank near the head was rectangular in section; but as the shank tapered, it became square in section, ending in a point.

Fe 33. Punch.                           Inv. No. W3-391.
Figs. 11-15 and 11-16.                    FCY-B (6A).
Pres. l. 0.097; shank pres. w. 0.009; shank pres.

th. 0.007.
Head missing. Silastic.

The shank was rectangular in section; as it tapered, it became round in section, ending in a blunt point.

These punches could have been used to make starting holes in wood for drill bits or to pierce metal.[26]

[26] Similar iron punches have been found at the Roman frontier post of Newstead, Scotland, and at Silchester, England (W. H. Manning, "Blacksmithing," in *Roman Crafts*, ed. D. Strong and D. Brown, p. 150, pls. 254–255).

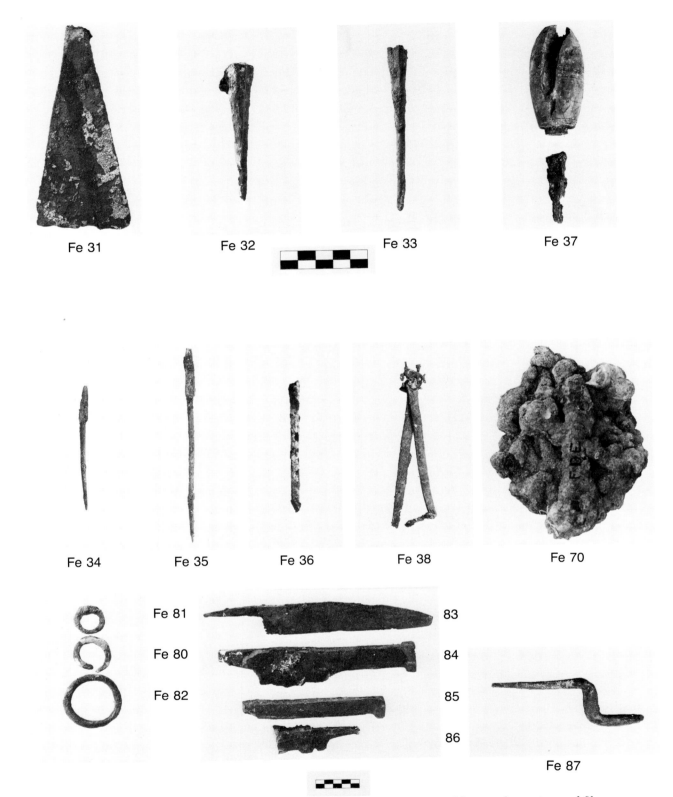

FIG. 11-16. Cast replicas of caulking iron, punches, bits, awl, carpenter's compass, nail bag, washers, ring, and files.

## Bits

Fe 34.  Bit.                            Inv. No. W3-394.
Figs. 11-15 and 11-16; Wreck Plan V*b*.
                    KZP-13 (6C—tool chest).
L. 0.149.
Whole. Smooth-On.

The tang of the bit was square in section; it tapered from a maximum size of 0.010 square at its juncture with the bit's shank to a minimum size of 0.005 square at its flat end. At the juncture of tang with shank the bit became round in section, diam. 0.006; it gradually narrowed, ending in a rounded point.[27]

Fe 35.  Bit.                            Inv. No. W3-395.
Figs. 11-15 and 11-16; Wreck Plan V*b*.
                    KZP-4 (6C—tool chest).
Pres. l. 0.232.
Point nicked. Smooth-On.

Similar to the preceding Fe 34; tang's maximum size 0.011 square and minimum size 0.006 square. Shank's max. diam. 0.007.

Fe 36.  Bit.                            Inv. No. W3-434.

Figs. 11-15 and 11-16.              FCT (8A).
Pres. l. 0.156; max. pres. diam. of shank 0.013.
Tang and top part of shank missing; one edge of point missing. Silastic.

The upper part of the shank was round in section; as it narrowed down its length, the shank became rectangular in section. Near its end the shank's faces tapered, and its sides flared out, max. pres. w. 0.014, and then narrowed, forming an arrowhead point.[28]

With their square-tapered tangs wedged into a stock, these bits were turned by a bow drill.[29] Since the back-and-forth action of a bow drill rotates a stock both clockwise and counterclockwise, such bits must be able to cut equally well in both directions. The simple points of Fe 34 and Fe 35 most probably would have been used to bore pilot holes, judging by the thinness of their shafts. With its sharpened sides Fe 36 would have cut a hole in excess of diam. 0.014, a size appropriate for the bolts used in the ship (see Fe 74–Fe 79, below).

## Awl

Fe 37.  Awl.                            Inv. No. W3-413.
Figs. 11-15 and 11-16; Wreck Plan V*b*.
                                    EL-2 (6B).
Pres. l. of shank 0.043; l. of handle 0.066.
Shank poorly preserved, both ends missing. Smooth-On.
Wood handle whole, but cracked.

The awl's shank was rectangular in section, max. pres. w. 0.008 and max. pres. th. 0.005. The handle is ellipsoidal in shape, round in section, max. diam. 0.031. There is a round projection, diam. 0.011 and l. 0.004, at one end of the handle into which the tang of the awl would have been inserted; the cutting for the tang measures w. 0.007, th. 0.003, and depth 0.032. Around this projection a ferrule of metal or leather would have been fitted to prevent the

handle from splitting as pressure was applied to the awl's blade. The handle is decorated by thirteen lathe-turned, shallow grooves which singly or in groups delineate bands of various width. In the widest band near the projection a graffito was scratched which may be read as ΔIMΛ. The first three letters form a ligature; the last character is separate. I am not able to provide any meaningful interpretation of this combination.[30]

An awl may be used in carpentry for scoring lines or boring grooves and holes in wood and in sailmaking for piercing eyelets in canvas.

[28] A similar bit with arrowhead point and square-tapered tang has been found at the Roman fort of Saalburg, Germany (Blümlein, *Bilder*, p. 85, fig. 265.15).

[29] A carpenter using a bow drill appears on the base of a late Roman, gilt glass bowl now in the Vatican Library (Richter, *Furniture*, p. 128, fig. 613; and Liversidge, "Woodwork," pp. 158–159, pl. 264). The brace does not appear until the fifteenth century (Mercer, *Ancient Carpenters' Tools*, p. 205; Goodman, *History of Woodworking Tools*, p. 175; and Salaman, *Dictionary of Tools*, p. 92).

[30] I am most grateful to Eugene Vanderpool and Colin N. Edmonson for their advice to me in my attempt to understand this graffito.

[27] Similar bits have been found in Compiègne and at Alise Ste. Reine, France (Champion, *RA*, 1916, no. 1, pp. 222–224, nos. 15901A and 60954, pl. V; and Reinach, *Catalogue illustré*, nos. 15901A and 60954, fig. 275). Another has been found at Silchester (Boon, *Roman Silchester*, p. 183, fig. 35.7).

## Carpenter's Compass

Fe 38.  Carpenter's Compass.          Inv. No. W3-445.
        Figs. 11-15 and 11-16; Wreck Plan V*b*.
                          KZP-14 (6C—tool chest).
        Pres. l. 0.196.
        Tips of both legs missing and heads poorly pre-
        served; imperfections in the mold caused excres-
        cences to be cast at the end of the shorter pre-
        served leg and between the heads. Smooth-On.

The legs were rectangular in section, their widths decreasing slightly towards the tips. The heads seem to have been circular in shape, and they appear to have been joined together by a rivet.[31]

The carpenter would have used this compass principally for transferring measurements.

## Fasteners

Fe 39.  Tack.                         Inv. No. W3-362.
        Figs. 11-17 and 11-18.                FAR (6A).
        L. 0.037; diam. of head 0.022; max. th. of shank
        0.007.
        Whole. Silastic.
        The circular head was slightly rounded on its
        top. The shank was square in section, tapering
        very gradually to a sudden, sharp point.

Fe 40.  Tack.                         Inv. No. W3-363.
        Fig. 3-31.                           FDD-1 (8B).
        Pres. l. 0.037; diam. of head 0.024; max. th. of
        shank 0.008.
        End of shank missing. Silastic.
        Similar to the preceding Fe 39.

Fe 41.  Tack.                         Inv. No. W3-364.
        Figs. 11-17 and 11-18.               KZM-B (6C).

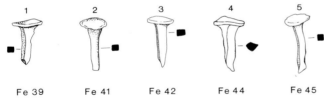

FIG. 11-17. Selection of iron tacks. *SWK*

FIG. 11-18. Cast replicas of (*left to right*) tacks Fe 39, Fe 41, Fe 42, Fe 44, and Fe 45.

L. 0.039; diam. of head 0.023; max. th. of shank 0.009.
Whole. Smooth-on.
        The circular head was flat on its top. The shank was square in section, tapering to a blunt point.

Fe 42.  Tack.                         Inv. No. W3-365.
        Figs. 11-17 and 11-18.                FAQ (5B).
        L. 0.041; diam. of head 0.021; max. th. of shank
        0.007.
        Whole. Silastic.
        The circular head was rounded on its top. The
        shank was square in section, tapering to a point.

Fe 43.  Tack.                         Inv. No. W3-366.
        Fig. 3-31.                           FAP-1 (5A).
        Pres. l. 0.042; diam. of head 0.021; max. th. of
        shank 0.007. End of shank missing. Only half of
        the tack's head and shank's thickness cast with
        Smooth-On.
        Similar to the preceding Fe 42.

Fe 44.  Tack.                         Inv. No. W3-367.
        Figs. 11-17 and 11-18.
                      FAA (lower right quadrant, 5C).
        L. 0.043; diam. of head 0.025; max. th. of shank
        0.009.
        Whole. Plaster.
        The circular head was slightly rounded on its
        top. The shank was roughly square in section,
        tapering to a point.

Fe 45.  Tack.                         Inv. No. W3-368.
        Figs. 11-17 and 11-18.                FAJ (5A).
        L. 0.047; diam. of head 0.021; max. th. of shank
        0.008.
        Whole. Smooth-On.
        Similar to Fe 39.

[31]For a similar carpenter's compass, see N. Walke, *Das römische Donaukastell Staubing-Sorviodurum*, pp. 61, 160, pl. 128.21.

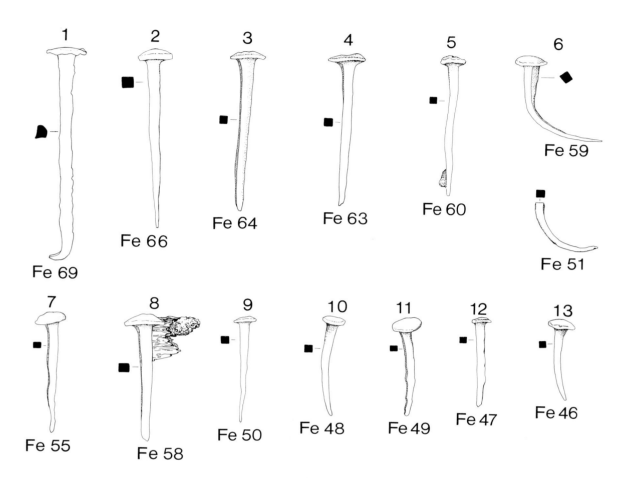

Fig. 11-19. Selection of iron nails and spikes. Cf. Fig. 3-30. 1:3. *SWK*

Fe 46. Nail.                          Inv. No. W3-369.
       Figs. 3-30 and 11-19.                  FAX (6A).
       L. 0.060; diam. of head 0.022; max. th. of shank
       0.008.
       Whole. Silastic.
          The circular head was slightly rounded on its
       top, but its peak was flat, giving it the ap-
       pearance of a truncated cone. The shank, bent
       slightly, was square in section, tapering to a
       point.
Fe 47. Nail.                          Inv. No. W3-370.
       Figs. 3-30 and 11-19.                  FBP (8A).
       L. 0.071; diam. of head 0.017; max. th. of shank
       0.007.
       Whole. Silastic.
          The small, circular head was very slightly
       rounded on its top. The shank was square in sec-
       tion, tapering to a point.

Fe 48. Nail.                          Inv. No. W3-371.
       Figs. 3-30 and 11-19.                  FAH (5A).
       L. 0.079; diam. of head 0.020; max. th. of shank
       0.008.
       Whole. Silastic.
          The circular head was flat on its top. The
       shank, bent slightly, was square in section, taper-
       ing to a point.
Fe 49. Nail.                          Inv. No. W3-372.
       Figs. 3-30 and 11-19.                  FAV (7C).
       L. 0.073; diam. of head 0.026; max. th. of shank
       0.008.
       Whole. Silastic.
          The circular head was slightly rounded on its
       top. The shank, bent slightly, was rectangular in
       section, tapering to a rounded point.
Fe 50. Nail.                          Inv. No. W3-373.
       Figs. 3-30 and 11-19.                        (?).

L. 0.086; diam. of head 0.021; max. th. of shank 0.008.

Whole. Silastic.

The circular head was slightly rounded on its top. The shank was square in section, tapering to a fine point.

Fe 51.  Nail shank.                          Inv. No. W3-387.
        Fig. 11-19.                              FAY (6B).
        Est. pres. l. of shank when straight 0.07; max. pres. th. of shank 0.007.

Head and top of shank missing. Silastic.

The bent shank was square in section, tapering to a fine point.

Fe 52.  Nail shank.                          Inv. No. W3-388.
        Not illustrated.                          FDH (7B).
        Est. pres. l. of shank when straight 0.085; max. pres. th. of shank 0.008.

Head and top of shank missing. Silastic.

The shank was square in section, tapering to a blunt point. The tip of the shank was bent.

Fe 53.  Nail.                                Inv. No. W3-374.
        Not illustrated.                          FDA (7B).
        L. 0.096; diam. of head 0.024; max. th. of shank 0.009.

Whole. Silastic.

The circular head was rounded on its top. The shank was rectangular in section, tapering to a point.

Fe 54.  Nail.                                Inv. No. W3-383.
        Not illustrated.           KZP-6 (6C—tool chest).
        Pres. l. 0.073; diam. of head 0.029; max. th. of shank 0.011.

End of shank missing. Smooth-On.

Similar to the preceding Fe 53.

Fe 55.  Nail.                                Inv. No. W3-376.
        Figs. 3-30 and 11-19.             FCX (bow area).
        L. 0.098; diam. of head 0.025; max. th. of shank 0.007.

Whole. Smooth-On.

Similar to Fe 53.

Fe 56.  Nail.                                Inv. No. W3-377.
        Not illustrated.                          FCJ (2C).
        L. 0.100; diam. of head 0.022; max. th. of shank 0.007.

Whole. Silastic.

The circular head was very slightly rounded on its top. The shank was roughly square in section, tapering to a point.

Fe 57.  Nail.                                Inv. No. W3-378.
        Not illustrated.                          KXD (2A).
        L. 0.102; diam. of head 0.023; max. th. of shank 0.008.

Whole. Plaster.

The roughly circular head was slightly rounded on its top. The shank was roughly rectangular in section, tapering to a point.

Fe 58.  Nail.                                Inv. No. W3-375.
        Figs. 3-30 and 11-19.                    KMG (4A).
        L. 0.103; diam. of head 0.032; max. th. of shank 0.011.

Whole. Silastic.

The circular head was rounded on its top, but its peak was flat, giving it the appearance of a truncated cone. The shank was square in section, tapering to a point. The nail's head and upper shank are still in contact with wood.

Fe 59.  Nail.                                Inv. No. W3-379.
        Figs. 3-30 and 11-19.                    FCH (1A).
        Est. l. of nail when straight 0.11; diam. of head 0.025; max. th. of shank 0.009.

Whole. Silastic.

The circular head was slightly rounded on its top, but its peak was flat, giving it the appearance of a truncated cone. The bent shank was square in section, tapering to a fine point.

Fe 60.  Nail.                                Inv. No. W3-380.
        Figs. 3-30 and 11-19.                    FCR (4B).
        L. 0.113; diam. of head 0.027; max. th. of shank 0.008.

Whole. Silastic.

The roughly circular head was rounded on its top. The shank was square in section, tapering to a point.

Fe 61.  Nail head.                           Inv. No. W3-392.
        Not illustrated.           KZP-9 (6C—tool chest).
        Diam. of head 0.024.

Head only. Smooth-On.

Similar to the preceding Fe 60.

Fe 62.  Nail shank.                          Inv. No. W3-427.
        Not illustrated.                         FCZ-2 (6D).
        Pres. l. 0.055; max. pres. th. of shank 0.009.

Shank broken off at both ends. Smooth-On.

Similar to Fe 60.

Fe 63.  Nail.                                Inv. No. W3-381.
        Figs. 3-30 and 11-19.                    KCE (6C).
        L. 0.124; diam. of head 0.030; max. th. of shank 0.009.

Whole. Silastic.

The circular head was slightly rounded on its top. The shank was square in section, tapering to a point.

Fe 64.  Nail.                                Inv. No. W3-382.
        Figs. 3-30 and 11-19.                    KFN (6A).

L. 0.129; diam. of head 0.030; max. th. of shank 0.010.

Whole. Silastic.

Similar to the preceding Fe 63.

Fe 65. Nail.                              Inv. No. W3-385.
Not illustrated.                         KXI (1C).
L. 0.129; diam. of head 0.031; max. th. of shank 0.012.

Whole. Plaster.

The circular head was rounded on its top. The shank was roughly rectangular in section, tapering to a point.

Fe 66. Spike.                            Inv. No. W3-384.
Figs. 3-30 and 11-19.                    (?).
L. 0.147; diam. of head 0.032; max. th. of shank 0.010.

Whole. Silastic.

The circular head was rounded on its top. The shank was square in section, tapering to a point.

Fe 67. Spike shank.                      Inv. No. W3-425.
Not illustrated.                         FDK-B-2 (6D).
Est. pres. l. of shank when straight 0.14; max. pres. th. of shank 0.008.

Shank broken off at both ends. Smooth-On.

The shank was square in section, tapering to one end; at the other end the shank was slightly bent.

Fe 68. Spike shank.                      Inv. No. W3-390.
Not illustrated.                         KZP-3 (6C—tool chest).
Pres. l. 0.155; max. pres. th. of shank 0.010.

Head and top of shank missing. Smooth-On.

The shank was rectangular in section, tapering to a round point.

Fe 69. Spike.                            Inv. No. W3-386.
Figs. 3-30 and 11-19.                    KXB (3A).
L. 0.171; diam. of head 0.034; max. th. of shank 0.012.

Whole. Plaster.

The roughly circular head was very slightly rounded on its top. The shank was roughly rectangular in section, tapering to a point. The tip of the shank was bent.

More than seventy encrusted nails were recovered in the excavation. The cataloged examples are representative of the different sizes. Their division into tacks, nails, and spikes—admittedly arbitrary—is based on their lengths: tacks measure less than 5 cm long, nails between 6 cm and 13 cm, and spikes greater than 14 cm. However, all of these items were of the same type: a "rose sharp" nail.[32] Hand-forged from an iron rod, the

[32] Mercer, *Ancient Carpenters' Tools*, p. 236, fig. 201.

shank had been squared and tapered to a point. Then the rose head was formed by four or more hammer hits. Found in virtually every area of the excavation, these nails (with the exception of Fe 54, Fe 61 and Fe 68, which were in the carpenter's tool chest) had been incorporated into various parts of the hull's construction (see chapter 3, pp. 56–57).

Fe 70. Nail bag.               Field identifications only.
Fig. 11-16; Wreck Plan V*b*.   FDE≡KZD (7C).
Max. diam. 0.235; max. h. 0.115.

Whole. No casts made.

A mass of encrusted nails was concreted together. The shape of the mass is roughly domical, and the bottom is roughly flat. At least fifteen separate nails can be distinguished on the surface.

Fe 71. Nail bag.               Field identification only.
Not illustrated.               KAS (8/9B).
No dimensions available.

Whole. No casts made.

Similar to the preceding Fe 70. At least twenty nails can be distinguished on the surface. This mass also yielded a bronze ring, MF 17.

Fe 72. Nail bag.               Field identification only.
Not illustrated.               FCQ (8C).
Max. diam. 0.283; max. h. 0.169.

Whole. No casts made.

Similar to Fe 70. At least thirty-three nails can be distinguished on the surface.

Fe 73. Nail bag.               Field identifications only.
Not illustrated.               FCC+FCL (6C).
Max. diam. 0.327; max. h. 0.215.

Two joined pieces form complete concretion. No casts made.

Similar to Fe 70. At least fifty-nine nails can be distinguished on the surface.

Casts have not been made from these four concretions because the dense, haphazard arrangement of nail molds makes the task most difficult, and the additional information retrieved would probably be minimal. As the size of the concretions increases, the number of encrusted nails visible on the surface also increases. Undoubtedly there are many more molds of nails inside these concretions that are not perceivable from the surface. Indeed, it is evident that the larger the concretion, the greater the number of nails it contained. Since Fe 71 yielded a bronze ring (MF 17, p. 274), it is possible that the other concretions also might contain a miscellany of small objects. The domical shape of these concretions suggests that the nails had been contained in bags, perhaps of leather or canvas. The original material has long ago disintegrated, but the shapes of the concretions still retain a baglike appearance. The flattish bottoms of these concretions indicate that the bags had been resting on a flat surface. Faint depressions on the bottom of Fe 70 suggest that this bag may have been reinforced by exterior bands that crossed at right angles at the bottom's center. The find spots of these concretions suggest that they had probably been stowed with the carpenter's tool chest.

Fe 74.  Bolt-end assembly.                    Inv. No. W3-469.
Figs. 3-31 and 11-20; Wreck Plan II.
                                          KBI+KTT (8B).
Pres. l. 0.122; max. pres. diam. of shaft at broken end 0.017.
Remainder of bolt missing; one end of key in slot broken off prior to shipwreck. Smooth-On.

The bolt shaft, round in section, tapered and became rectangular in section near its extremity; the tip was flat and slightly rounded. There was a slot (w. 0.003; l. between 0.016 and 0.023) with a key (pres. l. 0.045; max. pres. th. 0.007) a distance of 0.014 from the tip. A ring washer (outer diam. 0.040; inner diam. 0.026; th. 0.005) was around the shaft just below the slot. The key's intact end rested on the washer; the broken end was wedged against the washer's inner side. Wood adhered to the washer's underside. A tack (l. 0.039; max. diam. of head 0.020) had been driven into the wood inside the washer. The head rested on the washer and against the key's intact end.

Fe 75.  Bolt-end assembly.              Not inventoried.
Fig. 3-31.                                            (5A).
Pres. l. 0.060; broken end of shaft 0.016 square in section.
Assembly complete; remainder of bolt missing. Epoxy.

The assembly had a spring washer. Wood adhered to the washer's underside. The replica was not cataloged.

Fe 76.  Bolt.                                  Inv. No. W3-467.
Figs. 3-31 and 11-20; Wreck Plan II.
                                       KQH-A+KQH-B (1B).
L. 0.348; max. diam. of shaft, just below head, 0.022.
Bolt in two pieces which join imperfectly but certainly. Piece with bolt head not illustrated. One end of key and part of washer broken off. Smooth-On.

The bolt head (diam. 0.040; max. th. 0.008) was flat and circular. The shaft, round in section, tapered and became rectangular in section near its extremity; the tip was round and bulbous.

The slot (w. 0.004; l. 0.016) with key (pres. l. approx. 0.060; max. w. 0.015; max. pres. th. 0.003) was 0.015 from the tip. There was a spring washer (outer diam. 0.030; inner diam. 0.018; max. pres. th. 0.006) around the shaft just beneath the slot.

Fe 77.  Slotted bolt end.                     Inv. No. W3-472.
Figs. 3-31 and 11-20; Wreck Plan II. KQU-A (1C).
Pres. l. 0.102; max. pres. diam. of shaft 0.018.
Remainder of bolt missing. Silastic.

The shaft, round in section, tapered and became somewhat rectangular in section near its extremity; the tip was rounded. The slot (w. 0.006; l. 0.016) was 0.016 from the tip.

Fe 78.  Slotted bolt end with key.      Inv. No. W3-470.
Figs. 3-31 and 11-20; Wreck Plan II. KQU-B (1C).
Pres. l. 0.124; max. pres. diam. of shaft at broken end 0.014.
Remainder of bolt missing. Tip poorly preserved. Smooth-On.

The shaft, round in section, tapered and became rectangular in section near its extremity. The slot (w. 0.004; l. 0.019) with key (l. 0.067; max. w. 0.024; max. th. 0.003) was 0.014 from the tip.

Fe 79.  Slotted bolt end with key.      Inv. No. W3-471.
Figs. 3-31 and 11-20.                          FCV (3A).
Pres. l. 0.091; max. pres. diam. of shaft at broken end 0.015.
Remainder of bolt missing. One or both ends of key broken off. Smooth-On.

The shaft, slightly flattened on opposite sides at the broken end, tapered and became rectangular in section near its extremity. The slot (w. 0.004; l. 0.016) with key (pres. l. 0.037; max. w. 0.014; max. th. 0.001) was 0.012 from the tip.

Fe 80.  Spring washer.                        Inv. No. W3-401.
Figs. 3-31 and 11-16.                          FAP (5A).
Max. outer diam. 0.043; min. inner diam. 0.019. Whole. Silastic.

The spiral-shaped washer was square in section (max. th. 0.008), tapering slightly at both ends.

Fe 81.  Ring washer.                          Inv. No. W3-400.
Figs. 3-31 and 11-16; Wreck Plan II. FDD-2 (8B).
Max. outer diam. 0.035; min. inner diam. 0.019. Whole. Silastic.

The washer was roughly circular; it was rectangular in section, but the sectional dimensions varied from max. w. 0.010 and max. th. 0.008 to min. w. 0.007 and min. th. 0.003.

The same concretion yielded both ring washer

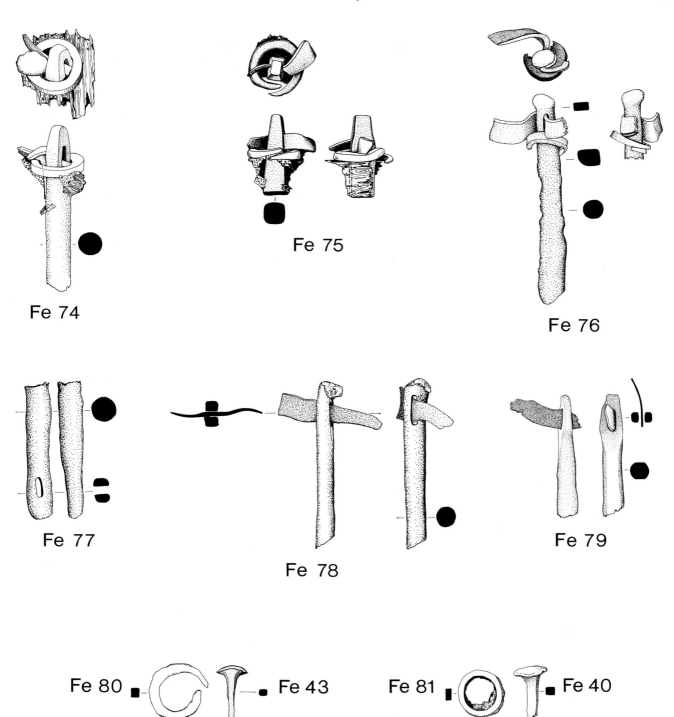

Fe 74

Fe 75

Fe 76

Fe 77

Fe 78

Fe 79

Fe 80 — Fe 43    Fe 81 — Fe 40

Cm    5

FIG. 11-20. Slotted bolts, bolt-end assemblies, and washers. Cf. Fig. 3-31. *SWK*

Fe 81 and tack Fe 40. Spring washer Fe 80 and tack Fe 43 were apparently found together, although this is not certain. Hence, these washers and tacks may have belonged to bolt-end assemblies.

Fe 82. Ring.                           Inv. No. W3-398.
       Figs. 11-15 and 11-16.          FAP-2 (5A).

Max. outer diam. 0.066; min. inner diam. 0.048. Whole. Smooth-On.

The circular ring was round in section; the sectional dimensions varied from max. diam. 0.011 to min. diam. 0.006.

Perhaps this ring had been part of the ship's rigging.

## Files

Fe 83. File.                           Inv. No. W3-428.
       Figs. 11-16 and 11-21; Wreck Plan V*b*.
                            KZP-11 (6C—tool chest).
       L. 0.264; max. w. 0.036; max. th. 0.013.
       Whole; blade's surface at the heel and one corner of the tip corroded. Smooth-On.

The file took the form of a thick knife. Its blade in section was an isosceles triangle and tapered to a flat end. The bottom edge was straight and sharp. The flat, narrow top ran slightly convex; this surface had been chiseled to form parallel filing ridges set on a slight diagonal to an edge. The broad faces were flat and chiseled in a herringbone pattern of five ranks. The tang, extending from the blade's top, was square in section, tapering to a blunt end.[33]

Fe 84. File.                           Inv. No. W3-429.
       Figs. 11-16 and 11-21; Wreck Plan V*b*.
                            FAS+FBA (7C).
       Pres. l. 0.223; max. w. 0.041; max. th. 0.019.
       Tang's end missing; portion of top and side faces badly corroded. Smooth-On.

The blade in section was an isosceles triangle; towards the tip it swelled to form a head with smooth faces and a flat end; towards the tang the blade widened to form a heel. Between the head and the heel the bottom edge was straight and sharp. The top was straight and flat; this surface had parallel filing ridges set perpendicular to an edge. The broad faces were flat and had filing ridges in a herringbone pattern of three ranks. The tang, extending from the blade's top, was trapezoidal in section, becoming rectangular as it tapered towards the end.

Fe 85. File.                           Inv. No. W3-430.
       Figs. 11-16 and 11-21.          FBH (8C).
       Pres. l. 0.163; max. w. 0.027; max. th. 0.015.

Most of tang missing. Silastic.

The blade in section was an isosceles triangle; towards the tip it flared beyond the bottom edge, forming a head with smooth faces and a flat end. The bottom edge was straight and sharp. The parallel top was straight and flat; its surface had no filing ridges. The broad faces were flat and had parallel filing ridges set on a slight diagonal to an edge. Only the initial curve of the tang from the heel of the blade was preserved.

Fe 86. File.                           Inv. No. W3-431.
       Figs. 11-16 and 11-21; Wreck Plan V*b*. KCV (6C).
       Pres. l. 0.099; max. w. 0.028; max. th. 0.017.
       Most of blade and end of tang missing; surfaces poorly preserved. Smooth-On.

The blade in section was an isosceles triangle. The bottom edge was straight and sharp. The parallel top was straight and flat; there was no trace of filing ridges on its surface. The broad faces were flat and did have parallel filing ridges set on a slight diagonal to an edge. Towards the tang the blade widened to form a heel; midway along the heel there was a V-shaped notch. The tang, extending from the blade's top, was trapezoidal in section and tapered towards the end.

Fe 87. File.                           Inv. No. W3-433.
       Figs. 11-16 and 11-21; Wreck Plan V*b*.
                            KZP-5 (6C—tool chest).
       L. 0.174.
       Blade's tip missing. Smooth-On.

The file had two dogleg bends, each of approximately 90°, so that the workman's hand would not scrape against the surface he was filing.[34] The shorter, file leg was roughly rectangular in section with rounded edges; unfortunately, no filing ridges were preserved on any of its surfaces. The longer, tang leg was also rectangular in section but with sharper edges; it tapered towards a flat

---

[33] For a similar knife-type file, see Champion, *RA*, 1916, no. 1, pp. 238–239, no. 50153, pl. XIII; and Reinach, *Catalogue illustré*, pp. 283–284, no. 50153, fig. 283.

[34] Similar dogleg files have been found at the Roman fort of Saalburg, Germany (Mercer, *Ancient Carpenters' Tools*, pp. 295–296, fig. 243).

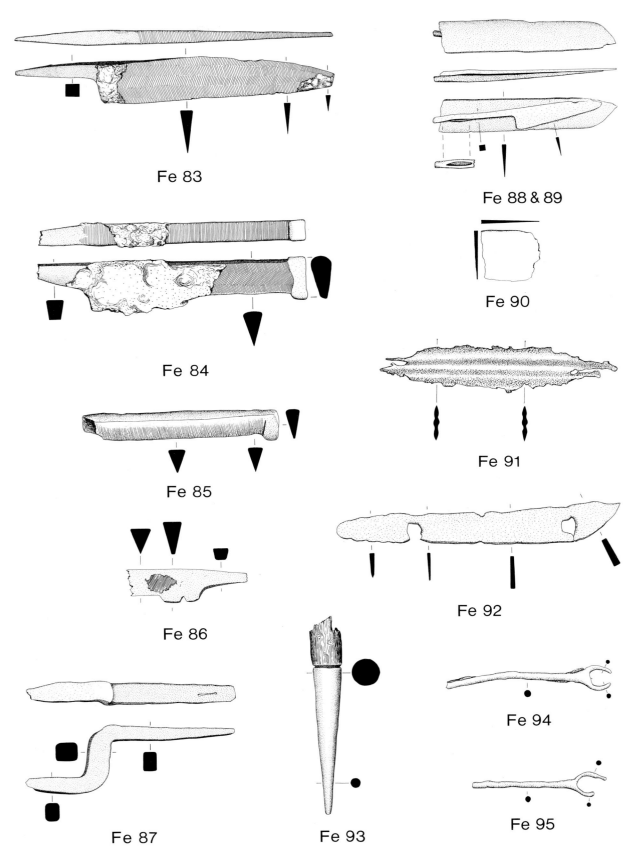

Fe 83

Fe 88 & 89

Fe 90

Fe 84

Fe 91

Fe 85

Fe 92

Fe 86

Fe 94

Fe 87          Fe 93          Fe 95

FIG. 11-21. Iron files, knives, pricker, and netting needles. approx. 1:3. *SWK*

end. Near this end the tang was pierced by a rectangular hole, l. 0.015 and w. 0.001. Possibly a thin pin was driven through the handle into this hole to aid in securing the handle to the tang.

Files present some of the finest examples of the ancient toolmaker's handicraft. After being shaped on the forge, their working surfaces were scored by a sharp-edged chisel struck with a heavy hammer. The files were then hardened by tempering and quenching. To achieve a series of closely spaced, parallel grooves required consummate coordination and control between hand and eye. It was a task to be undertaken by only the most experienced of craftsmen.

Fe 83 reveals the skill of just such an artisan. Its grooving was not only perfectly executed, but, to the best of my knowledge, the complex herringbone pattern—seen also on Fe 84—has not as yet been found on any other ancient files. Though less complicated, the grooving of Fe 85 and Fe 86 was rendered with equal precision.[35]

The head at the tip of Fe 84 and Fe 85 was probably a feature designed to facilitate the application of hand pressure there to increase the tool's friction against the worked surface. Files, which if used on wood rapidly lose their efficiency as their grooves clog, would mainly be used to shape and smooth metal. The rasp is much more effective in woodworking. Thus, files would be employed in sharpening tools, especially in filing sharp the teeth of saws. In fact, Fe 86 clearly was designated for sharpening saws, as the notch in its heel (Fe 84 probably also had a similar notch in its poorly preserved heel) was particularly used for setting saw teeth by twisting them alternately right and left to a desired angle.[36] No saw was found in the excavation. However, I believe that the notch in Fe 86 (and Fe 84?) presents enough evidence that we may infer that one or more saws were carried on board.

## Knives

Fe 88. Knife.                          Inv. No. W3-449.
Figs. 11-21 and 11-22.            FDM-C-2 (6C).
L. 0.142; max. w. 0.019; max. th. 0.005.
Whole. Silastic.

The knife's top was straight and flat. Its cutting edge, straight and sharp, converged with the top, forming a point and giving the blade a wedge-shaped profile. From the back of the blade the top continued to form a tang. Near the blade the tang was square in section, but it became round towards its end. Near this end in the tang's bottom was an indentation—l. 0.023, w. 0.004, and depth 0.002—of unknown purpose.

Fe 89. Knife blade.                    Inv. No. W3-448.
Figs. 11-21 and 11-22.            FDM-C-1 (6C).
Pres. l. 0.148; max. w. 0.027; max. th. 0.004.
Top edge chipped near point; handle end missing. Silastic.

The top edge was straight and flat. Almost parallel to it, the straight and sharp cutting edge curved up near the tip to form the knife's point.

Fe 90. Knife blade.                    Inv. No. W3-452.
Figs. 11-21 and 11-22.            FBG (8B).
Pres. l. 0.049; max. w. 0.044; max. th. 0.003.

Curved tip jagged; handle end missing. Silastic.

This small fragment suggests that the top edge was straight and flat, the parallel cutting edge was straight and sharp, and the blade ended in a curved tip.

Fe 91. Double-edged knife blade.       Inv. No. W3-451.
Figs. 11-21 and 11-22; Wreck Plan Ve. FDQ (8B).
Pres. l. 0.198; max. pres. w. 0.040; max. th. 0.005.
Edges badly preserved; ends not preserved. Smooth-On.

Both edges may have been convex and sharp. The ends were not sufficiently preserved to determine their shape, but at least one must have been pointed. Three parallel ribs ran down the length of the blade. No evidence survives to indicate how a handle was attached, but probably the central rib extended to form a tang.[37]

Fe 92. Knife tang?                     Inv. No. W3-450.
Figs. 11-21 and 11-22; Wreck Plan Vb.
KCU-A+KCU-B (5C).
Pres. l. 0.237; max. w. 0.033; max. th. 0.006.
Incompletely preserved. Smooth-On.

The edges were straight and flat over most of

---

[35] The closest analogy to the herringbone pattern is the "double-cut" grooving of modern files, and the simpler parallel pattern is identical to "single-cut" grooving (Salaman, *Dictionary of Tools*, p. 195, fig. 288*a*, *b*).

[36] Mercer, *Ancient Carpenters' Tools*, pp. 295–296, fig. 243.

[37] This blade might possibly have been part of a dagger; cf. J. Ward-Perkins and A. Claridge, *Pompeii A.D. 79*, fig. 310.

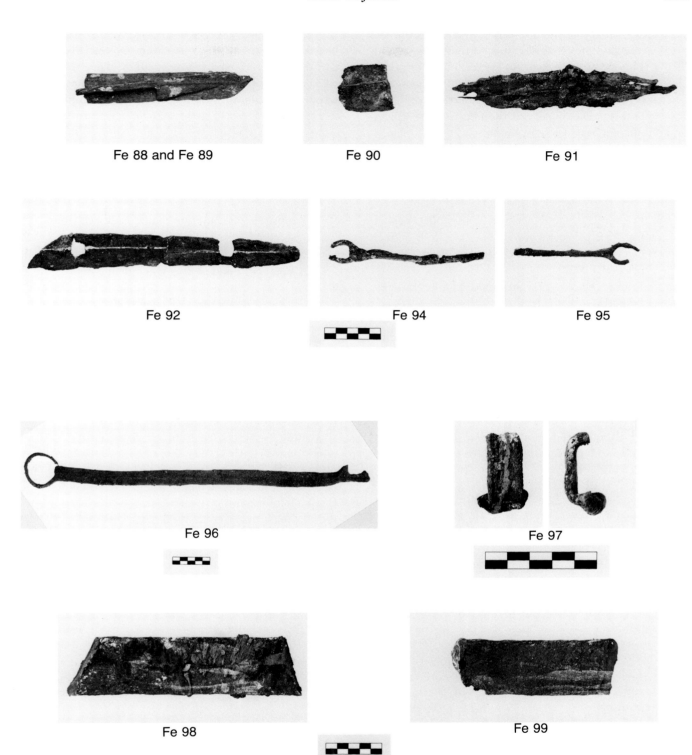

FIG. 11-22. Cast replicas of knives, netting needles, and miscellaneous iron objects.

the preserved length. They diverged from the rounded end towards the end that was pointed. The sides were flat and pierced by two poorly preserved holes, approx. diam. 0.012 and spaced 0.129 apart. These holes, possibly for rivets, suggest that the object was the tang for a wood handle of a large knife or cleaver.

## Mariners' Tools

Fe 93.  Pricker.                                    Inv. No. W3-426.
        Fig. 11-21; Wreck Plan V*b*.        FDK-B-3 (6B').
        Overall pres. l. 0.170; l. of pricker 0.126; diam. of pricker 0.023.
        Pricker whole; end of wood handle missing. Smooth-On.

        The pricker was round in section, tapering to a blunt point. In its top there was a socket in which the handle is set. The wood handle is round in section and does not appear to taper towards its broken end.

A pricker would have been used to open holes in canvas for eyelets and to separate strands of rope for splicing.[38] Although the point of Fe 93 was broad, it was not too large to have separated strands of twisted rope.

Fe 94.  Netting needle.                         Inv. No. W3-402.
        Figs. 11-21 and 11-22.                    FBQ (8A).
        Pres. l. 0.138; diam. of shaft 0.006.
        Shaft broken; therefore, second pair of prongs missing.
        Silastic.

        The shaft, round in section, bifurcated to form prongs. The two prongs curved slightly inward towards one another, and each was round in section.

Fe 95.  Netting needle.                         Inv. No. W3-403.
        Figs. 11-21 and 11-22; Wreck Plan V*e*.
                                                  FCT-B (8A).
        Pres. l. 0.112; diam. of shaft 0.005.
        Shaft broken; therefore, second pair of prongs missing. Tip of one of preserved prongs missing. Smooth-On.

        Similar to the preceding Fe 94.

Fe 94 and Fe 95 may represent two separate netting needles or fragments of one. They were recovered in the same area. The diameters at the broken ends of their shafts differ by less than 1 mm. If Fe 94 and Fe 95 were joined, the length of the restored needle would be in excess of 25 cm.[39] In any case, the netting needles should be restored so that one pair of prongs is perpendicular to the plane of the other. Fishermen use such netting needles to make and repair their nets.[40] Fe 94 and Fe 95 were located in the storage area aft of the ship's galley. There, lead weights for fishnets were also recovered (see chapter 13).

## Miscellaneous Iron Objects

Fe 96.  Ladle handle.                           Inv. No. W3-441.
        Figs. 11-22 and 11-23; Wreck Plan V*a*.
                                                  KZS-A+KZS-B (6B).
        Pres. l. 0.457; shank w. 0.020; shank th. 0.005.
        Ladle's bowl missing; attachment tongue of handle to bowl incomplete. Smooth-On.

        At its top the handle made a circular loop, diam. 0.040, which was rectangular in section. Its long, straight shank was also rectangular in section. Towards the bottom it thinned and became scooped to form the attachment tongue.

This scoop suggests the shape and size of the ladle's bowl, and although it is not clear, the poorly

---

[38] Salaman, *Dictionary of Tools*, p. 402; Tre Tryckare, *The Lore of Ships*, p. 125, fig. 3.

[39] W. Deonna, *Exploration archéologique de Délos*, vol. XVIII, *Le Mobilier délien*, p. 202, section 93, nos. B347 (length 30.5 cm) and B1301–6001 *bis* (length 26 cm), pl. LXIX.550, 1–12; and H. B. Walters, *Catalogue of the Bronzes, Greek, Roman, and Etruscan, in the Department of Greek and Roman Antiquities, British Museum*, p. 316, no. 2381 (length 11⅝ inches [29.5 cm]).

[40] Bronze netting needles have been found at Naukratis (E. A. Gardner, *Naukratis*, II, 86, pl. XVI.17); Harageh (Petrie, *Tools and Weapons*, p. 53, section 147, N 98, pl. LXV); Gaza (W. M. F. Petrie, *Ancient Gaza*, vol. IV, *Tell el Ajjūl*, p. 11, section 31, nos. 516–517, pl. XXXIV); Salamis (A. P. di Cesnola, *Salaminia [Cyprus]*, pl. IV.9.*E*); Dali (L. P. di Cesnola, *Cyprus*, p. 85, pl. IV; and L. P. di Cesnola, *A Descriptive Atlas of the Cesnola Collection of Cypriote Antiquities in the Metropolitan Museum of Art, New York*, III, pl. LXIV.2); Lindos

preserved tongue may have been attached to the bowl by two rivets. The bowl was more likely of thin copper than of iron (see MF 8, p. 272).

Judging from where it was found, the ladle was probably suspended from the galley's forward partition wall. There, it would have been above the hearth and within reach for serving from the large copper and pottery vessels used on board for cooking.

Fe 97.   Handle.                           Inv. No. W3-438.
Figs. 11-22 and 11-23; Wreck Plan V*f*. FBU (9A).
Pres. h. 0.037; w. 0.015; th. 0.004.
Broken off at the top, and broken from vase's wall at the bottom. Silastic.

Probably once part of a small jug, the handle would have been vertically placed. It was roughly rectangular in section and had a shallow median groove.

---

(C. Blinkenberg, *Lindos*, vol. I, *Les Petits objets*, p. 147, no. 406, pl. 15); Chios, Sanctuary of Apollo Phanaios (K. Kourouniotes, "Anaskaphai kai ereunai en Khio 2," *Deltion* 2 [1916]: 210, fig. 34); Panticapaeum (B. Pharmakowsky, "Archäologische Funde im Jahre 1913, Russland," *AA* 29 [1914]: 215–216, fig. 19); Olynthus (D. M. Robinson, *Excavations at Olynthus*, vol. X, *Metal and Minor Miscellaneous Finds*, pp. 364–365, nos. 1763–1787, pl. CXVI); Delos (Deonna, *Délos* XVIII); Halae (H. Goldman, "The Acropolis of Halae," *Hesperia* 9 [1940]: 418, fig. 61.3); Athens (Petrie, *Tools and Weapons*, p. 53, section 147, N 27, pl. LXII); Corinth (G. R. Davidson, *Corinth*, vol. XII, *The Minor Objects*, p. 177, no. 1273, pl. 79, "probably Byzantine period"); Messenia, Sanctuary of Apollo Korunthos (Ph. Bersakes, "To hieron tou Korunthou Apollonos," *Deltion* 2 [1916]: 95, no. 36, fig. 40.1–2); Olympia (A. Furtwängler, *Olympia*, vol. IV, *Die Bronzen und die übrigen kleineren Funde von Olympia*, p. 182, no. 1130, pl. LXV); Trichonion (G. Soteriades, "Ek taphon tes Aitolias," *ArchEph*, 1906, p. 78, fig. 2); Gradina (A. Colnago and J. Keil, "Archäologische Untersuchungen in Norddalmatien," *JOAIBeibl* 8 [1905]: 51, fig. 13c); Selinus (E. Gàbrici, "Il santuario della Malophoros a Selinunte," *MonAnt* 32 [1927]: 363, fig. 157a); Pompeii (C. Ceci, *Piccoli bronzi del Museo Nazionale di Napoli*, pl. VIII, no. 40; and Gusman, *Pompei*, p. 268); and Orvieto (Walters, *Catalogue of the Bronzes*, p. 316, no. 2381). For iron netting needles I can only cite publications of a pair of prongs from Tell Defenneh (Daphnae) in W. M. F. Petrie, *Tanis*, vol. II, *Nebesheh(am) and Defenneh (Tahpanhes)*, p. 79, pl. XXXVIII.7; and Petrie, *Tools and Weapons*, p. 53, section 147, N 26, pl. LXII; and my own observations of fishermen repairing their nets on the islands of Cyprus, Samos, and Lipari.

Fe 98.   Band.                             Inv. No. W3-411.
Figs. 11-22 and 11-23; Wreck Plan V*f*. KXA (4C).
Pres. l. 0.198; w. 0.049; max. th. 0.010; min. th. 0.005.
Broken at both ends. Silastic.

Curved band fragment (approx. 0.170 radius) trapezoidal in section. An irregular hole (0.010 × 0.005), near the fragment's center and passing through at an angle of approx. 45° with respect to its longitudinal axis, may only represent corrosion. Small bits of wood adhere to much of the inner face, the grain running across the width.

Fe 99.   Band.                             Inv. No. W3-410.
Figs. 11-22 and 11-23; Wreck Plan V*f*. FAC (4C).
Pres. l. 0.145; w. 0.049; max. th. 0.010; min. th. 0.005.
Broken at both ends. Silastic.

Curved band fragment, with a radius of curvature of approx. 0.140; trapezoidal in section.

The two fragments were found together in the lower left quadrant of sector 4C (Wreck Plan V*f*). Although they did not join, they very probably had been part of a single curved band with an overall radius of curvature somewhere in the neighborhood of 16 cm. Since the two fragments together represent only about one-third the circumference of a circle with this radius, it is uncertain whether or not the band extended full circle, but the wood adhering to the inner face of the larger fragment suggests that the band may have been a hoop for a cask, bucket, or tub of some kind.[41] However, it seems much too thick for such a purpose, particularly in view of its relatively small radius. Moreover, one wonders why fragments of other bands were not then found. A stronger possibility is that it has to do with some kind of fitting for one of the ship's spars. The fact that the fragments were found not far aft of midships offers some support to this possibility.

[41]Cf. C. Singer et al., eds., *A History of Technology*, II, 136.

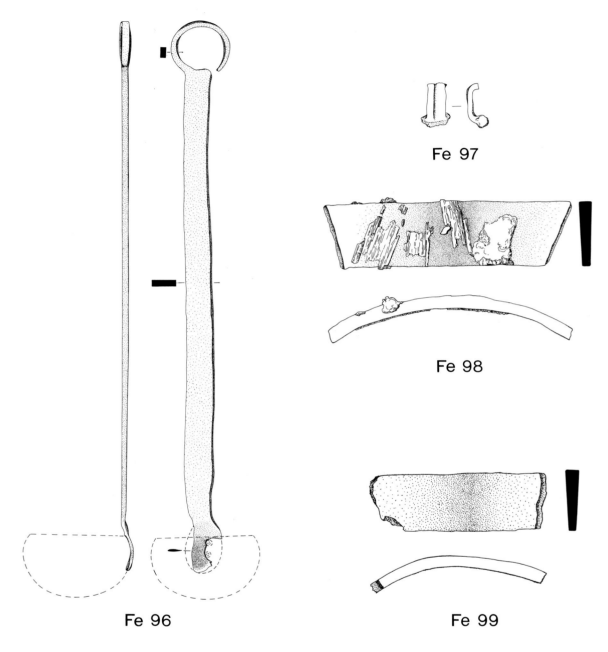

FIG. 11-23. Iron ladle handle, small handle, and band fragments. 1:3. *SWK*

## Summary

We recovered an unparalleled collection of agricultural implements and woodworking tools, consisting of the following:

| | |
|---|---|
| 1 | spade |
| 1 | hoe |
| 7 | billhooks |
| 4 | axes |
| 2 | mattocks |
| 5 | adzes |
| 4 | hammers |
| 6 | chisels |
| 2 | gouges |
| 1 | caulking iron |
| 2 | punches |
| 3 | bits |
| 1 | awl |
| 1 | carpenter's compass |
| 5 | files |
| 5 | knives |

Since the iron had decomposed, the source of the ore cannot be postulated. Furthermore, the tools' designs are so universal that their place of manufacture and purchase is beyond identification. Indeed, some of the tools are so similar to those used today that comparable examples can still be bought from a blacksmith in Bodrum (Fig. 11-24) or from one's local hardware store.

The tools were found concentrated in two distinguishable areas of the excavation: sectors 8A/B and 6B/C/C'. From areas 8A and 8B came the spade, Fe 1; three billhooks, Fe 3, Fe 4, and Fe 8; two axes, Fe 9 and Fe 11; and a mattock, Fe 12. Stowed between the galley and the sternpost, these tools would have been used by a shore party landed to replenish the ship's supply of fresh water, firewood, and food as well as to collect timber for hull repairs and brush dunnage for cargo storage. Here also the netting needles Fe 94 and Fe 95 and lead weights for fishing (see chapter 13) were recovered, and the grapnel anchor (see chapter 6) was found nearby. This group of objects and the ship's boat were the charge of the boatswain, ὁ καραβίτης, who, according to the Rhodian Sea-Law, would have received one and one-half shares of the voyage's profit.[42]

Clearly separated from the boatswain's stores, most of the woodworking tools were found forward and to the starboard of the galley. In the center of this second group (6C) was the carpenter's tool chest containing twelve objects: an adze, Fe 15; a chisel, Fe 23; gouge

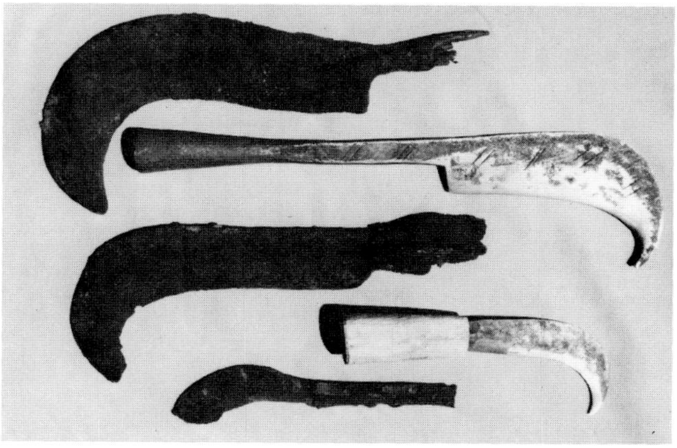

FIG. 11-24. Cast replicas of billhooks from the shipwreck compared with modern billhooks manufactured in Bodrum.

Fe 29; two bits, Fe 34 and Fe 35; carpenter's compass Fe 38; two files, Fe 83 and Fe 87; three nails, Fe 54, Fe 61, and Fe 68; and a bronze belt buckle, MF 21, which adds a personal touch. We know that about A.D. 900 every merchantman should have had on board a carpenter with all his tools.[43] So certainly was the case with the Byzantine ship some three centuries earlier. From city maritime statutes we also learn that the carpenter's tools might be kept on the deck.[44] This possibly was the case on the Byzantine ship, although it appears more probable that these tools were kept in a stores locker just forward of the galley (see chapter 5). Like the boatswain, the carpenter, ὁ ναυπηγός, would have received one and one-half shares of the profits.[45] His main duty was to keep the hull in good repair through fair and foul weather, and with the tools at hand he was excellently equipped for both routine maintenance as well as major storm damage. In fact, he had virtually all the tools necessary for the complete construction of a new hull.[46]

With such a complement of tools we have a well-found ship perfectly capable of independently resupplying and refitting herself during a sailing season in the seventh century A.D.

---

[42] W. Ashburner, *The Rhodian Sea-Law*, pp. 57–58.

[43] Leonis Imperatoris, *Tactica*, XIX, 5; see Ashburner, *Rhodian Sea-Law*, p. 58.

[44] Ashburner, *Rhodian Sea-Law*, p. clvii.

[45] Ibid., pp. 57–58.

[46] Cf. the scenes in a shipyard of the late Roman period shown in Richter, *Furniture*, p. 128, fig. 613; and Liversidge, "Woodwork," pp. 158–159, pl. 264. The base of the glass bowl shows a shipwright adzing a hull while his assistants are drilling, axing, sawing, chiseling, and planing.

# XII

## MISCELLANEOUS FINDS

### Susan Womer Katzev

### *The Censer*

MF 1.    Bronze censer.    Inv. No. W3-97.
Figs. 12-1 and 12-3; Wreck Plan V*c*.    RW (7B).
H. 0.086; max. diam. 0.068.
Cast in one piece and file-finished. Well preserved.

The lower part of the burner is octagonal and supported by three wide-splayed legs that terminate in claw feet. At the top is a rim in which the missing lid was seated. The lid was doubtless in openwork, most probably continuing the octagonal design of the base in pyramid fashion, surmounted by the bronze cross MF 2. Above the rim the censer walls taper inward for fitting down the lid; that they retain the eight-sided form is evidence that the lid was also octagonal. (A complete seven-sided censer in the Dumbarton Oaks Collection illustrates the lid shape suggested.)[1] Two closely spaced eyes project from the body at rim height to hinge the lid. Directly opposite the eyes, below the rim, is a small hole used in latching the lid.

MF 2.    Bronze cross.    Inv. No. W3-96.
Figs. 12-1 and 12-3; Wreck Plan V*c*.    TW (7B).
H. 0.076; max. w. 0.036.
Corroded. Appears to be more crudely cast than the censer.

The cross is supported on an orb atop a circular base with a concave bottom. Its find spot beside the incense burner suggests that it surmounted the censer lid, especially as the cross with orb is a common ornament on censers of this period.[2] There is a partially preserved hole at its top to receive a chain for suspension.[3]

The bronze incense burner with finial in the form of a cross strongly reinforces other evidence on board that the owner, captain, and crew of the ship were Byzantine Christians. The coins and weights that bear the customary signature of the Byzantine capital might as easily have been in the hands of Arab or Avaric merchants us-

Susan Womer Katzev completed a thorough study of artifacts assigned to her and submitted the manuscript for this chapter several years before publication. Several events caused the addition of new material to the chapter during the final editing of the book. First, van Doorninck, in the summer of 1977, made a last inspection of excavation finds stored in the Bodrum Museum and discovered several new joins among metal fragments that allowed the restoration of previously uncataloged vessels. Second, a number of lead bars, some triangular lead pieces, and a wooden cylinder were thought to have belonged to the ship herself instead of her contents. These items were therefore prepared for publication in a chapter written by van Doorninck, but because of uncertainty over their identification it was thought best by van Doorninck and Bass, during final editing, to list them simply as miscellaneous finds. Third, various bits of lead scrap and casting waste, probably for use in the manufacture of fishing weights, were removed from the material assigned to Peter Kuniholm for his study of the ship's fishing gear (chapter 13) and were placed, more conservatively, in this chapter. Fourth, the field notebooks reveal three fairly crude stone objects that were never cataloged. It seems clear now, after a study of the entire wreck and its contents, that these stones were artifacts carried for use in the ship. Finally, shells and bones had not been assigned to any author because of the unfulfilled hope that they might be studied in Bodrum by a specialist in animal remains.

Susan Katzev is in no way responsible for the original omission of the above from this chapter. Further, because she did not have the opportunity to study these finds personally in Bodrum before this book went to press, it did not seem fair that she be responsible for their interpretation. In order that the publication not be delayed further, however, I have added the above, with her kind permission, marking each item with an *.—G.F.B.

[1] M. C. Ross, *Catalogue of the Byzantine and Early Medieval Antiquities in the Dumbarton Oaks Collection*, I, pl. XXXIII, no. 48.

[2] Ibid., pl. XXXIII, nos. 46, 48, and 49; W. B. Emery and L. P. Kirwan, *The Royal Tombs of Ballana and Qustul: Mission Archéologique de Nubie, 1929–34*, II, pl. 97; O. Wulff, *Königliche Museen zu Berlin*, vol. III, part 1, *Altchristliche und mittelalterliche byzantinische und italienische Bildwerke*, pl. XLVI, nos. 977 and 978.

[3] Ross, *Catalogue of the Antiquities*, pl. XXXIII, nos. 46 and 48.

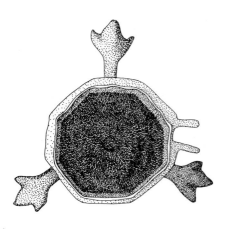

MF 1

MF 2

Fig. 12-1. Bronze censer and cross. *SWK*

ing the Byzantine standard. The censer, however, suggests that the Yassi Ada ship was Christian-operated and that some form of worship was performed on board.

It might be argued that the censer served only the mundane purpose of fumigating the galley or that it was brought out to enhance sailors' meals. As van Doorninck has pointed out, the censer's cruciform lid need not necessarily imply religious use.[4] Crosses, for example, appear on the handles of several of the ship's lamps but probably mean no more than that this was one style of decoration on lamps available at the time. However, in my opinion it would have been an unusual luxury for a working vessel such as the Byzantine merchantman to carry a censer purely for its aromatic function.

Let us consider the greater likelihood that this censer with its cruciform symbol served a combination of religious and legal uses. It is interesting to observe that in modern Greece, where custom and religion are so closely linked to the Byzantine past, incense is burned in the home—but *only* in a religious context. While saying their daily prayers, devout Christians swing a censer containing lighted charcoal and pellets of aromatic resin just as does a priest in the church. This is not considered by the Greek church as any usurpation of priestly function. Rather, it is an aid to worship by anyone. The scent is a purifier, thought to drive away the devil, while the smoke acts to carry the prayers of the faithful upward.[5]

In the sixth and early seventh centuries the use of censers outside of church ritual is documented by finds from tombs at Ballana[6] and from houses at Beth-Shan.[7] Writing of this period, Walter Emery says: "The burning of incense in the house is such a common practice in the Near East that it is unnecessary to consider the incense-burner or censer as essentially a piece of church furniture."[8]

Religious ceremonies on shipboard may be traced from at least Greek and Roman times, when wealthier ships carried images of their patron deities, to the modern era; even modest Roman merchantmen had some provision aft for an altar on which sacrifices were offered when the ship reached safe harbor.[9] A well-known relief

---

[4] F. H. van Doorninck, Jr., "The Seventh-Century Byzantine Ship at Yassi Ada: Some Contributions to the History of Naval Architecture" (Ph.D. diss., University of Pennsylvania, 1967), p. 192 and note 23. Van Doorninck points out: "Censers were used at dinner parties in antiquity, and are still so used in parts of the Arab world" (p. 192).

[5] I am indebted to Anna Kartsonis of Athens for her explanation of this custom which I observe daily from my apartment window in that city.

[6] Emery and Kirwan, *Royal Tombs* II, p. 168ff.

[7] G. M. Fitzgerald, *Beth-Shan Excavations 1921–1923*, vol. III, *The Arab and Byzantine Levels*, p. 42, pl. XXXVIII, no. 24.

[8] Emery and Kirwan, *Royal Tombs* II, p. 168.

[9] L. Casson, *Ships and Seamanship in the Ancient World*, p. 146 with figs. 125 and 130, and p. 182. Also see descriptions of the Aphrodite chapel on Hiero's third-century B.C. superfreighter *Syracusia* (pp. 181 and 196) and the altar and possible shrine remains from the late-second-century B.C. Spargi wreck (p. 182 n. 70). M. Amit (*Athens and the Sea: A Study in Athenian Sea-Power*, p. 12), referring to Aristophanes, *Acharnians*, ll. 544–547, mentions that fifth-century B.C. triremes carried statues of the gods of the cities to which they belonged, and it is such common practice on ships of all kinds in modern Greece to carry an icon of Saint Nicholas, patron saint of sailors, that it is entirely possible that the Byzantine ship also had such an image of its patron saint on board.

For example, in nineteenth-century Greece, "It was normal for a ship to have icons in the forecastle and the poop, and every member of the ship's company, to a greater or lesser extent, made it his business to see that there were always candles burning by them. At sunset one of the crew would incense the vessel, and every year on the feast of the Epiphany, the 'Feast of Lights,' the stern of the ship and the wheel were blessed. . . . A priest from Psara, Father Mikes Doukas, has left us a description of the religious customs practiced onboard that island's ships shortly before the War of Independence. Among other things, 'Whenever they were bound for Constantinople they fasted every eveof ca. A.D. 200 shows such a ceremony on a cargo ship entering the port of Rome.[10] Three people, perhaps the owner, his wife, and the captain, are gathered at the stern around what seems to be a portable altar set with a fire. The woman holds an incense box while the man at her right throws incense on the fire. In all likelihood, one or all of our Byzantine mariners used the censer in a similar ritual, offering prayers of thanks to their patron saint for safe passage. Although its find spot (sector 7B) is no proof that the censer was used in the stern of the ship, it shows that it was stored there, possibly in its own box on a shelf in the galley.[11]

The Rhodian Sea-Law suggests a second, legal purpose for the censer: "If a passenger comes on board, and he has gold or something else, let him deposit it with the captain. If he does not deposit it and says 'I have lost gold or silver,' no effect is to be given to what he says. But the captain and the sailors, all those on board together, are to take an oath upon the evangels."[12] This oath-taking seems intended to clear the captain and crew of responsibility for any valuables the passenger has not deposited. The ceremony would have taken place on the ship after the passenger had boarded, and the captain might well have used incense to "sanctify" the oath.

It is difficult to assign to the censer a place of manufacture. Its octagonal shape is, to my knowledge, unique. Polygonal censers, however—especially those with six sides that appear in Greece, Asia Minor, Syria, Palestine, Cyprus, and Egypt[13]—are common in the sixth and seventh centuries. A seven-sided example in the Dumbarton Oaks Collection[14] is the most comparable to the ship's censer and serves as an example for restoring its missing openwork lid; Marvin C. Ross assigns it an Egyptian origin.[15]

In Egypt, also, are found the best parallels for the lion feet that support the ship's censer. A Coptic workshop specializing in zoomorphic censers has been traced by Ross to the region of Thebes, and at least three polygonal examples with lion-claw feet were found there.[16] Thus, it is tempting to assign to the ship's piece a Theban origin. However, two features of our censer differ enough from the Egyptian models to cause concern. First, the feet are longer and very wide-splayed, a steadying design particularly suitable for use on shipboard. Second, the ship censer is thinly cast in comparison with the heavy Egyptian examples. It would thus appear to be made on a Theban model but in a workshop that had a tradition of finer sheet-metal craft, such as at Constantinople.

Two simple hexagonal censers found at Smyrna serve as stepping-stones to this conclusion.[17] One is lion-footed, the other plain. They are cast to a thickness midway between that of the Egyptian products and that of the ship's example. It is possible, therefore, that, like these examples from Smyrna, the censer carried on the ship took its original design from Egypt but that it was more likely produced in some city along the coast of Asia Minor.

---

ning. The steward would bring the icon of St. Nicholas out and place it on the capstan, and the ship's clerk or one of the sailors (if any of them was reasonably familiar with the liturgy) chanted the prayers, while the steward incensed the icon and the crew stood bareheaded. They prayed . . . for a following wind and a prosperous journey. . . . On their arrival in port the captain and crew went to confession before going on into the church to partake of the divine sacrament of the Eucharist. That day was always a holiday from any kind of work for the ship's company'"(A. I. Tzamtzis, in *The Greek Merchant Marine (1453–1850)*, ed. S. A. Papadopoulos, p. 59. This passage was kindly brought to my attention by Frederick van Doorninck).

[10] Casson, *Ships and Seamanship*, fig. 144. For a description of the scene, see p. 182 n. 69.

[11] A probable box hinge strap was found close by (see MF 12, below). However, the hinge could also be associated with a box for the set of inlaid weights from the galley.

[12] W. Ashburner, *The Rhodian Sea-Law*, Part III, chap. 13, p. 94, and Part II, chap. 14, p. 62. This section appears twice in the law, written in virtually identical language (see Ashburner's commentary, p. cc). Part III is quoted here in its entirety. It concludes with "are to take an oath." In Part II, the text concludes, "are to take an oath upon the evangels"; hence, I have taken the liberty of combining the two texts at that point.

[13] Typical hexagonal censers are shown in W. Deonna, *Exploration archéologique de Délos*, vol. XVIII, *Le Mobilier délien*, p. 391,

B1215–6030 *bis*, pl. CXIII, no. 1007; and A. Furtwängler, *Olympia*, vol. IV, *Die Bronzen und die übrigen kleineren Funde von Olympia*, p. 212, no. 1368, pl. LXXI (Greece); G. M. A. Hanfmann, *Sardis und Lydien*, pp. 534–535, pl. 16 (Asia Minor); Wulff, *Königliche Museen*, pl. XLVII, nos. 983, 985, and 986 (Asia Minor and Egypt); Ross, *Catalogue of the Antiquities*, p. 42, pl. XXXII, no. 45 (Syria); Fitzgerald, *Beth-Shan* III, 6 and 42, pl. XXXVIII, no. 24 (Palestine); and O. M. Dalton, *Byzantine Art and Archaeology*, p. 567, fig. 351 (Cyprus).

[14] Ross, *Catalogue of the Antiquities*, p. 44, with pl. XXXIII, no. 48.

[15] Ibid.

[16] M. C. Ross, "A Group of Coptic Incense Burners," *AJA* 46 (1942): 10–12. Lions are a favored subject at Thebes. One rectangular censer from Ross's group has a sculpted lioness finial and stands on four claw feet; it was found at the Monastery of Epiphanius, Thebes (p. 11, fig. 1). A second example, a simple box censer with feet identical to those on the ship's censer, was found in this same region at Luxor (Wulff, *Königliche Museen*, pl. XLVI, no. 990). Probably coming from Theban workshops as well are two bronze claw-footed vessels, one of them a six-sided censer (Wulff, *Königliche Museen*, pl. XLVII, no. 983) and the other a circular flask (Wulff, *Königliche Museen*, pl. LI, no. 1040), both of which are in the Berlin Museum. Their provenance is assigned thus far simply to Egypt.

[17] Wulff, *Königliche Museen*, pl. XLVII, nos. 985 and 986.

## Metal Vessels

MF 3.    Bronze or copper caldron.       Inv. No. W3-71.
Figs. 12-2 and 12-3; Wreck Plan V*a*. KL (8/9B).
H. 0.295; diam. of body 0.345; diam. of flange
0.375; diam. of bottom 0.380.
Metal badly corroded. Lid and parts of body
missing.

Hammered body, hourglass in shape with
convex bottom. A flange extends 0.028 out
from the body and then rises vertically 0.01. At
opposite sides of the flange are single holes.
Probably they once braced handle attachments
that were secured to the flange by the two
rivets preserved at either side of each hole.[18]
The interior of the flange is decorated with
beaten lines in an arrow-feather pattern. The
bottom of the vessel is a separate piece of
metal, tongued into the body by a horizontal
toothed join which is cold-hammered. No solder is visible. An illegible stamp appears beneath one handle attachment.

MF 4.*   Bronze or copper caldron fragment.
                                    Not inventoried.
Fig. 12-3; Wreck Plan V*a*.              PT (7B).

This is the only remnant, measuring 0.155 ×
0.20, of a caldron similar in size and shape to
MF 3. It preserves part of the lower side and
0.06 of the bottom edge's circumference; only a
tiny part of the bottom, projecting inward no
farther than 0.01, is preserved. Measured in
Bodrum Museum depot, but not inventoried
during excavation.

MF 5.    Bronze or copper pitcher.    Inv. No. W3-337.
Figs. 12-2 and 12-3; Wreck Plan V*c*.
                         MAJ (7C)+MCP (9C).
Est. h. 0.27; max. diam. of body 0.155; diam. of
base 0.130.
Badly corroded. Most of base missing. Upper
part of neck, with lip, located and found to join
in 1977 during a final inspection of metal fragments from the wreck stored in the Bodrum
Museum, is called MF 5*a*; it was originally
found in the wreck in area 7C (MAJ).

From a slightly convex bottom the body rises

cylindrically with a slight outward spread to a
sharply defined shoulder. Two short horizontal
steps between shoulder and base of neck. The
neck narrows before rising as a cylinder to a
splaying lip. No trace of handles. The vessel
is hammered and made in two pieces with a
toothed horizontal join cold-hammered 0.02
below the shoulder; no solder discernible in
join.

MF 6*a*.*Bronze or copper vessel.        Not inventoried.
Figs. 12-2 and 12-3; Wreck Plan V*c*.   GW (6B).
Pres. h. 0.196; diam. of base ca. 0.125.
Highly corroded and fragmentary.
See also MF 6*b*.

MF 6*b*.*Bronze or copper vessel.        Not inventoried.
Figs. 12-2 and 12-3; Wreck Plan V*c*.   GW (6B).
Pres. h. of handle 0.15.
Highly corroded and fragmentary.

MF 6*a* and MF 6*b* were found together on
the wreck, badly concreted, in a position which
suggested that they were the remains of a single two-handled vessel. Complete cleaning of
the fragments for photography in 1981, however, revealed that they are the remnants of
two similar but separate vessels: van Doorninck
notes that the height of their bases is not the
same; the body of MF 6*b* has horizontal ridges,
whereas MF 6*a* is plain; the base diameters differ; and the two handles differ not only in curvature but also in the configuration of their
lower ends.

MF 7.    Bronze or copper tray or baking pan.
                                    Inv. No. W3-161.
Figs. 12-2 and 12-3.   Raised before excavation.
Pres. l. 0.378; pres. w. 0.337; h. 0.044.
Extremely corroded, approximately one-half
preserved. In two joining pieces. Raised from
"cabin area" in 1958 preliminary investigation
of the wreck by Frost and Throckmorton;
shown as no. 23 on Fig. 1-4.[19]

Hammered rectangular tray. Flat bottom
with sides sloping up and outward to a slightly
flanged rim with a groove just below its top that
was probably for seating a lid. Approximately
midway up the shorter side are two rivet holes
for a handle, 0.025 down from the rim and centrally placed, 0.05 apart. The holes are 0.005 in

---

[18] For the method of attaching metal loops at this position to receive a suspension handle, see V. Hoffiller, "Antike Bronzegefässe aus
Sissek," *JOAIBeibl* 11 (1908): col. 119, no. 72, and col. 122, no. 75. As
suspension cooking is useless on board small ships, more likely the
caldron, even if it had a system of suspension, was also outfitted with
two fixed handles as restored in G. F. Bass, "New Tools for Undersea
Archaeology," *NatGeo* 134, no. 3 (September, 1968): 418–419.

[19] H. Frost, *Under the Mediterranean*, pp. 166 and 167; and
P. Throckmorton, *The Lost Ships*, p. 147.

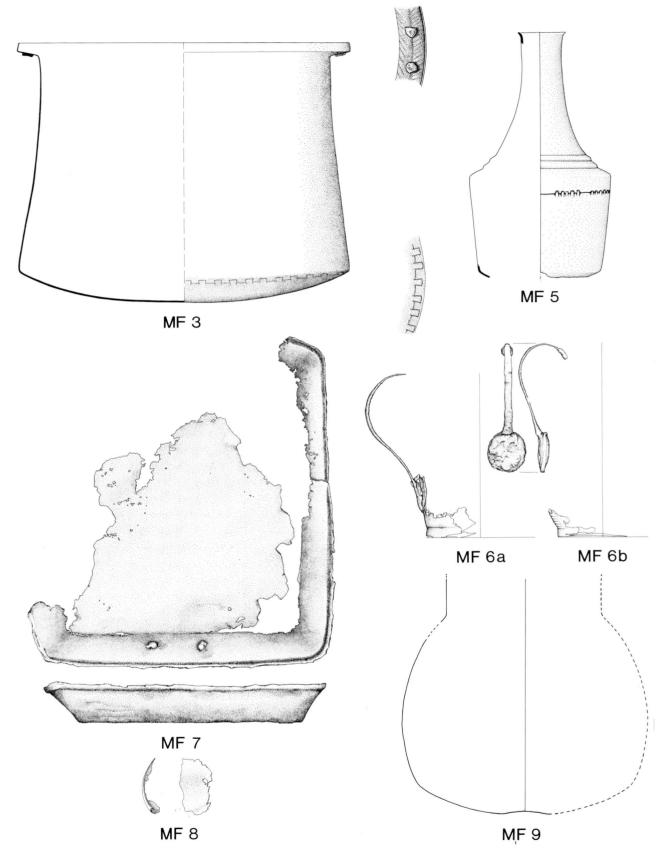

MF 3

MF 5

MF 7

MF 8

MF 6a

MF 6b

MF 9

FIG. 12-2. Bronze or copper caldron, pitcher, two-handled vessel, tray or baking pan, vessel fragment, and jug. 1:4. MF 3, MF 7, MF 8, *SWK*; MF 5, *NP*; MF 6a and MF 6b, *GG*; MF 9, *FHvD*

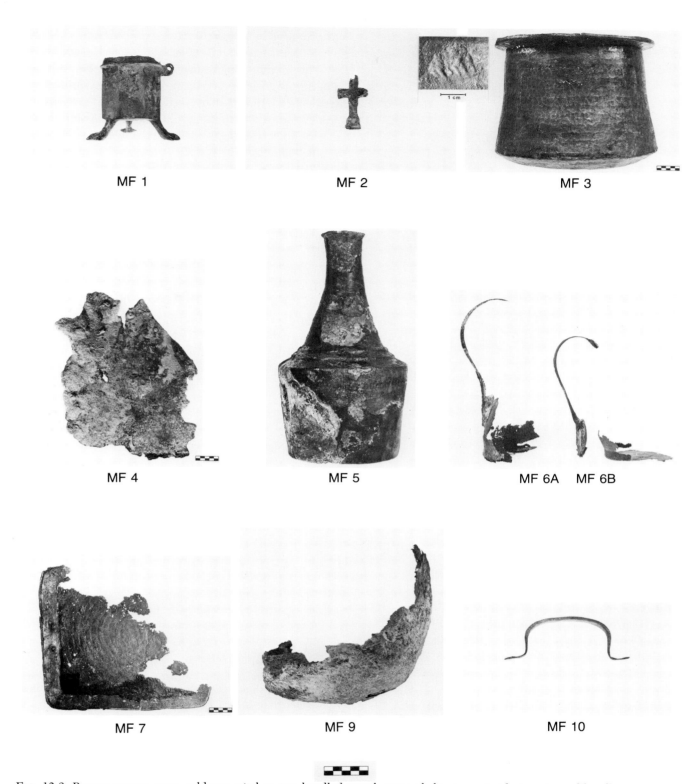

Fig. 12-3. Bronze censer, cross, caldrons, pitcher, two-handled vessel, tray or baking pan, jug fragments, and handle.

diam. Presumably the missing short side had the same provision for attachment of a handle. [Cleaning in 1980 revealed a pattern of concentric circles or ovals on the bottom.—GFB]

MF 8.    Bronze or copper vessel fragment.
                                    Not inventoried.
         Fig. 12-2.                          MBA (7A′).
         Pres. l. 0.063; pres. w. 0.036; th. 0.001.
         Very corroded with no finished edge. No evidence for rim or attachments.
             From a small, round-bodied object such as a ladle bowl (see Fe 96, p. 262), bowl, or cup.

MF 9.*   Bronze or copper jug fragments.
                                    Not inventoried.
         Figs. 12-2 and 12-3; Wreck Plan Vc.
             HM (7B), JM (6B), PY (7B), and CO (7C).
         Est. pres. h. 0.27; max. diam. approx. 0.27.
         In five fragments.
             Major piece (HM) preserves roughly one-third of bottom and one-quarter of body of vessel: pres. h. 0.198; max. diam. of vessel approx. 0.27; with shallow, circular depression at center of bottom approx. 0.05 in diam. Two fragments labeled JM; one preserves a small portion of the bottom and side of the vessel, and the other, if it belongs to the vessel, preserves part of a cylindrical neck with a diam. of approx. 0.175. The latter is a curved strip broken off on all four sides (pres. w. 0.045); midway along its length there is a straight vertical seam, and metal begins to curve outward along one long edge of the fragment, which measures 0.235 along circumference. Two fragments labeled PY; one appears to preserve a portion of body of vessel, and the other is a curved strip broken off on all four sides (pres. w. 0.05; l. along circumference 0.20), having the same radius as the second JM fragment and also curving outward along one long edge (the outward curves of the two long fragments seem to be remains of the vessel's shoulder). Fragment labeled CO on seabed was a piece of concretion that had detached from vessel bottom.

In the ship's galley were kept metal containers used in cooking and serving meals. First among them are the caldrons (MF 3 and MF 4), which could have been suspended over a shore fire or set on the ship's hearth grill and used for anything from boiling laundry to cooking soups and stews.[20] The flanged rim of the better-preserved caldron shows that it was designed originally with a lid (not preserved); the bronze or copper handle MF 10 (below) could have been the handle for such a lid.[21]

The caldrons' slightly hourglass profile with rounded bottom appears to be a shape originated by Byzantine metalworkers that has survived to this day. We find in earlier caldrons that the profile is straight-sided and tapers toward the base, as in a third-century example from Ballana.[22] A more contemporaneous bronze caldron from Beth-Shan,[23] however, exhibits a profile identical with that of the ship's examples. Since its origin, perhaps in the fifth or sixth century, the hourglass shape has lasted to the present day; identical caldrons of copper are made by hand in modern Turkey, and the coppersmiths of Bodrum even use the same toothed cuttings in hammering base to body.

It is curious that the walls of the Beth-Shan caldron, although hammered in metal, imitate the finger ridges of a wheel-thrown pot. On board the Byzantine ship was a smaller cooking pot (P 59, Fig. 8-15) very similar in shape to the ship's caldrons but made of terra-cotta. Thus, it can be seen that such utilitarian designs were exchanged freely at this time between metal smiths and potters.

We are fortunate to have pitcher MF 5 from the firmly dated context of the Yassi Ada merchantman, as its general type spans a period from at least the third century[24] to as late as the fourteenth century.[25] It might once have been equipped with a bronze or iron pouring handle of the type found on similar pitchers and flasks at Pergamon[26] and Olympia.[27] Such handles are attached by a metal band around the neck and are simply braced against, but not joined to, the lower body; thus, they leave no trace of their attachment.[28] The comparisons

---

[20] For a general discussion of the diet of the Middle Ages, see C. Singer et al., eds., *A History of Technology*, II, 123ff.

[21] This suggestion is discussed later, under "Metal Attachments and Miscellany."

[22] Emery and Kirwan, *Royal Tombs* II, 316, no. 641, pl. 76A.

[23] Fitzgerald, *Beth-Shan* III, pl. XXXVII, no. 14.

[24] An earlier example of the type is illustrated in Hoffiller, *JOAIBeibl* 11 (1908): cols. 133 and 134, fig. 19. Hoffiller refers to another Yugoslavian tankard from a Roman grave at Vinkovci that is identical in shape and three-piece construction to the piece from Sissek and is the source for his date in the second half of the third century.

[25] A very close parallel to the Yassi Ada example is a bronze pitcher from Corinth that is tooth-joined with bronze solder (G. R. Davidson, *Corinth*, vol. XII, *The Minor Objects*, p. 74, pl. 52, no. 559) and is dated by Waagé between the twelfth and fourteenth centuries on the basis of decoration and inscriptions on finds from the same cache (F. O. Waagé, "Bronze Objects from Old Corinth, Greece," *AJA* 39 [1935]: 86–91, fig. 9). The Yassi Ada pitcher differs only slightly in profile and is of similar measurement.

[26] A. Conze et al., *Altertümer von Pergamon*, I, part 2, 325. The pitcher, now exhibited in the Pergamon Museum, is not illustrated; however, a comparable piece in Athens is shown in fig. 117a.

[27] Furtwängler, *Olympia* IV, 213, no. 1372, pl. LXXI.

[28] Susan Womer Katzev did not have an opportunity to see the

cited here for MF 5 are described as bronze and have traces of solder on their toothed seams. The absence of solder in the Yassi Ada pitcher and caldron MF 3 suggests that they are either copper or a bronze made of

copper and tin only, which would be suitable for cold working.

I have yet to find parallels for the shallow baking pan (MF 7).

### Metal Attachments and Miscellany

MF 10.  Bronze handle.                     Inv. No. W3-91.
        Figs. 12-3 and 12-4.                       (7B/C).
        L. 0.134; w. 0.012.
        Well preserved.

        Detached handle, probably from a flat surface as indicated by the attitude of its flanges. Each flange neatly pierced for attachment.

MF 11.  Bronze or copper attachment. Inv. No. W3-231.
        Figs. 12-4 and 12-6; Wreck Plan V*f*.  MAC (9B).
        Max. h. 0.076; max. w. 0.045.
        Broken on one edge.

        Leaf-shaped attachment, somewhat spoon-shaped, with loop at upper end. Lead adhering to inside of attachment surface. The loop projects 0.023 from the leaf plate and has an inside diam. of 0.015; it is rectangular in section, 0.008 × 0.004 where best preserved.

MF 12.  Bronze hinge strap (?).         Inv. No. W3-94.
        Figs. 12-4 and 12-6.                        (7B).
        Pres. l. 0.118; max. w. 0.085; max. th. 0.003.
        Broken at one end; incompletely preserved at opposite end due to corrosion.

        As preserved, the strap curves at one end on both horizontal and vertical planes. At opposite end, half an attachment hole remains; a rivet or broken nail is in place 0.008 from this broken end.

MF 13.  Wick pin.                        Inv. No. W3-99.
        Figs. 12-4 and 12-6; Wreck Plan V*f*.   TM (7B).
        L. 0.059.
        Complete, but thin from corrosion.

        Bronze or brass pin with hooked end. Ring at opposite end 0.01 in diam. From ring, the pin's thickness tapers towards the curved end. Usually such metal pins are found connected to bronze lamps by a thin chain.[29] No bronze lamp was found in the Yassi Ada wreck. However,

with twenty-four terra-cotta lamps aboard, the presence of a wick pin is easily explained.

MF 14.  Unidentified metal fragment. Inv. No. W3-203.
        Figs. 12-4 and 12-6; Wreck Plan V*c*.   CI (7C).
        Max. pres. l. 0.033; w. of bar 0.010; th. 0.002.
        Fragmentary.

        Cast brass or bronze instrument fragment. Almost flat, but decorated equally on both sides. Deeply notched end of bar seems to be complete, but opposite end is broken. From a central axis, the two extremities are not symmetrical. At center of bar's upper edge is a raised knob of the same thickness, 0.004 wide at base and 0.003 at top; opposite this knob is an arch 0.003 deep and 0.013 across its widest span (there is a tiny notch, poorly preserved, at the apex of the arch). Bar's bottom edge is wavy. Symmetrically placed on either side of the arch, and on both sides of the bar, are circular indentations. Three incised vertical lines appear along the upper edge of the less well preserved end of the bar and also on both faces. These lines, combined with the notch at the apex of the arch and the symmetrical round indentations, suggest that this fragment could be the midpoint of some balancing instrument. On the other hand, it could be part of a key like an unpublished example (no. 13372) in the Benaki Museum, Athens, said to be "Medieval, Egyptian."

MF 15.  Bronze hinge part.               Inv. No. W3-214.
        Figs. 12-4 and 12-6.                         KI (8B).
        L. 0.022.
        Delicate workmanship, finely preserved.

        Spool-shaped, of three pieces; an axle, diamond-shaped in section and enlarged at its ends by hammering, with hollow knobs fixed at either end. Each knob is 0.007 high and 0.011 in diam. It is possible, but not certain, that the axle and knobs turned independently; they are now frozen together.

MF 16.  Bronze fragment.                 Inv. No. W3-213.
        Figs. 12-4 and 12-6; Wreck Plan V*f*.    LO (8C).
        Pres. l. 0.037; max. diam. 0.007.

---

upper neck fragment of MF 5, which was added to Fig. 12-2 shortly before publication of this book.—G.F.B.

[29] O. M. Dalton, *A Guide to the Early Christian and Byzantine Antiquities in the Department of British and Medieval Antiquities, British Museum*, p. 19, fig. 10, shows a fifth-century lamp with chain and pin. For pins from Corinth closer in design, see Davidson, *Corinth* XII, 194, nos. 1462 and 1463, with pl. 88.

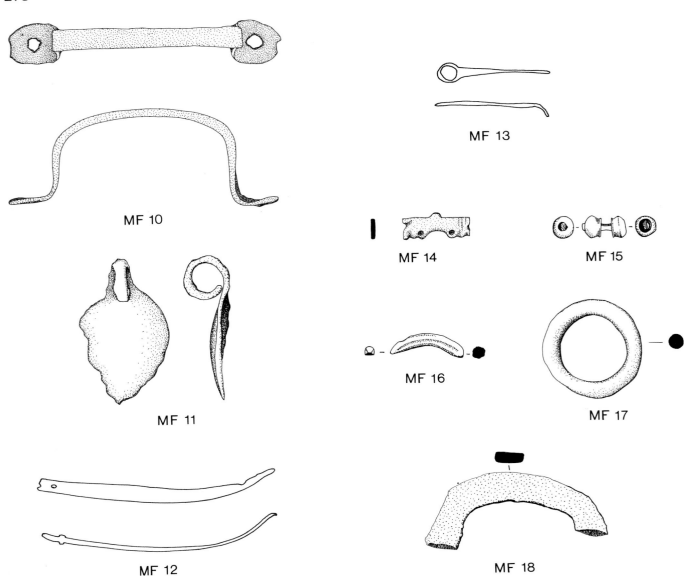

FIG. 12-4. Metal attachments and miscellany. approx. 1:2. *SWK*

Badly corroded. Broken and worn at both ends.

Arched bar, ending in blunt points, possibly fragment of a large ring. Hexagonal in section with grooves running its length.

MF 17.   Bronze ring.            Inv. No. W3-399.
           Figs. 12-4 and 12-6.           KAS (8/9B).
           Max. outer diam. 0.052; min. inner diam. 0.032.
           Whole.

The circular ring is round in section; the sectional dimensions vary from max. diam. 0.011 to min. diam. 0.007.

MF 18.   Iron lock handle (?) fragment. Inv. No. W3-437.
           Figs. 12-4 and 12-6.        FBM-B (8A).
           Pres. l. 0.092; pres. h. 0.039; th. 0.005.
           Incompletely preserved.

Curved bar, rectangular in section. Rubber cast from an iron concretion; hence, the finished appearance of the blunt ends is misleading, for the concretion mold was only preserved this far, and the replica was pared with a knife by its caster to remove excess pouring waste.

These isolated metal fixtures cannot be assigned with any certainty to their original contexts; I can simply speculate about three of them: MF 10–MF-12. The well-preserved handle (MF 10) may have been fixed to either a caldron, or a bake-tray lid, or it may have been used on a cupboard door.[30] Arguments for the latter possibility are that the handle's fastening flanges seem to be

[30] Bass, *NatGeo* 134, no. 3 (September, 1968): 418–419, shows an artist's preliminary reconstruction of the galley with the handle on the door.

bent for attachment to a flat surface and that the handle was not found in close association with the caldrons or tray. I would prefer to place this handle with the caldrons, however, for the following reasons. First, it is an elaborate and potentially dangerous fixture for use on a shipboard cabinet (with the overall crudeness of the ship's construction, one might expect instead simple wooden swivel latches of the type used on Mediterranean caiques today). Second, a handle identical to the Yassi Ada example appears on the lid of a bronze or copper caldron from Ballana dated to the third century.[31] Although the lid from Ballana is domed, it is not unreasonable to suggest that a Yassi Ada lid, made some four centuries later, was only slightly domed or even flat. Finally, the lid could easily have become separated from its caldron by its final placement in the galley, the ship's sinking, or the collapse of the stern that sent one caldron rolling some distance downhill.

The leaf-shaped attachment (MF 11) was found about 1 m from caldron MF 3. Lead on its joining surface indicates that it was soldered to some copper or bronze container.[32] A leaf-shaped discoloration of similar size appears below the rim flange of the caldron perpendicular to the axis of the vessel's riveted handles. Thus, it is possible that this leaf attachment held one end of a removable chain or solid loop handle for suspending the caldron. However, the Yassi Ada attachment would likely have been only a temporary replacement for a lost handle attachment, because of its dissimilar concave profile and the low melting point of the lead solder used to attach it. The leaf shape is common on Byzantine attachments that hold chains, rings, and drop handles,[33] and this piece could certainly have come from some other vessel, now lost.

No parallel has been found for the strip of bronze (MF 12) found in the galley area. Possibly it is the handle[34] for a lead spoon (MF 23) found 3 m distant. However, it closely resembles part of the hinge strap from a wooden box of the Byzantine period found at Corinth.[35] The distance of the preserved nail head from the broken hole suggests that this end of the strip might originally have terminated in a hinge along the top edge of a box, perhaps for the censer or for the set of inlaid weights (p. 205).

Bronze ring MF 17 was extracted from Fe 71, a bag of iron nails (p. 255). Why it was there is not known.

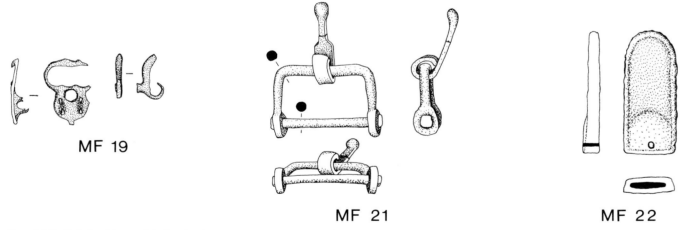

**MF 19**

**MF 21**

**MF 22**

FIG. 12-5. Belt buckles and belt tab. *SWK*

## Buckles

MF 19. Bronze belt buckle. Inv. No. W3-220.
Figs. 12-5 and 12-6. (5A).
Max. l. 0.0285; max. w. 0.020; plate th. 0.001; tongue l. 0.0195; tongue max. w. 0.011; tongue max. th. 0.003.

Cast bronze. Corroded. Tongue separated from buckle plate.

Buckle plate is shield-shaped and flat, without decoration. Hole centered near its top, 0.0055 in diam., is for attaching looped end of

---

[31] Emery and Kirwan, *Royal Tombs* II, 316, no. 641, with pl. 76A. In this example the relationship of handle length to the lid diameter is 1:4. For the ship's handle it would be 1:3.

[32] Bruce Barnby of the Ohio Metallurgical Service, Inc., Elyria, Ohio, informs me that lead with some mixture of tin in it would be suitable for joining bronze or copper in any combination.

[33] For examples, see Davidson, *Corinth* XII, 127, nos. 846 and 847, pl. 63; and 132, no. 899, pl. 66.

[34] D. M. Robinson, *Excavations at Olynthus*, vol. X, *Metal and Minor Miscellaneous Finds*, pl. LV, no. 667.

[35] Davidson, *Corinth* XII, 132 and 133, no. 906, pl. 67.

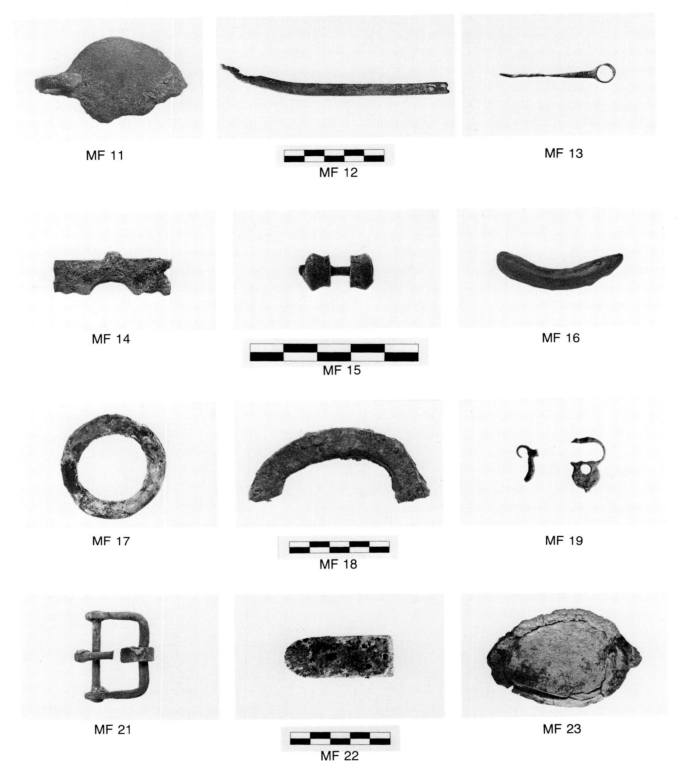

MF 11

MF 12

MF 13

MF 14

MF 15

MF 16

MF 17

MF 18

MF 19

MF 21

MF 22

MF 23

Fig. 12-6. Bronze attachment, hinge strap, wick pin, fragments, hinge part, ring, lock handle (?) fragment, belt buckles, belt tab, and spoon bowl.

the tongue. The tongue has a curious projecting knob on its upper edge, perhaps to prevent its bending back too far. Protruding from the reverse side of the plate are remnants of two loops for attaching the buckle to a leather or cloth belt.[36]

MF 20. Bronze belt buckle.              Inv. No. W3-346.
Fig. 12-7, Wreck Plan V*f*.              MCW (10B).
Pres. l. 0.025; max. w. 0.011; th. of plate approx. 0.003.

Corroded, missing tongue and clasp.

Oblong irregular profile, decorated on upper side with a facelike raised design. Eyebrows over the two eyes blend into a vertical nose which splits and flares upward in the lines of a mustache. Below this, slightly broken, is a circular outline that seems to contain some cruciform pattern, perhaps a monogram. Clasp is not preserved, but above the face a hole, 0.006 in diam., is preserved for attachment of the tongue. On the flat reverse surface are the remains of two loop attachments for securing the buckle plate to leather or cloth (see discussion below).

MF 21. Bronze buckle.                    Inv. No. W3-443.
Figs. 12-5 and 12-6; Wreck Plan V*b*.
                                                 KZP-10 (6C).
L. 0.046; w. 0.027.

Complete, except that tongue was sawn in two by excavators during the iron casting process (it was found inside a concretion of iron tools).

Hammered rectangular buckle in three pieces. Straight crossbar is round in section and 0.004 in diam. The buckle's frame is roughly round in section, 0.004 in diameter, and ends in two teardrop-shaped eyes through which the straight bar fits. Ends of bar are beaten over to rivet it tightly in place. The third piece, the tongue, is looped loosely around the frame's long side. It begins rectangular in section, 0.007 × 0.002, then narrows and ends in a slightly bulbous hook over the crossbar. Trace of a single punched circle decorates the tongue plate.

MF 22. Metal belt tab.                   Inv. No. W3-206.
Figs. 12-5 and 12-6; Wreck Plan V*f*.      FI (7A).
L. 0.054; w. 0.021; th. 0.004–0.008.

Badly encrusted. Probably hammered and

constructed in two pieces, upper and lower plates.[37]

Sheath, probably bronze, for the end of a leather belt. One end is squared, the other rounded. Flat on lower surface, hollow domed slot on upper face. Slot, for insertion of a leather strap end, is 0.014 wide, 0.003 high, and 0.017 deep, rounded at one end. A distance of 0.02 from the squared end is a pierced hole, 0.003 in diam., for securing the leather with a rivet. A ridge indented 0.002 from the edge is the only decoration on the upper face.

Though loop fixtures are universal on the backs of decorated Byzantine buckles, I have yet to find the attachment process explained. Small buckles such as MF 19 and MF 20 commonly have two projecting loops, while larger examples are equipped with three, spaced triangle-fashion. Within a given buckle, the orientation of the loops may vary by 90°. Hence, the use of a cross-pin through parallel loops is not always possible.

I would suggest that a leather strap end was cut with slits in the appropriate positions and then pressed down over the loop fixtures. A leather thong or string could then be laced through the projecting loops to hold the buckle fast. If the belt strap was to be of a heavy cloth, the same attachment method might apply, with the slits edged in a button-hole stitch to prevent tearing. An extra length of the cloth strap might be folded over and sewn down to hide the attachment. Such lightweight buckles as MF 19 and MF 20 could also simply be sewn directly onto cloth, using the loops, if the buckle was not intended to take much strain.

Presumably, the tab ends of such buckles were allowed to hang loose or were tucked back if used around the waist. Otherwise, the buckle decoration would be obscured.

The three bronze buckles and belt tab were found widely scattered, but all were aft of the ship's hold. One of the buckles (MF 21) may have been an item of carpentry gear. The other two and the tab would have come from leather belts belonging to passengers or crew.

[36] For an example of such loops fully preserved, see *AA* 59–60 (1944–1945): pl. 27, no. 4.

[37] For such two-piece construction in precious metals, see Ross, *Catalogue of the Antiquities* II, pls. XXXIV, no. 42*D*; XXXV, no. 44; and LXXXIII, no. 167. Many plainer examples are found in Hungary. See J. Hampel, *Alterthümer des frühen Mittelalters in Ungarn*, III, pls. 214, 219, and 247.

FIG. 12-7. Bronze belt buckle MF 20.

Since no skeletal remains were found with them, the buckles probably represent changes of clothing stored with their owners' bedrolls in the galley, most probably in its forward locker.[38]

We might expect the crew to have dressed as comfortably as possible on the ship—in bare feet and light sleeveless tunics tied at the waist[39] by rope belts or fabric girdles. On shore, however, a different type of belt was worn, at least by the fifth- and sixth-century working man. It was leather with a buckle, and through it was looped a second strap that ran, suspender style, over the left shoulder.[40] Hence, a shore-leave change of costume might be expected in the gear of a sailor who found this harness type of leather belt too encumbering to wear on shipboard.

The two dress buckles have their stylistic origins in the metal crafts of "barbaric" Europe.[41] However, finding their provenance is made difficult because the art of northern peoples is thoroughly intermingled with that of the Byzantine world by the early seventh century.[42] Buckle MF 19 is unusual in that there is no decoration on its shieldlike plate. However, in shape it compares favorably with those of an early-seventh-century group

known as "Syracusan." These buckles, usually found in graves, are widespread from England to Egypt and Carthage to South Russia. Originally it was thought that they came to be so scattered through the land migrations of northern tribes. However, Joachim Werner[43] has more recently argued convincingly that this and other "barbaric" buckle designs were made in gold at Constantinople,[44] were imitated throughout the empire in cast bronze, and were dispersed by sea trade throughout the seventh-century Byzantine world.

Werner has shown the geographical distribution of the Syracusan type.[45] His evidence thus far mitigates against any large-scale production of such buckles in bronze in Asia Minor. Aside from the ship's example, only one other of his main type has turned up in that region, and that in a private collection at Istanbul.[46] A variant of the Syracusan type that has openwork on the plate does occur in four examples from Pergamon,[47] suggesting a possible workshop there. The bulk of finds in the prime Syracusan style, however, is concentrated in Italy, Germany, Bulgaria, Yugoslavia, and particularly along the coasts of South Russia, where ten examples come from the Crimea.[48]

Perhaps it is not stretching imagination too far to suggest that one of the ship's crew was from the South Crimean coast, where grave finds indicate that both "barbaric" and Christian workshops mass-produced such buckles. And perhaps under pressure of Gothic incursions and the impending siege of Constantinople by Avars and Slavs, he signed onto our merchantman at some unknown port for a voyage through the Black Sea to safer ports in the south.

MF 19 is undecorated. It is also unusually small—less than two-thirds normal size.[49] Thus, it is probable that its owner was a boy. He could have been on board working his way in the service of a merchant for free passage,[50] or more likely as an apprentice deckhand. In

[38]The Rhodian Sea-Law indicates that passengers and crew brought their own bedding on board. See Ashburner, *Rhodian Sea-Law*, p. 87; space and weight allowances for bedding are discussed on pp. 59–60.

[39]L. M. Wilson, *The Clothing of the Ancient Romans*, p. 34.

[40]T. T. Rice, *Everyday Life in Byzantium*, p. 165.

[41]W. Holmqvist, "Europe, Barbarian," in *Encyclopedia of World Art*, V, 146–178.

[42]G. Ostrogorsky, "The Byzantine Empire in the World of the Seventh Century"; P. Charanis, "Ethnic Changes in the Byzantine Empire in the Seventh Century"; and R. S. Lopez, "The Role of Trade in the Economic Readjustment of Byzantium in the Seventh Century," all in *DOP* 13 (1959): 1–21, 23ff., 67ff.

[43]J. Werner, "Byzantinische Gürtelschnallen des 6. and 7. Jahrhunderts aus der Sammlung Diergardt," *KJVuF* 1 (1955): 36–47, with main "Syracusan" type of buckle illustrated in pl. 5, nos. 8, 9, 11, 12, and 14–16, and pl. 8, no. 14.

[44]Ross, *Catalogue of the Antiquities* II, pl. XI, no. 5A. See also M. C. Ross, "Byzantine Goldsmith-Work," in Greece, Office of the Minister to the Prime Minister, Department of Antiquities and Archaeological Restoration, *Byzantine Art, an European Art*, p. 361.

[45]Werner, *KJVuF* 1 (1955): 46, map.

[46]*AA* 59–60 (1944–1945): pl. 27, no. 3.

[47]Werner, *KJVuF* 1 (1955): pl. 8, nos. 1–4.

[48]Ibid., pp. 45–46, with map. The Crimean buckles are from Suuk-Su (six examples), Kerč (three) and Gursuff (one).

[49]Cf. example from Corinth in Davidson, *Corinth* XII, 271, no. 2185, pl. 114.

[50]Ashburner, *Rhodian Sea-Law*, p. 59. Ashburner also cites a twelfth-century contract in Amalric 357 in which a merchant offers his shipboard helper the price of the fare plus food, drink, and new tunics.

the Rhodian Sea-Law's description of the division of net profits due each member of a merchant crew,[51] last to be mentioned is the παρασχαρίτης, who received the smallest part—just half the share of an ordinary seaman. Ashburner translates the term as "ship's cook" but is quick to point out that such an important job should merit better wages.[52] Indeed, the presence on the Yassi Ada merchantman of a large galley, a hearth, and abundant cooking utensils bears out Ashburner's apprehension, for on this ship the cook's role must have been prestigious. Ashburner goes on to suggest that παρασχαρίτης might more reasonably refer to a young apprentice deckhand, for whom the half-pay would be more suitable. It may have been such a boy—perhaps from the Crimea—who stowed his change of clothes in the galley.

The second bronze buckle (MF 20) was found far astern in area 10B. Its plate bears an interesting and unusual design: an elongated human face whose nose splits into an upturned mustache; beneath the mustache, in place of a mouth, is a circle (incompletely preserved) which appears to frame a cruciform design, perhaps a monogram. The buckle's three circular motifs—the two eyes and large terminal circle—are carry-overs from the "northern" way of attaching cast buckles to leather by three round-headed rivets inserted at these points.[53] Hence, it was desirable in "barbaric" designs to use face-like motifs, whether lionesque, snakelike, or human, whose eyes and mouth would incorporate the rivets.

I have yet to find a convincing parallel for this buckle. Its decoration is certainly in the zoomorphic spirit of Migration Style metalwork that was spread from the Black Sea to Scandinavia and England during the sixth and seventh centuries[54] and was adapted freely by Byzantine artists. The human face is a motif found interwoven with plant and animal forms on precious metalwork of this period across Europe.[55] Since it is impossible, within my knowledge, to assign the buckle's manufacture to any single region, a few general observations are offered.

In shape, the Yassi Ada buckle plate MF 20 is not related to other contemporary Mediterranean types. Its

closest parallels are the catch ends on pagan Migration-Style fibulae.[56] On such fibulae the circular termination is quite common,[57] even containing a cruciform center[58] when no religious connotation was intended. If, however, we choose to interpret the ship's buckle as being of Christian manufacture with a cross, or even a cruciform monogram, there is also ample supporting evidence. Buckles of quite different shapes, yet in standard "barbaric" style, appear in firm Byzantine contexts at this time bearing Christian monograms inscribed on their circular ends.[59]

In any attempt to find a geographical connection between this far-flung Migration Style and the design on our ship's buckle, we must first ignore the bearded or mustached heads that are used in England and Scandinavia. In Hungary, however, much closer to the ship's possible route, we find excellent parallels for the design on metal belt tabs at the grave sites of Fenék and Fönlak. In the fifth-century example from Fenék,[60] two stylized faces, one with an upturned mustache, appear beard-to-beard divided by a cruciform design within a circle. On the much cruder seventh-century belt sheath from Fönlak[61] is incised a face form identical to that on the ship's buckle. Hence, this motif is established on belt tabs, if not on buckles, in Hungary. And from there it would have had ready access overland to the Adriatic or via the Danube to the Black Sea.

The rectangular buckle MF 21 is much larger and is of a utilitarian style commonly found on animal harnesses or weapon straps.[62] Within its type the buckle has two distinctive features: the tongue shape and the fact that the tongue is fitted on the opposite side from the crossbar to which one would expect to find it attached. An identical buckle exists from Delos;[63] on the basis of the Yassi Ada parallel it might now be redated from the "Roman period" to the early seventh century.

Buckle MF 21 was found concreted to a group of iron tools in sector 6C. There is little doubt that it was in the tool chest of the ship's carpenter (p. 265), together with an adze, a chisel, a wood gouge, files, nails, drill bits, and a carpenter's compass. One wonders why. Possibly it was scrap the carpenter was saving or even part

---

[51] Ibid., pp. 57–58.

[52] Ibid., p. 58.

[53] R. L. S. Bruce-Mitford, *The Sutton Hoo Ship Burial: A Handbook*, p. 103, fig. 79; Hampel, *Alterthümer* I, 292, fig. 719; and Holmqvist, "Europe, Barbarian," pl. 94 *right*.

[54] Holmqvist, "Europe, Barbarian," pl. 94 *right*.

[55] Ibid., pl. 91 *above left* (England); pl. 91 *below left and right* (Norway); pls. 85 *left* and 94 *left* (Sweden); and pl. 88 (Italy); Hampel, *Alterthümer* III, pl. 180, no. 8 (Hungary); and J. Werner, *Die langobardischen Fibelin aus Italien*, nos. A66, 77, 78, 81/82, and A68/69 on pl. A (Italy).

[56] Hampel, *Alterthümer* I, 320, fig. 802; B. Hougen, *The Migration Style of Ornament in Norway*, nos. 20 and 71.

[57] Hougen, *Migration Style*, nos. 9a, 17, 19, 54–57, 66, and 72.

[58] Ibid., no. 18.

[59] Werner, *KJVuF* 1 (1955): pl. 5, no. 1, and pl. 8, no. 13; see also Ross, *Catalogue of the Antiquities* II, pl. VII, no. 2C.

[60] Hampel, *Alterthümer* III, pl. 180, no. 8.

[61] Ibid., II, 750, no. 14.

[62] A. Maiuri, *La Casa del Menandro e il suo tesoro di argenteria*, p. 452, fig. 179; Hampel, *Alterthümer* I, 288–289.

[63] Deonna, *Délos* XVIII, 296, B1163, pl. LXXXVIII, no. 758.

of his own dress belt. It is much more probable, however, that it buckled a leather tool belt that the carpenter strapped to his waist just as sailors today commonly carry marlinspikes and other tools in leather cases on their belts. It is worth noting that a type of marlinspike known as a pricker (Fe 93) was found approximately 0.5

m from the probable tool chest.

Found in sector 7A was a metal tab (MF 22) that once sheathed the end of a leather strap. In size it would fit well with the carpenter's buckle, but as it was found more than 2.5 m distant from that buckle in the wreck, it could have belonged to another member of the crew.

## Lead Objects

MF 23.  Spoon bowl.          Inv. No. W3-308.
        Figs. 12-6 and 12-8.          MBD (8A).
        L. 0.072; w. 0.049; h. 0.015.
        Surface rough and cracked.

      Shallow metal bowl shaped like a modern tablespoon. On its flat bottom are traces of copper or bronze, perhaps related to such a metal inside or to the handle, which has disappeared. A handle stump remains at one end. Lead appears to be a surface coating over another metal.

The bowl of spoon MF 23 was among the finds scattered downslope from the galley. Its lead exterior is cracked and separating along the rim, suggesting that the spoon itself may be copper or bronze but that it was dipped into molten lead which formed a heavy crust. A folded sheet of lead (MF 38) and pieces of lead casting waste (MF 42–MF 48) were also on the ship. Together with the spoon, used for stirring and dipping hot metal, these finds indicate that simple lead objects such as net weights were possibly made by crew members as required on the voyage; MF 38 could also have been used for hull patches.

MF 24.  Lead seal impression.     Inv. No. W3-336.
        Fig. 12-9.              MCJ (9C).
        Pres. diam. 0.014; th. 0.0015; th. with knob 0.003.
        Edges and one letter missing.

      Fragmentary lead disc with small knob protruding on reverse, off-center. Circular impression with raised monogram A✝N . Letters A✝N preserved. Letter missing at bottom, probably ω, to form I[ω]ANNOY.

Tiny lead disc MF 24, stamped with the cruciform monogram reading "of Ioannis," is puzzling. A flattened knob projects from its plain reverse side. It is tempting to view it as a commercial seal placed on some part of the ship's cargo at a previous port. However, such seals on commodities are usually patterned on both sides and invariably show signs of a binding string or wire running

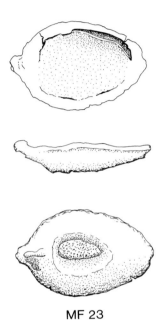

MF 23

FIG. 12-8. Lead-coated spoon bowl. 1:2. *SWK*

through them.[64] Alternatively, it could be suggested that an official named Ioannis was on the ship, serving either in the capacity of the Roman *magister nauis*[65] to handle all money exchanges or as the *scriba scriptor*,[66] who did the bookkeeping. This piece, then, would have been his certifying stamp, with its back knob imbedded in a small wooden handle. But in this interpretation, too, we are frustrated. Lead is an impractically soft metal to use as a stamp. Moreover, an impression made by the disc would read in the negative. We can be sure that this disc, how-

[64] Davidson, *Corinth* XII, pls. 128–133; G. Schlumberger, *Sigillographie de l'empire byzantin*, pp. 8–14. Forty-one different two-sided seals bearing some form of the name Ioannis in a monogram on the obverse, accompanied by a title or function on the reverse, have been found in Constantinople. They are thought to have come principally from official correspondence. See G. Zacos and A. Veglery, *Byzantine Lead Seals*, I, part 1, nos. 356–396, and pls. 52–54. I wish to thank George Bass for pointing out this publication.

[65] Ashburner, *Rhodian Sea-Law*, pp. cxxxvi–cxxxvii.

[66] Ibid., p. cxxxvii.

MF 24

FIG. 12-9. Lead seal or button. *SWK*

ever it was used, was the end product of a stamping.

The knob and flat back suggest that the monogram was once attached to another material and that the knob acted as a rivet. The outer surface of the knob is flared slightly at the edge, as if it had been struck with a downward blow. Identical knobs, albeit in harder metals, project at the backs of bronze studs used at this time to decorate leather straps.[67] Lacking evidence to the contrary, I suggest that the disc probably once had a second knob, also off-center, and that it was attached like a button by these "rivets" to clothing or leather as the personal seal of its owner. Certainly the name Ioannis was common enough in the Byzantine world that button merchants could stock dies for stamping this and other such monograms on cheap decorations.[68] Very likely, then, we have in the seal the name of one of the sailors, merchants, or passengers caught in the tragedy off Yassi Ada.

MF 25.* Lead bar.                              Inv. No. W3-189.
    Figs. 12-10 and 12-11; Wreck Plan V*f*.

                                               KZQ (6A).
L. 0.150; w. 0.063; max. th. 0.035; weight 2.310 kg.
Complete.

    Hole 0.027 from either end: one is square, the other round. Square hole measures 0.008 square at upper face and 0.007 square at under face; round nailhead impression, approx. 0.021 in diam. and sunk 0.001 into lead on side toward bar's center, encompasses hole on upper face. Round hole is 0.005 in diam. at upper face and 0.008 at under face; round nailhead impression, approx. 0.019 in diam. and sunk 0.002 into lead on side toward bar's center, encom-

passes hole on upper face. Upper face convex along longitudinal axis; under face nearly flat. Bar is 0.022 thick at square hole and 0.027 thick at round hole. Upper and lower faces curve together to meet at end with square hole; other end is very irregular. Both sides somewhat concave in section.

MF 26.* Lead bar.                              Inv. No. W3-177.
    Figs. 12-10 and 12-11; Wreck Plan V*f*.

                                               KXX (6A).
L. 0.191; w. 0.064; max. th. 0.037; weight 2.160 kg.
Complete.

    Square hole measuring 0.005 square at upper face and 0.007 square at under face occurs 0.065 from one end; slight circular depression approx. 0.001 in diam. encompasses hole on upper face. Round hole measuring 0.006 in diam. at upper face and 0.009 in diam. at under face occurs 0.048 from other end; slight, roughly square depression measuring approx. 0.015 on a side encompasses hole on upper face. Upper face is rounded, with a slight hump occurring at either hole; under face flat. Bar is 0.033 thick at square hole and 0.037 thick at round hole.

MF 27.* Lead bar.                              Inv. No. W3-124.
    Figs. 12-10 and 12-11; Wreck Plan V*f*.

                                               PW (7C).
L. 0.249; w. 0.043–0.046; th. 0.025–0.032; weight 2.975 kg.
Complete.

    Bar slightly tapered, becoming wider and thicker at one end. All faces fairly flat, but slight hump occurs at center on upper face. Square hole 0.036 in from either end. Roughly square depression measuring 0.018 on a side and 0.003 deep encompassed either hole on upper face, but depression at more slender end has been badly mashed. Hole at more slender end measures 0.006 × 0.009 at under face; hole at other end, 0.009 × 0.011 at under face.

MF 28.* Lead bar.                              Inv. No. W3-160.
    Figs. 12-10 and 12-11; Wreck Plan V*f*.

                                               KXL (5B).
L. 0.095; w. 0.060; th. 0.022.
Piece could not be located for weighing and reexamination.

    Upper and under faces flat; sides very rough and irregular. Photograph and drawing suggest that the lead may have been poured into some kind of cavity in wood.

MF 25, MF 26, and MF 28 were all uncovered

---

[67] Hampel, *Alterthümer* III, pls. 424 and 511.

[68] For example, the monogram appears on a buckle of the sixth century or later from Athens, now in the British Museum. See O. M. Dalton, *Catalogue of Early Christian Antiquities and Objects from the Christian East in the Department of British and Medieval Antiquities and Ethnography of the British Museum*, p. 115, no. 585.

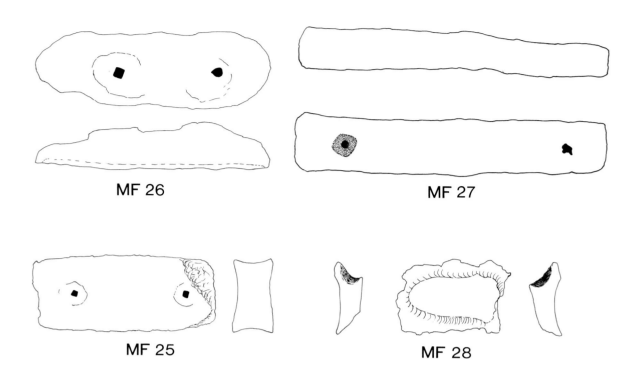

MF 26

MF 27

MF 25

MF 28

FIG. 12-10. Lead bars. 1:3. *SWK*

within a 1-m-square area overlapping the upper right quadrant of sector 6A and the lower left quadrant of sector 5B (Wreck Plan V*f*). MF 25 was found directly beneath a half-timber hull remnant whose precise original position within the hull is unknown (the remnant is marked with an X on Wreck Plan II), raising the possibility that the bar had already been outboard before the hull's breakup. Perhaps MF 25 and MF 26, and possibly MF 28 as well, were elements of the port steering-oar complex. The mount for this oar, we believe, would have come to rest on the seabed in the lower left quadrant of sector 5A.

MF 25 and MF 26 are very similar in design and were found within 0.30 of each other, suggesting a close structural and functional relationship. The axes of both the round and square holes in the bars can be brought into a fairly close alignment if one holds the two bars a few centimeters apart with their under faces turned toward each other. The two bars, therefore, might have had such a positional relationship, with a round metal shaft set in the round holes and riveted at either end, and with nails driven into an intervening piece of wood at the other end from the outer faces of the bars. It does not seem likely that a single nail ran through the two square holes, as the four corners of the holes are not in even approximate alignment. We cannot be certain that there were metal shafts in any of the holes at the time of

the ship's sinking, however, for no remains of such shafts were found. This is true also of MF 27.

MF 27 was uncovered in the lower left quadrant of 7C (Wreck Plan V*f*). While it may have served some function within the galley, its find spot does not preclude the possibility that it had been part of the starboard steering-oar complex.

MF 29.*Triangular lead piece.　　Inv. No. W3-251.
　　Figs. 12-11 and 12-12; Wreck Plan V*f*.
　　　　　　　　　　　　　　　　MAK (8A).
　　H. 0.065; base 0.053; th. 0.022; weight 245 g.
　　Right-hand portion of base corroded away (right side of rimmed face).

　　Corners rounded. One face slightly concave, the other outlined by very slight rim. Roughly oval hole (0.017 × 0.010) tangential to center of base on rimmed face; emerges on opposite face, 0.012 in from base, as narrow opening measuring 0.006 × 0.002.

MF 30.*Triangular lead piece.　　Inv. No. W3-320.
　　Figs. 12-11 and 12-12.　　　　MBJ (8A).
　　H. 0.055; base 0.048; th. 0.022; weight 335 g.
　　Bottom left corner (left of rimmed face) somewhat corroded.

　　Apex rather sharp; bottom corners rounded. One face flat, the other outlined by clearly defined rim. Hole 0.011 square, with slightly

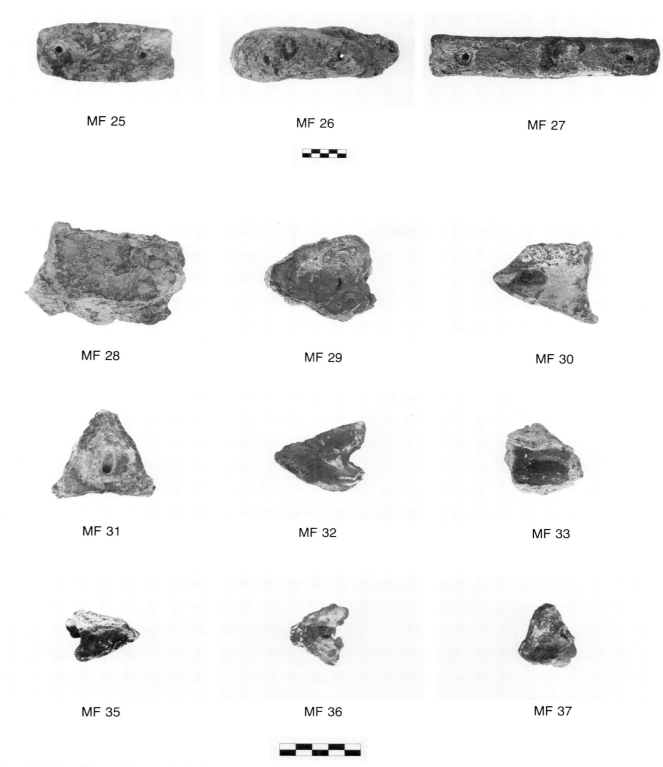

Fig. 12-11. Lead bars and triangular lead pieces.

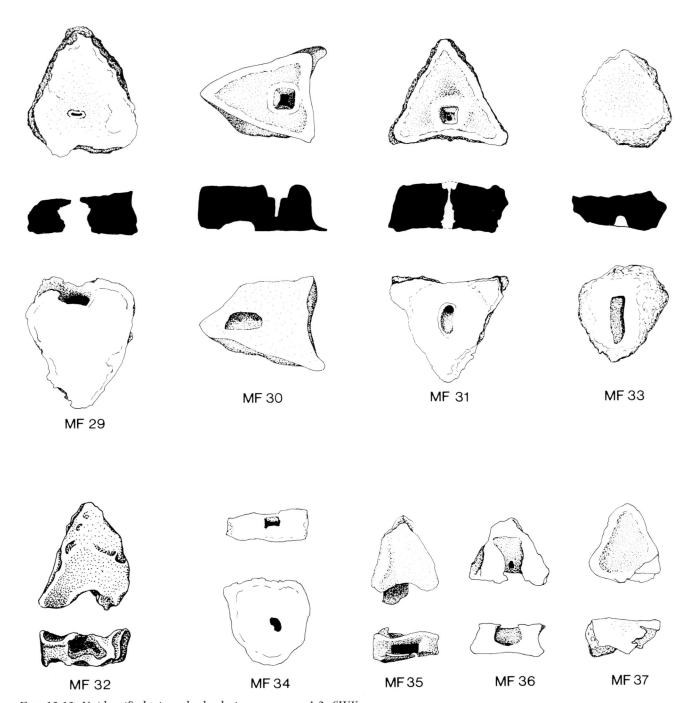

F ig. 12-12. Unidentified triangular lead pieces. approx. 1:2. *SWK*

raised rim, occurs 0.008 in from center of base on rimmed face and emerges on opposite face, 0.022 in from base, as oval hole (0.016 × 0.010). Hole partially filled with corroded lead.

MF 31.* Triangular lead piece.           Inv. No. W3-234. Figs. 12-11 and 12-12; Wreck Plan V*f*.

                                                        MAF (8B).

H. 0.054; base 0.058; th. 0.022; weight 288 g. White corrosion deposits on rimmed face;

green corrosion deposits on flat face.

Corners rounded. One face flat, the other outlined by clearly defined rim. Hole 0.008 square, with slightly raised rim, occurs 0.006 in from center of base on rimmed face and emerges on opposite face, 0.011 in from base, as oval hole (0.014 × 0.007). Very shallow circular impression, 0.035 in diam., encompasses oval hole.

MF 32.*Triangular lead piece.        Inv. No. W3-319.
Figs. 12-11 and 12-12                            (?).
H. 0.055; est. base 0.051; th. 0.019; weight
153 g.
Faces badly corroded. One corner and base corroded away.
   Apex and one bottom corner rounded. Hole
approx. 0.010 in diam. (perhaps similar to that
in MF 29) partially preserved at base.

MF 33.*Triangular lead piece.        Inv. No. W3-250.
Figs. 12-11 and 12-12.                    MAV (8A or 9A).
Est. original h. approx. 0.040; est. original base
approx. 0.038; th. 0.120; weight 108 g.
Badly corroded; corners and one face apparently not preserved.
   Roughly oval depression (0.023 × 0.008),
perhaps originally an emerging hole, occurs
0.015 in from center of base on preserved face;
it is 0.004 deep.

MF 34.*Triangular lead piece.        Not inventoried.
Fig. 12-12.                                      (?).
Pres. h. 0.045; pres. base 0.040; pres. th. 0.017;
weight 118 g.
Entire piece badly corroded.
   Roughly oval hole measuring 0.008 × 0.005
occurs near center of one face and emerges at
center of base, near other face, as roughly rectangular hole measuring 0.008 × 0.005.

MF 35.*Triangular lead piece.        Inv. No. W3-188.
Figs. 12-11 and 12-12; Wreck Plan V*f*.
                                               KXS (7B).
Pres. h. 0.046; pres. base 0.032; pres. th. 0.019.
Weight not recorded. Entire piece badly corroded and partly coated with white concretion.
   Roughly rectangular hole measuring 0.015 ×
0.005 penetrates into center of base, as presently preserved, to a depth of 0.027; for most of
this distance the hole is partially open on the
piece's front face.

MF 36.*Triangular lead piece.        Inv. No. W3-212.
Figs. 12-11 and 12-12; Wreck Plan V*f*.   MI (8B).
Pres. h. 0.034; pres. base 0.039; pres. th. 0.017.
Weight not recorded. Entire piece badly corroded.
   Roughly rectangular hole measuring 0.012 ×
0.008 penetrates into base, as presently preserved, to a depth of 0.024; hole is open on the
piece's one face.

MF 37.*Triangular lead piece.        Not inventoried.
Figs. 12-11 and 12-12; Wreck Plan V*f*.   (5A).
H. 0.039; est. original base 0.037; th. 0.019;
weight 70 g.

One face and one bottom corner corroded
away.
   Preserved face outlined by very slight rim.
Presence of hole not detected.

The precise find spots of five of the triangular lead
pieces are known and are indicated on Wreck Plan V*f*. At
least five of the nine pieces were found within sectors 8A
and 8B, possibly all within a 2-m-square area that in
large part overlaps the area in which the grapnel, fishing
gear, and tools for use on land were found. The five
pieces and MF 35 may all have been kept together
somewhere just aft of the galley. MF 35 was found only a
few centimeters forward of frame 4. MF 37, on the other
hand, was found 2 m forward of the galley, and it is perhaps significant that it was apparently the only triangular
lead that did not have a hole in it. It was found cemented
by iron concretion to the end of the wooden cylinder
MF 52 that had a single, centered hole. A faint outline of
the lead piece appears on the drawing of this end of the
cylinder, (Fig. 12-16, below), showing the position in
which it was concreted to the wood. However, it seemed
clear that the piece had not been originally attached to
the cylinder there, and it may be that the two objects
were in no way structurally or functionally related.

The pieces take the form of isosceles triangles when
complete. Many have one rimmed and one rimless face.
It is possible that the eight pieces with holes were all
similar in size and appearance. The shape of the holes
suggests they were for some kind of metal shaft. If so,
the metal involved remains unknown. Iron shafts seem
unlikely, because no trace of iron oxide was detected on
any of the eight pieces. The circular impression around
the oval hole and green corrosion deposits on the rimless
face of MF 31 suggest that the piece had been attached
to some object of copper or bronze, but none of the
other pieces yielded similar indications.

No convincing parallels have been found to support
an early hypothesis that the pieces were fishing weights
of some kind.

MF 38.  Lead sheet.                  Inv. No. W3-120.
Fig. 12-13; Wreck Plan V*b*.           JAF (7C).
L. approx. 0.56; w. 0.20; th. 0.004–0.005.
Folded in thirds.

MF 39.*Lead strips.                  Inv. No. W3-347.
Fig. 12-13; Wreck Plan V*f*.           MCT (8B).
Two strips.
*a*. L. 0.045; w. 0.019; th. 0.0015.
*b*. L. 0.035; w. 0.017; th. 0.0010.
Irregular hole punched through strip *a*.

MF 40.*Lead scrap.                   Inv. No. W3-312.
Figs. 12-13 and 12-14; Wreck Plan V*f*.
                                               MAI (2B).

MF 38

MF 39 A, B

MF 40

MF 41

MF 42

MF 43

MF 44

MF 45

Fig. 12-13. Lead sheet, strips, and scrap.

L. 0.136; w. approx. 0.045; th. 0.004.
Irregular band cut from a sheet and folded over.

MF 41.* Lead scrap.　　　　　　　Inv. No. W3-325.
　　　Figs. 12-13 and 12-14.　　　　　　　　(?).
　　　L. 0.068; w. 0.036; th. approx. 0.02.
　　　Lump which seems to have been cut roughly from a bar with rectangular section.

MF 42.* Lead casting waste.　　　　Inv. No. W3-352.
　　　Figs. 12-13 and 12-14; Wreck Plan V*f*.
　　　　　　　　　　　　　　　　MCZ (9/10A/B).
　　　L. 0.047; w. 0.029; h. 0.015.

MF 43.* Lead casting waste.　　　　Inv. No. W3-211.
　　　Figs. 12-13 and 12-14.　　　　　　　MO (?).
　　　L. 0.058; max. w. 0.018; th. 0.003–0.006.

MF 44.* Lead casting waste.　　　　Inv. No. W3-334.

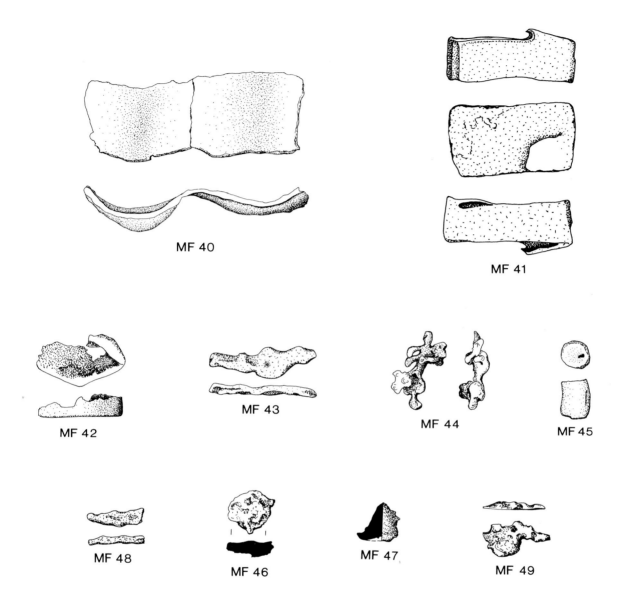

FIG. 12-14. Lead miscellany and scrap. 1:2. *SWK*

Figs. 12-13 and 12-14; Wreck Plan V*f*.
         MCA (9B).
  L. 0.045; w. 0.022.

MF 45.*Lead piece.     Inv. No. W3-248.
  Figs. 12-13 and 12-14.   MAW (8A).
  L. 0.021; diam. 0.015.
  Irregular cylindrical piece.

MF 46.*Lead casting waste (?).  Not inventoried.
  Fig. 12-14; Wreck Plan V*f*.   NO (8B).
  Approx. diam. 0.026; th. 0.01.

MF 47.*Lead casting waste (?).  Not inventoried.
  Fig. 12-14.       OG (8B).
  H. 0.021.

MF 48.*Lead casting waste (?).  Not inventoried.
  Fig. 12-14.        (?).
  L. 0.035; th. 0.005.

MF 49.*Lead scrap.     Not inventoried.
  Fig. 12-14.        (?).
  L. 0.03; th. 0.005.

Scraps of sheet lead were probably carried for the production of folded-over lead fishing weights; other scraps were possibly intended to be melted down and cast as fishing weights (see under MF 23).

## Wooden Objects

MF 50.  Wooden spool.                 Not inventoried.
        Fig. 12-16; Wreck Plan V*f*.        WAA (3B).
        Diam. 0.025; th. 0.0095.
        Lathe-turned. Complete except at edges. No longer preserved.
        Small disc from a single piece of wood, circumscribed by a **V**-shaped groove 0.004 deep.

MF 51.  Wooden padlock.               Not inventoried.
        Figs. 12-15 and 12-16; Wreck Plans V*b* and *c*.
                                              QM (7B).
        L. 0.076; w. 0.063; th. 0.041.
        No longer preserved.
        Rectangular block of wood, carved internally to receive moving parts. Iron concretion surrounding it indicates the wood was partially, if not completely, encased in iron plate.

FIG. 12-15. Wooden padlock MF 51.

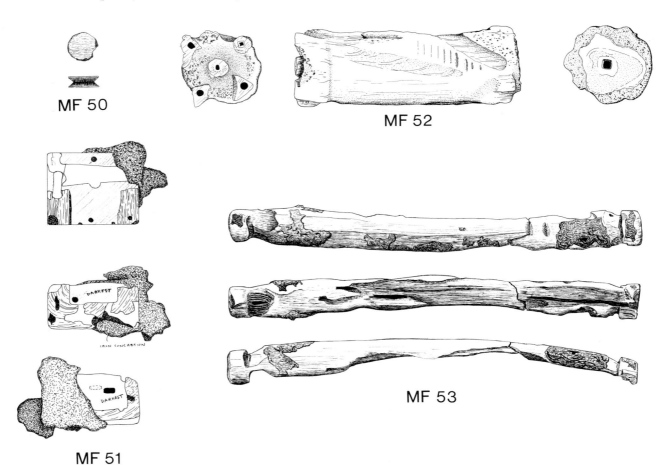

FIG. 12-16. Wooden spool, padlock, cylinder, and net spreader. approx. 1:3. *SWK*

Because adequate preservative chemicals were not available at the time, the expedition made every effort to care for small wooden items by drying them slowly. Unfortunately, the waterlogged wood distorted and was lost during storage at the Bodrum castle over the intervening winters. Thus, our evidence for the objects comes only from drawings made shortly after their discovery.

Wooden spool MF 50 was found in area 3B not far from the conjectured placement of the mast, and thus, despite its small size, it might have served in the rigging or in some mechanism at a point of minor stress. However, its V-shaped groove showed no signs of wear. Suggestions that it was a toggle worn on clothing or a reel to hold thin thread are equally unconvincing.

In the first year of excavation a wooden padlock was uncovered which I drew incompletely with hasty notations. It is regrettable that I did not better understand the piece at that time, for the wood has long since deteriorated, and the sense of the lock's workings was never made clear. However, in the hope that others may find some information in it, the original sketch is reproduced here unaltered (Fig. 12-16). This probably was a padlock instead of a lock fixed into a door, because concretion shows that it was bound on its sides by a casing of iron secured by nails. Also, a semicircular iron bar (MF 18) fits well in size and shape as the lock's spring handle, as compared to a preserved example from Corinth.[69]

The find spot of the lock suggests that it may have secured the forward locker in the galley (p. 93). In this locker may have been kept valuables delivered to the captain for safekeeping, as required by law (p. 316), as well as the ship's earnings and cash for revictualing.[70]

MF 52.* Wooden cylinder.                    Not inventoried.
    Fig. 12-16; Wreck Plan V*f*.           WAD (5/6A).
    L. 0.188; max. diam. 0.067.
    No longer preserved.

      Raised band 0.030 wide at either end. Diam. between bands 0.064. Series of narrow, shallow grooves spaced approx. 0.006 apart around cylinder's circumference between raised bands. Preserved areas of original surface at either end of cylinder flat and smooth. Centered hole 0.030 deep at one end; centered quincunx pattern of holes 0.016–0.020 deep at other end. Holes concreted with iron oxide.

MF 52 appears to have been either a handle or an axle or spool of some kind. It was found 0.5 m to port of MF 25 and MF 26 (Wreck Plan V*f*). Perhaps it, too, had something to do with the mounting or operation of the port steering oar. That it was the drum of a small winch is another possibility.

MF 53.    Wooden net spreader.           Not inventoried.
    Fig. 12-16; Wreck Plan V*f*.           KGQ (1C).
    L. 0.34; max. diam. 0.03.
    No longer preserved. One side badly decayed when found.

      A curved, round stick of wood deeply notched on both sides of either end.

MF 53 was thought, originally, to have come from the rigging of the ship, but modern parallels from fishing nets argue persuasively against that; I photographed a number of similar spreaders in use in Bodrum (Fig. 12-17; see also p. 307).

## Stone Objects

MF 54.    Stone mortar.           Inv. No. W3-83.
    Figs. 12-18 and 12-21; Wreck Plan V*a*.
                      NW (7B).
    H. 0.108; max. diam. of rim 0.240; diam. of base 0.135; th. of wall 0.024.
    Limestone, partly decomposed. More than half of rim missing, but traces of the third and fourth lugs project from the side walls.

      Crudely carved shallow bowl with flat bottom. Incised designs on the two preserved lugs: a palmette on one and a lotus bud on the other.[71]

MF 55.    Stone pestle.           Inv. No. W3-242.
    Figs. 12-19 and 12-21; Wreck Plan V*a*.
                      RI (6B′).
    Pres. l. 0.140; max. diam. 0.070; min. diam. 0.050.
    Well preserved except for small end, which is somewhat broken and decomposed. Hard, grey-white stone with some mica.

      Shape is that of a truncated cone, with rounded larger end.

MF 56.    Whetstone.           Inv. No. W3-178.
    Figs. 12-20 and 12-21; Wreck Plan V*f*.
                      KXY (6A).
    Pres. l. 0.155; w. 0.044–0.0485; th. 0.011–0.0175.

[69] Davidson, *Corinth* XII, 139–140, no. 1009, pl. 71.

[70] Ashburner, *Rhodian Sea-Law*, p. cl.

[71] For comparable pattern on a smaller Corinthian example dated "Late Roman," see Davidson, *Corinth* XII, 125, no. 827, pl. 61.

FIG. 12-17. Modern wooden net spreader. *SWK*

FIG. 12-18. Stone mortar MF 54.

FIG. 12-19. Stone pestle MF 55.

FIG. 12-20. Whetstone MF 56.

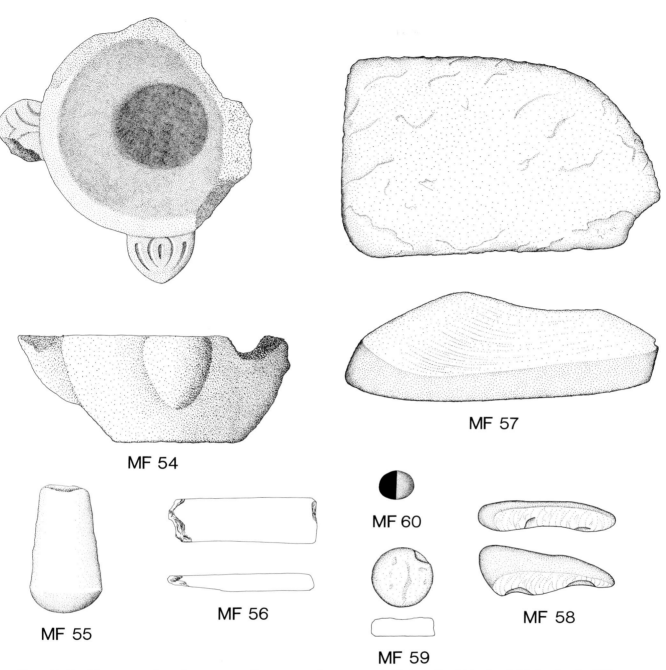

MF 57

MF 54

MF 60

MF 55

MF 56

MF 59

MF 58

FIG. 12-21. Mortar, pestle, whetstone, millstone, grinder, stone disc, and stone ball. 1:4. MF 54–MF 56, MF 60, *SWK*; MF 57–MF 59, *EBS after field sketches by LTJ*

Free of encrustation; one end broken. Fine-grained, dark grey slate.

One side is very smooth from wear, and the other is rough. Stone tapers towards broken end.

**MF 57.** * Millstone.                                Not inventoried.
Fig. 12-21; Wreck Plan V*a*.                IO (8A).
L. 0.32; w. 0.20; max. th. 0.075.
Whereabouts of this stone now unknown. The illustrations published here are based on measurements, and a sketch is recorded in the field notebook by L. Joline; the bottom also appears in a number of grid photographs taken under water.

Flat bottom. Top is worn smooth and hollowed out by use.

**MF 58.** * Stone grinder.                          Not inventoried.
Fig. 12-21.                                            OC (?).
L. 0.142; w. 0.054; h. 0.034.
This object, as was the case with MF 58, is known only from Joline's notebook sketches and measurements. He described it as "coarse, porous stone; bottom, top and ends—with exception of one fractured surface—worn smooth and rounded. Fits hand nicely." He further suggested that it may have been used with millstone MF 57.

**MF 59.** * Stone stopper (?).                     Not inventoried.
Fig. 12-21; Wreck Plan V*f*.                KZL (8A).
Diam. approx. 0.065; th. 0.03.
Known only from L. Joline's measurements and sketch in field notebook. A disc.

**MF 60.** Stone ball.                                 Not inventoried.
Fig. 12-21; Wreck Plan V*f*.                (7A).
Max. diam. 0.036; min. diam. 0.032.
Well preserved.

Slightly irregular, solid stone ball of unknown purpose.

The stone mortar and pestle in the galley were suitable for grinding ingredients for a meal.[72] The diet of a sailing crew probably consisted greatly of fresh fish, a cheap food then popular among working classes (see chapter 13); vegetables, breads, and soups and porridges thickened with ground beans or unmilled grain were also staples.[73] The mortar and pestle would also have served well for the rough grinding of cereals for making a Roman-style unleavened bread that could be cooked over coals in shallow pots or bake pans or even directly on a bed of charcoal. Saddle-shaped millstone MF 57 was probably also used in the preparation of food.

The whetstone could have been used by the ship's carpenter and/or cook for sharpening tools.

## Glass Objects

**MF 61*a*.** Blown glass bottle neck.        Inv. No. W3-321.
Figs. 12-22 and 12-25; Wreck Plan V*c*. SO (7C).
Pres. h. 0.091; max. pres. diam. 0.044; mouth diam. 0.027.
Most of body missing, some iridescence. Very pale green, almost clear in color. Bubbles and striations in glass.

Plain, cylindrical neck flares out very gently at mouth. From a slightly raised ridge at base of neck, the body curves outward, decorated with vertical indentations which twist diagonally. Thickest part of glass is just over 0.001 at lip; body thickness is only 0.0005.

**MF 61*b*.** Glass bottle base.              Inv. No. W3-321.
Figs. 12-23 and 12-25; Wreck Plan V*c*. SO (7C).
Base diam. 0.040; max. est. diam. 0.053.
Body missing. Color clear to very pale green.

Concave base, probably part of same vessel as neck fragment MF 61*a*; shows same swirling striations. Slightly less than 0.0005 thick, the glass is highly iridescent.

**MF 62.** Glass fragment.                      Inv. No. W3-198.
Figs. 12-24 and 12-25.                          Air-lifted.
L. 0.035; w. 0.032; th. of wall 0.0008.
Pitted on both sides; no finished edge preserved. Pale green. No weathering crust or iridescence present.

From a blown vessel. Remnant of applied strip of similar glass.

Discoveries of glass vessels on ancient shipwrecks show that even quite delicate pieces can survive, often intact.[74] Thus, we suspect that there simply was not much glass on the Byzantine ship.

[72] The presence of the pestle alleviates Davidson's suspicion, at least for Corinth Miscellaneous Find no. 827, that such stone vessels may not have been mortars (ibid., pp. 122–123).

[73] See Singer, *History of Technology* II, 123ff.

[74] G. D. Weinberg, "The Glass Vessels from the Antikythera Wreck," in *The Antikythera Shipwreck Reconsidered*, Transactions of the American Philosophical Society 55, Part 3 (1965) 30–39; G. F. Bass and F. H. van Doorninck, Jr., "A Fourth-Century Shipwreck at Yassi Ada," *AJA* 74 (1971): 37, pl. 3, fig. 37; G. F. Bass and F. H. van Doorninck, Jr., "An 11th Century Shipwreck at Serçe Liman, Turkey," *IJNA* 7 (1978): 124–131.

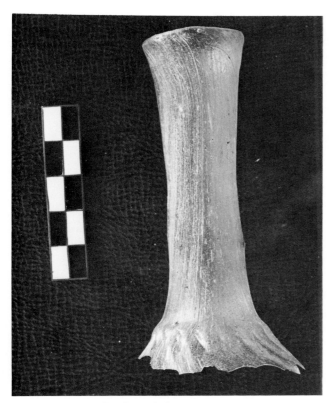

FIG. 12-22. Glass bottle neck fragment MF 61*a*.

FIG. 12-23. Glass bottle base fragment MF 61*b*.

FIG. 12-24. Glass fragment MF 62.

## Shells

Although countless shells, both broken and complete, were in the overburden covering the site, it is clear that a dozen or more mussel shells among them actually belonged to the ship in the seventh century (Fig. 12-26). Oktay Ercan first brought our attention to these shells in the wreck when he said that mussels, although common to the Bosporus, were not normally found in the region in which we were diving.

Closer inspection on the seabed then revealed that all of the mussel shells at Yassi Ada were from the same half of the original mussels, allowing them to be stacked quite neatly (a top and bottom valve from even the same

mussel will not fit inside one another, being mirror images); the range of size, from smaller to larger, aided this stacking.

Although whole mussels were originally taken on board most probably as food or fish bait (p. 308),[75] half of their shells had been kept, neatly stacked, for a secondary purpose, probably for spoons;[76] they were found near the galley hearth remains (three from 8B and the majority from the corner common to 5A/B and 6A/B). All are labeled MF 63 on Wreck Plan V*a*.

The origin of the shells was not necessarily the Bosporus, as was initially thought.[77] *Mytilus galloprovincialis*[78] is found from the Aegean islands to Smyrna to the Black Sea,[79] and Ephesus, not so far from Yassi Ada, was said in antiquity to have excellent mussels.[80]

[75] D'A. W. Thompson, *A Glossary of Greek Fishes*, pp. 166–167; I wish to thank Peter Kuniholm for this reference.

[76] Ibid., p. 167; cf. Dioscorides, *De Materia Medica*, I, 32–33.

[77] G. F. Bass, "A Byzantine Trading Venture," *Scientific American* 225, no. 2 (August, 1971): 31, reprinted in G. F. Bass, *Archaeology Beneath the Sea*, p. 141. It might be mentioned, however, that Ausonius (*Opuscula* 5. 35–41) in the fourth century praises the oysters of Byzantium. Peter Kuniholm suggests that that praise, although Ausonius calls the shellfish *ostrea* in the same breath that he refers to the oysters of Britain, could probably be applied better to the mussels of Byzantium.

[78] The Yassi Ada shells were identified for Laurence Joline of the expedition staff by the Philadelphia Academy of Natural Science.

[79] H. C. Weinkauff, *Die Conchylich des Mittelmeers*, I, 225.

[80] Thompson, *Glossary of Greek Fishes*, p. 166.

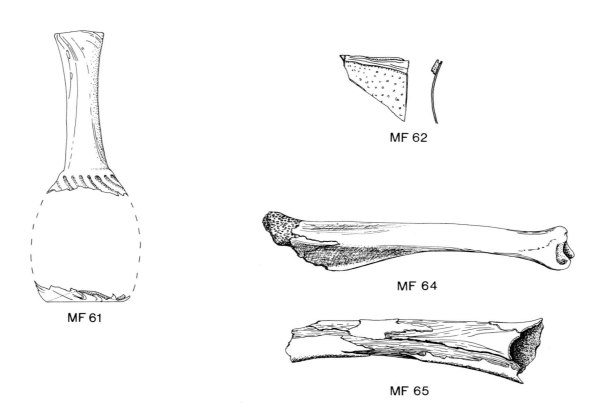

FIG. 12-25. Glass fragments and bones. 1:2. *SWK*

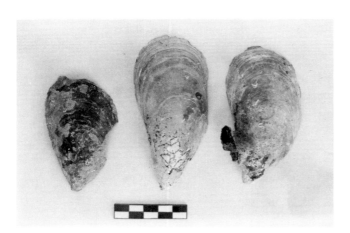

FIG. 12-26. Some of the mussel shells (MF 63) found in the shipwreck.

### Bones

MF 64.* Bone.                                    Inv. No. W3-20.
     Fig. 12-25; Wreck Plan V*a*.            CM (6A).
     Pres. l. 0.16.
     Apparently the tibia from a small ruminant (goat?).[81]

MF 65.* Bone.                                    Not inventoried.
     Fig. 12-25; Wreck Plan V*a*.            UI (7B).
     Pres. l. 0.136.
     Probably the radius and ulna from a small ruminant.[82]

MF 66.* Bone.                                    Inv. No. W3-100.
     Not illustrated.                        JW (8A).
     Probably another ruminant bone.

[81] Kindly identified by A. G. Kemler of the School of Veterinary Science at Texas A&M University. Kemler had only the drawings for examination.
[82] Ibid.

## Summary

On the Byzantine ship was a variety of small finds whose principal value is that they represent a diversity of common household items that now can be dated securely to the end of the first quarter of the seventh century A.D. Domestic items such as these are often difficult to date, even to the nearest century, when excavated on land; their appearance on the antiquities market or in private collections, out of excavated context, further complicates their dating.

Apart from its value for dating, however, the ship's miscellany serves to illuminate the daily life of the crew on board a modest trading ship. The censer suggests that this was a Christian ship whose sailors held ceremonies on board in some combination of worship, contract sealing, and thanksgiving for safe passage. From their scattered buckles and belt tab we can assume that at least three mariners were on board, with the carpenter being a fourth. To "Georgios, Senior Sea Captain" (see p. 314), we may add the name of another sailor, "Ioannis," whose lead button bore his monogram. Perhaps a young boy from the Black Sea left the smallest of the buckles to mark his presence as an apprentice seaman.

The surviving metal vessels from the galley, when combined with the great volume of pottery for storing, cooking, and serving food, tell us that mealtime must have been a major event. While the caldrons seem to have been a necessity, a bake pan, three pitchers, and the remnants of several other metal vessels lend a certain sense of luxury to the ship's equipment.

Where they can be traced, the small finds also offer some clue to the ship's route. They point away from the western Mediterranean to a voyage not touching farther west than Delos, and they indicate that the merchantman could have set out somewhere in the Black Sea before sailing south along the Asia Minor coast to her ultimate fate at Yassi Ada.

# XIII

## THE FISHING GEAR

### Peter Ian Kuniholm

DISCUSSION of Byzantine fishing in the seventh century is limited by the fact that no contemporary accounts survive. The late ninth-century ordinances of Leo VI concern the activities of fishmongers (ἰχθυσπράται) and the regulation of prices rather than the actual techniques of catching fish,[1] and the thirteenth- to fourteenth-century Byzantine manuscript entitled "The Fishbook" (ψαρο-λόγος) is more properly a series of humorous anecdotes about personified fish.[2] A brief discussion of Byzantine fishing by Phaidon I. Koukoules lists the extant references.[3] Evidence suggests, however, that methods of fishing in the Aegean did not change significantly from the time of Homer until after World War II, when steel and nylon lines came into general use along with deep-water trawls, dynamite, and sonar for fish detection. Thus, for our seventh-century fishing weights, interpolation from a combination of classical, late antique, mediaeval, and modern sources is necessary.[4]

Although the uses of some of the Yassi Ada lead objects are ambiguous, the following groupings of the weights should provide the reader with a convenient means of identification and comparison: (1) conical, piriform, and spherical weights; (2) sphendonoidal weights; (3) crescentic weights; (4) a triangular weight; and (5) folded-over strips of lead sheet.

In addition, the wreck contained lead weights almost certainly used for weighing (see chapter 10) and miscellaneous lead pieces, including cylindrical and round pieces, amorphous lumps, casting waste, and large and small sheets which may have been the stock from which smaller weights were made. Although some or many of the miscellaneous pieces were probably used in the manufacture of fishing weights, they are cataloged in chapter 12.

There are also nonlead items, such as an iron net

---

[1] *The Book of the Eparch*, tr. E. H. Freshfield (Cambridge, 1938).

[2] K. Krumbacher, "Das mittelgriechische Fischbuch," *SBMünchen*, 1903, pp. 345–380.

[3] Ph. I. Koukoules, "Ek tou halieutikou biou ton Buzantinon," *Epet* 18 (1948): 28–41.

[4] The best introduction to fishing techniques and gear is W. Radcliffe, *Fishing from the Earliest Times*, 2d ed.; a reprint of the first edition (1921) is now available (Chicago: Ares Publishers, 1974) which unfortunately omits the superb bibliography of the second edition. The basic bibliographies are by T. Westwood and T. Satchell, *Bibliotheca Piscatoria*, citing 1,500 authors and 2,148 fishing works; R. B. Marston, *Supplement to the Bibliotheca Piscatoria*, listing 1,200 authors; L. R. Albee, *A List of Books on Angling, Fishes, and Fish Culture in Harvard College Library*; and J. Turrell, *Ancient Angling Authors*.

The best guide to the often confused nomenclature of fish and fishing is D'A. W. Thompson, *A Glossary of Greek Fishes*, supplemented by a modern Turkish study of fish nomenclature: F. Akşıray, *Türkiye Deniz Balıkları: Tâyin Anahtarı*.

The principal discussion of fishing surviving from antiquity is

Oppian, *Halieutica*, tr. A. W. Mair. A recent summary of the archaeological evidence is H.-G. Buchholz, G. Jöhrens, and I. Maull, "Jagd und Fischfang," *Archaeologia Homerica*, II.

The standard work on modern Greek fishing is N. Ch. Apostolides, *La Pêche en Grèce*. The second, revised edition of 1907 was not available to me, although many European writers quote it at length. For modern Turkey the authoritative reference is K. Devedjian, *Pêche et pêcheries en Turquie*. See also G. L. Faber, *The Fisheries of the Adriatic*; H. Höppener, *Halieutica: Bijdrage tot de kennis der Oud-Grieksche Visscherij*; and *RE*, suppl. IV, *s.v.* "Fischereigewerbe."

Modern classifications of fishing gear are best summed up, with a key in six languages, by A. von Brandt in H. Kristjonsson, ed., *Modern Fishing Gear of the World*, pp. 274–296. See also A. von Brandt's *Fish Catching Methods of the World*, with excellent bibliography, and I. N. Gabrielson, ed., *The Fisherman's Encyclopedia*.

I am indebted to the librarians of the Rockey Collection at Princeton University and of the Daniel B. Fearing Collection at Harvard University, each a collection of over five thousand books on fish and fishing, for their kind help; also to the curators of the Index of Christian Art at Princeton University for their assistance in locating early representations of fishermen.

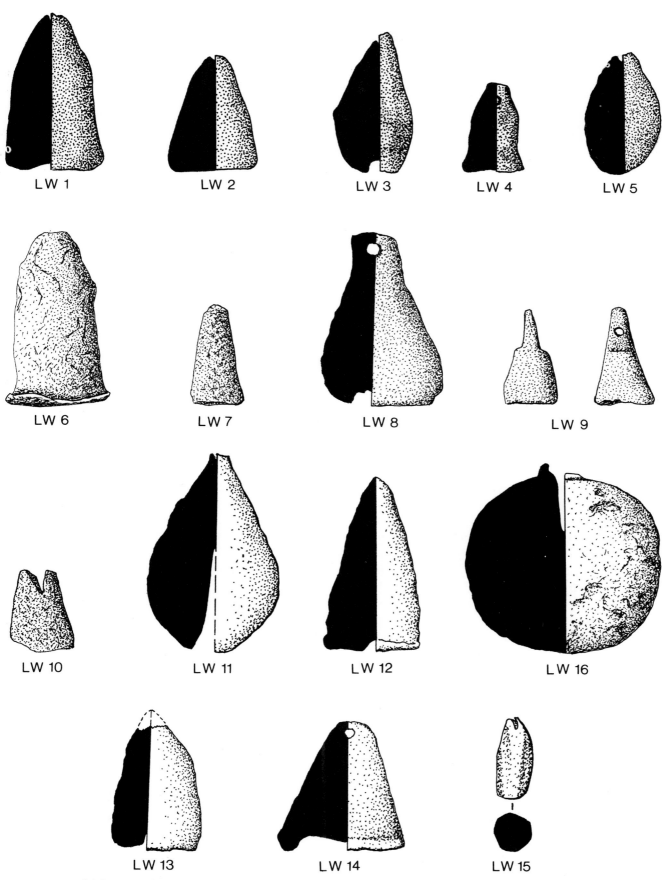

FIG. 13-1. Lead fishing weights. 1:1. *SWK*; LW 19, *NP*

fork, a wooden spreader, and a spoon used for casting or pouring molten lead, that had to do with fishing. These

are discussed below, although they, too, are cataloged in chapters 11 and 12.

## Conical, Piriform, and Spherical Weights

LW 1.    Lead weight.                          Inv. No. W3-86A.
         Figs. 13-1 and 13-2; Wreck Plan V*e*.          (7A).
         H. 0.04; w. at base 0.025; weight 146 g.
         Irregular cone. Flat bottom has slight indentation from pouring of lead. Small hole in top.

LW 2.    Lead weight.                          Inv. No. W3-86B.
         Figs. 13-1 and 13-2; Wreck Plan V*e*.          (7A).
         H. 0.033; w. at base 0.024; weight 87 g.
         Irregular cone. Flat bottom without indentation. Small hole in top.

LW 3.    Lead weight.                          Inv. No. W3-86C.
         Figs. 13-1 and 13-2; Wreck Plan V*e*.          (8A).
         H. 0.037; w. at thickest part 0.02; weight 76 g.
         Irregular teardrop. Bottom hollowed from mold.

LW 4.    Lead weight.                          Inv. No. W3-86D.
         Figs. 13-1 and 13-2; Wreck Plan V*e*.          (6B).
         H. 0.024; w. at base 0.016; weight 27 g.
         Irregular cone. Small hole near the bottom and two holes drilled near top.

LW 5.    Lead weight.                          Inv. No. W3-86E.
         Figs. 13-1 and 13-2; Wreck Plan V*e*.          (6B).
         H. 0.033; w. at thickest part 0.02; weight 74 g.
         Teardrop. Cataloged as having concave bottom and being small at top, but illustration does not show concavity; I have not been able to resolve this conflict.

LW 6.    Lead weight.                          Inv. No. W3-86F.
         Figs. 13-1 and 13-2; Wreck Plan V*e*. KNC (5C).
         H. 0.044; w. at base 0.029; weight 172 g.
         Irregular cone. Flat bottom splayed out wider than body, perhaps from lead overflow in mold or from being hammered. Top slightly flattened on two opposite sides.

LW 7.    Lead weight.                          Inv. No. W3-86G.
         Figs. 13-1 and 13-2; Wreck Plan V*e*. KXU (7B).
         H. 0.028; w. at base 0.013–0.015; weight 26 g.
         Irregular cone. Flat bottom with slight indentation. Weight is bent to one side.

LW 8.    Lead weight.                          Inv. No. W3-159.
         Figs. 13-1 and 13-2; Wreck Plan V*e*.
                                               KXR (4/5C).
         H. 0.049; w. at base 0.034; weight 249.5 g.
         Cone with flattened top. Pierced with horizontal hole, diam. 0.005. Rough impression on base, max. depth 0.007.

Identified and published in a preliminary report as "a conical sounding lead, with a hollow for the tallow or wax that picked up samples of the bottom."[5] Although the lead is suitably shaped for this purpose, it is too light for use in any but the shallowest of waters, and I think it is more probably a fishing weight.

LW 9.    Lead weight.                          Inv. No. W3-186.
         Figs. 13-1 and 13-2; Wreck Plan V*e*. KXW (6A).
         H. 0.0275; w. at base 0.0165; weight 22 g.
         Cone, flattened on top, and pierced by a hole (diam. 0.0035) 0.005 from top. On two sides to a distance of 0.011 from top the lead has been cut away to leave a straight-sided projection above a truncated cone. This projection tapers upward from w. 0.003 to 0.002. Base is irregular and has a slight indentation. Most of the surface is covered with a white oxide.

LW 10.   Lead weight.                          Inv. No. W3-205.
         Figs. 13-1 and 13-2; Wreck Plan V*e*.    EI (7B).
         H. 0.021; w. at base 0.017.
         Very irregular cone with concave base. Split open at top and covered with white oxide.

LW 11.   Lead weight.                          Inv. No. W3-210.
         Figs. 13-1 and 13-2; Wreck Plan V*e*.    LI (8C).
         H. 0.054; max. w. 0.035; weight 308 g.
         Piriform. Max. w. is 0.017 above base. Top of conical upper section broken away. May have had ring or hole for line. Bottom section is truncated cone with a tapering hole 0.034 deep in center. Hole is vertical but does not seem to reach top. Hole is 0.008 square in section at bottom of weight.

LW 12.   Lead weight.                          Inv. No. W3-246.
         Figs. 13-1 and 13-2.                       MAQ (7A′).
         H. 0.05; max. w. 0.027; weight 142 g.
         Irregular cone with irregular depression in base as if made by nail.

LW 13.   Lead weight.                          Inv. No. W3-247.
         Figs. 13-1 and 13-2.                       MAU (8A).
         H. 0.035; max. w. 0.024; weight 118 g.
         Same as LW 12 except that tip has broken off.

LW 14.   Lead weight.                          Inv. No. W3-310.
         Figs. 13-1 and 13-2; Wreck Plan V*e*. MBQ (9B).

[5] G. F. Bass, "A Byzantine Trading Venture," *Scientific American* 225, no. 2 (August, 1971): 27.

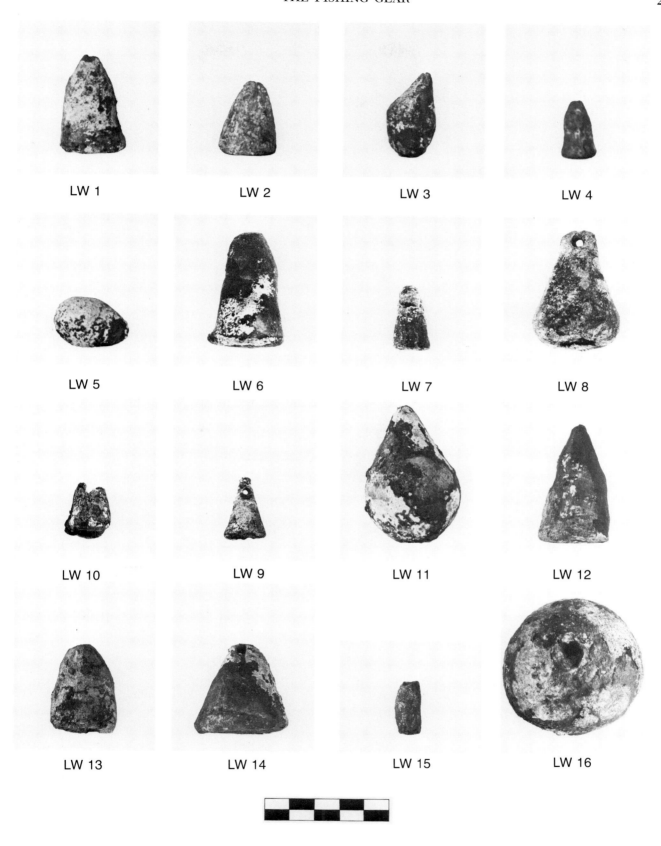

FIG. 13-2. Conical, piriform, and spherical lead fishing weights.

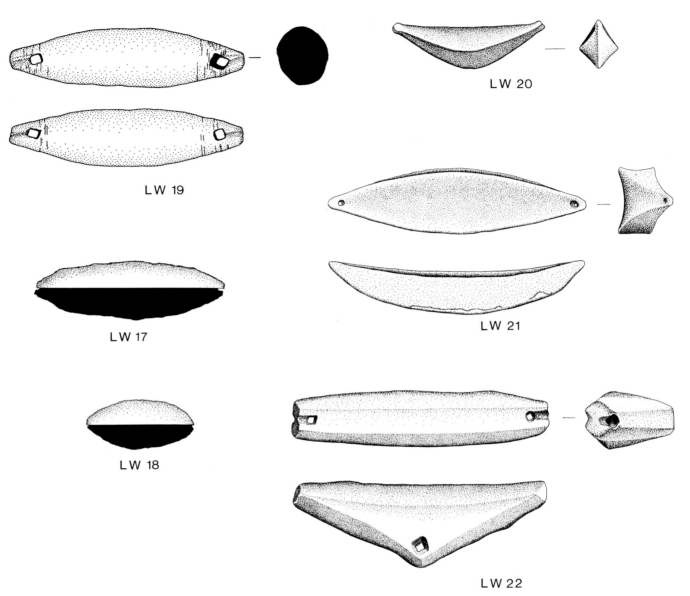

FIG. 13-3. Lead fishing weights. 1:2. *SWK*

H. 0.037; max. w. 0.035; weight 162 g.

Cone with roughly concave base and horizontal hole, diam. 0.0035, piercing blunt top.

LW 15.  Lead weight.                    Inv. No. W3-318.
Figs. 13-1 and 13-2; Wreck Plan V*e*.  MBO (6B).
H. 0.022; max. w. 0.01; weight 35 g.

Crude cone, roughly cylindrical, slightly pointed at one end, with a notch cut into the pointed end.

LW 16.  Lead weight.                    Inv. No. W3-345.

Figs. 13-1 and 13-2; Wreck Plan V*e*.  MCS (8B).
Diam. 0.05.
Missing hook (?).

Spherical. Crude ball of lead with hole 0.013 deep and 0.003 in diam. with jagged edge. The shape is unique among the fishing weights, but the piece is cataloged here, rather than as a possible counterweight for a steelyard (chapter 10), because it was found in a cluster of certain fishing weights.

## Sphendonoidal Weights

LW 17. Lead weight. Inv. No. W3-232.
Figs. 13-3 and 13-4; Wreck Plan V*e*. MAB (8B).
L. 0.101; max. diam. 0.03 tapering to approx.
0.007 at each end; weight 503 g.
Surface corroded and pitted, with white oxidation in spots.
Elongated sphendonoid. Traces of a hole, diam.
approx. 0.003, remain in each end. These are
now only 0.003–0.005 deep, but may have gone
through the length of the object.

LW 18. Lead weight. Inv. No. W3-238.
Figs. 13-3 and 13-4; Wreck Plan V*e*.
MAG (8B/C).
L. 0.058; max. diam. 0.025 tapering to 0.004 at
each end; weight 202 g.
Surface corroded and pitted; white oxidation.
Slightly irregular sphendonoid. Traces of a
hole, diam. approx. 0.002, in each end. These

are now only 0.0015 deep, but may have gone
through the length of the object.

LW 19. Lead weight.[6] Inv. No. W3-339.
Figs. 13-3 and 13-4; Wreck Plan V*e*.
MCF (9B/C).
L. 0.123; max. diam. 0.032 tapering to 0.01 at
each end; weight 623 g.
Irregular sphendonoid. Pierced by rectangular holes, approximately 0.005 on a side.
Grooves to pointed ends connect outer sides of
each hole.
In redrawing the weight in 1980, Netia Piercy
noted grooves cut around the tapering ends,
possibly to prevent cord from slipping off; on
one side she noted an impression of three
strands of whipping cord side by side, each
strand impression being just over 0.0005 wide.

## Crescentic Weights

LW 20. Lead weight. Inv. No. W3-348.
Figs. 13-3 and 13-4; Wreck Plan V*e*. MCS (8B).
L. 0.08; max. w. 0.22 tapering to 0.005 at each
end; max. th. 0.02 tapering to 0.005 at each
end; weight 107 g.
Four-sided piece, each face of which is an
isosceles triangle about 0.015 high. Two faces
are flat; two are curved.

LW 21. Lead weight. Inv. No. W3-349.
Fig. 13-3; Wreck Plan V*e*. MCQ (8B).
L. 0.135; w. 0.034; max. th. 0.025; weight 479 g.
Boat-shaped, with flat base and slightly concave top. Rises to two pointed ends, each
pierced by a vertical stringhole 0.004 and 0.005
from ends. Diam. of holes approx. 0.002. No
grooves as on LW 19.

## Triangular Weight

LW 22. Lead weight.[7] Inv. No. W3-350.
Figs. 13-3 and 13-4; Wreck Plan V*e*. MCR (8B).
L. 0.132; h. 0.048; max. th. 0.03 tapering to
0.0125 at ends; weight 918 g.
Triangular. Both triangular faces are beveled
on all three sides to the flat surfaces which connect the two triangles. Rectangular stringholes
at each corner, the two at the base parallel to
the two triangular faces and the one at the apex

connecting the triangular faces. The holes are
approximately 0.004 on a side, and one end of
each hole is connected to the other end by a
groove or channel around the outside of the
piece. Thus, a line could have been threaded
through each hole and then made fast with a
knot.

[6] Ibid., p. 32, upper fig.
[7] Ibid., lower fig.

LW 17

LW 18

LW 19

LW 20

LW 22

LW 25

LW 26

LW 27

FIG. 13-4. Sphendonoidal, crescentic, triangular, and folded-over lead fishing weights.

## Folded-over Strips of Lead

LW 23. Lead weight.            Inv. No. W3-123A.
       Not illustrated.                         (?).
       L. 0.072; diam. 0.014; th. 0.003.
       Curved sheet of lead, U-shaped in section.

LW 24. Lead weight.            Inv. No. W3-123B.
       Not illustrated.                         (?).
       L. 0.063; diam. 0.016; th. 0.002–0.003.
       Curved sheet of lead.

LW 25. Lead weight.            Inv. No. W3-123C.
       Figs. 13-4 and 13-5; Wreck Plan Ve. KXO (5A).
       L. 0.08; max. diam. 0.022; th. 0.003.
       Curved sheet of lead.

LW 26. Lead weight.            Inv. No. W3-204.
       Figs. 13-4 and 13-5; Wreck Plan Ve.    GI (7A).
       L. 0.038; w. 0.008; th. 0.002.
       Plain, irregular, but almost rectangular strip of lead, slightly bent at one end.

LW 27. Lead weight.            Inv. No. W3-313.
       Figs. 13-4 and 13-5; Wreck Plan Ve. MBF (5B).
       L. 0.076; diam. 0.015; th. approx. 0.003.
       Strip of lead folded over into rough tube, open on one side.

LW 28. Lead weight.            Inv. No. W3-314.
       Figs. 13-5 and 13-6; Wreck Plan Ve.
                              MAP (6B').
       L. 0.075; diam. 0.016–0.01; th. approx. 0.003.
       Same as LW 27 except that tube has been smashed flat.

LW 29. Lead weight.            Inv. No. W3-315.
       Figs. 13-5 and 13-6; Wreck Plan Ve.
                              MAL (7B').
       L. 0.095; th. 0.002.
       Made of two pieces, one a curved lead sheet like LW 27 (l. 0.069; w. 0.012) mashed and closed over another strip of lead (l. 0.086; w. 0.016; th. approx. 0.0015); the strip has been scored lengthwise in places. It is hard to tell whether these were originally one piece or two.

LW 30. Lead weight.            Inv. No. W3-316.
       Figs. 13-5 and 13-6; Wreck Plan Ve.
                              MAM (7B').
       L. 0.034; w. 0.025–0.01; th. 0.001–0.002.
       Fragment of a curved lead sheet like LW 27. Mashed nearly flat.

LW 31. Lead weight.            Inv. No. W3-317.
       Figs. 13-5 and 13-6.             MAS (7A').
       L. 0.057; diam. 0.025; th. 0.001–0.002.
       Curved sheet similar to LW 27, but mashed somewhat irregularly. The exterior surface is partially covered with an irregular grid of raised lines, with grid squares averaging 0.015 square.

LW 32. Lead sheet.             Inv. No. W3-187.
       Figs. 13-5 and 13-6; Wreck Plan Ve.
                              KAW (7C).
       Sides 0.036 × 0.041 × 0.039 × 0.037; th. 0.002. Completely coated with white oxide; black substance covers this on one side.
       Nearly flat, almost square lead sheet; 0.036 of edge curves upward, probably the result of cutting. One surface has an irregular grid of lines, slightly raised in places where a black substance covers them, but lower than the surface because of a lack of oxide covering where not coated with black. The black substance covers part of side with grid and all of reverse. Grid squares average 0.015 square, suggesting that this sheet was part of the stock from which LW 31 was made.

LW 33. Lead weight.            Inv. No. W3-333.
       Figs. 13-5 and 13-6; Wreck Plan Ve. MBZ (9B).
       L. 0.035; max. w. 0.015; th. 0.002; weight 21 g.
       Folded lead strip, V-shaped in section.

LW 34. Lead weight.            Inv. No. W3-340.
       Figs. 13-5 and 13-6.             MCH (8C).
       L. 0.043; w. 0.017; th. 0.002; weight 22 g.
       Folded lead strip, one side longer than the other, with a raised ridge running perpendicular to the length on the inside of the longer side. This ridge may be a trace of the raised grid noted on LW 31 and LW 32.

LW 35. Lead weight.            Inv. No. W3-341.
       Figs. 13-5 and 13-6; Wreck Plan Ve.
                              MCE (9B).
       L. 0.032; w. 0.01; th. 0.001; weight 6 g.
       Strip of folded lead.

LW 36. Lead weight.            Inv. No. W3-342.
       Figs. 13-5 and 13-6; Wreck Plan Ve.
                              MCG (9B).
       L. 0.083; w. 0.017; th. 0.001; weight 19 g.
       Strip of folded lead.

LW 37. Lead weight.            Inv. No. W3-344.
       Figs. 13-5 and 13-6; Wreck Plan Ve.
                              MCU (8B).
       L. 0.05; w. 0.025; th. 0.003; weight 54 g.
       Strip of lead folded over roughly and mashed together.

LW 38. Lead weight.            Inv. No. W3-351.
       Figs. 13-5 and 13-6; Wreck Plan Ve.

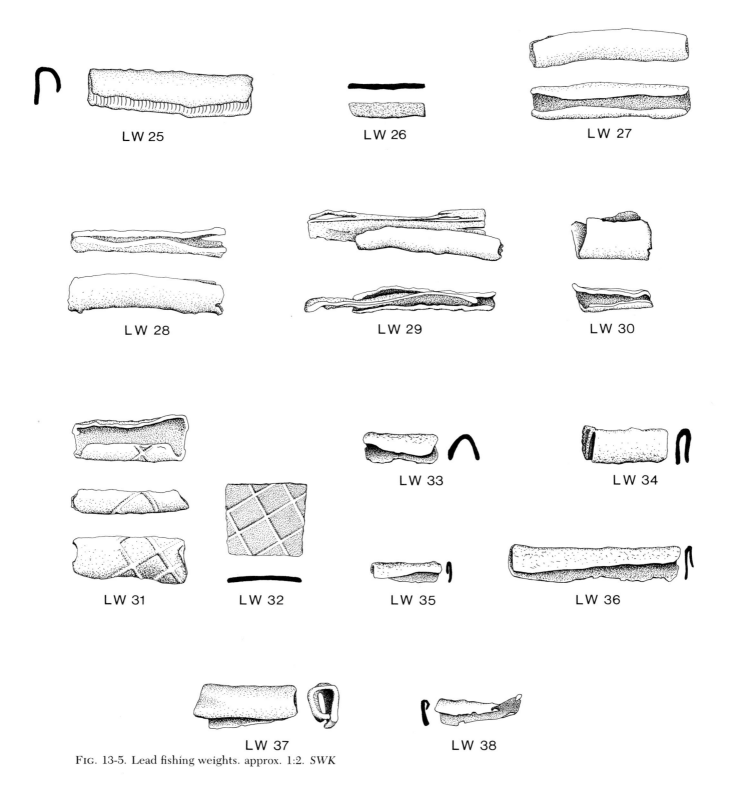

FIG. 13-5. Lead fishing weights. approx. 1:2. *SWK*

L 28

L 29

L 30

L 31

L 32

L 33

L 34

L 35

L 36

L 37

L 38

FIG. 13-6. Folded-over lead strip and sheet fishing weights.

MCX (9C).
L. 0.044; w. 0.013; th. 0.001; weight 6 g.
Folded strip of lead.

Note that the stock from which the above folded-over weights were cut seems to have varied in thickness from 1 to 3 mm. Allowing for crudities in the preparation of lead, the rough treatment accorded fishing implements, thirteen hundred years' exposure to seawater (and the vagaries of measurement), it is possible that all were made from the same piece. The method of preparation that resulted in cross-hatchings has not been determined.

## Traditional Fishing Practices

The traditions of fishing in the Aegean appear to have been well established from the earliest times. Homer mentions the catching of fish with bent hooks (*Odyssey* 12. 331), and the companions of Odysseus are snatched by Scylla and compared with fish caught on a long pole and flung out upon the shore (*Odyssey* 12. 251). Since most of these references occur in similes, the implication is that the art of fishing was well known to Homeric audiences despite Athenaeus' comment that the catching and cleaning of fish lacks dignity and elevation and is hence unsuited to Homeric characters (*Deipnosophistae* 1. 26*d*). Thus, in the sixth century B.C., when the soothsayer Amphilytus spoke to Peisistratus about the casting of fishing nets and the darting of tunnies through the sea on a moonlit night (Herodotus *Historiae* 1. 62), Peisistratus understood the oracle to be predicting a successful attack on the Athenians.

Aside from the many literary references, some of which border on the extravagant or absurd (which is to say that fish stories are not a new phenomenon), much of the surviving ancient commentary on fish and fishing appears to be borne out by modern observation. While fishing from a small rowboat on the Bosporus, I have found the currents and the channel along the European shore to be as they were described by Procopius about A.D. 560 (*Buildings* 1. 5. 2–13; 1. 8. 2–11; 1. 9. 2–4). Moreover, specialists at Istanbul University's Hydrobiological Research Institute at Baltaliman say that Aristotle's descriptions of fish, their breeding habits, and their annual migrations from the Aegean to the Black Sea and back (*Historia Animalium* 5.9 [543*a*]), are remarkably accurate.[8] I have used a dry fly (red hackle), tied according to Aelian's specifications (*De Animalium* 15. 1), successfully for trout in the mountain streams of Bithynia, and in a more ambitious experiment J. W. Hills found that eleven of the twelve flies described by Dame Juliana Berners[9] in 1496 could be identified and that six of them are still killers.[10]

Oppian mentions four implements for catching fish (*Halieutica* 3. 72ff.): the net (nine types), the hook, the weel or wickerwork basket, and the trident.[11] The Yassi Ada leads suggest that both a simple net and various hook-and-line rigs were used on the ship.

### NETS

The number and size of the weights on the wreck indicate that they belonged to a rather small net or nets, unless, of course, a large number of them were lost overboard before the sinking. The limited manpower available on board also excludes the larger varieties of nets. The possible nets on the Yassi Ada ship are the following:

*Casting-net* (Oppian's type 2, ἀμφίβληστρον, or type 9, σφαιρῶν; modern Gk. πεζόβολος or ἀπλάδια; Turk. *saçma* or *serpme*; Fr. *épervier*; Ger. *wurfnetz*). This is a one-man net suitable for mackerel, horse mackerel, and other surface fish. On the circular rim of the casting-net is a line on which are attached at regular intervals small lead weights, often split buckshot (whence the Turkish word *saçma*, or "buckshot," for the net) or the folded-over type. I have never seen a casting-net on which conical weights were employed, although fishermen along the Bosporus insist that such nets are not uncommon and that the weights tangle after the cast is made, thereby trapping the fish. It would appear at best a nuisance to have to untangle the weights before making each cast, and I would prefer to reserve judgment on the use of conical weights on this type of net until I see one in use. Another drawback to putting our conical, piriform, and spherical weights on a casting-net is their

---

[8] Dr. Tekin Mengi very kindly examined the drawings of the Yassi Ada weights, producing from his collection a modern counterpart for almost every one. His appreciation, from a modern hydrobiologist's point of view, of Aristotle's observations was particularly enlightening.

[9] Dame Juliana Berners, *The Treatyse of Fysshynge with an Angle*. A new critical edition of Dame Berners' treatise is J. McDonald, *The Origins of Angling*, which shows modern copies of these flies on pp. 115ff. An earlier version of the text, the Wagstaff manuscript at Yale University, dated ca. 1450, is also included.

[10] J. W. Hills, *A History of Fly Fishing*, 25; modern copies of these flies are shown in color in McDonald, *Origins of Angling*, pp. 115ff.

[11] For a detailed discussion of each type of net, see the introduction by Mair to his translation of the Loeb Library edition of Oppian, *Halieutica*, pp. xl–xlvi.

unevenness of size. A uniform spread of the thrown net requires a uniform distribution of weights along the circumference, and we do not have enough similar weights from that group for such distribution. The folded-over leads may possibly have been used on a casting-net, though the longer weights would be rather inflexible for this kind of rig. I have seen folded-over weights ranging in length from 2 cm to 5 cm in use on a modern casting-net in Bodrum harbor.

Casting-nets are shown on a lamp in the Hermitage Museum;[12] in a Roman mosaic at Sousse;[13] on a fourth-century glass dish from Bardo;[14] and by Devedjian,[15] Faber,[16] and Siemenz and Fischer.[17]

*Draw-net* (Oppian's type 3, γρῖφος; modern Gk. γριπαρόλι or κωλοβρέχτης; also a small seine, σαγήνη, sometimes called τράτα). This type of net is suitable for grey mullet and other shore fish. Only the smaller nets of this category (worked by one to four men) are conceivable for use on our ship. I have seen as many as forty men hauling in the larger varieties of this type of net.

The draw-net is stretched between two horizontal cords or lines. The upper or float line (σαρδούνας) is hung with corks (φελλοί). The lower or lead line is hung with lead (μολυβίθρες) at equal intervals. The two lines are kept separate from one another by two vertical spreaders (σταλίκια), one at either end of the net. The notched piece of wood MF 53 (p. 289) is probably such a spreader.[18] From each end of the spreader stick a cord (χαλινός) runs to the main line by which the net is hauled in, thus forming a triangle (Fig. 12-17).

The draw-net can use any kind of lead weight. If the net has a pocket or bag at the center (usually only on the larger types), the heavier weights, even pierced stones, are concentrated there. The shortness of the Yassi Ada spreader stick (30 cm from notch to notch) suggests that the net was rather small, entirely in keeping with the total weight of lead available for distribution on the lead line. Any or all of the conical, piriform, spherical, sphendonoidal, and folded-over weights could have been used on such a net.

Draw-nets are depicted in the early-fourteenth-century St. Florian manuscript (complete with leads),[19] as reproduced in Fig. 13-7; the Twenty-Sixth Dynasty tomb of Aba at Deir el Gebrâwi (also complete with leads);[20] and on any number of mosaics, some of the best of which are at Aquileia (fourth century),[21] Leptis Magna (second century),[22] Hippo-Diarrhytus,[23] Antioch (fifth century),[24] and the church of S. Apollinare Nuovo in Ravenna (fifth–sixth century).[25]

*Drift-net* (μανώμενα; Turk. *difana* or *çifte fanyalı ağı*). A final possibility is that some kind of drift-net may have been used. While the ship was at anchor in a roadstead or in a bay through which pelagic fish were passing, the net would have been shot at night and recovered the next morning (modern Gk. ἀπὸ στατοῦ). Such a net would have to have been a compound or trammel net consisting of a finely meshed net between two with larger meshes.[26] Sphendonoidal weights such as LW 17, LW 18, and LW 19 are commonly used on these tangle nets.

## LINE-FISHING

The second most likely use of the Yassi Ada leads is for line-fishing, either with a hand line or, if a rod was used, with a tight line as opposed to a running line (that is, there were no reels, and the line was not free to run when a fish struck at the lure). Indeed, line-fishing may have enjoyed a priority over net-fishing (Plutarch *De Sollertia Animalium* 26). The most thorough surviving premodern description of the making of hook, line, and sinker, together with a listing of the necessary tools, is by Dame Juliana Berners. After a splendid account of

[12] M.-L. Bernhard, "Topographie d'Alexandrie: Le Tombeau d'Alexandre et mausolée d'Auguste," *RA* 47 (1956): 135, fig. 3, after M. Mathieu, *Griekorimskiy i wizantiykiy Egipiet*, sal. 207, no. 2.

[13] P. Gauckler, "Les Mosaïques de l'arsenale a Sousse," *RA* 3, no. 31 (1897): 8–22 and pl. xi.

[14] J. Villette, "Une Coupe chrétienne, en verre gravé, trouvée à Carthage," *MonPiot* 46 (1952): pl. XV opp. p. 136.

[15] Devedjian, *Pêche et pêcheries*, pp. 352, fig. 182, and 353, fig. 183.

[16] Faber, *Fisheries*, pl. 24, "rizzajo."

[17] P. Siemenz and F. Fischer, *Zeitschrift für Fischerei und deren Hilfswissenschaften*, XI, 240–242, s.v. "wurfnetz," and figs. 471–472.

[18] The *tratta* with spreader sticks is shown in use by Faber, *Fisheries*, pl. 17, and by Devedjian, *Pêche et pêcheries*, p. 320, fig. 176.

[19] G. Schmidt, *Die Malerschule von S. Florian*, pl. 52; Stiftsbibliothek, III, 204, Gradual-Sacramentary, fol. 212vo., ca. A.D. 1320–1325. (Professor Schmidt kindly informs me that this scene from the border of the manuscript "was not painted by an Austrian but by a Bolognese illuminator, possibly drawing on a Byzantine model.")

[20] N. de G. Davies, *The Rock Tombs of Deir el Gebrâwi*, pp. 12–14, pl. III.

[21] G. C. Menis, *I mosaici cristiani de Aquileia*, pl. 54.

[22] S. Aurigemma, *L'Italia in Africa: Tripolitania*, vol. I, *I monumenti d'arte decorativa, parte prima—I mosaici*, pls. 94, 96, 97, 110.

[23] P. Gauckler, *Catalogue du Musée Alaoui (Supplément)*, p. 5, pl. V (mosaic no. 231); O. Keller, *Die Antike Tierwelt*, II, 323, fig. 117b.

[24] D. Levi, *Antioch Mosaic Pavements*, I, 323ff.

[25] G. Bovini, *Mosaici di S. Apollinare Nuovo di Ravenna: Il ciclo cristologico*, pl. III (A.D. 429–596), "The Calling of St. Peter and St. Andrew." Note for all references to depictions in mosaics that the quality of representation, especially where putti are shown hauling in the nets, is often very sketchy. The maker of the mosaic cannot be presumed to have had a first-hand acquaintance with the details of net construction.

[26] For details of net construction, see D. B. Hull, *Hounds and Hunting in Ancient Greece*, pp. 10–18 and p. 203 for technical terms. See also Devedjian, *Pêche et pêcheries*, pp. 297–353; and Faber, *Fisheries*, pp. 104–110, pl. 10.

FIG. 13-7. Fishing scene from the St. Florian manuscript.

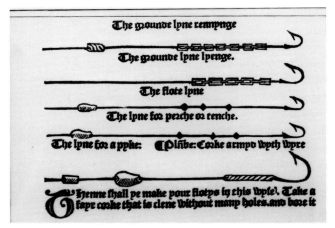

FIG. 13-8. Descriptions of fishing lines from Dame Juliana Berners.

how different sizes of needles are to be selected for all the types of hooks and of how the tempering is to be accomplished, she continues:

> Your lynes muſt be plumbid wyth lede: and ye ſhall wyte yᵗ the nexte plube vnto the hoke ſhall be therfro a large fote and more. And euery plumbe of a quantyte to the gretnes of the lyne. There be thre manere of plubis for a grounde lyne rennynge. And for the flote ſet vpon the grounde lyenge x plumbes joynynge all togider. On the grounde lyne rennynge ix or x ſmalle. The flote plube ſhall be ſo heuey yᵗ the leeſt plucke of ony fyſſhe maye pull it doune in to yᵉ water. And make your plubis rounde and ſmoythe yᵗ they stycke not on ſtonys or on wedys. And for the more vnderſtondynge to theym, here in fygure. [Fig. 13-8][27]

Conical leads (μολυβίθρης) were used on the free end of the line,[28] sometimes attached to a horsehair leader (παράμωλα). For deep-swimming sea perch or sea bream, and for bottom feeders, a plummet (κάθετος; Lat. *perpendiculum*) was used at the end of the line, with the weight resting on the sea bottom (thus the term *ground-line*) and the lure attached to a leader some distance up the line.[29] Multiple horsehair leaders and hooks (four to eight) off the same line, known as ledgers, may be the same rig as that which Oppian calls πολυαγκίστρον, or "many-hooked" (*Halieutica* 3. 78), and which, according to Apostolides, is favored by "amateurs de pêche, dans leurs moments de loisir."[30] (Apostolides' observation could be interpreted as a favorable comment about the quality of a seaman's life aboard our Byzantine ship!)

Only one hook was found in the Yassi Ada wreck, and that, according to the field notebooks, was lost while being carried to the surface; the indirect evidence for the use of hooks is nevertheless strong. Aelian (*De Animalium Natura* 15. 10), while describing the capture of a pelamyd, explains how one of the crew sitting at the stern lets down on either side of the ship lines with hooks (πολυαγκίστρα). Such hooks need to be baited, which may explain the presence of the mussels on board the Yassi Ada ship (p. 293). Since only one side of each mussel shell was present, the mussels may have been opened in advance and one side of the shell of each discarded so that the bait could be attached to the hooks without delay. Given the variety of lead-and-line rigs in use in the Aegean, almost any of the Yassi Ada leads could have been used for some kind of line-fishing.[31]

### LEAD LURES

Perhaps the most interesting weight at Yassi Ada, in that we may with considerable precision suggest its use, is LW 20. This boat-shaped or leaf-shaped lure is identical to modern types used for catching *torik* (Turk.), the 3.5- to 5.5-kg (summer) or 4.5- to 7.0-kg (winter) variant of the pelamyd or bonito (Turk. *palamut*; modern Gk. παλαμύδα; ancient Gk. πηλαμύς or ἀμία).[32] Oppian de-

---

[27] Berners, *Treatyse of Fysshynge*, pp. 57–59 (1832 ed.)

[28] Apostolides, *La Pêche en Grèce*, pp. 57–58.

[29] Mair's commentary on Oppian, *Halieutica*, p. 351.

[30] Apostolides, *La Pêche en Grèce*, p. 58. A further note about horsehair: white horsehair was favored over black as it casts no shadow. Moreover, a stallion's hair was favored over a mare's, the urination of the mare being thought to weaken the hair (Plutarch *De Sollertia Animalium* 24).

[31] A sinker has a threefold purpose: to weight a lure or bait so that it may be cast to a particular spot, to carry the lure or bait to the bottom, and to hold it on the bottom. Round and dipsy sinkers are good over rocky bottoms; pyramid sinkers hold best on sandy bottoms. See R. Scharff, *Standard Handbook of Salt-Water Fishing*, pp. 43, 90, 106.

[32] The nomenclature of this fish is confusing, as it is often confused with the tunny. It is *Thynnus pelamys* (Cuv.) as well as *Pelamys sarda* (C., V. and Bl.). Thus, Turkish *palamut* is to *torik* as Aristotle's pelamyd is to his tunny (*Historia Animalum* 571*a*9). See Thompson, *Glossary of Greek Fishes*, *s.v.* "pelamys," and the discussion by Devedjian, *Pêche et pêcheries*, pp. 16–23, with illustration.

scribes how this fish bites off the hook (*Halieutica* 3. 144) unless, of course, the hook is protected by a wire leader or metal jig such as we have here.[33] The hook in LW 20 is no longer preserved. The lure imitates *Trachurus trachurus*, or scad. It could also be mistaken for a small mackerel (Turk. *istavrit*; modern Gk. σαβρίδι) or an anchovy. It is sometimes augmented by feathers and used for bluefish (*Temnodon saltator* [Cuv.]; Turk. *lüfer*) with a ground-line below the lure and a 40- to 50-g weight at the bottom.[34]

Modern practice is to whirl this lure around one's head and sling it out as much as 25 to 30 m. In the days before nylon, a horsehair line of eighteen to twenty-four strands was used. The lure is retrieved as quickly as possible, arm-length by arm-length. After the strike, the line is retrieved so that the fish is close enough to be hand-netted or harpooned.[35] In an experiment conducted several years ago, Yalçın Koç, a student of mine at Robert College in Istanbul, using precisely this type of lure and this technique, caught about two dozen of these fish in one and one-half hours. Modern practice on the Bosporus and in the Black Sea is to rub mercury on the lures with one's finger several times a day to make them more visible and attractive. The cost of a high shine is, unfortunately, a high level of mercury poisoning. The Yassi Ada leads have not been examined to see if traces of mercury can be found.

LW 21 is possibly a similar type of lure (if a hook had been fitted into one of the small holes at either end). It is

one of the standard sizes in use on the Bosporus. When a small white feather or two is added to such a lead, it can be trailed behind a caique for the flying gurnard (*Trigla lyra*; Turk. *kırlangıç*; modern Gk. φιλομήλα or φιλομήλιτζα; ancient Gk. κόκκυξ).[36] Alternatively it may have been used as are keel-shaped weights and swivels today—as an anti-kink device, particularly necessary when multiple lines and spreaders are in use,[37] as in heavy-duty trolling for tuna.

### THE SPREADER

Often when fishing for red mullet (*Mullus surmuletus*; Turk. *barbunya*; modern Gk. μπαρμπούνι), Aegean fishermen employ a fork-cast (Turk. *çatal köstek*), a spreader which allows the angler to troll or jig two lines from one. Although most modern fork-casts are of wire, examples still exist of heavy lead. LW 22 appears to be such a spreader. The line to the fisherman's hand would be tied through the hole at the top of the triangle. The lines to the two hooks would trail about 13 cm apart, each one tied through a hole at one of the acute angles of the triangle and bedded in the shallow grooves described in the catalog. A similar lead spreader is shown by Devedjian.[38] Not long ago on the Bosporus nine to fourteen braided hairs from a stallion's tail were used to attach a hook to such a spreader. The stiff horsehair would hold the hooks away from the spreader and from each other. The grooves thus serve a practical purpose in keeping the lines parallel.[39]

## *Manufacture of the Fishing Leads*

At Yassi Ada, downslope from the galley, was found a bronze or possibly copper spoon (MF 23), heavily encrusted with lead, the exterior of which is cracked and separated from the rim, suggesting that the spoon may have been dipped into molten lead. This spoon, together with the folded sheet of lead (MF 38) and pieces of casting waste, indicates that lead objects such as the fishing weights were probably cast by crew members as needed to replenish their supply. In Great Britain mussel shells

such as those found at Yassi Ada are still used, embedded in damp sand, for the casting of lead weights (hollowed-out halves of raw potatoes also serve the purpose).[40] Since none of the weights recovered is of mussel-shell shape, some other form of molding must have been used. The lead sheet which appears to be the stock from which the folded-over leads were made is thin enough to be cut with a heavy knife.

[33] See Buchholz, Jöhrens, and Maull, "Jagd und Fischfang," J.171, hook *m*, a four-part jointed leader of twisted wire from Mallia. In the depot at Herculaneum are unpublished parallels, one example of which, with a three-part jointed wire leader, is 35 cm long.

[34] Devedjian, *Pêche et pêcheries*, pp. 37 and 357ff., with fig.

[35] Ibid., pp. 357ff., and p. 362, fig. 191, for illustration of the hand-line rig.

[36] Ibid., p. 363.

[37] L. R. Hardy, ed., *Hardy's Angler's Guide: Coronation Number*, pp. 139ff.

[38] Devedjian, *Pêche et pêcheries*, p. 364, fig. 192; W. E. Davies, *The Techniques of Sea Fishing*, p. 27 (note his three-boom wire paternoster); and Scharff, *Standard Handbook*, pp. 94ff.

[39] Bosporus fishermen, personal communication.

[40] Davies, *Techniques of Sea Fishing*, pp. 25ff., as informed by the commodore of the Dreadnought (London) Sea Anglers' Society.

## Net Making and Net Repair

Fe 94 and Fe 95 (p. 262) are either parts of two net mending forks of iron or two parts of the same fork. Fishermen probably spend more time mending nets than using them. The presence of these forks or needles at Yassi Ada is evidence that nets were indeed in use on the Byzantine ship and in their usual need of repair. The netting needles from Herculaneum on display in the Museo Nazionale in Naples and in the storerooms at Herculaneum are identical to those at Yassi Ada.[41] Moreover, an inspection of Roman nets demonstrates that even the same type of knot was used in antiquity as today.[42]

[41] My thanks to Prof. Dr. Alfonso De Franciscis for providing access to this material. J. J. Diess, *Herculaneum*, p. 102, provides a photograph of some nets and bronze net mending instruments.

[42] The tying of the knot is best shown in Faber, *Fisheries*, pl. 9 and accompanying discussion. See also "Rybolovstvo na Russkom Severe," *Sbornik Muzeya Antropologii i Etnografii* 28 (1972): 75, fig. 2a; and A. Gruvel, *La Pêche dans la préhistoire*, p. 39, fig. 29.

# XIV

## CONCLUSIONS

### George F. Bass

*Some readers of this book will be interested mainly in the economics of Byzantine trade and may have little knowledge of ship construction or its specialized terminology. Others, primarily concerned with details of ship construction, on the other hand, may be unfamiliar with terms commonly used by students of ancient Greek or classical archaeology. In this chapter I attempt to summarize, in language familiar to all, the story of a seventh-century ship as revealed by the evidence detailed in the preceding chapters. Thus, with apology to purists, I will use here such common, though improper, terms as ribs, for I will at the same time use such familiar terms as* pitchers *and* water jar *for oinochoai and pithos. Footnotes are reserved generally for material not previously discussed. It is my hope that a reader studying, say, only anchors will, through this chapter, be able to understand the context of the Yassi Ada anchors without necessarily reading the chapters on pottery or coins, and that an archaeologist using the Yassi Ada pottery for comparative purposes will not have to learn the finer points of hull design.*

Not long before A.D. 625, probably during the first quarter of the seventh century, a cypress keel about 12 m long was set on stocks in an unidentified shipyard.[1] The keel was joined to a high, curving sternpost of the same wood; a stem may also have been of cypress, but it did not last until modern times.

Once the spine of the hull had been completed, the shipwrights went on to construct the sides. They did not, as we would do today, first build a complete skeleton by adding frames (ribs) to the spine and then nail planking to the skeleton. They began, instead, by following the Greco-Roman practice of building up the hull one strake, or strip of planking, at a time, shaping each plank with adzes to fit closely to adjoining ones, and fastening the planks together with mortise-and-tenon joints. The tenons in this ship, however, were not as large, tightly fitted, or closely spaced as those used in earlier Greek and Roman ships, nor were they held in place by wooden pegs driven through them. The shipwrights cut the mortises every 30 to 50 cm near the stern, but up to 90 cm apart elsewhere, and fastened the pine planks together edge to edge by inserting loosely fitted tenons made of oak.

After the hull was built up from the keel in this fashion, one strake at a time, for several rows of planking, elm floors, or short "ribs," were placed inside and secured with iron nails driven through the pine planks from outside. Another four or five strakes were added to bring the hull to the turn of the bilge, and longer floors were inserted. The shell was then completed to the waterline, and the remainder of the ribbing was added. Internal hull planking (ceiling) was installed next, and finally the heavy-timbered hull sides were completed by four pairs of heavier strakes, or wales, bolted to the ribs, with the spaces between them filled by additional planks nailed to the ribs without mortise-and-tenon joining.

---

This chapter was originally written as a talk for a colloquium on ancient trade organized by the Center for Ancient History at the University of Pennsylvania in 1971 and was published, with editorial improvements, in *Scientific American* 225, no. 2 (August, 1971): 22–33. A few changes resulted from further research before the article was reprinted as a chapter in my *Archaeology Beneath the Sea*. It is slightly revised in this, the first annotated version.

[1] We unfortunately have no dates for the wood from which the ship was constructed and thus cannot estimate the hull's age at the time of loss (see chapter 2, p. 31). The areas in which the ship probably was constructed did not lack for forests (H. Antoniadis-Bibicou, *Études d'histoire maritime de Byzance à propos du "thème des caravisiens,"* pp. 22–23).

This transitional stage between ancient and modern hull construction methods was not a sudden development. The hull of a ship built in the fourth century, about 225 years earlier,[2] was made with carefully mortised planking up to the deck level and possibly all the way to the gunwale, and its planks were fixed to the ribs with treenails—long wooden dowels—instead of iron nails; smaller wooden pegs held each tenon securely in place. Even by then, however, the mortise-and-tenon joints were spaced more than 15 cm apart, nearly twice as far apart as those of ships from the turn of the millennium. The seventh-century ship's construction shows, therefore, a continuing decrease, begun two or three centuries earlier, in the amount of labor that ship builders were able or willing to put into their work. The seventh-century shipwright made a further savings of labor and money by using rough half-timbers—halves of trees sawn once lengthwise—both for wales and for part of the inside lining, or ceiling, of his hull.

This use of unfinished timbers and the drift away from mortise-and-tenon construction may reflect the modest amounts private entrepreneurs could invest in shipping;[3] the seventh-century ship was only half the size of ships considered small when Imperial Roman grain carriers plying between Alexandria and Rome carried more than 1,200 tons.[4] The trend was destined to continue. The practice of fastening planks to ribs with iron nails and omitting mortise-and-tenon joints, a building technique found only above the waterline in the seventh-century ship, advanced until the strength of a hull came to depend exclusively on the bonds between the ribs and the planking, as is true today, and mortise-and-tenon hull stiffening disappeared.[5]

Deck beams ran across the width of the seventh-century merchantman's hull, supported at their ends by short L-shaped timbers, or knees, of pine. The ship was completely decked except for the galley area at the stern and a hatch aft of the centrally located mast; there may also have been a smaller hatch forward. Certain deck beams projected through the hull on each side of the ship to form a pair of rectangular structures where the steering oars were mounted.

The finished ship (Fig. 14-1) was just under 20 m long, with a streamlined hull and a beam of only 5.22 m, resulting in a length-to-width ratio of four to one, which is quite slender for a cargo vessel. The fourth-century vessel mentioned above had been beamier; its ratio was roughly two and one-half to one. Swifter merchant vessels were needed in the seventh century, it is believed, to outrun the increased number of hostile ships on the sea.[6]

About the time the slim merchantman was ready for launching, her owner needed the various pieces of gear necessary for outfitting his new vessel. For this purpose he probably visited ship chandlers close to the waterfront in large, vaulted shops, if we may take the nearly contemporaneous harbor facility at the Black Sea port of Tomis as an example. There he could have found his needs—among them, stacked against a wall, iron anchors with removable stocks.[7] The owner bought at least eleven anchors and also obtained a clawlike grapnel, probably for the ship's boat.

Why did he need so many anchors? The likelihood of their theft[8] was not the only reason. Because they

---

[2] G. F. Bass and F. H. van Doorninck, Jr., "A Fourth-Century Shipwreck at Yassi Ada," *AJA* 75 (1971): 27–37; G. F. Bass and F. H. van Doorninck, Jr., "Excavation of a Late Roman Shipwreck at Yassi Ada, Turkey," in *National Geographic Research Reports, 1969 Projects*, pp. 1–11; F. H. van Doorninck, Jr., "The 4th Century Wreck at Yassi Ada: An Interim Report on the Hull," *IJNA* 5 (1976): 115–131; and F. H. van Doorninck, Jr., "Byzantium, Mistress of the Sea: 330–641," in *A History of Seafaring Based on Underwater Archaeology*, ed. G. F. Bass, pp. 137–139.

[3] R. S. Lopez, "The Role of Trade in the Economic Readjustment of Byzantium in the Seventh Century," *DOP* 13 (1959): 79–84, for the rise of independent traders in the seventh century and some of the economic reasons behind their importance. It is my understanding that in the grain fleets, at least, hereditary ship masters were replaced by independent merchants only later in the century, however, after the Arab conquest of Egypt; thus, economic causes for the type of construction used in the Yassi Ada ship should not necessarily outweigh simple technical advances.

[4] L. Casson, "The Size of Ancient Merchant Ships," in *Studi in onore di Aristide Calderini e Roberto Paribeni*, I, 232–238; J. R. Steffy calculates the Yassi Ada ship to have been of about 60 tons burden (p. 86).

[5] The earliest known seagoing vessel built in the "frame-first"

manner without mortise-and-tenon joints is the eleventh-century ship being excavated at Serçe Liman, Turkey (G. F. Bass and F. H. van Doorninck, Jr., "An 11th Century Shipwreck at Serçe Liman, Turkey," *IJNA* 7 [1978]: 119–132); and G. F. Bass, "A Medieval Islamic Merchant Venture," *Archaeological News* 8, nos. 2 and 3 (1979): 84–94. For the social background for this change, see B. M. Kreutz, "Ships, Shipping, and the Implications of Change in the Early Medieval Mediterranean," *Viator* 7 (1976): 79–109.

[6] "To what extent this [the development of smaller, swifter ships] was a direct answer to the small and fast Slavonic monoxyle and Arab dhow, and to what extent it depended on the fact that commercial cargoes were no longer very large, we cannot tell" (Lopez, *DOP* 13 [1959]: 71). The year 626, in which the Yassi Ada ship may have sunk, saw Slavs taking part in an unsuccessful Avar attack on Constantinople (D. Obolensky, "The Empire and Its Northern Neighbors, 565–1018," *CMH* IV, part 1, 482).

[7] V. Canarache, *The Mosaic-Floored Edifice of Tomi*; and V. Canarache, *The Archaeological Museum of Constantza*, pp. 78–85. Due to the untimely death of Mr. Canarache, these two guidebooks (available in a number of languages from the Regional Archaeological Museum of Dobrudja) were the only publications of the site when I visited it in 1970. Now, however, see A. V. Radulescu, "Amfore cu inscriptii de la edificiul roman cu mozaic," *Pontica* 6 (1973): 193–207, for contents of the vaults.

[8] W. Ashburner, *The Rhodian Sea-Law*, pp. cxliii–cxliv, 10–12, 71, 77–80.

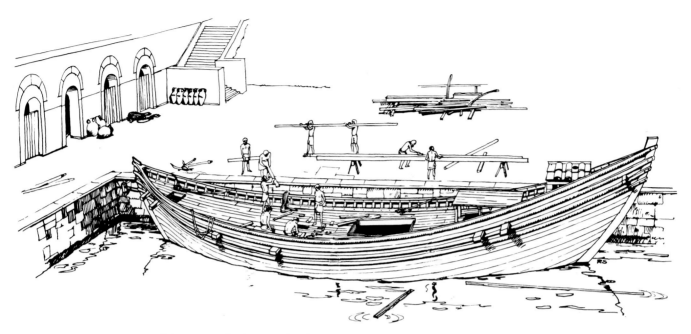

FIG. 14-1. Reconstruction of the Yassi Ada ship. *Richard Schlecht*

were extremely light, the captain must have occasionally found it necessary to use four bower anchors, carried ready for use in the forward quarter of the ship, simultaneously. The shanks and arms of the anchors were quite thin and the flukes poorly developed, so such anchors were undoubtedly often broken. Consequently, the captain carried four spare bowers stacked on the deck nearby. At the bottom of the stack lay three heavier sheet anchors to be used as a last resort. The uniformity of the weights of the anchors suggests that statutes required vessels of various classes to carry a minimum number of anchors of specified sizes, as in later times.

The chandlery patronized by the owner, if it was like that at Tomis, also offered a variety of resins for sale. The ship had already been coated with resin below the waterline, inside and out, but her owner at some point obtained smaller amounts of resin to be melted on board in a cheap cooking pot and applied as needed to seal the pores of clay pitchers and other containers for wine. The Tomis chandler also offered pigments for paint and jars full of iron nails. We do not know whether the owner painted his ship, although ships of earlier times were often described as brightly colored,[9] but we do know that he bought several bags of nails, probably with shipboard repairs in mind. Literary accounts of the period mention skins for covering deck cargo in foul weather as well as sails and hemp rope, and all of these items the owner may have bought at the chandlery.[10] We are certain that he acquired twenty-four oil lamps, perhaps made from molds kept on hand in the chandlery, as was done at Tomis.[11]

The preceding account of the construction and outfitting of the ship is based on archaeological evidence. What can archaeological evidence suggest concerning the ship's crew? The seventh-century or slightly later Rhodian Sea-Law lists a regular ship's company of the day and assigns to each member his proper share in the profits of a successful venture.[12] First is the *naukleros*, the shipowner or captain or both, who receives two shares. Next are the *kybernetes*, the helmsman; the *proreus*, the "prow officer"; the *naupegos*, the ship's carpenter; and the *karabites*, the boatswain. Each of these officers receives a share and one-half. The *nautai*, or seamen, who follow on the roster receive a single share each. Last is the lowliest member of the crew, the *paraskharites*, possibly the cook;[13] his stake in the voyage is

[9] L. Casson, *Ships and Seamanship in the Ancient World*, pp. 211–212.

[10] Ashburner, *Rhodian Sea-Law*, pp. clxxxiv–clxxxv, 80–81, 92.

[11] It is interesting that molds for making lamps were found in what I consider to be a chandlery at Tomis, for although today a chandler is most often thought of as one who supplies ships with their needs, he is primarily one who makes or sells candles. The importance of lamps to ancient mariners is suggested by the numbers of them on excavated shipwrecks.

[12] Ashburner, *Rhodian Sea-Law*, pp. clxvi ff., 1, 57–59; the shares might vary and were paid by the shipowner.

[13] Ibid., pp. 58–59, states that there is no proof that the *para-*

only half a share. A merchant could also have on board two boys, but only if he paid their fare.[14]

The *naukleros* of the Yassi Ada vessel was named Georgios. The finest scale on the ship, a bronze balance of the kind called a steelyard, had his name punched in it in Greek letters to read, "Georgiou Presbyterou Nauklerou," which can be translated to mean that the steelyard belonged to "Georgios Elder (or Senior), Owner/ Sea Captain." This inscription presents problems in spite of its simplicity. Christianity was a strong element in every aspect of Byzantine life; was Captain Georgios a *presbyteros*, an elder in the church? Or does the word have some other meaning here? Several passages in the Rhodian Sea-Law indicate that sometimes there was more than one *naukleros* aboard a vessel.[15] How would one have distinguished between two captains? Should Georgios' title perhaps be read as "Georgios, Senior Sea Captain"? In the previous century the name of one Nicholas Naukleros Mesatos had been inscribed on a baptismal basin in a church in southwestern Asia Minor. *Mesatos* is derived from *mesos*, meaning "middle," and it has been suggested that Nicholas might have been something such as an "intermediate sea captain"—that is, an officer junior to a senior sea captain.[16] In support of this theory it should be noted that *mesonautai* are mentioned in the literature of the sixth century, and it is believed that the term was applied to a junior grade of *nautai*, or regular seamen;[17] today, of course, we have lieutenant commanders and commanders, rear admirals and vice admirals.

The next officer listed in the sea-law, the helmsman, possibly stood on a high wooden platform just forward of the galley in order to man the giant steering oars, whose positions we know. The prow officer, if one was on board, may have had charge of the anchors.

The ship's carpenter stored his tools in a locker in the galley's forward partition wall. These tools included adzes, hammers, chisels, gouges, a caulking iron, punches, drill bits, a compass or dividers, files, an awl, nails, and a bronze belt buckle that may have been used on a tool belt. With these tools the carpenter was equipped with everything needed for jobs ranging from minor repairs to the construction of a new hull. A folded sheet of lead and some waste from lead casting suggest that various fittings and patches, as well as additional fishing weights, were made on board the ship.

If Byzantine boatswains were responsible for the ship's boat, then the grapnel stowed aft of the galley is evidence of a kind that Georgios' crew included a boatswain, who also would have been responsible for rigging and cables. Near the grapnel were kept fishing gear and, clearly separated from the carpenter's kit, another group of iron tools: axes, a spade, three billhooks, and a mattock. These last items appear to be boatswain's stores that would have been needed by a landing party to collect firewood for the cook and to enlarge springs to obtain fresh water.

As for ordinary seamen who may have served on board, we can not guess. In American days of sail, square-rigged ships only slightly smaller than Georgios' merchantman often had a crew of no more than three men and a boy.[18] There may not have been many ordinary seamen in the crew to eat further into the profits of the venture. Indeed, there may have been none.

The poorly paid cook, if that is what the *paraskharites* was, worked in a cramped galley located at the extreme stern of the ship and set as low as possible within the hull, with an overall floor area barely 1.5 m by less than 3 m. The galley had a deckhouse superstructure roofed with tiles, including one tile with a circular hole to let the smoke from the galley fire escape. The precise arrangement of the hearth where the fire burned is not reconstructed with certainty. We do know that it was built of square tiles and iron bars, and it stood in the port half of the galley. Probably its tiles formed a low firebox open at the top and covered by a grill of iron rods that supported the round-bottomed cooking pots. All of the cooking would have been done here, for the Rhodian

*skharites* was the cook, and he questions the low pay. The word means literally "the one by the grill or hearth (ἐσχάρα)," however, and the Yassi Ada ship surely had such a grill or hearth in its galley. Thus, there is little doubt in my mind about the identification. I thank Eustathius Katsaros-Liossis for bringing this to my attention in an ancient seafaring seminar at Texas A&M University.

[14] Ibid., pp. 2, 59.

[15] Ibid., pp. 14, 26–27, 85, 105.

[16] On January 26, 1962, R. M. Harrison wrote to me from Bryn Mawr College: "In June 1959 I discovered a 6th-century monastery church at Karabel in central Lycia (reported in *ILN*, 20th August, 1960, and in *Anatolian Studies* X [1960], pp. 26–28; yet another reference, with a correction concerning the inscription in *Anatolian Studies* XI [1961], p. 6); a dedicatory inscription on the baptismal basin refers to a Nicholas 'ΝΑΥΚΛΗΡΟC MECATOC.'" In that letter Professor Harrison suggested to me that MECATOC is rank and simply a cognate form of MECOC. However, on January 21, 1963, he wrote to me from Lincoln College, Oxford, that he then felt the inscription should be translated "of Nicholas the sea-captain, son of Mesatos." He went on to say, "There was a 5th century B.C. Tragedian called Mesatos (cf. A. Lesky, in *Hermes* [1954], pp. 1 ff.)." I am deeply grateful to Professor Harrison for bringing all of this to my attention, even though in the case of Nicholas he no longer feels that MECATOC denotes rank.

[17] J. Rougé, *Recherches sur l'organisation du commerce maritime en Méditerranée sous l'empire romain*, p. 216; Seymour Mann, student in a course on ancient seafaring I gave at the University of Houston, asked if *mesonautai* might be "midshipmen."

[18] Personal communication from J. Richard Steffy regarding sizes of crews of later sailing ships.

Sea-Law stipulates that passengers were not to chop fire-wood or fry fish on board.[19]

The possible presence of passengers is suggested by the large number of cooking utensils, usually supplied by crew and passengers,[20] found in the galley. The cook had at his disposal more than twenty cooking pots, many fire-blackened, stowed near the hearth; the lamps in use on board were kept in the same area. Elsewhere in the galley, on shelves and perhaps also in the galley's for-ward locker, was a quantity of dining wares. Someone on board was evidently not laggard in the fashions of the day: four of the bowls are the oldest precisely dated ex-amples of Byzantine lead-glazed pottery. Besides these bowls there were eight or nine plain red plates or dishes, three cups, from three to six jars with spouts (two with lids), and eighteen pitchers. Most of the pitchers were coated inside with resin, which indicates that they were used to hold wine. A further array of seventeen storage jars of various shapes and sizes, doubtless including one or two filled with lamp oil, and possibly the ship's large water jar were kept on the starboard side of the galley.

The galley also contained a number of copper pitch-ers and a copper tray or bake pan, a stone mortar and pestle, a millstone, a whetstone, a spoon with a lead-coated bowl, and three steelyards. More valuable items, including a supply of money, a set of balance-pan weights, glassware, a bronze censer (possibly for provid-ing incense with meals or for sanctifying the ship as we know was done in more recent times), and unused lamps were most likely stored in the galley's forward locker, which may have been fitted with an iron-sheathed wooden padlock.

The coarser jugs and pitchers and two copper cal-drons were stowed in a storage section at the very stern of the galley, near the grapnel and probable boatswain's stores. There, too, were three bronze belt buckles and a metal belt-tip sheath, perhaps from changes of clothing.

We have seen the ship constructed and outfitted, and we have seen evidence of her personnel. What can be said of the ship's last voyage?

Georgios, in addition to being the captain, may have been the owner and a merchant-venturer as well.[21] The basis for this conjecture is the fact that the steelyard bearing his name is an item of merchant's equipment. It should be mentioned that later Venetian statutes re-quired that shipowners supply every vessel with a weighing device;[22] perhaps even during Byzantine times a captain, merchant or not, may have needed to carry his own balance to show that his freight charges were cor-rect. If we may assume, however, that Georgios was the owner as well as master, we can calculate with some con-fidence his total investment in the ship and all its stores.

The Rhodian Sea-Law indicates that the seventh-century cost of fully outfitted shipping ran about 50 so-lidi per six and one-half tons' capacity.[23] On this basis Georgios' investment would have been some 460 solidi, a substantial sum in times when a shipyard caulker might earn 18 solidi for a year's work and less skilled la-borers might receive only 7 or 8 solidi.[24] Might this in-vestment have been all Georgios could afford, leaving him with no capital to invest in a cargo? A shipload of wine, for example, would have cost 70 or so solidi at then-current prices.[25]

One piece of evidence suggested, at first, that such was the case. A possible lead seal on board bears a cru-ciform monogram of the name Ioannis, or John. An em-poros, or merchant, aboard Georgios' ship, traveling with him to pay the freight charge and handle the sale of goods at the vessel's destination, would have needed

[19]Ashburner, *Rhodian Sea-Law*, pp. cxlix, cl, 2, 61. These pas-sages of the sea-law suggest to Ashburner (p. cl) that "the passenger supplied himself with food and did his own cooking." This does not seem necessarily to be the case. Why does fish, and no other food, deserve such a rule, presumably to prevent fire aboard ship? Countless times in the Mediterranean I have seen sailors, passengers, and mem-bers of my own staff fish from small boats or the diving barge. These fishermen take pride in preparing their limited catches as tidbits for themselves and their friends, although all of their other meals are pre-pared and eaten communally. Fresh fish is considered a special treat and is often cooked separately.

[20]Ibid., pp. 87–88.

[21]Ashburner writes: "In the Roman empire as in modern times the parties to the maritime adventure are sharply distinguished. The shipowner employs the mariners and lets the ship to the merchant. What makes it so difficult sometimes to understand the medieval au-thorities is that these positions are continually melting into one an-other. The shipowners are often themselves the mariners, and, while in their capacity of mariners they divide one part of the profits, where that system of payment existed, in their capacity of owners they share the other part. The mariners again may be themselves merchants: they, or some of them, load the ship with their own goods, so that you may have a case where the ship is owned, navigated, and freighted by substantially the same persons" (ibid., p. cxxix). See also ibid., p. cxxxii for four different meanings of the word *naukleros*. The same overlap-ping of roles is described in A. H. M. Jones, *The Later Roman Em-pire, 284–602*, II, 866.

[22]Ashburner, *Rhodian Sea-Law*, p. clxxxviii.

[23]Ibid., pp. clii–clv, 3, 63–64; Jones, *Later Roman Empire* II, 868.

[24]Antoniadis-Bibicou, *Études d'histoire maritime*, p. 25, gives salaries for the early eighth century. They are similar to those of the sixth century, when a laborer or a private soldier earned about 7 solidi a year (Jones, *Later Roman Empire* II, 858). Thus, it would seem that they are fairly representative of seventh-century salaries as well.

[25]A fairly accurate estimate of the total volume of wine in the cargo, based on the assumption that all amphoras were full, is 74,000 pints (35,000 l). Prices for wine in the fifth and sixth centuries are found in Jones, *Later Roman Empire* I, 446–447: 200 *sextarii* (pints) to the solidus (a rather high price in countries that produced little wine). However, see Antoniadis-Bibicou, *Études d'histoire maritime*, p. 129, for risks of converting medieval measures into modern units.

such a seal. If John was indeed a merchant or merchant's agent, he would have been required by law to ask other merchants who had sailed with Georgios whether or not the ship was in good condition.[26] When he heard that it was, he and Georgios would have entered into a contract. Georgios then would have been allowed to take on board only water, provisions, and necessary ship's gear, unless there were spare room for additional cargo after John had loaded the ship.[27]

This attractive theory rests on the slight possibility that the seal was for official use.[28] More probably it was a button that could have belonged to any passenger or crew member. No other archaeological evidence points to the presence or absence of an *emporos* on board. Thus, Georgios could have acted as merchant as well as captain.

One can visualize next, regardless of his source of capital, Georgios supervising a procession of porters carrying aboard the cargo of more than 850 amphoras and passing them down through the hatch into the hold.[29] Most of the jars were large and globular, a relatively new shape that was difficult to handle but which was made practical by the newly introduced wine-thief. These globular jars held wine, some of it possibly spiced. Other jars were smaller and more elongated; we do not know if they contained wine or another commodity. We assume that all the jars were full when placed on board, but we cannot be certain;[30] not all of them were lined with resin, the customary method of waterproofing porous clay, and only a hundred or so stoppers were found (admittedly the remaining stoppers could have been of perishable material).[31] However, if all the jars were filled

with liquid, say wine, the cargo would have weighed some 37 tons.

The cook's stores probably would have been loaded at the same time. Presumably the cook saw to it that his largest jar had been filled with the common store of fresh water[32] and checked his supply of lamp oil. Perhaps at the same time, or later on the voyage, he took on goat or sheep meat, perhaps live animals to be butchered on board. Fresh rations also included a basketful of mussels; their empty shells, carefully nested within one another, were later set aside for some unknown use.

The ship could now be under way. The prow officer—if such was his responsibility—lashed a pair of anchors to the port gunwale and another to the starboard gunwale near the bow and stacked the remaining seven just forward of the mast. Although there is no archaeological evidence for it, we may assume, from seventh-century practice, that port taxes were paid and that the ship soon passed a customs point where export duty was charged.[33]

Meanwhile, the captain had placed in the galley certain valuables, including a money purse or two. These held at least sixty copper folles (coins worth a small fraction of a solidus) and sixteen small gold pieces; the total value of the coins was just a little more than 7 solidi. Was this a ship's fund or money deposited by a passenger? The Rhodian Sea-Law declares: "If a passenger comes on board and has gold, let him deposit it with the captain. If he does not deposit it and says 'I have lost gold or silver,' no effect is to be given to what he says, since he did not deposit it with the captain."[34] If one is to try to answer the question, one needs to know something about the purchasing power of the solidus.

Seven solidi represented a year's wage for some kinds of labor at slightly earlier and later dates; early in the eighth century, for example, a blacksmith earned three-quarters of a solidus per month.[35] Early in the seventh century a cloak might cost from 1 to 3 solidi, and later in the century 1 solidus would buy four cheap blankets.[36] Food was much less dear. One sixth-century figure gives 5 solidi as the cost of a year's rations for one man; in the years when our ship made its final voyage, a loaf of bread cost 3 folles.[37] The money found in the purses would have fed a crew of fifteen for a month with something left over, not even taking into consideration

[26] Ashburner, *Rhodian Sea-Law*, pp. clxxxii, 18–19, 91–93.

[27] Ibid., pp. cl, 25, 102.

[28] An almost identical seal is published by V. Laurent, "Bulletin de sigillographie byzantine," *Byzantion* 6 (1931): 827, fig. 12. For use of seals for merchandise, see H. Antoniadis-Bibicou, *Recherches sur les douanes à Byzance: L'"Octava," le "kommerkion," et les commerciaires*, pp. 158, 165; and also G. Schlumberger, *Sigillographie de l'empire byzantin*, pp. 10–11.

[29] In medieval times, at least, longshoremen protected their jobs as zealously as they do today. Stevedores, rather than seamen, packed cargoes in ships' holds, with *naukleroi* making certain that the lading did not endanger their ships (Ashburner, *Rhodian Sea-Law*, pp. clviii, clxxvi).

[30] Although the contents of only sixteen randomly selected globular amphoras were sieved for organic remains in 1980, nine contained grape seeds, suggesting that most or all globular amphoras carried wine. All of the smaller, elongated amphoras were cleaned of mud long before we learned to detect seeds in them.

[31] See A. Tchernia, P. Pomey, and A. Hesnard, *L'Épave romaine de la Madrague de Giens (Var.)*, p. 38, for a brief discussion of the conditions under which cork stoppers were preserved on another wreck. H. E. Winlock, in his work with W. E. Crum, *The Monastery of Epiphanius at Thebes*, I, 79–80, describes Coptic amphora stoppers of black earth and chopped straw.

[32] Ashburner, *Rhodian Sea-Law*, pp. cl, cli.

[33] Antoniadis-Bibicou, *Recherches sur les douanes*, pp. 78, 81, 85, 91–92.

[34] Ashburner, *Rhodian Sea-Law*, pp. 3, 19–20, 62, 94.

[35] Antoniadis-Bibicou, *Études d'histoire maritime*, p. 25.

[36] Jones, *Later Roman Empire* I, 445–448.

[37] A. N. Stratos, *Byzantium in the Seventh Century*, p. 176.

the evidence that the ship's company supplemented its provisions en route with fresh fish. It therefore seems likely that the coins were the ship's victualing money; with port and customs taxes already paid, there would have been no need to risk more cash at sea.[38]

The seventy-odd coins enable us today to pinpoint the date of the voyage at about A.D. 625 or 626. A dozen of the coins were too badly preserved to allow identification. Of the remainder, only two were minted earlier than the reign of Emperor Heraclius (A.D. 610–641). The latest coin in the group was minted in the sixteenth year of the emperor's reign—that is, in A.D. 625/626. We may safely assume that the ship last sailed in the same year or quite soon thereafter.

The weighing equipment for the voyage was also stowed in the galley cupboard or close to it. The balance-pan weights, made of bronze inlaid with silver, came in a wooden tray that held them in a graduated series in cylindrical pockets. Seven of the original nine weights were recovered; in addition, we found what may be a fragment of the balance itself. The bronze steelyard beam that bears Georgios' name was one of three scales of this kind on board.

Georgios' steelyard beam is decorated with a boar's head at one end and the head of another animal, possibly a dog or lion, at the other. It has two fulcrum points and two calibrated scales, one each for heavy and for light loads; the counterweight is a lead-filled bust of the goddess Athena similar to those carried on ships lost off Sicily and in the Dardanelles during the same period.[39] This bronze steelyard beam, and another that is in good enough condition to be legible, are calibrated in terms of a pound that was equal to 315 g (our pound troy, which is 373 g, is the closest modern equivalent; our pound avoirdupois is 453 g), seemingly the same lightweight pound used as the unit of measurement for the ship's anchors. The same unit is very close to one determined earlier

from weights of fifth-century and sixth-century Byzantine times.

Curiously, the balance-pan weights represent an entirely different system. Most are clearly marked; they include a 1-*libra*, or 1-pound, weight; a 6-*unciae*, or 6-ounce, weight; and 3-ounce, 2-ounce, and 1-ounce weights. Two smaller weights are unmarked: one of 3 *nomismata* (6 *nomismata* normally equaled 1 *uncia*) and the other of 1 *nomisma*. This is possibly the most complete set of Byzantine weights in existence, and their pound is not the standard "light" 315-g one, but an extremely low pound of 284 g. Furthermore, it is a pound divided into fourteen ounces instead of the customary twelve, and its ounce is divided into seven *nomismata* instead of six.

These unusual values are not the result of any alteration in the original weights as a consequence of their long submersion. Each of the weights in the set, give or take a fraction of a gram, is consistent with all the others; in every case the ounce is 20.45 g. It happens that an ounce of this weight was the Byzantine standard for gold coinage; the standard was established in the time of Constantine the Great (A.D. 272–337) on the basis of the old Roman pound (327.45 g). In this coinage-weight system, however, there were sixteen ounces to the pound instead of fourteen. Only one other 14-ounce pound is known: during the fourth century a "heavy" pound divided into fourteen ounces instead of twelve was used in the mining of gold in order to increase state revenues from mine leases. All of this, however, can have nothing to do with the standard of the balance-pan weights on the ship. At present that standard remains unexplained.

The ship carried one more balance weight—a small pendant of yellow glass that is pierced for stringing. It is so similar in appearance to other Byzantine glass weights that it must have been one. The pendant is shaped like a coin, and pressed into the glass is another cruciform monogram, this one giving the name Theodoros. Such weights are thought to have been used to weigh gold coins, although the weights of the glass pieces seldom correspond to the weights of any coins then in circulation. The discrepancy is explained on the grounds that the glass pieces have lost weight as a result of corrosion.[40]

With all of these valuables stored safely, the ship continued her voyage. It seems safe to state, on the basis of the coins alone, that the voyage was from north to

---

[38] On these points I am in disagreement with most numismatists I have consulted. No ancient merchant ship yet excavated, to my knowledge, has yielded any substantial number of coins; the Yassi Ada seventh-century ship seems an exception because it yielded more than most. It seems unlikely that in each of dozens of cases the crews escaped with most or all of the money on board at the times of disaster. It would seem, instead, that little cash was risked at sea. However, Joan Fagerlie, in fn. 10 in chapter 7, provides a strong argument against my opinion.

[39] F. Papò, "Lo Scandaglio come una bomba," *Mondo Sommerso*, September, 1963, pp. 123–124. Metropolitan Museum of Art Acc. No. 61.112; "According to the vendor this was found in the Dardanelles" (personal communication from Thomas P. F. Hoving, February 26, 1962; I thank Mr. Hoving for furnishing unpublished photographs of the piece at that time). For a more recent study of similar weights, see C. W. J. Eliot, "A Bronze Counterpoise of Athena," *Hesperia* 45 (1976): 163–170.

[40] The presence of this glass weight on board should eventually be evaluated in comparison with the dozen or more Arab glass weights that have appeared on the eleventh-century wreck at Serçe Liman, Turkey (see Bass and van Doorninck, *IJNA* 7 [1978]: 126, for the four weights excavated during the 1977 campaign).

south. All the identifiable coins but one, a very early coin from Alexandretta ad Issum on what is now the Levantine coast of Turkey, were minted in the north at Constantinople, Thessalonica, Nicomedia, and Cyzicus. Although these mints were major ones whose coins might be found in any ship, their overwhelmingly northern provenance suggests that the home port of the ship was also a northern one.

The pottery in the galley strengthens this assumption. Fully half the lamps are Asia Minor types, with their best parallels coming from Ephesus, Miletus, Samos, Smyrna, Troy, and Delos; similar lamps have also been found on Chios. Seven of the lamps are of a type common to western Bulgaria, Romania, Thrace, and the Hellespont; a number of counterparts for this type exist also from excavations in Constantinople. The remainder of the two dozen lamps cannot yet be assigned a provenance, but, as with the coins, none of them seems to have come from west, south, or east of the point where the ship sank.

Other wares from the galley also find their best parallels to the north. The lead-glazed bowls speak of Constantinople, and other pottery is similar to the ware of Chios and of two Black Sea ports: Histria and Tomis. The plain red plates are believed to be African in origin, but such plates were so popular and widespread in the Mediterranean that they were available almost anywhere.[41]

The cargo amphoras on board seem also to have a northern origin, although their exact place of manufacture remains unknown. The best parallels for all the amphora types in the ship are found in sites along the western coast of the Black Sea, but there they are considered to be imports from another region. The amphoras which held resins, iron nails, and pigments at the Tomis chandlery are similar, but not identical, to those on the ship; the slight differences are perhaps explained by their slightly earlier date. Is there a region which exported these products as well as wine? Or were old wine containers simply reused for shipping other materials after their original contents had been drained? In fact, how far and wide were empty amphoras, whether new or used, shipped? Today one sees vessels plying the Aegean whose holds and decks are crowded with pottery containers. The pots are empty; they are the cargo. The rather large number of tile-carrying and plate-carrying

shipwrecks in the Mediterranean, some from the Byzantine period, prove that other ceramic products were shipped instead of being fabricated where they were needed. Why do we assume that all amphoras found on ancient wrecks were full at the time the ships sank? Is it not plausible that empty containers were also shipped from manufacturing centers, in this case perhaps Constantinople where many fragments of the Yassi Ada types have been excavated? Future analyses of clays used in Byzantine times may answer these questions.

A major clue to the route of the ship remains. The vessel, beyond any reasonable doubt, was sailing in a southeasterly direction before a *meltem* wind when she hit the reef at Yassi Ada, tore a hole in her bottom, and sank almost immediately on the southeast side of the reef.

The ship's destination is less certain. She was sailing toward Cos, Cnidus, and Rhodes, all wine-producing centers, yet grape seeds in her amphoras suggest a cargo of wine.[42] Maybe she carried some special wine from the north, perhaps from Thasos, where similar amphoras are well known from excavations.

Regardless of her destination, the final moments of the ship can be imagined with near certainty.[43] As she sailed southward along the western coast of Asia Minor, her sail swelled by a following *meltem*, Halicarnassus was only a few hours away.

The helmsman steered a course that would keep him as near the small, flat island as he felt was safe. From his low ship he could not see the change of color in the water ahead. Whitecaps camouflaged the breakers in their midst.[44] The ship hit the reef, tearing a hole in her bottom, but continued her course to the reef's far side.

The helmsman probably tried to steer directly for the island, little more than a hundred meters away. But already his vessel was under the lee of its shore. Her sails must have fallen slack. She lost her way in deep water less than a hundred meters from the shallow bottom on which she might have settled.

She drifted downward and landed on an even keel, still pointing her bow toward the island. Then she listed to port. Shipworms began their attack on her unprotected starboard side. Eventually the starboard an-

---

[41] All of these clues, based on similarities in pottery, depend on the fortunes of excavation and publication; some of the best parallels were excavated within a few years before my study of the pottery in 1969, changing tentative conclusions I had reached in the early 1960's when I first sought parallels; perhaps other parallels in other places have been excavated more recently. Future analyses of clays may further indicate that pottery types common to a region were not manufactured there but were imported from elsewhere.

[42] Supra, n. 30.

[43] The voyage most probably took place between the end of May and the end of September and almost certainly between early March and early November. See Jones, *Later Roman Empire* II, 843 (citing Vegetius) and 1353 n. 45 for the sailing seasons.

[44] The description is not as fanciful as it might seem, for it is based on my own near sinking of a similar-sized vessel, Mehmet Turguttekin's 20-m trawler *Kardeshler*, on the same reef in 1967. Only Captain Mehmet's prompt action in taking the wheel from me and steering between Yassi Ada and the reef averted disaster.

chors, held high above the seabed, broke free and dropped to the sand. The hearth tiles fell to the tilting galley floor and slid into a heap along its port edge. The galley roof, as its wooden supports were eaten away, collapsed, spilling its tiles below. The forward wall of the galley remained long enough for the cargo in the hold to become stabilized, but when it finally came apart, the contents of the cupboards built into it fell into the wreckage. At last no exposed wood remained, and sand drifted over the small objects from the galley. The cargo of amphoras, a pile of anchors, and terra-cotta tiles were all that remained visible.

# DESCRIPTION OF THE BALLAST STONES

## John A. Gifford

Field study of the ballast stones (chapter 3, pp. 63–64) indicates that the three most common rock types recovered include
1. A yellowish grey (5 Y 8/1) partly recrystalized microcrystalline limestone (calcilutite or micrite).
2. A well-indurated, medium grey (N 5) shale containing laminae of darker (N 3) carbonaceous shale averaging 1 mm in thickness.
3. A greenish grey (5 G 5/1) calcareous subgraywacke composed of well-sorted, medium sand–sized quartz, mica, and feldspar grains and occasional angular rock fragments in a calcareous/feruginous matrix.

Two less common types noted are
1. A slightly metamorphosed dark grey (N 3) limestone containing secondary hydrothermal calcite veins (low-grade marble).
2. A greyish yellow green (5 GY 7/2) feldspathic sandstone.

All these rock types are most commonly present as compact, well-rounded, large cobbles (128–256 mm diameter). No attempt was made to determine quantitatively the depositional environment of these rocks (by grain size and sorting measurements), since the recovered sample, while more than large enough for statistical treatment, may well have been biased toward a particular size range either when the rocks were originally collected for placement in the hold or, to a lesser degree, during the disintegration of the wreck before its burial. However, the size and shape of the recovered ballast stones only admit two possible high-energy depositional environments: a cobble beach or the coarse alluvial fill characteristic of the outwash deposits of many intermittent stream valleys of eastern Mediterranean coastlines.

Assuming these five rock types were collected at the same locality, it might be possible to determine their source area if some definitive petrographic attribute were present, such as a distinctive suite of minerals in the sandstones or diagnostic microfossils in the limestones. These rocks are notably nondistinctive, however. Based on available geological information from Greece and Turkey, the ballast stones could have come from any number of coastal localities, excepting several Aegean islands that would not, in any event, intuitively be considered as likely ports of call. Moreover, a detailed survey of coastal areas for the source of the ballast stones could only be undertaken with the assumption that that source had not been dispersed by coastal processes or buried by more recent sedimentary deposits.

# ANCHOR METALLURGY

## D. E. DELWICHE

THE iron sample taken from An 1 was studied metallographically and was analyzed for composition in the hope of characterizing the material well enough to identify the method of manufacture and possible source of the iron. A microstructural examination and compositional analyses by both a wet chemical method and a spectrographic technique revealed the iron to be a wrought material of high purity. With a density of 7.807 g/cm$^3$, it is the product of a well-developed Roman iron-making technology which remained essentially unchanged until well into the seventeenth century. Attempts to speculate on the source of the metal or the ore from which the metal was smelted were not successful. Iron composition is strongly influenced by many process variables, including (1) processing temperature, (2) fire-brick (refractory material) contamination, (3) the puddling techniques used, and (4) the composition of the flux used for slag removal.

The sample was an irregularly shaped mass of oxidized ferrous material perhaps 15 cm long by about 5 cm wide. Three sections, 1.5–2 cm thick, were cut from one end of the sample for use in metallurgical studies (Fig. B-1). Sectioning revealed that the sample had been heavily oxidized, with perhaps only three-fourths of the total mass being metallic iron. Three properties of particular interest were microstructure, material density, and chemical composition. The first slice was used for optical micrography, while the remaining two slices were also observed by optical microscope to check for microstructural uniformity. The second slice was subjected to a spectrographic analysis for the determination of trace metals, and the third slice was used for both a rough density measurement and wet chemical analysis.

Initial studies were made by microscopic examination. The sample wafers were ground, polished, and

FIG. B-1. Sample sections of unoxidized anchor iron from An 1.

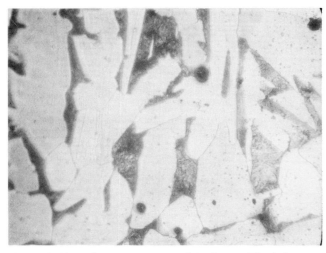

FIG. B-2. Typical microstructure of An 1 iron. The light areas are ferrite and the dark regions are pearlite. The structure is that of a hand-puddled wrought iron remarkably free of slag inclusions.

etched to reveal the microstructure under the metallurgical microscope. Fig. B-2 is a typical microphotograph taken at 300X. It reveals that the material has a pearlitic and ferritic structure with a wide range of grain sizes, the result of the hand puddling process at temperatures of 1100°–1150° C. The material appears to be quite free of slag inclusions. The microstructure is that of a wrought iron with a characteristically low carbon content, typical of an iron produced by technology in use before the seventeenth century. There is no evidence of quench hardening, as one would expect, since this sample came from the core of the original iron mass and would have been unaffected by any rapid surface cooling process.

In order to estimate the original weight of the anchors of known general dimensions, it was necessary to determine the density of the iron. An initial rough check was made to determine the density by weight and volume measurements. To prepare the sample, the lower-density iron oxide was carefully chipped away from the iron core. The density was estimated to be 7.22 g/cm³, a value which was unexpectedly low since the material has a microstructure relatively free of included slag. The low value undoubtedly was due to the inadequate separation of the oxide from the sample. This value was not used in the final weight calculations; a more reliable density figure was derived from composition calculations.[1]

Chemical analysis of the iron was determined by two techniques: a conventional wet chemical analysis for major constituents and a more qualitative nondestructive spectrographic laser technique for determination of trace elements.[2] The wet chemical analysis resulted in the following determination: carbon, 0.07 percent; manganese, <0.01 percent; phosphorus, 0.06 percent; sulfur, 0.008 percent; and silicon, 0.14 percent.

The spectrographic technique identified trace elements, thus supplementing the findings of the wet chemical method. Its results are presented in the first row of Table B-1. Although the determinations of trace elements are rather qualitative, the findings are felt to be quite representative. For comparison, the anchor iron is listed together with the compositions of two other ancient irons and two irons dating from more recent times. The anchor iron by comparison is a wrought material of high purity. The manganese content is low, indicating that no deliberate attempt was made to harden the material by adding a manganese ore to the furnace charge. The analysis of Table B-1 was used to derive the density figure for the anchor iron of 7.807 g/cm³, which has a high confidence level and was used to calculate the weights of the original anchors.

There is much information in the literature on the ancient art of iron smelting that describes the processes by which iron was manufactured and the techniques that were used to forge it into utilitarian shapes.[3] This information indicates that the Byzantine anchor iron is not unique in any way but represents a sample of iron similar to known Roman types. The iron was found to be a relatively pure wrought material with irregularly shaped grains in a wide range of sizes typical of hand-puddled iron produced at temperatures in the neighborhood of 1150° C. Only gross composition information is reported in the literature with frequency; information on trace elements is very sketchy. With the information available, analyses which include trace elements are presently of restricted value because of the process variables which tend to obscure any useful source information. Attempts to use data on trace elements to gain insight into the origin of metals or the patterns of iron trade of the ancient world have met with frustration. However, it is hoped that the information presented here will make some contribution to eventual successes in attempts at identifying the sources of iron used by the ancients.

---

[1] This value of 7.22 g/cm³ was used, however, for the calculated weights of the anchors given in G. F. Bass, ed., *A History of Seafaring Based on Underwater Archaeology*, p. 140.

[2] The analyses were conducted by Jeanine Bonini of the Jarrell-Ash Division of the Fisher Scientific Company.

[3] L. Aitchison, *A History of Metals*, I, 111; R. J. Forbes, *Metallurgy in Antiquity*, p. 35; G. Agricola, *De Re Metallica*, trans. H. C. Hoover and L. H. Hoover, pp. 420–427; H. R. Schubert, *History of the British Iron and Steel Industry from c. 450 B.C. to A.D. 1775*, pp. 26–28; and O. Davies, *Roman Mines in Europe*, pp. 228–244.

TABLE B-1. Chemical Analyses of Wrought Irons.

| Iron Source | Constituent (percentage) | | | | | | | | | |
|---|---|---|---|---|---|---|---|---|---|---|
| | C | P | S | Si | Na | Mg | Al | Ca | Ti | V |
| Seventh-century anchor* | .07 | .06 | .008 | .14 | .005 | .005 | .05 | .005 | .005 | .01 |
| Roman bloom— ca. A.D. 300[†] | .097 | .044 | .025 | .046 | | | | | .38 | |
| Fourth-century Roman axe[‡] | .05–.6 | .061 | .007 | trace | | | | | | |
| Recent hand-puddled iron[§] | .06 | .086 | .009 | .101 | | | | | | |
| Recent wrought iron[§] | .08 | .115 | .045 | .183 | | | | | | |

| Iron Source | Constituent (percentage) | | | | | | | | | | | |
|---|---|---|---|---|---|---|---|---|---|---|---|---|
| | Cr | Mn | Co | Ni | Cu | Zr | Ag | As | N | Mo | Slag | Fe |
| Seventh-century anchor* | .1 | .007 | 1.0 | .5 | .005 | .5 | .0005 | | | | | remainder |
| Roman bloom— ca. A.D. 300[†] | | .040 | | | .010 | | | .049 | | | | remainder |
| Fourth-century Roman axe[‡] | | .013 | | .033 | .015 | | | .071 | .0065 | .020 | | remainder |
| Recent hand-puddled iron[§] | | .045 | | | | | | | | | 1.97 | remainder |
| Recent wrought iron[§] | | .029 | | | | | | | | | 2.85 | remainder |

*This composition information represents a best-estimate analysis based on a wet chemical and spectrographic analysis by Jarrell-Ash Division, Fisher Scientific Company.

[†] Sample obtained from the remains of an ancient Roman bloomery. See L. Aitchison, *A History of Metals*, I, 208.

[‡] Found at Silchester, England. This iron composition is thought to have been obtained from the reduction of siderite ore, as shown by the arsenic content. See H. R. Schubert, *History of the British Iron and Steel Industry from c. 450 B.C. to A.D. 1775*, p. 56.

[§] Source, American Society for Metals, *Metals Handbook*.

Appendix C

# ANALYSIS OF AN IRON CONCRETION

## Michael L. Katzev

A section from the concretion of a nail was mounted and polished by Alfred Spitalieri. Robert Maddin analyzed this specimen through a microscope and determined that the original nail had decomposed into iron oxides, particularly magnetite. Henry Katz performed X-ray diffraction and fluorescence analyses of samples taken from this concretion. His report, dated May 31, 1966, follows:

The samples for X-ray diffraction were run in a 114.6 mm. diameter Philips powder camera using chromium $K\alpha$ radiation with a vanadium filter at forty kilovolts and twenty milliamperes with exposure times ranging from twelve to fifteen hours. A description of the samples is given below:

I. Scrapings were made on the surface of the concretion surrounding the nail.

II. A sample was taken of the black material found on the surface of the concretion.

III. A sample was taken of the yellow material found on the surface of the concretion.

IV. A sample was taken of the material surrounding the polished cross-section of the nail.

The substances found in each of the samples are given below in order of decreasing positiveness of identification:

Sample I.

A. $FeS_2$ (pyrite); $Fe_3O_4$ (magnetite)—Both positively identified.

B. The aragonite and calcite crystalline forms of $CaCO_3$.

The author received a National Science Foundation grant (GP-4776), administered jointly by the Department of Metallurgical Engineering and the Applied Science Center for Archaeology at the University Museum of the University of Pennsylvania, to study this material during the autumn of 1965.

C. The $\alpha$ $SiO_2$ crystalline form of quartz.

D. NaCl—Identification based on only one line.

Sample II.

A. $FeS_2$; $Fe_3O_4$—Both positively identified.

Sample III.

A. $FeS_2$; $FeCO_3$ (siderite)—Both positively identified.

B. NaCl.

C. $\alpha$ $SiO_2$—Identification based on only two lines.

D. $Fe_3O_4$—Identification based on only one line.

Sample IV.

A. $Fe_3O_4$—Positively identified.

B. $FeCO_3$—Most probably present.

Not all of the lines in the powder diffraction patterns of the four samples above were identified; however, in all cases, the unidentified lines were of low intensity.

A fluorescence pattern was also obtained on Sample I using a Philips X-ray spectrograph with a lithium fluoride analyzing crystal, scintillation counter and a tungsten tube for sample excitation. The lithium fluoride crystal allows detection of elements down to potassium. The fluorescence analysis showed the definite presence of iron, the most probable presence of calcium, and the probable presence of strontium. The reasons that the X-ray diffraction analysis of Sample I did not show any strontium compound could probably be that the strontium is present in the two forms of calcium carbonate by substituting for calcium, or the strontium compound is amorphous.

Independent of this study John D. Milliman and Frank T. Manheim have analyzed another nail concretion.[1]

[1]"Submarine Encrustation of a Byzantine Nail," *Journal of Sedimentary Petrology*, September, 1968, pp. 950–953.

Appendix D

# DENDROCHRONOLOGY OF THE KEEL

## Peter Ian Kuniholm

A sawn section of the Yassi Ada ship's keel was examined at the laboratory of the Aegean Dendrochronology Project at Cornell University.[1] For the present, no dendrochronological date can be given. The keel was fashioned from a whole log, the sample of which is oval in section with maximum dimensions of 28 × 18 cm. A maximum of fifty-seven annual growth rings, commencing with the pith, is present on one radius (rad. = 15.6 cm). No signs of the original squared exterior of the timber are evident. Thus, an unknown number of tree rings are missing, and if a dendrochronological date is ever derived for the wood, it will have to be a *terminus post quem* date. The ring measurements (in hundredths of millimeters) of this longest radius are as follows:

[1]The only published dendrochronological study on Byzantine material is P. I. Kuniholm and C. L. Striker, "The Tie-Beam System in the Nave Arcade of St. Eirene: Structure and Dendrochronology," *Istanbuler mitteilungen Beiheft* 18 (1977): 229–240. For progress in constructing an absolute master chronology for the Aegean, see P. I. Kuniholm, "Dendrochronology in the Aegean and the Near East," in *Deforestation, Erosion, and Ecology in the Ancient Mediterranean and Middle East* (proceedings of a symposium at the Smithsonian Institution, April 19, 1978, in press). An important synopsis of recent European work is J. Fletcher, ed., *Dendrochronology in Europe: Principles, Interpretations, and Applications to Archaeology and History*, British Archaeological Reports, International Series 51 (1978). As of January, 1981, the longest master chronology in pine for Greece extends from 1979 to 1255. In advance of its publication in *To Dasos*, copies may be obtained from P. I. Kuniholm, Department of Classics, Cornell University, Ithaca, New York.

| Ring No. | 0 | 1 | 2 | 3 | 4 | 5 | 6 | 7 | 8 | 9 |
|---|---|---|---|---|---|---|---|---|---|---|
| 0 | 664 | 498 | 275 | 203 | 373 | 390 | 378 | 407 | 439 | 350 |
| 10 | 266 | 381 | 364 | 355 | 383 | 352 | 240 | 214 | 164 | 225 |
| 20 | 305 | 270 | 361 | 359 | 325 | 276 | 213 | 301 | 214 | 231 |
| 30 | 165 | 195 | 170 | 375 | 292 | 139 | 218 | 189 | 246 | 162 |
| 40 | 202 | 147 | 207 | 227 | 194 | 271 | 217 | 139 | 188 | 207 |
| 50 | 136 | 165 | 147 | 200 | 214 | 273 | (last ring unmeasurable) | | | |

Previous investigations of Aegean wood have shown that if one hundred rings or more are preserved on a specimen, there is a reasonably good chance that it can be cross-dated with other pieces. With only one-half century's worth of rings preserved on a single specimen, the Yassi Ada ship has only a slight chance of ever being dated by its tree rings. Moreover, cypress is a notoriously difficult wood to analyze. False rings are common, and, in the absence of a master tree-ring chronology for the seventh century, it is entirely possible that we were deceived by some of these rings. The measurements are presented here, however, in the hope that other researchers will be inspired to submit additional material for study. Only by the patient collection and analysis of more groups of wood and charcoal specimens from the seventh to the thirteenth centuries will we be able to extend the Aegean master tree-ring chronology to the range which will help date this ship.

Appendix E

# PRELIMINARY ANALYSIS OF AMPHORA CONTENTS

Vaughn M. Bryant, Jr., and Robert E. Murry, Jr.

CONTENTS of the sixteen amphoras recovered in 1980 were tested. Each of these amphoras was recovered unbroken, but none of them were found with their stoppers still in place. Approximately 10–20 cc of liquid and solid debris, collected mostly from the bottommost portion of each amphora, were forwarded to the Texas A&M University Archeobotany Laboratory in separate sterile plastic vials; this amount was only a fraction of the total collected and inspected visually at Yassi Ada.

The sediment in the bottommost portion of each amphora was selected for analysis in hopes that the samples might reveal information concerning the original contents of each vessel. Each of the sixteen amphoras had filled with solid and liquid debris over the years since the shipwreck occurred. Thus, the excavators knew that most (if not all) of the contents in each amphora would represent material from the surrounding sea-bottom environment rather than from the original ship's cargo. However, it was hoped that in each case some of the amphora's original contents might still be preserved in the bottom portion beneath the subsequent trapped deposits.

Once samples were removed from the amphoras, special care was taken to avoid letting the samples dry. This was necessary because rapid drying of tiny waterlogged seeds or pieces of wood can sometimes cause irreversible damage which makes later identification impossible.

Each of the sixteen samples was processed at our Texas A&M University laboratory in the same manner using laboratory techniques perfected for the recovery of delicate plant fragments from archaeological sites on land. The specific laboratory steps that were taken include the following:

1. Each sample was emptied onto a large brass screen with openings of 150 microns. The sample was then rinsed with distilled water until only the debris larger than 150 microns remained on top of the screen. Plant pollen and phytoliths (plant crystals) are the most durable types of plant remains and can sometimes offer clues to the past presence of plants even when all other parts of a plant have deteriorated. Both pollen and phytoliths are smaller than 150 microns and pass easily through a brass screen like the one we used. Thus, we made a routine search for these types of remains in the liquid that passed through the screen, but found none.

2. The material trapped on the top of the brass screen was placed in a petri dish and was examined through a dissecting microscope. All items of plant origin were separated and treated with polyvinyl acetate to prevent them from cracking and warping when they dried.

3. Items of paleoethnobotanical importance were photographed, measured, weighed, analyzed, and then stored for future reference.

As mentioned above, none of the sixteen samples we examined came from amphoras which were still sealed when they were found. Each sample contained mostly material which represented postdepositional contamination. Common items found in each of the sixteen samples included tiny pieces of crustacean exoskeletons, broken pieces of bivalve and univalve seashells, pieces of calcium carbonate, fragments of small rocks and coral, broken pieces of sponge spicules, and fragments of calcareous algae. Each sample also contained a small portion of plant debris which consisted mainly of algae and tiny pieces of unidentifiable plant remains.

Twelve of the sixteen amphora samples contained botanical remains of plants which may reflect part of the

TABLE E-1. Botanical Contents of Amphoras.

| Amphora | Grape Seeds | Olive Pits | Pine Seed Hulls | Umbelliferae Seeds | Other Botanical Remains |
|---------|-------------|------------|-----------------|--------------------|-------------------------|
| X-1  | 2  |   |   |   | Charcoal fragments (3), seaweed fragment, small lump of resin |
| X-2  |    |   |   |   | One round seed, seaweed fragments |
| X-3  | 35 | 1 | 1 | 5 | Seed fragment, plant stem or twig, small charcoal fragment |
| X-4  | 5  |   |   |   | Seaweed and wood fragments |
| X-5  |    |   |   |   | Wood fragments |
| X-6  | 5  | 2 |   | 1 | Seaweed and small wood fragments |
| X-7  |    |   |   |   | Seaweed |
| X-8  | 69 | 1 | 1 |   | One round seed, seaweed |
| X-9  |    |   |   |   | Seaweed and wood fragments |
| X-10 | 3  | 1 |   |   | Seaweed |
| X-11 | 4  |   |   |   | Seed fragments, seaweed? |
| X-12 | 49 |   |   | 1 | Seaweed and wood fragments |
| X-13 |    |   |   |   | One flat seed (cf. *Helianthus*) |
| X-14 |    |   |   |   | Seaweed and wood fragments |
| X-15 |    |   |   |   | Seaweed |
| X-16 | 2  |   |   |   | Wood fragments |

ship's original cargo. Nine of the twelve amphoras contained a total of 174 grape (*Vitis*) seeds, four amphoras contained a total of five olive (*Olea*) pits, three of the amphoras contained a total of seven Umbelliferae seeds, and two of the amphoras contained a total of two pine (*Pinus*) seed hulls (Table E-1). It is also worth noting that in each of the amphoras containing olive pits, pine seeds, or Umbelliferae seeds, grape seeds were also present.

## Grape Seeds and Olive Pits

The easiest and simplest explanation for the presence of 174 grape seeds in these samples is that part of the ship's original cargo may have been amphoras filled with wine. If we follow that line of reasoning, then other questions arise. For example, was it common not to remove all of the grape seeds and other kinds of impurities from wine being shipped or stored in amphoras? Were there different grades of wine? In the making and transport of cheaper wines, was only minimal care taken to remove impurities such as seeds?

Other explanations can be suggested for the presence of grape seeds in these amphora samples. Archaeological records suggest that sometimes olives may have been preserved and shipped in wine to prevent spoilage.[1] Raisins also may have been a cargo item. Perhaps they were stored in the amphoras we examined, and the recovered seeds represent all that now remains of them. And finally, it is possible that some of the amphoras may have carried fresh grapes or grape must destined for

wine making at some port that the ship never reached.

Although each of the above suggestions is possible, we feel that the recovered evidence of grapes and olives is not sufficient to support any of these possibilities except that the ship carried a cargo of wine. If olives were being stored in wine, then we would have expected to find more than only one or two pits in each amphora sample. Olives and their pits are fairly large items, and we do not believe that underwater currents would have been strong enough to remove more than a few of the olives through the small opening at the mouth of each amphora. If raisins were stored in any of the amphoras, we suspect that hundreds, or even thousands, of grape seeds should have remained behind in those amphoras. Although grape seeds are smaller and lighter than olive pits, we doubt that underwater currents could have removed more than a few of the raisins or the resulting grape seeds through the small opening of each of these amphoras. Like raisins, an amphora cargo of fresh grapes or grape must should have produced hundreds of seeds as residue. Once in residue form, most of the grape seeds should have remained preserved in the bottom

[1]G. Charlin, J. Gassend, and R. Lequément, "L'Épave antique de la Baie de Cavalière," *Archaeonautica*, No. 2 (1978): 24.

sediments of those amphoras. Since that does not seem to have happened, we suspect that none of the amphoras we examined carried an original cargo of either grapes or grape must. Thus, the only reasonable explanation at this time seems to be our original suggestion that the remains of grape seeds reflect evidence of a wine cargo. Similar finds of grape seeds in amphoras from underwater shipwrecks dating from the Hellenistic period through late Byzantine times have been recovered on numerous occasions in recent years and seem to suggest original cargoes of wine.[2]

The origin of the five olive pits found in four of the amphoras remains an unanswered mystery. As mentioned earlier, we doubt that their origin can be linked to the storage of olives in any of the suspected wine-carrying amphoras we examined. Thus, our only reasonable conclusion is that the olive pits probably represent some type of contamination that occurred after the Yassi Ada ship sank. Perhaps the isolated olive pits came from

other amphoras on board the ship or from perishable sacks or baskets stored above the amphoras, or perhaps the pits were discarded into the bilge of the ship before it sank. Later the olive pits may have dropped into the amphoras, or during storms, the accompanying underwater turbulence may have carried a few of the olive pits into four of the amphoras. This type of hypothesis might explain the presence of so few olive pits in the amphora samples we have examined. An alternate possibility is that the olive pits may have originated from modern sponge divers who routinely picked sponges around the Yassi Ada reef and are known to discard olive pits over the sides of their sponge boats. If such an assumption is correct, then perhaps five of the discarded pits may have eventually found their way into the narrow openings of four different amphoras, although this idea seems less plausible than that the olives were originally on the Byzantine ship.

## Pine Seeds

A single pine seed hull was found in each of two of the amphoras we examined from the shipwreck site. Pine seeds have long been used as a source of supplemental food in the Mediterranean area. Perhaps pine seeds were being stored in amphoras other than the ones we actually examined in this study or were in perishable containers. If so, then maybe two of the seeds were carried by underwater currents into the two amphora vessels we examined. The only other reasonable explana-

tion for the presence of pine seed hulls at this wreck site is that they, like the olive pits, may have been cast from a modern sponge boat moving above the shipwreck site. We seriously doubt that pine seeds were actually a part of the original cargo stored in any of the sixteen amphoras we examined, since a cargo of that type would have left a large number of pine seeds and hulls as residue instead of only one pine seed hull in each of two vessels.

## Umbelliferae Seeds

The identity of the Umbelliferae seeds found in three of the samples cannot be determined precisely. We know the seeds are definitely from an umbelliferous plant, yet many different species of this plant family have been used by man for over two thousand years. The seeds of Umbelliferae plant species such as cumin (*Cuminum cyminum*), fennel (*Foeniculum vulgare*), dill (*Anethum graveolens*), coriander (*Coriandrum sativum*) and anise (*Pimpinella anisum*) were known and widely used by the Greeks, Romans, and Arabs as spices and for their suspected medicinal benefits.[3] The ancient Greeks also

used the seeds of an herb called silphium, which was exported in great amounts from Cyrene to Greece. By the first century A.D. the plant was reported to have become extinct. No clear trace of this plant or its seeds remains today, yet some botanists believe it was *Ferula tingitana*, a rare umbelliferous plant still found in Cyrenaica.[4]

When the seeds recovered from these three samples were compared to the seeds of known umbelliferous plants, they revealed the closest match to the seeds of the modern anise plant. We feel that the recovered seeds are probably those of anise, yet we cannot be certain, since some differences still exist between the re-

---

[2] G. F. Bass, personal communications. Texas A&M graduate student Donald H. Keith should be credited with first sieving amphora contents for seeds at Serçe Liman, Turkey, in 1977.

[3] J. W. Parry, *The Story of Spices*, pp. 49–50.

[4] F. Rosengarten, Jr., *The Book of Spices*, p. 27.

covered seeds and modern seed specimens of anise. Although the seeds from these amphoras and the modern examples of anise are similar in size (2–5 mm × 1–2 mm), shape, and overall morphology, the ancient seed specimens lack the typical short body hairs found on modern examples of anise seeds.[5] On the other hand, the absence of hairs on these ancient seeds may be due to the seeds' long exposure to abrasion and other forces of mechanical destruction while trapped in the bottoms of the amphoras.

The probability that these seeds may represent an early use of anise seeds in the making of wine or as trade items stored in the amphoras on board the seventh-century wreck is enhanced by the known historical use and distribution of the anise plant. A native of Egypt and of the nearby coastal areas in the Mediterranean region, anise flourished as a wild annual and later as a cultivated herb. Clay tablets found in Ninevah dating from the eleventh century B.C. contain Assyrian praises for the anise seed as a powerful medicinal plant. In the sixth century B.C. Pythagoras recommended anise as an antidote for scorpion stings and as a cure for attacks of epilepsy. During the Roman era, Pliny the Elder recorded additional medicinal uses of the anise plant. He noted that drinking anise tea and rubbing on anise oil would restore a youthful appearance, that attaching pouches of it to a pillow would ward off evil dreams, and that chewing the seeds would freshen one's breath. Other early writers noted that anise tea could be used as an aphrodisiac or as a refresher to revive weary travelers.[6] Dioscorides (*ca.* A.D. 40–90), an early Greek physician who traveled with the armies of Nero, commented that anise was a useful cure for ailments such as calculi of the bladder, headache, dysentery, and sneezing.[7] Finally, references from early Greek and Roman literature also mention that anise was a favored spice used to flavor wine, cakes, and various types of bread.[8]

## Other Miscellaneous Plant Remains

In addition to the identified materials we have already mentioned, we also found other fragments of plant origin that remained unidentified. In some cases the botanical remains were too poorly preserved to permit accurate identification. In other cases our modern plant reference collection for the Mediterranean region was not as extensive as it perhaps should be. Thus, in a few instances we had to classify an item as tentative even though it was preserved sufficiently for purposes of identification.

Some of the items in the miscellaneous category include plant remains that we suspect are tiny fragments of seaweeds or small pieces of wood (2–6 mm × 2–3 mm) from the hull of the ship or from the plant packing materials used to cushion the amphora cargo. Other miscellaneous items include a single flat seed (sample X-13) of unknown origin. The seed most closely resembles the seeds of wild sunflowers (*Helianthus* spp.); however, until we can obtain modern examples of sunflower seeds native to the Mediterranean region, our identification must remain tentative at best. Several sizes of small, round seeds were also found in a few of the amphora samples. All either were charred or were naturally black in color. Severe surface abrasion had distorted their identifiable morphological characteristics, and thus an accurate identification is not possible. Other botanical items from the amphoras included several small twig fragments, one round fragment of pitch (2 mm in diameter), and one small lump of charcoal.

[6] H. S. Redgrove, *Spices and Condiments*, p. 225; M. W. Liebman, *From Caravan to Casserole: Herbs and Spices in Legend, History, and Recipes*, pp. 19–20.
[7] J. W. Parry, *Spices* I, pp. 49–50.
[8] M. Grieve, *Culinary Herbs and Condiments*, p. 33.

[5] J. W. Parry, *Spices: Their Morphology, Histology and Chemistry*, p. 99.

## *Summary*

The paleoethnobotanical analysis of the sixteen amphoras recovered from the seventh-century A.D. wreck at Yassi Ada does not offer any positive clues to that ship's last cargo. On the other hand, the large number of grape seeds found in many of the amphoras suggests that wine was probably one of the main cargo items. At present we cannot be certain of this hypothesis, since none of the examined amphoras were still sealed when they were found on the wreck site. Thus, because the amphoras were open, there exists the possibility that certain contaminants and even some seeds may have entered each amphora after the ship sank. Aside from grape seeds, the other recovered botanical remains such as olive pits, pine seed hulls, and Umbelliferae seeds each may reflect a part of the ship's original cargo stored in amphoras or other containers besides the ones we examined. The alternate hypothesis is that many, or all, of the seed remains that were not from grape seeds may have come solely from sources other than the ship's original cargo.

Although the sieving for seeds and other botanical remains at Yassi Ada was a start, more could be learned from future sites if the contents of amphoras and other types of ceramic vessels were studied stratigraphically, if it were noted in each case whether the mouth of a sunken amphora pointed upwards or downwards, and if fine screening and flotation methods were employed to recover even the tiniest botanical remains from amphoras. However, future searches for botanical clues should not be limited only to the contents of amphoras and other types of ceramic vessels. Searches of the sediments along the inside portion of the keel might contain the scattered remains of cargoes that spilled from their containers as the ship sank or discarded items that were thrown into the ship's bilge before it sank. Identification of wooden remains at wreck sites could provide valuable information about the types of materials used in ship construction and types of woods that may have been used as cargo packing material. And finally, a search for fibers, fragments of rope, caulking materials, resins used to waterproof ceramic vessels, cloth used for sails or clothing, and other types of similar remains will give us a much richer understanding of ancient maritime activities and the civilizations they helped to build.

# SHIPBUILDING GLOSSARY

## J. Richard Steffy

BATTEN. A long strip of wood which is bent around molds or frames of a ship's hull to determine hull shape or fairness of curvature.

BEARDING LINE. The line at which the keel and inner garboard face meet.

CEILING (Fig. 4-24). The internal lining of a ship's hull. Made up of varying widths and thicknesses of planking, the ceiling was fastened to the inside faces of the frames. It served to keep the heavy cargo from wearing against the outside planking and prevented foreign matter from entering the bilges. Some ceiling strakes also served as structural members by stiffening the hull at selected locations.

CLAMP (Fig. 4-28). A heavy ceiling strake, usually located adjacent to a wale, that served to stiffen the hull internally along the sides.

COAMING (Fig. 4-29). A raised wooden curb bordering a hatch to keep out water.

DECK BEAM (Fig. 4-27). A timber mounted athwartships to support the deck.

ENTRY (Fig. 4-30). The foremost underwater portion of a ship's hull.

FALSE POST. An outer protective timber attached to stem or sternpost. Since it absorbed any damage to the ends of the hull, this member was attached for easy replacement.

FLOORS. Extended across the bottom of the hull, floors were usually centered on the keel and attached to it, with their arms extending approximately equidistant from this centerline. See also FRAMES.

FRAMES. Single or composite members mounted perpendicularly to the keel whose function is that of strengthening the hull and maintaining its shape. Frames are often erroneously called ribs. The frames of this ship were composed of four different types of members: FLOORS, FUTTOCKS, HALF-FRAMES, and TOP-TIMBERS.

FUTTOCKS. On ancient ships, futtocks were usually separate upper pieces of a frame that extended the frame coverage beyond the practical limits of a floor or half-frame. Unlike latter-day frames, these futtocks were not necessarily scarphed to and often did not even butt the floors or half-frames with which they combined to form frames.

GARBOARD (Figs. 4-10, 4-11). The lowest outer hull strake, one side of which was attached to the keel. Garboards were often thicker than their adjacent planks.

HALF-FRAMES. Commencing on or near the keel and terminating well up the side of the hull, half-frames only covered one side of the hull and were therefore used in pairs, sometimes butting in the center of the keel. They always covered the area of transition from hull bottom to hull side.

HANGING KNEE (Fig. 4-32). An anglular piece cut from that part of the tree where a large branch or root joined the trunk. Used to brace the juncture of a deck beam with the ship's side, its trunk arm was attached to the ceiling and its branch arm to the beam.

HOGGING. Hull distortion in which the ends of the hull droop while its midsection arches.

KEELSON (Fig. 4-21). An internal keel, mounted atop the floors directly above the keel. It was fastened to both floors and keel to increase bottom stiffness.

LATEEN RIGGING. The arrangement in which a three-cornered sail is attached to a yard which obliquely crosses a low, forward-raking mast.

LIMBER BOARDS (Fig. 4-24). Removable planks which permit access to the bilges.

LIMBER HOLES. Notches or flats cut into the lower faces of the floor timbers on either side of the keel to permit free passage of bilge water.

LINES (Fig. 4-4). Graphic expressions of the various shapes of the ship's hull. For a good explanation of the interpretation of ships' lines, see Howard I. Chapelle, *The History of American Sailing Ships*, pp. 19–23.

MOLDED HEIGHT. The distance between the upper surfaces of the limber boards adjacent to the keelson and the bottom of the deck beams at the section in question; *depth of hold* refers to this distance at the midship section.

MOLD LOFTING. The laying out of a ship's lines in full size, usually on a large floor, whereby measurements and frame shapes could be directly transferred to the hull under construction.

RABBET (Fig. 4-10). A groove cut into the keel or other member for the purpose of seating planking edges. Rabbets permitted more rigidity by increasing the surface area at the point of contact between keel and plank. They also helped prevent leakage at this important junction.

READY SHEET ANCHOR. The heaviest anchor in the ship, required to be kept in ready reserve in case of emergency.

RIDER. A timber mounted across the inner surface of ceiling strakes to aid in the bracing of deck beams or other opposing timbers.

SCANTLING. A set of specified dimensions for constructing the principal parts of a ship's hull; collectively, the finished major hull timbers.

SCARPH JOINTS. A joint by which two pieces of timber were connected. Two types of scarph joints were recovered from this wreck—a hook scarph between keel and sternpost, and diagonal scarphs in the planking.

SHELF CLAMP. The ceiling strake upon which the deck beams rested.

SHOE. A thin, replaceable piece of wood attached to the bottom of the keel to protect it from damage.

SPAWLS. Temporary braces intended for stiffening the frames during the installation of planking, wales, etc.

STEALER (Fig. 4-17). A short extra plank inserted into the hull to fill out the wider areas of its sides.

STEM. The piece extending forward from the keel and forming the upright post to which the two sides of the bow were attached.

STERNPOST. The piece extending aft and upward from the keel to which the sides of the stern were attached.

STRAKE. A row of planking made up of one piece or several pieces scarphed together.

THROUGH-BEAM (Fig. 4-26). An athwartships beam which penetrates the outer hull planking.

TOP-TIMBERS. On the seventh-century Yassi Ada ship, the futtocks above the half-frames. They covered only the area above the shell and were installed after the wales.

WALE (Fig. 4-26). A heavy piece of outer planking strategically placed to gird the upper part of the hull. The wales acted as bands which bound the upper part of the hull together.

# BIBLIOGRAPHY

Adelson, H. L. *Light Weight Solidi and Byzantine Trade During the Sixth and Seventh Centuries*. ANSNNM, no. 138. New York, 1957.

Agricola, G. *De Re Metallica*. Trans. H. C. Hoover and L. H. Hoover. New York, 1950.

Aitchison, L. *A History of Metals*. London, 1960.

Akşıray, F. *Türkiye Deniz Balıkları: Tâyin Anahtarı*. İstanbul Üniversitesi Fen Fakültesi, Hidrobioloji Araştırma Enstitüsü Yayınlarından Seri 1. Istanbul, 1954.

Albee, L. R. *A List of Books on Angling, Fishes, and Fish Culture in Harvard College Library*. Cambridge, Mass., 1896.

Alexander, M. A. "The Symbolism of Christianity." *Archaeology* 3 (1950): 242–247.

American Society for Metals. *Metals Handbook*. 7th ed. Cleveland, 1948.

Amit, M. *Athens and the Sea: A Study in Athenian Sea-Power*. Collection Latomus, vol. 74. Brussels, 1965.

Antoniadis-Bibicou, H. *Études d'histoire maritime de Byzance à propos du "thème des caravisiens."* Paris, 1966.

————. *Recherches sur les douanes à Byzance: L' "Octava," le "kommerkion" et les commerciaires*. Cahiers des Annales, vol. 20. Paris, 1963.

Apostolides, N. Ch. *La Pêche en Grèce*. Athens, 1883.

*Archaeologia Homerica*, Vol. II. Göttingen, 1968.

Ashburner, W. *The Rhodian Sea-Law*. Oxford, 1909.

*Atti del II Congresso Internazionale di Archeologia Sottomarina, Albenga, 1958*. Bordighera, 1961.

Aurigemma, S. *L'Italia in Africa: Tripolitania*, vol. I, *I monumenti d'arte decorativa, parte prima—I mosaici*. Rome, 1960.

Barnea, I. "L'Incendie de la cité de Dinogetia au VIᵉ siècle." *Dacia*, n.s. 10 (1966): 237–259.

Bass. G. F. *Archaeology Beneath the Sea*. New York, 1975.

————. *Archaeology Under Water*. 2d ed. Harmondsworth, Eng., and Baltimore, 1970.

————. "A Byzantine Trading Venture." *Scientific American* 225, no. 2 (August, 1971): 22–33.

————. *Cape Gelidonya: A Bronze Age Shipwreck*. Transactions of the American Philosophical Society, n.s. vol. 57, pt. 8. Philadelphia, 1967.

————. "Glass Treasure from the Aegean." *NatGeo* 153, no. 6 (June, 1978): 768–793.

————. "A Medieval Islamic Merchant Venture." *Archaeological News* 8, nos. 2 and 3 (1979): 84–94.

————. "New Tools for Undersea Archaeology." *NatGeo* 134, no. 3 (September, 1968): 402–423.

————. "Turkey: Survey for Shipwrecks, 1973." *IJNA* 3 (1974): 335–338.

————. "The Turkish Aegean: Proving Ground for Underwater Archaeology." *Expedition* 10, no. 3 (Spring, 1968): 2–10.

————. "Underwater Archaeology: Key to History's Warehouse." *NatGeo* 124, no. 1 (July, 1963): 138–156.

————. "Underwater Archeological Expedition to Turkey." In *National Geographic Society Research Reports, 1963 Projects*, pp. 21–34. Washington, D.C., 1968.

————. "Underwater Archeological Expedition to Turkey, 1961–1962." In *National Geographic Society Research Reports, 1961–1962 Projects*, pp. 11–20. Washington, D.C., 1970.

————. "Underwater Excavations at Yassi Ada: A Byzantine Shipwreck." *AA* 77 (1962): 537–564.

————, ed. *A History of Seafaring Based on Underwater Archaeology*. London and New York, 1972.

————, and M. L. Katzev. "Tools for Underwater Archaeology." *Archaeology* 21 (1968): 164–173.

————, and D. M. Rosencrantz. "The Asherah—A Pioneer in Search of the Past." In *Submersibles and Their Use in Oceanography and Ocean Engineering*. Ed. R. A. Geyer, pp. 335–351. Amsterdam, Oxford, and New York, 1977.

————, and ————. *A Diversified Program for the Study of Shallow Water Searching and Mapping Techniques*. Office of Naval Research Report, no. AD 686 487. Springfield, Va., 1968.

————, and ————. "Submersibles in Underwater Search and Photogrammetric Mapping." In *Underwater Archaeology: A Nascent Discipline*. Museums and Monuments, vol. 13, pp. 271–283. Paris, 1972.

————, and P. Throckmorton. "Excavating a Bronze Age Shipwreck." *Archaeology* 14 (1961): 78–87.

————, and F. H. van Doorninck, Jr. "An 11th Century Shipwreck at Serçe Liman, Turkey." *IJNA* 7 (1978): 119–132.

————, and ————. "Excavation of a Late Roman Shipwreck at Yassi Ada, Turkey." In *National Geographic Society Research Reports, 1969 Projects*, pp. 1–11. Washington, D.C., 1978.

————, and ————. "Excavations of a Byzantine Shipwreck at Yassi Ada, Turkey." In *National Geographic Society Research Reports, 1964 Projects*, pp. 9–20. Washington, D.C., 1969.

————, and ————. "A Fourth-Century Shipwreck at Yassi Ada." *AJA* 75 (1971): 27–37.

Bassett, S. E. "The Cave at Vari: VI. The Terra-Cotta Lamps." *AJA* 7 (1903): 338–349.

Bates, G. E. *Archaeological Exploration of Sardis*, vol. I, *Byzantine Coins, 1958–1968*. Cambridge, Mass., 1971.

————. "A Byzantine Hoard from Coelesyria." *ANSMN* 14 (1968): 67–109.

Becatti, G. *Scavi di Ostia*, vol. IV, *Mosaici e pavimenti marmorei*. Rome, 1961.

Bell, H. W. *Sardis*, vol. XI, *Coins, 1910–1914*. Leiden, 1916.

Bellinger, A. R. *Catalogue of the Byzantine Coins in the Dumbarton Oaks Collection and in the Whittemore Collection*, vol. I, *Anastasius to Maurice, 491–602*. Washington, D.C., 1966.

Benoît, F. *L'Épave du Grand Congloué à Marseille. Gallia* Supplement 14. Paris, 1961.

————. "Jas d'ancre et pièces d'outillage des épaves de Provence." *RStLig* 21 (1955): 117–128.

————. "Nouvelles épaves de Provence (II)." *Gallia* 18 (1960): 41–56.

Berners, Dame Juliana. *The Treatyse of Fysshynge with an Angle*. Westminster, Eng., 1496 (University of Pennsylvania facsimile ed., [n.p., n.d.]). Reprint, London, 1832.

Bernhard, M.-L. *Lampki starozytne*. Warsaw, 1955.

————. "Topographie d'Alexandrie: Le Tombeau d'Alexandre et le mausolée d'Auguste." *RA* 47 (1956): 129–156.

Bersakes, Ph. "To hieron tou Korunthou Apollonos." *Deltion* 2 (1916): 65–118.

Blackman, D. J., ed. *Marine Archaeology*. Colston Papers, no. 23. London and Hamden, Conn., 1973.

Blinkenberg, C. *Lindos*, vol. I, *Les Petits objets*. Berlin, 1931.

Blümlein, C. *Bilder aus dem römisch-germanischen Kulturleben*. Munich, 1926.

Blümner, H. *Technologie und Terminologie der Gewerbe und Künste bei Griechen und Römern*. Leipzig, 1875–1887.

Boon, G. C. *Roman Silchester*. London, 1957.

Bovini, G. *Mosaici di S. Apollinare Nuovo di Ravenna: Il ciclo cristologico*. Florence, 1958.

————. "Principali restauri compiuti nel secolo scorso da Felice Kibel nei mosaici di S. Apollinare Nuovo di Ravenna." *Corsi di cultura sull'arte Ravennate e Bizantina* 13 (1966).

Brants, J. *Antieke Terra-Cotta Lampen uit het Rijksmuseum van Oudheden te Leiden*. Leiden, 1913.

Bridge, R. N., and P. D. Whitting. "A Hoard of Early Heraclius Folles." *NumCirc* 74, no. 5 (May, 1966): 131–132.

Broneer, O. *Corinth*, vol. IV, part 2, *Terracotta Lamps*. Cambridge, Mass., 1930.

————. "Excavations in Corinth, 1934." *AJA* 39 (1935): 53–75.

————. "Excavations on the North Slope of the Acropolis, 1937." *Hesperia* 7 (1938): 161–263.

Bruce-Mitford, R. L. S. *The Sutton Hoo Ship Burial: A Handbook*. 3rd ed. London, 1979.

Bruneau, P. *Exploration archéologique de Délos*, vol. XXVI, *Les Lampes*. Paris, 1965.

Bruyère, B., et al. *Tell Edfou*. 3 vols. Cairo, 1937–1950.

Buchholz, H.-G., G. Jöhrens, and I. Maull. "Jagd und Fischfang." In *Archaeologia Homerica*, II. Göttingen, 1973.

Burford, A. *Craftsmen in Greek and Roman Society*. London, 1972.

Butzer, K. W. *Environment and Archaeology: An Introduction to Pleistocene Geography*. 2d ed. Chicago, 1970.

Callender, M. H. *Roman Amphorae*. London and New York, 1965.

Canarache, V. *The Archaeological Museum of Constantza*. Bucharest, n.d. (ca. 1967).

————. *The Mosaic-Floored Edifice of Tomi*. Constanţa, n.d.

Čangova, J. "Amphores du Moyen Age en Bulgarie." *BIABulg* 22 (1959): 243–262.

Carrazé, F. "L'Épave 'Grand Ribaud A.'" *CahArchSub* 4 (1975): 19–58.

Casson, L. *The Ancient Mariners*. New York, 1959; London, 1960.

————. *Illustrated History of Ships and Boats*. Garden City, N.Y., 1964.

————. "More Sea-Digging." *Archaeology* 10 (1957): 248–257.

————. *Ships and Seamanship in the Ancient World*. Princeton, 1971.

————. "The Size of Ancient Merchant Ships." In *Studi in onore di Aristide Calderini e Roberto Paribeni*. Vol. I, pp. 231–238. Milan, 1956.

Catling, H. W. "An Early Byzantine Pottery Factory at Dhiorios in Cyprus." *Levant* 4 (1972): 1–82.

————. "Minoan and Mycenaean Pottery: Composition and Provenance." *Archaeometry* 6 (1963): 1–9.

————, et al. "Correlations between Composition and Provenance of Mycenaean and Minoan Pottery." *BSA* 58 (1963): 94–115.

Ceci, C. *Piccoli bronzi del Museo Nazionale di Napoli*. Naples, 1873.

Cesnola, A. P. di. *Salaminia (Cyprus)*, 2d ed. London, 1884.

Cesnola, L. P. di. *Cyprus*. London, 1877.

————. *A Descriptive Atlas of the Cesnola Collection of Cypriote Antiquities in the Metropolitan Museum of Art, New York*. Boston, 1885–1903.

Champion, B. "Outils en fer du Musée de Saint-Germain." *RA*, 1916, no. 1, pp. 211–246.

Champollion-Figeac, M. *Documents historiques inédits tirés des collections manuscrites de la Bibliothèque Royale et des archives ou des bibliothèques des departements*. Vols. 1 and 2. Paris, 1841.

Chantraine, H. "Uncia." *RE* 9, A, 1 (1961): 604–665.

Chapelle, H. I. *The History of American Sailing Ships*. New York, 1935.

Charanis, P. "Ethnic Changes in the Byzantine Empire in the Seventh Century." *DOP* 13 (1959): 23–44.

Charlin, G., J. Gassend, and R. Lequément. "L'Épave antique de la Baie de Cavalière." *Archaeonautica*, Part 2 (1978): 9–93.

Cloché, P. *Les Classes, les métiers, le trafic*. Paris, 1931.

Colnago, A., and J. Keil. "Archäologische Untersuchungen in Norddalmatien." *JOAIBeibl* 8 (1905): 31–60.

Condurachi, E., et al. *Histria*. Vol. I. Bucharest, 1954.

Conference for National Cooperation in Aquatics. *The New*

*Science of Skin and Scuba Diving*. New York, 1957.

Conze, A., et al. *Altertümer von Pergamon*. Vol. I, part 2. Berlin, 1913.

Cox, D. H. *Coins from the Excavations at Curium, 1932–1953*. ANSNNM, no. 145. New York, 1959.

Dalton, O. M. *Byzantine Art and Archaeology*. Oxford, 1911.

———. *Catalogue of Early Christian Antiquities and Objects from the Christian East in the Department of British and Medieval Antiquities and Ethnography of the British Museum*. London, 1901.

———. *A Guide to the Early Christian and Byzantine Antiquities in the Department of British and Mediaeval Antiquities, British Museum*. Oxford, 1903; 2d ed., Oxford, 1921.

Daremberg, C., and E. Saglio. *Dictionnaire des antiquités grecques et romaines*. Paris, 1877–1919.

Daux, G. "Chronique des fouilles 1964, Thasos." *BCH* 89 (1965): 919–978.

Davey, N. *A History of Building Materials*. London, 1961.

Davidson, G. R. *Corinth*, vol. XII, *The Minor Objects*. Princeton, 1952.

Davies, N. de G. *The Rock Tombs of Deir el Gebrâwi*. London, 1902.

Davies, O. *Roman Mines in Europe*. Oxford, 1935.

Davies, W. E. *The Techniques of Sea Fishing*. London, 1953.

Davis, C. *The Ship Model Builder's Assistant*. New York, 1955.

Delougaz, P., and R. C. Haines. *A Byzantine Church at Khirbat al-Karak*. OIP, no. 85, Chicago, 1960.

Deonna, W. *Exploration archéologique de Délos*, vol. XVIII, *Le Mobilier délien*. Paris, 1938.

———. "Ex-voto déliens." *BCH* 56 (1932): 410–490.

Devedjian, K. *Pêche et pêcheries en Turquie*. Constantinople, 1926.

Diess, J. J. *Herculaneum*. New York, 1960.

Dimitrov, D. P., et al. "Archeologicheskie raskopki v vostochnom sektore nove v 1962 gody." *BIABulg* 27 (1964): 217–235.

———. "Archeologicheskie raskopki v zapadnom sektore nove v 1965 g." *BIABulg* 30 (1967): 59–74.

———. "Archeologicheskie raskopki v vostochnom sektore nove v 1965 g." *BIABulg* 30 (1967): 75–100.

Dioscorides. *De Materia Medica*. Ed. Max Wellmann. n.p., 1958.

Donald, P. J., and P. D. Whitting. "A VIIth Century Hoard from Cyprus." *NumCirc* 75, no. 6 (June, 1967): 162–165.

Dumas, F. *Deep-Water Archaeology*. Trans. H. Frost. London, 1962.

Dürr, N. "Catalogue de la Collection Lucien Naville au Cabinet de Numismatique du Musée d'Art et d'Histoire de Genève. *Genava* 12 (1964): 1–42.

Edwards, K. M. *Corinth*, vol. VI, *Coins, 1896–1929*. Cambridge, Mass., 1933.

Eliot, C. W. J. "A Bronze Counterpoise of Athena." *Hesperia* 45 (1976): 163–170.

Emery, W. B. *Nubian Treasure: An Account of the Discoveries at Ballana and Qustul*. London, 1948.

———, and L. P. Kirwan. *The Royal Tombs of Ballana and Qustul: Mission Archéologique de Nubie, 1929–34*. 2 vols. Cairo, 1938.

Erentoz, K. "A Brief Review of the Geology of Anatolia (Asia Minor)." *Geotectonics* 2 (1967): 85–95.

Evans, J. "On Some Iron Tools and Other Articles Formed of Iron Found at Silchester in the Year 1890." *Archaeologia* 54 (1894): 139–156.

Faber, G. L. *The Fisheries of the Adriatic*. London, 1883.

Fiori, P., and J.-P. Joncheray. "Mobilier métallique (outils, armes, pièces de greement) provenant de fouilles sous-marines." *CahArchSub* 2 (1973): 73–94.

Fitzgerald, G. M. *Beth-Shan Excavations 1921–1923*, vol. III, *The Arab and Byzantine Levels*. Philadelphia, 1931.

———. *A Sixth Century Monastery at Beth-Shan (Scythopolis)*. Philadelphia, 1939.

Forbes, R. J. *Metallurgy in Antiquity*. Leiden, 1950.

Frey, D., F. Hentschel, and D. Keith. "Deepwater Archaeology: The Capistello Wreck Excavation, Lipari, Aeolian Islands." *IJNA* 7 (1978): 279–300.

Frost, H. "First Season of Excavation on the Punic Wreck in Sicily." *IJNA* 2 (1973): 33–49.

———. "The Punic Wreck in Sicily: 1. Second Season of Excavation." *IJNA* 3 (1974): 35–42.

———. *Under the Mediterranean*. London and Englewood Cliffs, N.J., 1963.

Furtwängler, A. *Olympia*, vol. IV, *Die Bronzen und die übrigen kleineren Funde von Olympia*. Berlin, 1890.

Gàbrici, E. "Il santuario della Malophoros a Selinunte." *MonAnt* 32 (1927): 5–420.

Gabrielson, I. N., ed. *The Fisherman's Encyclopedia*. New York, 1950.

Gardner, E. A. *Naukratis*. Vol. II. London, 1888.

Gargallo, P. "Anchors of Antiquity." *Archaeology* 14 (1961): 31–35.

Gauckler, P. *Catalogue du Musée Alaoui (Supplément)*. Paris, 1910.

———. "Les Mosaïques de l'arsenale à Sousse." *RA* 3, no. 31 (1897): 8–22.

Goldman, H. "The Acropolis of Halae." *Hesperia* 9 (1940): 381–514.

———, et al. *Excavations at Gözlü Kule, Tarsus*, vol. I, *The Hellenistic and Roman Periods*. Princeton, 1950.

Goodman, W. L. *The History of Woodworking Tools*. London, 1964.

Greece, Office of the Minister to the Prime Minister, Department of Antiquities and Archaeological Restoration. *Byzantine Art, an European Art*. 2d ed. Athens, 1964.

Green, J. N. "Cape Andreas." *IJNA* 1 (1972): 190.

———. "An Underwater Archaeological Survey of Cape Andreas, Cyprus, 1969–70." In *Marine Archaeology*, ed. D. J. Blackman, pp. 141–179. Colston Papers, no. 23. London and Hamden, Conn., 1973.

Grierson, P. *Catalogue of the Byzantine Coins in the Dumbarton Oaks Collection and in the Whittemore Collection*, vol. II, part 1, *Phocas and Heraclius (602–641)*. Washington, D.C., 1968.

———. "The *Tablettes Albertini* and the Value of the *Solidus* in the Fifth and Sixth Centuries A.D." *JRS* 49 (1959): 73–80.

Grieve, M. *Culinary Herbs and Condiments*. New York, 1934.

Gruvel, A. *La Pêche dans la préhistoire*. Paris, 1928.

Gültekin, H., and P. Throckmorton. "Preliminary Report of Exploration for Ancient Wrecks in the Turkish Aegean." Unpublished report, 1958.

Gummerus, H. "Darstellungen aus dem Handwerk auf römischen Grab- und Votivsteinen in Italien." *JdI* 28 (1913): 63–126.

Gusman, P. *Pompei*. Paris, 1899.

Hamilton, D. L. *Conservation of Metal Objects from Underwater Sites: A Study in Methods*. Publication of the Texas Antiquities Committee, no. 1, and Miscellaneous Papers of the Texas Memorial Museum, no. 4. Austin, 1976.

Hampel, J. *Alterthümer des frühen Mittelalters in Ungarn*. 3 vols. Brunswick, Germany, 1905.

Hanfmann, G. M. A. *Sardis und Lydien*. Abhandlungen der geistes- und sozialwissenschaftlichen Klasse, 1960, no. 6, Akademie der Wissenschaften und der Literatur in Mainz. Wiesbaden, 1960.

Hardy, L. R., ed. *Hardy's Angler's Guide: Coronation Number*. 55th ed. Alnwick, Eng., 1937.

Hayes, J. W. "Excavations at Saraçhane in Istanbul: A Seventh-Century Pottery Group." *DOP* 22 (1968): 195–216.

———. *Late Roman Pottery*. London, 1972.

Hill, D. K. "When Romans Went Shopping." *Archaeology* 5 (1952): 51–55.

Hills, J. W. *A History of Fly Fishing*. London, 1921.

*Histria*. Vol. I. Bucharest, 1954. See also Condurachi.

Höppener, H. *Halieutica: Bijdrage tot de kennis der Oud-Grieksche Visscherij*. Amsterdam, 1931.

Hoffiller, V. "Antike Bronzegefässe aus Sissek." *JOAIBeibl* 11 (1908): 117–134.

Holmqvist, W. "Europe, Barbarian." In *Encyclopedia of World Art*. Vol. V. New York, Toronto, and London, 1958.

Hougen, B. *The Migration Style of Ornament in Norway*. 2d ed. Oslo, 1967.

Hull, D. B. *Hounds and Hunting in Ancient Greece*. Chicago, 1964.

Iacobson, A. L. "Srednevekovye amfory severnogo prichernomor'ya." *SovArch* 15 (1951): 325–344.

Iconomu, C. *Opaițe greco-romane*. Constanța, 1967.

Isler, H. P. "Heraion von Samos: Eine frühbyzantinische Zisterne." *AthMitt* 84 (1969): 202–230.

Joncheray, J.-P. *L'Épave "C" de la Chrétienne*. Frejus, 1975.

———. "Une Épave du Bas Empire: Dramont F." *CahArchSub* 4 (1975): 91–140.

———. "Étude de l'épave Dramont D, dite 'des pelvis.'" *CahArchSub* 3 (1974): 21–48.

———. "Étude de l'épave Dramont D: IV, les objets métalliques." *CahArchSub* 4 (1975): 5–18.

Jones, A. H. M. *The Later Roman Empire, 284–602*. 2 vols. Oxford and Norman, Okla., 1964.

Jones, T. B. *In the Twilight of Antiquity: The R. S. Hoyt Memorial Lectures (1973)*. Minneapolis, 1978.

Kapitän, G. "The Church Wreck off Marzamemi." *Archaeology* 22 (1969): 122–133.

———. "Greco-Roman Anchors and the Evidence for the One-Armed Wooden Anchor in Antiquity." In *Marine Archaeology*, ed. D. J. Blackman. Colston Papers, no. 23. London and Hamden, Conn., 1973.

Karius, R., P. Merifield, and D. Rosencrantz. "Stereo-Mapping of Underwater Terrain from a Submarine." In *Ocean Science and Engineering: Transactions of the Joint Conference, Marine Technology Society and American Society of Limnology and Oceanography, Washington, D.C.*, June, 1965, pp. 1167–1177.

Katzev, M. L., and F. H. van Doorninck, Jr. "Replicas of Iron Tools from a Byzantine Shipwreck." *Studies in Conservation* 11, no. 3 (1966): 133–142.

Katzev, S. W., and M. L. Katzev. "Last Harbor for the Oldest Ship." *NatGeo* 146, no. 5 (November, 1974): 618–625.

Kebabian, P. B., and D. Witney. *American Woodworking Tools*. Boston, 1978.

Keller, O. *Die Antike Tierwelt*. Vol. II. Leipzig, 1913.

Kisch, B. *Scales and Weights: A Historical Outline*. New Haven and London, 1965.

Koukoules, Ph. I. "Ek tou halieutikou biou ton Buzantinon." *Epet* 18 (1948): 28–41.

Kourouniotes, K. "Anaskaphai kai ereunai en Khio 2." *Deltion* 2 (1916): 190–215.

Kraeling, C. H. *Ptolemais, City of the Libyan Pentapolis*. Chicago, 1962.

Kreutz, B. M. "Ships, Shipping, and the Implications of Change in the Early Medieval Mediterranean." *Viator* 7 (1976): 79–109.

Kristjonsson, H., ed. *Modern Fishing Gear of the World*. London, 1957.

Krumbacher, K. "Das mittelgriechische Fischbuch." *SB-München*, 1903, pp. 345–380.

Laser, S. "Hausrat." In *Archaeologia Homerica*. Vol. II. Göttingen, 1968.

Laurent, V. "Bulletin de sigillographie byzantine." *Byzantion* 6 (1931): 771–829.

Lazzarini, M. "Le Bilance romane del Museo Nazionale e dell' Antiquarium Comunale di Roma." *RendLinc*, 8th ser., 3 (1948): 221–254.

Leuthold, E. "Monete bizantine rinvenute in Siria." *RIN*, 5th ser., 54–55 (1952–1953): 31–49.

Levi, D. *Antioch Mosaic Pavements*. Vol. I. Princeton, 1947.

Libertini, G. *Il Museo Biscari*. Milan and Rome, 1930.

Liebman, M. W. *From Caravan to Casserole: Herbs and Spices in Legend, History, and Recipes*. Miami, Fla., 1977.

Lindenschmit, L. "Ein Massenfund römischer Eisengeräte." In *Die Altertümer unserer heidnischen Vorzeit*. Vol. V, pp. 255–264. Mainz, 1858–1911.

Liou, B. "Direction des recherches archéologiques sous-marines." *Gallia* 31 (1973): 571–608.

———. "Direction des recherches archéologiques sous-marines." *Gallia* 33 (1975): 571–605.

———. "L'Épave romaine de l'anse Gerbal à Port-Vendres." *CRAI*, 1974, pp. 414–433.

Liversidge, J. "Woodwork." In *Roman Crafts*. Ed. D. Strong and D. Brown. London, 1976.

Lopez, R. S. "The Role of Trade in the Economic Readjustment of Byzantium in the Seventh Century." *DOP* 13 (1959): 67–85.

Maiuri, A. *La casa del Menandro e il suo tesoro di argenteria*. Rome, 1933.

McDonald, J. *The Origins of Angling*. New York, 1963.

Majewski, K. "Novae—Sektor Zachodni, 1967." *Archeologia* 20 (1969): 119–190.

Marsden, P. "The County Hall Ship." *Transactions of the London and Middlesex Archaeological Society* 21 (1965): 109–117.

Marston, R. B. *Supplement to the Bibliotheca Piscatoria*. London, 1901.

Mathieu, M. *Griekorimskiy i wizantiykiy Egipiet*. Leningrad,

1939.

Menis, G. C. *I mosaici cristiani de Aquileia*. Udine, 1965.

Menzel, H. *Antike Lampen in Römisch-Germanischen Zentralmuseum zu Mainz*. Mainz, 1954.

Mercer, H. C. *Ancient Carpenters' Tools*. Doylestown, Pa., 1960.

Milliman, J. D., and F. T. Manheim. "Submarine Encrustation of a Byzantine Nail." *Journal of Sedimentary Petrology*, September, 1968, pp. 950–953.

Miltner, F. *Forschungen in Ephesos*, vol. IV, part 2, *Das Coemeterium der sieben Schläfer*. Baden, 1937.

Mitten, D. G., and S. F. Doeringer. *Master Bronzes from the Classical World*. Mainz, 1967.

Mommsen, T. *Geschichte des römischer Münzwesens*. Berlin, 1860.

———, and P. M. Meyer. *Codex Theodosianus*. Berlin, 1905.

Moody, E. A., and M. Clagett. *The Medieval Science of Weights*. Madison, 1952.

Mordtmann, Dr. "Byzantinische Glasstempel." *BZ* 7 (1898): 603–608.

Muratori, S. *Il R. Museo Nazionale di Ravenna*. Rome, 1937.

Negrel, J. "Une Coque du Bas-Empire dans la rade de Marseille." *Archéologia* 55 (February, 1973): 59–65.

Neppi-Mòdona, A. "Ancora antica." *NSc*, 1932, pp, 434–436.

Neuburger, A. *Die Technik des Altertums*. Leipzig, 1919.

Neville, R. C. "Description of a Remarkable Deposit of Roman Antiquities of Iron, Discovered at Great Chesterford, Essex, in 1854." *Archaeological Journal* 13 (1856): 1–13.

Nowotny, E. "Zur Mechanik der Antiken Wage." *JOAIBeibl* 16 (1913): 5–36.

Oppian. *Halieutica*. Tr. A. W. Mair. Cambridge, 1963.

Ostrogorsky, G. "The Byzantine Empire in the World of the Seventh Century." *DOP* 13 (1959): 1–21.

Oxé, A. "Kor und Kab. antike Hohlmasse und Gewichte in neuer Beleuchtung." *BonnJbb* 147 (1942): 191.

Palladion. *Antike Kunst: Katalog 1976*. Basel, 1976.

Papadopoulos, S. A., ed. *The Greek Merchant Marine (1453–1850)*. Athens, 1972.

Papò, F. "Lo Scandaglio come una bomba." *Mondo Sommerso*, September, 1963, pp. 123–124.

Parry, J. W. *Spices*. Vol. I. New York, 1969.

———. *Spices: Their Morphology, Histology and Chemistry*. New York, 1962.

———. *The Story of Spices*. New York, 1953.

Pelichet, E. "A Propos des amphores romaines trouvées à Nyon." *ZSchwAKg* 8 (1946): 189–202.

Perlzweig, J. *The Athenian Agora*, vol. VII, *Lamps of the Roman Period*. Princeton, 1961.

Pernice, E. *Griechische Gewichte*. Berlin, 1894.

Peterson, M. *History Under the Sea*. Washington, D.C., 1965.

Petrie, W. M. F. *Ancient Gaza*, vol. IV, *Tell el Ajjūl*. BSAE, no. 56. London, 1934.

———. *Tanis*, vol. II, *Nebesheh (am) and Defenneh (Tahpanhes)*. London, 1888.

———. *Tools and Weapons*. London, 1917.

Pharmakowsky, B. "Archäologische Funde im Jahre 1913, Russland." *AA* 29 (1914): 205–292.

Picard, O., and J.-P. Sodini. "Sondage Delcos-Valma." *BCH* 96 (1972): 936–949.

Pink, K. *Römische und byzantinische Gewichte in österreichischen Sammlungen*. Sonderschriften des österreichischen

archäologischen Institutes in Wien, vol. 12. Vienna, 1938.

Quennell, M., and C. H. B. Quennell. *Everyday Life in Roman and Anglo-Saxon Times*. London, 1959.

Radcliffe, W. *Fishing from the Earliest Times*, 2d ed. London, 1926.

Radulescu, A. V. "Amfore cu inscriptii de la edificiul roman cu mozaic." *Pontica* 6 (1973): 193–207.

Reinach, S. *Catalogue illustré du Musée des Antiquités Nationales au Chateau de Saint-Germain-en-Laye*. Paris, 1917.

Rice, T. T. *Everyday Life in Byzantium*. London and New York, 1967.

Richter, G. M. A. *The Furniture of the Greeks, Etruscans, and Romans*. London, 1966.

———. *Greek, Etruscan and Roman Bronzes*. New York, 1915.

Robinson, D. M. *Excavations at Olynthus*, vol. X, *Metal and Minor Miscellaneous Finds*. Baltimore, 1941.

Robinson, H. S. *The Athenian Agora*, vol. V, *Pottery of the Roman Period: Chronology*. Princeton, 1959.

Romanelli, P., and P. Nordhagen. *S. Maria Antiqua*. Rome, 1964.

Rosencrantz, D. M. "Underwater Photography and Photogrammetry." In *Photography in Archaeological Research*. Ed. E. Harp, pp. 265–309. Albuquerque, 1975.

Rosengarten, F., Jr. *The Book of Spices*. Philadelphia, 1969.

Ross, M. C. *Catalogue of the Byzantine and Early Medieval Antiquities in the Dumbarton Oaks Collection*. Vol. I. Washington, D.C., 1962.

———. "A Group of Coptic Incense Burners." *AJA* 46 (1942): 10–12.

Rougé, J. *Recherches sur l'organisation du commerce maritime en Méditerranée sous l'empire romain*. Paris, 1966.

Ryan, E., and G. F. Bass. "Underwater Surveying and Draughting—A Technique." *Antiquity* 36 (1962): 252–261.

"Rybolovstvo na Russkom Severe," *Sbornik Muzeya Antropologii i Etnografii* 28 (1972): 75.

Salaman, R. A. *Dictionary of Tools*. London, 1975.

Sanders, J. E. "Diver-operated Simple Hand Tools for Coring Nearshore Sands." *Journal of Sedimentary Petrology* 38 (1968): 1381–1386.

Scharff, R. *Standard Handbook of Salt-Water Fishing*. Rev. ed. New York, 1971.

Schilbach, E. *Byzantinische Metrologie: Handbuch der Altertumswissenschaft*. Vol. XII, part 4. Munich, 1970.

Schlumberger, G. "Poids de verre étalons monétiformes d'origine byzantine." *REG* 8 (1895): 59–76.

———. *Sigillographie de l'empire byzantin*. Paris, 1884.

Schmidt, G. *Die Malerschule von S. Florian*. Linz, 1962.

Schneider, A. M. "Samos in frühchristlicher und byzantinischer Zeit." *AthMitt* 54 (1929): 97–141.

Schubert, H. R. *History of the British Iron and Steel Industry from c. 450 B.C. to A.D. 1775*. London, 1957.

Scorpan, C. "Sapaturile arheologice de la Sacidava." *Pontica* 6 (1973): 267–331.

*Second Report upon the Excavations Carried Out in and near the Hippodrome of Constantinople in 1928 on Behalf of the British Academy*. London, 1929.

Severeanu, G. "Lampes en terre-cuite appartenant aux collections du Musée Municipal de Bucarest et du Dr. Severeanu." *Bucureştii* 2, nos. 1–2 (1936): 39–87.

Siemenz, P., and F. Fischer. *Zeitschrift für Fischerei und deren Hilfswissenschaften*. Vol. XI. Berlin, 1903.

Singer, C., et al., eds. *A History of Technology*. 2d ed. 5 vols. Oxford, 1954–1958.

Sloane, E. *A Museum of Early American Tools*. New York, 1964.

Smith, H. R. B. *Blacksmiths' and Farriers' Tools at Shelburne Museum*. Shelburne, Vt., 1966.

Sokol'skii, N. I. "Gorodishche Il'ichevskoye." *SovArch*, 1966, pt. 4, pp. 125–140.

Soteriades, G. "Ek taphon tes Aitolias," *ArchEph*, 1906, pp. 67–88.

Stefan, Gh. "Dinogetia I." *Dacia*, 1st ser., 7–8 (1937–1940): 401–425.

Sténuit, R. "The Wreck of the Pink *Evstafii*." *IJNA* 5 (1976): 221–243, 317–331.

Stevenson, R. B. K. *The Great Palace of the Byzantine Emperors*. Oxford, 1947.

Stoian, I. "La città pontica di Tomis." *Dacia*, n.s. 5 (1961): 233–274.

Stratos, A. N. *Byzantium in the Seventh Century*. Amsterdam, 1968.

Strong, D., and D. Brown, eds. *Roman Crafts*. London, 1976.

Strzygowski, J. *Koptische Kunst*. Vienna, 1904.

Tchernia, A., P. Pomey, and A. Hesnard. *L'Épave romaine de la Madrague de Giens (Var)*. *Gallia* Supplement 34. Paris, 1978.

Testaguzza, O. *Portus: Illustrazione dei porti di Claudio e Traiano e della citta di Porto a Fiumicino*. Rome, 1970.

Thomas, A. C. "Imported Pottery in Dark-Age Western Britain." *Medieval Archaeology* 3 (1959): 89–111.

Thompson, D'A. W. *A Glossary of Greek Fishes*. London, 1947.

Thompson, M. *The Athenian Agora*, vol. II, *Coins from the Roman through the Venetian Period*. Princeton, 1954.

Throckmorton, P. *The Lost Ships*. Boston, 1964.

———. "Thirty-three Centuries Under the Sea." *NatGeo* 117, no. 5 (May, 1960): 682–703.

———, and J. Bullitt. "Underwater Surveys in Greece: 1962." *Expedition* 5, no. 2 (Winter, 1963): 16–23.

———, and J. Throckmorton. "The Roman Wreck at Pantano Longarini." *IJNA* 2 (1973): 243–266.

———, H. Frost, C. Martin, et al. *Surveying in Archaeology Underwater*. Colt Archaeological Institute Monograph No. 5. London, 1969.

*Traditional Tools of the Carpenter and Other Craftsmen*. Christie's Sale No. CA794/5T, April 23–24, 1979. London, 1979.

Tre Tryckare. *The Lore of Ships*. New York, 1975.

Tudor, D. *Oltenia Romana*. Bucharest, 1958.

———. *Sucidava: Une Cité daco-romaine et byzantine en Dacie*. Collection Latomus, vol. 80. Brussels, 1965.

———. "Sucidava II." *Dacia*, 1st ser., 7–8 (1937–1940): 359–400.

———. "Sucidava III." *Dacia*, 1st ser., 11–12 (1945–1947): 145–208.

Turrell, J. *Ancient Angling Authors*. London, 1910.

Ucelli, G. *Le Navi di Nemi*. 2d ed. Rome, 1950.

U.S. Department of Defense, Defense Mapping Agency Hydrographic Center. N.O. Chart no. BHA 54418.

U.S. Naval Oceanographic Office. *Sailing Directions for the Mediterranean*, vol. V, *The Aegean Sea*. 2d ed. Hydrographic Office Publication No. 56. Washington, D.C., 1952.

U.S. Navy. *Diving Manual*. NAVSHIPS 250-538. Washington, D.C., 1959.

van Doorninck, F. H., Jr. "Byzantium, Mistress of the Sea, 330–641." In *A History of Seafaring Based on Underwater Archaeology*. Ed. G. F. Bass. London and New York, 1972.

———. "The 4th Century Wreck at Yassi Ada: An Interim Report on the Hull." *IJNA* 5 (1976): 115–131.

———. "The Seventh-Century Byzantine Ship at Yassi Ada: Some Contributions to the History of Naval Architecture. Ph.D. diss., University of Pennsylvania, 1967.

van Nouhuys, J. "The Anchor." *MM* 37 (1951): 17–47.

Varoqueaux, C. "L'Épave du Musée des Docks à Marseille." *Publications universitaires des lettres et sciences humaines d'Aix-en-Provence: Études classiques* 3 (1968–70): 25–50.

"The Victor Merlo Collection." *Los Angeles Museum Bulletin*, July, 1932.

Villette, J. "Une Coupe chrétienne, en verre gravé, trouvée à Carthage." *MonPiot* 46 (1952): 131–151.

Visquis, A. "Premier inventaire du mobilier de l'épave dite 'des jarres' à Agay." *CahArchSub* 2 (1973): 157–166.

von Brandt, A. *Fish Catching Methods of the World*. London, 1964.

Vrsalović, D. *Istraživanja i Zaštita Podmorskih Arheoloških Spomenika u SR Hrvatskoj*. Zagreb, 1974.

Vulpe, R., and I. Barnea. *Din Istoria Dobrogei*, vol. II, *Romanii la Dunărea de Jos*. Bucharest, 1968.

Waagé, D. B. *Antioch-on-the-Orontes*, vol. IV, part 2, *Greek, Roman, Byzantine and Crusaders' Coins*. Princeton, 1952.

Waagé, F. O. *Antioch-on-the-Orontes*, vol. IV, part 1, *Ceramics and Islamic Coins*. Princeton, 1948.

———. "Bronze Objects from Old Corinth, Greece." *AJA* 39 (1935): 79–91.

Walke, N. *Das römische Donaukastell Straubing-Sorviodurum*. Berlin, 1965.

Walters, H. B. *Catalogue of the Bronzes, Greek, Roman, and Etruscan, in the Department of Greek and Roman Antiquities, British Museum*. London, 1899.

Ward-Perkins, J., and A. Claridge. *Pompeii A.D. 79*. London, 1976.

Weinberg, G. D., et al. *The Antikythera Shipwreck Reconsidered*. Transactions of the American Philosophical Society, n.s. vol. 55, pt. 3. Philadelphia, 1965.

Weinkauff, H. C. *Die Conchylien des Mittelmeers*. Vol. I. Kassel, 1867.

Werner, J. "Byzantinische Gürtelschnallen des 6. und 7. Jahrhunderts aus der Sammlung Diergardt." *KJVuF* 1 (1955): 36–47.

———. *Die langobardischen Fibelin aus Italien*. Berlin, 1950.

Westwood, T., and T. Satchell. *Bibliotheca Piscatoria*. London, 1883.

White, K. D. *Agricultural Implements of the Roman World*. Cambridge, 1967.

Whitehouse, D. "The Medieval Glazed Pottery of Lazio." *BSR* 35, n.s. 22 (1967): 40–86.

Wiegand, T., and H. Schrader. *Priene*. Berlin, 1904.

Wildung, F. H. *Woodworking Tools at Shelburne Museum*. Shelburne, Vt., 1957.

Wilson, L. M. *The Clothing of the Ancient Romans*. The Johns Hopkins University Studies in Archaeology, no. 24. Baltimore, 1938.

Winlock, H. E., and W. E. Crum. *The Monastery of Epiphanius at Thebes*. Vol I. Publications of the Metropolitan Museum of Art Egyptian Expedition, no. 3. New York, 1926.

Wroth, W. *Catalogue of the Imperial Byzantine Coins in the British Museum*. 2 vols. London, 1908.

Wulff, O. *Königliche Museen zu Berlin*, vol. III, part 1, *Altchristliche und mittelalterliche byzantinische und italienische Bildwerke*. Berlin, 1909.

Zacos, G., and A. Veglery, *Byzantine Lead Seals*. 1 vol. in 4 parts. Basel, 1972.

# INDEX